Down to Earth Sociology

Introductory Readings
TWELFTH EDITION

JAMES M. HENSLIN
Editor

THE FREE PRESS

New York London Toronto Sydney Singapore

THE FREE PRESS
A Division of Simon & Schuster, Inc.
1230 Avenue of the Americas
New York, NY 10020

First Free Press trade paperback edition 2003

Designed by Publications Development Company

Manufactured in the United States of America

10 9 8 7 6 5 4 3 2

Library of Congress Cataloging-in-Publication Data

Down to earth sociology : introductory readings / James M. Henslin, editor.—12th ed.
     p. cm.
    Includes bibliographical references and index.
     1. Sociology.   2. United States—Social conditions.   I. Henslin, James M.
  HM586 .D68 2003
  301—dc21
                                                                    2002040821

ISBN 0-7432-4716-7

Credits and Acknowledgments

35 Reprinted by permission of *Zmagazine.*

36 Reprinted by permission of the author and publisher from *Signs 16*:3, pp. 485–501.

37 Reprinted by permission of Center for Media Literacy.

38 From *Human Nature Magazine* 1 (2), pp. 28, 30–36, February 1978. Copyright © by Human Nature, Inc.

39 Reprinted by permission of the author and publisher from *Beyond Caring: Hospitals, Nurses and the Social Organization of Ethics*, University of Chicago Press. Copyright © 1996. All rights reserved.

40 Jennifer Hunt, *Urban Life*, Vol. 13, No. 4 (January 1985) Copyright © 1985 by Sage Publications, Inc. Reprinted by permission of Sage Publications, Inc.

41 From *War: Past, Present, and Future* by Gwynne Dyer, copyright © 1985 by Media Resources. Used by permission of Crown Publishers, a division of Random House, Inc.

42 Excerpts reprinted by permission from pp. 44–52, 53–55, 60, 65, 72–76, 82–85 of *Fast Food, Fast Talk: Service Work and the Routinization of Everyday Life,* Robin Leidner. Copyright © 1993 The Regents of the University of California.

43 Reprinted by permission of the Lancaster Mennonite Historical Society, from *Pennsylvania Mennonite Heritage*, Vol. 13, No. 3, July 1990.

44 "Not Just Weapons of the Weak" by Laura L. Miller. Reprinted by permission of the author and publisher from *Social Psychology Quarterly,* 60 (1), March 1997, excerpts from various pages. Copyright © 1997 by the American Sociological Association.

45 From *Journal of Contemporary Ethnography*, 24 (3). Copyright ©1995 by Sage Publications. Reprinted by permission.

In Memory of

Erving Goffman
1922–1982

and

William Foote Whyte
1914–2000

Whose Examples Are Our Legacy

Contents

Preface to the Twelfth Edition

Sociology has the marvelous capacity to open new windows of perception on our familiar worlds, leaving no aspect of our lives untouched.

—Author

IT IS WITH PLEASURE that I introduce the twelfth edition of *Down to Earth Sociology,* a pleasure akin to seeing a dear friend reach another cheerful milestone in his or her life. Adopters of earlier editions will find themselves at home, I believe, in this latest edition. They will see many selections that they have already used successfully in the classroom, and I trust they will welcome the many newcomers.

Following the suggestions of those who have used earlier editions of *Down to Earth Sociology,* I have strived to continue to present down to earth articles in order to make the student's introduction to sociology enjoyable as well as meaningful. These selections narrate the first-hand experiences of their authors—researchers who put a human voice on sociological experiences—those who have "been there" and who, with a minimum of jargon and quantification, insightfully share their experiences with the reader.

Focusing on social interaction in everyday activities and situations, these selections share some of the fascination of sociology. They reflect both the individualistic and the structural emphases of our discipline. They make clear how social structure is not simply an abstract fact of life, but vitally affects our lives. These selections help students become more aware of how the decisions of the rich, the politically powerful, and the bureaucrats provide social constraints that augment those dictated by birth, social class, and other circumstances. They help students understand how their location in a social structure lifts or limits their vision of life, closes or opens their chances of success, and, ultimately, brings tears and laughter, hope and despair.

So much of sociology, however, goes about its business as though data were unconnected to people, as though the world consisted of abstract social facts. Yet from our own experiences in social life, we know how far these suppositions are from the truth—how divorced they are from real life. Consequently, I have sought to include authors who are able to share the realities that directly affect people's lives. As I see it, sociology is the most fascinating of the social sciences, and it is this fascination that these selections are designed to convey.

It is my hope that I have succeeded in accomplishing this goal, because sociology has the marvelous capacity to open new windows of perception on our familiar worlds, leaving no aspect of our lives untouched. If these readings even come close to this goal, I am indebted to the many adopters of earlier editions, whose reactions and suggestions have helped give shape to this one. To all of you, a sincere and fond thank you.

I owe a special debt of gratitude to the instructors who shared with me their experiences with earlier editions. Their sharing proved invaluable in shaping this present version. I wish to acknowledge the help of

Richard Ambler, Southern Arkansas University
Julie E. Artis, DePaul University
Joe Bishop, Dakota State University
John Bowman, University of North Carolina at Pembroke
Tom Boyd, Berea College
Suzanne Brandon, College of St. Catherine
John C. Bridges, Immaculata College
Grace Budrys, DePaul University
Meryl Cozart, Towson University
Rolf Diamon, University of Southern Maine
Merl Dirksen, Lee University
Robert B. Enright, Jr., University of Wisconsin–Stevens Point
David C. Erickson, Northwest College
Kerry Ferris, Bradley University
Richard Gendron, Assumption College
Frank Glamser, University of Southern Mississippi
Peter R. Grahame, Mount Saint Mary's College
Susan F. Greenwood, University of Maine–Orono
Larry D. Hall, Spring Hill College
Terrell A. Hayes, Davis & Elkins College
Ines W. Jindra, Bethany Lutheran College
Cathryn Johnson, Emory University
Susan L. Johnson, Carl Sandburg College
James W. Jordan, Longwood College
Quintus Joubeve, Rutgers University
Mariame Kaba, Northeastern Illinois University
Meg Wilkes Karraker, University of St. Thomas
Margot Kempers, Fitchburg State College
Marilyn Krogh, Loyola University of Chicago
Anthony Lack, Lee College
Helene M. Lawson, University of Pittsburgh

Bill Lockhart, New Mexico State University
Jerry Lowney, Carroll College
Philip Luck, Georgia State University
Kristin Marsh, Emory University
Tina Martinez, Blue Mountain Community College
R. Robin Miller, Drury University
Sharon L. Miller, Hope College
Janine Minkler, Northern Arizona University
Elizabeth J. Mitchell, Rutgers University
Thomas S. Moore, University of Wisconsin–Milwaukee
Christopher W. Mullins, Southwestern Illinois College
Peter F. Parilla, University of St. Thomas
Kristin Park, Westminster College
Tim Pippert, Augsburg College
Paul-Jahi Price, Pasadena City College
Pam Rosenberg, Gettysburg College
Richard Rubinson, Emory University
Ross T. Runfola, Medaille College
Allen Scarboro, Augusta State University
Richard Senter, Jr., Central Michigan University
Ryan Sheppard, King's College
Rick L. Shifley, Montserrat College of Art
Thomas Soltis, Westmoreland County Community College
Marybeth C. Stalp, University of Georgia
Judith Stepan-Norris, University of California–Irvine
Jordan J. Titus, University of Alaska
Kathy Trosen, Muscatine Community College
Suzanne Tuthill, Delaware Technical and Community College
Judy C. Vaughan, Arkansas Tech University
Anita Veit, University of North Carolina
Abram Lawrence Wehmiller, Greenhill School
Clovis L. White, Oberlin College
Fred Zampa, Macon State College

One of the more interesting tasks in preparing this book is to gather information on the contributors' backgrounds. In addition to biographical data concerning their education, teaching, and publishing, this section also contains their statements telling us why they like sociology or became sociologists. You may want to assign this section with the articles to help personalize the readings and increase the student's awareness of biographical factors that go into the choice to become a sociologist.

The selections in this edition continue to be organized to make them compatible with most introductory textbooks. Through subjects that are inherently interesting, we cover the major substantive areas of sociology. Part I, an introduction to the sociological perspective, invites students to view the world in a new way by participating in this exciting enterprise we call sociology. Part II is designed to answer the basic question of how sociologists do research. Part III examines the cultural underpinnings of social life, those taken-for-granted assumptions and contexts that provide the contours of our everyday lives. Part IV focuses on that essential component of our beings, gender and sexuality. There we look at both the process by which we assume the social identity of male or female and how those identities provide the basis for interaction among adults.

In Part V, we examine social groups and social structure, looking behind the scenes to reveal how people's assumptions, their location on social hierarchies, and the features of social settings establish both constraints and freedoms in human relationships. In Part VI, we consider the relativity of deviance and the process of becoming deviant, especially the social context that shapes deviance. We also examine features of social control, those aspects of social groups that are designed to minimize deviance. In Part VII, we focus on social stratification, beginning with the micro level of physical appearance and then looking at gender, race–ethnicity, poverty, wealth, and power as dimensions of social inequality. In Part VIII, we analyze the social institutions of economics, marriage and family, education, sports, the mass media, religion, medicine, law, and the military. In this edition, we add an analysis of science, examining how myth creeps into its "objective" knowledge. We conclude the book with a look at social change, the focus of Part IX. After examining how everyday life is being rationalized in a process called McDonaldization, we look at resistance to social change—how the Amish withdraw from mainstream society and how male soldiers undermine the integration of women in the military. We then conclude the book with a look at how people adjust to the aftermath of a hurricane.

These selections bring the reader face-to-face with the dual emphases of contemporary sociological research: the focus on the individual's experiences, and the analysis of social structure. Uncovering the basic expectations that underlie routine social interactions, these articles emphasize the ways in which social institutions are interrelated. It is to their authors' credit that we lose sight of neither the people who are interacting nor the structural base that so directly influences the form and content of their interactions.

In some of the selections written before stylistic changes occurred in our language, "he," "his," "him," "himself," "man," "world of men," and so on, are generic, referring to both males and females. Although the linguistic style is outdated, the ideas are not.

Jim Henslin
December 2002

About the Contributors

Linda Liske Belgrave (article 45), who earned her Ph.D. from Case Western Reserve University, is Associate Professor of Sociology at the University of Miami. Using a qualitative approach, she has published in sociology journals, primarily on gerontology, health care, and collective behavior.

Belgrave took her first course in sociology because "the pickings were slim, and sociology happened to fit my schedule. I was an older student, with a family and a job, and sociology addressed important issues in a way that 'rang true.' Sociology opened new worlds, and it felt 'like coming home.' Before the quarter was over, I was hooked, and I immediately changed my major to sociology. Without ever having said, 'I want to be a sociologist,' I found that I became one." Belgrave, a political activist, is also a ballet student.

Peter L. Berger (article 1) received his Ph.D. in Sociology from the New School for Social Research. He is Professor of Sociology and Theology at Boston University, where he is also Director of the Institute for the Study of Economic Culture. He is the author of numerous books, including *The Social Construction of Reality: A Treatise in the Sociology of Knowledge* (with Thomas Luckmann), *A Far Glory: The Quest for Faith in an Age of Credulity,* and *Invitation to Sociology,* from which his selection in this book is taken.

Berger says, "I was born in Austria and came to the United States with my parents after the war. You might say that I became a sociologist by accident. I took some courses in sociology and liked them. I have always been curious about what makes people tick, and that is what sociology is all about."

Mae A. Biggs (article 18) earned her M.A. in Sociology at Southern Illinois University, Edwardsville, and is an associate of the Masters-Johnson Institute (Biological Research Institute) in St. Louis, Missouri.

Theodore Caplow (article 10) earned his Ph.D. in Sociology at the University of Minnesota. He is Professor of Sociology at the University of Virginia. Among his books are *Systems of War and Peace* (with Louis Hicks), *The First Measured Century: An Illustrated Guide to Trends in America 1900–2000,* and *Middletown Families: Fifty Years of Change and Continuity* (with Howard Bahr, Bruce Chadwick, Reuben Hill, and Margaret Williamson).

Caplow says, "As an undergraduate at Columbia, I planned to become a historian. But a friend invited me to sit in on a course he was taking with Professor Robert Lynd, and I was captivated. Years later, I followed his footsteps to Middletown."

Karen A. Cerulo (article 21), who earned her Ph.D., at Princeton University, is Associate Professor of Sociology at Rutgers University. She wrote *Deciphering Violence: The Cognitive Order of Right and Wrong, Culture in Mind: Toward a Sociology of Culture and Cognition,* and (with Janet Ruane) *Second Thoughts: Seeing Conventional Wisdom Through the Sociological Eye,* from which her selection in this book is taken.

When asked why she became a sociologist, Cerulo said, "I started my academic career as a psychology student. When I took my first sociology course, I realized that the discipline offered so much more than psychology did. The multifaceted lens with which sociologists view the world won me over."

Napoleon A. Chagnon (article 8) earned his Ph.D. in Anthropology at the University of Michigan. He is Professor Emeritus of Anthropology at the University of California at Santa Barbara and the author of *Yąnomamö: The Last Days of Eden; Yąnomamö Warfare, Social Organization and Marriage Alliances;* and the book from which his selection is taken, *Yąnomamö: The Fierce People.*

Daniel F. Chambliss (article 39), who received his Ph.D. from Yale University, is Sidney Wertimer Professor at Hamilton College. He has published *Champions: The Making of Olympic Swimmers* and *Beyond Caring: Hospitals, Nurses, and the Social Organization of Ethics,* the book from which his selection is adapted.

Chambliss, who does management consulting, also loves to coach competitive swimmers. He says, "Sociology was intellectually the freest discipline I encountered in college. You could study math or philosophy or psychology and apply them all in sociology. It is the broadest of the social sciences. There are no artificial limits."

William J. Chambliss (article 24) received his Ph.D in Sociology at Indiana University and is Professor of Sociology at George Washington University. His books include *On the Take: From Petty Crooks to Presidents, Law, Order and Power,* and *Power, Politics, and Crime.* Professor Chambliss is a past President of the American Society of Criminology (1987–88) and a past President of the Society for the Study of Social Problems (1992–93).

Chambliss says, "I became a sociologist out of an interest in doing something about crime. I remained a sociologist because it became clear to me that until we have a greater understanding of the political and economic conditions that lead some societies to have excessive amounts of crime we will never be able to do anything about the problem. Sociology is a beautiful discipline that affords an opportunity to investigate just about anything connected with human behavior and still claim an identity with a discipline. This is its strength, its promise, and why I find it thoroughly engaging, enjoyable, and fulfilling."

John R. Coleman (article 19) was the President of Haverford College from 1967 to 1977 and then President of the Edna McConnell Clark Foundation in New York City. He decided to try his hand at business and now runs "The Inn at Long Last" in Chester, Vermont.

Kingsley Davis (article 12) received his Ph.D. in Sociology at Harvard University and is Distinguished Professor of Sociology at the University of Southern California and Senior Research Fellow at the Hoover Institution on War, Revolution and Peace at Stanford University. His books include *Human Society, The Population of India and Pakistan,* and *Below-Replacement Fertility in Industrial Societies: Causes, Consequences, Policy.*

Davis, who often travels to remote places on the globe, likes sociology because "first, sociology deals with all aspects of society, not just economic behavior or political matters; second, in regard to social change, sociology takes a longer view than most other social science fields. I became a sociologist because I wanted to write and decided that I had better learn something to write, so I elected to learn sociology. Also, I wanted to know how the social system works. We were in the Great Depression at the time, so a social science should be able to analyze and explain that terrible catastrophe."

Gwynne Dyer (article 41) is a London-based independent journalist. Writing on current social issues, his articles appear in many newspapers and magazines.

Donna Eder (article 14), who earned her Ph.D. in Sociology at the University of Wisconsin, is Professor of Sociology at Indiana University. She has written *School Talk: Gender and Adolescent Culture,* the book from which her selection is taken.

When asked why she became a sociologist, Eder said, "I thought that by understanding school dynamics we could change society through improving our schools. I have since found that sociological research often focuses too much on social problems. Now I am trying to study solutions to social problems, not just the problems."

Barbara Ehrenreich (article 32) is a freelance writer and political satirist who has published widely. Her books include *Debating P.C.: The Controversy over Political Correctness on College Campuses; Fear of Falling: The Inner Life of the Middle Class,* and *Nickel and Dimed: On (Not) Getting by in America,* from which her selection in this book is taken.

D. Stanley Eitzen (article 35), who received his Ph.D. from the University of Kansas, is Professor Emeritus in the Department of Sociology at Colorado State University. Among his many books, he has edited *Experiencing Poverty: Voices from the Bottom* (with Kelly Eitzen Smith) and has written, *Sociology of North American Sport* (with George Sage) and *Diversity in Families* (with Maxine Baca Zinn).

Herbert J. Gans (article 30) received his Ph.D. in City Planning and Sociology from the University of Pennsylvania. He is Robert S. Lynd Professor of Sociology at Columbia University and has written such books as *The Urban Villagers; The War against the Poor: The Underclass and Antipoverty Policy;* and *Popular Culture and High Culture: An Analysis and Evaluation of Taste.* Professor Gans is a past President of the American Sociological Association (1987–88).

Gans "finds sociology more interesting than hobbies." He says: "When I was in high school, I thought I would become a journalist, but then when I got to college I discovered that the articles I enjoyed writing most were sociology. From then on I was pretty sure I would become a sociologist." He adds, "The deeper reason I became a sociologist is because I am a refugee from Nazi Germany, and ever since I came to the United States as a teenager in 1940, I have been trying to understand the country which took me in." Whenever possible—and his family agrees—Gans rents an apartment for a month in a European city or medieval town and "explores it, living in it fully."

Erving Goffman (article 11) earned his Ph.D. in Sociology at the University of Chicago and at the time of his death in 1982 was Director of the Center for Urban Ethnography at the University of Pennsylvania. His many books include *Stigma: Notes on the Management of a Spoiled Identity; Behavior in Public Places: Notes on the Social Organization of Gatherings;* and the book from which his selection is taken, *The Presentation of Self in Everyday Life.*

Harry L. Gracey (article 34) received his Ph.D. in Sociology at the New School for Social Research. He is in private practice in organizational development in Cambridge, Massachusetts, and has published *Curriculum or Craftsmanship?: Elementary School Teacher in a Bureaucratic System,* and *Readings in Introductory Sociology* (with Dennis H. Wrong).

Gracey says, "What led me to study sociology was a curiosity about how things work, which in my case got focused on the world of social life, rather than on the physical or biological world. Sociology, uniquely among the social sciences, I think, 'lifts the veil of ideology' on the working of society to see what is really going on—and who is doing it and how it is being done."

Edward T. Hall (article 9) was awarded his Ph.D. at Columbia University. He is Emeritus Professor of Anthropology at Northwestern University. His books include *The Silent Language, The Hidden Dimension,* and *Beyond Culture.*

Mildred R. Hall (article 9) received her B.A. from Barnard College and (with Edward T. Hall) has written *The Fourth Dimension in Architecture; Hidden Differences: Doing Business with the Japenese;* and *Understanding Cultural Differences: German, French, and American.*

Marvin Harris (article 38) received his Ph.D. from Columbia University. He was Graduate Research Professor of Anthropology at the University of Florida until his death in 2001. Following his primary interest, cultural anthropology, Harris searched for the practical reasons that underlie customs that on the surface seem unreasonable or even bizarre. His numerous writings include *Cows, Pigs, Wars, and Witches: The Riddles of Culture; Cannibals and Kings: The Origins of Cultures;* and *Good to Eat: Riddles of Food and Culture.*

James M. Henslin (articles 2, 4, 13, 18, and 23) earned his Ph.D. in Sociology at Washington University in St. Louis. He is Professor Emeritus of Sociology at Southern Illinois University, Edwardsville. His many books include *Social Problems; Sociology: A Down-to-Earth Approach;* and *Essentials of Sociology: A Down-to-Earth Approach.*

Henslin says, "My early childhood was marked by poverty. I was born in a rented room in a minister's parsonage. Then my parents made a leap in their economic status—we moved into our own home, a converted garage, with no running water or indoor plumbing! My parents continued their climb in status, and when I was thirteen they built one of the nicest houses in town. These experiences helped make me keenly aware of the significance of 'place' and opportunity in social life." He adds, "I like sociology because of its tremendous breadth—from social class and international stratification to the self and internal conflicts. No matter how diverse your curiosities, you can follow them and they are still part of sociology. Everything that is part of the landscape of human behavior comes under the lens of sociology."

Stephen Higley (article 31) received his Ph.D. in Geography from the University of Illinois at Urbana-Champaign. He is Associate Professor of Geography at the University of Montevallo. Higley wrote *Privilege, Power, and Place: The Geography of the American Upper Class*, the book from which his selection is taken.

As an urban social geographer, Higley's approach to geography is close to sociology. He stresses the consequences of the stratification (or geographical structure) of U.S. metropolitan areas on school systems, public amenities, social services, and even for stereotyping people from different social classes. He says, "The upper class has the means and the influence to create a distinct style of life that minimizes their contact with other social classes. One of the most important vehicles for this separation is where they live and how they control it (of course, with the help of the upper middle class)."

Arlie Russell Hochschild (article 33) received her Ph.D. in Sociology from the University of California, Berkeley, where she is now Professor of Sociology. She has published *The Managed Heart: Commercialization of Human Feeling; The Second Shift: Inside the Two-Job Marriage;* and *The Time Bind: When Work Becomes Home and Home Becomes Work*, the book from which her selection is taken.

Hochschild says, "I majored in international relations at Swarthmore College (a combination of history, economics, and political science) in the early sixties when my college had no sociology department. By chance I discovered David Riesman's *The Lonely Crowd*, his *Individualism Reconsidered*, and C. Wright Mills' *People, Politics and Power*. It was between the covers of these exciting books that I decided that there was a powerful lens through which to see the world—and I wanted to get on the other side of it."

Robert A. Hummer (article 28), who received his Ph.D. from Florida State University, is Associate Professor in the Department of Sociology at the University of Texas, Austin. He has published (with Richard Rogers and Charles Nam) *Living and Dying in the U.S.A.: Behavioral, Health, and Social Differentials of Adult Mortality*.

Hummer says he became a sociologist because "sociology provides me a better way of understanding the complex world in which I live." He enjoys traveling with his wife and daughter, fishing, and watching the Detroit Tigers.

Jennifer Hunt (article 40) received her Ph.D. in Sociology from the City University of New York and is Professor of Sociology at Montclair State University. She is also a research candidate in the clinical training program at the Psychoanalytic Institute at the New York University Medical Center.

Hunt has written *Psychoanalytic Aspects of Fieldwork*. She likes sociology because "it provides an unusual opportunity to explore other cultural worlds by doing in-depth fieldwork."

Bruce A. Jacobs (article 6), who received his Ph.D. in Sociology from the University of Southern California, is Associate Professor in the Department of Criminology and Criminal Justice at the University of Missouri at St. Louis. He is the author of *Robbing Drug Dealers: Violence Beyond the Law* and *Dealing Crack: The Social World of Streetcorner Selling*, the book from which his selection is taken.

Sidney Katz (article 27), who earned a Bachelor in Social Sciences from Carleton University and a Master of Social Work at the University of Toronto, is a professional writer. He has published hundreds of articles and two books and has done considerable radio and TV broadcasting. He has been a columnist, a feature writer, and an editor at the *Toronto Star* and at *Maclean's Magazine*. He says, "I have retired several times, but it hasn't stuck."

Jean Kilbourne (article 37) received her Ed.D. from Boston University, with a focus on Humanistic and Behavioral Studies. As a lecturer, media critic, filmmaker, and writer, she travels around the country giving lectures on college campuses and for conferences and organizations. She is the author of *Can't Buy My Love: How Advertising Changes the Way We Think and Feel* (originally published as *Deadly Persuasion: Why Women and Girls Must Fight the Addictive Power of Advertising*).

Kilbourne says that she "has always enjoyed sociology because it helps us to see how utterly similar and how completely unique human beings are. I've always been interested in understanding what makes us tick, individually and in communities and societies. I may have been the first person to examine the image of women in advertising and the advertising of alcohol and tobacco." Kilbourne, who is an avid reader of fiction, poetry, and mysteries, lives in Boston with her 15-year-old daughter. They enjoy bike-riding, rollerblading, skiing, and traveling.

Helene M. Lawson (article 17) earned her Ph.D. at Loyola University. She is Associate Professor of Sociology at the University of Pittsburgh at Bradford. She has written *Ladies on the Lot: Women, Car Sales, and the Pursuit of the American Dream,* the book from which her selection is taken.

Lawson says, "I decided to become a sociologist after getting a B.A. in Elementary Education and two M.A. degrees, one in Early Childhood and one in Gerontology. I was teaching people about human behavior, but I was not content with the explanations I gained from psychology, biology, or education. There was so much unhappiness. Sociology gave me a broader view of social institutions and the motivations for individual behavior, and, through its encompassing view of human institutions, even a vision of progress in which I find hope." Lawson's interests are broad, and, as she says, "My writings range from stories about gender equality in blue-collar families to what it's like to work on hair, and even the interactions of conservation officers with hunted animals." She is now doing research on the world of Internet courtship.

Robin Leidner (article 42), who earned her Ph.D. at Northwestern University, is Associate Professor in the Department of Sociology at the University of Pennsylvania.

Leidner says, "I became a sociologist after concluding that acting was unlikely to be my life's work. I have carried my interest in acting into sociology, and I am now doing research on work, identity, and scripts in professional theater. Questions about how much acting is asked of workers in other jobs, and about how people reconcile who they want to be with what they have to do to make a living, are central to my sociological work."

Zella Luria (article 15) received her Ph.D. in Psychology at Indiana University and is Professor of Psychology at Tufts University. She is the author of *The Psychology of Human Sexuality* (with Mitchel D. Rose) and *Human Sexuality* (with S. Friedman and Mitchel D. Rose).

Luria says, "What I appreciate about sociology is its exquisite attention to the group context for explanations of behavior."

Joseph Marolla (article 5) earned his Ph.D. in Sociology at the University of Denver. He is Professor of Sociology at Virginia Commonwealth University. He has published articles in social psychology, criminology, sociology of education, symbolic interaction, and self-esteem.

Marolla says, "I suppose, as much as anything else, I became a sociologist because my draft lottery number was 315 in the winter of 1969—which meant that I would not be going to Vietnam. At the time, I had given very little thought to life beyond the war. Once handed the option, school seemed the reasonable thing to do since I had been doing it for a while. I was an English major, and I moved to sociology because I thought it would broaden my creative writing. . . . What I most like about sociology is that it provides a broad picture and helps us see through the facade of life as we live it. This was appealing to me, and still is. Our research on rape is an example. Psychologists are convinced that rape is due to psychological dysfunction. We have demonstrated that rape is dramatically embedded in the culture."

Emily Martin (article 36), who received her Ph.D. in Anthropology from Cornell University, is Professor of Anthropology at New York University. Her books include *The Woman in the Body: A Cultural Analysis of Reproduction, The Cult of the Dead in a Chinese Village,* and *Flexible Bodies: Tracking Immunity in American Culture from the Days of Polio to the Age of AIDS.*

Patricia Yancey Martin (article 28), who received her Ph.D. from Florida State University, is Professor of Sociology at Florida State University. Her books include *Feminist Organizations: Harvest of the New Women's Movement* (with Myra M. Ferree) and *The Social Environment: Open Systems Applications* (with Gerald O'Connor).

Martin, whose favorite activity outside of teaching, gardening, and the arts, is traveling to Europe, says that she majored in English literature, but didn't like it enough to pursue it after the bachelor's degree. She thought she might be interested in sociology, and tried graduate school. "After I was in sociology a few years," she says, "I came to see the power of the sociological perspective." She adds, "I love trying to observe and explain the social world around me."

Philip Meyer (article 22) earned an M.A. in Political Science at the University of North Carolina at Chapel Hill, where he is now Knight Chair in Journalism. His books include *Precision Journalism: A Reporter's Introduction to Social Science Methods; Ethical Journalism: A Guide for Students, Practitioners, and Consumers;* and (with Edmund Tambeth and Esther Thorson) *Assessing Public Journalism.*

Meyer says, "I became interested in sociology because, as a journalist, I envied its research tools. I spent a postgraduate year at Harvard learning about those tools and thinking of ways to apply them to news reporting. In the course of that work, I learned about the Milgram experiments."

Laura L. Miller (article 44), who received her Ph.D. from Northwestern University, is Assistant Professor of Sociology at the University of California at Los Angeles. In addition to articles, she also has published *New Opportunities for*

Military Women: Effects Upon Readiness, Cohesion, and Morale (with Margaret C. Harrell).

Miller, whose primary focus is human relations in the military, has done research on peacekeeping operations in Somalia, Macedonia, Haiti, and Bosnia. She also enjoys snowboarding, international travel, live music, and playing at the beach. She says, "In college I was interested in so many different subjects. Sociology was the answer for me, because as a sociologist I can study anything I want and never have to change jobs."

C. Wright Mills (article 3) received his Ph.D. in Sociology from the University of Wisconsin. His scathing criticisms of U.S. society in such books as *White Collar, The Causes of World War III*, as well as the book from which his article is taken, *The Sociological Imagination*, made him one of the most controversial sociologists in the United States. At the time of his death in 1962, he was Professor of Sociology at Columbia University.

Horace Miner (article 7) earned his Ph.D. in Social Anthropology at the University of Chicago. He is Professor Emeritus of Anthropology at the University of Michigan. His books include *The Primitive City in Timbuctoo, St. Denis: A French Canadian Parish,* and *The City in Modern Africa.*

Miner says, "It was by accident that I became a sociologist. Having received my degree in social anthropology, it was easy to teach sociology when I received an offer. My courses were listed in both anthropology and sociology."

Clarence Page (article 29) is the editor of *A Foot in Each World: Essays and Articles* (with Leanita McClain), and the author of *Freedom's Champion: Elijah Lovejoy* (with Paul Simon), and *Showing My Color: Impolite Essays on Race and Identity*, the book from which his selection is taken.

Page says, "My interest in sociology dates back to my high school years. It is grounded in the same curiosity that informed my book of essays on race." He adds, "I like sociology because it tries to analyze and explain the group behaviors, attitudes, and relationships that raise the sort of questions I try to answer in my book."

David L. Rosenhan (article 26), who received his Ph.D. in Psychology from Columbia University, is Professor Emeritus of Psychology and Law at Stanford University. His books include *Foundations of Abnormal Psychology* (with Perry London), *Theory and Research in Abnormal Psychology*, and (with Martin Seligman and Elaine Walker) *Abnormal Psychology.*

Janet M. Ruane (article 21), who received her Ph.D. in Sociology at Rutgers University, is Associate Professor of Sociology at Montclair State University. She wrote *Essentials of Research Methods* and (with Karen Cerulo) *Second Thoughts: Seeing Conventional Wisdom Through the Sociological Eye,* from which her selection in this book is taken.

When I asked Ruane, who teaches courses in social research and the sociology of deviance and social control, why she became a sociologist, she said, "I was fortunate to stumble into sociology in high school. An enlightened history teacher introduced us to some classic works by Riesman and Coser. I was hooked, and I knew that sociology would be a part of my future studies and life work. In fact, my interest in teaching sociology is sustained by the satisfaction I derive from introducing new cohorts of students to the sense that sociology can make in our lives."

Jerry Savells (article 43) received his Ph.D. in Sociology at Louisiana State University. He is Professor of Sociology at Wright State University. He has edited (with Larry Cross) *The Changing Family: Making Way for Tomorrow,* and *Marriage and the Family in a Changing Society.*

Savells, whose favorite activity outside of teaching and doing sociology is fishing, earned his bachelor's degree in chemistry and biology at Murray State University. He says, "After working for a few years, I found the chemistry laboratory too confining. I decided that I wanted to move into an area where I could have more impact on people, and I returned to graduate school and studied sociology. I also served as an officer in the army, where I did some teaching, and thought that I would like to teach in an academic setting. I am fascinated with human behavior, with how people get together in social groups, and I have focused on families, especially on how families respond to social change."

Diana Scully (article 5) earned her Ph.D. in Sociology at the University of Illinois. She is Professor of Sociology and Coordinator of Women's Studies at Virginia Commonwealth University. She has written *Understanding Sexual Violence: A Study of Convicted Rapists,* and *Men Who Control Women's Health: The Miseducation of Obstetrician Gynecologists.*

Scully says, "I changed my undergraduate major to sociology on the day that Martin Luther King was assassinated. I felt then and continue to believe that because of its focus on social structure sociology has a greater potential than other disciplines for understanding complex problems, such as racism and sexism, and therefore can be used as a tool for accomplishing change that is meaningful collectively and individually."

Kenneth J. Smith (article 45), who received his Ph.D. from Duke University, is Associate Professor of Sociology at the University of Miami. He has published articles in sociology on qualitative methods, mental illness, and collective behavior.

Smith says, "I was an undergraduate during the civil rights period and a graduate student during the Vietnam years. Sociology addressed the burning issues of the time. My 'left-Christian-peace-and-justice' background also influenced my decision to be a sociologist. Ultimately the purpose of sociology and the obligation of sociologists (as well as everyone else) is to improve the human condition. Becoming a sociologist is a decision I've never regretted." An active member in church and secular organizations devoted to human rights, Smith shares his sons' interests in sports cars and motorcycles.

Deborah Tannen (article 16) earned a Ph.D. in English literature at the University of California at Berkeley. After teaching English at several universities in the U.S. and Greece, she joined the Linguistics Department at Georgetown University, where she is University Professor. Her books include *Talking from 9 to 5; You Just Don't Understand: Women and Men in Conversation;* and *That's Not What I Meant: How Conversational Style Makes or Breaks Relationships.*

William Thompson (article 20) earned his Ph.D. in Sociology at Oklahoma State University and is Professor of Sociology and Criminal Justice at Texas A&M University at Commerce. He has edited *Juvenile Delinquency: Classic and Contemporary Readings* (with Jack E. Bynum) and written *Juvenile Delinquency: A Sociological Approach* (with Jack E. Bynum), and *Society in Focus* (with Joseph V. Hickey).

Coming from a working-class background, Thompson is the first in his immediate family to graduate from high school. He says that he is attracted to sociology because "sociology makes the entire world your laboratory."

Barrie Thorne (article 15) earned her Ph.D. in Sociology at Brandeis University. She is Professor of Sociology and of Women's Studies at the University of California at Berkeley. Thorne is the author of *Gender Play: Girls and Boys in School,* and (with Barbara Laslett) the editor of *Feminist Sociology: Life Histories of a Movement,* and *Language, Gender and Society.*

When asked why she became a sociologist, Thorne said, "Existing arrangements aren't fixed; they're the result of and can be changed by human action. Sociology provides tools for digging beneath the surface of the 'given'—such as arrangements of schooling. This helps us see underlying structures of inequality, enabling us to learn more about the perspectives of groups, like women and children, who have historically been relatively invisible in knowledge. Critical sociological perspectives connect empirical inquiry with visions of justice—a useful path for both understanding and action."

Philip G. Zimbardo (article 25) earned his Ph.D. in Social Psychology at Yale University and is Professor of Social Psychology at Stanford University. His books include *Psychology and Life* (with Richard J. Gerrig), *The Shy Child: Overcoming and Preventing Shyness from Infancy to Adulthood* (with Shirley Radl), and (with Michael R. Leippe) *The Psychology of Attitude Change and Social Influence.*

Zimbardo, who has taught in Italy and enjoys collecting and studying the arts and crafts of the Native Americans of the Northwest and Southwest, says that he likes sociology because of "the scope of the significant questions it raises about human behavior."

The Sociological Perspective

Sociology is an invitation to look behind the scenes of the social world—a passport, as it were, to a different way of viewing life.

—the author

I WOULD LIKE TO BEGIN this first introduction on a personal note. Since my early school days, reading has been one of my favorite pastimes. I used to read almost anything I could lay my hands on, but I was especially fascinated by books that explored people's lives—especially novels that described their life situations, thoughts, relationships, hopes and dreams, challenges and obstacles. Without knowing it, I was gaining an appreciation for understanding the social context in which people live out their lives—for seeing how important that context is in determining what people are like.

When I went to college, I discovered that there was a name for my interests: *sociology*. What an exciting revelation: I had found an entire academic discipline centered on understanding the general context in which people live and analyzing how their lives are influenced by it! I could not help wanting to read sociology, to take more courses, to immerse myself in it. I was hooked—so thoroughly, in fact, that eventually I decided to become a sociologist and spend my life in this fascinating endeavor.

The intention of this book is fourfold. First, I want to share some of the excitement and fascination of sociology. Then, through these readings, I want to make more visible the context of social life that affects us all. Third, if this is successful, you will gain a better understanding not only of people in general, but of your own self as well. Finally, I hope to whet your appetite for more sociology.

As Peter Berger says in the opening selection, the discovery of sociology can change your life. It can help you to understand the social forces you confront, the forces that constrain and free you as you go about living your life.

This understanding offers a liberating potential: To gain insight into how these social forces influence your life allows you to stand somewhat apart from at least some of them, and thereby to exert more creative control over your own life.

But just what is sociology? In my teaching I have found that introductory students often find this a vexing question. To provide a better grasp of what sociology is, then, in the second selection I compare sociology with the other social sciences. One of the main points of this article is that sociology casts an intellectual net that provides an unparalleled approach to understanding social life.

In the third and last article in Part I, C. Wright Mills turns again to this liberating potential that sociology offers. As he points out, this capacity centers on understanding three main issues: (1) the structure of society—that is, how society's components are interrelated; (2) where one's society stands in human history and the changes that are occurring in it; and 3) what type of people prevail in one's society, how they are selected for prevalence, and what types are coming to prevail.

Thinking of life in these terms, says Mills, is a quality of mind that we should strive for. This *sociological imagination,* to use his term for the sociological perspective, allows us to peer beyond our immediate confines, to seek out and understand the broader social and historical forces at work in our lives. One of the rewarding consequences of this perspective, he says, is that it enables us to see ourselves in a different light.

It is the goal of Part I, then, to let you dip your feet in the sociological waters, to challenge you to venture into sociology, and, while venturing, to stimulate your sociological imagination.

1 Invitation to Sociology

PETER L. BERGER

Motivated by an intense desire to know what is "really happening," what goes on "behind the scenes," sociologists study almost every aspect of life in society. As Berger indicates, nothing is too sacred or too profane to be spared the sociologist's scrutiny. But when you penetrate the surface and peer behind the masks that individuals and organizations wear, you find a reality quite unlike the one that is so carefully devised and, just as carefully, put forward for public consumption.

This changed angle of vision, however, is dangerous. Once you have peered behind the scenes and viewed life in a new light, it is nearly impossible to revert to complacent assumptions. The old, familiar, and so very comfortable ways of looking at life become upset when your angle of vision changes. This potential of sociology is also part of its attraction.

THE SOCIOLOGIST (that is, the one we would really like to invite to our game) is a person intensively, endlessly, shamelessly interested in the doings of men. His natural habitat is all the human gathering places of the world, wherever men come together. The sociologist may be interested in many other things. But his consuming interest remains in the world of men, their institutions, their history, their passions. And since he is interested in men, nothing that men* do can be altogether tedious for him. He will naturally be interested in the events that engage men's ultimate beliefs, their moments of tragedy and grandeur and ecstasy. But he will also be fascinated by the commonplace, the everyday. He will know reverence, but this reverence will not prevent him from wanting to see and to understand. He may sometimes feel revulsion or contempt. But this also will not deter him from wanting to have his questions answered. The sociologist, in his quest for understanding, moves through the world of men without respect for the usual lines of demarcation. Nobility and degradation, power and obscurity, intelligence and folly—these are equally *interesting* to him, however unequal they may be in his personal values or tastes. Thus his questions may lead him to all possible levels of society, the best and the least known places, the most respected and the most

*Some of the classic articles in this book were written when "men" was generic, when it commonly referred to both men and women. So it is with "he, his, him," and so on. Although the writing style has changed, the sociological ideas have not.

despised. And, if he is a good sociologist, he will find himself in all these places because his own questions have so taken possession of him that he has little choice but to seek for answers.

It would be possible to say the same things in a lower key. We could say that the sociologist, but for the grace of his academic title, is the man who must listen to gossip despite himself, who is tempted to look through keyholes, to read other people's mail, to open cabinets. Before some otherwise unoccupied psychologist sets out now to construct an aptitude test for sociologists on the basis of sublimated voyeurism, let us quickly say that we are speaking merely by way of analogy. Perhaps some little boys consumed with curiosity to watch their maiden aunts in the bathroom later become inveterate sociologists. This is quite uninteresting. What interests us is the curiosity that grips any sociologist in front of a closed door behind which there are human voices. If he is a good sociologist he will want to open that door, to understand these voices. Behind each closed door he will anticipate some new facet of human life not yet perceived and understood.

The sociologist will occupy himself with matters that others regard as too sacred or as too distasteful for dispassionate investigation. He will find rewarding the company of priests or of prostitutes, depending not on his personal preferences but on the questions he happens to be asking at the moment. He will also concern himself with matters that others may find much too boring. He will be interested in the human interaction that goes with warfare or with great intellectual discoveries, but also in the relations between people employed in a restaurant or between a group of little girls playing with their dolls. His main focus of attention is not the ultimate significance of what men do, but the action in itself, as another example of the infinite richness of human conduct.

In these journeys through the world of men the sociologist will inevitably encounter other professional Peeping Toms. Sometimes these will resent his presence, feeling that he is poaching on their preserves. In some places the sociologist will meet up with the economist, in others with the political scientist, in yet others with the psychologist or the ethnologist. Yet chances are that the questions that have brought him to these places are different from the ones that propelled his fellow-trespassers. The sociologist's questions always remain essentially the same: "What are people doing with each other here?" "What are their relationships to each other?" "How are these relationships organized in institutions?" "What are the collective ideas that move men and institutions?" In trying to answer these questions in specific instances, the sociologist will, of course, have to deal with economic or political matters, but he will do so in a way rather different from that of the economist or the political scientist. The scene that he contemplates is the same human scene that these other scientists concern themselves with. But the sociologist's angle of vision is different. When this is understood, it becomes clear that it makes little sense to try to stake out a special enclave within which the sociologist will carry on business in his own right. Like Wesley the sociologist will have to confess that his parish is the world. But unlike some latter-day Wesleyans he will gladly share this parish with others. There is, however, one traveler whose path the sociologist will cross more often than anyone else's on his journeys. This is the historian. Indeed, as soon as the sociologist turns from the present to the past, his preoccupations are very hard indeed to distinguish from those of the historian. [T]he sociological journey will be much impoverished unless it is punctuated frequently by conversation with that other particular traveler.

Any intellectual activity derives excitement from the moment it becomes a trail of discovery. . . . The excitement of sociology is [not always to penetrate] worlds that had previously been quite unknown . . . for instance, the world of crime, or the world of some bizarre religious sect, or the world fashioned by the exclusive concerns of some group such as medical specialists or military leaders or advertising executives. [M]uch of the time the sociologist moves in sectors of experience that are familiar to him and to most people in his society. He investigates communities, institutions, and activities that one can read about every day in the newspapers. Yet there is another excitement of discovery beckoning in his investigations. It is not the excitement of finding the familiar becoming transformed in it. The fascination of sociology lies in the fact that its perspective makes us see in a new light the very world in which we have lived all of our lives. This also constitutes a transformation of consciousness. Moreover, this transformation is more relevant existentially than that of many other intellectual disciplines, because it is more difficult to segregate in some special compartment of the mind. The astronomer does not live in the remote galaxies, and the nuclear physicist can, outside his laboratory, eat and laugh and marry and vote without thinking about the insides of the atom. The geologist looks at rocks only at appropriate times, and the linguist speaks English with his wife. The sociologist lives in society, on the job and off it. His own life, inevitably, is part of his subject matter. Men being what they are, sociologists too manage to segregate their professional insights from their everyday affairs. But it is a rather difficult feat to perform in good faith.

The sociologist moves in the common world of men, close to what most of them would call real. The categories he employs in his analyses are only refinements of the categories by which other men live—power, class, status, race, ethnicity. As a result, there is a deceptive simplicity and obviousness about some sociological investigations. One reads them, nods at the familiar scene, remarks that one has heard all this before and don't people have better things to do than to waste their time on truisms—until one is suddenly brought up against an insight that radically questions everything one had previously assumed about this familiar scene. This is the point at which one begins to sense the excitement of sociology.

Let us take a specific example. Imagine a sociology class in a Southern college where almost all the students are white Southerners. Imagine a lecture on the subject of the racial system of the South. The lecturer is talking here of matters that have been familiar to his students from the time of their infancy. Indeed, it may be that they are much more familiar with the minutiae of this system than he is. They are quite bored as a result. It seems to them that he is only using more pretentious words to describe what they already know. Thus he may use the term "caste," one commonly used now by American sociologists to describe the Southern racial system. But in explaining the term he shifts to traditional Hindu society, to make it clearer. He then goes on to analyze the magical beliefs inherent in caste tabus, the social dynamics of commensalism and connubium, the economic interests concealed within the system, the way in which religious beliefs relate to the tabus, the effects of the caste system upon the industrial development of the society and vice versa—all in India. But suddenly India is not very far away at all. The lecture then goes back to its Southern theme. The familiar now seems not quite so familiar any more. Questions are raised that are new, perhaps raised angrily, but raised all the same. And at least some of the students have begun to understand that there are functions involved in this business of race that they have not read about in the newspapers (at least not those in their hometowns) and that their parents have not told them—partly, at least, because neither the newspapers nor the parents knew about them.

It can be said that the first wisdom of sociology is this—things are not what they seem. This too is a deceptively simple statement. It ceases to be simple after a while. Social reality turns out to have many layers of meaning. The discovery of each new layer changes the perception of the whole.

Anthropologists use the term "culture shock" to describe the impact of a totally new culture upon a newcomer. In an extreme instance such shock will be experienced by the Western explorer who is told, halfway through dinner, that he is eating the nice old lady he had been chatting with the previous day—a shock with predictable physiological if not moral consequences. Most explorers no longer encounter cannibalism in their travels today. However, the first encounters with polygamy or with puberty rites or even with the way some nations drive their automobiles can be quite a shock to an American visitor. With the shock may go not only disapproval or disgust but a sense of excitement that things can *really* be that different from what they are at home.

To some extent, at least, this is the excitement of any first travel abroad. The experience of sociological discovery could be described as "culture shock" minus geographical displacement. In other words, the sociologist travels at home—with shocking results. He is unlikely to find that he is eating a nice old lady for dinner. But the discovery, for instance, that his own church has considerable money invested in the missile industry or that a few blocks from his home there are people who engage in cultic orgies may not be drastically different in emotional impact. Yet we would not want to imply that sociological discoveries are always or even usually outrageous to moral sentiment. Not at all. What they have in common with exploration in distant lands, however, is the sudden illumination of new and unsuspected facets of human existence in society. . . .

People who like to avoid shocking discoveries, who prefer to believe that society is just what they were taught in Sunday School, who like the safety of the rules and the maxims of what Alfred Schutz has called the "world-taken-for-granted," should stay away from sociology. People who feel no temptation before closed doors, who have no curiosity about human beings, who are content to admire scenery without wondering about the people who live in those houses on the other side of that river, should probably stay away from sociology. They will find it unpleasant or, at any rate, unrewarding. People who are interested in human beings only if they can change, convert, or reform them should also be warned, for they will find sociology much less useful than they hoped. And people whose interest is mainly in their own conceptual constructions will do just as well to turn to the study of little white mice. Sociology will be satisfying, in the long run, only to those who can think of nothing more entrancing than to watch men and to understand things human.

It may now be clear that we have, albeit deliberately, understated the case in the title of this chapter. [The chapter title from which this selection is taken is "Sociology as an Individual Pastime."] To be sure, sociology is an individual pastime in the sense that it interests some men and bores others. Some like to observe human beings, others to experiment with mice. The world is big enough to hold all kinds and there is no logical priority for one interest as against another. But the word "pastime" is weak in describing what we mean. Sociology is more like a passion. The sociological perspective is more like a demon that possesses one, that drives one compellingly, again and again, to the questions that are its own. An introduction to sociology is, therefore, an invitation to a very special kind of passion.

2 What Is Sociology? Comparing Sociology and the Social Sciences

JAMES M. HENSLIN

Introductory students often wrestle with the question of what sociology is. If you continue your sociological studies, however, that vagueness of definition—"Sociology is the study of society" or "Sociology is the study of social groups"—that frequently so bothers introductory students will come to be appreciated as one of sociology's strengths and one of its essential attractions. That sociology encompasses almost all human behavior is, indeed, precisely the appeal that draws many to sociology.

To help make clearer at the outset what sociology is, however, Henslin compares and contrasts sociology with the other social sciences. After examining similarities and differences in their approaches to understanding human behavior, he looks at how social scientists from these related academic disciplines would approach the study of juvenile delinquency.

Science and the Human Desire for Explanation

HUMAN BEINGS ARE FASCINATED with the world in which they live, and they aspire to develop ways to explain their experiences. People appear to have always felt this fascination—along with the intense desire to unravel the world's mysteries—for people in ancient times also attempted to explain their worlds. Despite the severe limitations that confronted them, the ancients explored the natural or physical world, constructing explanations that satisfied them. They also developed an understanding of their social world, the world of people with all their activities and myriad ways of dealing with one another. The ancients, however, mixed magic and superstition to explain their observations.

Today, we are no less fascinated with the world within which we live out our lives. We also investigate both the mundane and the esoteric. We cast a quizzical eye at the common rocks we find embedded in the earth, as well as at some rare variety of insect found only in an almost inaccessible region of remote Tibet. We subject our contemporary world to the constant probings of the instruments and machines we have developed to extend our senses. In our attempts to decipher our observations, we no longer are satisfied with traditional explanations of origins or of relationships. No longer do we unquestioningly accept explanations that earlier generations took for granted. Making observations with the aid of our new technology—such as electronic microscopes, satellites, and the latest generation of computers and software—we derive testable conclusions concerning the nature of our world.

As the ancients could only wish to do, we have been able to expand our objective study of the world beyond the confines of this planet. In our relentless pursuit after knowledge, we no longer are limited to speculation concerning the nature of the stars and planets. In the last couple of centuries the telescope has enabled us to make detailed and repetitive observations of the planets and other heavenly bodies. From these observations we have reached conclusions startlingly different from those which people traditionally drew concerning the relative place of the earth in our galaxy and the universe. In just the past few years, by means of space technology, we have been able to extend our senses, as it were, beyond anything we had before dreamed possible. We now are able to reach out by means of our spaceships, observational satellites, and space platforms to record data from other planets and—by means of computer-enhanced graphics—to gain a changing vision of our physical world. We have also been able to dig up and return to the earth samples of soil from the surface of the moon as well as to send probes to the radiation and magnetic belts of Jupiter, over a distance so great (or, we could say, with our technology still so limited) that they must travel eighteen months before they can send reports back to earth. Having discovered evidence of water and recent volcanic activity on Mars, we have begun to draw up plans to dig into its surface to find out if life exists on our "sister" planet.

A generation or so ago such feats existed only in the minds of "mad" scientists, who at that time seemed irrelevant to the public but whose ideas today are producing fascinating and frequently fearful consequences for our life on earth. Some of those scientists are giving serious thought to colonizing space, opening still another area of exciting exploration, but one whose consequences probably will be only inadequately anticipated. Others are drawing plans for real space wars, with potential outcomes so terrifying we can barely imagine them. For good and evil, science directly impinges on our contemporary life in society, leaving none of us unaffected.

The Natural and the Social Sciences

In satisfying our basic curiosities about the world, we have developed two parallel sets of sciences, each identified by its distinct subject matter. The first is called the *natural sciences,* the intellectual-academic endeavors designed to comprehend, explain, and predict the events in our natural environment. The endeavors of the natural scientists are divided into specialized fields of research and are given names on the basis of their particular subject matter—such as biology, geology, chemistry, and physics. These fields of knowledge are further subdivided into even more highly specialized areas, each with a further narrowing of content—biology into botany and zoology, geology into mineralogy and geomorphology, chemistry into its organic and inorganic branches, and physics into biophysics and quantum mechanics. Each of these divisions, in turn, is subdivided into further specialized areas. Each specialized area of investigation examines a particular "slice" of the natural world.

In their pursuit of a more adequate understanding of their world, people have not limited themselves to investigating nature. They have also developed a second primary area of science that focuses on the social world. These, the *social sciences,* examine human relationships. Just as the natural sciences are an attempt to understand objectively the world of nature, so the social sciences are an attempt to understand objectively the social world. Just as the world of nature contains ordered (or lawful) relationships that are not obvious but must be abstracted from nature through controlled observations, so the ordered relationships of the human or social world are not obvious but must be abstracted by means of controlled and repeated observations.

Like the natural sciences, the social sciences also are divided into specialized fields based on their subject matter. The usual or typical divisions of the social sciences are anthropology, economics, political science, psychology, and sociology, with history sometimes included in the enumeration, depending primarily on the preference of the person drawing the list. To be inclusive, I shall count history as a social science.

Like the natural sciences, the social sciences also are divided into further specialized fields, with these branches being named on the basis of their particular focus. Anthropology is divided into cultural and physical anthropology, economics into its macro and micro specialties, history into ancient and modern, political science into theoretical and applied, psychology into clinical and experimental, while sociology has its quantitative and qualitative branches. Except for sociology, we shall not be concerned with these finer divisions.

Sociology Contrasted with the Other Social Sciences

Since our focus is sociology, we shall take a brief look at each of the social sciences and contrast each with sociology. I should point out that the differences

I shall elaborate are not always so clear in actual practice, for much that so-cial scientists do as they practice their crafts greatly blurs the distinctions I am making.

Let's begin with *history,* the social science focusing on past events. His-torians attempt to unearth the facts surrounding some event that they feel is of social significance. They attempt to establish the context, or social milieu, of the event—the important people, ideas, institutions, social movements, or preceding events that in some way appear to have influenced the outcome they desire to explain. From this context, which they reconstruct from records of the past, they abstract what they consider to be the most important ele-ments, or *variables,* that caused the event. By means of those "causal" factors or variables, historians "explain" the past.

Political science focuses on politics or government. The political scientist studies the ways people govern themselves—the various forms of government, their structures, and their relationships to other institutions of society. The political scientist is especially interested in how people attain ruling positions in their society, how they maintain those positions once they secure them, and the consequences of the activities of rulers for those who are governed. In studying a government that has a constitutional electorate, such as ours, the political scientist is especially concerned with voting behavior.

Economics is another discipline in the social sciences that concentrates on a single social institution. Economists study the production, distribution, and allocation of the material goods and services of a society. They want to know what goods are being produced at what rate at what cost, and the variables that determine who gets what. They are also interested in the choices that under-lie production—for example, why with limited resources a certain item is being produced instead of another. Some economists, but not nearly enough in my judgment, also are interested in the consequences for human life of the facts of production, distribution, and allocation of goods and services.

The traditional focus of *anthropology* has been on tribal and peasant peo-ples. Although there are other emphases, the primary concern of anthropol-ogists is to understand *culture,* the total way of life of a group of people. Culture includes (1) the artifacts people produce, such as their tools, art, and weapons; (2) the group's structure, that is, the hierarchy and other group pat-terns that determine people's relationships to their fellow members; (3) ideas and values, especially the belief system of a people, and their effects on peo-ple's lives; and (4) their forms of communication, especially their language. The anthropologists' traditional focus on past societies and contemporary tribal peoples has widened, and some anthropologists study groups in indus-trialized and post-industrialized settings. Anthropologists who focus on con-temporary societies are practically indistinguishable from sociologists.

Psychology concentrates on processes occurring within the individual, within what they call the "skin-bound organism." The psychologist is primarily concerned with what is sometimes referred to as the "mind." Although still regularly used by the public, this term is used with reservation by some psychologists, probably, among other reasons, because no physical entity can be located that exactly corresponds to "mind." Psychologists typically study such phenomena as perception, attitudes, and values. They are also especially interested in personality, in mental aberration (or mental illness), and in how individuals cope with the problems they face.

Sociology is like history in that sociologists also attempt to establish the social contexts that influence people. Sociology is also similar to political science in that sociologists, too, study how people govern one another, especially the consequences for people's lives of various forms of government. Sociology is like economics in that sociologists also are highly interested in what happens to the goods and services of a society, especially the social consequences of production and distribution. Sociology is similar to anthropology in that sociologists also study culture and are particularly interested in the social consequences of material goods, group structure, and belief systems, as well as how people communicate with one another. Sociology is like psychology in that sociologists also study how people adjust to the problems and challenges they face in life.

With these overall similarities, then, where are the differences? Unlike historians, sociologists are primarily concerned with events in the present. Unlike political scientists and economists, sociologists do not concentrate on only a single social institution. Unlike anthropologists, sociologists primarily focus on contemporary societies. And unlike psychologists, to determine what influences people sociologists stress variables external to the individual.

The Example of Juvenile Delinquency

Because all the social sciences focus on human behavior, they differ from one another not so much in the content of what each studies but, rather, in what the social scientists look for when they conduct their studies. It is basically their approaches, their orientations, or their emphases that differentiate the social sciences. Accordingly, to make clearer the differences between them, it might be helpful to look at how different social scientists might approach the same topic. We shall use juvenile delinquency as our example.

Historians interested in juvenile delinquency would examine juvenile delinquency in some particular past setting, such as New York City in the 1920s or Los Angeles in the 1950s. The historian would try to interpret the delinquency by stressing the social context (or social milieu) of the period. For example, if delinquent gangs in New York City in the 1920s were the focus, historians might emphasize the social disruption caused by World War I; the problems of unassimilated, recently arrived ethnic groups; competition and rivalry for social standing among those ethnic groups; intergenerational conflict; the national, state, and local political and economic situation; and so on. The historian might also document the number of gangs, as well as their ethnic makeup. He or she would then produce a history of juvenile delinquency in New York City in the 1920s.

Political scientists are less likely to be interested in juvenile delinquency. But if they were, they would want to know how the existence of juvenile gangs is related to politics. For example, are the children of people who have less access to political decision making more likely to join gangs? Or political scientists might study the power structure within a particular gang by identifying its leaders and followers. They might then compare one gang with another, perhaps even drawing analogies with the political structure of some legitimate group.

Economists also are not likely to study delinquent gangs or juvenile delinquency. But if they did, they, of course, would emphasize the economic aspects of delinquency. They might determine how material goods, such as "loot," are allocated within a gang. But they would be more inclined to focus on delinquency in general, emphasizing the relationship of gangs to economic factors in the country. Economists might wish to examine the effects of economic conditions, such as booms and busts, on the formation of gangs or on the incidence or prevalence of delinquency. They might also wish to determine the cost of juvenile delinquency to the nation in terms of property stolen and destroyed and wages paid to police and social workers.

Anthropologists are likely to be highly interested in studying juvenile delinquency and the formation of juvenile gangs. If anthropologists were to study a particular gang, they might examine the implements of delinquency, such as tools used in car theft or in burglary. They would focus on the social organization of the gang, perhaps looking at its power structure. They would study the belief system of the group to see how it supports the group's delinquent activities. They would also concentrate on the ways in which group members communicate with one another, especially their *argot,* or special language. Anthropologists would stress the larger cultural context in order to see what it is about a culture, such as the ways in which it marks entry into manhood, that leads to the formation of such groups. They would compare their findings with what anthropologists have discovered about delinquency in other cultures. In making such a *cross-cultural comparison,* they probably would note that juvenile delinquency is not a universal phenomenon but is largely a characteristic of industrialized and post-industrialized societies. They would point out that these societies require many years of formal education for their youth. This postpones the age at which young men and women are allowed to assume the role of adults, and it is during this "in-between status" that delinquency occurs. The emphasis given by anthropologists in such a study, then, would be true to their calling; that is, anthropologists would be focusing on culture.

Psychologists also have high interest in juvenile delinquency. When psychologists approach the subject, however, they tend to focus on what exists *within* the delinquent. They might test the assumption (or *hypothesis*) that, compared with their followers, gang leaders have more outgoing personality traits, or greater hostility and aggressiveness. Psychologists might also compare the personality traits of adolescent males who join gangs with boys from the same neighborhood or in the general population who do not become gang members. They might give a series of tests to determine whether gang members are more insecure, dominant, hostile, or aggressive than nonmembers.

Sociologists are also interested in most of the aspects emphasized by the other social scientists. Sociologists, however, ordinarily are not concerned with a particular gang from some past period, as historians might be, although they, too, try to identify the relevant social context. Sociologists focus on the power structure of gangs, as would political scientists, and they also are interested in certain aspects of property, as an economist might be. But sociologists would be more interested in the gang members' attitudes toward property, why delinquents feel it is legitimate to steal and vandalize, and how they divide up the property they steal.

Sociologists would also approach delinquency in a way quite similar to that of anthropologists and be interested in the same sorts of things. But sociologists would place strong emphasis on *social class* (which is based on occupation, income, and education). They would want to know if there is greater likelihood that a person will join a gang if his or her parents have little education, and how gang membership varies with income. If sociologists found that delinquency varies with education, age, sex, religion, income, or race–ethnicity, they would want to know the reasons for this. Do children of unskilled workers have a greater chance of becoming delinquent than the children of doctors and lawyers? If so, why?

The sociologists' emphases also separate them from psychologists. Sociologists are inclined to ignore personality, the primary focus of psychologists, and instead to stress the effects of social class on recruitment into delinquency. Sociologists also examine group structure and interaction. For example, both sociologists and psychologists would be interested in differences between a gang's leaders and followers. To discover these, however, sociologists are not likely to give paper-and-pencil tests. They are much more likely to observe *face-to-face interaction* among gang members (what they do in each other's presence). Sociologists would want to see if leaders and followers uphold the group's values differently; who suggests their activities; and who does what when they do them—whether the activity be simply some form of recreation or a criminal act. For example, do leaders maintain their leadership by committing more acts of daring and bravery than their followers?

Compared with other social scientists, sociologists are more likely to emphasize the routine activities of the police, the courts, and changing norms. The police approach their job with preconceived ideas about who is likely to commit crimes and who is not. Their ideas are based on what they have experienced "on the streets," as well as on stereotypes nurtured within their occupation. The police typically view some people (usually lower-class males living in some particular area of the city) to be more apt to commit crimes than males from other areas of the city, males from a higher social class, or females in general. How do the police develop their ideas? How are such stereotypes supported in their occupational subculture? What effects do they have on the police and on those whom they encounter? In other words, sociologists are deeply interested in finding out how the police define people and how those definitions help to determine whom the police arrest.

Sociologists are also interested in what occurs following an arrest. Prosecutors wield much discretion. For the same act they can level a variety of charges. They can charge an individual with first degree burglary, second degree burglary, breaking and entering, or merely trespassing. Sociologists want to know how such decisions are made, as well as their effects on the lives of those charged with crimes. Sociologists also study what happens when an individual comes before a judge, especially the outcome of the trial by the type of offense and the sex, age, or race–ethnicity of the offender. They also focus on the effects of detention and incarceration, as well as how people adjust when they are released back into the community.

Norms, the behaviors that people expect of others, obviously change over time. What was considered proper behavior a generation ago is certainly not the same as what is considered proper today. Consequently, the law changes, and acts considered to be law violations at one time are not necessarily considered criminal at another time. Similarly, acts not now considered criminal may become law violations at a later date. For example, at one point in our history drinking alcohol in public at age sixteen was within the law in many communities, while today it would be an act of delinquency. In the same way, a person under sixteen who is on the streets after 10 P.M. unaccompanied by an adult is breaking the law in some communities. But if the law is changed or if the sixteen-year-old has a birthday or moves to a different community, the same act is not a violation of the law. With marijuana, the case is similar. Millions of Americans break the law when they smoke grass, but for several years Alaska allowed possession of marijuana for personal use, a legal right later revoked.

Perhaps more than any of the other social scientists, the sociologist maintains a crucial interest in the effects of changing legal definitions in determining what people are arrested for and charged with. In effect, sociologists are interested in what juvenile delinquency is in the first place. They take the definition of delinquency not as obvious but as problematic, something to be studied in the context of lawmaking, lawbreaking, and the workaday world of the judicial system.

By means of this example of juvenile delinquency, it is easy to see that the social sciences greatly overlap one another. Sociology, however, is an *overarching* social science, because sociologists are, for the most part, interested in the same things that other social scientists are interested in. They are, however, not as limited in their scope or focus as are the others. Except for its traditional concerns with tribal societies, anthropology is similarly broad in its treatment of human behavior.

Types of Sociology: Structural and Interactional

As sociologists study human behavior, they focus on people's *patterned* relationships; that is, sociologists study the recurring aspects of human behavior. This leads them to focus on two principal aspects of life in society: (1) *group membership* (including the *institutions* of society, the customary arrangements by which humans attempt to solve their perennial problems, such as the need for social order or dealing with sickness and death) and (2) *face-to-face interaction,* that is, what people do when they are in one another's presence. These twin foci lead to two principal forms of sociology, the structural and the interactional.

In the first type of sociology, *structural,* the focus is placed on the *group.* Structural sociologists are interested in determining how membership in a group, such as a religion, influences people's behavior and attitudes, such as how they vote, or perhaps how education affects the stand they take on social issues. For example, are there voting differences among Roman Catholics, Lutherans, Jews, Baptists, and charismatics? If so, on what issues? And within the same religion, do people's voting patterns differ according to their income and education?

Also of interest to sociologists who focus on group memberships would be how people's attitudes toward social issues (or their voting) differ according to their age, sex, occupation, race or ethnicity, or even geographical residence—

both by region of the country and by urban or rural setting. As you probably have gathered, the term "group" is being used in an extended sense. People do not have to belong to an actual group to be counted; sociologists simply "group" together people who have similar characteristics, such as age, height, weight, education, or, if it is thought relevant, even those who take their vacations in the winter versus those who take them during the summer. These are known as *aggregates*, people grouped together for the purpose of social research because of characteristics they have in common.

Note that sociologists with this first orientation concentrate on how group memberships affect people's attitudes and behavior. Ordinarily they do not simply want to know the proportion of Roman Catholics who vote Democratic (or, in sociological jargon, "the correlation between religious-group membership and voting behavior") but may try to determine what difference being a Roman Catholic makes in people's dating practices, in premarital sex, in birth control, in abortion, in what they do for recreation, or in how they treat their spouses and rear their children.

In the second type of sociology, the *interactional*, greater emphasis is placed on individuals. Some sociologists with this orientation focus on what people do when they are in the presence of one another. They directly observe their behavior, recording the interaction by taking notes or by using tape, video, or film. Other sociologists tap people's attitudes and behaviors more indirectly by interviewing them. Still others examine social records—from diaries and letters to court transcripts, even memorabilia of pop culture from *Playboy* and *Playgirl* to science fiction and comic books. They may systematically observe soap operas, children's cartoons, police dramas, situation comedies, or MTV. Sociologists who focus on interaction develop ways of classifying the *data*—what they have observed, read, recorded, or been told. From their direct and indirect observations of people, they draw conclusions about their attitudes and what significantly affects their lives.

Types of Sociology: Qualitative and Quantitative

Another important division among sociologists is based on the *methods* they use to study people. Some sociologists are statistically oriented, attempting to determine *numbers* to represent people's patterns of behavior. They stress that proper measurement by the use of statistical techniques is necessary if one is to understand human behavior. Many refer to this emphasis as *quantitative* sociology.

A group of sociologists who strongly disagree with this position concentrate instead on the *meaning* of what is happening to people. They focus on how people construct their worlds, how they develop their ideas and attitudes, and how they communicate with one another. They attempt to determine how people's meanings (called symbols, mental constructs, ideas, and stereotypes) affect their ideas about the self and their relationships to one another. Many refer to this emphasis as *qualitative* sociology.

Conclusion

From chicken to sociology, there are many ways of dividing up anything in life. And just as those most familiar with chicken may disagree about the proper way of cutting up a chicken, so those most familiar with sociology will disagree about how to slice up sociology. From my experiences, however, the divisions I have presented here appear to reflect accurately what is taking place in sociology today. Inevitably, however, other sociologists would disagree with this classification and probably would present another way of looking at our discipline. Nonetheless, I think you will find this presentation helpful for visualizing sociology.

It is similarly the case when it comes to evaluating the divisions within sociology. These are *not* neutral matters for sociologists. For example, almost all sociologists *feel strongly* about whether a qualitative or quantitative approach is the *proper* way to study human behavior.

Certainly my own biases strongly favor qualitative sociology. For me, there simply is no contest. I see qualitative sociology as more accurately reflecting people's lives, as being more closely tied into the realities that people experience—how they make sense of their worlds, how they cope with their problems, and how they try to maintain some semblance of order in their lives. Because I find this approach fascinatingly worthwhile, the qualitative approach is stressed in this book. You should note, however, that many sociologists find the quantitative approach to be the most rewarding way to study social life.

Wherever and whenever people come into one another's presence, there are potential data for the sociologist. Sunday School and the bar, the street and the classroom—even the bedroom—all provide material for sociologists to observe and analyze. Nothing is really taboo for them. Sociologists regularly raise questions about most aspects of social life. Simply overhearing an ordinary conversation—or catching a glimpse of some unusual happening—is enough to whet the curiosity of many sociologists. In following that curiosity, they can simply continue to "overhear" conversations, but this time purposely, or they can conduct an elaborate study with a scientifically selected random sample backed by huge fundings from some agency. What sociologists study can be as socially significant as an urban riot or as common but personally significant as two people greeting with a handshake or parting with a kiss.

In this sense, then, the world belongs to the sociologist—for to the sociologist everything is fair game. The all-inclusiveness of sociology, indeed, is what makes sociology so intrinsically fascinating for many: Sociology offers a framework that provides a penetrating perspective on almost everything that we do in life.

Some of you who are being introduced to sociology through this essay may find the sociological approach to understanding human life rewarding enough to take other courses in sociology and, after college, to be attracted to books of sociological content. A few, perhaps, may even make sociology your life's vocation and thus embark on a lifelong journey that takes you to the far corners of human endeavor, as well as to people's more familiar pursuits. Certainly some of us, already captivated by sociology's enchantment, have experienced an unfolding panorama of intellectual delight in the midst of an intriguing exploration of the social world. And, in this enticing process, we have the added pleasure of constantly discovering and rediscovering our changing selves.

3 The Promise

C. WRIGHT MILLS

The *sociological imagination* is seeing how the unique historical circumstances of a particular society affect people and, at the same
time, seeing how people affect history. Every individual lives out his
or her life in a particular society, with the historical circumstances of
that society greatly influencing what that individual becomes. People
thus shaped by their society contribute, in turn, to the formation of
their society and to the course of its history.

It is this quality of mind (termed the *sociological imagination* by
Mills and the *sociological perspective* by others) that is presented for
exploration in the readings of this book. As this intersection of biography and history becomes more apparent to you, your own sociological imagination will grow, bringing you a deepened and broadened
understanding of social life—and of your own place within it.

NOWADAYS, MEN OFTEN FEEL that their private lives are a se-
ries of traps. They sense that, within their everyday worlds, they cannot overcome their troubles, and, in this feeling, they are quite correct: What ordinary
men are directly aware of and what they try to do are bounded by the private
orbits in which they live; their visions and their powers are limited to the close-
up scenes of job, family, neighborhood; in other milieux, they move vicariously and remain spectators. And the more aware they become, however
vaguely, of ambitions and of threats that transcend their immediate locales,
the more trapped they seem to feel.

Underlying this sense of being trapped are seemingly impersonal changes
in the very structure of continent-wide societies. The facts of contemporary
history are also facts about the success and the failure of individual men and
women. When a society is industrialized, a peasant becomes a worker; a feudal lord is liquidated or becomes a businessman. When classes rise or fall, a
man is employed or unemployed; when the rate of investment goes up or
down, a man takes new heart or goes broke. When wars happen, an insurance
salesman becomes a rocket launcher; a store clerk, a radar man; a wife lives
alone; a child grows up without a father. Neither the life of an individual nor
the history of a society can be understood without understanding both.

Yet, men do not usually define the troubles they endure in terms of historical change and institutional contradiction. The well-being they enjoy, they

do not usually impute to the big ups and downs of the societies in which they live. Seldom aware of the intricate connection between the patterns of their own lives and the course of world history, ordinary men do not usually know what this connection means for the kinds of men they are becoming and for the kinds of history-making in which they might take part. They do not possess the quality of mind essential to grasp the interplay of man and society, of biography and history, of self and world. They cannot cope with their personal troubles in such ways as to control the structural transformations that usually lie behind them.

Surely, it is no wonder. In what period have so many men been so totally exposed at so fast a pace to such earthquakes of change? That Americans have not known such catastrophic changes as have the men and women of other societies is due to historical facts that are now quickly becoming "merely history." The history that now affects every man is world history. Within this scene and this period, in the course of a single generation, one-sixth of mankind is transformed from all that is feudal and backward into all that is modern, advanced, and fearful. Political colonies are freed; new and less visible forms of imperialism, installed. Revolutions occur; men feel the intimate grip of new kinds of authority. Totalitarian societies rise, and are smashed to bits—or succeed fabulously. . . . After two centuries of hope, even formal democracy is restricted to a quite small portion of mankind. Everywhere in the underdeveloped world, ancient ways of life are broken up and vague expectations become urgent demands. Everywhere in the overdeveloped world, the means of authority and of violence become total in scope and bureaucratic in form. . . .

The very shaping of history now outpaces the ability of men to orient themselves in accordance with cherished values. And which values? Even when they do not panic, men often sense that older ways of feeling and thinking have collapsed, and that newer beginnings are ambiguous to the point of moral stasis. Is it any wonder that ordinary men feel they cannot cope with the larger worlds with which they are so suddenly confronted? That they cannot understand the meaning of their epoch for their own lives? That—in defense of selfhood—they become morally insensible, trying to remain altogether private men? Is it any wonder that they come to be possessed by a sense of the trap?

It is not only information that they need—in this Age of Fact, information often dominates their attention and overwhelms their capacities to assimilate it. It is not only the skills of reason that they need—although their struggles to acquire these often exhaust their limited moral energy.

What they need, and what they feel they need, is a quality of mind that will help them to use information and to develop reason in order to achieve lucid summations of what is going on in the world and of what may be happening within themselves. It is this quality, I am going to contend, that journalists and scholars, artists and publics, scientists and editors are coming to expect of what may be called the sociological imagination.

The sociological imagination enables its possessor to understand the larger historical scene in terms of its meaning for the inner life and the external career of a variety of individuals. It enables him to take into account how individuals, in the welter of their daily experience, often become falsely conscious of their social positions. Within that welter, the framework of modern society is sought, and within that framework the psychologies of a variety of men and women are formulated. By such means, the personal uneasiness of individuals is focused upon explicit troubles, and the indifference of publics is transformed into involvement with public issues.

The first fruit of this imagination—and the first lesson of the social science that embodies it—is the idea that the individual can understand his own experience and gauge his own fate only by locating himself within his period, that he can know his own chances in life only by becoming aware of those of all individuals in his circumstances. In many ways, it is a terrible lesson; in many ways, a magnificent one. We do not know the limits of man's capacities for supreme effort or willing degradation, for agony or glee, for pleasurable brutality or the sweetness of reason. But in our time we have come to know that the limits of "human nature" are frighteningly broad. We have come to know that every individual lives, from one generation to the next, in some society; that he lives out a biography, and that he lives it out within some historical sequence. By the fact of his living he contributes, however minutely, to the shaping of this society and to the course of its history, even as he is made by society and by its historical push and shove.

The sociological imagination enables us to grasp history and biography and the relations between the two within society. That is its task and its promise. To recognize this task and this promise is the mark of the classic social analyst. It is characteristic of Herbert Spencer—turgid, polysyllabic, comprehensive; of E. A. Ross—graceful, muckraking, upright; of Auguste Comte and Emile Durkheim; of the intricate and subtle Karl Mannheim. It is the quality of all that is intellectually excellent in Karl Marx; it is the clue to Thorstein Veblen's brilliant and ironic insight, to Joseph Schumpeter's many-sided constructions of reality; it is the basis of the psychological sweep of W. E. H. Lecky no less than of the profundity and clarity of Max Weber. And it is the signal of what is best in contemporary studies of man and society.

No social study that does not come back to the problems of biography, of history, and of their intersections within a society has completed its intellectual journey. Whatever the specific problems of the classic social analysts, however limited or however broad the features of social reality they have examined, those who have been imaginatively aware of the promise of their work have consistently asked three sorts of questions:

1. What is the structure of this particular society as a whole? What are its essential components, and how are they related to one another? How does it differ from other varieties of social order? Within it, what is the meaning of any particular feature for its continuance and for its change?

2. Where does this society stand in human history? What are the mechanics by which it is changing? What is its place within, and its meaning for, the development of humanity as a whole? How does any particular feature we are examining affect, and how is it affected by, the historical period in which it moves? And this period—what are its essential features? How does it differ from other periods? What are its characteristic ways of history-making?

3. What varieties of men and women now prevail in this society and in this period? And what varieties are coming to prevail? In what ways are they selected and formed, liberated and repressed, made sensitive and blunted? What kinds of "human nature" are revealed in the conduct and character we observe in this society in this period? And what is the meaning for "human nature" of each and every feature of the society we are examining?

Whether the point of interest is a great power state or a minor literary mood, a family, a prison, a creed—these are the kinds of questions the best social analysts have asked. They are the intellectual pivots of classic studies of man in society—and they are the questions inevitably raised by any mind possessing the sociological imagination. For that imagination is the capacity to shift from one perspective to another—from the political to the psychological; from examination of a single family to comparative assessment of the national budgets of the world; from the theological school to the military establishment; from considerations of an oil industry to studies of contemporary poetry. It is the capacity to range from the most impersonal and remote transformations to the most intimate features of the human self—and to see the relations between the two. Back of its use, there is always the urge to know the social and historical meaning of the individual in the society and in the period in which he has his quality and his being.

That, in brief, is why it is by means of the sociological imagination that men now hope to grasp what is going on in the world, and to understand what is happening in themselves as minute points of the intersections of biography and history within society. In large part, contemporary man's self-conscious view of himself as at least an outsider, if not a permanent stranger, rests upon an absorbed realization of social relativity and of the transformative power of history. The sociological imagination is the most fruitful form of this self-consciousness. By its use, men whose mentalities have swept only a series of limited orbits often come to feel as if suddenly awakened in a house with which they had only supposed themselves to be familiar. Correctly or incorrectly, they often come to feel that they can now provide themselves with adequate summations, cohesive assessments, comprehensive orientations. Older decisions that once appeared sound now seem to them products of a mind unaccountably dense. Their capacity for astonishment is made lively again. They acquire a new way of thinking; they experience a transvaluation of values. In a word, by their reflection and by their sensibility, they realize the cultural meaning of the social sciences.

Perhaps the most fruitful distinction with which the sociological imagination works is between the "personal troubles of milieu" and the "public issues of social structure." This distinction is an essential tool of the sociological imagination and a feature of all classic work in social science.

Troubles occur within the character of the individual and within the range of his immediate relations with others; they have to do with his self and with those limited areas of social life of which he is directly and personally aware. Accordingly, the statement and the resolution of troubles properly lie within the individual as a biographical entity and within the scope of his immediate milieu—the social setting that is directly open to his personal experience and, to some extent, his willful activity. A trouble is a private matter: Values cherished by an individual are felt by him to be threatened.

Issues have to do with matters that transcend these local environments of the individual and the range of his inner life. They have to do with the organization of many such milieu into the institutions of a historical society as a whole, with the ways in which various milieu overlap and interpenetrate to form the larger structure of social and historical life. An issue is a public matter: Some value cherished by publics is felt to be threatened. Often, there is a debate about what that value really is and about what it is that really threatens it. This debate is often without focus, if only because it is the very nature of an issue, unlike even widespread trouble, that it cannot very well be defined in terms of the immediate and everyday environments of ordinary men. An issue, in fact, often involves a crisis in institutional arrangements, and often, too, it involves what Marxists call "contradictions" or "antagonisms."

In these terms, consider unemployment. When, in a city of 100,000, only one man is unemployed, that is his personal trouble, and for its relief we properly look to the character of the man, his skills, and his immediate opportunities. But when, in a nation of 50 million employees, 15 million men are unemployed, that is an issue, and we may not hope to find its solution within the range of opportunities open to any one individual. The very structure of opportunities has collapsed. Both the correct statement of the problem and range of possible solutions require us to consider the economic and political institutions of the society, and not merely the personal situation and character of a scatter of individuals.

Consider war. The personal problem of war, when it occurs, may be how to survive it or how to die in it with honor; how to make money out of it; how to climb into the higher safety of the military apparatus; or how to contribute to the war's termination. In short, according to one's values, to find a set of milieux and within it to survive the war or make one's death in it meaningful. But the structural issues of war have to do with its causes; with what types of men its throws up into command; with its effects upon economic and political, family and religious institutions; with the unorganized irresponsibility of a world of nation-states.

Consider marriage. Inside a marriage, a man and a woman may experience personal troubles; but, when the divorce rate during the first four years of marriage is 250 out of every 1,000 attempts, this is an indication of a structural issue having to do with the institutions of marriage and the family and other institutions that bear upon them.

Or consider the metropolis—the horrible, beautiful, ugly, magnificent sprawl of the great city. For many upper-class people, the personal solution to the problem of the city is to have an apartment with private garage under it in the heart of the city, and forty miles out, a house by Henry Hill, garden by Garrett Eckbo, on a hundred acres of private land. In these two controlled environments—with a small staff at each end and a private helicopter connection—most people could solve many of the problems of personal milieux caused by the facts of the city. But all this, however splendid, does not solve the public issues that the structural fact of the city poses. What should be done with this wonderful monstrosity? Break it all up into scattered units, combining residence and work? Refurbish it as it stands? Or, after evacuation, dynamite it and build new cities according to new plans in new places? What should those plans be? And who is to decide and to accomplish whatever choice is made? These are structural issues; to confront them and to solve them requires us to consider political and economic issues that affect innumerable milieux.

Insofar as an economy is so arranged that slumps occur, the problem of unemployment becomes incapable of personal solution. Insofar as war is inherent in the nation-state system and in the uneven industrialization of the world, the ordinary individual in his restricted milieu will be powerless— with or without psychiatric aid—to solve the troubles this system or lack of system imposes upon him. Insofar as the family as an institution turns women into darling little slaves and men into their chief providers and unweaned dependents, the problem of a satisfactory marriage remains incapable of purely private solution. Insofar as the overdeveloped megalopolis and the overdeveloped automobile are built-in features of the overdeveloped society, the issues of urban living will not be solved by personal ingenuity and private wealth.

What we experience in various and specific milieu, I have noted, is often caused by structural changes. Accordingly, to understand the changes of many personal milieu, we are required to look beyond them. And the number and variety of such structural changes increase as the institutions within which we live become more embracing and more intricately connected with one another. To be aware of the idea of social structure and to use it with sensibility is to be capable of tracing such linkages among a great variety of milieu. To be able to do that is to possess the sociological imagination.

What are the major issues for publics and the key troubles of private individuals in our time? To formulate issues and troubles, we must ask what values are cherished yet threatened, and what values are cherished and supported, by the characterizing trends of our period. In the case both of threat and of support, we must ask what salient contradictions of structure may be involved.

When people cherish some set of values and do not feel any threat to them, they experience *well-being*. When they cherish values but *do* feel them to be threatened, they experience a *crisis*—either as a personal trouble or as a public issue. And, if all their values seem involved, they feel the total threat of panic.

But suppose people are neither aware of any cherished values nor experience any threat? That is the experience of *indifference*, which, if it seems to involve all their values, becomes apathy. Suppose, finally, they are unaware of any cherished values, but still are very much aware of a threat? That is the experience of *uneasiness*, of anxiety, which, if it is total enough, becomes a deadly, unspecified malaise.

Ours is a time of uneasiness and indifference—not yet formulated in such ways as to permit the work of reason and the play of sensibility. Instead of troubles—defined in terms of values and threats—there is often the misery of vague uneasiness; instead of explicit issues, there is often merely the beat feeling that all is somehow not right. Neither the values threatened nor whatever threatens them has been stated; in short, they have not been carried to the point of decision. Much less have they been formulated as problems of social science. . . .

We are frequently told that the problems of our decade, or even the crises of our period, have shifted from the external realm of economics and now have to do with the quality of individual life—in fact, with the question of whether there is soon going to be anything that can properly be called individual life. Not child labor but comic books, not poverty but mass leisure, are at the center of concern. Many great public issues as well as many private troubles are described in terms of "psychiatric"—often, it seems in a pathetic attempt to avoid the large issues and problems of modern society. Often, this statement seems to rest upon a provincial narrowing of interest to the Western societies, or even to the United States—thus ignoring two-thirds of mankind; often, too, it arbitrarily divorces the individual life from the larger institutions within which that life is enacted, and which on occasion bear upon it more grievously than do the intimate environments of childhood.

Problems of leisure, for example, cannot even be stated without considering problems of work. Family troubles over comic books cannot be formulated as problems without considering the plight of the contemporary family in its new relations with the newer institutions of the social structure. Neither leisure nor its debilitating uses can be understood as problems without recognition of the extent to which malaise and indifference now form the social and personal climate of contemporary American society. In this climate, no problems of the "private life" can be stated and solved without recognition of the crisis of ambition that is part of the very career of men at work in the incorporated economy.

It is true, as psychoanalysts continually point out, that people do often have the "increasing sense of being moved by obscure forces within themselves that they are unable to define." But it is *not* true, as Ernest Jones asserted, that "man's chief enemy and danger is his own unruly nature and the dark forces pent up within him." On the contrary: "Man's chief danger" today lies in the unruly forces of contemporary society itself, with its alienating methods of production, its enveloping techniques of political domination, its international anarchy—in a word, its pervasive transformations of the very "nature" of man and the conditions and aims of his life.

It is now the social scientist's foremost political and intellectual task—for here the two coincide—to make clear the elements of contemporary uneasiness and indifference. It is the central demand made upon him by other cultural workmen—by physical scientists and artists, by the intellectual community in general. It is because of this task and these demands, I believe, that the social sciences are becoming the common denominator of our cultural period, and the sociological imagination, our most needed quality of mind.

PART II Doing Sociological Research

Iɴ Part I, ʏᴏᴜ ʟᴇᴀʀɴᴇᴅ that sociologists are fascinated with the unknown—how we constantly want to peer behind locked doors to better understand social life. Part II will show you how sociologists open those doors. I wrote the first selection in this Part to give you an overview of the research methods that sociologists use. Diana Scully and Joseph Marolla then follow with an article based on interviewing in a difficult situation. Bruce Jacobs closes Part II with a review of his first attempts at field work. These last two articles give you a glimpse of the intriguing—and sometimes dangerous— worlds that sociologist explore.

As we begin to pry open some of the doors that people so carefully lock, you will be able to catch a glimpse of what goes on behind them. For example, from Scully's and Marolla's research, you will better understand why men rape, and, from Jacobs' article, why people sell illegal drugs. In and of itself, such an understanding is valuable, but the selections in this Part have an additional purpose—to introduce you to the two major activities of sociologists: (1) conducting empirical research and (2) constructing a theoretical base. Let's look at each of these activities.

When sociologists do their craft, these twin tasks merge. They are so joined to one another that neither is more important than the other—nor does one necessarily come before the other. For the sake of presentation, however, let's say that the *first* task of sociology is to conduct empirical research. *Empirical* means "based on objective observations." Sociologists cannot draw conclusions based on guesswork, hunches, custom, superstition, common sense, or how they would like the world to be. They must gather information that represents people's attitudes and behaviors accurately. Then they must report their observations openly, spelling out in detail how they conducted their studies so that others can test their conclusions.

Sociologists use a variety of methods to do their research, several of which are represented by articles in this book. To mention a few: an experiment (article 22, on compliance to authority), interviewing (article 44, on women in the military), and documents or secondary sources (article 12, the classic report on abused children, Anna and Isabelle). Article 13, on childhood, is even based on a method for which we have no standard name. We could make up a fancy term such as *post-event reflexivity*, or we could simply call it recall and analysis.

As sociologists do their research, they sometimes find that using just one method is not enough to accomplish their goals, and they combine methods. The studies of how doctors and nurses deal with patients (article 39) and how rookie cops learn from seasoned officers *their* distinction between brutality and justifiable force (article 40), for example, are based on interviewing combined with participant observation. Most of the articles in this book, however, are based on participant observation, which you will read about in the selection that opens this Part (as well as a more detailed analysis in the opening to Part V).

Because no specific reading summarizes the *second* task of sociology, constructing a theoretical base, I shall provide an overview at this point.

The word *theory* sometimes scares students. It shouldn't, for *all of us are theorists*. To see what I mean by this, let's start with a basic point—how we make sense out of life. Facts never interpret themselves; yet we constantly want to know the meaning of the things that happen to us. To find this meaning, we place our experiences (our "facts") into a conceptual framework. That is, we take a "fact" (which can be someone's behavior, something we see on television—anything that happened to us) and compare it with what we know about "that kind of thing." We then use "what we know" to interpret that "fact."

Doing this gives us an understanding of what that event or "fact" of life means. Whether our understanding is right or wrong is not the point. The point is that we all do this as a regular part of our everyday lives. We feel a need to know how "events" are related to one another. By placing them into "frameworks" that we carry around in our heads, we arrive at that meaning. This process can be called "everyday theorizing." In essence, then, all of us are theorists all the time.

So why be scared of theory? We all know how to "do" theory. Now let's consider how sociologists "do" theory.

Like the events of everyday life, sociological "facts" (the observations, measurements, or research results of sociologists) do not come with built-in meanings. They, too, must be interpreted. To make sense of them, sociologists place their findings into conceptual frameworks that they have developed. These frameworks provide explanations of how pertinent "facts" are related to one another. The basic difference between sociological theory and everyday-life theory is that sociological theory is more rigorous. Sociologists constantly check to see how the "empirical" (the things observed) match a theory—and then refine the theory to match the real world.

A *theory*, then, is a conceptual framework that interprets "facts," that shows how they are related to one another. Because each theory provides a framework that interprets sociological observations, it offers a unique explanation of reality. This will become clearer as we examine the three dominant theories of sociology. You will see how each theory reveals a contrasting picture of social life.

The *first* theory is called *symbolic interactionism* (or *symbolic interaction*). It stresses what you already know quite well—that you live in a world filled with meaning. You are surrounded by *people* who mean something to you (from your parents to your friends), by *objects* that represent something special (your clothing, your pet, your car, your room), and by *events* that are filled with meaning (first kiss, first date, first job, birthdays, holidays, anniversaries). The term *symbol* refers to the meanings that such things have for us. And symbols are what *symbolic* interactionists focus on—how we construct meanings, how we use symbols to communicate with one another, and how symbols are the foundation of our social world.

Symbolic interactionism has three major themes: (1) human beings have a self; (2) people construct meanings, and act on the basis of those meanings; and (3) people take into account the possible reactions of others. Let's look at each of these points.

1. *Human beings have a self.* This means that we have the capacity to think, to talk about, and to reflect on our own actions (what we have done), future actions (what we plan to do), even our thoughts and feelings about our actions (such as what we regret or are pleased at having done). We are even able to tell others what was going on in our mind when we did something. That is, just as we can reflect on the actions and motives of others, so we can reflect on our own actions, analyze our own motives, and evaluate how we feel about what we did or what happened to us. This is called "making the self an object."

2. *People construct meanings, and act on the basis of those meanings.* We reflect on our experiences, and we interpret (or give meaning to) what happens to us. As we evaluate how others react to us and to events, we further refine those meanings. The significance of this human trait is

that the meanings we give to our experiences (the objects, the important events—the "facts" of our life) become the basis for how we act.

This sounds abstract and vague, but all of us do this all the time.
For example, if someone makes physical contact with us, we want to
know what it means. If we interpret the contact as an "accidental
bump," it requires nothing but a mumbled apology—but if we interpret it as a "push" or a "stomp," our reactions are quite different. The
actual act is the same in either case, but our *interpretation* determines
what it means for us, as well as indicating what our "appropriate" reaction should be. Note that the basis for our "appropriate" reaction
does not depend on the act, but on the symbols we apply—that is, how
we interpret (or define) the act.

How we interpret (or "symbolize") life's events is actually a good
deal more complicated than I have just sketched. While we all place
our experiences into categories, the categories we use differ from individual to individual. Even an accidental bump, for example, has different meanings to people of different backgrounds. I am reminded
of this by Kody Scott's fascinating book, *Monster*, in which, among
gang members, an accidental bump can be an invitation to death.

3. *People take into account the possible reactions of others*. We are aware
of how others might react to something that we are thinking about
doing, and we take those anticipated reactions into account as we make
decisions about what to do. This is called *taking the role of others*,
which simply means that we adjust our behavior according to how we
think people might react.

As is apparent, taking the role of others is a regular part of everyday life.
We take the role of individuals ("specific others") and of groups of people ("the
generalized other"). For example, if a Chicago Bulls player were tempted to accept a bribe, he might think, "What would my coach or mom [a specific other]
think if I took this?" He probably would also think, "What would my team and
the American public [a generalized other] think of me if they found out?"

In sum: Central to symbolic interactionism is the principle that to understand people's behavior we must understand their symbolic worlds. That is,
we must understand how people think about life, how they mentally construct
their worlds. Accordingly, sociologists study the meanings that people give to
things, to events, and to other people, for symbols hold the key to understanding both our attitudes and our behavior.

The *second* theory is called *functionalism*. Functionalists stress that society is an integrated system made up of many parts. When working properly,
each part contributes to the stability of society: that is, each part fulfills a

function that helps keep society going. Sometimes, however, a part fails to work correctly; that is, it becomes *dysfunctional*. This creates problems for other parts of the system, for they were depending on it. In short, functionalists stress how the parts of society are interrelated, and how a change in one part of society affects its other parts.

To illustrate functionalism, let's consider why divorce is so prevalent in U.S. society. Functionalists first point out that the family performs important functions for the entire society. Over the millennia, the family's traditional functions have been economic production, the distribution of property, the socialization of children, reproduction, recreation, sexual control of its members, and taking care of its sick, injured, and aged. During the past couple of hundred years (especially the last hundred), as society industrialized profound changes occurred that have left no aspect of social life untouched.

The consequences for family life have been especially remarkable. Consider how industrialization has eroded the family's traditional functions. For example, medical personnel now take care of the family's sick and injured, often the family's elderly are placed in homes for the aged, and almost all economic production has moved from family to factories. As its basic functions have been at least partially taken over by other units of society, the family has weakened. Simply put, the "ties that bind" became fewer—and with fewer functions holding them together, husbands and wives became more prone to break up.

The *third* dominant theory in sociology is *conflict theory*. From this perspective, society is viewed as a system in which its various parts are in conflict. For their survival and to improve their relative position in society, each group competes for resources. There are not enough resources to satisfy each group; each group tends to want more power, more wealth, more prestige, and so on. Consequently, groups compete with one another for a larger share of these limited resources. Those groups that already have more than their share are not about to redistribute what they have willingly. Instead, they hold on to it for dear life, while trying to enlarge what they already have. Conflict is the inevitable result.

As a consequence, say conflict theorists, society is not like a smoothly running machine, as the functionalists picture it, with each part contributing to the well-being of the other parts. Rather, society is more like an imbalanced machine running wildly out of kilter and ready to break apart. The results of this inherent conflict show up as racism, with one racial–ethnic group pitted against another; sexism, with men and women squared off in the struggle for dominance; social class conflict, with the exploitation of the powerless by a ruling elite; ageism, with a struggle for finances (Social Security) dividing the generations of workers; and so on.

Due to space limitations, I can provide only this brief sketch of these three theories that dominate sociology today. Among the many examples of *symbolic interactionism* in this book, you might look at selections by Goffman (11), Lawson (17), and Henslin and Biggs (18). The readings by Gans (30), Harris (38), and Savells (43) provide examples of *functionalism*, while the one by Gracey (34) is an example of *conflict theory*. The dominant orientation of this book is symbolic interactionism.

Part II of the book, then, builds upon the first Part. I hope that it will help you to better appreciate how sociologists do their research and how they interpret what they find.

4　How Sociologists Do Research

JAMES M. HENSLIN

Guesswork does not go very far in helping us to understand our social world. Some of our guesses, hunches, and ideas that pass for common sense are correct. Others are not. And we seldom know the difference.

Sociologists must gather data in such a way that what they report is objective—presenting information that represents what is really "out there." To do so, they must use methods that other researchers can repeat (*replicate*) to check their findings. They also must tie their findings into what other researchers have already reported and into sociological theory. In this overview of *research methods,* Henslin outlines the procedures that sociologists use to gather data.

———————

Renée had never felt fear before—at least not like this. It had begun as a vague feeling that something was out of place. Then she felt it creep up her spine, slowly tightening as it clawed its way upward. Now it was like a fist pounding inside her skull.

Renée never went anywhere with strangers. Hadn't her parents hammered that into her head since she was a child? And now, at 19, she wasn't about to start breaking *that* rule.

And yet here she was, in a car with a stranger. He seemed nice enough. And it wasn't as though he were some strange guy on the side of the road or anything. She had met George at Patricia's party, and. . . .

Renée had first been attracted by his dark eyes. They seemed to light up his entire face when he smiled. And when he asked her to dance, Renée felt flattered. He was a little older, a little more sure of himself than most of the guys she knew. Renée liked that: It was a sign of maturity.

As the evening wore on and he continued to be attentive to her, it seemed natural to accept his offer to take her home.

But then they passed the turn to her dorm. She didn't understand his mumbled reply about "getting something." And as he turned off on the country road, that clawing at the back of her neck had begun.

As he looked at her, his eyes almost pierced the darkness. "It's time to pay, Babe," he said, as he clawed at her blouse.

Renée won't talk about that night. She doesn't want to recall anything that happened then.

IN THIS PAPER we examine how sociologists do research. To better understand how they gather data, it is useful to focus on a single topic. Let's try to answer this question: How can we gather reliable information on rape—which is to say on both rapists *and* their victims?

Sociology and Common Sense

Common sense will give us some information. From common sense (a kind of knowledge not based on formal investigation, but on ideas that we pick up from our groups, mixed with abstractions from our own experiences), we know that Renée's rape was a significant event in her life. And from common sense we know that rape has ongoing effects, that it can trigger fears and anxieties, and that it can make women distrust men.

It so happens that these ideas are true. But many other common-sense ideas, even though glaringly obvious to us, are *not* true, and so we need research to test the validity and accuracy of our ideas. For example, common sense also tells us that one reason men rape is the revealing clothing that some women wear. And common sense may tell us that men who rape are sexually deprived. These common-sense ideas, however, are not on target. Researchers have found that men who rape don't care what a woman is wearing. Most don't even care who the woman is. She is simply an object for their lust, drives for power and exploitation, and, sometimes, frustration and anger. Researchers have also found that rapists may or may not be sexually deprived—the same as with men who do not rape. For example, many rapists have wives or girlfriends with whom they have an ongoing sexual relationship.

If it is neither provocative clothing nor sexual deprivation, then, what *does* cause rape? And what effects does rape have on victims? Phrasing the matter this way—instead of assuming that we know the answers—not only opens up our minds but also underscores the pressing need for sociological research. We need to search for empirical findings that will take us completely out of the realm of guesswork and well beyond common sense.

Let's see how sociologists do their research. We shall look first at a research model, and then at the research methods used in sociology.

A Research Model

As shown in Figure 4.1, eight basic steps are involved in social research. As you look at each of these steps, be aware that this is an ideal model. In some research these steps are collapsed, in others their order may be rearranged, while in still others one or more steps may be omitted.

1. SELECTING A TOPIC

The first step is to select a topic. What is it that you want to know more about? Many sociologists simply follow their curiosity, their drive to know. They

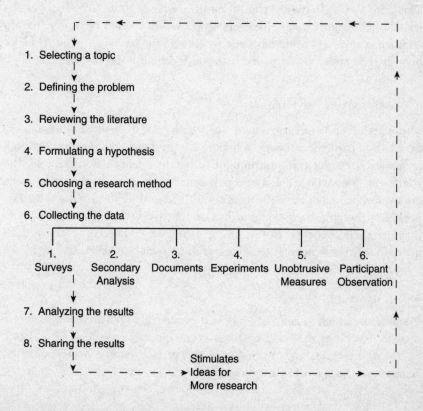

Figure 4.1   The Research Model (*Modification of Fig. 2.2 in Schaefer and Lamm 1998.*)

become interested in a particular topic, and they pursue it. Sometimes sociologists choose a topic simply because funds are available. At other times, some social problem, such as rape, has become a pressing issue and the sociologist wants to gather data that will help people better understand—and perhaps help solve it.

2. DEFINING THE PROBLEM

The second step is to define the problem, to determine what you want to learn about the topic. To develop a researchable question, you need to focus on a specific area or problem. For example, you may want to determine the education and work experiences of rapists, or the average age of their victims.

3. REVIEWING THE LITERATURE

The third step is to review the literature. Nobody wants to rediscover the wheel. If the question has already been answered, you want to know that. In addition, a review of what has been written on the topic can stir your ideas, help sharpen your questions, and help you accomplish the next step.

4. FORMULATING A HYPOTHESIS

The fourth step is to formulate a *hypothesis,* a statement of what you expect to find based on a theory. A hypothesis predicts a relationship between or among *variables* (factors thought to be significant). For example, the statement "Men who are more socially isolated are more likely to rape than are men who are more socially integrated" is an example of a hypothesis. Hypotheses (the plural) need *operational definitions*—that is, precise ways to measure their concepts. In this example, you would need operational definitions for three concepts: social integration, social isolation, and rape.

5. CHOOSING A RESEARCH METHOD

The ways by which sociologists collect data are called *research methods.* You need to select a method that will answer the questions you have formulated. (In the next section, beginning on page 40, I go into detail concerning the six research methods used by sociologists.)

6. COLLECTING THE DATA

The next step is to gather the data. Great care needs to be taken to assure that the data are both valid and reliable. *Validity* means the extent to which the operational definitions measure what you intend to measure. In other words, do your definitions or measures of social isolation and integration *really* measure these concepts and not something else?

The concept of rape is not as simple to define (or operationalize) as it may seem. For example, there are various degrees of sexual assault. Look at Table 4.1, which depicts a variety of forced sexual activities. Deciding which of these constitute rape for the purposes of your research project is an example of the difficulties of developing operational definitions. Certainly not all of these acts are rape—and, therefore, not all of those who did them are rapists.

Reliability refers to the extent to which your measures and studies give consistent results. Inadequate operational definitions and sampling (covered later) will prevent reliability. For example, if other researchers want to replicate (repeat) your study but your measure of rape is inadequate, they will exclude acts that you included, and include acts that you excluded. In that case, how can you compare the results?

TABLE 4.1   Date Rape and Other Unwanted Sexual Activities Experienced by College Undergraduates

UNWANTED SEXUAL ACTIVITY	WOMEN WHO REPORTED THIS HAD HAPPENED TO THEM (%)	MEN WHO REPORTED THEY HAD DONE THIS (%)
He kissed without tongue contact	3.7	2.2
He kissed with tongue contact	12.3	0.7
He touched/kissed her breasts through her clothes	24.7	7.3
He touched/kissed her breasts under her clothes	22.6	13.1
He touched her genitals through her clothes	28.8	15.3
He touched her genitals under her clothes	28.4	13.9
He performed oral sex on her	9.9	8.8
He forced her to touch his genitals through his clothes	2.9	0.7
He forced her to touch his genitals under his clothes	5.8	2.2
He forced her to perform oral sex on him	2.5	4.4
He forced her to have sexual intercourse	20.6	15.3

These are the results of a survey of 380 women and 368 men enrolled in introductory psychology courses at Texas A&M University. Percentages add up to more than 100 because often more than one unwanted sexual activity occurred on the same date.

Source: Based on Muehlenhard and Linton 1987:190.

7. ANALYZING THE RESULTS

After the data are gathered, it is time to analyze them. Sociologists have specific techniques for doing this, each of which requires special training. They range from statistical tests (of which there are many, each with its own rules for application) to *content analysis* (examining the content of something in order to identify its themes—in this case perhaps magazine articles and television reports about rape, or even diaries kept by women who have been raped). If a hypothesis has been part of the research (and not all social research has hypotheses), it is during this step that it is tested.

8. SHARING THE RESULTS

Now it is time to wrap up the research. In this step, you write a report that shares your findings with the scientific community. You relate your findings to the literature, to show how they are connected to what has previously been discovered. You explain your research procedures so others can *replicate* them—i.e., can repeat the study to test its findings. In this way science slowly builds, adding finding to finding.

Now let's look in greater detail at the fifth step to examine the research methods that sociologists use.

Six Research Methods

Sociologists use six *research methods* (also called research designs). These *procedures for gathering data* are surveys, secondary analysis, documents, experiments, unobtrusive measures, and participant observation.

SURVEYS

Let's suppose that you want to know how many women are raped each year. The *survey*—having people answer a series of questions—would be an appropriate method to use.

Before using this method, however, you have to decide whom you will survey. What is your *population;* that is, what is the target group that you want to learn about? Is it all females in the world? Only U.S. or Canadian females? The females in a particular state, county, or city? Only females above a certain age? Or only women on your college campus?

Let's suppose that your research interest is modest—that you want only to know the extent of rape on your campus. Ideally, you would survey all women students. But let's also suppose that your college enrollment is large, making this impractical. To get at the answer, then, you must select a smaller group, a *sample* of individuals, from whom you can generalize to the entire campus. How you choose your sample is crucial, for it will affect the results of your study. For example, you will get different results if you survey only freshmen or seniors—or only women taking introductory sociology or advanced physics classes.

What kind of sample will allow you to *generalize* to the entire campus? The best is a *random* sample. This does *not* mean that you stand on some campus corner and ask questions of whomever happens to walk by. *In a random sample everyone in the population has the same chance of being included in the study.* In this case, since the population is all women taking classes at your college, all such women must have the same chance of being included in your research—whether they are freshmen, sophomores, juniors, seniors, or graduate students. It also means that such factors (*variables*) as a woman's choice of major, her grade point average, or whether she is a day or evening student cannot affect her chances of being a part of your sample.

To obtain a random sample, you would need a list of all women currently enrolled in your college. To determine which students become part of the sample, you might assign a number to each name on the list and then use random numbers to determine which particular women become part of the sample. (Random numbers are available on tables in statistics books, and can be generated by computer.)

Because a random sample represents the population (in this case women students at your college), you can generalize your findings to all the women students on your campus, whether they were part of the sample or not.

In some surveys, *questionnaires,* a list of questions, are mailed to people. Although such *self-administered questionnaires* allow a large number of people to be sampled at a lower cost, control is lost. For example, under what conditions did people (*respondents*) fill them out? Who influenced their answers?

Other surveys use *interviews:* Respondents are asked questions directly. This is usually done on a face-to-face basis, although some interviews are conducted over the telephone. The advantage of this type of survey is that the researchers bring control to the situation. They know the conditions under which the interviews took place and that each question was asked in precisely the same way. Its disadvantages include not only the more limited number of questionnaires that can be completed, and the increased cost, but also *interviewer bias,* the effects that interviewers can have on respondents that lead to biased answers. For example, although respondents may be willing to write an anonymous answer, they may not want to express their opinions to another person directly. Some even try to make their answers match what they think the interviewer wants to hear.

Sociologists sometimes use *closed-ended questions,* called *structured interviews.* Each question is followed by a list of possible answers. The advantages are that these are faster to administer, and make it easier for the answers to be *coded* (categorized) so they can be fed into a computer for analysis. If you use closed-ended questions, you will have to be careful to make sure that they represent people's opinions. For example, if you were to ask "What do you think should be done to rapists?" and the only choices you provide are to castrate or kill them, you would not be taking accurate measurements of people's opinions. Similarly, if you begin a question with, "Don't you agree that" ("rapists should be locked up for life"—or whatever you want to add), you would tilt the results toward agreement with a particular position.

Questions, then, must be carefully worded so they do not slant answers— because biased findings are worthless. It takes a great deal of training to construct questions that are free of bias, and sociologists are extremely critical of both how questions are worded and how they are administered (given).

To better tap the depth and diversity of people's experiences and attitudes, you may wish to use *open-ended questions,* called *unstructured interviews,* that allow people to answer in their own words. The primary advantage of this type of interview is that it allows people to express their full range of opinions. The major disadvantage is that it is difficult to compare people's answers. For example, how would you compare these answers to the question "What do you think causes rape?"

"They haven't been raised right."
"I think they must have had problems with their mother."
"We ought to kill every one!"
"They're all sick."
"I don't want to talk about it."

The research topic we are considering also brings up another significant item. Let's suppose that you want to interview rape victims. Would they really give honest answers? Will a woman even admit to a stranger that she has been raped, much less talk about it? Wouldn't all your efforts be futile?

If you were to simply walk up to a stranger on the street and ask if she had ever been raped, you can guess the results—and they certainly would give little basis for placing confidence in your findings. Researchers must establish *rapport* (pronounced ruh–pour), a feeling of trust, with their respondents. When it comes to sensitive topics, areas about which people may feel embarrassment, shame, hostility, or other deep emotions, rapport is all the more important.

Once rapport is gained (often through building trust by explaining the significance of the research, assuring anonymity, and first asking nonsensitive questions), victims usually will talk about rape. For example, each year researchers conduct a national crime survey in which they interview a random sample of 49,000 households—about 90,000 Americans. They find that most rape victims will talk about their experiences. These national crime surveys show that rape is three times as high as the official statistics, and that most rape is committed by someone the victim knows (*Statistical Abstract of the United States* 2001: page 180).

SECONDARY ANALYSIS

In *secondary analysis,* the second research method we shall consider, the researcher analyzes data already collected by others. For example, if you were to examine the basic data gathered by the interviewers who did the national crime survey just mentioned, you would be doing secondary analysis.

Ordinarily, researchers prefer to gather their own data, but lack of resources, especially time and money, may make this preference impossible to fulfill. In addition, data already gathered may contain a wealth of information not pertinent to the purposes of those who did the original study. It simply lies there, waiting to be analyzed.

While this approach can solve problems of access, it also poses its own problems. Not having directly carried out the research, how can you be sure that the data were systematically gathered and accurately recorded, and biases avoided? That may not be an easy task, especially if the original data were gathered by numerous researchers, not all of whom were equally qualified.

DOCUMENTS

The use of *documents,* written sources, is a third research method employed by sociologists. To investigate social life, sociologists examine such diverse sources as books, newspapers, diaries, bank records, police reports, immigration records, household accounts, and records kept by schools, hospitals, and other organizations. (Although they are not commonly called documents, also included here are movies, television programs, videotapes, computer disks, and CD-ROMs.)

To apply this method to the study of rape, you might examine police reports. They may reveal what proportion of all arrests are for rape; how many of the men arrested go to trial; what proportion is convicted, put on probation, sent to prison; and so forth. If these are your questions, police statistics could be valuable.

But for other questions, police records would be useless. For example, if you want to know about the adjustment of rape victims, they would tell you nothing. Other documents, however, may lend themselves to this question. If your campus has a rape crisis center, for example, it might have records that would provide key information. Or you may obtain diaries kept by victims, and search them for clues to their reactions—especially how their orientations change over time. If you couldn't find such diaries, you might contact a sample of rape victims and ask them to keep diaries. Locating that sample is extremely difficult—but, again, the rape crisis center could be the key. Their personnel might ask victims to keep the diaries. (To my knowledge, however, no sociologist has yet studied rape in this way.)

I am writing, of course, about an ideal case, as though the rape crisis center is opening its arms to you. In actual fact it may not cooperate at all, refusing to ask victims to keep diaries and not even letting you near their records. Access, then, is another problem researchers constantly face. Simply put, you can't study something unless you can gain access to it.

EXPERIMENTS

A fourth research method is the *experiment*. This is the classic method of the natural sciences. Sociologists seldom use it, however, because they are more likely to be interested in broad features of society and social behavior, or in studying a social group in a natural setting, neither of which lends itself to an experiment.

The basic purpose of an experiment is to identify cause-and-effect relationships—to find out what causes what. Ordinarily, experiments are used to test a hypothesis. Experiments involve *independent variables* (those factors that cause a change in something) and *dependent variables* (those factors that are changed). Before the experiment, you must measure the dependent variable. Then, after introducing the independent variable, you again measure the dependent variable in order to see what change has occurred.

Let's assume, for example, that you want to test the hypothesis that pornography creates attitudes that favor rape. The independent variable would be pornography, the dependent variable attitudes toward rape. You can measure a group of men's attitudes toward rape and then use random numbers to divide the men into two subgroups. To one group, the *experimental group,* you introduce the independent variable (such as violent pornographic movies). The other group, the *control group,* is not exposed to the independent variable (that is, they are not shown these movies). You then measure the dependent variable in both groups. Changes in the dependent variable (in this case attitudes toward rape) are due to what only the experimental group received, the independent variable (in this case, the pornography).

Because there is always some chance that unknown third variables have not been evenly distributed among the groups, you would need to retest your results by repeating the experiment with other groups of men.

UNOBTRUSIVE MEASURES

The fifth method we shall consider is *unobtrusive measures:* observing people's behavior when they do not know they are being studied. For example, social researchers have studied the level of whiskey consumption in a "dry" town by counting empty bottles in trash cans; the degree of fear induced through telling ghost stories by measuring the shrinking diameter of a circle of seated children; and the popularity of exhibits at Chicago's Museum of Science and Industry by the wear upon tiles in front of the various displays (Webb et al. 1966; Lee 2000).

Unobtrusive measures could also be used to study rape. For example, you could observe rapists in prison when they do not know they are being watched. You might arrange for the leader of a therapy group for rapists to be called out of the room. During his absence, you could use a one-way mirror to observe the men's interactions, and video cameras to preserve what they say and do. You might even have a stooge bring up a certain topic. Such an approach would probably tell you more about the men's real attitudes than most other techniques.

Professional ethics, however, would disallow such a study. And I know of no research that has applied this method to the study of rape.

PARTICIPANT OBSERVATION (FIELD WORK)

Let's turn to my favorite method, one that involves the researcher in the most direct way. In *participant observation* (or field work) the researcher *participates* in a research setting while *observing* what is happening in that setting.

How is it possible to study rape by participant observation? It would seem that this method would not apply. If one considers being present during rape, it certainly does not. But there are many other questions about rape that can be answered by participant observation, answers that cannot be gained as adequately by any other method.

Let's suppose that your interest is the adjustment of rape victims. You would like to learn how the rape has affected their behavior and their orientations to the world. For example, how has their victimization affected their hopes and goals, their dating patterns, their ideas about men and intimacy? Participant observation can provide detailed answers to such questions.

Let's go back to your campus again. Assume that your campus has a rape crisis intervention center. This setting lends itself to participant observation, for here you can observe rape victims from the time they first report the attack to their later participation in individual and group counseling. With good rapport, you can even spend time with victims outside this setting, observing how it affects other aspects of their lives.

Participant observation has the added benefit of allowing you to study whatever happens to occur while you are in the setting. In this instance, you would also be able to study the operation of the rape crisis center. As you observe counselors at work, you could also study *their* attitudes and behaviors.

As you may have noticed, in participant observation the personal characteristics of the researcher are important. Could a man, for example, conduct such research? Technically, the answer is yes. Properly introduced and with the right attitudes, men could do this research. But granted the topic, and especially the emotional states of females who have been brutally victimized by males, it may be more appropriate for women sociologists to conduct this research. Their chances of success are likely to be higher.

In conducting research, then, sociologists must be aware of such variables as the sex, age, race–ethnicity, personality, and even height and weight of the researcher (Henslin 1990). While important in all research methods (for example, in surveys men who are being interviewed may be more talkative to young, shapely women than to obese men with bad breath), these variables are especially important in participant observation.

Participant observers face a problem with generalizability. Although they look for principles of human behavior, it is difficult to know the extent to which their findings apply beyond the setting in which they occur. Consequently, most participant observation is exploratory in nature: The findings document in detail what people in a particular setting are experiencing and how they are reacting to those experiences, suggesting that other people who face similar situations will react in similar ways.

I find participant observation the most exciting of the methods. It is the type of sociology that I like to do and the type I like to read about. From these studies, I gain a depth of understanding of settings that I want to know more about but for whatever reason am not able to study, and in some cases am not even able to enter. If I were a woman, for example, I might have volunteered for work in my campus's rape crisis center—a technique often used by sociologists to solve the problem of access.

Conclusion: A Note on Choosing Research Methods

As you have seen, a crucial factor in choosing a research method is the questions you wish to answer. Each method lends itself much better to answering particular interests or questions than do other methods. You also have seen that access to subjects is crucial in deciding which research method to use. Two other factors are significant in this choice: the resources available to the researcher, and the researcher's background or training. For example, a researcher who prefers to conduct a survey may find that finances will not permit it, and instead turn to the study of documents. The researcher's background is similarly significant in this choice. Researchers who have been trained in *quantitative techniques* (an emphasis on measurement, numbers, statistics) are more likely to use surveys, while researchers who have been trained in *qualitative techniques* (generally, making direct observations of what people do and say) lean toward participant observation. The particular training that sociologists receive in graduate school, which sometimes depends on capricious events, orients them toward certain research methods. They feel comfortable with those, and tend to continue to use them throughout their careers.

References

Henslin, James M. (1990). "It's not a lovely place to visit, and I wouldn't want to live there." In Robert G. Burgess (ed.), *Studies in Qualitative Methodology II*: 51–76. Greenwich, CT: JAI Press.

Lee, Raymond (2000). *Unobtrusive Methods in Social Research*. Philadelphia: Open University Press.

Muehlenhard, Charlene L., and Melaney A. Linton (1987). "Date rape: Familiar strangers." *Journal of Counseling Psychology 34:* 186–96.

Schaefer, Richard T., and Robert P. Lamm (1998). *Sociology.* 6th ed. New York: McGraw-Hill.

Statistical Abstract of the United States. Washington, D.C.: U.S. Government Printing Office, 2001.

Webb, Eugene J., Donald T. Campbell, Richard D. Schwartz, and Lee Sechrest (1966). *Unobtrusive Measures: Nonreactive Research in the Social Sciences.* Chicago: Rand McNally.

5

"Riding the Bull at Gilley's": Convicted Rapists Describe the Rewards of Rape

DIANA SCULLY
JOSEPH MAROLLA

As we saw in the previous reading, sociologists can choose from a variety of research methods. Rape was used as the example to illustrate the various ways in which sociologists collect data. In this selection, you can see how two sociologists used the research method known as unstructured interviewing to gather data on rape. What prompted their research was a question that many people wonder about: "Just why do men rape?"

Scully and Marolla interviewed a sample of men who had been sent to prison for rape. In what was a difficult situation, they established enough *rapport* that the men felt free to talk about their motives. From this selection, you should gain an understanding of the reasons why men commit this violent act. To determine how widespread (representative) these motives are, we need more studies, preferably with both convicted and unconvicted rapists. Perhaps you, now a student reading this book in the introductory course, will become a sociologist who will build on this study.

OVER THE PAST SEVERAL DECADES, rape has become a "medicalized" social problem. That is to say, the theories used to explain rape are predicated on psychopathological models. They have been generated from clinical experiences with small samples of rapists, often the therapists' own clients. Although these psychiatric explanations are most appropriately applied to the atypical rapist, they have been generalized to all men who rape and have come to inform the public's view on the topic.

Two assumptions are at the core of the psychopathological model: that rape is the result of idiosyncratic mental disease and that it often includes an uncontrollable sexual impulse (Scully and Marolla, 1985). For example, the presumption of psychopathology is evident in the often cited work of Nicholas Groth (1979). While Groth emphasizes the nonsexual nature of rape (power, anger, sadism), he also concludes, "Rape is always a symptom of some psychological dysfunction, either temporary and transient or chronic and repetitive" (Groth, 1979:5). Thus, in the psychopathological view, rapists lack the ability to control their behavior; they are "sick" individuals from the "lunatic fringe" of society.

In contradiction to this model, empirical research has repeatedly failed to find a consistent pattern of personality type or character disorder that reliably discriminates rapists from other groups of men (Fisher and Rivlin, 1971; Hammer and Jacks, 1955; Rada, 1978). Indeed, other research has found that fewer than 5 percent of men were psychotic when they raped (Abel et al., 1980).

Evidence indicates that rape is not a behavior confined to a few "sick" men, but many men have the attitudes and beliefs necessary to commit a sexually aggressive act. In research conducted at a midwestern university, Koss and her coworkers reported that 85 percent of men defined as highly sexually aggressive had victimized women with whom they were romantically involved (Koss and Leonard, 1984). A survey quoted in *The Chronicle of Higher Education* estimates that more than 20 percent of college women are the victims of rape and attempted rape (Meyer, 1984). These findings mirror research published several decades earlier which also concluded that sexual aggression was commonplace in dating relationships (Kanin, 1957, 1965, 1967, 1969; Kirkpatrick and Kanin, 1957). In their study of 53 college males, Malamuth, Haber, and Feshback (1980) found that 51 percent indicated a likelihood that they, themselves, would rape if assured of not being punished.

In addition, the frequency of rape in the United States makes it unlikely that responsibility rests solely with a small lunatic fringe of psychopathic men. Johnson (1980), calculating the lifetime risk of rape to girls and women aged twelve and over, makes a similar observation. Using Law Enforcement Assistance Association and Bureau of Census Crime Victimization Studies, he calculated that, excluding sexual abuse in marriage and assuming equal risk to all women, 20 to 30 percent of girls now 12 years old will suffer a violent sexual attack during the remainder of their lives. Interestingly, the lack of empirical support for the psychopathological model has not resulted in the demedicalization of rape, nor does it appear to have diminished the belief that rapists are "sick" aberrations in their own culture. This is significant because of the implications and consequences of the model.

A central assumption in the psychopathological model is that male sexual aggression is unusual or strange. This assumption removes rape from the realm of the everyday or "normal" world and places it in the category of "special" or "sick" behavior. As a consequence, men who rape are cast in the role of outsider and a connection with normative male behavior is avoided. Since, in this view, the source of the behavior is thought to be within the psychology of the individual, attention is diverted away from culture or social structure as contributing factors. Thus, the psychopathological model ignores evidence which links sexual aggression to environmental variables and which suggests that rape, like all behavior, is learned.

Cultural Factors in Rape

Culture is a factor in rape, but the precise nature of the relationship between culture and sexual violence remains a topic of discussion. Ethnographic data from pre-industrial societies show the existence of rape-free cultures (Broude and Green, 1976; Sanday, 1979), although explanations for the phenomenon differ. Sanday (1979) relates sexual violence to contempt for female qualities and suggests that rape is part of a culture of violence and an expression of male dominance. In contrast, Blumberg (1979) argues that in pre-industrial societies women are more likely to lack important life options and to be physically and politically oppressed where they lack economic power relative to men. That is, in pre-industrial societies relative economic power enables women to win some immunity from men's use of force against them.

Among modern societies, the frequency of rape varies dramatically, and the United States is among the most rape-prone of all. In 1980, for example, the rate of reported rape and attempted rape for the United States was eighteen times higher than the corresponding rate for England and Wales (West, 1983). Spurred by the Women's Movement, feminists have generated an impressive body of theory regarding the cultural etiology of rape in the United States. Representative of the feminist view, Griffin (1971) called rape "The All American Crime."

The feminist perspective views rape as an act of violence and social control which functions to "keep women in their place" (Brownmiller, 1975; Kasinsky, 1975; Russell, 1975). Feminists see rape as an extension of normative male behavior, the result of conformity or overconformity to the values and prerogatives which define the traditional male sex role. That is, traditional socialization encourages males to associate power, dominance, strength, virility, and superiority with masculinity, and submissiveness, passivity, weakness, and inferiority with femininity. Furthermore, males are taught to have expectations about their level of sexual needs and expectations for corresponding female accessibility which function to justify forcing sexual access. The justification for forced sexual access is buttressed by legal, social, and religious definitions of women as male property and sex as an exchange of goods (Bart, 1979). Socialization prepares women to be "legitimate" victims and men to be potential offenders (Weis and Borges, 1973). Herman (1984) concludes that the United States is a rape culture because both genders are socialized to regard male aggression as a natural and normal part of sexual intercourse.

Feminists view pornography as an important element in a larger system of sexual violence; they see pornography as an expression of a rape-prone culture where women are seen as objects available for use by men (Morgan, 1980; Wheeler, 1985). Based on his content analysis of 428 "adults only" books, Smith (1976) makes a similar observation. He notes that, not only is rape presented as part of normal male/female sexual relations, but the woman, despite her terror, is always depicted as sexually aroused to the point of cooperation. In the end, she is ashamed but physically gratified. The message—women desire and enjoy rape—has more potential for damage than the image of the violence *per se*.

The fusion of these themes—sex as an impersonal act, the victim's uncontrollable orgasm, and the violent infliction of pain—is commonplace in the actual accounts of rapists. Scully and Marolla (1984) demonstrated that many convicted rapists denied their crime and attempted to justify their rapes by arguing that their victim enjoyed herself despite the use of a weapon and the infliction of serious injuries, or even death. In fact, many argued, they had been instrumental in making *her* fantasy come true.

The images projected in pornography contribute to a vocabulary of motive which trivializes and neutralizes rape and which might lessen the internal controls that otherwise would prevent sexually aggressive behavior. Men who rape use this culturally acquired vocabulary to justify their sexual violence.

Another consequence of the application of psychopathology to rape is that it leads one to view sexual violence as a special type of crime in which the motivations are subconscious and uncontrollable rather than overt and deliberate as with other criminal behavior. Black (1983) offers an approach to the analysis of criminal and/or violent behavior which, when applied to rape, avoids this bias. Black suggests that it is theoretically useful to ignore that crime is criminal in order to discover what such behavior has in common with other kinds of conduct. From his perspective, much of the crime in modern societies, as in pre-industrial societies, can be interpreted as a form of "self help" in which the actor is expressing a grievance through aggression and violence. From the actor's perspective, the victim is deviant and his own behavior is a form of social control in which the objective may be conflict management, punishment, or revenge. For example, in societies where women are considered the property of men, rape is sometimes used as a means of avenging the victim's husband or father (Black, 1983). In some cultures rape is used as a form of punishment. Such was the tradition among the puritanical, patriarchal Cheyenne, where men were valued for their ability as warriors. It was Cheyenne custom that a wife suspected of being unfaithful could be "put on the prairie" by her husband. Military confreres then were invited to "feast" on the prairie (Hoebel, 1954; Llewellyn and Hoebel, 1941). The ensuing mass rape was a husband's method of punishing his wife.

Black's (1983) approach is helpful in understanding rape because it forces one to examine the goals that some men have learned to achieve through sexually violent means. Thus, one approach to understanding why some men rape is to shift attention from individual psychopathology to the important question of what rapists gain from sexual aggression and violence in a culture seemingly prone to rape. In this paper, we address this question using data from interviews conducted with 114 convicted, incarcerated rapists.

Methods

SAMPLE

During 1980 and 1981 we interviewed 114 convicted rapists. All of the men had been convicted of the rape or attempted rape of an adult woman and subsequently incarcerated in a Virginia prison. Men convicted of other types of sexual offense were omitted from the sample.

In addition to their convictions for rape, 39 percent of the men also had convictions for burglary or robbery, 29 percent for abduction, 25 percent for sodomy, 11 percent for first or second degree murder, and 12 percent had been convicted of more than one rape. The majority of the men had previous criminal histories, but only 23 percent had a record of past sex offenses and only 26 percent had a history of emotional problems. Their sentences for rape and accompanying crimes ranged from ten years to seven life sentences plus 380 years for one man. Twenty-two percent of the rapists were serving at least one life sentence. Forty-six percent of the rapists were white, 54 percent black. In age, they ranged from 18 to 60 years, but the majority were between 18 and 35 years. Based on a statistical profile of felons in all Virginia prisons prepared by the Virginia Department of Corrections, it appears that this sample of rapists was disproportionately white and, at the time of the research, somewhat better educated and younger than the average inmate.

All participants in this research were volunteers. In constructing the sample, age, education, race, severity of current offense, and past criminal record were balanced within the limitations imposed by the characteristics of the volunteer pool. Obviously the sample was not random and thus may not be typical of all rapists, imprisoned or otherwise.

How Offenders View the Rewards of Rape

REVENGE AND PUNISHMENT

As noted earlier, Black's (1983) perspective suggests that a rapist might see his act as a legitimized form of revenge or punishment. Additionally, he asserts that the idea of "collective liability" accounts for much seemingly random violence. "Collective liability" suggests that all people in a particular category are held accountable for the conduct of each of their counterparts. Thus, the victim of a violent act may merely represent the category of individual being punished.

These factors—revenge, punishment, and the collective liability of women—can be used to explain a number of rapes in our research. Several cases will illustrate ways in which these factors combined in various types of rape. Revenge-rapes were among the most brutal and often included beatings, serious injuries, and even murder.

Typically, revenge-rapes included the element of collective liability. That is, from the rapist's perspective, the victim was a substitute for the woman on whom he wanted revenge. As explained elsewhere (Scully and Marolla, 1984), an upsetting event, involving a woman, preceded a significant number of rapes. When they raped, these men were angry because of a perceived indiscretion, typically related to a rigid, moralistic standard of sexual conduct, which they required from "their woman" but, in most cases, did not abide by themselves. Over and over these rapists talked about using rape "to get even" with their wives or some other significant woman. Typical is a young man who, prior to the rape, had a violent argument with his wife over what eventually proved to be her misdiagnosed case of venereal disease. She assumed the disease had been contracted through him, an accusation that infuriated him. After fighting with his wife, he explained that he drove around "thinking about hurting someone." He encountered his victim, a stranger, on the road where her car had broken down. It appears she accepted his offered ride because her car was out of commission. When she realized that rape was pending, she called him "a son of a bitch," and attempted to resist. He reported flying into a rage and beating her, and he confided,

> I have never felt that much anger before. If she had resisted, I would have killed her. . . . The rape was for revenge. I didn't have an orgasm. She was there to get my hostile feelings off on.

Although not the most common form of revenge-rape, sexual assault continues to be used in retaliation against the victim's male partner. In one such case, the offender, angry because the victim's husband owed him money, went to the victim's home to collect. He confided, "I was going to get it one way or another." Finding the victim alone, he explained, they started to argue about the money and,

> I grabbed her and started beating the hell out of her. Then I committed the act. I knew what I was doing. I was mad. I could have stopped, but I didn't. I did it to get even with her and her husband.

Griffin (1971) points out that when women are viewed as commodities, "In raping another man's woman, a man may aggrandize his own manhood and concurrently reduce that of the other man" (p. 33).

Revenge-rapes often contained an element of punishment. In some cases, while the victim was not the initial object of the revenge, the intent was to punish her because of something that transpired after the decision to rape had been made or during the course of the rape itself. This was the case with a young man whose wife had recently left him. Although they were in the process of reconciliation, he remained angry and upset over the separation. The night of the rape, he met the victim and her friend in a bar where he had gone to watch a fight on TV. The two women apparently accepted a ride from him, but after taking her friend home, he drove the victim to his apartment. At his apartment, he found a note from his wife indicating she had stopped by to watch the fight with him. This increased his anger because he preferred his wife's company. Inside his apartment, the victim allegedly remarked that she was sexually interested in his dog, which, he reported, put him in a rage. In the ensuing attack, he raped and pistol-whipped the victim. Then he forced a vacuum cleaner hose, switched on suction, into her vagina and bit her breast, severing the nipple. He stated:

> I hated at the time, but I don't know if it was her (the victim). (Who could it have been?) My wife? Even though we were getting back together. I still didn't trust her.

During his interview, it became clear that this offender, like many of the men, believed men have the right to discipline and punish women. In fact, he argued that most of the men he knew would also have beaten the victim because "that kind of thing (referring to the dog) is not acceptable among my friends."

Finally, in some rapes, both revenge and punishment were directed at victims because they represented women whom these offenders perceived as collectively responsible and liable for their problems. Rape was used "to put women in their place" and as a method of proving their "manhood" by displaying dominance over a female. For example, one multiple rapist believed his actions were related to the feeling that women thought they were better than he was.

> Rape was a feeling of total dominance. Before the rapes, I would always get a feeling of power and anger. I would degrade women so I could feel there was a person of less worth than me.

Another, especially brutal, case involved a young man from an upper middle class background, who spilled out his story in a seven-hour interview conducted in his solitary confinement cell. He described himself as tremendously angry, at the time, with his girlfriend, who he believed was involved with him in a "storybook romance," and from whom he expected complete fidelity. When she went away to college and became involved with another man, his revenge lasted eighteen months and involved the rape and murder of five women, all strangers who lived in his community. Explaining his rape-murders, he stated:

> I wanted to take my anger and frustration out on a stranger, to be in control, to do what I wanted to do. I wanted to use and abuse someone as I felt used and abused. I was killing my girl friend. During the rapes and murders, I would think about my girl friend. I hated the victims because they probably messed men over. I hated women because they were deceitful and I was getting revenge for what happened to me.

AN ADDED BONUS

Burglary and robbery commonly accompany rape. Among our sample, 39 percent of the rapists had also been convicted of one or the other of these crimes committed in connection with rape. In some cases, the original intent was rape, and robbery was an afterthought. However, a number of men indicated that the reverse was true in their situation. That is, the decision to rape was made subsequent to their original intent, which was burglary or robbery.

This was the case with a young offender who stated that he originally intended only to rob the store in which the victim happened to be working. He explained that when he found the victim alone,

> I decided to rape her to prove I had guts. She was just there. It could have been anybody.

Similarly, another offender indicated that he initially broke into his victim's home to burglarize it. When he discovered the victim asleep, he decided to seize the opportunity "to satisfy an urge to go to bed with a white woman, to see if it was different." Indeed a number of men indicated that the decision to rape had been made after they realized they were in control of the situation. This was also true of an unemployed offender who confided that his practice was to steal whenever he needed money. On the day of the rape, he drove to a local supermarket and paced the parking lot, "staking out the situation." His pregnant victim was the first person to come along alone and "she was an easy target." Threatening her with a knife, he reported the victim as saying she would do anything if he didn't harm her. At that point, he decided to force her to drive to a deserted area, where he raped her. He explained:

> I wasn't thinking about sex. But when she said she would do anything not to get hurt, probably because she was pregnant, I thought, "why not?"

The attitude of these men toward rape was similar to their attitude toward burglary and robbery. Quite simply, if the situation is right, "why not?" From the perspective of these rapists, rape was just another part of the crime—an added bonus.

SEXUAL ACCESS

In an effort to change public attitudes that are damaging to the victims of rape and to reform laws seemingly premised on the assumption that women both ask for and enjoy rape, many writers emphasize the violent and aggressive character of rape. Often such arguments appear to discount the part that sex plays in the crime. The data clearly indicate that from the rapists' point of view, rape is in part sexually motivated. Indeed, it is the sexual aspect of rape that distinguishes it from other forms of assault.

Rape as a means of sexual access also shows the deliberate nature of this crime. When a woman is unwilling or seems unavailable for sex, the rapist can seize what isn't volunteered. In discussing his decision to rape, one man made this clear.

> . . . a real fox, beautiful shape. She was a beautiful woman and I wanted to see what she had.

The attitude that sex is a male entitlement suggests that when a woman says "no," rape is a suitable method of conquering the "offending" object. If, for example, a woman is picked up at a party or in a bar or while hitchhiking (behavior which a number of the rapists saw as a signal of sexual availability), and the woman later resists sexual advances, rape is presumed to be justified. The same justification operates in what is popularly called "date rape." The belief that sex was their just compensation compelled a number of rapists to insist they had not raped. Such was the case of an offender who raped and seriously beat his victim when, on their second date, she refused his sexual advances.

> I think I was really pissed off at her because it didn't go as planned. I could have been with someone else. She led me on but wouldn't deliver. . . . I have a male ego that must be fed.

The purpose of such rapes was conquest, to seize what was not offered.

Despite the cultural belief that young women are the most sexually desirable, several rapes involved the deliberate choice of a victim relatively older than the assailant. Since the rapists were themselves rather young (26 to 30 years of age on the average), they were expressing a preference for sexually experienced, rather than elderly, women. Men who chose victims older than themselves often said they did so because they believed that sexually experienced women were more desirable partners. They raped because they also believed that these women would not be sexually attracted to them.

Finally, sexual access emerged as a factor in the accounts of black men who consciously chose to rape white women. The majority of rapes in the United States are intraracial. However, for the past 20 years, according to national data based on reported rapes as well as victimization studies, which include unreported rapes, the rate of black on white (B/W) rape has significantly exceeded the rate of white on black (W/B) rape (La Free, 1982). Indeed, we may be experiencing a historical anomaly, since, as Brownmiller (1975) has documented, white men have freely raped women of color in the past. The current structure of interracial rape, however, reflects contemporary racism and race relations in several ways.

First, the status of black women in the United States today is relatively lower than the status of white women. Further, prejudice, segregation, and other factors continue to militate against interracial coupling. Thus, the desire for sexual access to higher status, unavailable women, an important function in B/W rape, does not motivate white men to rape black women. Equally important, demographic and geographic barriers interact to lower the incidence of W/B rape. Segregation as well as the poverty expected in black neighborhoods undoubtedly discourages many whites from choosing such areas as a target for housebreaking or robbery. Thus, the number of rapes that would occur in conjunction with these crimes is reduced.

Reflecting in part the standards of sexual desirability set by the dominant white society, a number of black rapists indicated they had been curious about white women. Blocked by racial barriers from legitimate sexual relations with white women, they raped to gain access to them. They described raping white women as "the ultimate experience" and "high status among my friends. It gave me a feeling of status, power, macho." For another man, raping a white woman had a special appeal because it violated a "known taboo," making it more dangerous, and thus more exciting to him, than raping a black woman.

IMPERSONAL SEX AND POWER

The idea that rape is an impersonal rather than an intimate or mutual experience appealed to a number of rapists, some of whom suggested it was their preferred form of sex. The fact that rape allowed them to control rather than care encouraged some to act on this preference. For example, one man explained,

> Rape gave me the power to do what I wanted to do without feeling I had to please a partner or respond to a partner. I felt in control, dominant. Rape was the ability to have sex without caring about the woman's response. I was totally dominant.

Another rapist commented:

> Seeing them laying there helpless gave me the confidence that I could do it. . . . With rape, I felt totally in charge. I'm bashful, timid. When a woman wanted to give in normal sex, I was intimidated. In the rapes, I was totally in command, she totally submissive.

During his interview, another rapist confided that he had been fantasizing about rape for several weeks before committing his offense. His belief was that it would be "an exciting experience—a new high." Most appealing to him was the idea that he could make his victim "do it all for him" and that he would be in control. He fantasized that she "would submit totally and that I could have anything I wanted." Eventually, he decided to act because his older brother told him, "forced sex is great, I wouldn't get caught and, besides, women love it." Though now he admits to his crime, he continues to believe his victim "enjoyed it." Perhaps we should note here that the appeal of impersonal sex is not limited to convicted rapists. The amount of male sexual activity that occurs in homosexual meeting places as well as the widespread use of prostitutes suggests that avoidance of intimacy appeals to a large segment of the male population. Through rape men can experience power and avoid the emotions related to intimacy and tenderness. Further, the popularity of violent pornography suggests that a wide variety of men in this culture have learned to be aroused by sex fused with violence (Smith, 1976). Consistent with this observation, experimental research conducted by Malamuth et al. (1980) demonstrates that men are aroused by images that depict women as orgasmic under conditions of violence and pain. They found that, for female students, arousal was high when the victim experienced an orgasm and *no* pain, whereas male students were highly aroused when the victim experienced an orgasm *and* pain. On the basis of their results, Malamuth et al. suggest that forcing a woman to climax despite her pain and abhorrence of the assailant makes the rapist feel powerful; he has gained control over the only source of power historically associated with women, their bodies. In the final analysis, dominance was the objective of most rapists.

RECREATION AND ADVENTURE

Among gang rapists, most of whom were in their late teens or early twenties when convicted, rape represented recreation and adventure, another form of delinquent activity. Part of rape's appeal was the sense of male camaraderie engendered by participating collectively in a dangerous activity. To prove one's self capable of "performing" under these circumstances was a substantial challenge and also a source of reward. One gang rapist articulated this feeling very clearly.

> We felt powerful; we were in control. I wanted sex, and there was peer pressure. She wasn't like a person, no personality, just domination on my part. Just to show I could do it—you know, macho.

Our research revealed several forms of gang rape. A common pattern was hitchhike-abduction for the purpose of having sex. Though the intent was rape, a number of men did not view it as such because they were convinced that women hitchhiked primarily to signal sexual availability and only secondarily as a form of transportation. In these cases, the unsuspecting victim was driven to a deserted area, raped, and in the majority of cases physically injured. Sometimes, the victim was not hitchhiking; she was abducted at knife or gun point from the street, usually at night. Some of these men did not view this type of attack as rape either, because they believed a woman walking alone at night to be a prostitute. In addition, they were often convinced "she enjoyed it."

"Gang date" rape was another popular variation. In this pattern, one member of the gang would make a date with the victim. Then, without her knowledge or consent, she would be driven to a predetermined location and forcibly raped by each member of the group. One young man revealed this practice was so much a part of his group's recreational routine, they had rented a house for the purpose. From his perspective, the rape was justified because "usually the girl had a bad reputation, or we knew it was what she liked."

During his interview, another offender confessed to participating in twenty or thirty such "gang date" rapes because his driver's license had been revoked, making it difficult for him to "get girls." Sixty percent of the time, he claimed, "they were girls known to do this kind of thing," but "frequently, the girls didn't want to have sex with all of us." In such cases, he said, "It might start out as rape, but, then, they (the women) would quiet down and none ever reported it to the police." He was convicted for a gang rape, which he described as "the ultimate thing I ever did," because unlike his other rapes, the victim, in this case, was a stranger whom the group abducted as she walked home from the library. He felt the group's past experience with "gang date" rape had prepared them for this crime in which the victim was blindfolded and driven to the mountains where, though it was winter, she was forced to remove her clothing. Lying on the snow, she was raped by each of the four men several times before being abandoned near a farm house. This young man continued to believe that if he had spent the night with her, rather than abandoning her, she would not have reported it to the police.

Solitary rapists also used terms like "exciting," "a challenge," "an adventure" to describe their feelings about rape. Like the gang rapists, these men found the element of danger made rape all the more exciting. Typifying this attitude was one man who described his rape as intentional. He reported:

> It was exciting to get away with it (rape), just being able to beat the system, not women. It was like doing something illegal and getting away with it.

Another rapist confided that for him "rape was just more exciting and compelling" than a normal sexual encounter because it involved forcing a stranger. A multiple rapist asserted, "It was the excitement and fear and the drama that made rape a big kick."

FEELING GOOD

When the men were asked to recall their feelings immediately following the rape, only eight percent indicated that guilt or feeling bad was part of their emotional response. The majority said they felt good, relieved, or simply nothing at all. Some indicated they had been afraid of being caught or felt sorry for themselves. Only two men out of 114 expressed any concern or feeling for the victim. Feeling good or nothing at all about raping women is not an aberration limited to men in prison. Smithyman (1978), in his study of "undetected rapists"—rapists outside of prison—found that raping women had no impact on their lives, nor did it have a negative effect on their self-image.

Significantly, a number of men volunteered the information that raping had a positive impact on their feelings. For some, the satisfaction was in revenge. For example, the man who had raped and murdered five women:

> It seems like so much bitterness and tension had built up, and this released it. I felt like I had just climbed a mountain and now I could look back.

Another offender characterized rape as habit forming: "Rape is like smoking. You can't stop once you start." Finally, one man expressed the sentiments of many rapists when he stated,

> After rape, I always felt like I had just conquered something, like I had just ridden the bull at Gilley's.

Conclusions

This paper has explored rape from the perspective of a group of convicted, incarcerated rapists. The purpose was to discover how these men viewed sexual violence and what they gained from their behavior.

We found that rape was frequently a means of revenge and punishment. Implicit in revenge-rapes was the notion that women were collectively liable for the rapists' problems. In some cases, victims were substitutes for significant women on whom the men desired to take revenge. In other cases, victims were thought to represent all women, and rape was used to punish, humiliate, and "put them in their place." In both cases women were seen as a class, a category, not as individuals. For some men, rape was almost an afterthought, a bonus added to burglary or robbery. Other men gained access to sexually unavailable or unwilling women through rape. For this group of men, rape was a fantasy come true, a particularly exciting form of impersonal sex which enabled them to dominate and control women, by exercising a singularly male form of power. These rapists talked of the pleasures of raping—how for them it was a challenge, an adventure, a dangerous and "ultimate" experience. Rape made them feel good and, in some cases, even elevated their self-image.

The pleasure these men derived from raping reveals the extreme to which they objectified women. Women were seen as sexual commodities to be used or conquered rather than as human beings with rights and feelings. One young man expressed the extreme of the contemptful view of women when he confided to the female researcher.

> Rape is a man's right. If a woman doesn't want to give it, the man should take it. Women have no right to say no. Women are made to have sex. It's all they are good for. Some women would rather take a beating, but they always give in; it's what they are for.

This man murdered his victim because she wouldn't "give in."

Undoubtedly, some rapes, like some of all crimes, are idiopathic [caused by a condition of unknown origin]. However, it is not necessary to resort to pathological motives to account for all rape or other acts of sexual violence. Indeed, we find that men who rape have something to teach us about the cultural roots of sexual aggression. They force us to acknowledge that rape is more than an idiosyncratic act committed by a few "sick" men. Rather, rape can be viewed as the end point in a continuum of sexually aggressive behaviors that reward men and victimize women. In the way that motives for committing any criminal act can be rationally determined, reasons for rape can also be determined. Our data demonstrate that some men rape because they have learned that in this culture, sexual violence is rewarding. Significantly, the overwhelming majority of these rapists indicated they never thought they would go to prison for what they did. Some did not fear imprisonment because they did not define their behavior as rape. Others knew that women frequently do not report rape and of those cases that are reported, conviction rates are low, and therefore they felt secure. These men perceived rape as a rewarding, low-risk act. Understanding that otherwise normal men can and do rape is critical to the development of strategies for prevention.

We are left with the fact that all men do not rape. In view of the apparent rewards and cultural supports for rape, it is important to ask why some men do not rape. Hirschi (1969) makes a similar observation about delinquency. He argues that the key question is not "Why do they do it?" but rather "Why don't we do it?" (p. 34). Likewise, we may be seeking an answer to the wrong question about sexual assault of women. Instead of asking men who rape "Why?" perhaps we should be asking men who don't "Why not?"

References

Abel, G., J. Becker, and L. Skinner (1980). "Aggressive behavior and sex." *Psychiatric Clinics of North America* 3: 133–51.

Bart, P. (1979). "Rape as a paradigm of sexism in society—victimization and its discontents." *Women's Studies International Quarterly* 2: 347–57.

Black, D. (1983). "Crime as social control." *American Sociological Review* 48: 34–45.

Blumberg, R. L. (1979). "A paradigm for predicting the position of women: Policy implications and problems." Pp. 113–42 in J. Lipman-Blumen and J. Bernard (eds.), *Sex Roles and Social Policy*. London: Sage Studies in International Sociology.

Broude, G., and S. Green (1976). "Cross-cultural codes on twenty sexual attitudes and practices." *Ethnology* 15: 409–28.

Brownmiller, S. (1975). *Against Our Will*. New York: Simon & Schuster.

Fisher, G., and E. Rivlin (1971). "Psychological needs of rapists." *British Journal of Criminology* 11: 182–85.

Griffin, S. (1971, September). "Rape: The all American crime." *Ramparts* 10: 26–35.

Groth, N. (1979). *Men Who Rape*. New York: Plenum Press.

Hammer, E., and I. Jacks (1955). "A study of Rorschach flexnor and extensor human movements." *Journal of Clinical Psychology* 11: 63–67.

Herman, D. (1984). "The rape culture." Pp. 20–39 in J. Freeman (ed.), *Women: A Feminist Perspective*. Palo Alto, CA: Mayfield.

Hirschi, T. (1969). *Causes of Delinquency*. Berkeley: University of California Press.

Hoebel, E. A. (1954). *The Law of Primitive Man*. Boston: Harvard University Press.

Johnson, A. G. (1980). "On the prevalence of rape in the United States." *Signs* 6: 136–46.

Kanin, E. (1957). "Male aggression in dating-courtship relations." *American Journal of Sociology 63:* 197–204.

___ (1965). "Male sex aggression and three psychiatric hypotheses." *Journal of Sex Research 1:* 227–29.

___ (1967). "Reference groups and sex conduct norm violation." *Sociological Quarterly 8:* 495–504.

___ (1969). "Selected dyadic aspects of male sex aggression." *Journal of Sex Research* 5: 12–28.

Kasinsky, R. (1975, September). "Rape: A normal act?" *Canadian Forum,* pp. 18–22.

Kirkpatrick, C., and E. Kanin (1957). "Male sex aggression on a university campus." *American Sociological Review 22:* 52–58.

Koss, M. P., and K. E. Leonard (1984). "Sexually aggressive men: Empirical findings and theoretical implications." Pp. 213–32 in N. M. Malamuth and E. Donnerstein (eds.), *Pornography and Sexual Aggression*. New York: Academic Press.

LaFree, G. (1980). "The effect of sexual stratification by race on official reactions to rape." *American Sociological Review 45:* 824–54.

___ (1982). "Male power and female victimization: Towards a theory of interracial rape." *American Journal of Sociology 88:* 311–28.

Llewellyn, K. N., and E. A. Hoebel (1941). *The Cheyenne Way: Conflict and Case Law in Primitive Jurisprudence*. Norman: University of Oklahoma Press.

Malamuth, N., S. Haber, and S. Feshback (1980). "Testing hypotheses regarding rape: Exposure to sexual violence, sex difference, and the 'normality' of rapists." *Journal of Research in Personality 14:* 121–37.

Malamuth, N., M. Heim, and S. Feshback (1980). "Sexual responsiveness of college students to rape depictions: Inhibitory and disinhibitory effects." *Social Psychology 38:* 399–408.

Meyer, T, J. (1984, December 5). "'Date rape': A serious problem that few talk about." *Chronicle of Higher Education*.

Morgan, R. (1980). "Theory and practice: Pornography and rape." Pp. 134–40 in L. Lederer (ed.), *Take Back the Night: Women on Pornography*. New York: William Morrow.

Rada, R. (1978). *Clinical Aspects of Rape*. New York: Grune & Stratton.

Russell, D. (1975). *The Politics of Rape*. New York: Stein & Day.

Sanday, P. R. (1979). *The Socio-Cultural Context of Rape*. Washington, D.C.: U.S. Dept. of Commerce, National Technical Information Service.

Scully, D., and J. Marolla (1984). "Convicted rapists' vocabulary of motive: Excuses and justifications." *Social Problems 31:* 530–44.

___ (1985). "Rape and psychiatric vocabulary of motive: Alternative perspectives." Pp. 294–312 in A. W. Burgess (ed.), *Rape and Sexual Assault: A Research Handbook*. New York: Garland Publishing.

Smith, D. (1976). "The social context of pornography." *Journal of Communications* 26: 16–24.

Smithyman, S. (1978). *The Undetected Rapist*. Unpublished dissertation. Claremont Graduate School.

West, D. J. (1983). "Sex offenses and offending." Pp. 1–30 in M. Tonry and N. Morris (eds.), *Crime and Justice: An Annual Review of Research*. Chicago: University of Chicago Press.

Weis, K., and S. Borges (1973). "Victimology and rape: The case of the legitimate victim." *Issues in Criminology 8:* 71–115.

Wheeler, H. (1985). "Pornography and rape: A feminist perspective." Pp. 374–91 in A. W. Burgess (ed.), *Rape and Sexual Assault: A Research Handbook*. New York: Garland Publishing.

6 Dealing Crack: Doing Research with Streetcorner Dealers

BRUCE A. JACOBS

Let's suppose that you want to study streetcorner drug dealing. How would you go about it? You could pass out questionnaires, but to whom? Considering how they might be filled out, what confidence could you have in the answers? You could interview people who have been charged with selling illegal drugs, but how would you know if they are similar to dealers who have not been arrested? If you decide to conduct a survey, whom would you survey?

Jacobs faced this dilemma. He wanted accurate information on drug dealing, but how was he to get it? His solution was to go where the action was. He talked to dealers on the streetcorners and observed how they sold drugs. He learned about their lives and why they engage in such risky behavior. Getting dealers to open up wasn't easy, however, for this sociologist was a stranger to them—and his questions seemed too nosey. On top of this, his looks and speech marked him as someone who was not part of their world. At first, the dealers thought that he was from the police, not exactly a comfortable identity in this setting. In this selection, the author focuses on how he overcame these obstacles.

Setting and Respondents

LIKE OTHER POST–WORLD WAR II rustbelt cities of its general size and type, St. Louis has suffered rapid deindustrialization, population loss, resource deprivation, and urban decay. Mobility to surrounding suburbs is high and continues unabated, taking important tax revenue and social capital with it. Since 1990, St. Louis has lost 15 percent of its population; 9,000 residents left in 1997 alone. The city's base of 341,000 makes the impact of such trends acute. St. Louis is developing a concentrated population of the truly disadvantaged—people with scarce resources and abundant social service needs that cannot be met and are getting worse. Such conditions provide an ideal context for drug use, drug selling, and other serious criminality.

Historically, St. Louis has had one of the largest illicit drug markets in the midwestern United States. In many neighborhoods, crack, heroin, marijuana, and PCP are sold openly and are available throughout the day—particularly on the troubled north side, where social disorganization and urban decay are most pronounced. St. Louis arrestees persistently have high rates of cocaine-, opiate-, and marijuana-positive urine specimens; they are among the highest of the twenty-four cities measured in the Drug Use Forecasting program. Emergency room cases involving cocaine and heroin mirror other large metropolitan areas and indicate a high degree of street drug institutionalization. Though street gangs neither control nor direct drug sales in St. Louis, the nearly 1,500 members of forty-five different gangs facilitate them by providing the microstructural networks and mass of contacts necessary for the trade to thrive.

Among the most socially distressed and impoverished areas in the St. Louis metropolitan area, the study neighborhood generally outranks other local sectors in the percentage of people living at or below poverty, proportions of citizens unemployed or on welfare, dropout rates of children of school age, drug arrests, substance abuse rates, and various indicators of poor health. The study neighborhood and contiguous blocks have all the earmarks of an "urban dead zone"—abandoned buildings, burned-out tenements, garbage-strewn vacant lots, and graffiti-splashed walls. Groups of young men collect on the street, selling crack, "insulting one another's sexual prowess, getting high, and looking for an opportunity to make some fast cash."

The study population is made up of curbside (streetcorner) distributors, consisting of persons who "routinely sell crack in the same areas, [though] each is a freelancer with his own supplier and responsible for his own profits and losses." These sellers are gang affiliated but not gang directed. This book, therefore, is not about street gang members who sell crack but about crack sellers who happen to be street gang members. Though the public widely perceives gangs to drive street drug selling, research has consistently demonstrated the rarity of such a phenomenon. Inner-city street gangs do not have exclusive control over crack distribution, and many street distributors are not gang members. Gang membership and crack selling correlate but in a facilitating way: gangs provide the connections and criminal capital necessary to do business. Street gangs, however, are unable to develop and implement hierarchical, functionally interdependent structures that would allow a formal business of selling to happen.

As freelancers, the offenders in my sample are rarely fronted supplies (given crack to sell and allowed to pay for it later), sell for their own individual profit, and generally are in constant competition for a small number of compulsively addicted daily smokers who always try to negotiate the price down. Not infrequently, a number of sellers work the same street, corner, or vacant lot at the same time. Though not always blatant or obtrusive, transactions may easily be observed if looked for. Any organization between or among sellers tends to be crude, primitive, and fleeting. House sales are uncommon because the offenders usually lack access to private dwellings in which to do business. Their "collective orientation" as street gang members also is far too weak to support a social organization conducive to selling from private dwellings.

Entering the Setting

Studying active drug dealers is difficult and challenging precisely because their activity is criminal. Active offenders are generally "hard to locate because they find it necessary to lead clandestine lives. Once located, they are reluctant, for similar reasons, to give accurate and truthful information about themselves." By definition, criminological fieldworkers seek to explore the lives of those engaged in felonies where exposure could mean hard prison time. Outside observers represent a potential legal threat, a fact that impedes a good deal of ethnographic work. The more illegal the behavior, the more offenders have to lose if found out. Individuals may refuse to cooperate or may give less than reliable answers to protect their privacy. It is no surprise that outsiders—such as researchers—are often perceived as narcotics officers seeking to obtain damaging evidence for juridical purposes. Indeed, the most common suspicion that subjects have about fieldworkers is that they are spies of some sort.

I began frequenting a neighborhood known for open street-level crack sales. . . . For weeks, I would either walk or slowly drive through the area to try to be recognized, attempting to capitalize on what Goffman has called second seeings: "under some circumstances if he and they see each other seeing each other, they can use this fact as an excuse for an acquaintanceship greeting upon next seeing." Unfortunately, this process did not go as easily as Goffman suggests. When I drove by, crack dealers yelled "SCAT" at me, screams accentuated with derisive looks and obscene gestures. *SCAT* is an acronym for "street-corner apprehension team." This fifteen-man undercover team is charged with curbing street-level drug sales by apprehending dealers immediately after sales to one of their "buy" officers. Hiding nearby in unmarked cars, personnel swoop down on offenders in an attempt to catch them with the marked money just given to them by purchasing officers. This money has either traceable dye or serial numbers previously recorded that link dealers to undercover transactions. SCAT units were both feared and loathed, being reportedly merciless in their arrest procedures, which involved strip searches and no breaks.

A few more weeks passed and more trips, but I had yet to make any direct contact. Finally, I decided to get out of my car and approach the individuals I had seen dealing. Though this classic ethnographic technique of approaching strangers and initiating dialogue is said to be ineffective with drug dealers, I tried anyway. I told the dealers who I was and that I wished to take a few minutes out of their day to interview them about street life. Predictably they scoffed, accused me of being "the poh-lice," and instructed me to "get the hell out of here." Two days later, I tried again. I showed the dealers my university identification and told them that the interviews would be confidential and anonymous and that they would be paid for their time and effort. It was the money that was critical in generating their interest—even the modest sum that I offered. On the streets, money talks; nobody does anything for nothing.

Though I had made contact, making that contact stick proved difficult because dealers still suspected that I was tied to law enforcement in some way. Ironically, the police gave me my biggest credibility boost.

Police and Credibility

Hanging out with offenders on street corners, driving them around in my car, and visiting their homes must have been a curious sight. My appearance is somewhat like that of a college student. Shorts, t-shirts, casual boots, and baseball caps with rounded brims—"just like SCAT wear them," as one dealer put it—are my typical attire. Further, I am white, clean-cut, and affect a middle-class appearance—traits the relatively poor, African American respondents associate with the police.

To offenders who hadn't gotten to know me well or were waiting to pass judgment, I was seen as being on a deep-cover assignment designed to unearth their secrets and put them in jail. To cops on the beat, I was just another college boy driving down to crackville with a user in tow to buy for him. Such relations are commonplace in the street-level drug scene and have generalized subcultural currency: users serve as middlemen and funnel unfamiliar customers to dealers for a finder's fee, usually in drugs and without the customer's consent (for being "taxed," that is) but generally with his or her tacit permission. When cops see a nicely dressed, clean-shaven white boy, wearing a baseball cap, with a black street person in the passenger seat of a late-model car (a car with out-of-state plates, I might add), they scent that business is in the offering. . . .

My first run-in came two weeks after making initial contact with offenders. I was driving a field contact (an active crack seller) through a crack-filled neighborhood—a neighborhood that also happened to have the highest murder rate in a city with the fourth-highest murder rate in the nation. We were approaching a group of ten midteen youths and were about to stop when a St. Louis City patrol car pulled behind. Should I stop, as I planned on doing, get out, and talk with these youth (some of whom the field contact marginally knew), or would that place them in imminent danger of arrest? Or should I continue on as if nothing was really going on, even though I had been driving stop and go, under ten miles an hour, prior to and during the now slow-speed pursuit? I opted for the latter, accelerating slowly in a vain attempt to reassert a "normal appearance."

Sirens went on. I pulled over and reassured my field contact there was nothing to worry about since neither of us had contraband (I hoped). As officers approached, I thought about what to tell them. Should I say I was a university professor doing field research on crack dealers (a part I clearly didn't look), lie, or say nothing at all? "What you doin' down here?" one of the officers snapped. "Exit the vehicle, intertwine your fingers behind your heads, and kneel with your ankles crossed," he commanded. The searing June sidewalk was not conducive to clear thinking, but I rattled something off. "We used to work together at _____ . I waited tables, he bussed, and we been friends since. I'm a sociology major up at _____ and he said he'd show me around the neighborhood sometime. Here I am." "Yeah right," the cop snapped again while searching for the crack he thought we already had purchased. Three other police cars arrived, as the cop baited my field contact and me as to how we really knew each other, what each other's real names were (which neither of us knew at the time), and what we were doing here. Dissatisfied with my answers, a sergeant took over, lecturing me on the evils of crack and how it would destroy a life others in this very neighborhood wished they had. I found no fault with the argument, listened attentively, and said nothing. After a final strip search in the late afternoon sun revealed nothing, they let us go, said I was lucky, and vowed to take me in if I ever showed my face again.

On a second occasion, my field contact and one of his crack-selling friends were in my car when we pulled up to a local liquor store. The two offenders became nervous on seeing two suits in a "tec" (detective) car parked at the phone booth. I told the two to wait while I went into the store. As I exited, the two men approached me and showed their badges. "What you doin' with these guys? Do you know 'em?" "Yes," I said, deciding to tell them who I *really* was and what I was doing. "Mind if we search your car?" one asked. "No problem," I replied. "Go right ahead." As one searched my car (for crack, guns, or whatever else he thought he'd find), his partner cuffed both of the offenders and ran warrants. As I soon learned, both detectives knew the two as repeat violent offenders with long rap sheets. "I respect what you're doing," the searching officer said as he finished and approached, "but you don't know who you're dealing with. These guys are no good." I told him thanks and promptly left. . . .

I did not realize it at the time, but these episodes with the police were absolutely essential to my research. Police provided the test I desperately needed to pass if my study were to be successful. The differential enforcement practices of these officers—where young minority males are singled out as the "symbolic assailants" and "suspicious characters" deserving of attention—benefited me immensely. Police detained me because I was with them. Driving alone in these same areas at the same time—though suspicious—would not likely have attracted nearly as much attention. I was "guilty by association" and "deserving" of the scrutiny young black males in many urban locales receive consistently. For my research, at least, this differential enforcement was anything but negative.

Police had treated me like just another user and did so with offenders present. This treatment provided the "actions" for me, the picture that spoke a thousand words. Offenders' accounts of my treatment spread rapidly through the grapevine, solidifying my credibility for the remainder of the project, and setting up the snowball sampling procedure I would use to recruit additional respondents.

Why police never attempted to confiscate my notes during these pullovers, I'll never know. Perhaps it was because they appeared to be indecipherable by anyone but me. Perhaps it was because they didn't reveal anything the cops did not already know or at least thought they knew. Regardless, the law is clearly against ethnographers, who can be held in contempt and sent to jail for protecting sources and withholding information. This, of course, says nothing about issues of guilty knowledge or guilty observation. Being aware of dealing operations and watching transactions take place make one an accessory to their commission, a felony whether one participates or not. Criminological fieldworkers almost inevitably will be coconspirators, no matter their motive or intent. "If one is effectively to study adult criminals in their natural settings," Polsky concludes, "he must make the moral decision that in some ways he will break the law himself."

Chain Referral and Data Collection

The first five respondents were recruited directly from the dealers I initially approached. Four of these five became contacts and provided six additional referrals. Three of these six then referred nine additional respondents. This chain referral method was carried out to secure a forty-person sample. Two contacts in particular proved critical for recruiting work. Snowball samples, after all, are only as good as the gatekeepers on the chain. These two had multiple contacts in the study neighborhood and in neighborhoods nearby with similar characteristics, forms of sales organization, and leader-customer/dealer-dealer relations. Roughly half of the forty respondents moved in different sets and lived in different parts of the city, providing the opportunity to address the problem that chain referral methods can have in creating a sample of like-minded offenders that offers limited response variance.

Contacts were given eligibility criteria before referring someone to me. Rather broad ranging and reflective of the variable and often vague nature of participation street-level crack dealing involves, these criteria called for someone who trafficked on streets and public thruways one or more days a week, who had done so for at least six months to several different customers per day (six to fifteen), and who grossed between $300 and $2,000 a month for all activity relevant to street crack sales (that is, selling crack, carrying drugs for someone, steering customers, or other assisting activities).

The first set of forty interviews focused on the social organization of street sales as it pertained to risk perception and detection avoidance. An additional fourteen interviews were structured to explore more systematically the areas that comprise the topical focus of this book—motivation, functions and roles, transactional security, and other core issues in the social organization of streetcorner crack sales. My "intensive fourteen" provided the richest source of data and primary stock of information on which the present study is based.

Ten of the fourteen were new subjects but similar to the original forty respondents on variables such as age, race, gang membership, amount of crack sold, number of hours per day and per week spent selling it, contact in which they sold it, level in the crack distribution hierarchy at which they dealt, and forms of sales activity and social organization in which they participated. I am confident that these fourteen are representative of the original sample and of similar sellers situated in other parts of the city in which streetcorner crack dealing is performed. More on the data's internal and external validity is provided below.

The intensive fourteen's self-reported estimates for the categories listed below were as follows: average gross monthly income per respondent, $1,787; average number of days per week spent selling, six; average grade completion, tenth; average age, 17.5. For the original forty, these estimated averages were as follows: gross monthly income, $2,300; days per week spent selling, 5.5; grade completion, tenth; average age, twenty. Estimations are based on respondent reports and must be interpreted with care, as independent validation of such figures is inherently difficult. All members of the intensive fourteen were African American males. All members of the original forty were African American. Thirty-four of the forty were male, and six were female.

Data were collected using an open-ended interview format guided by specific category and subject headings. This technique allows subjects a measure of latitude and flexibility in their responses. It also helps to make interviews flow much like a conversation, creating a comfort zone between researcher and respondent that facilitates collection of valid and reliable data. Most important, it permits the researcher to study crack sellers without actually becoming one, yielding descriptive data about the dealing subculture and insights into the ways in which sellers "observe, classify, and describe their own life experiences." Interviews were not tape recorded because respondents tended to link recording devices to undercover police. Extensive notes were taken, and further details were filled in immediately after interviews had finished. Interviews took place in private rooms or secluded areas.

Though skeptical at first, interviewees relaxed and opened up soon after interviews had begun. They talked with ease and comfort, apparently trusting the guarantee of anonymity and confidentiality I had given them. Offenders also seemed to enjoy speaking with someone "straight" about their criminal experiences; it may have provided some sort of outlet for them to share their expertise and teach me, someone supposedly "smarter" than them (in terms of academic degrees), a thing or two about street life. Respondents also may see something in the research that benefits them or define it as an opportunity to correct faulty impressions of what it is they do. Finally, the legitimation from my field contacts was critical; if they told others that it was "cool" to talk to me and that participants would not be "burned" as a result, it tended to be believed.

How reliable and valid are my data? Here I was intruding into the lives of individuals engaged in felonies for which they could receive long sentences. How could I know they were giving me the straight story? How could it have been in their interest to provide incisive, accurate comments about their lives when divulging such details might undermine their success as dealers? To begin, though the inclusion criteria seem fairly straightforward, they are inherently difficult to apply in the real world of street dealing. Some respondents may have lied about their dealing status. Others may have failed to meet the specified eligibility requirements: it seemed a waste, however, to turn away potentially valuable respondents for the sake of adhering to a somewhat arbitrary operational definition of eligibility in the first place. I tried to compensate for possible mistakes by using unobtrusive observational measures— a very revealing strategy. In one case, a respondent interrupted our interview to run to a nearby restroom so that he could regurgitate two $20 rocks he had swallowed ten minutes before in an attempt to avoid arrest. This is one among a number of such stories. I impressed on my contacts the importance of having referrals meet the criteria and, of course, asked specifically targeted questions designed to screen out those who were inappropriate for the study. That I may not have been able to match every offender to the specified criteria need not be devastating. As Van Maanen notes, imperfections are an inevitable part of fieldwork, given the complexity of the enterprise.

Though participants in the drug market have an image of lying or evading the truth more than others (both nonoffending citizens and other offenders), there is little evidence to support this claim. Self-report data have been carefully assessed by a number of researchers, all of whom conclude that drug dealers are among the best, if not the best, source of information about the behaviors being studied. The most accurate self-report designs are those that ask questions regarding serious criminality and those that involve face-to-face data collection—my technique—rather than surveys administered impersonally. Offender reports are not always immune from "exaggerations, intentional distortions, lies, self-serving rationalizations, or drug-induced forgetfulness," but they may be less susceptible than some might think.

The fact that responses became repetitious indicated sufficient topical coverage, although such repetition could have been an artifact of the sampling design itself. Dealers may have conspired to respond only in a certain way, but their separation from each other in the interview process—both contextually and in many cases over periods of time—makes this unlikely. Reasonable effort was made to question every offender about every issue, but the nature of open-ended qualitative interviewing is such that not all topics could be anticipated and not all offenders could be asked the same questions about issues that emerged later, often serendipitously, during the research process.

The unobtrusive observation I engaged in of drug sales and interactions among dealers over the twenty-two-month research period, though unsystematic, confirmed many of the issues reported in the interviews. I have supplemented these interview and observational data with information collected during the course of several years of field research on the use, distribution, and control of street drugs—preceding and including the study period—from persons and places relevant to the present topic. Eight months of ride-alongs with officers from an elite gun and drug unit in the St. Louis City Police Department form part of this experiential reservoir. The researcher is the research instrument in qualitative research, and such experiences can be key to the form, content, and structure of the work produced.

PART III

The Cultural Context of Social Life

WHAT IS CULTURE? The concept is easier to grasp by description than by definition. For example, when we meet someone from a different culture, that person's culture is immediately evident to us. We see it in his or her clothing, jewelry, and gestures. We hear it when that person speaks a different language—or, when speaking our language, the individual uses awkward expressions and unusual pronunciation. The individual may also voice attitudes and opinions unlike ours. We may even smell it in unfamiliar perfumes and body lotions. These characteristics, especially when they contrast sharply with our own, alert us to broad differences in the way that person was reared—to that person's culture.

Culture consists of *material* things, such as buildings, art, weapons, utensils, machines, clothing, and jewelry. Culture is also *nonmaterial*, consisting of the beliefs and patterns of behavior common to a group of people. Nonmaterial (or *symbolic*) culture is of primary interest to sociologists, for it provides the broad framework that people use to interpret life. Culture is the lens through which we see the world, the basis on which we construct reality and make our decisions.

Understanding how culture affects people's lives is essential to attaining a sociological imagination. But while we may become aware of culture's pervasive influence when we meet someone from a different culture, our perception of *our own* culture is quite another matter. We usually take *our* speech, *our* body language, *our* beliefs, and *our* ways of doing things for granted. We assume that these are normal or natural, and almost without exception we perform them without question. As Ralph Linton said, "The last

75

thing a fish would ever notice would be water." So it is with us: Except for unusual circumstances, the effects of our own culture generally remain imperceptible to us.

Yet culture's significance is profound—not only for our behavior, but also for our orientations to life, and, ultimately, for our very being. It would be difficult to identify any aspect of who and what we are that is untouched by culture. We came into this life without a language, without values, with no ideas about religion, education, war, money, jobs, friendship, love, truth, honesty, honor, humor, family relationships, and so on. At birth, we possessed no such fundamental orientations to social life—which are so essential in determining the type of people we are. Yet now we take them for granted. This, we might say, is culture *within* us.

These learned and shared ways of believing and of doing things (another way to define culture) penetrate our being at an early age. They become part of our basic assumptions about what normal is. They form the screen through which we perceive and evaluate our world. Seldom do we question these assumptions, because like water for a fish, they form our framework for viewing life but remain beyond our ordinary perception.

On occasion, however, some unusual event may challenge our background assumptions. This makes our assumptions more visible to us, and, if we are fortunate, it even makes us aware of how arbitrary they are. For example, when several Americans converge at a ticket booth they usually line up on the basis of time of arrival. The ticket seller, who shares the same culture, also assumes the normalcy of this behavior and expects to sell tickets on a "first come, first served" basis. To us, this seems the natural way of doing things, and we engage in this behavior routinely, and without thought.

But in northern Africa, where people's ideas of how to use space sharply contrast with ours, when several people want a ticket each pushes his or her way toward the ticket booth. With no idea similar to our "first come, first served" notion, the ticket seller first dispenses tickets to the noisiest, the pushiest, and (not incidentally) those with the longest arms.

When I traveled in northern Africa, I found this part of their culture most upsetting. It violated my basic expectations of how people *ought* to act—expectations that I did not even know I held until they were challenged so abruptly. At that point I experienced *culture shock*, the sudden inability to depend on the basic orientations to everyday life learned in childhood. That I was several inches taller than most Arabs, however, and was able to outreach almost everyone, helped me to adjust (partially) to this different way of doing things. I never did get used to the idea that pushing ahead of others was "right," though, and always felt guilty about using the accident of my height to receive preferential treatment.

It is to sensitize us to this aspect of life in society—to how cultural factors so fundamentally influence our lives—that the selections in this third Part are directed. Each reading introduces us to aspects of our social lives that ordinarily go unquestioned and unnoticed. Horace Miner helps make visible our basic assumptions about taking care of the body; Napoleon Chagnon exposes our taken-for-granted assumptions about sharing, making requests, and how to treat strangers and guests; Edward and Mildred Hall illustrate how culture influences our posture, gestures, eye contact, and use of space in face-to-face interaction; Theodore Caplow uncovers the cultural rules, many hidden beneath our consciousness, that govern our giving of Christmas gifts; and Erving Goffman helps us to see how our nonverbal communications are intricate ways by which we attempt to manipulate people's opinions of us. These analyses of culture can serve as starting points from which we can begin to analyze other assumptions of reality that we unquestioningly hold, and thus gain a startlingly different perspective of social life—and of our own roles in it.

7 Body Ritual Among the Nacirema

HORACE MINER

As part of their culture, all peoples develop ideas about proper ways to care for their bodies. The Nacirema, however, have advanced these ideas to an extraordinary degree, and they spend a good deal of their time, energy, and income following the rituals prescribed by their culture. Taking care of the body in the prescribed manner is so important to these people that even a good part of their childrearing revolves around instructing their children in the precise manner of fulfilling their cultural rituals. With intense and prolonged training, accompanied by punishing children who fail to conform while shunning nonconforming adults, it is no wonder that almost all members of the Nacirema culture unquestioningly conform to their prescribed body rituals and dutifully pass them on to their own children.

A better understanding of the Nacirema culture might possibly shed some light on our own way of life.

THE ANTHROPOLOGIST HAS BECOME so familiar with the diversity of ways in which different peoples behave in similar situations that he is not apt to be surprised by even the most exotic customs. In fact, if all of the logically possible combinations of behavior have not been found somewhere in the world, he is apt to suspect that they must be present in some yet undescribed tribe. This point has, in fact, been expressed with respect to clan organization by Murdock. In this light, the magical beliefs and practices of the Nacirema present such unusual aspects that it seems desirable to describe them as an example of the extremes to which human behavior can go.

Professor Linton first brought the ritual of the Nacirema to the attention of anthropologists twenty years ago, but the culture of this people is still very poorly understood. They are a North American group living in the territory between the Canadian Cree, the Yaqui and Tarahumare of Mexico, and the Carib and Arawak of the Antilles. Little is known of their origin, although tradition states that they came from the east.

Nacirema culture is characterized by a highly developed market economy which has evolved in a rich natural habitat. While much of the people's time is devoted to economic pursuits, a large part of the fruits of these labors and a considerable portion of the day are spent in ritual activity. The focus of this activity is the human body, the appearance and health of which loom as a dominant concern in the ethos of the people. While such a concern is certainly not unusual, its ceremonial aspects and associated philosophy are unique.

The fundamental belief underlying the whole system appears to be that the human body is ugly and that its natural tendency is to debility and disease. Incarcerated in such a body, people's only hope is to avert these characteristics through the use of the powerful influences of ritual and ceremony. Every household has one or more shrines devoted to this purpose. The more powerful individuals in the society have several shrines in their houses and, in fact, the opulence of a house is often referred to in terms of the number of such ritual centers it possesses. Most houses are of wattle and daub construction, but the shrine rooms of the more wealthy are walled with stone. Poorer families imitate the rich by applying pottery plaques to their shrine walls.

While each family has at least one such shrine, the rituals associated with it are not family ceremonies but are private and secret. The rites are normally only discussed with children, and then only during the period when they are being initiated into these mysteries. I was able, however, to establish sufficient rapport with the natives to examine these shrines and to have the rituals described to me.

The focal point of the shrine is a box or chest which is built into the wall. In this chest are kept the many charms and magical potions without which no native believes he could live. These preparations are secured from a variety of specialized practitioners. The most powerful of these are the medicine men, whose assistance must be rewarded with substantial gifts. However, the medicine men do not provide the curative potions for their clients, but decide what the ingredients should be and then write them down in an ancient and secret language. This writing is understood only by the medicine men and by the herbalists who, for another gift, provide the required charm.

The charm is not disposed of after it has served its purpose, but is placed in the charm-box of the household shrine. As these magical materials are specific for certain ills, and the real or imagined maladies of the people are many, the charm-box is usually full to overflowing. The magical packets are so numerous that people forget what their purposes were and fear to use them again. While the natives are very vague on this point, we can only assume that the idea in retaining all the old magical materials is that their presence in the charm-box, before which the body rituals are conducted, will in some way protect the worshipper.

Beneath the charm-box is a small font. Each day every member of the family, in succession, enters the shrine room, bows his head before the charm-box, mingles different sorts of holy water in the font, and proceeds with a brief rite of ablution. The holy waters are secured from the Water Temple of the community, where the priests conduct elaborate ceremonies to make the liquid ritually pure.

In the hierarchy of magical practitioners, and below the medicine men in prestige, are specialists whose designation is best translated "holy-mouth-men." The Nacirema have an almost pathological horror of and fascination with the mouth, the condition of which is believed to have a supernatural influence on all social relationships. Were it not for the rituals of the mouth, they believe that their teeth would fall out, their gums bleed, their jaws shrink, their friends desert them, and their lovers reject them. They also believe that a strong relationship exists between oral and moral characteristics. For example, there is a ritual ablution of the mouth for children which is supposed to improve their moral fiber.

The daily body ritual performed by everyone includes a mouth-rite. Despite the fact that these people are so punctilious about care of the mouth, this rite involves a practice which strikes the uninitiated stranger as revolting. It was reported to me that the ritual consists of inserting a small bundle of hog hairs into the mouth, along with certain magical powders, and then moving the bundle in a highly formalized series of gestures.

In addition to the private mouth-rite, the people seek out a holy-mouth-man once or twice a year. These practitioners have an impressive set of paraphernalia, consisting of a variety of augers, awls, probes, and prods. The use of these objects in the exorcism of the evils of the mouth involves almost unbelievable ritual torture of the client. The holy-mouth-man opens the client's mouth and, using the above mentioned tools, enlarges any holes which decay may have created in the teeth. Magical materials are put into these holes. If there are no naturally occurring holes in the teeth, large sections of one or more teeth are gouged out so that the supernatural substance can be applied. In the client's view, the purpose of these ministrations is to arrest decay and draw friends. The extremely sacred and traditional character of the rite is evident in the fact that the natives return to the holy-mouth-men year after year, despite the fact that their teeth continue to decay.

It is to be hoped that, when a thorough study of the Nacirema is made, there will be careful inquiry into the personality structure of these people. One has but to watch the gleam in the eye of a holy-mouth-man, as he jabs an awl into an exposed nerve, to suspect that a certain amount of sadism is involved. If this can be established, a very interesting pattern emerges, for most of the population shows definite masochistic tendencies. It was to these that Professor Linton referred in discussing a distinctive part of the daily body ritual which is performed only by men. This part of the rite involves scraping and lacerating the surface of the face with a sharp instrument. Special women's rites are performed only four times during each lunar month, but what they lack in frequency is made up in barbarity. As part of this ceremony, women bake their heads in small ovens for about an hour. The theoretically interesting point is that what seems to be a preponderantly masochistic people have developed sadistic specialists.

The medicine men have an imposing temple, or *latipso,* in every community of any size. The more elaborate ceremonies required to treat very sick patients can only be performed at this temple. These ceremonies involve not only the thaumaturge but a permanent group of vestal maidens who move sedately about the temple chambers in distinctive costume and headdress.

The *latipso* ceremonies are so harsh that it is phenomenal that a fair proportion of the really sick natives who enter the temple ever recover. Small children whose indoctrination is still incomplete have been known to resist attempts to take them to the temple because "that is where you go to die." Despite this fact, sick adults are not only willing but eager to undergo the protracted ritual purification, if they can afford to do so. No matter how ill the supplicant or how grave the emergency, the guardians of many temples will not admit a client if he cannot give a rich gift to the custodian. Even after one has gained admission and survived the ceremonies, the guardians will not permit the neophyte to leave until he makes still another gift.

The supplicant entering the temple is first stripped of all his or her clothes. In everyday life the Nacirema avoids exposure of his body and its natural functions. Bathing and excretory acts are performed only in the secrecy of the household shrine, where they are ritualized as part of the body-rites. Psychological shock results from the fact that body secrecy is suddenly lost upon entry into the *latipso.* A man whose own wife has never seen him in an excretory act, suddenly finds himself naked and assisted by a vestal maiden while he performs his natural functions into a sacred vessel. This sort of ceremonial treatment is necessitated by the fact that the excreta are used by a diviner to ascertain the course and nature of the client's sickness. Female clients, on the other hand, find their naked bodies are subjected to the scrutiny, manipulation, and prodding of the medicine men.

Few supplicants in the temple are well enough to do anything but lie on their hard beds. The daily ceremonies, like the rites of the holy-mouth-men, involve discomfort and torture. With ritual precision, the vestals awaken their miserable charges each dawn and roll them about on their beds of pain while performing ablutions, in the formal movements of which the maidens are highly trained. At other times they insert magic wands in the supplicant's mouth or force him to eat substances which are supposed to be healing. From time to time the medicine men come to their clients and jab magically treated needles into their flesh. The fact that these temple ceremonies may not cure, and may even kill the neophyte, in no way decreases the people's faith in the medicine men.

There remains one other kind of practitioner, known as a "listener." This witchdoctor has the power to exorcise the devils that lodge in the heads of people who have been bewitched. The Nacirema believe that parents bewitch their own children. Mothers are particularly suspected of putting a curse on children while teaching them the secret body rituals. The counter-magic of the witchdoctor is unusual in its lack of ritual. The patient simply tells the "listener" all his troubles and fears, beginning with the earliest difficulties he can remember. The memory displayed by the Nacirema in these exorcism sessions is truly remarkable. It is not uncommon for the patient to bemoan the rejection he felt upon being weaned as a babe, and a few individuals even see their troubles going back to the traumatic effects of their own birth.

In conclusion, mention must be made of certain practices which have their base in native esthetics but which depend upon the pervasive aversion to the natural body and its functions. There are ritual fasts to make fat people thin and ceremonial feasts to make thin people fat. Still other rites are used to make women's breasts larger if they are small, and smaller if they are large. General dissatisfaction with breast shape is symbolized in the fact that the ideal form is virtually outside the range of human variation. A few women afflicted with almost inhuman hyper-mammary development are so idolized that they make a handsome living by simply going from village to village and permitting the natives to stare at them for a fee.

Reference has already been made to the fact that excretory functions are ritualized, routinized, and relegated to secrecy. Natural reproductive functions are similarly distorted. Intercourse is taboo as a topic and scheduled as an act. Efforts are made to avoid pregnancy by the use of magical materials or by limiting intercourse to certain phases of the moon. Conception is actually very infrequent. When pregnant, women dress so as to hide their condition. Parturition takes place in secret, without friends or relatives to assist, and the majority of women do not nurse their infants.

Our review of the ritual life of the Nacirema has certainly shown them to be a magic-ridden people. It is hard to understand how they have managed to exist so long under the burdens which they have imposed upon themselves. But even such exotic customs as these take on real meaning when they are viewed with the insight provided by Malinowski when he wrote:

> Looking from far and above, from our high places of safety in the developed civilization, it is easy to see all the crudity and irrelevance of magic. But without its power and guidance early man could not have mastered his practical difficulties as he has done, nor could man have advanced to the higher stages of civilization.

8 Doing Fieldwork Among the Yąnomamö

NAPOLEON A. CHAGNON

As stated in the second reading, the primary difference between sociology and anthropology is the choice of research setting. That is, sociologists usually study people living in industrialized and post-industrialized societies, while anthropologists usually focus on tribal and peasant groups. The distinction does not always hold, however, because some anthropologists do research in urban settings, and occasionally a sociologist wanders into peasant society. Consequently, it makes little difference that the fieldwork reported here was done by an anthropologist, for if a sociologist had done participant observation among the Yąnomamö, he or she would have written a similar account of those experiences. (Sociologists, however, are considerably less interested in kinship and genealogy.)

Note how the culture of the Yąnomamö sets the stage for their behaviors. Although from our perspective their behaviors are strange, this is the way of life that the Yąnomamö take for granted. What they experience is as natural for them as our way of life is for us. But, as Chagnon discovered firsthand, for someone from our culture to experience Yąnomamö life is to encounter an alien world. Chagnon experienced *culture shock*—that is, the fundamentals of life that he had learned and lived with from childhood no longer applied, and he was most uncomfortable with what he confronted. How would you have felt in his place?

THE YĄNOMAMÖ INDIANS live in southern Venezuela and the adjacent portions of northern Brazil. Some 125 widely scattered villages have populations ranging from 40 to 250 inhabitants, with 75 to 80 people the most usual number. In total numbers their population probably approaches 10,000 people, but this is merely a guess. Many of the villages have not yet been contacted by outsiders, and nobody knows for sure exactly how many uncontacted villages there are, or how many people live in them. By comparison to African or Melanesian tribes, the Yąnomamö population is small. Still, they are one of the largest unacculturated tribes left in all of South America.

But they have a significance apart from tribal size and cultural purity: The Yąnomamö are still actively conducting warfare. It is in the nature of man to fight, according to one of their myths, because the blood of "Moon" spilled on this layer of the cosmos, causing men to become fierce. I describe the Yąnomamö as "the fierce people" because that is the most accurate single phrase that describes them. That is how they conceive themselves to be, and that is how they would like others to think of them.

I spent nineteen months with the Yąnomamö, during which time I acquired some proficiency in their language and, up to a point, submerged myself in their culture and way of life. The thing that impressed me most was the importance of aggression in their culture. I had the opportunity to witness a good many incidents that expressed individual vindictiveness on the one hand and collective bellicosity on the other. These ranged in seriousness from the ordinary incidents of wife beating and chest pounding to dueling and organized raiding by parties that set out with the intention of ambushing and killing men from enemy villages. One of the villages was raided approximately twenty-five times while I conducted the fieldwork, six times by the group I lived among. . . .

This is not to state that primitive man everywhere is unpleasant. By way of contrast, I have also done limited fieldwork among the Yąnomamö's northern neighbors, the Carib-speaking Makiritare Indians. This group was very pleasant and charming, all of them anxious to help me and honor bound to show any visitor the numerous courtesies of their system of etiquette. In short, they approached the image of primitive man that I had conjured up, and it was sheer pleasure to work with them. . . .

My first day in the field illustrated to me what my teachers meant when they spoke of "culture shock." I had traveled in a small, aluminum rowboat propelled by a large outboard motor for two and a half days. This took me from the Territorial capital, a small town on the Orinoco River, deep into Yąnomamö country. On the morning of the third day we reached a small mission settlement, the field "headquarters" of a group of Americans who were working in two Yąnomamö villages. The missionaries had come out of these villages to hold their annual conference on the progress of their mission work, and were conducting their meetings when I arrived. We picked up a passenger at the mission station, James P. Barker, the first non-Yąnomamö to make a sustained, permanent contact with the tribe (in 1950). He had just returned from a year's furlough in the United States, where I had earlier visited him before leaving for Venezuela. He agreed to accompany me to the village I had selected for my base of operations to introduce me to the Indians. This village was also his own home base, but he had not been there for over a year and did not plan to join me for another three months. Mr. Barker had been living with this particular group about five years.

We arrived at the village, Bisaasi-teri, about 2:00 P.M. and docked the boat along the muddy bank at the terminus of the path used by the Indians to fetch their drinking water. It was hot and muggy, and my clothing was soaked with perspiration. It clung uncomfortably to my body, as it did thereafter for the remainder of the work. The small, biting gnats were out in astronomical numbers, for it was the beginning of the dry season. My face and hands were swollen from the venom of their numerous stings. In just a few moments I was to meet my first Yąnomamö, my first primitive man. What would it be like? I had visions of entering the village and seeing 125 social facts running about calling each other kinship terms and sharing food, each waiting and anxious to have me collect his genealogy. I would wear them out in turn. Would they like me? This was important to me; I wanted them to be so fond of me that they would adopt me into their kinship system and way of life, because I had heard that successful anthropologists always get adopted by their people. I had learned during my seven years of anthropological training at the University of Michigan that kinship was equivalent to society in primitive tribes and that it was a moral way of life, "moral" being something "good" and "desirable." I was determined to work my way into their moral system of kinship and become a member of their society.

My heart began to pound as we approached the village and heard the buzz of activity within the circular compound. Mr. Barker commented that he was anxious to see if any changes had taken place while he was away and wondered how many of them had died during his absence. I felt into my back pocket to make sure that my notebook was there and felt personally more secure when I touched it. Otherwise, I would not have known what to do with my hands.

I looked up and gasped when I saw a dozen burly, naked, filthy, hideous men staring at us down the shafts of their drawn arrows! Immense wads of green tobacco were stuck between their lower teeth and lips making them look even more hideous, and strands of dark-green slime dripped or hung from their noses. We arrived at the village while the men were blowing a hallucinogenic drug up their noses. One of the side effects of the drug is a runny nose. The mucus is always saturated with the green powder and the Indians usually let it run freely from their nostrils. My next discovery was that there were a dozen or so vicious, underfed dogs snapping at my legs, circling me as if I were going to be their next meal. I just stood there holding my notebook, helpless and pathetic. Then the stench of the decaying vegetation and filth struck me and I almost got sick. I was horrified. What sort of a welcome was this for the person who came here to live with you and learn your way of life, to become friends with you? They put their weapons down when they recognized Barker and returned to their chanting, keeping a nervous eye on the village entrances.

We had arrived just after a serious fight. Seven women had been abducted the day before by a neighboring group, and the local men and their guests had just that morning recovered five of them in a brutal club fight that nearly ended in a shooting war. The abductors, angry because they lost five of the seven captives, vowed to raid the Bisaasi-teri. When we arrived and entered the village unexpectedly, the Indians feared that we were the raiders. On several occasions during the next two hours the men in the village jumped to their feet, armed themselves, and waited nervously for the noise outside the village to be identified. My enthusiasm for collecting ethnographic curiosities diminished in proportion to the number of times such an alarm was raised. In fact, I was relieved when Mr. Barker suggested that we sleep across the river for the evening. It would be safer over there.

As we walked down the path to the boat, I pondered the wisdom of having decided to spend a year and a half with this tribe before I had even seen what they were like. I am not ashamed to admit, either, that had there been a diplomatic way out, I would have ended my fieldwork then and there. I did not look forward to the next day when I would be left alone with the Indians; I did not speak a word of their language, and they were decidedly different from what I had imagined them to be. The whole situation was depressing, and I wondered why I ever decided to switch from civil engineering to anthropology in the first place. I had not eaten all day, I was soaking wet from perspiration, the gnats were biting me, and I was covered with red pigment, the result of a dozen or so complete examinations I had been given by as many burly Indians. These examinations capped an otherwise grim day. The Indians would blow their noses into their hands, flick as much of the mucus off that would separate in a snap of the wrist, wipe the residue into their hair, and then carefully examine my face, arms, legs, hair, and the contents of my pockets. I asked Mr. Barker how to say "Your hands are dirty"; my comments were met by the Indians in the following way: They would "clean" their hands by spitting a quantity of slimy tobacco juice into them, rub them together, and then proceed with the examination.

Mr. Barker and I crossed the river and slung our hammocks. When he pulled his hammock out of a rubber bag, a heavy, disagreeable odor of mildewed cotton came with it. "Even the missionaries are filthy," I thought to myself. Within two weeks everything I owned smelled the same way, and I lived with the odor for the remainder of the fieldwork. My own habits of personal cleanliness reached such levels that I didn't even mind being examined by the Indians, as I was not much cleaner than they were after I had adjusted to the circumstances.

So much for my discovery that primitive man is not the picture of nobility and sanitation I had conceived him to be. I soon discovered that it was an enormously time-consuming task to maintain my own body in the manner to which it had grown accustomed in the relatively antiseptic environment of the northern United States. Either I could be relatively well fed and relatively comfortable in a fresh change of clothes and do very little fieldwork, or, I could do considerably more fieldwork and be less well fed and less comfortable.

It is appalling how complicated it can be to make oatmeal in the jungle. First, I had to make two trips to the river to haul the water. Next, I had to prime my kerosene stove with alcohol and get it burning, a tricky procedure when you are trying to mix powdered milk and fill a coffee pot at the same time: the alcohol prime always burned out before I could turn the kerosene on, and I would have to start all over. Or, I would turn the kerosene on, hoping that the element was still hot enough to vaporize the fuel, and not start a small fire in my palm-thatched hut as the liquid kerosene squirted all over the table and walls and ignited. It was safer to start over with the alcohol. Then I had to boil the oatmeal and pick the bugs out of it. All my supplies, of course, were carefully stored in Indian-proof, ratproof, moisture-proof, and insect-proof containers, not one of which ever served its purpose adequately. Just taking things out of the multiplicity of containers and repacking them afterward was a minor project in itself. By the time I had hauled the water to cook with, unpacked my food, prepared the oatmeal, milk, and coffee, heated water for dishes, washed and dried the dishes, repacked the food in the containers, stored the containers in locked trunks and cleaned up my mess, the ceremony of preparing breakfast had brought me almost up to lunch time.

Eating three meals a day was out of the question. I solved the problem by eating a single meal that could be prepared in a single container, or, at most, in two containers, washed my dishes only when there were no clean ones left, using cold river water, and wore each change of clothing at least a week to cut down on my laundry problem, a courageous undertaking in the tropics. I was also less concerned about sharing my provisions with the rats, insects, Indians, and the elements, thereby eliminating the need for my complicated storage process. I was able to last most of the day on *café con leche,* heavily sugared espresso coffee diluted about five to one with hot milk. I would prepare this in the evening and store it in a thermos. Frequently, my single meal was no more complicated than a can of sardines and a package of crackers. But at least two or three times a week I would do something sophisticated, like make oatmeal or boil rice and add a can of tuna fish or tomato paste to it. I even saved time by devising a water system that obviated the trips to the river. I had a few sheets of zinc roofing brought in and made a rain-water trap. I caught the water on the zinc surface, funneled it into an empty gasoline drum, and then ran a plastic hose from the drum to my hut. When the drum was exhausted in the dry season, I hired the Indians to fill it with water from the river.

I ate much less when I traveled with the Indians to visit other villages. Most of the time my travel diet consisted of roasted or boiled green plantains that I obtained from the Indians, but I always carried a few cans of sardines with me in case I got lost or stayed away longer than I had planned. I found peanut butter and crackers a very nourishing food, and a simple one to prepare on trips. It was nutritious and portable, and only one tool was required to prepare the meal, a hunting knife that could be cleaned by wiping the blade on a leaf. More importantly, it was one of the few foods the Indians would let me eat in relative peace. It looked too much like animal feces to them to excite their appetites.

I once referred to the peanut butter as the dung of cattle. They found this quite repugnant. They did not know what "cattle" were, but were generally aware that I ate several canned products of such an animal. I perpetrated this myth, if for no other reason than to have some peace of mind while I ate. Fieldworkers develop strange defense mechanisms, and this was one of my own forms of adaptation. On another occasion I was eating a can of frankfurters and growing very weary of the demands of one of my guests for a share in my meal. When he asked me what I was eating, I replied: "Beef." He then asked, "What part of the animal are you eating?" to which I replied, "Guess!" He stopped asking for a share.

Meals were a problem in another way. Food sharing is important to the Yąnomamö in the context of displaying friendship. "I am hungry," is almost a form of greeting with them. I could not possibly have brought enough food with me to feed the entire village, yet they seemed not to understand this. All they could see was that I did not share my food with them at each and every meal. Nor could I enter into their system of reciprocities with respect to food; every time one of them gave me something "freely," he would dog me for months to pay him back, not with food, but with steel tools. Thus, if I accepted a plantain from someone in a different village while I was on a visit, he would most likely visit me in the future and demand a machete as payment for the time that he "fed" me. I usually reacted to these kinds of demands by giving a banana, the customary reciprocity in their culture—food for food— but this would be a disappointment for the individual who had visions of that single plantain growing into a machete over time.

Despite the fact that most of them knew I would not share my food with them at their request, some of them always showed up at my hut during mealtime. I gradually became accustomed to this and learned to ignore their persistent demands while I ate. Some of them would get angry because I failed to give in, but most of them accepted it as just a peculiarity of the subhuman foreigner. When I did give in, my hut quickly filled with Indians, each demanding a sample of the food that I had given one of them. If I did not give all a share, I was that much more despicable in their eyes.

A few of them went out of their way to make my meals unpleasant, to spite me for not sharing; for example, one man arrived and watched me eat a cracker with honey on it. He immediately recognized the honey, a particularly esteemed Yąnomamö food. He knew that I would not share my tiny bottle and that it would be futile to ask. Instead, he glared at me and queried icily, "Shaki![1] What kind of animal semen are you eating on that cracker?" His question had the desired effect, and my meal ended.

Finally, there was the problem of being lonely and separated from your own kind, especially your family. I tried to overcome this by seeking personal friendships among the Indians. This only complicated the matter because all my friends simply used my confidence to gain privileged access to my cache of steel tools and trade goods, and looted me. I would be bitterly disappointed that my "friend" thought no more of me than to finesse our relationship exclusively with the intention of getting at any locked up possessions, and my depression would hit new lows every time I discovered this. The loss of the possession bothered me much less than the shock that I was, as far as most of them were concerned, nothing more than a source of desirable items; no holds were barred in relieving me of these, since I was considered something subhuman, a non-Yąnomamö.

The thing that bothered me most was the incessant, passioned, and aggressive demands the Indians made. It would become so unbearable that I would have to lock myself in my mud hut every once in a while just to escape from it: Privacy is one of Western culture's greatest achievements. But I did not want privacy for its own sake; rather, I simply had to get away from the begging. Day and night for the entire time I lived with the Yąnomamö I was plagued by such demands as: "Give me a knife, I am poor!"; "If you don't take me with you on your next trip to Widokaiya-teri, I'll chop a hole in your canoe!"; "Don't point your camera at me or I'll hit you!"; "Share your food with me!"; "Take me across the river in your canoe and be quick about it!"; "Give me a cooking pot!"; "Loan me your flashlight so I can go hunting tonight!"; "Give me medicine . . . I itch all over!"; "Take us on a week-long hunting trip with your shotgun!"; and "Give me an axe, or I'll break into your hut when you are away visiting and steal one!" And so I was bombarded by such demands day after day, months on end, until I could not bear to see an Indian.

It was not as difficult to become calloused to the incessant begging as it was to ignore the sense of urgency, the impassioned tone of voice, or the intimidation and aggression with which the demands were made. It was likewise difficult to adjust to the fact that the Yąnomamö refused to accept "no" for an answer until or unless it seethed with passion and intimidation—which it did after six months. Giving in to a demand always established a new threshold; the next demand would be for a bigger item or favor, and the anger of the Indians even greater if the demand was not met. I soon learned that I had to become very much like the Yąnomamö to be able to get along with them on their terms: sly, aggressive, and intimidating.

Had I failed to adjust in this fashion I would have lost six months of supplies to them in a single day or would have spent most of my time ferrying them around in my canoe or hunting for them. As it was, I did spend a considerable amount of time doing these things and did succumb to their outrageous demands for axes and machetes, at least at first. More importantly, had I failed to demonstrate that I could not be pushed around beyond a certain point, I would have been the subject of far more ridicule, theft, and practical jokes than was the actual case. In short, I had to acquire a certain proficiency in their kind of interpersonal politics and to learn how to imply subtly that certain potentially undesirable consequences might follow if they did such and such to me. They do this to each other in order to establish precisely the point at which they cannot goad an individual any further without precipitating retaliation. As soon as I caught on to this and realized that much of their aggression was stimulated by their desire to discover my flash point, I got along much better with them and regained some lost ground. It was sort of like a political game that everyone played, but one in which each individual sooner or later had to display some sign that his bluffs and implied threats could be backed up. I suspect that the frequency of wife beating is a component of this syndrome, since men can display their ferocity and show others that they are capable of violence. Beating a wife with a club is considered to be an acceptable way of displaying ferocity and one that does not expose the male to much danger. The important thing is that the man has displayed his potential for violence and the implication is that other men better treat him with respect and caution.

After six months, the level of demand was tolerable in the village I used for my headquarters. The Indians and I adjusted to each other and knew what to expect with regard to demands on their part for goods, favors, and services. Had I confined my fieldwork to just that village alone, the field experience would have been far more enjoyable. But, as I was interested in the demographic pattern and social organization of a much larger area, I made regular trips to some dozen different villages in order to collect genealogies or to recheck those I already had. Hence, the intensity of begging and intimidation was fairly constant for the duration of the fieldwork. I had to establish my position in some sort of pecking order of ferocity at each and every village.

For the most part, my own "fierceness" took the form of shouting back at the Yąnomamö as loudly and as passionately as they shouted at me, especially at first, when I did not know much of their language. As I became more proficient in their language and learned more about their political tactics, I became more sophisticated in the art of bluffing. For example, I paid one young man a machete to cut palm trees and make boards from the wood. I used these to fashion a platform in the bottom of my dugout canoe to keep my possessions dry when I traveled by river. That afternoon I was doing informant work in the village; the long-awaited mission supply boat arrived, and most of the Indians ran out of the village to beg goods from the crew. I continued to work in the village for another hour or so and went down to the river to say "hello" to the men on the supply boat. I was angry when I discovered that the Indians had chopped up all my palm boards and used them to paddle their own canoes across the river. I knew that if I overlooked this incident I would have invited them to take even greater liberties with my goods in the future. I crossed the river, docked amidst their dugouts, and shouted for the Indians to come out and see me. A few of the culprits appeared, mischievous grins on their faces. I gave a spirited lecture about how hard I had worked to put those boards in my canoe, how I had paid a machete for the wood, and how angry I was that they destroyed my work in their haste to cross the river. I then pulled out my hunting knife and, while their grins disappeared, cut each of their canoes loose, set them into the current, and let them float away. I left without further ado and without looking back.

They managed to borrow another canoe and, after some effort, recovered their dugouts. The headman of the village later told me with an approving chuckle that I had done the correct thing. Everyone in the village, except, of course, the culprits, supported and defended my action. This raised my status.

Whenever I took such action and defended my rights, I got along much better with the Yąnomamö. A good deal of their behavior toward me was directed with the forethought of establishing the point at which I would react defensively. Many of them later reminisced about the early days of my work when I was "timid" and a little afraid of them, and they could bully me into giving goods away.

Theft was the most persistent situation that required me to take some sort of defensive action. I simply could not keep everything I owned locked in trunks, and the Indians came into my hut and left at will. I developed a very effective means for recovering almost all the stolen items. I would simply ask a child who took the item and then take that person's hammock when he was not around, giving a spirited lecture to the others as I marched away in a faked rage with the thief's hammock. Nobody ever attempted to stop me from doing this, and almost all of them told me that my technique for recovering my possessions was admirable. By nightfall the thief would either appear with the stolen object or send it along with someone else to make an exchange. The others would heckle him for getting caught and being forced to return the item.

With respect to collecting the data I sought, there was a very frustrating problem. Primitive social organization is kinship organization, and to understand the Yąnomamö way of life I had to collect extensive genealogies. I could not have deliberately picked a more difficult group to work with in this regard: They have very stringent name taboos. They attempt to name people in such a way that when the person dies and they can no longer use his name, the loss of the word in the language is not inconvenient. Hence, they name people for specific and minute parts of things, such as "toenail of some rodent," thereby being able to retain the words "toenail" and "(specific) rodent," but not being able to refer directly to the toenail of that rodent. The taboo is maintained even for the living: One mark of prestige is the courtesy others show you by not using your name. The sanctions behind the taboo seem to be an unusual combination of fear and respect.

I tried to use kinship terms to collect genealogies at first, but the kinship terms were so ambiguous that I ultimately had to resort to names. They were quick to grasp that I was bound to learn everybody's name and reacted, without my knowing it, by inventing false names for everybody in the village. After having spent several months collecting names and learning them, this came as a disappointment to me: I could not cross-check the genealogies with other informants from distant villages.

They enjoyed watching me learn these names. I assumed, wrongly, that I would get the truth to each question and that I would get the best information by working in public. This set the stage for converting a serious project into a farce. Each informant tried to outdo his peers by inventing a name even more ridiculous than what I had been given earlier, or by asserting that the individual about whom I inquired was married to his mother or daughter, and the like. I would have the informant whisper the name of the individual in my ear, noting that he was the father of such and such a child. Everybody would then insist that I repeat the name aloud, roaring in hysterics as I clumsily pronounced the name. I assumed that the laughter was in response to the violation of the name taboo or to my pronunciation. This was a reasonable interpretation, since the individual whose name I said aloud invariably became angry. After I learned what some of the names meant, I began to understand what the laughter was all about. A few of the more colorful examples are: "hairy vagina," "long penis," "feces of the harpy eagle," and "dirty rectum." No wonder the victims were angry.

I was forced to do my genealogy work in private because of the horseplay and nonsense. Once I did so, my informants began to agree with each other and I managed to learn a few new names, real names. I could then test any new informant by collecting a genealogy from him that I knew to be accurate. I was able to weed out the more mischievous informants this way. Little by little I extended the genealogies and learned the real names. Still, I was unable to get the names of the dead and extend the genealogies back in time, and even my best informants continued to deceive me about their own close relatives. Most of them gave me the name of a living man as the father of some individual in order to avoid mentioning that the actual father was dead.

The quality of a genealogy depends in part on the number of generations it embraces, and the name taboo prevented me from getting any substantial information about deceased ancestors. Without this information, I could not detect marriage patterns through time. I had to rely on older informants for this information, but these were the most reluctant of all. As I became more proficient in the language and more skilled at detecting lies, my informants became better at lying. One of them in particular was so cunning and persuasive that I was shocked to discover that he had been inventing his information. He specialized in making a ceremony out of telling me false names. He would look around to make sure nobody was listening outside my hut, enjoin me to never mention the name again, act very nervous and spooky, and then grab me by the head to whisper the name very softly into my ear. I was always elated after an informant session with him, because I had several generations of dead ancestors for the living people. The others refused to give me this information. To show my gratitude, I paid him quadruple the rate I had given the others. When word got around that I had increased the pay, volunteers began pouring in to give me genealogies.

I discovered that the old man was lying quite by accident. A club fight broke out in the village one day, the result of a dispute over the possession of a woman. She had been promised to Rerebawa, a particularly aggressive young man who had married into the village. Rerebawa had already been given her older sister and was enraged when the younger girl began having an affair with another man in the village, making no attempt to conceal it from him. He challenged the young man to a club fight, but was so abusive in his challenge that the opponent's father took offense and entered the village circle with his son, wielding a long club. Rerebawa swaggered out to the duel and hurled insults at both of them, trying to goad them into striking him on the head with their clubs. This would have given him the opportunity to strike them on the head. His opponents refused to hit him, and the fight ended. Rerebawa had won a moral victory because his opponents were afraid to hit him. Thereafter, he swaggered around and insulted the two men behind their backs. He was genuinely angry with them, to the point of calling the older man by the name of his dead father. I quickly seized on this as an opportunity to collect an accurate genealogy and pumped him about his adversary's ancestors. Rerebawa had been particularly nasty to me up to this point, but we became staunch allies: We were both outsiders in the local village. I then asked about other dead ancestors and got immediate replies. He was angry with the whole group and not afraid to tell me the names of the dead. When I compared his version of the genealogies to that of the old man, it was obvious that one of them was lying. I challenged his information, and he explained that everybody knew that the old man was deceiving me and bragging about it in the village. The names the old man had given me were the dead ancestors of the members of a village so far away that he thought I would never have occasion to inquire about them. As it turned out, Rerebawa knew most of the people in that village and recognized the names.

I then went over the complete genealogical records with Rerebawa, genealogies I had presumed to be in final form. I had to revise them all because of the numerous lies and falsifications they contained. Thus, after five months of almost constant work on the genealogies of just one group, I had to begin almost from scratch!

Discouraging as it was to start over, it was still the first real turning point in my fieldwork. Thereafter, I began taking advantage of local arguments and animosities in selecting my informants, and used more extensively individuals who had married into the group. I began traveling to other villages to check the genealogies, picking villages that were on strained terms with the people about whom I wanted information. I would then return to my base camp and check with local informants the accuracy of the new information. If the informants became angry when I mentioned the new names I acquired from the unfriendly group, I was almost certain that the information was accurate. For this kind of checking I had to use informants whose genealogies I knew rather well: They had to be distantly enough related to the dead person that they would not go into a rage when I mentioned the name, but not so remotely related that they would be uncertain of the accuracy of the information. Thus, I had to make a list of names that I dared not use in the presence of each and every informant. Despite the precautions, I occasionally hit a name that put the informant into a rage, such as that of a dead brother or sister that other informants had not reported. This always terminated the day's work with that informant, for he would be too touchy to continue any further, and I would be reluctant to take a chance on accidentally discovering another dead kinsman so soon after the first.

These were always unpleasant experiences, and occasionally dangerous ones, depending on the temperament of the informant. On one occasion I was planning to visit a village that had been raided about a week earlier. A woman whose name I had on my list had been killed by the raiders. I planned to check each individual on the list one by one to estimate ages, and I wanted to remove her name so that I would not say it aloud in the village. I knew that I would be in considerable difficulty if I said this name aloud so soon after her death. I called on my original informant and asked him to tell me the name of the woman who had been killed. He refused, explaining that she was a close relative of his. I then asked him if he would become angry if I read off all the names on the list. This way he did not have to say her name and could merely nod when I mentioned the right one. He was a fairly good friend of mine, and I thought I could predict his reaction. He assured me that this would be a good way of doing it. We were alone in my hut so that nobody could overhear us. I read the names softly, continuing to the next when he gave a negative reply. When I finally spoke the name of the dead woman he flew out of his chair, raised his arm to strike me, and shouted: "You son-of-a-bitch![2] If you ever say that name again, I'll kill you!" He was shaking with rage, but left my hut quietly. I shudder to think what might have happened if I had said the name unknowingly in the woman's village. I had other, similar experiences in different villages, but luckily the dead person had been dead for some time and was not closely related to the individual into whose ear I whispered the name. I was merely cautioned to desist from saying any more names, lest I get people angry with me.

I had been working on the genealogies for nearly a year when another individual came to my aid. It was Kaobawa, the headman of Upper Bisaasi-teri, the group in which I spent most of my time. He visited me one day after the others had left the hut and volunteered to help me on the genealogies. He was poor, he explained, and needed a machete. He would work only on the condition that I did not ask him about his own parents and other very close kinsmen who were dead. He also added that he would not lie to me as the others had done in the past. This was perhaps the most important single event in my fieldwork, for out of this meeting evolved a very warm friendship and a very profitable informant-fieldworker relationship.

Kaobawa's familiarity with his group's history and his candidness were remarkable. His knowledge of details was almost encyclopedic. More than that, he was enthusiastic and encouraged me to learn details that I might otherwise have ignored. If there were things he did not know intimately, he would advise me to wait until he could check things out with someone in the village. This he would do clandestinely, giving me a report the next day. As I was constrained by my part of the bargain to avoid discussing his close dead kinsmen, I had to rely on Rerebawa for this information. I got Rerebawa's genealogy from Kaobawa.

Once again I went over the genealogies with Kaobawa to recheck them, a considerable task by this time: they included about two thousand names, representing several generations of individuals from four different villages.

Rerebawa's information was very accurate, and Kaobawa's contribution enabled me to trace the genealogies further back in time. Thus, after nearly a year of constant work on genealogies, Yąnomamö demography and social organization began to fall into a pattern. Only then could I see how kin groups formed and exchanged women with each other over time, and only then did the fissioning of larger villages into smaller ones show a distinct pattern. At this point I was able to begin formulating more intelligent questions because there was now some sort of pattern to work with. Without the help of Rerebawa and Kaobawa, I could not have made very much sense of the plethora of details I had collected from dozens of other informants.

Kaobawa is about 40 years old. I say "about" because the Yąnomamö numeration system has only three numbers: one, two, and more-than-two. He is the headman of Upper Bisaasi-teri. He has had five or six wives so far and temporary affairs with as many more women, one of which resulted in a child. At the present time he has just two wives, Bahimi and Koamashima. He has had a daughter and a son by Bahimi, his eldest and favorite wife. Koamashima, about 20 years old, recently had her first child, a boy. Kaobawa may give Koamashima to his youngest brother. Even now the brother shares in her sexual services. Kaobawa recently gave his third wife to another of his brothers because she was beshi: "horny." In fact, this girl had been married to two other men, both of whom discarded her because of her infidelity. Kaobawa had one daughter by her; she is being raised by his brother.

Kaobawa's eldest wife, Bahimi, is about thirty-five years old. She is his first cross-cousin. Bahimi was pregnant when I began my fieldwork, but she killed the new baby, a boy, at birth, explaining tearfully that it would have competed with Ariwari, her nursing son, for milk. Rather than expose Ariwari to the dangers and uncertainty of an early weaning, she killed the new child instead. By Yąnomamö standards, she and Kaobawa have a very tranquil household. He only beats her once in a while, and never very hard. She never has affairs with other men.

Kaobawa is quiet, intense, wise, and unobtrusive. He leads more by example than by threats and coercion. He can afford to be this way as he established his reputation for being fierce long ago, and other men respect him. He also has five mature brothers who support him, and he has given a number of his sisters to other men in the village, thereby putting them under some obligation to him. In short, his "natural" following (kinsmen) is large, and he does not have to constantly display his ferocity. People already respect him and take his suggestions seriously.

Rerebawa is much younger, only about twenty-two years old. He has just one wife by whom he has had three children. He is from Karohi-teri, one of the villages to which Kaobawa's is allied. Rerebawa left his village to seek a wife in Kaobawa's group because there were no eligible women there for him to marry.

Rerebawa is perhaps more typical than Kaobawa in the sense that he is concerned about his reputation for ferocity and goes out of his way to act tough. He is, however, much braver than the other men his age and backs up his threats with action. Moreover, he is concerned about politics and knows the details of intervillage relationships over a large area. In this respect he shows all the attributes of a headman, although he is still too young and has too many competent older brothers in his own village to expect to move easily into the position of leadership there.

He does not intend to stay in Kaobawa's group and has not made a garden. He feels that he has adequately discharged his obligations to his wife's parents by providing them with fresh game for three years. They should let him take the wife and return to his own village with her, but they refuse and try to entice him to remain permanently in Bisaasi-teri to provide them with game when they are old. They have even promised to give him their second daughter if he will stay permanently.

Although he has displayed his ferocity in many ways, one incident in particular shows what his character is like. Before he left his own village to seek a wife, he had an affair with the wife of an older brother. When he was discovered, his brother attacked him with a club. Rerebawa was infuriated so he grabbed an axe and drove his brother out of the village after soundly beating him with the flat of the blade. The brother was so afraid that he did not return to the village for several days. I recently visited his village with him. He made a point to introduce me to this brother. Rerebawa dragged him out of his hammock by the arm and told me, "This is the brother whose wife I had an affair with," a deadly insult. His brother did nothing and slunk back into his hammock, shamed, but relieved to have Rerebawa release the vise-grip on his arm.

Despite the fact that he admires Kaobawa, he has a low opinion of the others in Bisaasi-teri. He admitted confidentially that he thought Bisaasi-teri was an abominable group: "This is a terrible neighborhood! All the young men are lazy and cowards and everybody is committing incest! I'll be glad to get back home." He also admired Kaobawa's brother, the headman of Monou-teri. This man was killed by raiders while I was doing my fieldwork. Rerebawa was disgusted that the others did not chase the raiders when they discovered the shooting: "He was the only fierce one in the whole group; he was my close friend. The cowardly Monou-teri hid like women in the jungle and didn't even chase the raiders!"

Even though Rerebawa is fierce and capable of being quite nasty, he has a good side as well. He has a very biting sense of humor and can entertain the group for hours on end with jokes and witty comments. And, he is one of few Yąnomamö that I feel I can trust. When I returned to Bisaasi-teri after having been away for a year, Rerebawa was in his own village visiting his kinsmen. Word reached him that I had returned, and he immediately came to see me. He greeted me with an immense bear hug and exclaimed, "Shaki! Why did you stay away so long? Did you know that my will was so cold while you were gone that at times I could not eat for want of seeing you?" I had to admit that I missed him, too.

Of all the Yąnomamö I know, he is the most genuine and the most devoted to his culture's ways and values. I admire him for that, although I can't say that I subscribe to or endorse these same values. By contrast, Kaobawa is older and wiser. He sees his own culture in a different light and criticizes aspects of it he does not like. While many of his peers accept some of the superstitions and explanatory myths as truth and as the way things ought to be, Kaobawa questions them and privately pokes fun at some of them. Probably, more of the Yąnomamö are like Rerebawa, or at least try to be.

Notes

1. "Shaki," or, rather, "Shakiwa," is the name they gave me because they could not pronounce "Chagnon." They like to name people for some distinctive feature when possible. *Shaki* is the name of a species of noisome bees; they accumulate in large numbers around ripening bananas and make pests of themselves by eating into the fruit, showering the people below with the debris. They probably adopted this name for me because I was also a nuisance, continuously prying into their business, taking pictures of them, and, in general, being where they did not want me.

2. This is the closest English translation of his actual statement, the literal translation of which would be nonsensical in our language.

9   The Sounds of Silence

EDWARD T. HALL
MILDRED R. HALL

When we refer to communication, we generally think about words. People who are talking, however, use much more than words to communicate with one another. *How* they say things is just as important— sometimes more so—than *what* they say. Their inflections, tones, pauses, cadence, and volume also convey meanings. If people are speaking face-to-face, their gestures, expressions, mannerisms, and use of space also contain significant messages.

Nonverbal communication is especially significant in conveying feelings and attitudes. Through ways so subtle that they lie beyond even our own perception—and ways so obvious that no one can miss the message—we communicate feelings of comfort and discomfort, trust and distrust, pleasure or tension, suspicions, uncertainties, desires, and a host of other feelings and concerns.

Yet we seldom think about our nonverbal communications. Our body language, for example, usually seems to be "just doing what is natural." Researchers, however, have found little that is "natural" about it. Like our speech, our body language and other forms of nonverbal communication are acquired. Thus, the specific ways by which people communicate these messages vary from one group to another, as the Halls make evident in this selection.

BOB LEAVES HIS APARTMENT at 8:15 A.M. and stops at the corner drugstore for breakfast. Before he can speak, the counterman says, "The usual?" Bob nods yes. While he savors his Danish, a fat man pushes onto the adjoining stool and overflows into his space. Bob scowls, and the man pulls himself in as much as he can. Bob has sent two messages without speaking a syllable.

Henry has an appointment to meet Arthur at 11:00 A.M.; he arrives at 11:30. Their conversation is friendly, but Arthur retains a lingering hostility. Henry has unconsciously communicated that he doesn't think the appointment is very important or that Arthur is a person who needs to be treated with respect.

George is talking to Charley's wife at a party. Their conversation is entirely trivial, yet Charley glares at them suspiciously. Their physical proximity and the movements of their eyes reveal that they are powerfully attracted to each other.

José Ybarra and Sir Edmund Jones are at the same party, and it is important for them to establish a cordial relationship for business reasons. Each is trying to be warm and friendly, yet they will part with mutual distrust, and their business transaction will probably fall through. José, in Latin fashion, moves closer and closer to Sir Edmund as they speak, and this movement is being miscommunicated as pushiness to Sir Edmund, who keeps backing away from this intimacy, which in turn is being miscommunicated to José as coldness. The silent languages of Latin and English cultures are more difficult to learn than their spoken languages.

In each of these cases, we see the subtle power of nonverbal communication. The only language used throughout most of the history of humanity (in evolutionary terms, vocal communication is relatively recent), it is the first form of communication you learn. You use this preverbal language, consciously and unconsciously, every day to tell other people how you feel about yourself and them. This language includes your posture, gestures, facial expressions, costume, the way you walk, even your treatment of time and space and material things. All people communicate on several different levels at the same time but are usually aware of only the verbal dialogue and don't realize that they respond to nonverbal messages. But when a person says one thing and really believes something else, the discrepancy between the two can usually be sensed. Nonverbal communication systems are much less subject to the conscious deception that often occurs in verbal systems. When we find ourselves thinking, "I don't know what it is about him, but he doesn't seem sincere," it's usually this lack of congruity between a person's words and his behavior that makes us anxious and uncomfortable.

Few of us realize how much we all depend on body movement in our conversation or are aware of the hidden rules that govern listening behavior. But we know instantly whether or not the person we're talking to is "tuned in," and we're very sensitive to any breach in listening etiquette. In white middle-class American culture, when someone wants to show he is listening to someone else, he looks either at the other person's face or, specifically, at his eyes, shifting his gaze from one eye to the other.

If you observe a person conversing, you'll notice that he indicates he's listening by nodding his head. He also makes little "Hmm" noises. If he agrees with what's being said, he may give a vigorous nod. To show pleasure or affirmation, he smiles; if he has some reservations, he looks skeptical by raising an eyebrow or pulling down the corners of his mouth. If a participant wants to terminate the conversation, he may start shifting his body position, stretching his legs, crossing or uncrossing them, bobbing his foot, or diverting his gaze from the speaker. The more he fidgets, the more the speaker becomes aware that he has lost his audience. As a last measure, the listener may look at his watch to indicate the imminent end of the conversation.

Talking and listening are so intricately intertwined that a person cannot do one without the other. Even when one is alone and talking to oneself, there is part of the brain that speaks while another part listens. In all conversations, the listener is positively or negatively reinforcing the speaker all the time. He may even guide the conversation without knowing it, by laughing or frowning or dismissing the argument with a wave of his hand.

The language of the eyes—another age-old way of exchanging feelings— is both subtle and complex. Not only do men and women use their eyes differently, but there are class, generational, regional, ethnic, and national cultural differences. Americans often complain about the way foreigners stare at people or hold a glance too long. Most Americans look away from someone who is using his eyes in an unfamiliar way because it makes them self-conscious. If a man looks at another man's wife in a certain way, he's asking for trouble, as indicated earlier. But he might not be ill-mannered or seeking to challenge the husband. He might be a European in this country who hasn't learned our visual mores. Many American women visiting France or Italy are acutely embarrassed because, for the first time in their lives, men really look at them—their eyes, hair, nose, lips, breasts, hips, legs, thighs, knees, ankles, feet, clothes, hairdo, even their walk. These same women, once they have become used to being looked at, often return to the United States and are overcome with the feeling that "No one ever really looks at me anymore."

Analyzing the mass of data on the eyes, it is possible to sort out at least three ways in which the eyes are used to communicate: dominance vs. submission, involvement vs. detachment, and positive vs. negative attitude. In addition, there are three levels of consciousness and control, which can be categorized as follows: (1) conscious use of the eyes to communicate, such as the flirting blink and the intimate nosewrinkling squint; (2) the very extensive category of unconscious but learned behavior governing where the eyes are directed and when (this unwritten set of rules dictates how and under what circumstances the sexes, as well as people of all status categories, look at each other); and (3) the response of the eye itself, which is completely outside both awareness and control—changes in the cast (sparkle) of the eye and the pupillary reflex.

The eye is unlike any other organ of the body, for it is an extension of the brain. The unconscious pupillary reflex and the cast of the eye have been known by people of Middle Eastern origin for years—although most are unaware of their knowledge. Depending on the context, Arabs and others look directly at the eyes or deeply *into* the eyes of their interlocutor. We became aware of this in the Middle East several years ago while looking at jewelry. The merchant suddenly started to push a particular bracelet at a customer and said, "You buy this one." What interested us was that the bracelet was not the one that had been consciously selected by the purchaser. But the merchant, watching the pupils of the eyes, knew what the purchaser really wanted to buy. Whether he specifically knew *how* he knew is debatable.

A psychologist at the University of Chicago, Eckhard Hess, was the first to conduct systematic studies of the pupillary reflex. His wife remarked one evening, while watching him reading in bed, that he must be very interested in the text because his pupils were dilated. Following up on this, Hess slipped some pictures of nudes into a stack of photographs that he gave to his male assistant. Not looking at the photographs but watching his assistant's pupils, Hess was able to tell precisely when the assistant came to the nudes. In further experiments, Hess retouched the eyes in a photograph of a woman. In one print, he made the pupils small, in another, large; nothing else was changed. Subjects who were given the photographs found the woman with the dilated pupils much more attractive. Any man who has had the experience of seeing a woman look at him as her pupils widen with reflex speed knows that she's flashing him a message.

The eye-sparkle phenomenon frequently turns up in our interviews of couples in love. It's apparently one of the first reliable clues in the other person that love is genuine. To date, there is no scientific data to explain eye sparkle; no investigation of the pupil, the cornea, or even the white sclera of the eye shows how the sparkle originates. Yet we all know it when we see it.

One common situation for most people involves the use of the eyes in the street and in public. Although eye behavior follows a definite set of rules, the rules vary according to the place, the needs and feelings of the people, and their ethnic background. For urban whites, once they're within definite recognition distance (sixteen to thirty-two feet for people with average eyesight), there is mutual avoidance of eye contact—unless they want something specific: a pickup, a handout, or information of some kind. In the West and in small towns generally, however, people are much more likely to look and greet one another, even if they're strangers.

It's permissible to look at people if they're beyond recognition distance, but once inside this sacred zone, you can only steal a glance at strangers. You *must* greet friends, however; to fail to do so is insulting. Yet, to stare too fixedly even at them is considered rude and hostile. Of course, all of these rules are variable.

A great many blacks, for example, greet each other in public even if they don't know each other. To blacks, most eye behavior of whites has the effect of giving the impression that they aren't there, but this is due to white avoidance of eye contact with anyone in the street.

Another very basic difference between people of different ethnic backgrounds is their sense of territoriality and how they handle space. This is the silent communication, or miscommunication, that caused friction between Mr. Ybarra and Sir Edmund Jones in our earlier example. We know from the research that everyone has around himself an invisible bubble of space that contracts and expands depending on several factors: his emotional state, the activity he's performing at the time, and his cultural background. This bubble is a kind of mobile territory that he will defend against intrusion. If he is accustomed to close personal distance between himself and others, his bubble will be smaller than that of someone who's accustomed to greater personal distance. People of northern European heritage—English, Scandinavian, Swiss, and German—tend to avoid contact. Those whose heritage is Italian, French, Spanish, Russian, Latin American, or Middle Eastern like close personal contact.

People are very sensitive to any intrusion into their spatial bubble. If someone stands too close to you, your first instinct is to back up. If that's not possible, you lean away and pull yourself in, tensing your muscles. If the intruder doesn't respond to these body signals, you may then try to protect yourself, using a briefcase, umbrella, or raincoat. Women—especially when traveling alone—often plant their pocketbooks in such a way that no one can get very close to them. As a last resort, you may move to another spot and position yourself behind a desk or a chair that provides screening. Everyone tries to adjust the space around himself in a way that's comfortable for him; most often, he does this unconsciously.

Emotions also have a direct effect on the size of a person's territory. When you're angry or under stress, your bubble expands and you require more space. New York psychiatrist Augustus Kinzel found a difference in what he calls body-buffer zones between violent and nonviolent prison inmates. Dr. Kinzel conducted experiments in which each prisoner was placed in the center of a small room, and then Dr. Kinzel slowly walked toward him. Nonviolent prisoners allowed him to come quite close, while prisoners with a history of violent behavior couldn't tolerate his proximity and reacted with some vehemence.

Apparently, people under stress experience other people as looming larger and closer than they actually are. Studies of schizophrenic patients have indicated that they sometimes have a distorted perception of space, and several psychiatrists have reported patients who experience their body boundaries as filling up an entire room. For these patients, anyone who comes into the room is actually inside their body, and such an intrusion may trigger a violent outburst.

Unfortunately, there is little detailed information about normal people who live in highly congested urban areas. We do know, of course, that the noise, pollution, dirt, crowding, and confusion of our cities induce feelings of stress in most of us, and stress leads to a need for greater space. The man who's packed into a subway, jostled in the street, crowded into an elevator, and forced to work all day in a bull pen or in a small office without auditory or visual privacy is going to be very stressed at the end of his day. He needs places that provide relief from constant overstimulation of his nervous system. Stress from overcrowding is cumulative, and people can tolerate more crowding early in the day than later; note the increased bad temper during the evening rush hour as compared with the morning melee. Certainly one factor in people's desire to commute by car is the need for privacy and relief from crowding (except, often, from other cars); it may be the only time of the day when nobody can intrude.

In crowded public places, we tense our muscles and hold ourselves stiff, and thereby communicate to others our desire not to intrude on their space and, above all, not to touch them. We also avoid eye contact, and the total effect is that of someone who has "tuned out." Walking along the street, our bubble expands slightly as we move in a stream of strangers, taking care not to bump into them. In the office, at meetings, in restaurants, our bubble keeps changing as it adjusts to the activity at hand.

Most white middle-class Americans use four main distances in their business and social relations: intimate, personal, social, and public. Each of these distances has a near and a far phase and is accompanied by changes in the volume of the voice. Intimate distance varies from direct physical contact with another person to a distance of six to eighteen inches and is used for our most private activities—caressing another person or making love. At this distance, you are overwhelmed by sensory inputs from the skin, the fragrance of perfume, even the sound of breathing—all of which literally envelop you. Even at the far phase, you're still within easy touching distance. In general, the use of intimate distance in public between adults is frowned on. It's also much too close for strangers, except under conditions of extreme crowding.

In the second zone—personal distance—the close phase is one and a half to two and a half feet: it's at this distance that wives usually stand from their husbands in public. If another woman moves into this zone, the wife will most likely be disturbed. The far phase—two and a half to four feet—is the distance used to "keep someone at arm's length" and is the most common spacing used by people in conversation.

The third zone—social distance—is employed during business transactions or exchanges with a clerk or repairman. People who work together tend to use close social distance—four to seven feet. This is also the distance for conversation at social gatherings. To stand at this distance from someone who is seated has a dominating effect (e.g., teacher to pupil, boss to secretary). The far phase of the third zone—seven to twelve feet—is where people stand when someone says, "Stand back so I can look at you." This distance lends a formal tone to business or social discourse. In an executive office, the desk serves to keep people at this distance.

The fourth zone—public distance—is used by teachers in classrooms or speakers at public gatherings. At its farthest phase—twenty-five feet and beyond—it is used for important public figures. Violations of this distance can lead to serious complications. During his 1970 U.S. visit, the president of France, Georges Pompidou, was harassed by pickets in Chicago, who were permitted to get within touching distance. Since pickets in France are kept behind barricades a block or more away, the president was outraged by this insult to his person, and President Nixon was obliged to communicate his concern as well as offer his personal apologies.

It is interesting to note how American pitchmen and panhandlers exploit the unwritten, unspoken conventions of eye and distance. Both take advantage of the fact that once explicit eye contact is established, it is rude to look away, because to do so means to brusquely dismiss the other person and his needs. Once having caught the eye of his mark, the panhandler then locks on, not letting go until he moves through the public zone, the social zone, the personal zone and, finally, into the intimate sphere, where people are most vulnerable.

Touch also is an important part of the constant stream of communication that takes place between people. A light touch, a firm touch, a blow, a caress are all communications. In an effort to break down barriers among people, there's been a recent upsurge in group-encounter activities, in which strangers are encouraged to touch one another. In special situations such as these, the rules for not touching are broken with group approval, and people gradually lose some of their inhibitions.

Although most people don't realize it, space is perceived and distances are set not by vision alone but with all the senses. Auditory space is perceived with the ears, thermal space with the skin, kinesthetic space with muscles of the body, and olfactory space with the nose. And, once again, it's one's culture that determines how his senses are programmed—which sensory information ranks highest and lowest. The important thing to remember is that culture is very persistent. In this country, we've noted the existence of culture patterns that determine distance between people in the third and fourth generations of some families, despite their prolonged contact with people of very different cultural heritages.

Whenever there is great cultural distance between two people, there are bound to be problems arising from differences in behavior and expectations. An example is the American couple who consulted a psychiatrist about their marital problems. The husband was from New England and had been brought up by reserved parents who taught him to control his emotions and to respect the need for privacy. His wife was from an Italian family and had been brought up in close contact with all the members of her large family, who were extremely warm, volatile, and demonstrative.

When the husband came home after a hard day at the office, dragging his feet and longing for peace and quiet, his wife would rush to him and smother him. Clasping his hands, rubbing his brow, crooning over his weary head, she never left him alone. But when the wife was upset or anxious about her day, the husband's response was to withdraw completely and leave her alone. No comforting, no affectionate embrace, no attention—just solitude. The woman became convinced her husband didn't love her, and in desperation she consulted a psychiatrist. Their problem wasn't basically psychological but cultural.

Why has man developed all these different ways of communicating messages without words? One reason is that people don't like to spell out certain kinds of messages. We prefer to find other ways of showing our feelings. This is especially true in relationships as sensitive as courtship. Men don't like to be rejected, and most women don't want to turn a man down bluntly. Instead, we work out subtle ways of encouraging or discouraging each other that save face and avoid confrontations.

How a person handles space in dating others is an obvious and very sensitive indicator of how he or she feels about the other person. On a first date, if a woman sits or stands so close to a man that he is acutely conscious of her physical presence—inside the intimate-distance zone—the man usually construes it to mean that she is encouraging him. However, before the man starts moving in on the woman, he should be sure what message she's really sending; otherwise, he risks bruising his ego. What is close to someone of northern European background may be neutral or distant to someone of Italian heritage. Also, women sometimes use space as a way of misleading a man, and there are few things that put men off more than women who communicate contradictory messages, such as women who cuddle up and then act insulted when a man takes the next step.

How does a woman communicate interest in a man? In addition to such familiar gambits as smiling at him, she may glance shyly at him, blush, and then look away. Or she may give him a real come-on look and move in very close when he approaches. She may touch his arm and ask for a light. As she leans forward to light her cigarette, she may brush him lightly, enveloping him in her perfume. She'll probably continue to smile at him, and she may use what ethologists call preening gestures—touching the back of her hair, thrusting her breasts forward, tilting her hips at she stands, or crossing her legs if she's seated, perhaps even exposing one thigh or putting a hand on her thigh and stroking it. She may also stroke her wrists as she converses or show the palm of her hand as a way of gaining his attention. Her skin may be unusually flushed or quite pale, her eyes brighter, the pupils larger.

If a man sees a woman whom he wants to attract, he tries to present himself by his posture and stance as someone who is self-assured. He moves briskly and confidently. When he catches the eye of the woman, he may hold her glance a little longer than normal. If he gets an encouraging smile, he'll move in close and engage her in small talk. As they converse, his glance shifts over her face and body. He too, may make preening gestures—straightening his tie, smoothing his hair, or shooting his cuffs.

How do people learn body language? The same way they learn spoken language—by observing and imitating people around them as they're growing up. Little girls imitate their mothers or an older female. Little boys imitate their fathers or a respected uncle or a character on television. In this way, they learn the gender signals appropriate for their sex. Regional, class, and ethnic patterns of body behavior are also learned in childhood and persist throughout life. . . .

Nonverbal communications signal to members of your own group what kind of person you are, how you feel about others, how you'll fit into and work in a group, whether you're assured or anxious, the degree to which you feel comfortable with the standards of your own culture, as well as deeply significant feelings about the self, including the state of your own psyche. For most of us, it's difficult to accept the reality of another's behavioral system. And, of course, none of us will ever become fully knowledgeable of the importance of every nonverbal signal. But as long as each of us realizes the power of these signals, the society's diversity can be a source of great strength rather than a further—and subtly powerful—source of division.

10 The Rules for Giving Christmas Gifts

THEODORE CAPLOW

Our lives are bound by rules. I'm not referring to just the laws of the land or the official policies of your college. As important as these are, they pale into insignificance when we compare them with the rules of everyday life. From the time we wake up in the morning to the time we go to bed at night, our lives are governed by a complex system of norms or expectations. These rules govern not only what we do, including what we say and how we say it, but even the look on our face as we say it.

You might think that I'm being extreme in this statement, that as a sociologist I'm getting carried away with my subject matter. We seem to experience freedom, and we think that we think independent thoughts and have independent feelings—but do we? Consider the implications of this article. In his study of Middletown (Muncie, Indiana), Caplow and his research team found that the residents of this town followed highly detailed rules in their Christmas giving. These rules were so powerful that almost everyone followed them—yet people could not verbalize these rules. We, too, follow implicit rules in our everyday lives, not just in giving gifts, but in *everything* we do. As with the residents of Muncie, these background assumptions (or rules) are so embedded in our consciousness that we, too, would have a difficult time telling someone what they were. Yet we and others follow them, which allows interaction to flow and group life to exist. Such is the power of socialization into culture.

THE CELEBRATION OF CHRISTMAS, the high point of the [holiday cycle in Middletown], mobilizes almost the entire population for several weeks, accounts for about 4% of its total annual expenditures, and takes precedence over ordinary forms of work and leisure. In order to include this large phenomenon, we interviewed a random sample of 110 Middletown adults. . . . The survey included an inventory of all Christmas gifts given and received by these respondents. . . . The total number of gifts inventoried was 4,347, a mean of 39.5 per respondent.

How are the rules that appear to govern Christmas gift-giving in Middletown communicated and enforced? There are no enforcement agents and little indignation against violators. Nevertheless, the level of participation is very high. Here are some typical gift-giving rules that are enforced effectively in Middletown without visible means of enforcement and indeed without any widespread awareness of their existence:

The Tree Rule

> Married couples with children of any age should put up Christmas trees in their homes. Unmarried persons with no living children should not put up Christmas trees. Unmarried parents (widowed, divorced, or adoptive) may put up trees but are not required to do so.

Conformity with the Tree Rule in our survey sample may be fairly described as spectacular.

Nobody in Middletown seems to be consciously aware of the norm that requires married couples with children of any age to put up a Christmas tree, yet the obligation is so compelling that, of the 77 respondents in this category who were at home for Christmas, only one failed to so. Few of the written laws that agents of the state attempt to enforce with endless paperwork and threats of violence are so well obeyed as this unwritten rule that is promulgated by no identifiable authority and backed by no evident threat. Indeed, the existence of the rule goes unnoticed. People in Middletown think that putting up a Christmas tree is an entirely voluntary act. They know that it has some connection with children, but they do not understand that married couples with children of any age are effectively required to have trees and that childless unmarried people are somehow prevented from having them.

The Wrapping Rule

> Christmas gifts must be wrapped before they are presented.

A subsidiary rule requires that the wrapping be appropriate, that is, emblematic, and another subsidiary rule says that wrapped gifts are appropriately displayed as a set but that unwrapped gifts should not be so displayed. Conformity with these rules is exceedingly high. An unwrapped object is so clearly excluded as a Christmas gift that Middletown people who wish to give something at that season without defining it as a Christmas gift have only to leave the object unwrapped. Difficult-to-wrap Christmas gifts, like a pony or a piano, are wrapped symbolically by adding a ribbon or bow or card and are hidden until presentation.

In nearly every Middletown household, the wrapped presents are displayed under or around the Christmas tree as a glittering monument to the family's affluence and mutual affection. Picture taking at Christmas gatherings is clearly a part of the ritual; photographs were taken at 65% of the recorded gatherings. In nearly all instances, the pile of wrapped gifts was photographed; and individual participants were photographed opening a gift, ideally at the moment of "surprise."

The Decoration Rule

Any room where Christmas gifts are distributed should be decorated by affixing Christmas emblems to the walls, the ceiling, or the furniture. This is done even in nondomestic places, like offices or restaurant dining rooms, if gifts are to be distributed there. Conformity to this rule was perfect in our sample of 366 gatherings at which gifts were distributed, although, once again, the existence of the rule was not recognized by the people who obeyed it.

The same lack of recognition applies to the interesting subsidiary rule that a Christmas tree should not be put up in an undecorated place, although a decorated place need not have a tree. Unmarried, childless persons normally decorate their homes, although they have no trees, and decorations without a tree are common in public places, but a Christmas tree in an undecorated room would be unseemly.

The Gathering Rule

Christmas gifts should be distributed at gatherings where every person gives and receives gifts.

Compliance with this rule is very high. More than nine-tenths of the 1,378 gifts our respondents received, and of the 2,969 they gave, were distributed in gatherings, more than three-quarters of which were family gatherings. Most gifts mailed or shipped by friends and relatives living at a distance were double wrapped, so that the outer unceremonious wrappings could be removed and the inner packages could be placed with other gifts to be opened at a gathering. In the typical family gathering, a number of related persons assemble by prearrangement at the home of one of them where a feast is served; the adults engage in conversation; the children play; someone takes photographs; gifts are distributed, opened, and admired; and the company then disperses. The average Middletown adult fits more than three of these occasions into a 24–hour period beginning at Christmas Eve, often driving long distances and eating several large dinners during that time.

The Dinner Rule

> Family gatherings at which gifts are distributed include a "traditional Christmas dinner."

This is the rule that participants in Middletown's Christmas ritual may disregard if they wish, but it is no less interesting because compliance is only partial. Presumably, this rule acquired its elective character because the pattern of multiple gatherings described above requires many gatherings to be scheduled at odd hours when dinner either would be inappropriate or, if the dinner rule were inflexible, would require participants to overeat beyond the normal expectations of the season. However, 65% of the survey respondents had eaten at least one traditional Christmas dinner the previous year.

There appears to be a subsidiary rule that traditional Christmas dinners served in homes should be prepared exclusively by women. There was not a single reported instance in this survey of a traditional Christmas dinner prepared by a man.

The Gift Selection Rules

> A Christmas gift should (a) demonstrate the giver's familiarity with the receiver's preferences; (b) surprise the receiver, either by expressing more affection—measured by the aesthetic or practical value of the gift—than the receiver might reasonably anticipate or more knowledge than the giver might reasonably be expected to have; (c) be scaled in economic value to the emotional value of the relationship.

The economic values of any giver's gifts are supposed to be sufficiently scaled to the emotional values of relationships that, when they are opened in the bright glare of the family circle, the donor will not appear to have disregarded either the legitimate inequality of some relationships by, for example, giving a more valuable gift to a nephew than to a son, or the legitimate equality of other relationships by, for example, giving conspicuously unequal gifts to two sons.

Individuals participating in these rituals are not free to improvise their own scales of emotional value for relationships. The scale they are supposed to use, together with its permissible variations, is not written down anywhere but is thoroughly familiar to participants. From analysis of the gifts given and received by our survey respondents, we infer the following rules for scaling the emotional value of relationships.

The Scale

(a) A spousal relationship should be more valuable than any other for both husband and wife, but the husband may set a higher value on it than the wife.

(b) A parent-child relationship should be less valuable than a spousal relationship but more valuable than any other relationship. The parent may set a higher value on it than the child does.

(c) The spouse of a married close relative should be valued as much as the linking relative.

(d) Parents with several children should value them equally throughout their lives.

(e) Children with both parents still living, and still married to each other, may value them equally *or* may value their mothers somewhat more than their fathers. A married couple with two pairs of living, still-married parents should value each pair equally. Children of any age with divorced, separated, *or* remarried parents may value them unequally.

(f) Siblings should be valued equally in childhood but not later. Adult siblings who live close by and are part of one's active network should be equally valued, along with their respective spouses, but siblings who live farther away may be valued unequally.

(g) Friends of either sex, aside from sexual partners treated as quasi-spouses, may be valued as much as siblings but should not be valued as much as spouses, parents, or children.

(h) More distant relatives—like aunts *or* cousins—may be valued as much as siblings but should not be valued as much as spouses, parents, or children.

It is a formidable task to balance these ratios every year and to come up with a set of Christmas gifts that satisfies them. Small wonder that Middletown people complain that Christmas shopping is difficult, and fatiguing. But although they complain, they persist in it year after year without interruption. People who are away from home for Christmas arrange in advance to have their gifts distributed to the usual receivers and to open their own gifts ceremoniously. People confined by severe illness delegate others to do shopping and wrapping. Although our random sample of Middletown adults included several socially isolated persons, even the single most isolated respondent happened to have an old friend with whom he exchanged expensive gifts.

Given the complexity of the rules, errors and failures in gift selection can be expected to occur, and they frequently do. Indeed, the four or five shopping days immediately after Christmas are set aside in Middletown stores for return or exchange of badly selected gifts. A number of respondents described relatives who make a point of being impossible to please. The standard disappointing gift is an article of clothing in the wrong size. Women are particularly resentful of oversized items that seem to say the giver perceives them as "fat." Children are often insulted by inattentive relatives who give them toys that are too "young." The spouse's or lover's gift that is disliked by the receiver is a sign of alienation. Two of the five couples in our sample for whom such gifts were reported at Christmas 1978 had separated by the time of the interview several weeks later.

Fitness Rules

Rules about the fitness of gifts (e.g., women should not give cut flowers to men) are too numerous to specify, but one deserves passing attention. Money is an appropriate gift from senior to junior kin, but an inappropriate gift from junior to senior kin, regardless of the relative affluence of the parties. This is another rule which appears to be unknown to the people who obey it. Of 144 gifts of money given by persons in our sample to those in other generations, 94% went to junior kin, and of the 73 money gifts respondents received from persons in other generations, 93% were from senior kin. A gift certificate may be given to a parent or grandparent to whom an outright gift of money would be improper. . . .

The Reciprocity Rule

Participants in this gift system should give (individually or jointly) at least one Christmas gift every year to their mothers, fathers, sons, daughters; to the current spouses of these persons; and to their own spouses.

By the operation of this rule, participants expect to receive at least one gift in return from each of these persons excepting infants. Conformity runs about 90% for each relationship separately and for the aggregate of all such relationships. Gifts to grandparents and grandchildren seem to be equally obligatory if these live in the same community or nearby, but not at greater distances.

The Reciprocity Rule does not require reciprocated gifts to be of equal value. Parents expect to give more valuable and more numerous gifts to their minor children and to their adult children living at home than they receive in return. This imbalance is central to the entire ritual. The iconography of

Middletown's secular Christmas emphasizes unreciprocated giving to children by the emblematic figure of Santa Claus, and the theme of unreciprocated giving provides one of the few connections between the secular and religious iconography of the festival—the Three Wise Men coming from a distant land to bring unreciprocated gifts to a child.

Equivalence of value tends to be disregarded in gift-giving between husbands and wives and between parents and their adult children. Husbands often give more valuable gifts to wives than they receive from them. The gifts of parents to adult children are approximately balanced in the aggregate—about the same number of substantial gifts are given in each direction—but there is no insistence on equivalence in particular cases, and when we examine such relationships one by one, we discover many unbalanced exchanges, which seem to be taken for granted.

Only in the relationship between siblings and sibling couples do we find any active concern that the gifts exchanged be of approximately equal value, and even there it is more important to give gifts of approximately equal value to several siblings than to exchange gifts of equal value with each of them.

Empirically, the gift-giving between adults and children in our sample was highly unbalanced, in both quantity and value. Respondents gave 946 gifts to persons under 18 and received 145 in return; 89 of these were of substantial value and six of the return gifts were. In about one-third or these relationships, no gift was returned to the adult either by the child or in the child's name. In most of the remaining relationships, the child returned a single gift of token or modest value.

Discussion

Since the problem is to account for the uniformities of gift-giving behavior revealed by the data, speaking of rules begs the question to some extent. Although we infer from the uniformities observed in Middletown's Christmas gift-giving that, somewhere in the culture, there must be statements to which the observed behavior is a response, the crucial point is that we cannot find those statements in any explicit form. Indeed, they are not recognized by participants in the system. In effect, the rules of the game are unfamiliar to the players, even though they can be observed to play meticulously by the rules. Instructions for Christmas gift-giving are not found in administrative regulations or popular maxims or books of etiquette; they are not *promulgated*.

Gift exchange, in effect, is a language that employs objects instead of words as its lexical elements. In this perspective, every culture has a language of presentation [i.e., the obligatory exchange of objects] to express important interpersonal relationships on special occasions, just as it has a verbal language to create and manage meaning for other purposes. The language of presentation, like the verbal language, begins to be learned in early childhood and is used with increasing assurance as the individual matures and acquires social understanding. The problem of accounting for the enforcement of gift-giving rules without visible means is simplified if we take them to be linguistic rules, or at least as similar to them, because linguistic rules, for the most part, are enforced among native speakers of a language without visible means and without being recognized explicitly.

Visualizing Christmas gift-giving as a language or, more precisely, as a dialect or code, helps to explain, among other matters, the preference for the simultaneous exchange of gifts at family gatherings rather than in private.

In most cases such a gathering is composed of a parent-child unit containing one or two parents and one or more children together with other persons who are tied to that unit by shared membership in another parent-child unit, such as children's children, children's spouses, parents' siblings, or parents' parents. Although there is room at a family gathering for a friend or distant relative who otherwise might be solitary at Christmas, there is no convenient way of including any large number of persons to whom no gift messages are owed.

Under the Scaling Rules, gift messages are due from every person in a parent-child relationship to every other. The individual message says "I value you according to the degree of our relationship" and anticipates the response "I value you in the same way." But the compound message that emerges from the unwrapping of gifts in the presence of the whole gathering allows more subtle meanings to be conveyed. It permits the husband to say to the wife "I value you more than my parents" or the mother to say to the daughter-in-law "I value you as much as my son so long as you are married to him" or the brother to say to the brother "I value you more than our absent brothers, but less than our parents and much less than my children."

These statements, taken together, would define and sustain a social structure, if only because, by their gift messages, both parties to each dyadic relationship confirm that they have the same understanding of the relationship, and the bystanders, who are interested parties, endorse that understanding by tacit approval. The compound messages would have a powerful influence even if they were idiosyncratic and each parent-child unit had its own method of scaling relationships. In fact, there are some observable differences in scaling from one Middletown family to another and from one subcultural group to another, but the similarities are much more striking than the differences. We attribute this commonality to the shared dialect of Christmas gift-giving, hyper-developed in Middletown and elsewhere in the

United States in response to commercial promotion, stresses in the family institution, and constant reiteration by the mass media. Once the dialect is
known, these factors continue to enlarge its vocabulary and its domain.

Another circumstance facilitating the standardization of the dialect is
that nearly every individual in this population belongs to more than one
parent-child unit for Christmas gift-giving purposes. Because these units are
linked and cross-linked to other units in a network that ultimately includes
the larger part of the community, they would probably tend to develop a common set of understandings about appropriate kinship behavior, even without
the reinforcement provided by domestic rituals.

The most powerful reinforcement remains to be mentioned. In the dialect of Christmas gift-giving, the absence of a gift is also a lexical sign, signifying either the absence of a close relationship, as in the Christmas contact
of cousins, or the desire to terminate a close relationship, as when a husband
gives no gift to his wife. People who have once learned the dialect cannot
choose to forget it, nor can they pretend to ignore messages they understand.
Thus, without any complicated normative machinery, Middletown people find
themselves compelled to give Christmas gifts to their close relatives, lest they
inadvertently send them messages of hostility. In this community, where most
people depend on their relatives for emotional and social support, the consequences of accidentally sending them a hostile message are too serious to contemplate, and few are willing to run the risk.

In sum, we discover that the participants in this gift-giving system are
themselves the agents who enforce its complex rules, although they do so unknowingly and without conscious reference to a system. The dialect, once
learned, imposes itself by linguistic necessity, and the enforcement of its rules
is the more effective for being unplanned.

11 The Presentation of Self in Everyday Life

ERVING GOFFMAN

All the world's a stage
And all the men and women merely players.
They have their exits and their entrances;
And one man in his time plays many parts. . . .
> William Shakespeare
> *As You Like It,* Act 2, Scene 7

This quotation from Shakespeare could well serve as the keynote for the following selection. Taking Shakespeare's statement seriously, Goffman presents a dramaturgical model of human life and uses it as the conceptual framework for understanding life-in-society. In this view, people in everyday life are actors on stage, the audience consists of those persons who observe what others are doing, the parts are the roles that people play (whether occupational, familial, friendship roles, or whatever), the dialogue consists of ritualized conversational exchanges ("Hi. How ya doin'?"; "Hey, bro', wha's hapnin'?"; "How's it goin'?"; the hellos, the goodbyes, and the in-betweens), while the costuming consists of whatever clothing happens to be in style.

Goffman's insightful analysis provides a framework from which we can gain a remarkably different perspective of what we do in life—at home, at school, with friends, while on a date, or while shopping. When understood properly, however, you may find this approach to understanding human behavior disturbing. For example, if we are all actors playing roles on the stage of life, where is the "real me"? Is all of life merely a "put-on," play acting, a masquerade of some sort? Does not this framework for understanding human interaction constitute an essentially cynical and manipulative approach to life, a sort of everyday Machiavellianism?

WHEN AN INDIVIDUAL ENTERS the presence of others, they commonly seek to acquire information about him or to bring into play information about him already possessed. They will be interested in his general socio-economic status, his conception of self, his attitude toward them, his competence, his trustworthiness, etc. Although some of this information seems to be sought almost as an end in itself, there are usually quite practical reasons for acquiring it. Information about the individual helps to define the situation, enabling others to know in advance what he will expect of them and what they may expect of him. Informed in these ways, the others will know how best to act in order to call forth a desired response from him.

For those present, many sources of information become accessible and many carriers (or "sign-vehicles") become available for conveying this information. If unacquainted with the individual, observers can glean clues from his conduct and appearance which allow them to apply their previous experience with individuals roughly similar to the one before them or, more important, to apply untested stereotypes to him. They can also assume from past experience that only individuals of a particular kind are likely to be found in a given social setting. They can rely on what the individual says about himself or on documentary evidence he provides as to who and what he is. If they know, or know of, the individual by virtue of experience prior to the interaction, they can rely on assumptions as to the persistence and generality of psychological traits as a means of predicting his present and future behavior.

However, during the period in which the individual is in the immediate presence of the others, few events may occur which directly provide the others with the conclusive information they will need if they are to direct wisely their own activity. Many crucial facts lie beyond the time and place of interaction or lie concealed within it. For example, the "true" or "real" attitudes, beliefs, and emotions of the individual can be ascertained only indirectly, through his avowals or through what appears to be involuntary expressive behavior. Similarly, if the individual offers the others a product or service, they will often find that during the interaction there will be no time and place immediately available for eating the pudding that the proof can be found in. They will be forced to accept some events as conventional or natural signs of something not directly available to the senses. In Ichheiser's terms,[1] the individual will have to act so that he intentionally or unintentionally *expresses* himself, and the others will in turn have to be *impressed* in some way by him.

The expressiveness of the individual (and therefore his capacity to give impressions) appears to involve two radically different kinds of sign activity: the expression that he *gives,* and the expression that he *gives off.* The first involves verbal symbols or their substitutes which he uses admittedly and solely to convey the information that he and the others are known to attach to these symbols. This is communication in the traditional and narrow sense. The second involves a wide range of action that others can treat as symptomatic of the actor, the expectation being that the action was performed for reasons other than the information conveyed in this way. As we shall have to see, this distinction has an only initial validity. The individual does of course intentionally convey misinformation by means of both of these types of communication, the first involving deceit, the second feigning.

Taking communication in both its narrow and broad sense, one finds that when the individual is in the immediate presence of others, his activity will have a promissory character. The others are likely to find that they must accept the individual on faith, offering him a just return while he is present before them in exchange for something whose true value will not be established until after he has left their presence. (Of course, the others also live by inference in their dealings with the physical world, but it is only in the world of social interaction that the objects about which they make inferences will purposely facilitate and hinder this inferential process.) The security that they justifiably feel in making inferences about the individual will vary, of course, depending on such factors as the amount of information they already possess about him, but no amount of such past evidence can entirely obviate the necessity of acting on the basis of inferences. As William I. Thomas suggested:

> It is also highly important for us to realize that we do not as a matter of fact lead our lives, make our decisions, and reach our goals into everyday life either statistically or scientifically. We live by inference. I am, let us say, your guest. You do not know, you cannot determine scientifically, that I will not steal your money or your spoons. But inferentially I will not, and inferentially you have me as a guest.[2]

Let us now turn from the others to the point of view of the individual who presents himself before them. He may wish them to think highly of him, or to think that he thinks highly of them, or to perceive how in fact he feels toward them, or to obtain no clearcut impression; he may wish to ensure sufficient harmony so that the interaction can be sustained, or to defraud, get rid of, confuse, mislead, antagonize, or insult them. Regardless of the particular objective which the individual has in mind and of his motive for having this objective, it will be in his interests to control the conduct of the others, especially their responsive treatment of him.[3] This control is achieved largely by influencing the definition of the situation which the others come to formulate, and he can influence this definition by expressing himself in such a way as to give them the kind of impression that will lead them to act voluntarily in accordance with his own plan. Thus, when an individual appears in the presence of others, there will usually be some reason for him to mobilize his activity so that it will convey an impression to others which it is in his interests to convey. Since a girl's dormitory mates will glean evidence of her popularity from the calls she receives on the phone, we can suspect that some girls will arrange for calls to be made, and Willard Waller's finding can be anticipated.

It has been reported by many observers that a girl who is called to the telephone in the dormitories will often allow herself to be called several times, in order to give all the other girls ample opportunity to hear her paged.[4]

Of the two kinds of communication—expressions given and expressions given off—this report will be primarily concerned with the latter, with the more theatrical and contextual kind, the non-verbal, presumably unintentional kind, whether this communication be purposely engineered or not. As an example of what we must try to examine, I would like to cite at length a novelistic incident in which Preedy, a vacationing Englishman, makes his first appearance on the beach of his summer hotel in Spain:

> But in any case he took care to avoid catching anyone's eye. First of all, he had to make it clear to those potential companions of his holiday that they were of no concern to him whatsoever. He stared through them, round them, over them—eyes lost in space. The beach might have been empty. If by chance a ball was thrown his way, he looked surprised; then let a smile of amusement lighten his face (Kindly Preedy), looked round dazed to see that there *were* people on the beach, tossed it back with a smile to himself and not a smile *at the* people, and then resumed carelessly his nonchalant survey of space.
>
> But it was time to institute a little parade, the parade of the Ideal Preedy. By devious handlings he gave any one who wanted to look a chance to see the title of the book—a Spanish translation of Homer, classic thus, but not daring, cosmopolitan too—and then gathered together his beachwrap and bag into a neat sand-resistant pile (Methodical and Sensible Preedy), rose slowly to stretch at ease his huge frame (Big-Cat Preedy), and tossed aside his sandals (Carefree Preedy, after all).
>
> The marriage of Preedy and the sea! There were alternative rituals. The first involved the stroll that turns into a run and a dive straight into the water, thereafter smoothing into a strong splashless crawl towards the horizon. But of course not really to the horizon. Quite suddenly he would turn on to his back and thrash great white splashes with his legs, somehow thus showing that he could have swum further had he wanted to, and then would stand up a quarter out of water for all to see who it was.
>
> The alternative course was simpler; it avoided the cold-water shock, and it avoided the risk of appearing too high-spirited. The point was to appear to be so used to the sea, the Mediterranean, and this particular beach, that one might as well be in the sea as out of it. It involved a slow stroll down and into the edge of the water—not even noticing his toes were wet, land and water all the same to *him!*—with his eyes up at the sky gravely surveying portents, invisible to others, of the weather (Local Fisherman Preedy).[5]

The novelist means us to see that Preedy is improperly concerned with the extensive impressions he feels his sheer bodily action is giving off to those around him. We can malign Preedy further by assuming that he has acted merely in order to give a particular impression, that this is a false impression, and that the others present receive either no impression at all, or worse still, the impression that Preedy is affectedly trying to cause them to receive. But the important point for us here is that the kind of impression Preedy thinks he is making is in fact the kind of impression that others correctly and incorrectly glean from someone in their midst.

I have said that when an individual appears before others his actions will influence the definition of the situation which they come to have. Sometimes the individual will act in a thoroughly calculating manner, expressing himself in a given way solely in order to give the kind of impression to others that is likely to evoke from them a specific response he is concerned to obtain. Sometimes the individual will be calculating in his activity but be relatively unaware that this is the case. Sometimes he will intentionally and consciously express himself in a particular way, but chiefly because the traditions of his group or social status require this kind of expression and not because of any particular response (other than vague acceptance or approval) that is likely to be evoked from those impressed by the expression. Sometimes the traditions of an individual's role will lead him to give a well-designed impression of a particular kind and yet he may be neither consciously nor unconsciously disposed to create such an impression. The others, in their turn, may be suitably impressed by the individual's efforts to convey something, or may misunderstand the situation and come to conclusions that are warranted neither by the individual's intent nor by the facts. In any case, in so far as the others act *as if* the individual had conveyed a particular impression, we may take a functional or pragmatic view and say that the individual has "effectively" projected a given definition of the situation and "effectively" fostered the understanding that a given state of affairs obtains.

There is one aspect of the others' response that bears special comment here. Knowing that the individual is likely to present himself in a light that is favorable to him, the others may divide what they witness into two parts: a part that is relatively easy for the individual to manipulate at will, being chiefly his verbal assertions, and a part in regard to which he seems to have little concern or control, being chiefly derived from the expressions he gives off. The others may then use what are considered to be the ungovernable aspects of his expressive behavior as a check upon the validity of what is conveyed by the governable aspects. In this a fundamental asymmetry is demonstrated in the communication process, the individual presumably being aware of only one stream of his communication, the witness of this stream and one other. For example, in Shetland Isle one crofter's wife, in serving native dishes to a visitor from the mainland of Britain, would listen with a polite smile to his polite claims of liking what he was eating; at the same time she would take note of the rapidity with which the visitor lifted his fork or spoon to his mouth, the eagerness with which he passed food into his mouth, and the gusto expressed in chewing the food, using these signs as a check on the stated feelings of the eater. The same woman, in order to discover what one acquaintance (A) "actually" thought of another acquaintance (B), would wait until B was in the presence of A but engaged in conversation with still another person (C). She would then covertly examine the facial expressions of A as he regarded B in conversation with C. Not being in conversation with B, and not being directly observed by him, A would sometimes relax usual constraints and tactful deceptions, and freely express what he was "actually" feeling about B. This Shetlander, in short, would observe the unobserved observer.

Now given the fact that others are likely to check up on the more controllable aspects of behavior by means of the less controllable, one can expect that sometimes the individual will try to exploit this very possibility, guiding the impression he makes through behavior felt to be reliably informing.[6] For example, in gaining admission to a tight social circle, the participant observer may not only wear an accepting look while listening to an informant, but may also be careful to wear the same look when observing the informant talking to others; observers of the observer will then not as easily discover where he actually stands. A specific illustration may be cited from Shetland Isle. When a neighbor dropped in to have a cup of tea, he would ordinarily wear at least a hint of an expectant warm smile as he passed through the door into the cottage. Since lack of physical obstructions outside the cottage and lack of light within it usually made it possible to observe the visitor unobserved as he approached the house, islanders sometimes took pleasure in watching the visitor drop whatever expression he was manifesting and replace it with a sociable one just before reaching the door. However, some visitors, in appreciating that this examination was occurring, would blindly adopt a social face a long distance from the house, thus ensuring the projection of a constant image.

This kind of control upon the part of the individual reinstates the symmetry of the communication process, and sets the stage for a kind of information game—a potentially infinite cycle of concealment, discovery, false revelation, and rediscovery. It should be added that since the others are likely to be relatively unsuspicious of the presumably unguided aspect of the individual's conduct, he can gain much by controlling it. The others of course may sense that the individual is manipulating the presumably spontaneous aspects of his behavior, and seek in this very act of manipulation some shading of conduct that the individual has not managed to control. This again provides a check upon the individual's behavior, this time his presumably uncalculated behavior, thus re-establishing the asymmetry of the communication process.

Here I would like only to add the suggestion that the arts of piercing an individual's effort at calculated unintentionality seem better developed than our capacity to manipulate our own behavior, so that regardless of how many steps have occurred in the information game, the witness is likely to have the advantage over the actor, and the initial asymmetry of the communication process is likely to be retained.

When we allow that the individual projects a definition of the situation when he appears before others, we must also see that the others, however passive their role may seem to be, will themselves effectively project a definition of the situation by virtue of their response to the individual and by virtue of any lines of action they initiate to him. Ordinarily the definitions of the situation projected by the several different participants are sufficiently attuned to one another so that open contradiction will not occur. I do not mean that there will be the kind of consensus that arises when each individual present candidly expresses what he really feels and honestly agrees with the expressed feelings of the others present. This kind of harmony is an optimistic ideal and in any case not necessary for the smooth working of society. Rather, each participant is expected to suppress his immediate heartfelt feelings, conveying a view of the situation which he feels the others will be able to find at least temporarily acceptable. The maintenance of this surface of agreement, this veneer of consensus, is facilitated by each participant concealing his own wants behind statements which assert values to which everyone present feels obliged to give lip service. Further, there is usually a kind of division of definitional labor. Each participant is allowed to establish the tentative official ruling regarding matters which are vital to him but not immediately important to others, e.g., the rationalizations and justifications by which he accounts for his past activity. In exchange for this courtesy he remains silent or noncommittal on matters important to others but not immediately important to him. We have then a kind of interactional *modus vivendi*. Together, the participants contribute to a single over-all definition of the situation which involves not so much a real agreement as to what exists but rather a real agreement as to whose claims concerning what issues will be temporarily honored. Real agreement will also exist concerning the desirability of avoiding an open conflict of definitions of the situation.[7] I will refer to this level of agreement as a "working consensus." It is to be understood that the working consensus established in one interaction setting will be quite different in content from the working consensus established in a different type of setting. Thus, between two friends at lunch, a reciprocal show of affection, respect, and concern for the other is maintained. In service occupations, on the other hand, the specialist often maintains an image of disinterested involvement in the problem of the client, while the client responds with a show of respect for the competence and integrity of the specialist. Regardless of such differences in content, however, the general form of these working arrangements is the same.

In noting the tendency for a participant to accept the definitional claims made by the others present, we can appreciate the crucial importance of the information that the individual *initially* possesses or acquires concerning his fellow participants, for it is on the basis of this initial information that the individual starts to define the situation and starts to build up lines of responsive action. The individual's initial projection commits him to what he is proposing to be and requires him to drop all pretenses of being other things. As the interaction among the participants progresses, additions and modifications in this initial informational state will of course occur, but it is essential that these later developments be related without contradiction to, and even built up from, the initial positions taken by the several participants. It would seem that an individual can more easily make a choice as to what line of treatment to demand from and extend to the others present at the beginning of an encounter than he can alter the line of treatment that is being pursued once the interaction is under way.

In everyday life, of course, there is a clear understanding that first impressions are important. Thus, the work adjustment of those in service occupations will often hinge upon a capacity to seize and hold the initiative in the service relation, a capacity that will require subtle aggressiveness on the part of the server when he is of lower socio-economic status than his client. W. F. Whyte suggests the waitress as an example:

> The first point that stands out is that the waitress who bears up under pressure does not simply respond to her customers. She acts with some skill to control their behavior. The first question to ask when we look at the customer relationship is, "Does the waitress get the jump on the customer, or does the customer get the jump on the waitress?" The skilled waitress realizes the crucial nature of this question. . . .
>
> The skilled waitress tackles the customer with confidence and without hesitation. For example, she may find that a new customer has seated himself before she could clear off the dirty dishes and change the cloth. He is now leaning on the table studying the menu. She greets him, says, "May I change the cover, please?" and, without waiting for an answer, takes his menu away from him so that he moves back from the table, and she goes about her work. The relationship is handled politely but firmly, and there is never any question as to who is in charge.[8]

When the interaction that is initiated by "first impressions" is itself merely the initial interaction in an extended series of interactions involving the same participants, we speak of "getting off on the right foot" and feel that it is crucial that we do so. Thus, one learns that some teachers take the following view:

You can't ever let them get the upper hand on you or you're through. So I start out tough. The first day I get a new class in, I let them know who's boss. . . . You've got to start off tough; then you can ease up as you go along. If you start out easy-going, when you try to be tough, they'll just look at you and laugh.[9]

Similarly, attendants in mental institutions may feel that if the new patient is sharply put in his place the first day on the ward and made to see who is boss, much future difficulty will be prevented.[10]

Given the fact that the individual effectively projects a definition of the situation when he enters the presence of others, we can assume that events may occur within the interaction which contradict, discredit, or otherwise throw doubt upon this projection. When these disruptive events occur, the interaction itself may come to a confused and embarrassed halt. Some of the assumptions upon which the responses of the participants had been predicted become untenable, and the participants find themselves lodged in an interaction for which the situation has been wrongly defined and is now no longer defined. At such moments the individual whose presentation has been discredited may feel ashamed while the others present may feel hostile, and all the participants may come to feel ill at ease, nonplussed, out of countenance, embarrassed, experiencing the kind of anomy that is generated when the minute social system of face-to-face interaction breaks down.

In stressing the fact that the initial definition of the situation projected by an individual tends to provide a plan for the cooperative activity that follows—in stressing this action point of view—we must not overlook the crucial fact that any projected definition of the situation also has a distinctive moral character. It is this moral character of projections that will chiefly concern us in this report. Society is organized on the principle that any individual who possesses certain social characteristics has a moral right to expect that others will value and treat him in an appropriate way. Connected with this principle is a second, namely that an individual who implicitly or explicitly signifies that he has certain social characteristics ought in fact to be what he claims he is. In consequence, when an individual projects a definition of the situation and thereby makes an implicit or explicit claim to be a person of a particular kind, he automatically exerts a moral demand upon the others, obliging them to value and treat him in the manner that persons of his kind have a right to expect. He also implicitly forgoes all claims to be things he does not appear to be[11] and hence forgoes the treatment that would be appropriate for such individuals. The others find, then, that the individual has informed them as to what is and as to what they *ought* to see as the "is."

One cannot judge the importance of definitional disruptions by the frequency with which they occur, for apparently they would occur more frequently were not constant precautions taken. We find that preventive practices are constantly employed to avoid these embarrassments and that corrective practices are constantly employed to compensate for discrediting occurrences that have not been successfully avoided. When the individual employs these strategies and tactics to protect his own projections, we may refer to them as "defensive practices"; when a participant employs them to save the definition of the situation projected by another, we speak of "protective practices" or "tact." Together, defensive and protective practices comprise the techniques employed to safeguard the impression fostered by an individual during his presence before others. It should be added that while we may be ready to see that no fostered impression would survive if defensive practices were not employed, we are less ready perhaps to see that few impressions could survive if those who received the impression did not exert tact in their reception of it.

In addition to the fact that precautions are taken to prevent disruption of projected definitions, we may also note that an intense interest in these disruptions comes to play a significant role in the social life of the group. Practical jokes and social games are played in which embarrassments which are to be taken unseriously are purposely engineered.[12] Fantasies are created in which devastating exposures occur. Anecdotes from the past—real, embroidered, or fictitious—are told and retold, detailing disruptions which occurred, almost occurred, or occurred and were admirably resolved. There seems to be no grouping which does not have a ready supply of these games, reveries, and cautionary tales, to be used as a source of humor, a catharsis for anxieties, and a sanction for inducing individuals to be modest in their claims and reasonable in their projected expectations. The individual may tell himself through dreams of getting into impossible positions. Families tell of the time a guest got his dates mixed and arrived when neither the house nor anyone in it was ready for him. Journalists tell of times when an all-too-meaningful misprint occurred, and the paper's assumption of objectivity or decorum was humorously discredited. Public servants tell of times a client ridiculously misunderstood form instructions, giving answers which implied an unanticipated and bizarre definition of the situation.[13] Seamen, whose home away from home is rigorously he-man, tell stories of coming back home and inadvertently asking mother to "pass the fucking butter."[14] Diplomats tell of the time a near-sighted queen asked a republican ambassador about the health of his king.[15]

To summarize, then, I assume that when an individual appears before others he will have many motives for trying to control the impression they receive of the situation.

Notes

1. Gustav Ichheiser, "Misunderstandings in Human Relations," Supplement to *The American Journal of Sociology*, 55 (September, 1949):6–7.

2. Quoted in E. H. Volkart, editor, *Social Behavior and Personality, Contributions of W. I. Thomas to Theory and Social Research* (New York: Social Science Research Council, 1951), p. 5.

3. Here I owe much to an unpublished paper by Tom Burns of the University of Edinburgh. He presents the argument that in all interaction a basic underlying theme is the desire of each participant to guide and control the responses made by the others present. A similar argument has been advanced by Jay Haley in a recent unpublished paper, but in regard to a special kind of control, that having to do with defining the nature of the relationship of those involved in the interaction.

4. Willard Waller, "The Rating and Dating Complex," *American Sociological Review,* 2:730.

5. William Sansom, *A Contest of Ladies* (London: Hogarth, 1956), pp. 230–32.

6. The widely read and rather sound writings of Stephen Potter are concerned in part with signs that can be engineered to give a shrewd observer the apparently incidental cues he needs to discover concealed virtues the gamesman does not in fact possess.

7. An interaction can be purposely set up as a time and place for voicing differences in opinion, but in such cases participants must be careful to agree not to disagree on the proper tone of voice, vocabulary, and degree of seriousness in which all arguments are to be phrased, and upon the mutual respect which disagreeing participants must carefully continue to express toward one another. This debaters' or academic definition of the situation may also be invoked suddenly and judiciously as a way of translating a serious conflict of views into one that can be handled within a framework acceptable to all present.

8. W. F. Whyte, "When Workers and Customers Meet," Chap. VII, *Industry and Society,* ed. W. F. Whyte (New York: McGraw-Hill, 1946), pp. 132–33.

9. Teacher interview quoted by Howard S. Becker, "Social Class Variations in the Teacher-Pupil Relationship," *Journal of Educational Sociology,* 25:459.

10. Harold Taxel, "Authority Structure in a Mental Hospital Ward" (unpublished Master's thesis, Department of Sociology, University of Chicago, 1953).

11. This role of the witness in limiting what it is the individual can be has been stressed by Existentialists, who see it as a basic threat to individual freedom. See Jean-Paul Sartre, *Being and Nothingness,* trans. by Hazel E. Barnes (New York: Philosophical Library, 1956), pp. 365 ff.

12. Erving Goffman, "Communication Conduct in an Island Community" (unpublished Ph.D. dissertation, Department of Sociology, University of Chicago, 1953), pp. 319–27.

13. Peter Blau, *Dynamics of Bureaucracy: A Study of Interpersonal Relationships in Two Government Agencies,* 2nd ed. (Chicago: University of Chicago Press, 1963).

14. Walter M. Beattie, Jr., "The Merchant Seaman" (unpublished M. A. Report, Department of Sociology, University of Chicago, 1950), p. 35.

15. Sir Frederick Ponsonby, *Recollections of Three Reigns* (New York: Dutton, 1952), p. 46.

Socialization
and Gender

ESSENTIAL TO OUR SURVIVAL following birth is *sociali-zation*—learning to become full-fledged members of a human group. As we saw in Part III, this learning involves such fundamental, taken-for-granted aspects of group life as ideas about health and morality, and the many nuances of nonverbal communication. We saw that socialization involves learning rules (what we should and should not do under different circumstances) and values (what is considered good or bad, desirable or undesirable), as well as expectations about how we should present the self in different social settings.

The *agents of socialization* include our parents, brothers and sisters and other relatives, friends and neighbors, as well as clergy and schoolteachers. They also include people we do not know and never will know, such as clerks and shoppers who, by their very presence—and the expectations we know they have of us—influence our behavior in public settings, and thereby shape it for similar situations in the future. Through this process of socialization each of us develops a *personality*, the tendency to behave in particular ways, which distinguishes us from others.

Essential to our forming an identity is socialization into gender—that is, learning how to be masculine or feminine. The term *sex* refers to biological characteristics, while the term *gender* refers to what is expected of people because of those characteristics. We inherit our sex, but we learn our gender.

Although we come into this world with the biological equipment of a male or a female, these physical organs do not determine what we shall be like as a male or a female. Whether or not we defer to members of the opposite sex, for example, is not an automatic result of our particular sexual equipment but is due to what we learn is proper for us because of the particular biological equipment we possess. This learning process is called *gender* or *sex role socialization*.

Our gender extends into almost every area of our lives, even into situations for which it may be quite irrelevant. For example, if we are grocery clerks, by means of our clothing, language, and gestures we communicate to others that we are *male* or *female* clerks. Because gender cuts across most aspects of social life, sociologists refer to gender as a *master trait*.

Challenged for generations (the women's movement was active before our grandparents were born), the expectations attached to the sexes have undergone substantial modification in recent years. One can no longer safely assume particular behavior on the part of another simply because of that person's sex. Despite such changes, however, most Americans follow rather traditional lines as they socialize their children. Changes in something as basic as gender take place slowly, and male dominance remains a fact of social life.

What would we humans be like if we were untouched by culture? Although there is much speculation, no one knows the answer to this question, for any behavior or attitude that we examine is embedded within cultural learning. The closest we can come to answering the question is to observe those children who have received the least introduction to their culture—as Kingsley Davis does in the opening selection. Even isolated children, such as Anna and Isabelle, however, have been exposed to a culture, even though minimally. One really cannot think of humanity apart from culture, then, for culture shapes humanity.

In the past, an occasional naked, wild-looking child was discovered living alone in the wilderness. They could not speak, walked and crawled on all fours, and pounced on small animals, devouring them raw while emitting guttural sounds. Such *feral* ("wild") *children* were thought to have been raised by animals and to be untouched by human culture. Although documented cases of feral children exist—one boy discovered in 1798 was even studied intensely by scientists—the presumption today is that feral children had been abandoned by their parents because they were mentally handicapped. If so, the study of feral children does not answer the question of what humans would be like if they were untouched by culture. If it did, the answer certainly would not be encouraging—granted their lack of language, pouncing on and devouring small animals, and so on.

It is through our association with other humans, then, not some inborn instincts, that we learn what it means to be human. To provide a context for appreciating the implications of this fundamental aspect of life, this part opens with a classic article by Kingsley Davis, in which he relates the story of Anna. Essential to our becoming human is our socialization into gender, the primary focus of Part IV. Here we explore the question of how we learn gender, the sex roles we are socially destined to play. Memories of childhood may surface while reading my analysis of some of the processes by which boys are socialized into social dominance. Focusing on childhood, I examine experiences that direct boys into a world distinct from the female world, that often lead boys and men to think of themselves as superior, and that later make it difficult for men and women to communicate in depth and to maintain "significant relationships" with each other. Donna Eder continues this focus on children's experiences. The interactions of the girls she observed in middle school reveal another emphasis on superficiality, how appearance (or attractiveness) becomes an essential orientation of the self. Barrie Thorne and Zella Luria continue to place the sociological spotlight on the world of children, examining how schoolchildren separate their activities and friendships on the basis of sex and engage in forms of play that help to maintain male dominance in society. Deborah Tannen closes this Part with an analysis of how men and women express themselves. She highlights communication styles that not only hinder communication between men and women but which also may reflect underlying gender differences in orientations to social life.

Taken together, these articles help us to better understand how gender pervades our lives. They ought to provide considerable insight into your own socialization into gender—how you became masculine or feminine—and, once propelled into that role, how your ongoing experiences in society continue to influence your attitudes and behaviors.

12 Extreme Isolation

KINGSLEY DAVIS

What could the editor possibly mean by this article's heading in the table of contents: "Learning to be human"? Isn't it obvious that we humans are born human? Certainly this is true concerning our *biological* characteristics, that is, our possession of arms, legs, head, and torso, as well as our internal organs.

But to act like other people, to think the way others think—and perhaps even the ability to think—are *learned* characteristics. These are the result of years of exposure to people living in groups, especially the acquisition of language.

Just how much does biology contribute to what we are, and how much is due to social life? (Or, in Davis' terms, what are the relative contributions of the biogenic and the sociogenic factors?) Although this question has intrigued many, no one has yet been able to unravel its mystery. According to the findings reported here, however, the contributions of the social group reach much farther and are of greater fundamental consequence than most of us imagine. Our speech, for example, helps shape our basic attitudes and orientations to life. As indicated in this article, however, the social group may even contribute characteristics that we ordinarily presume are biological, such as our ability to walk. Although this selection will not present any "final answers" to this age-old question, it should stir up your sociological imagination.

EARLY IN 1940 THERE APPEARED . . . an account of a girl called Anna.[1] She had been deprived of normal contact and had received a minimum of human care for almost the whole of her first six years of life. At this time observations were not complete and the report had a tentative character. Now, however, the girl is dead, and with more information available,[2] it is possible to give a fuller and more definitive description of the case from a sociological point of view.

Anna's death, caused by hemorrhagic jaundice, occurred on August 6, 1942. Having been born on March 1 or 6,[3] 1932, she was approximately ten and a half years of age when she died. The previous report covered her development up to the age of almost eight years; the present one recapitulates the earlier period on the basis of new evidence and then covers the last two and a half years of her life.

Early History

The first few days and weeks of Anna's life were complicated by frequent changes of domicile. It will be recalled that she was an illegitimate child, the second such child born to her mother, and that her grandfather, a widowed farmer in whose house her mother lived, strongly disapproved of this new evidence of the mother's indiscretion. This fact led to the baby's being shifted about.

Two weeks after being born in a nurse's private home, Anna was brought to the family farm, but the grandfather's antagonism was so great that she was shortly taken to the house of one of her mother's friends. At this time a local minister became interested in her and took her to his house with an idea of possible adoption. He decided against adoption, however, when he discovered that she had vaginitis. The infant was then taken to a children's home in the nearest large city. This agency found that at the age of only three weeks she was already in a miserable condition, being "terribly galled and otherwise in very bad shape." It did not regard her as a likely subject for adoption but took her in for a while anyway, hoping to benefit her. After Anna had spent nearly eight weeks in this place, the agency notified her mother to come and get her. The mother responded by sending a man and his wife to the children's home with a view to their adopting Anna, but they made such a poor impression on the agency that permission was refused. Later the mother came herself and took the child out of the home and then gave her to this couple. It was in the home of this pair that a social worker found the girl a short time thereafter. The social worker went to the mother's home and pleaded with Anna's grandfather to allow the mother to bring the child home. In spite of threats, he refused. The child, by then more than four months old, was next taken to another children's home in a near-by town. A medical examination at this time revealed that she had impetigo, vaginitis, umbilical hernia, and a skin rash.

Anna remained in this second children's home for nearly three weeks, at the end of which time she was transferred to a private foster-home. Since, however, the grandfather would not, and the mother could not, pay for the child's care, she was finally taken back as a last resort to the grandfather's house (at the age of five and a half months). There she remained, kept on the second floor in an attic-like room because her mother hesitated to incur the grandfather's wrath by bringing her downstairs.

The mother, a sturdy woman weighing about 180 pounds, did a man's work on the farm. She engaged in heavy work such as milking cows and tending hogs and had little time for her children. Sometimes she went out at night, in which case Anna was left entirely without attention. Ordinarily, it seems,

Anna received only enough care to keep her barely alive. She appears to have been seldom moved from one position to another. Her clothing and bedding were filthy. She apparently had no instruction, no friendly attention.

It is little wonder that, when finally found and removed from the room in the grandfather's house at the age of nearly six years, the child could not talk, walk, or do anything that showed intelligence. She was in an extremely emaciated and undernourished condition, with skeletonlike legs and a bloated abdomen. She had been fed on virtually nothing except cow's milk during the years under her mother's care.

Anna's condition when found, and her subsequent improvement, have been described in the previous report. It now remains to say what happened to her after that.

Later History

In 1939, nearly two years after being discovered, Anna had progressed, as previously reported, to the point where she could walk, understand simple commands, feed herself, achieve some neatness, remember people, etc. But she still did not speak, and, though she was much more like a normal infant of something over one year of age in mentality, she was far from normal for her age.

On August 30, 1939, she was taken to a private home for retarded children, leaving the county home where she had been for more than a year and a half. In her new setting she made some further progress, but not a great deal. In a report of an examination made November 6 of the same year, the head of the institution pictured the child as follows:

> Anna walks about aimlessly, makes periodic rhythmic motions of her hands, and, at intervals, makes guttural and sucking noises. She regards her hands as if she had seen them for the first time. It was impossible to hold her attention for more than a few seconds at a time—not because of distraction due to external stimuli but because of her inability to concentrate. She ignored the task in hand to gaze vacantly about the room. Speech is entirely lacking. Numerous unsuccessful attempts have been made with her in the hope of developing initial sounds. I do not believe that this failure is due to negativism or deafness but that she is not sufficiently developed to accept speech at this time. . . . The prognosis is not favorable. . . .

More than five months later, on April 25, 1940, a clinical psychologist, the late Professor Francis N. Maxfield, examined Anna and reported the following: large for her age; hearing "entirely normal"; vision apparently normal; able to climb stairs; speech in the "babbling stage" and "promise for developing intelligible speech later seems to be good." He said further that "on the

Merrill–Palmer scale she made a mental score of 19 months. On the Vineland social maturity scale she made a score of 23 months.[4]

Professor Maxfield very sensibly pointed out that prognosis is difficult in such cases of isolation. "It is very difficult to take scores on tests standardized under average conditions of environment and experience," he wrote, "and interpret them in a case where environment and experience have been so unusual." With this warning he gave it as his opinion at that time that Anna would eventually "attain an adult mental level of six or seven years."[5]

The school for retarded children, on July 1, 1941, reported that Anna had reached 46 inches in height and weighed 60 pounds. She could bounce and catch a ball and was said to conform to group socialization, though as a follower rather than a leader. Toilet habits were firmly established. Food habits were normal, except that she still used a spoon as her sole implement. She could dress herself except for fastening her clothes. Most remarkable of all, she had finally begun to develop speech. She was characterized as being at about the two-year level in this regard. She could call attendants by name and bring in one when she was asked to. She had a few complete sentences to express her wants. The report concluded that there was nothing peculiar about her, except that she was feebleminded—"probably congenital in type."[6]

A final report from the school made on June 22, 1942, and evidently the last report before the girl's death, pictured only a slight advance over that given above. It said that Anna could follow directions, string beads, identify a few colors, build with blocks, and differentiate between attractive and unattractive pictures. She had a good sense of rhythm and loved a doll. She talked mainly in phrases but would repeat words and try to carry on a conversation. She was clean about clothing. She habitually washed her hands and brushed her teeth. She would try to help other children. She walked well and could run fairly well, though clumsily. Although easily excited, she had a pleasant disposition.

Interpretation

Such was Anna's condition just before her death. It may seem as if she had not made much progress, but one must remember the condition in which she had been found. One must recall that she had no glimmering of speech, absolutely no ability to walk, no sense of gesture, not the least capacity to feed herself even when the food was put in front of her, and no comprehension of cleanliness. She was so apathetic that it was hard to tell whether or not she could hear. And all this at the age of nearly six years. Compared with this condition, her capacities at the time of her death seem striking indeed, though they do not amount to much more than a two-and-a-half-year mental level. One conclusion therefore seems safe, namely, that her isolation prevented a considerable amount of mental development that was undoubtedly part of her capacity. Just what her original capacity was, of course, is hard to say; but her development after her period of confinement (including the ability to walk and run, to play, dress, fit into a social situation, and, above all, to speak) shows that she had at least this capacity—capacity that never could have been realized in her original condition of isolation.

A further question is this: What would she have been like if she had received a normal upbringing from the moment of birth? A definitive answer would have been impossible in any case, but even an approximate answer is made difficult by her early death. If one assumes, as was tentatively surmised in the previous report, that it is "almost impossible for any child to learn to speak, think, and act like a normal person after a long period of early isolation," it seems likely that Anna might have had a normal or near-normal capacity, genetically speaking. On the other hand, it was pointed out that Anna represented "a marginal case, [because] she was discovered before she had reached six years of age," an age "young enough to allow for some plasticity."[7] While admitting, then, that Anna's isolation *may* have been the major cause (and was certainly a minor cause) of her lack of rapid mental progress during the four and a half years following her rescue from neglect, it is necessary to entertain the hypothesis that she was congenitally deficient.

In connection with this hypothesis, one suggestive though by no means conclusive circumstance needs consideration, namely, the mentality of Anna's forebears. Information on this subject is easier to obtain, as one might guess, on the mother's than on the father's side. Anna's maternal grandmother, for example, is said to have been college educated and wished to have her children receive a good education, but her husband, Anna's stern grandfather, apparently a shrewd, hard-driving, calculating farmowner, was so penurious that her ambitions in this direction were thwarted. Under the circumstances her daughter (Anna's mother) managed, despite having to do hard work on the farm, to complete the eighth grade in a country school. Even so, however, the daughter was evidently not very smart. "A schoolmate of [Anna's mother] stated that she was retarded in school work; was very gullible at this age; and that her morals even at this time were discussed by other students." Two tests administered to her on March 4, 1938, when she was thirty-two years of age, showed that she was mentally deficient. On the Standard Revision of the Binet–Simon Scale her performance was equivalent to that of a child of eight years, giving her an I.Q. of 50 and indicating mental deficiency of "middle-grade moron type."[8]

As to the identity of Anna's father, the most persistent theory holds that he was an old man about seventy-four years of age at the time of the girl's birth. If he was the one, there is no indication of mental or other biological deficiency, whatever one may think of his morals. However, someone else may actually have been the father.

To sum up: Anna's heredity is the kind that *might* have given rise to innate mental deficiency, though not necessarily.

Comparison with Another Case

Perhaps more to the point than speculations about Anna's ancestry would be a case for comparison. If a child could be discovered who had been isolated about the same length of time as Anna but had achieved a much quicker recovery and a greater mental development, it would be a stronger indication that Anna was deficient to start with.

Such a case does exist. It is the case of a girl found at about the same time as Anna and under strikingly similar circumstances. A full description of the details of this case has not been published, but in addition to newspaper reports, an excellent preliminary account by a speech specialist, Dr. Marie K. Mason, who played an important role in the handling of the child, has appeared.[9] Also the late Dr. Francis N. Maxfield, clinical psychologist at Ohio State University, as was Dr. Mason, has written an as yet unpublished but penetrating analysis of the case.[10] Some of his observations have been included in Professor Zingg's book on feral man.[11] The following discussion is drawn mainly from these enlightening materials. The writer, through the kindness of Professors Mason and Maxfield, did have a chance to observe the girl in April, 1940, and to discuss the features of her case with them.

Born apparently one month later than Anna, the girl in question, who has been given the pseudonym Isabelle, was discovered in November, 1938, nine months after the discovery of Anna. At the time she was found she was approximately six and a half years of age. Like Anna, she was an illegitimate child and had been kept in seclusion for that reason. Her mother was a deaf-mute, having become so at the age of two, and it appears that she and Isabelle had spent most of their time together in a dark room shut off from the rest of the mother's family. As a result Isabelle had no chance to develop speech; when she communicated with her mother, it was by means of gestures. Lack of sunshine and inadequacy of diet had caused Isabelle to become rachitic. Her legs in particular were affected; they "were so bowed that as she stood erect the soles of her shoes came nearly flat together, and she got about with a skittering gait."[12] Her behavior toward strangers, especially men, was almost that of a wild animal, manifesting much fear and hostility. In lieu of speech she made only a strong croaking sound. In many ways she acted like an infant. "She was apparently utterly unaware of relationships of any kind. When presented with a ball for the first time, she held it in the palm of her hand, then reached out and stroked my face with it. Such behavior is comparable to that of a child of six months."[13] At first it was even hard to tell whether or not she could hear, so unused were her senses. Many of her actions resembled those of deaf children.

It is small wonder that, once it was established that she could hear, specialists working with her believed her to be feeble-minded. Even on nonverbal tests her performance was so low as to promise little for the future. Her first score on the Stanford–Binet was 19 months, practically at the zero point of the scale. On the Vineland social maturity scale her first score was 39, representing an age level of two and a half years.[14] "The general impression was that she was wholly uneducable and that any attempt to teach her to speak, after so long a period of silence, would meet with failure."[15]

In spite of this interpretation, the individuals in charge of Isabelle launched a systematic and skillful program of training. It seemed hopeless at first. The approach had to be through pantomime and dramatization, suitable to an infant. It required one week of intensive effort before she even made her first attempt at vocalization. Gradually she began to respond, however, and, after the first hurdles had at last been overcome, a curious thing happened. She went through the usual stages of learning characteristic of the years from one to six not only in proper succession but far more rapidly than normal. In a little over two months after her first vocalization she was putting sentences together. Nine months after that she could identify words and sentences on the printed page, could write well, could add to ten, and could retell a story after hearing it. Seven months beyond this point she had a vocabulary of 1,500–2,000 words and was asking complicated questions. Starting from an educational level of between one and three years (depending on what aspect one considers), she had reached a normal level by the time she was eight and a half years old. In short, she covered in two years the stages of learning that ordinarily require six.[16] Or, to put it another way, her I.Q. trebled in a year and a half.[17] The speed with which she reached the normal level of mental development seems analogous to the recovery of body weight in a growing child after an illness, the recovery being achieved by an extra fast rate of growth for a period after the illness until normal weight for the given age is again attained.

When the writer saw Isabelle a year and a half after her discovery, she gave him the impression of being a very bright, cheerful, energetic little girl. She spoke well, walked and ran without trouble, and sang with gusto and accuracy. Today she is over fourteen years old and has passed the sixth grade in a public school. Her teachers say that she participates in all school activities as normally as other children. Though older than her classmates, she has fortunately not physically matured too far beyond their level.[18]

Clearly the history of Isabelle's development is different from that of Anna's. In both cases there was exceedingly low, or rather blank, intellectual level to begin with. In both cases it seemed that the girl might be congenitally feeble-minded. In both a considerably higher level was reached later on. But the Ohio girl achieved a normal mentality within two years, whereas Anna was still markedly inadequate at the end of four and half years. This difference in achievement may suggest that Anna had less initial capacity. But an alternative hypothesis is possible.

One should remember that Anna never received the prolonged and expert attention that Isabelle received. The result of such attention, in the case of the Ohio girl, was to give her speech at an early stage, and her subsequent rapid development seems to have been a consequence of that. "Until Isabelle's speech and language development, she had all the characteristics of a feeble-minded child." Had Anna, who, from the standpoint of psychometric tests and early history, closely resembled this girl at the start, been given a mastery of speech at an earlier point by intensive training, her subsequent development might have been much more rapid.[19]

The hypothesis that Anna began with a sharply inferior mental capacity is therefore not established. Even if she were deficient to start with, we have no way of knowing how much so. Under ordinary conditions she might have been a dull normal or, like her mother, a moron. Even after the blight of her isolation, if she had lived to maturity, she might have finally reached virtually the full level of her capacity, whatever it may have been. That her isolation did have a profound effect upon her mentality, there can be no doubt. This is proved by the substantial degree of change during the four and a half years following her rescue.

Consideration of Isabelle's case serves to show, as Anna's case does not clearly show, that isolation up to the age of six, with failure to acquire any form of speech and hence failure to grasp nearly the whole world of cultural meaning, does not preclude the subsequent acquisition of these. Indeed, there seems to be a process of accelerated recovery in which the child goes through the mental stages at a more rapid rate than would be the case in normal development. Just what would be the maximum age at which a person could remain isolated and still retain the capacity for full cultural acquisition is hard to say. Almost certainly it would not be as high as age fifteen; it might possibly be as low as age ten. Undoubtedly various individuals would differ considerably as to the exact age.

Anna's is not an ideal case for showing the effects of extreme isolation, partly because she was possibly deficient to begin with, partly because she did not receive the best training available, and partly because she did not live long enough. Nevertheless, her case is instructive when placed in the record with numerous other cases of extreme isolation. This and the previous article about her are meant to place her in the record. It is to be hoped that other cases will be described in the scientific literature as they are discovered (as unfortunately they will be), for only in these rare cases of extreme isolation is it possible "to observe *concretely separated* two factors in the development of human personality which are always otherwise only analytically separated, the biogenic and the sociogenic factors."[20]

Notes

1. Kingsley Davis, "Extreme Social Isolation of a Child," *American Journal of Sociology,* XLV (January, 1940), 554–65.

2. Sincere appreciation is due to the officials in the Department of Welfare, Commonwealth of Pennsylvania, for the kind cooperation in making available the records concerning Anna and discussing the case frankly with the writer. Helen C. Hubbell, Florentine Hackbusch, and Eleanor Mecklenburg were particularly helpful, as was Fanny L. Matchette. Without their aid neither of the reports on Anna could have been written.

3. The records are not clear as to which day.

4. Letter to one of the state officials in charge of the case.

5. *Ibid.*

6. Progress report of the school.

7. Davis, *op. cit.,* p. 564.

8. The facts set forth here as to Anna's ancestry are taken chiefly from a report of mental tests administered to Anna's mother by psychologists at a state hospital where she was taken for this purpose after the discovery of Anna's seclusion. This excellent report was not available to the writer when the previous paper on Anna was published.

9. Marie K. Mason, "Learning to Speak after Six and One-Half Years of Silence," *Journal of Speech Disorders,* VII (1942), 295–304.

10. Francis N. Maxfield, "What Happens When the Social Environment of a Child Approaches Zero." The writer is greatly indebted to Mrs. Maxfield and to Professor Horace B. English, a colleague of Professor Maxfield, for the privilege of seeing this manuscript and other materials collected on isolated and feral individuals.

11. J. A. L. Singh and Robert M. Zingg, *Wolf-Children and Feral Man* (New York: Harper & Bros., 1941), pp. 248–51.

12. Maxfield, unpublished manuscript cited above.

13. Mason, *op. cit.*, p. 299.

14. Maxfield, unpublished manuscript.

15. Mason, *op. cit.*, p. 299.

16. *Ibid.*, pp. 300–304.

17. Maxfield, unpublished manuscript.

18. Based on a personal letter from Dr. Mason to the writer, May 13, 1946.

19. This point is suggested in a personal letter from Dr. Mason to the writer, October 22, 1946.

20. Singh and Zingg, *op. cit.*, pp. xxi–xxii, in a foreword by the writer.

13 On Becoming Male: Reflections of a Sociologist on Childhood and Early Socialization

JAMES M. HENSLIN

Although relations between men and women are enveloped in social change, men still dominate our social institutions: law, politics, business, religion, education, the military, medicine, science, sports, and in many ways, even marriage and family. Despite far-reaching social change, women often find themselves in the more backstage, nurturing, and supportive roles—and those roles generally are supportive of the more dominant roles men play.

Why? Is this a consequence of genetic heritage—boys and girls being born with different predispositions? Or is it due to culture, because boys are socialized into dominance? While there is considerable debate among academics on this matter, sociologists side almost unanimously with the proponents of socialization. In this article, Henslin analyzes some of the socialization experiences that place boys in a distinctive social world and prepare them for dominance. This selection is an attempt to penetrate the taken-for-granted, behind-the-scenes aspects of socialization into masculine sexuality. Whether male or female, you might find it useful to contrast your experiences in growing up with those the author describes.

ACCORDING TO THE PREVAILING sociological perspective, our masculinity or femininity is not biologically determined. Although our biological or genetic inheritance gives each of us the sex organs of a male or female, how our "maleness" or "femaleness" is expressed depends on what we learn. Our masculinity or femininity, that is, what we are like as sexual beings—our orientations and how we behave as a male or a female—does not depend on biology but on social learning. It can be said that while our gender

is part of our biological inheritance, our sexuality (or masculinity or femininity) is part of our social inheritance.

If this sociological position is correct—that culture, not anatomy, is our
destiny—how do we become the "way we are"?[1] What factors shape or influence us into becoming masculine or feminine? If our behaviors do not come
from our biology, how do we end up having behaviors that are typically associated with our gender? If they *are* learned, how do our behaviors, attitudes,
and other basic orientations come to be felt by us as natural and essential to
our identity? (And they are indeed essential to our identity.) In what ways is
the process of "becoming" related to the social structure of society?

Not only would it take volumes to answer these questions fully, but it
would also be impossible, since the answers are only now slowly being unrav-
eled by researchers. In this short and rather informal article, I will be able to
indicate only some of the basics underlying this foundational learning. I will
focus exclusively on being socialized into masculinity, and will do this by reflecting on (1) my own experience in "becoming"; (2) my observations as a
sociologist of the experiences of others; and (3) what others have shared with
me concerning their own experiences. The reader should keep in mind that
this article is meant to be neither definitive nor exhaustive, but is designed to
depict general areas of male socialization and thereby to provide insight into
the acquisition of masculinity in our culture.

In the Beginning . . .

Except for a few rare instances,[2] each of us arrives in this world with a clearly
definable physical characteristic that sets us apart from about half the rest of the
world. This characteristic makes a literal world of difference. Our parents become excited about whether we have been born with a penis or a vagina. They
are usually either happy or disappointed about which organ we possess, seldom
feeling neutral about the matter. They announce it to friends, relatives, and sometimes to complete strangers ("It's a boy!" "It's a girl!"). Regardless of how they
feel about it, on the basis of our possessing a particular physical organ they purposely, but both consciously and subconsciously, separate us into two worlds.
Wittingly and unwittingly, they thereby launch us onto a career that will en-
compass almost every aspect of our lives—and will remain with us until death.

Colors, Clothing, and Toys

While it is not inherently more masculine or feminine than red, yellow, pur-
ple, orange, white, or black, the color blue has become associated arbitrarily

with infantile masculinity. After what is usually a proud realization that the neonate possesses a penis (which marks him as a member of the overlords of the universe), the inheritor of dominance is wrapped in blue. This color is merely an arbitrary choice, as originally any other would have done as well. But now that the association is made, no other will do. The announcing colors maintain their meaning for only a fairly short period, gradually becoming sexually neutralized.[3] Pink, however, retains at least part of its meaning of sexuality, for even adult males tend to shy away from it.

Our parents gently and sometimes not so gently push us onto a predetermined course. First they provide clothing designated appropriate to our masculine status. Even as infants our clothing displays sexual significance, and our parents are extremely careful that we never are clothed in either dresses or ruffles. For example, while our plastic panties are designed to keep mothers, fathers, and their furniture and friends dry, our parents make absolutely certain that ours are never pink with white ruffles. Even if our Mom had run out of all other plastic panties, she would rather stay home than take us out in public wearing ruffled pinkies. Mom would probably feel a twinge of guilt over such cross-dressing even in private.[4]

So both Mom and Dad are extremely cautious about our clothing. Generally plain, often simple, and usually sturdy, our clothing is designed to take the greater "rough and tumble" that they know boys are going to give it. They also choose clothing that will help groom us into future adult roles; depending on the style of the period, they dress us in little sailor suits, miniature jogging togs, or two-piece suits with matching ties. Although at this early age we could care less about such things, and their significance appears irrelevant to us, our parents' concern is always present. If during a supermarket expedition even a stranger mistakes our sexual identity, this agitates our parents, challenging their sacred responsibility to maintain the reality-ordering structure of the sex worlds. Such mistaken identification forces them to rethink their activities in proper sex typing, their deep obligation to make certain that their offspring is receiving the right start in life. They will either ascribe the mistake to the stupidity of the stranger or immediately forswear some particular piece of clothing.

Our parents' "gentle nudging" into masculinity does not overlook our toys. These represent both current activities thought sexually appropriate and those symbolic of our future masculinity of courage, competition, daring—and of violence. We are given trucks, tanks, and guns. Although our mother might caution us about breaking them, it is readily apparent by her tone and facial expressions that she does not mean what she says. We can continue to bang them together roughly, and she merely looks at us—sometimes quite uncomprehendingly, and occasionally muttering something to the effect that boys will be boys. We somehow perceive her sense of confirmation and we bang them all the more, laughing gleefully at the approval we know it is bringing.

Play and the Sexual Boundaries of Tolerance

We can make all sorts of expressive sounds as we play. We can shout, grunt, and groan on the kitchen floor or roll around in the sandbox. As she shoves us out the door, Mom always cautions us not to get dirty, but when we come in filthy her verbal and gestural disapproval is only mild. From holistic perception, of which by now we have become young masters, we have learned that no matter what Mom's words say, they do not represent the entirety of her feelings.

When we are "all dressed up" before going somewhere, or before company comes, Mom acts differently. We learn that at those times she means what she says about not getting dirty. If we do not want "fire in our pants," we'd better remain clean—at least for a while, for we also learn that after company has come and has had a glimpse of the neat and clean little boy (or, as they say, "the nice little gentleman" or the "fine young man"), we can go about our rough and tumble ways. Pushing, shouting, running, climbing, and other expressions of competition, glee, and freedom then become permissible. We learn that the appearance required at the beginning of a visit is quite unlike that which is passable at the end of the visit.

Our more boisterous and rougher play continues to help us learn the limits of our parents' tolerance. As we continuously test those limits, somewhat to our dismay we occasionally find that we unwittingly have crossed beyond them. Through what is at times painful trial and error, we learn both the limits and how they vary with changed circumstance. We eventually learn those edges extremely well and know, for example, precisely how much more we can "get away with" when company comes than when only the immediate family is present, when Mom and Dad are tired or when they are arguing.

As highly rational beings, who are seldom adequately credited by adults for our keen cunning, we learn to calculate those boundaries exceedingly carefully. We eventually come to the point where we know precisely where the brink is—that one more word of back talk, one more quarrel with our brother, sister, or friend, even a small one, or even one more whine will move our parents from words to deeds, and their wrath will fall abruptly upon us with full force. Depending on our parents' orientation to childrearing (or often simply upon their predilection of the moment, for at these times theory tends to fly out the window), this will result in either excruciating humiliation in front of our friends accompanied by horrible (though momentary) physical pain, or excruciating humiliation in front of our friends accompanied by the horrifying (and longer) deprivation of a privilege (which of course we know is really a "right" that is being unjustifiably withheld from us).

On Freedom and Being

As we calculate those boundaries of tolerance (or in the vernacular used by our parents and well understood by us, find out how much they can "stand"), we also learn something about our world vis-à-vis that of those strange female creatures who coinhabit our space. We learn that we can get dirtier, play rougher, speak louder, act more crudely, wander farther from home, stay away longer, and talk back more.

We see that girls live in a world foreign to ours. Theirs is quieter, neater, daintier, and in general more subdued. Sometimes our worlds touch, but then only momentarily. We learn, for example, that while little sisters might be all right to spend an occasional hour with on a rainy afternoon, they are, after all, "only girls." They cannot really enter our world, and we certainly do not want to become part of theirs, with its greater restrictions and fewer challenges. Occasionally, we even find ourselves delighting in this distinction as we taunt them about not being able to do something because it is "not for girls."

If we sometimes wonder about the reason for the differences between our worlds, our curiosity quickly runs its course, for we know deep down that these distinctions are proper. They are *girls,* and, as our parents have told us repeatedly, we are NOT girls. We have internalized the appropriateness of our worlds; some things are right for us, others for them. Seldom are we sorry for the tighter reins placed on girls. We are just glad that we are not one of "them." We stick with "our own kind" and immensely enjoy our greater freedom. Rather than lose ourselves in philosophical reflections about the inequalities of this world (greatly beyond our mental capacities at this point anyway), we lose ourselves in exultation over our greater freedom and the good fortune that made us boys instead of girls.

That greater freedom becomes the most prized aspect of our existence. Before we are old enough to go to school (and later, during summer or weekends and any other nonschool days), when we awaken in the morning we can hardly wait to get our clothes on. Awaiting us is a world of adventure. If we are up before Mom, we can go outside and play in the yard. Before venturing beyond voice distance, however, we have to eat our "wholesome" breakfast, one that somehow is always in the process of "making a man" out of us. After this man-producing breakfast, which might well consist of little more than cereal, we are free to roam, to discover, to experience. There are no dishes to do, no dusting, sweeping, or cleaning. Those things are for sisters, mothers, and other females.

Certainly we have spatial and associational restrictions placed on us, but they are much more generous than those imposed on girls of our age. We know how many blocks we can wander and whom we are allowed to see. But just as significant, we know how to go beyond that distance without getting caught and how to play with the "bad boys" and the "too big boys" without Mom ever being the wiser. So long as we are home within a certain time limit, despite verbal restrictions we really are free to come and go.

We do learn to accept limited responsibility in order to guard our freedom, and we are always pestering other mothers for the time or, when we are able, arranging for them to tell us when it is "just about noon" so we can make our brief appearance for lunch—and then quickly move back into the exciting world of boy activities. But we also learn to lie a lot, finding out that it is better to say anything plausible rather than to admit that we violated the boundaries and be "grounded," practically the worst form of punishment we can receive. Consequently, we learn to deny, to avoid, to deceive, to tell half-truths, and to involve ourselves in other sorts of subterfuge rather than to admit violations that might restrict our freedom of movement.

Our freedom is infinitely precious to us, for whether it is cops and robbers or space bandits, the Lone Ranger or Darth Vader, ours is an imaginary world filled with daring and danger. Whether it is six-shooters with bullets or space missiles with laser disintegrators, we are always shooting or getting shot. There are always the good guys and the bad guys. Always there is a moral victory to be won. We are continuously running, shouting, hiding, and discovering. The world is filled with danger, with the inopportune and unexpected lurking just around the corner. As the enemy stalks us, the potential of sudden discovery and the sweet joys of being undetected are unsurpassable. Nothing in adulthood, despite its great allure, its challenges and victories yet to be experienced, will ever be greater than this intense bliss of innocence—and part of the joy of this period lies in being entirely unaware of that savage fact of life.

. . . And the Twain Shall Never Meet

Seldom do we think about being masculine. Usually we are just being. The radical social differences that separate us from girls have not gone unnoticed, of course. Rather, these essential differences in life-orientations not only have penetrated our consciousness but also have saturated our very beings. Our initial indifference to things male and female has turned to violent taste and distaste. We have learned our lessons so well that we sometimes end up teaching our own mothers lessons in gender. For example, we would rather be caught dead than to wear sissy clothing, and our tantrums will not cease until our mothers come to their senses and relent concerning putting something on us that we consider sissified.

We know there are two worlds, and we are grateful for the one we are in. Ours is superior. The evidence continually bombards us, and we exult in masculine privilege. We also protect our sexual boundaries from encroachment and erosion. The encroachment comes from tomboys who strive to become part of our world. We tolerate them—up to a point. But by excluding them from some activities, we let them know that there are irrevocable differences that forever separate us.

The erosion comes from sissies. Although we are not yet aware that we are reacting to a threat to our developing masculine identity, we do know that sissies make us uncomfortable. We come to dislike them intensely. To be a sissy is to be a traitor to one's very being. It is to be "like a girl," that which we are not—and that which we definitely never will be.

Sissies are to be either pitied or hated. While they are not girls, neither are they real boys. They look like us, but they bring shame on us because they do not represent anything we are. We are everything they are not. Consequently, we separate ourselves from them in the most direct manner possible. While we may be brutal, this breach is necessary, for we must define clearly the boundaries of our own existence—and one way that we know who we are is by knowing what we are not.

So we shame sissies. We make fun of anyone who is not the way he "ought" to be. If he hangs around the teacher or girls during recess instead of playing our rough and tumble games, if he will not play sports because he is afraid of getting dirty or being hurt, if he backs off from a fight, if he cries or whines, or even if he gets too many A's, we humiliate and ridicule him. We gather around him in a circle. We call him a sissy. We say, "Shame! Shame!" We call him gay, fag, and queer. We tell him he is a girl and not fit for us.

And as far as we are concerned, he never will be fit for us. He belongs to some strange status, not quite a girl and not quite a boy. Whatever he is, he certainly is not one of us. WE don't cry when we are punished or hurt. WE don't hang around girls. WE are proud of our average grades. WE play rough games. WE are not afraid of getting hurt. (Or if we are, we would never let it show.) WE are not afraid of sassing the teacher—or at least of calling the teacher names when his or her back is turned. We know who we are. We are boys.

The Puberty Shock

We never know, of course, how precarious our gender identity is. From birth we have been set apart from females, and during childhood we have severely separated ourselves both from females and from those who do not match our standards of masculinity. Our existence is well defined, our world solid. By the end of grade school, the pecking order is clear. For good or ill, each of us has been locked into a system of well-honed, peer-determined distinctions, our destiny determined by a heavily defended social order. Our masculine world seems secure, with distinct boundaries that clearly define "us" from "them." We know who we are, and we are cocky about it.

But then comes puberty, and overnight the world undergoes radical metamorphosis. Girls suddenly change. Right before our eyes the flat chests we have always taken for granted begin to protrude. Two little bumps magically appear, and while we are off playing our games, once in a while we cast quizzical glances in the direction of the girls. Witnessing a confusing, haunting change, we shrug off the dilemma and go back to our games.

Then the change hits us. We feel something happening within our own bodies. At first the feeling is vague, undefined. There is no form to it. We just know that something is different. Then we begin to feel strange stirrings within us. These stirrings come on abruptly, and that abruptness begins to shake everything loose in our secure world. Until this time our penis has never given us any particular trouble. It has just "been there," appended like a finger or toenail. It has been a fact of life, something that "we" had and "they" didn't. But now it literally springs to life, taking on an existence of its own and doing things that we once could not even imagine would ever take place. This sometimes creates embarrassment, and there are even times when, called to the blackboard to work out some problem, we must play dumb because of the bulge that we never willed.

It is a new game. The girls in our class are different. We are different. And never will we be the same.

We are forced into new concepts of masculinity. We find this upsetting, but fortunately we do not have to begin from scratch. We can build on our experiences, for mostly the change involves just one area of our lives, girls, and we are able to keep the rest intact. We can still swagger, curse, sweat, get dirty, and bloody ourselves in our games. While the girls still watch us admiringly from the sidelines as we "do our manly thing," we also now watch them more closely as they "do their womanly thing" and strut before us in tight sweaters and blouses.

While the girls still admire our toughness, a change is now demanded. At times we must show gentleness. We must be cleaner and watch our language more than before. We must even show consideration. Those shifting requirements are not easy to master, but we have the older, more experienced boys to count on—and they are more than willing to initiate us into this new world and, while doing so, to demonstrate their (always) greater knowledge and skills in traversing the social world.

The Transition into Artificiality

It is with difficulty that we make the transition. A new sexuality is really required, and such radical change could be easy for no one. We already have been fundamentally formed, and what we really learn at this point is to be more adept role-players. We behave one way when we are with the guys. This is the "natural" way, the way we feel. It is relaxed and easy. And we learn to act a different way while we are around girls. This form of presentation we find more contrived and artificial, for it requires greater politeness, consideration, and gentleness. In other words, it is contrary to what we have learned previously, to what we have become.

Consequently we hone our acting skills, the ability to put on expected performances. We always have been actors; it is just that we learned our earlier role at a more formative period, and, *having formed us,* this role now provides greater fit. And acting differently while we are around females is nothing new. We have been practicing this since we were at our mother's knee. But now the female expectations are more pressing as our worlds more frequently intersect. Although we become fairly skilled at meeting these expectations, they never become part of our being. Always they consist of superficial behaviors added onto what is truly and, by this time, "naturally" us.

This lesson in artificiality reinforces our many exercises in manipulation. We learn that to get what we want, whether that be an approving smile, a caress, a kiss, or more, we must meet the expectations of the one from whom we desire something. We are no strangers to this foundational fact of life, of course, but the masks we must wear in these more novel situations, our uncomfortable gestures and the requisite phrasing, make us awkward strangers to ourselves. We wonder why we are forced into situations that require such constant posing and posturing.

But awkward or not (and as we become more proficient at the game, much of the initial discomfort leaves), we always come back for more. By now sports and games with the fellows are no longer enough. Females seemingly hold the key to our happiness. They can withhold or grant as they see fit. And for favors to be granted, this demanding intersexual game must be played.

The Continuing Masculine World—and Marriage

Eventually we become highly adept players in this intersexual game. We even come to savor our maturing manipulative abilities as the game offers highly stimulating physical payoffs. Our growing skills let us determine if a particular encounter will result in conquest, and thus calculate if it is worth the pursuit. To meet the challenge successfully provides yet another boost to our masculinity.

The hypocrisies and deceits the game requires sometimes disturb us. We really want to be more honest than the game allows. But we do not know how to bring this about—and still succeed at the game *and* our masculinity.

Discomforts arising from the game, especially the intimate presence of the female world, must be relieved. Manly activities provide us refuge from this irritant, endeavors in which we men can truly understand one another, where we share a world of aspiration, conflict, and competition. Here we can laugh at the same things and talk the way we really feel with much less concern about the words we choose. We know that among men our interests, activities, and desires form an essential part of a shared, self-encapsulating world.

To continue to receive the rewards offered by females, on occasion we must leave our secure world of manliness momentarily to penetrate the conjoint world occupied by our feminine counterparts. But such leave-takings remain temporary, never a "real" part of us. Always waiting for us are the "real" conversations that reflect the "real" world, that exciting realm whose challenging creativity, competition, and conflict help make life worth living.

And we are fortunate in having at our fingertips a socially constructed semi-imaginary masculine world, one we can summon at will to retreat into its beckoning confines. This world of televised football, baseball, basketball, wrestling, boxing, hockey, soccer, and car racing is part of the domain of men. At least here is a world, manly and comfortable, that offers us refuge from that threatening feminine world, allowing us to withdraw from its suffocating demands of sharing and intimacy. This semi-imaginary world offers continual appeal because it summons up subconscious feelings from our childhood, adolescence, and, eventually as we grow older, early manhood.

Many of us would not deny that the characteristics we males learn or, if you prefer, the persons we tend to become, fail to provide an adequate basis for developing fulfilling intersexual relationships. But those characteristics, while underlying what is often the shallowness of our relationships with women, are indeed us. They are the logical consequence of our years of learning our culture. We have become what we painstakingly have been shaped to become. Although willing participants in our social destiny, we are heirs of a culture that long preceded our arrival on the social scene.

Some of us, only with great difficulty, have overcome our masculine socialization into intersexual superficiality and have developed relationships with wives and girlfriends that transcend the confines of those cultural dictates. But such relearning, painfully difficult, comes at a price, leaving in its wake much hurt and brokenness.

Hardly any aspect of this process of becoming a man in our society augurs well for marriage. The separateness of the world that we join at birth signals our journey into an intricate process whereby we become a specific type of being. Our world diverges in almost all aspects from the world of females. Not only do we look different, not only do we talk differently and act differently, but our fundamental thinking and orientations to life sharply contrast with theirs. This basic divergence is difficult for women to grasp and, when grasped, is often accompanied by a shudder of disbelief and distaste at the revelatory insight into such dissimilar reality. Yet we are expected to unite permanently with someone from this contradispositional world and, despite our essential differences, not only to share a life space but also to unite our goals, hopes, dreams, and aspirations.

Is it any wonder, then, that in the typical case men remain strangers to women, and women to men, with marriage a crucible of struggle?

Notes

1. The diversity of opinion among sociologists regarding the nature/nurture causes of behavioral differences of males and females is illustrated in *Society* magazine (September/October 1986:4–39). The connection between ideology and theoretical interpretation of data is especially apparent in this heated exchange. I also discuss this topic in my introductory textbooks, *Sociology: A Down-to-Earth Approach* and *Essentials of Sociology: A Down-to-Earth Approach,* both published by Allyn & Bacon of Boston, and both in many editions.

2. Of about one in every 30,000 births, the sex of a baby is unclear. A genetic disorder called congenital adrenal hyperplasis results in the newborn having parts of both male and female genitals (*St. Louis Globe-Democrat,* March 10–11, 1979, p. 3D).

3. When people (almost exclusively women) are invited to a baby shower and the expectant mother has not yet given birth (or if they wish to take advantage of a

sale and buy a gift in advance of the delivery), they find themselves in a quandary. The standard solution to this problem of not knowing the sex of the child (at least in the Midwest) is to purchase either clothing of yellow color or a "sex neutral" item. With ultrasound and other technology that can determine the sex of fetuses, the surprise factor has been eliminated for many parents—as well as for their friends.

4. Duly noted, of course, are the historical arbitrariness and relativity of the gender designation of clothing, with the meaning of ruffles and other stylistic variations depending on the historical period.

14 On Becoming Female: Lessons Learned in School

DONNA EDER

In the previous article, we focused on how socialization puts boys on a distinct road in life. We saw how boys' experiences give them distinct orientations to the world, including what they feel they can reasonably expect out of life—and how those orientations become a divisive factor in marriage and other male–female relationships. In this article, we turn the focus on girls' experiences in peer groups. We examine further how peer groups vitally influence our orientations, even how we view the self.

The author of this article headed a research team that explored the social world of girls in middle school. This is a vital age, for at this point in life girls are developing a more precise sexual identity. Eder watched and listened as the girls interacted with one another, and as they interacted with boys, about whom they were ambivalent. Their statements, which disclose inner feelings, conflicts, rivalries, and jealousies, reveal the ongoing formation of a self. Note especially the role that peers play in the developing identity of the girls—and how the peer interactions focus on the superficialities of appearance. How do you think this emphasis on appearance and attractiveness becomes part of women's orientations to life and influences their interactions?

ATTRACTIVENESS has long been part of the construction of femininity. . . . Preoccupation [with appearance] among American women prevents them from focusing on more constructive aspects of themselves, such as who they are or what they are capable of accomplishing. It is becoming more and more clear that this is one of the main areas in which women are hindered by stereotypical notions of femininity.

At Woodview [Middle School], concerns about attractiveness were promoted primarily through the high-status activity of cheerleading. This focus was most evident during the cheerleading tryouts. The teacher who organized the tryouts told the judges to keep [appearance] in mind as they selected the candidates.

> She also told them to pay attention to the person's weight, saying, "If you don't like the way they look, you wouldn't like them to stand in front of you."

This message conveys the essence of cheerleaders as adornments to a team as well as promoters of team enthusiasm and support. The fact that cheerleaders are seen as team representatives makes their appearance salient in the context of a culture that places a high value on female beauty. To be the best representatives, they should be highly attractive as well as capable of promoting school spirit.

Officially, appearance was included in the judging of cheerleaders under the category of "sparkle." Ten of the fifty total points a candidate could obtain were allotted to this category, as the cheerleading coach explained to the candidates during one of the practice sessions prior to the tryouts.

> At one point, Mrs. Tolson started to tell them what they were going to be judged on, saying they would get ten points for sparkle, which was their smile, personality, bubbliness, appearance, attractiveness—not that all cheerleaders had to be attractive, but it was important to have a clean appearance, not to be sloppy, have messy or greasy hair, because that doesn't look like a cheerleader.

Throughout the practice sessions girls were reminded to wear a clean, neat outfit for tryouts and to have clean, neatly combed hair. This emphasis on neatness continued despite the physical nature of this activity, which includes cartwheels and backflips. It was important to have the skills to do these gymnastic routines, but it was equally important to find ways to maintain a neat, feminine appearance throughout the performance. This again conveys the message to girls that how they look is as important as what they do.

Another way in which cheerleading candidates were encouraged to enhance their looks was by remembering to smile. Smiling was considered an important part of the cheerleading role—something that made you "look like a cheerleader." Girls were encouraged to smile to cover up feelings that might accompany their efforts, such as pain and concentration.

> When they were doing a stunt, she [the coach] said she wanted them to smile through the pain. Later on, when they were practicing the stunts in front of the eighth-graders, Karla [an eighth-grade cheerleader] continually reminded them to smile as they were working on their jumps. The way Karla put it was, "Smile the whole time."

The judges themselves evaluated the candidates' appearance during the decision-making process. Both neatness and cuteness were mentioned, as were the quality of their smiles. For example, one judge noted that the girl they were discussing had a cute smile. Another judge disagreed, indicating through imitation that the girl's smile was forced. This judge rated her more negatively than did the first one. Although weight was taken into account, one year some girls who were considered overweight were selected. The judges suggested that they be put on diets, preserving the idea that thinness is an important aspect of cheerleaders' appearance.

The high profile given to cheerleading means that traits that are valued in cheerleaders also have a greater impact on the school's informal peer culture.

Boys' Focus on Girls' Appearance in Peer Interaction

Many Woodview boys focused their evaluation of girls on their attractiveness. In fact, male interest in their bodies as being sexual and appealing could arouse the deepest level of appearance anxiety in girls. For example, one day a group of eighth-grade girls discussed a male ranking of female peers.

> Penny said that she had seen a list some boys had made which rated girls in the class. Karla was at the top, then Sara, then Peggy or Darlene. They said that they had told these guys, "Thanks a lot" for not including them on the list. Bonnie said, "Did you notice that all of those girls are early figure people?" indicating that the reason she thought they were rated highly was because they have a figure already. Then they pointed to Sara and said, "There she is. She's the one with the big hips. You can't miss her."

Informal rankings such as this remind girls that they are being evaluated on a daily basis, even when they haven't entered formal beauty contests or cheerleading tryouts.

Boys frequently referred to the physical appearance of girls they knew, both in their presence and when the girls were absent. For example, one day a boy announced at lunch, "Any girl who thinks she's beautiful, stand up." The appearance of someone's girlfriend was a typical topic of conversation, usually implying that some feature of hers was unattractive or that she was ugly in general. Even some of the prettiest girls in the school, cheerleaders and other high-status-group members, were criticized by boys for having ugly faces or deficient bodies.

The Role of Girls' Gossip

Even when girls are by themselves, their conversations are often dominated by cultural standards and male perspectives that highlight the importance of good looks. Girls themselves contribute to this, especially through gossip about the looks and dress of other girls. When we first told students we were interested in finding out what they did during their free time, some girls told us that mainly they talked about other girls. Given the frequency of this activity, many girls were constantly confronted with the topic of female appearance.

It was evident from the girls' comments that the continual focus on other girls' looks further added to their anxieties about their own appearance.

> There was an interesting discussion between Peggy and Lisa about the girl that Bob is taking to the dance. They talked about whether she was cute or not and ended up agreeing that she was a stack of bones. That generated some discussion about weight and Lisa said that she [Lisa] was fat. Peggy said that she wasn't. Then Wendy wondered if she was a stack of bones and Lisa told her that no, she was just right—that she wasn't skinny and she wasn't fat either. [Stephanie's notes]

While these girls got reassurance from their friends that they were neither too fat nor too thin, in most cases girls did not openly reveal their concerns and thus did not receive such assurance. Instead, many girls were likely to remain self-conscious and insecure about their body type and weight. Girls from lower-working-class backgrounds often couldn't afford to buy name-brand clothes and shoes, and their attire was often subject to criticism by girls who could afford nicer clothes. Comments about people's clothes were often made loudly enough for the targets to hear.

> As Lynn walked by they jeered at her and made fun of her. . . . One of these girls was going, "Oooh, look at those pants! Ohh, how could you wear those?" [Stephanie's notes]

At other times people were directly ridiculed.

> She also said that the cheerleaders made fun of people if they didn't wear Nike or Adidas shoes. They'd look at her and say, "Oh, where did you get your shoes?" She said that she just wears plain old tennis shoes. [Cathy's notes]

Besides being appraised on the basis of their attire, girls were also evaluated for their body weight and type. Girls who were particularly overweight were frequent targets of gossip, as in this extensive discussion of an isolate by several sixth-graders.

> A large part of what these girls did today was make fun of one girl, Gloria. One girl would say, "Here is the airplane; the pilot says, 'Will somebody please come up front,' and all of a sudden somebody walks up front," showing with her hands how the plane dives. Then somebody else says, "Or here's the plane flying," and she shows it flying lopsided with her hands. "Then Gloria walks over to the other side and it flips the other way." Or, "Here's the airplane and there's a weak spot in the middle, and Gloria walks down the aisle and she falls through." [Stephanie's notes]

This episode continued with other jokes about Gloria, including using her as a trampoline in gym class and how she could serve as a windblock for all of them at once.

It was not just overweight girls who were made fun of and evaluated, however. Girls who were too skinny were also criticized, as were girls who had large hips or large breasts. Girls have no control over most of these physical characteristics. Perhaps because of the extensive nature of this type of gossip, girls often try to increase their control over their weight by dieting, which leads, in more severe cases, to eating disorders such as anorexia and bulimia. Although this focus on body weight may seem obsessive, it makes sense in light of the frequency of body critiques in girls' evaluative talk and in the media.

Given the importance of good looks for gaining status among peers and avoiding negative evaluations, it is not surprising that girls devote so much attention to their appearance. Ironically, another relatively frequent theme of gossip was negatively judging others for putting too much emphasis on their looks. Girls seemed particularly critical of girls who tried to stand out in some manner, either by dressing in a unique fashion or by making themselves "too attractive" or "too sexy."

A group of sixth-graders spent much of one lunch period making fun of a popular girl for wearing a particularly unusual outfit to school.

> There was a long discussion throughout lunch about Jane, who I have been told before is the most popular girl in the sixth grade. Today she was wearing a khaki outfit, matching pants and a shirt—sort of a safari look. The first thing that got the conversation going was that Ilene started talking about a girl that had a "jungle suit" on. And Nicki, Jesse, and Kristy all sort of joined in with this conversation, and even Andrea played along with it for a while. They started out by saying that they'd seen her in the hall, given her the Tarzan yell, and she'd turned around and looked at them and they'd said, "Where'd you get the jungle outfit?" And they wondered if she was going to give the Tarzan yell back. They started talking about it as though she was Tarzan's monkey, Cheetah, and then the conversation sort of strayed from clothes and went to how she won the dog contest—how she's the number one dog of the school, which is the exact opposite since she's so popular. She does look older. She had her hair up, and had quite a bit of makeup on. [Stephanie's notes]

In another case, a group of eighth-grade girls was critical of a local beauty pageant contestant of high school age who visited the school to collect money for her campaign. In this case, they claimed that she used makeup to give a false image of beauty, and that underneath she was really ugly.

Eighth-Grade
PENNY: I'm not giving it to her.
CINDY: The only thing that makes her look anything is all the makeup and [unclear]
PENNY: She had a picture and she's standing there like this, she's going [Poses with one hand on her hip and one by her head]

CINDY: Her face is probably this skinny but it looks that big cuz of all the makeup she has on it.
PENNY: She's *ugly,* ugly, ugly! [In a low voice]
BONNIE: She looks like a cow.

This girl was criticized for her attempts to be "too attractive" and "too sexy." In her case, a flirtatious pose in one of her photographs was seen as evidence of trying to be too sexy.

These different themes of gossip add to the already confusing message girls receive about their appearance. On the one hand they are continually faced with media messages that emphasize the importance of using makeup and fashionable attire to enhance their attractiveness and their sexuality. If they do succeed in looking, acting, or dressing like the models they see in the media, however, they are likely to be accused of portraying false images or wanton sexuality. Furthermore, this practice of criticizing the objects of sexual gaze deflects criticism away from boys and men for viewing girls in this limited manner. Thus, girls blame each other for drawing sexual attention to themselves rather than criticizing the social practices that promote a view of girls and women as sexual objects.

Attractiveness as an Increasing Concern for Girls

Appearance is already a salient concern among these students, and it is likely to increase in importance for many as they get older. The number of school-sponsored contests that emphasize attractiveness increases in high school as girls are selected for pompon teams, cheerleading, baton twirlers in marching bands, and so on. In most of these cases, girls choose to enter these contests, although sometimes this "choice" may be the result of maternal pressure. A more powerful form of school-sponsored competition is the selection of prom queens, homecoming queens, and attendants in which girls are annually evaluated on their attractiveness, often without ever volunteering to enter such competitions. Generally, school officials assume that every girl in the school wants to enter, which implies that all girls wish to be judged on the basis of their appearance. At the same time, diverse subcultures often develop within large high schools, some of which places less emphasis on stereotypical gender concerns such as appearance.

[Conclusion]

[These experiences] send girls a strong message that what they do and who they are is less important then how they look. Even girls in achievement roles, such as basketball team members, continue to receive messages about the importance of appearance. Such an emphasis prepares girls for adult careers and occupations where appearance continues to be an explicit or implicit basis for hiring and retaining employees. . . .

Girls and women continue to be viewed as sexual objects within the media as well as other arenas from cheerleading and pompon teams to swimsuit competitions. Increasingly, adult female models are portrayed as innocent and childlike in their sexual allure, while young girls are depicted as erotic and seductive. Since girls are cast as sexual objects at such an early age, they often internalize this image as a central aspect of their identity. It then becomes extraordinarily difficult for them to move beyond this self-image to develop a greater sense of their own erotic potential as well as their general creative life force. This denial contributes to such largely female maladies as anorexia and bulimia as well as a growing obsession with plastic surgery among adolescent girls.

Through objectification, women are denied their sense of totality. To be viewed primarily as a physical and sexual object is to experience denial of self as a whole person with thoughts, feelings, and actions. Women must struggle to overcome a perception of self as object rather than subject before they can begin the process of self-definition as total and complete human beings. Only then can they develop their unique interests and have a real impact on the world around them.

15 Sexuality and Gender in Children's Daily Worlds

BARRIE THORNE
ZELLA LURIA

In this selection, the researchers focus on children's play, examining its implications for relations between men and women. Their observations are likely to bring back many memories of your own childhood. You will also become aware that children's play is not simply play, but has serious sociological meaning—in this instance, the fierce maintenance of social boundaries between males and females.

To gather their data, Thorne and Luria studied fourth- and fifth-graders in four schools within three states. They found that the children usually are very careful to separate their friendships and activities on the basis of sex. Girls of this age are more concerned about "being nice," while the interests of boys center on sports and testing the limits of rules. The larger groups into which they band provide each boy a degree of protection and anonymity. The sociological significance of children's play is that both boys and girls are helping to socialize one another into primary adult gender roles, girls being more concerned with intimacy, emotionality, and romance, and boys with independence and sexuality. They are writing the "scripts" that they will follow as adults.

THE AMBIGUITIES OF "SEX"—a word used to refer to biological sex, to cultural gender, and also to sexuality—contain a series of complicated questions. Although our cultural understandings often merge these three domains, they can be separated analytically; their interrelationships lie at the core of the social organization of sex and gender. In this paper we focus on the domains of gender and sexuality as they are organized and experienced among elementary school children, especially nine- to eleven-year-olds. This analysis helps illuminate age-based variations and transitions in the organization of sexuality and gender.

We use "gender" to refer to cultural and social phenomena—divisions of labor, activity, and identity which are associated with but not fully determined by biological sex. The core of sexuality, as we use it here, is desire and arousal. Desire and arousal are shaped by and associated with socially learned activities and meanings which Gagnon and Simon (1973) call "sexual scripts." Sexual scripts—defining who does what, with whom, when, how, and what it means—are related to the adult society's view of gender (Miller and Simon, 1981). Nine- to eleven-year-old children are beginning the transition from the gender system of childhood to that of adolescence. They are largely defined (and define themselves) as children, but they are on the verge of sexual maturity, cultural adolescence, and a gender system organized around the institution of heterosexuality. Their experiences help illuminate complex and shifting relationships between sexuality and gender.

First we explore the segregated gender arrangements of middle childhood as contexts for learning adolescent and adult sexual scripts. We then turn from their separate worlds to relations *between* boys and girls, and examine how fourth- and fifth-grade children use sexual idioms to mark gender boundaries. Separate gender groups and ritualized, asymmetric relations between girls and boys lay the groundwork for the more overtly sexual scripts of adolescence.

The Daily Separation of Girls and Boys

Gender segregation—the separation of girls and boys in friendships and casual encounters—is central to daily life in elementary schools. A series of snapshots taken in varied school settings would reveal extensive spatial separation between girls and boys. When they choose seats, select companions for work or play, or arrange themselves in line, elementary school children frequently cluster into same-sex groups. At lunchtime, boys and girls often sit separately and talk matter-of-factly about "girls' tables" and "boys' tables." Playgrounds have gendered spaces: boys control some areas and activities, such as large playing fields and basketball courts; and girls control smaller enclaves like jungle-gym areas and concrete spaces for hopscotch or jump-rope. Extensive gender segregation in everyday encounters and in friendships has been found in many other studies of elementary- and middle-school children. Gender segregation in elementary and middle schools has been found to account for more segregation than race (Schofield, 1982).

Gender segregation is not total. Snapshots of school settings would also reveal some groups with a fairly even mix of boys and girls, especially in games like kickball, dodgeball, and handball, and in classroom and playground activities organized by adults. Some girls frequently play with boys, integrating their groups in a token way, and a few boys, especially in the lower grades, play with groups of girls. In general, there is more gender segregation when children are freer to construct their own activities.

Most of the research on gender and children's social relations emphasizes patterns of separation, contrasting the social organization and cultures of girls' groups with those of boys. In brief summary: Boys tend to interact in larger and more publicly visible groups; they more often play outdoors, and their activities take up more space than those of girls. Boys engage in more physically aggressive play and fighting; their social relations tend to be overtly hierarchical and competitive. Organized sports are both a central activity and a major metaphor among boys; they use a language of "teams" and "captains" even when not engaged in sports.

Girls more often interact in smaller groups or friendship pairs, organized in shifting alliances. Compared with boys, they more often engage in turn-taking activities like jump-rope and doing tricks on the bars, and they less often play organized sports. While boys use a rhetoric of contests and teams, girls describe their relations using language which stresses cooperation and "being nice." But the rhetorics of either group should not be taken for the full reality. Girls *do* engage in conflict, although it tends to take more indirect forms than the direct insults and challenges more often found in interactions among boys, and between girls and boys.

Interaction Among Boys

In daily patterns of talk and play, boys in all-male groups often build towards heightened and intense moments, moments one can describe in terms of group arousal with excited emotions. This especially happens when boys violate rules.

Dirty words are a focus of rules, and rule breaking, in elementary schools. Both girls and boys know dirty words, but flaunting of the words and risking punishment for their use was more frequent in boys' than in girls' groups in all the schools we studied. In the middle-class Massachusetts public school, both male and female teachers punished ballplayers for [their dirty words]. But teachers were not present after lunch and before school, when most group-directed play took place. A female paraprofessional, who alone managed almost 150 children on the playground, never intervened to stop bad language in play; the male gym teacher who occasionally appeared on the field at after-lunch recess always did. Boys resumed dirty talk immediately after he passed them. Dirty talk is a staple part of the repertoire of the boys' groups (also see Fine, 1980). Such talk defines their groups as, at least in part, outside the reach of the school's discipline.

Some of the dirty talk may be explicitly sexual, as it was in the Massachusetts public school when a group of five fifth-grade boys played a game called "Mad Lib" (also described in Luria, 1983). The game consisted of a paragraph (in this case, a section of a textbook discussing the U.S. Constitution) with key words deleted, to be filled in by the players. Making the paragraph absurd and violating rules to create excitement seemed to be the goal of the game. The boys clearly knew that their intentions were "dirty": They requested the field observer not to watch the game.

Sports, dirty words, and testing the limits are part of what boys teach boys how to do. The assumption seems to be: Dirty words, sports interest and knowledge, and transgression of politeness are closely connected.

RULE TRANSGRESSION: COMPARING GIRLS' AND BOYS' GROUPS

Rule transgression in *public* is exciting to boys in their groups. Boys' groups are attentive to potential consequences of transgression, but, compared with girls, groups of boys appear to be greater risk-takers. Adults tending and teaching children do not often undertake discipline of an entire boys' group; the adults might lose out and they cannot risk that. Girls are more likely to affirm the reasonableness of rules, and, when it occurs, rule-breaking by girls is smaller scale. This may be related to the smaller size of girls' groups and to adults' readiness to use rules on girls who seem to believe in them. It is dubious if an isolated pair of boys (a pair is the model size of girls' groups) could get away with the rule-breaking that characterizes the larger male group. A boy may not have power, but a boys' *group* does. Teachers avoid disciplining whole groups of boys, partly for fear of seeming unfair. Boys rarely identify those who proposed direct transgressions and, when confronted, they claim (singly), "I didn't start it; why should I be punished?"

Boys are visibly excited when they break rules together—they are flushed as they play, they wipe their hands on their jeans, some of them look guilty. The Mad Lib game described above not only violates rules, it also evokes sexual meanings within an all-male group. Arousal is not purely individual; in this case, it is shared by the group. . . . The audience for the excitement is the gender-segregated peer group, where each boy increases the excitement by adding still a "worse" word. All of this takes place in a game ("rules") context, and hence with anonymity despite the close-up contact of the game.

While we never observed girls playing a Mad Lib game of this sort, some of our female students recall playing the game in grade school but giving it up after being caught by teachers, or out of fear of being caught. Both boys and girls may acquire knowledge of the game, but boys repeatedly perform it because their gender groups give support for transgression.

These instances all suggest that boys experience a shared, arousing context for transgression, with sustained gender group support for rule-breaking. Girls' groups may engage in rule-breaking, but the gender group's support for repeated public transgression is far less certain. The smaller size of girls' gender groupings in comparison with those of boys, and girls' greater susceptibility to rules and social control by teachers, make girls' groups easier to control. Boys' larger groups give each transgressor a degree of anonymity. Anonymity—which means less probability of detection and punishment—enhances the contagious excitement of rule-breaking.

The higher rates of contagious excitement, transgression, and limit-testing in boys' groups means that when they are excited, boys are often "playing" to male audiences. The public nature of such excitement forges bonds among boys. This kind of bonding is also evident when boys play team sports, and when they act aggressively toward marginal or isolated boys. Such aggression is both physical and verbal (taunts like "sissy," "fag," or "mental"). Sharing a target of aggression may be another source of arousal for groups of boys.

THE TIE TO SEXUALITY IN MALES

When Gagnon and Simon (1973) argued that there are gender-differentiated sexual scripts in adolescence, they implied what our observations suggest: the gender arrangements and subcultures of middle childhood prepare the way for the sexual scripts of adolescence. Fifth- and sixth-grade boys share pornography, in the form of soft-core magazines like *Playboy* and *Penthouse,* with great care to avoid confiscation. Like the Mad Lib games with their forbidden content, soft-core magazines are also shared in all-male contexts, providing explicit knowledge about what is considered sexually arousing and about attitudes and fantasies. Since pornography is typically forbidden for children in both schools and families, this secret sharing occurs in a context of rule-breaking.

While many theorists since Freud have stressed the importance of boys loosening ties and identification with females (as mother surrogates), few theorists have questioned why "communally aroused" males do not uniformly bond sexually to other males. If the male groups of fifth and sixth grade are the forerunners of the "frankly" heterosexual gender groups of the junior and high school years, what keeps these early groups from open homosexual expression? Scripting in same-gender peer groups may, in fact, be more about gender than about sexual orientation. Boys, who will later view themselves as having homosexual or heterosexual preferences, are learning patterns of masculinity. The answer may also lie in the teaching of homophobia.

By the fourth grade, children, especially boys, have begun to use homophobic labels—"fag," "faggot," "queer"—as terms of insult, especially for marginal boys. They draw upon sexual allusions (often not fully understood, except for their negative and contaminating import) to reaffirm male hierarchies and patterns of exclusion. As "fag" talk increases, relaxed and cuddling patterns of touch decrease among boys. Kindergarten and first-grade boys touch one another frequently and with ease, with arms around shoulders, hugs, and holding hands. By fifth grade, touch among boys becomes more constrained, gradually shifting to mock violence and the use of poking, shoving, and ritual gestures like "give five" (flat hand slaps) to express bonding. The tough surface of boys' friendships is no longer like the gentle touching of girls in friendship.

Interaction Among Girls

In contrast with the larger, hierarchical organization of groups of boys, fourth- and fifth-grade girls more often organize themselves in pairs of "best friends" linked in shifting coalitions. These pairs are not "marriages"; the pattern is more one of dyads moving into triads, since girls often participate in two or more pairs at one time. This may result in quite complex social networks. Girls often talk about who is friends with or "likes" whom; they continually negotiate the parameters of friendships.

For example, in the California school, Chris, a fifth-grade girl, frequently said that Kathryn was her "best friend." Kathryn didn't proclaim the friendship as often; she also played and talked a lot with Judy. After watching Kathryn talk to Judy during a transition period in the classroom, Chris went over, took Kathryn aside, and said with an accusing tone, "You talk to Judy more than me." Kathryn responded defensively, "I talk to you as much as I talk to Judy."

In talking about their relationships with one another, girls use a language of "friends," "nice," and "mean." They talk about who is most and least "liked," which anticipates the concern about "popularity" found among junior high and high school girls (Eder, 1985). Since relationships sometimes break off, girls hedge bets by structuring networks of potential friends. The activity of constructing and breaking dyads is often carried out through talk with third parties. Some of these processes are evident in a sequence recorded in a Massachusetts school:

> The fifth-grade girls, Flo and Pauline, spoke of themselves as "best friends," while Flo said she was "sort of friends" with Doris. When a lengthy illness kept Pauline out of school, Flo spent more time with Doris. One day Doris abruptly broke off her friendship with Flo and began criticizing her to other girls. Flo, who felt very badly, went around asking others in their network, "What did I do? Why is Doris being so mean? Why is she telling everyone not to play with me?"

On school playgrounds girls are less likely than boys to organize themselves into team sports. They more often engage in small-scale, turn-taking kinds of play. When they jump rope or play on the bars, they take turns performing and watching others perform in stylized movements which may involve considerable skill. Sometimes girls work out group choreographies, counting and jumping rope in unison, or swinging around the bars. In other synchronized body rituals, clusters of fifth- and sixth-grade girls practice cheerleading routines or dance steps. In interactions with one another, girls often use relaxed gestures of physical intimacy, moving bodies in harmony, coming close in space, and reciprocating cuddly touches. We should add that girls also poke and grab, pin one another from behind, and use hand-slap rituals like "giving five," although less frequently than boys.

In other gestures of intimacy, which one rarely sees among boys, girls stroke or comb their friends' hair. They notice and comment on one another's physical appearance such as haircuts or clothes. Best friends monitor one another's emotions. They share secrets and become mutually vulnerable through self-disclosure, with an implicit demand that the expression of one's inadequacy will induce the friend to disclose a related inadequacy. In contrast, disclosure of weakness among boys is far more likely to be exposed to others through joking or horsing around.

IMPLICATIONS FOR SEXUALITY

Compared with boys, girls are more focused on constructing intimacy and talking about one-to-one relationships. Their smaller and more personal groups provide less protective anonymity than the larger groups of boys. Bonding through mutual self-disclosure, especially through disclosure of vulnerability, and breaking off friendships by "acting mean," teach the creation, sustaining, and ending of emotionally intimate relations. Girls' preoccupation with who is friends with whom, and their monitoring of cues of "nice" and "mean," liking and disliking, teach them strategies for forming and leaving personal relationships. In their interactions girls show knowledge of motivational rules for dyads and insight into both outer and inner realities of social relationships. Occasionally, girls indicate that they see boys as lacking such "obvious" knowledge.

Girls' greater interest in verbally sorting out relationships was evident during an incident in the Massachusetts public school. The fifth-grade boys often insulted John, a socially isolated boy who was not good at sports. On one such occasion during gym class, Bill, a high status boy, angrily yelled "creep" and "mental" when John fumbled the ball. The teacher stopped the game and asked the class to discuss the incident. Both boys and girls vigorously talked about "words that kill," with Bill saying he was sorry for what he said, that he had lost control in the excitement of the game. The girls kept asking, "How could anyone do that?" The boys kept returning to, "When you get excited, you do things you don't mean." Both girls and boys understood and verbalized the dilemma, but after the group discussion the boys dropped the topic. The girls continued to converse, with one repeatedly asking, "How could Bill be so stupid? Didn't he know how he'd make John feel?"

When talking with one another, girls use dirty words much less often than boys do. The shared arousal and bonding among boys which we think occurs around public rule-breaking has as its counterpart the far less frequent giggling sessions of girls, usually in groups larger than three. The giggling often centers on carefully guarded topics, sometimes, although not always, about boys.

The sexually related discourse of girls focuses less on dirty words than on themes of romance. In the Michigan school, first- and second-grade girls often jumped rope to rhymes about romance. A favorite was, "Down in the Valley Where the Green Grass Grows," a saga of heterosexual romance which, with the name of the jumper and a boy of her choice filled in, concludes: ". . . along came Jason, and kissed her on the cheek . . . first comes love, then comes marriage, then along comes Cindy with a baby carriage." In the Michigan and California schools, fourth- and fifth-grade girls talked privately about crushes and about which boys were "cute," as shown in the following incident recorded in the lunchroom of the Michigan school:

> The girls and boys from one of the fourth-grade classes sat at separate tables. Three of the girls talked as they peered at a nearby table of fifth-grade boys, "Look behind you," one said. "Ooh," said the other two. "That boy's named Todd." "I know where my favorite guy is . . . there," another gestured with her head while her friends looked.

In the Massachusetts private school, fifth-grade girls plotted about how to get particular boy–girl pairs together.

As Gagnon and Simon (1973) have suggested, two strands of sexuality are differently emphasized among adolescent girls and boys. Girls emphasize and learn about the emotional and romantic before the explicitly sexual. The sequence for boys is the reverse; commitment to sexual acts precedes commitment to emotion-laden, intimate relationships and the rhetoric of romantic love. Dating and courtship, Gagnon suggests, are processes in which each sex teaches the other what each wants and expects. The exchange, as they point out, does not always go smoothly. Indeed, in heterosexual relationships among older adults, tension often persists between the scripts (and felt needs) of women and of men.

Children's Sexual Meanings and the Construction of Gender Arrangements

Girls and boys, who spend considerable time in gender-separate groups, learn different patterns of interaction which, we have argued, lay the groundwork for the sexual scripts of adolescence and adulthood. However, sexuality is not simply delayed until adolescence. Children engage in sexual practices—kissing, erotic forms of touch, masturbation, and sometimes intercourse. As school-based observers, we saw only a few overt sexual activities among children, mostly incidents of public, cross-gender kissing, surrounded by teasing, chasing, and laughter.

HETEROSEXUAL TEASING AND THE IMPORTANCE OF THIRD PARTIES

The special loading of sexual words and gestures makes them useful for accomplishing non-sexual purposes. Sexual idioms provide a major resource which children draw upon as they construct and maintain gender segregation. Through the years of elementary school, children use with increasing frequency heterosexual idioms—claims that a particular girl or boy "likes," "has a crush on," or is "goin' with" someone from the other gender group.

Children's language for heterosexual relationships consists of a very few, often repeated, and sticky words. In a context of teasing, the charge that a particular boy "likes" a particular girl (or vice versa) may be hurled like an insult. The difficulty children have in countering such accusations was evident in a conversation between the observer and a group of third-grade girls in the lunchroom at the Michigan school:

> Susan asked me what I was doing, and I said I was observing the things children do and play. Nicole volunteered, "I like running when boys chase all the girls. See Tim over there? Judy chases him all around the school. She likes him." Judy, sitting across the table, quickly responded, "I hate him. I like him for a friend." "Tim loves Judy," Nicole said in a loud, sing-song voice.

Sexual and romantic teasing marks social hierarchies. The most popular children and the pariahs—the lowest status, excluded children—are most frequently mentioned as targets of "liking." Linking someone with a pariah suggests shared contamination and is an especially vicious tease.

When a girl or boy publicly says that she or he "likes" someone or has a boyfriend or girlfriend, that person defines the romantic situation and is less susceptible to teasing than those targeted by someone else. Crushes may be secretly revealed to friends, a mark of intimacy, especially among girls. The entrusted may then go public with the secret ("Wendy likes John"), which may be experienced as betrayal, but which also may be a way of testing the romantic waters. Such leaks, like those of government officials, can be denied or acted upon by the original source of information.

Third parties—witnesses and kibbitzers—are central to the structure of heterosexual teasing. The teasing constructs dyads (very few of them actively "couples"), but within the control of larger gender groups. Several of the white fifth-graders in the Michigan and California schools and some of the black students in the Massachusetts schools occasionally went on dates, which were much discussed around the schools. Same-gender groups provide launching pads, staging grounds, and retreats for heterosexual couples, both real and imagined. Messengers and emissaries go between groups, indicating who likes whom and checking out romantic interest. By the time "couples" actually get together (if they do at all), the groups and their messengers have provided a network of constructed meanings, a kind of agenda for the pair. As we have argued, gender-divided peer groups sustain different meanings of the sexual. They also regulate heterosexual behavior by helping to define the emerging sexual scripts of adolescence (who "likes" whom, who might "go with" whom, what it means to be a couple).

HETEROSEXUALLY CHARGED RITUALS

Boundaries between boys and girls are also emphasized and maintained by heterosexually charged rituals like cross-sex chasing. Formal games of tag and informal episodes of chasing punctuate life on playgrounds. The informal episodes usually open with a provocation—taunts like "You can't get me!" or "Slobber monster!"; bodily pokes; or the grabbing of possessions like a hat or scarf. The person who is provoked may ignore the taunt or poke, handle it verbally ("Leave me alone!"), or respond by chasing. After a chasing sequence, which may end after a short run or a pummeling, the chaser and chased may switch roles.

Chasing has a gendered structure. When boys chase one another, they often end up wrestling or in mock fights. When girls chase girls, they less often wrestle one another to the ground. Unless organized as a formal game like "freeze tag," same-gender chasing goes unnamed and usually undiscussed. But children set apart cross-gender chasing with special names—"girls chase the boys," "boys chase the girls"; "the chase"; "chasers"; "chase and kiss"; "kiss-chase"; "kissers and chasers"; "kiss or kill"—and with animated talk about the activity. The names vary by region and school, but inevitably contain both gender and sexual meanings.

When boys and girls chase one another, they become, by definition, separate teams. Gender terms override individual identities, especially for the other team: "Help, a girl's chasin' me!"; "C'mon Sarah, let's get that boy"; "Tony, help save me from the girls." Individuals may call for help from, or offer help to, others of their gender. In acts of treason they may also grab someone of their gender and turn them over to the opposing team, as when, in the Michigan school, Ryan grabbed Billy from behind, wrestled him to the ground, and then called, "Hey girls, get 'im."

Names like "chase and kiss" mark the sexual meanings of cross-gender chasing. The threat of kissing—most often girls threatening to kiss boys—is a ritualized form of provocation. Teachers and aides are often amused by this form of play among children in the lower grades. They are more perturbed by cross-gender chasing among fifth- and sixth-graders, perhaps because at those ages some girls "have their development" (breasts make sexual meanings seem more consequential), and because of the more elaborate patterns of touch and touch avoidance in chasing rituals among older children. The principal of one Michigan school forbade the sixth-graders from playing "pom-pom," a complicated chasing game, because it entailed "inappropriate touch."

Cross-gender chasing is sometimes structured around rituals of pollution, such as "cooties," where individuals or groups are treated as contaminating or "carrying germs." Children have rituals for transferring cooties (usually touching someone else and shouting "You've got cooties!"), for immunization (e.g., writing "CV" for "cootie vaccination" on their arms), and for eliminating cooties (e.g., saying "no gives" or using "cootie catchers" made of folded paper). Boys may transmit cooties, but cooties usually originate with girls. One version of cooties played in Michigan is called "girl stain." Although cooties is framed as play, the import may be serious. Female pariahs—the ultimate school untouchables by virtue of gender and some added stigma such as being overweight or from a very poor family—are sometimes called "cootie queens" or "cootie girls." Conversely, we have never heard or read about "cootie kings" or "cootie boys."

In these cross-gender rituals girls are defined as sexual. Boys sometimes threaten to kiss girls, but it is girls' kisses and touch which are deemed especially contaminating. Girls more often use the threat of kissing to tease boys and to make them run away, as in this example recorded among fourth-graders on the playground of the California school:

> Smiling and laughing, Lisa and Jill pulled a fourth-grade boy along by his hands, while a group of girls sitting on the jungle-gym called out, "Kiss him, kiss him." Grabbing at his hair, Lisa said to Jill, "Wanna kiss Jonathan?" Jonathan got away, and the girls chased after him. "Jill's gonna kiss your hair," Lisa yelled.

The use of kisses as a threat is double-edged, since the power comes from the threat of pollution. A girl who frequently uses this threat may be stigmatized as a "kisser."

Gender-marked rituals of teasing, chasing, and pollution heighten the boundaries between boys and girls. They also convey assumptions which get worked into later sexual scripts: (1) that girls and boys are members of distinctive, opposing, and sometimes antagonistic groups; (2) that cross-gender contact is potentially sexual and contaminating, fraught with both pleasure and danger; and (3) that girls are more sexually defined (and polluting) than boys.

Conclusion

Social scientists have often viewed the heterosexual dating rituals of adolescence—when girls and boys "finally" get together—as the concluding stage after the separate, presumably non-sexual, boys' and girls' groups that are so prevalent in childhood. We urge a closer look at the organization of sexuality and of gender in middle and late childhood. The gender-divided social worlds of children are not totally asexual. And same-gender groups have continuing import in the more overtly sexual scripts of adolescence and adulthood.

From an early age "the sexual" is prescriptively heterosexual and male homophobic. Children draw on sexual meanings to maintain gender segregation—to make cross-gender interaction risky and to mark and ritualize boundaries between "the boys" and "the girls." In their separate gender groups, girls and boys learn somewhat different patterns of bonding—boys sharing the arousal of group rule-breaking; girls emphasizing the construction of intimacy, and themes of romance. Coming to adolescent sexual intimacy from different and asymmetric gender subcultures, girls and boys bring somewhat different needs, capacities, and types of knowledge.

References

Eder, Dona (1985). "The cycle of popularity: interpersonal relations among female adolescents." *Sociology of Education* 58: 154–65.

Fine, Gary Alan (1980). "The natural history of preadolescent male friendship groups." Pp. 293–320 in Hugh C. Foot, Antony J. Chapman, and Jean R. Smith (eds.), *Friendship and Social Relations in Children.* New York: Wiley.

Gagnon, John H., and William Simon (1973). *Sexual Conduct.* Chicago: Aldine.

Luria, Zella (1983). "Sexual fantasy and pornography: two cases of girls brought up with pornography." *Archives of Sexual Behavior 11:* 395–404.

Miller, Patricia Y., and William Simon (1981). "The development of sexuality in adolescence." Pp. 383–407 in Joseph Adelson (ed.), *Handbook of Adolescent Psychology.* New York: Wiley.

Schofield, Janet (1982). *Black and White in School.* New York: Praeger.

16 "But What Do You Mean?" Women and Men in Conversation

DEBORAH TANNEN

We seldom realize how precarious social interaction is between men and women. For the most part, we manage to get our ideas across to one another with little difficulty. Sometimes, however, communication across gender lines leaves us headshakingly confused that "the other" could have said that, thought that, done that—giving us a glimmer that our worlds really are different. Sociologically, men and women represent distinct worlds of socialization—with all the differences this implies, from ideas about sex and love to the best ways to get ahead in life.

Are these statements exaggerations? Or are there really such major differences in male/female communications? You be the judge, as you read Tannen's summary of how women and men communicate. Compare her analysis with your own experiences. You might also consider the implications of this analysis for problems experienced by couples "going together," as well as for difficulties between husbands and wives.

CONVERSATION IS A RITUAL. We say things that seem obviously the thing to say, without thinking of the literal meaning of our words, any more than we expect the question "How are you?" to call forth a detailed account of aches and pains.

Unfortunately, women and men often have different ideas about what's appropriate, different ways of speaking. Many of the conversational rituals common among women are designed to take the other person's feelings into account, while many of the conversational rituals common among men are designed to maintain the one-up position, or at least avoid appearing one-down. As a result, when men and women interact—especially at work—it's often women who are at the disadvantage. Because women are not trying to avoid the one-down position, that is unfortunately where they may end up.

Here, the biggest areas of miscommunication.

175

1. Apologies

Women are often told they apologize too much. The reason they're told to stop doing it is that, to many men, apologizing seems synonymous with putting oneself down. But there are many times when "I'm sorry" isn't self-deprecating, or even an apology; it's an automatic way of keeping both speakers on an equal footing. For example, a well-known columnist once interviewed me and gave me her phone number in case I needed to call her back. I misplaced the number and had to go through the newspaper's main switchboard. When our conversation was winding down and we'd both made ending-type remarks, I added "Oh, I almost forgot—I lost your direct number, can I get it again?" "Oh, I'm sorry," she came back instantly, even though she had done nothing wrong and *I* was the one who'd lost the number. But I understood she wasn't really apologizing; she was just automatically reassuring me she had no intention of denying me her number.

Even when "I'm sorry" *is* an apology, women often assume it will be the first step in a two-step ritual: I say "I'm sorry" and take half the blame, then you take the other half. At work, it might go something like this:

A. When you typed this letter, you missed this phrase I inserted.
B. Oh, I'm sorry. I'll fix it.
A. Well, I wrote it so small it was easy to miss.

When both parties share blame, it's a mutual face-saving device. But if one person, usually the woman, utters frequent apologies and the other doesn't, she ends up looking as if she's taking the blame for mishaps that aren't her fault. When she's only partially to blame, she looks entirely in the wrong.

I recently sat in on a meeting at an insurance company where the sole woman, Helen, said "I'm sorry" or "I apologize" repeatedly. At one point she said, "I'm thinking out loud. I apologize." Yet the meeting was intended to be an informal brain-storming session, and *everyone* was thinking out loud.

The reason Helen's apologies stood out was that she was the only person in the room making so many. And the reason I was concerned was that Helen felt the annual bonus she had received was unfair. When I interviewed her colleagues, they said that Helen was one of the best and most productive workers—yet she got one of the smallest bonuses. Although the problem might have been outright sexism, I suspect her speech style, which differs from that of her male colleagues, masks her competence.

Unfortunately, not apologizing can have its price too. Since so many women use ritual apologies, those who don't may be seen as hard-edged.

What's important is to be aware of how often you say you're sorry (and why), and to monitor your speech based on the reaction you get.

2. Criticism

A woman who co-wrote a report with a male colleague was hurt when she read a rough draft to him and he leapt into a critical response—"Oh, that's too dry! You have to make it snappier!" She herself would have been more likely to say, "That's a really good start. Of course, you'll want to make it a little snappier when you revise."

Whether criticism is given straight or softened is a matter of convention. In general, women use more softeners. I noticed this difference when talking to an editor about an essay I'd written. While going over changes she wanted to make, she said, "There's one more thing. I know you may not agree with me. The reason I noticed the problem is that your other points are so lucid and elegant." She went on hedging for several more sentences until I put her out of her misery: "Do you want to cut that part?" I asked—and of course she did. But I appreciated her tentativeness. In contrast, another editor (a man) I once called summarily rejected my idea for an article by barking, "Call me when you have something new to say."

Those who are used to ways of talking that soften the impact of criticism may find it hard to deal with the right-between-the-eyes style. It has its own logic, however, and neither style is intrinsically better. People who prefer criticism given straight are operating on an assumption that feelings aren't involved. "Here's the dope. I know you're good; you can take it."

3. Thank-Yous

A woman manager I know starts meetings by thanking everyone for coming, even though it's clearly their job to do so. Her "thank-you" is simply a ritual.

A novelist received a fax from an assistant in her publisher's office; it contained suggested catalogue copy for her book. She immediately faxed him her suggested changes and said, "Thanks for running this by me," even though her contract gave her the right to approve all copy. When she thanked the assistant, she fully expected him to reciprocate: "Thanks for giving me such a quick response." Instead, he said, "You're welcome." Suddenly, rather than an equal exchange of pleasantries, she found herself positioned as the recipient of a favor. This made her feel like responding, "Thanks for nothing!"

Many women use "thanks" as an automatic conversation starter and closer; there's nothing literally to thank you for. Like many rituals typical of women's conversation, it depends on the goodwill of the other to restore the balance. When the other speaker doesn't reciprocate, a woman may feel like someone on a seesaw whose partner abandoned his end. Instead of balancing in the air, she has plopped to the ground, wondering how she got there.

4. Fighting

Many men expect the discussion of ideas to be a ritual fight—explored through verbal opposition. They state their ideas in the strongest possible terms, thinking that if there are weaknesses someone will point them out, and by trying to argue against those objections, they will see how well their ideas hold up.

Those who expect their own ideas to be challenged will respond to another's ideas by trying to poke holes and find weak links—as a way of *helping*. The logic is that when you are challenged you will rise to the occasion: Adrenaline makes your mind sharper, you get ideas and insights you would not have thought of without the spur of battle.

But many women take this approach as a personal attack. Worse, they find it impossible to do their best work in such a contentious environment. If you're not used to ritual fighting, you begin to hear criticism of your ideas as soon as they are formed. Rather than making you think more clearly, it makes you doubt what you know. When you state your ideas, you hedge in order to fend off potential attacks. Ironically, this is more likely to *invite* attack because it makes you look weak.

Although you may never enjoy verbal sparring, some women find it helpful to learn how to do it. An engineer who was the only woman among four men in a small company found that as soon as she learned to argue, she was accepted and taken seriously. A doctor attending a hospital staff meeting made a similar discovery. She was becoming more and more angry with a male colleague who'd loudly disagreed with a point she'd made. Her better judgment told her to hold her tongue, to avoid making an enemy of this powerful senior colleague. But finally she couldn't hold it any longer, and she rose to her feet and delivered an impassioned attack on his position. She sat down in a panic, certain she had permanently damaged her relationship with him. To her amazement, he came up to her afterward and said, "That was a great rebuttal. I'm really impressed. Let's go out for a beer after work and hash out our approaches to this problem."

5. Praise

A manager I'll call Lester had been on his new job six months when he heard that the women reporting to him were deeply dissatisfied. When he talked to them about it, their feelings erupted; two said they were on the verge of quitting because he didn't appreciate their work, and they didn't want to wait to be fired. Lester was dumbfounded: He believed they were doing a fine job. Surely, he thought, he had said nothing to give them the impression he didn't like their work. And indeed he hadn't. That was the problem. He had said *nothing*—and the women assumed he was following the adage "If you can't say something nice, don't say anything." He thought he was showing confidence in them by leaving them alone.

Men and women have different habits in regard to giving praise. For example, Deidre and her colleague William both gave presentations at a conference. Afterward, Deidre told William, "That was a great talk." He thanked her. Then she asked, "What did you think of mine?" and he gave her a lengthy and detailed critique. She found it uncomfortable to listen to his comments. But she assured herself that he meant well, and that his honesty was a signal that she, too, should be honest when he asked for a critique of his performance. As a matter of fact, she had noticed quite a few ways in which he could have improved his presentation. But she never got a chance to tell him because he never asked—and she felt put down. The worst part was that it seemed she had only herself to blame, since she *had* asked what he thought of her talk.

But had she really asked for his critique? The truth is, when she asked for his opinion, she was expecting a compliment, which she felt was more or less required following anyone's talk. When he responded with criticism, she figured, Oh, he's playing "Let's critique each other"—not a game she'd initiated, but one which she was willing to play. Had she realized he was going to criticize her and not ask her to reciprocate, she would never have asked in the first place.

It would be easy to assume that Deidre was insecure, whether she was fishing for a compliment or soliciting a critique. But she was simply talking automatically, performing one of the many conversational rituals that allow us to get through the day. William may have sincerely misunderstood Deidre's intention—or may have been unable to pass up a chance to one-up her when given the opportunity.

6. Complaints

"Troubles talk" can be a way to establish rapport with a colleague. You complain about a problem (which shows that you are just folks) and the other person responds with a similar problem (which puts you on equal footing). But while such commiserating is common among women, men are likely to hear it as a request to solve the problem.

One woman told me she would frequently initiate what she thought would be pleasant complaint-airing sessions at work. She'd just talk about situations that bothered her just to talk about them, maybe to understand them better. But her male office mate would quickly tell her how she could improve the situation. This left her feeling condescended to and frustrated. She was delighted to see this very impasse in a section in my book *You Just Don't Understand,* and showed it to him. "Oh," he said, "I see the problem. How can we solve it?" Then they both laughed, because it had happened again: He short-circuited the detailed discussion she'd hoped for and cut to the chase of finding a solution.

Sometimes the consequences of complaining are more serious: A man might take a woman's lighthearted griping literally, and she can get a reputation as a chronic malcontent. Furthermore, she may be seen as not up to solving the problems that arise on the job.

7. Jokes

I heard a man call in to a talk show and say, "I've worked for two women and neither one had a sense of humor. You know, when you work with men, there's a lot of joking and teasing." The show's host and the guest (both women) took his comment at face value and assumed the women this man worked for were humorless. The guest said, "Isn't it sad that women don't feel comfortable enough with authority to see the humor?" The host said, "Maybe when more women are in authority roles, they'll be more comfortable with power." But although the women this man worked for *may* have taken themselves too seriously, it's just as likely that they each had a terrific sense of humor, but maybe the humor wasn't the type he was used to. They may have been like the woman who wrote to me: "When I'm with men, my wit or cleverness seems inappropriate (or lost!) so I don't bother. When I'm with my women friends, however, there's no hold on puns or cracks and my humor is fully appreciated."

The types of humor women and men tend to prefer differ. Research has shown that the most common form of humor among men is razzing, teasing, and mock-hostile attacks, while among women it's self-mocking. Women often mistake men's teasing as genuinely hostile. Men often mistake women's mock self-deprecation as truly putting themselves down.

Women have told me they were taken more seriously when they learned to joke the way the guys did. For example, a teacher who went to a national conference with seven other teachers (mostly women) and a group of administrators (mostly men) was annoyed that the administrators always found reasons to leave boring seminars, while the teachers felt they had to stay and take notes. One evening, when the group met at a bar in the hotel, the principal asked her how one such seminar had turned out. She retorted, "As soon as you left, it got much better." He laughed out loud at her response. The playful insult appealed to the men—but there was a trade-off. The women seemed to back off from her after this. (Perhaps they were put off by her using joking to align herself with the bosses.)

There is no "right" way to talk. When problems arise, the culprit may be style differences—and *all* styles will at times fail with others who don't share or understand them, just as English won't do you much good if you try to speak to someone who knows only French. If you want to get your message across, it's not a question of being "right"; it's a question of using language that's shared—or at least understood.

Social Groups and Social Structure

N o one is only a member of humanity in general; each of us is also a member of particular social groups. We live in a certain country and in a particular neighborhood. We belong to a family and are members of a gender and a racial–ethnic group. We have certain *peers*—like–minded people, often close to us in age—with whom we identify. Most of us work at a job and have friends, and many of us go to school or belong to churches, clubs, or other social organizations. The articles in this Part are meant to sensitize us to how social groups and social structure have far-reaching effects on our lives. Let's see what some of those effects are.

No fact of social life is more important than group membership. *To belong to a group is to yield to others the right to make certain decisions about our behavior, while assuming obligations to act according to the expectations of those others.* This is illustrated by a parent saying to a teenage daughter or son, "As long as you are living under my roof, you had better be home by midnight." In this instance, the parents are saying that as long as the daughter or son wants to remain a member of the social group known as the household, her or his behavior must conform to their expectations. So it is with *all* the groups to which we belong: By our membership and participation in them, we relinquish to others at least some control over our own lives.

Those groups that come with our birth are called *involuntary memberships* or *associations*. These include our family and our sexual, ethnic, and racial groups. In contrast, those groups which we choose to join are called *voluntary memberships* or *associations*. The Boy and Girl Scouts, professional associations, church groups, clubs, friendship cliques, and work groups are examples. In certain instances we willingly, sometimes even gladly, conform to their rules and expectations in order to become members. In all groups, we must modify some of our behaviors in order to remain members in good standing.

Not all memberships in voluntary associations involve the same degree of willingness to yield to others a measure of control over our lives. There even are groups, as in some jobs, where we can hardly bear to remain a member but feel that, under the circumstances, we cannot quit. Sociologists still use the term *voluntary association* to refer to such memberships. *Both* voluntary and involuntary memberships have deep effects on our lives, for our participation in a group, whether it is willing or unwilling, shapes not only our behaviors but also our ideas about life.

It is easy to see that social groups have far-reaching effects on our lives— for, as stressed in Part IV, we would not even be "human" without group membership. But what about the second term in the title of this Part? What does *social structure* mean? By this term, sociologists mean that the various social groups that make up our lives are not simply a random collection of components; rather, they are interrelated, and, taken together, they form a significant unit that surrounds us.

I know that if any term in sociology sounds vague and irrelevant, it is *social structure*. This term, however, also refers to highly significant matters—for *the social organization that underlies your life determines your relationships with others*. To better see what this term means, we can note that "social structure" encompasses five "levels." As I summarize them, I shall go from the broadest to the narrowest level.

The first two levels are *inter*societal; that is, they refer to international relationships. *First*, on the broadest level, social structure refers to relationships among blocs (or groups) of nations. Examples are the West's dependence on the Middle East for much of its oil, and the domination of the poor, Least Industrialized Nations by the wealthy, Most Industrialized Nations. The *second* level, the next broadest, refers to relationships between particular nations, such as the extensive role that the United States plays in the Canadian economy. These first two levels—the international dimensions of social structure—sensitize us to relationships based on historical events as well as current balances of power and the division of resources among nations.

The next three levels are *intra*societal; that is, they refer to relationships *within* a society. The *first* level is quite broad. It refers to how the social institutions within a society are related to one another. This level sensitizes us to how political decisions affect the military, how economic booms and busts affect families, and the like. The *second*, a narrower level, refers to patterns between social groups, such as the relationship between McDonald's and other firms in the fast-food business. The *third*, the narrowest level, deals with such matters as how people are organized within a particular group—such as an individual's role as leader or follower, or the parents' authority over their young children that empowers them to determine what the children eat, where they live, what schools they attend, and how they are to be disciplined.

This Part opens with an unusual focus, that of car selling. Helene Lawson, who interviewed men and women who sell cars, details how the socialization we stressed in Part IV shows up in distinct sales styles. (Another way of phrasing this is that gender is part of the social structure of the automobile industry—just as it is part of our own experience of social life, whatever corner of society we find ourselves in.) In the next article, Mae Biggs and I look at how vaginal examinations are organized. We use Erving Goffman's dramaturgical model to uncover the means by which nonsexuality is sustained during pelvic examinations. John Coleman then focuses on city life, pinpointing the debilitating isolation of the urban homeless. In the final selection, William Thompson reports on an unusual occupation, undertaking. He focuses on how morticians cope with the stigma that attaches to their work.

A DIGRESSION ON PARTICIPANT OBSERVATION

Because several articles in this Part—and many in the book itself—are based on participant observation, it is useful to take a closer look at this research method. Lawson observed car salespeople at work (and also interviewed them). For years, before Biggs went to graduate school in sociology, she worked as a gynecological nurse. Coleman, who became concerned about homeless people, slept in their shelters and wandered the streets of New York City. As these researchers *participated* in the lives of the people they were studying, they systematically *observed* what was happening; hence the term *participant observation*.

To gather their data, participant observers sometimes place greater emphasis on observing people, at other times on participating in their lives. Lawson's focus was observation of the car salespeople, and she did little participation. In contrast, because Biggs didn't go to graduate school until after many years of work as a gynecological nurse, her emphasis was almost solely on participation. This is also the basis of Coleman's study of the homeless. Regardless of whether participation or observation receives the greater emphasis, when a researcher reports on personal observations of a social setting, the term *participant observation* is used to describe this method of studying social life. (The terms *field research*, *fieldwork*, *ethnographic research*, and *qualitative research* are also used to refer to this technique of studying people.)

Participant observation allows researchers to provide rich, detailed descriptions that, by retaining some of the "flavor" of the settings, bring the reader close to the events that occurred. Thus, in the article on the homeless you can sense the crushing despair of people living on the streets. Although participant observation lends itself to such rich, insightful descriptions, it is not the method, of course, but the author who does the communicating. We depend on an author's skills for learning what life is like in some group, even for gaining a sense of being there. Consequently, in article 22, the account of the experiment on conformity, although it is far from participant observation, you will feel the dilemma faced by the experimenter's victims.

As I stressed in my article on research methods in Part II, a chief concern of sociologists is to gather accurate information about the people they study. To do this, sociologists try to be objective, to leave their biases behind both when they gather data and as they interpret those data for books, articles, and other reports they write. A primary distinction between research methods is whether they are *quantitative* or *qualitative*. Participant observation is an example of a qualitative method, and is exploratory or descriptive. Quantitative methods place the emphasis on measuring precise differences between individuals and groups.

Through their training and experience, sociologists come to prefer some particular method of gathering data. They also associate with one another, both on the basis of the subject matter they are interested in *and* on the basis of the research methods they employ. Consequently, the qualitative and quantitative approaches to social research have become major identifiers among sociologists. Although sociologists have their preferences, and sometimes feel strongly that one approach is vastly superior, both qualitative and quantitative methods are valid means with which to gather data about social life.

In this book, the emphasis is on studies based on the qualitative approach. These selections impart the meanings and experiences of the groups being studied, sometimes even the "flavor" of being a member of these groups. This approach best imparts the excitement of sociological discovery.

17 Attacking Nicely: Women Selling Cars

HELENE M. LAWSON

The articles in the preceding Part stressed how boys and girls experience childhood differently. These differences are not a superficial matter, something that has little or no consequence for later life. We don't simply fold childhood away, shutting it up in some drawer as we would a discarded toy. Rather, we carry these experiences with us for the rest of our lives. Our distinct socialization as boys or girls equips us with specific sets of attitudes, behaviors, and orientations. These become an essential part of how we approach the world, helping to set us on different roads in life's journey

The result is not that all women act one way and all men another. Sociologists don't make such a claim. Rather, they say that because of our socialization, women and men tend to show distinct approaches to life's tasks. These differences are often subtle, but they show up in almost everything we do. As Lawson analyzes people who sell cars, some of these distinctions become apparent. None of these characteristics is inevitable, the unvarying consequence of biology, or socialization, or a combination thereof. As socialization changes, then, we can expect to see these behaviors—and even feelings—similarly change.

IN OUR SOCIETY car sales work goes against the norms of trust in human relations. Customers are aware that salespersons are trained in impression management techniques based on empathy to win confidence or on aggressive intimidation to overcome resistance to high prices (Oda 1983; Prus 1989). In addition, the car business is unstable; salesman and customers will probably never see each other again. This makes for transient relationships and an environment where the building of trust is problematic. In fact, throughout the whole social structure of sales interactions, there is little trust.

Researchers find that persons who enter this occupation cope with dishonesty, distrust and immoral dealings in various ways. One way is to concentrate on monetary goals as a measure of success and status (Leidner 1991). A second way is to suppress reflections on the unethical tasks they perform (Oakes 1990). A third way is to claim innocence through apparent unawareness of illicit doings. A fourth way is to claim one was merely following orders. And lastly, workers blame the recipients or victims of their services for negative interactions (Hughes 1962).

Working under these conditions is especially problematic for women who have been socialized as mothers and care takers to be concerned with the needs of others and to maintain honesty in relations (Dinnerstein 1976; Mead 1934; Chodorow 1978; Gilligan 1982). Although few articles have been written about women's experience in the field of high commission sales, there is research on women in other high pressure, male-dominated fields such as management (Kanter 1977) and the military (Rustad 1984). These studies find that women take on stereotypical male or female roles to adapt to a structure in which they experience inherent role conflict (Turner 1990).

My research examines how women handle the conflict between their socialized roles and their adopted role of car salesperson. I will describe both how the women themselves change and how they are also changing the interactions within the workplace, shaping new definitions of what it is to be a car salesperson. This study, therefore, analyzes modes of personal adaption as well as modes of social change. To provide a framework for understanding these changes, I have identified a concept—adapting to an incompatible status through role making—as well as five categories of this concept, "Innocents," "Ladies," "Tough Guys," "Reformers," and "Retreaters." I use these categories to describe how women deal with co-workers and customers when they enter the field, and the changes that emerge as they progress along their career paths, from selling their first cars to becoming experienced salespersons. In an effort to explore the ways in which gender roles operate in the bartering and negotiations endemic to selling cars, the article focuses on saleswomen's initial values and attitudes toward co-workers and customers, the adaptations they make as they become more experienced, and finally, the ways in which some women change the dealership itself.

Data Collection and Sample

I collected the data for this study from in-depth interviews with and observations with 35 car saleswomen and 15 car salesmen at car agencies and restaurants in the Chicago metropolitan area, over a period of three years. The informants were recontacted at intervals in order to follow their career paths. In two instances, I became a customer out of necessity because I needed a car, buying automobiles from women who did not know I was doing research until after the purchases were completed. An additional male informant was a personal friend who began selling on a commission basis about the same time I started to do my research and who spoke with me about his progress on a daily basis.

How Women Come In

An examination of the work women did before beginning car sales shows that most had traditional women's careers, such as teaching, waitressing, social work, retail sales and secretarial jobs. These occupations primarily involved service to others and paid low wages. Although ex-teachers complained that students were discipline problems, "little monsters" and "heathens," and ex-sales clerks and beauticians said customers were "pains in the ass," because they returned used merchandise or couldn't make up their minds about how they wanted their hair done, the women basically liked what they did in these jobs, especially the supportive relationships they had with co-workers. However, these women found it difficult to make a living and support families. Such women, with no previous sales experience, were usually encouraged to try car sales by male friends or family members who stressed the possibility of better pay. When they entered car sales, many assumed they would be able to make friends and establish good co-worker relations as they had done at their previous work. Nina commented:

> I used to cashier at a discount drug store, The pay was bad, but I got a real break on formula for the baby and make-up and stuff like that. Mostly, I stayed because the other saleswomen were terrific. We laughed a lot. . . . told each other our problems. When the store closed, I decided to try car sales. I figured, "What the hell. People like me. I shouldn't have a problem." And I was excited to work for commission.

The hours are very long in car sales and salesmen, for the most part, socialize during slow times, telling each other how well they are doing, commiserating over losses, telling jokes or "kibitzing." To further cement friendships, many salesmen go drinking together after work. Most had been in car sales before so they knew others in the field. But even male novices to car sales said they were accepted by one clique or another. Newcomer women also attempted to befriend salesmen and socialize during slow times. They want to talk about a customer who gave them a hard time, family life, or even the weather. But when they approached the men, the women were usually rejected or harassed. Nina related:

When I would try to make conversation with other salesman they were very gross. They swear. They pat you on the butt like this. If I did well, the guys would say, "What do you need to sell a car, a bra?" If I was five minutes late, the boss would send me home. The guys would laugh. They made me an example.

Women who attempted to go to bars with salesmen after working hours developed a bad reputation. Evelyn observed:

You have to be careful. Women learn quick around here. You don't party. You don't hang out with the guys after work. Those who do are called "sluts" or "whores."

Co-worker relations between men and women were strained, and since there were usually only one or two saleswomen at most dealerships, women could not form their own cliques. Interactions between the two sexes remained an area of conflict, and probably will continue as such until there is a more equal balance between women and men car salespersons.

There are, however, more important areas than co-worker relations on which women must concentrate. If they are to succeed, saleswomen must interact well with customers. Yet, all 35 saleswomen remembered many initial contact experiences with male customers as upsetting and negative. These women agreed that most "older" men reacted in a rude, insulting manner when approached. Some openly refused to deal with women. Sara said these men "did not want to answer questions about their income or credit rating, or even discuss cars with a woman." Arlene said some "older men used foul language," or were so abrasive that saleswomen ended up "turning them over to a salesman." Because new saleswomen generally began work with no car sales experience, this rejection added to their self doubt and caused them to feel they needed to learn more about cars in order to sell them.

The car has traditionally been identified with men, and most saleswomen said they knew "little" about automobiles. They did not grow up fixing cars, talking about them with friends, or understanding how they operate. Therefore, at the beginning, many of the women said they thought it was most important to become technically knowledgeable about cars. Joyce had been in car sales for two months:

I think it is important to be able to talk to a customer about the vehicle—to understand how the engine works and what benefits the make has over others. I watch videos. I listen to other salesmen. I read all the pamphlets. I want to learn as much as I can.

To make maters more difficult, salespersons were not given much training. Newcomers were usually "thrown out on the floor" and had to figure out what to do on their own. Newcomers, men or women, had a hard time closing their first sales, because they lacked experience. Novices were generally hired by the type of dealership salespersons called "green pea stores." This is an agency which usually hires inexperienced salespersons and has managers close sales in the final stages of bargaining. Larry, a general manager, explained the social arrangements of these types of sales which function to shelter newcomers from the guilt and pressure of customer relations:

> They [management] try to keep new salespeople in the dark as far as gross cost on cars. They think it makes them more believable to customers. If the manager tells you, "no, you can't sell that car for this amount," for whatever reason, "this is the price you got to sell it for," you have to go out there, and that is what you do.

Ann, whose father owned a car dealership, said that even more experienced salespersons only got to see the front page of an invoice:

> There's an invoice that they [the dealership] can show you [the salesperson] and a customer can buy the car, usually for $100 over the invoice. But, you [the salesperson] will never see the back page which is all their profit. When they [the dealership] sell a car for invoice there is like about $1,200 usually in that figure. If you're talking Cadillac, it's more like $5,000.

Once newcomers in green pea stores had been at work a month or so, management expected them to begin to close on their own. Although salespersons were told by management at the beginning of their careers that making money for the dealership was paramount, the first steps most salespersons, men or women, took was to try to sell the customer a car close to the amount he or she wanted to pay. Generally this was lower than management would like, and meant a smaller commission for the salesperson. However, most women said pleasing the customer through a cheap price made them feel good because they felt they were helping someone.

> At the beginning I believed I didn't need to be greedy because there was a price I could sell at that would make everybody happy—the customer, my manager and myself. If you sell enough cars, you are going to make money anyway.

How Women Change

Yet, what women said about first sales in which they made high commissions show how their values were affected by their work. Fran discussed her new attitude:

> I'll tell you about my first big sale because that one I remember very well. I was working for about a couple [of] weeks, and it was right after the auto show, and a young dentist came in with his wife, and he had his hands in his pockets jingling his money, and he goes, "I want to buy a Spider [Alfa Romeo]." I found out what the list price was and I wrote it down. I got a $5,000 deposit from him and he took his credit out and I knew nothing. I went into the boss and he almost died. So he goes, "Don't lose this one!" I sold that car way over cost and I didn't even know I was doing it. It was the most exciting thing I had ever done. When he [the customer] came in to pick up the car, he said, "I wanted that car so bad, and I guess I really got screwed." At the beginning I believed it was wrong to ask for too much money—that it was greedy. After that, I started going for the buck.

This sale was exciting for many reasons. It was unexpected, the manager was pleased, and the saleswoman made a large commission. But most of all, selling seemed so easy, as though it were done through luck or magic. Therefore, the saleswoman did not need to blame herself for "screwing" the customer. Events like this became a turning point in women's careers, when attitudes and values toward making lots of money at others' expense became fun.

And in order to sell themselves, women developed roles. They made tools of their personalities and gender traits in order to coerce customers into buying cars, distancing themselves from their potential disloyalty to the other in the relationship.

Innocents

Probably because the first high commission sale made by most newcomers was painless and negotiated in ignorance, many women continued on in the role of the Innocent. Innocents did not use crude language or insider argot. They employed dress and demeanor to portray their particular role. Denise, a younger woman, played school girl:

> I've got a baby face and I do not pose a threat to anybody who walks in—young, old, seasoned buyer, first timer. I put people at ease. I don't scare anybody. I've sold many campers wearing sweats with sorority letters on the bottom. I have a face that will show people I'm honest.

Innocents continued to view their success as "luck" or "magic," both factors out of their control. They said that most customers would sell themselves a car if they [the saleswomen] said little. Innocents adapted through avoidance. They wore blinders so they did not see the dubious dealings going on around them and could deny being a party to the transactions. The woman who sold me my most recent car exemplified this orientation. She originally described the car as having been a manufacturer representative's car, a "brass hat." A week after I purchased the car, I dropped my pen and was feeling around underneath the front seat, when I felt a small plastic object. This turned out to be a key chain from a car rental agency in Florida. It had my car's identification number on it.

I called the rental agency and they verified that the car had indeed been theirs but they had recently sold it to Mazda. I do not think I would have bought this car if I had known it was previously used as a rental car. When I confronted Phyllis with the key chain, she replied:

> Is that true? I never asked too many questions. I know I saw literature on the car. . . . that it came from an auction. I know they buy when Mazda is having auctions. I thought is was a manufacturer rep's car.

Other experienced Innocents in my study told me when sales are slow they "dummy up" [use ignorance to sell cars], because customers believed that newcomers did not possess the ability to devise ways of cheating them. The greater trust in the saleswoman made the customers less resistant to her pitches.

Ladies

Women who wished to remain in the field, but were uncomfortable with the Innocent role, had several options. One was to become Ladies, taking on exaggerated feminine characteristics. Ladies said customers were more easily manipulated through forms of stereotypical feminine behavior than through aggressive "pushy" tactics. They cajoled and nurtured male customers in order to deter sexual harassment and to sell cars. Their work relationships became patterned to fit relationships men have experienced in families. Ann, a 52-year-old grandmother, described how she used the goodness of her maternal role to gain trust and respect from her customers: "I tell them, 'Look at these pictures on my desk. I am a mother. I am a grandmother. I wouldn't hurt you, now would I?'"

Ladies helped customers feel comfortable, served them coffee, listened with apparent interest to their problems and generally treated them with familial warmth and hospitality. Rita labeled this method of sales "attacking nicely":

> You have to be nice and talk to the [customers] and make them feel at home before you can sell them a car. It is usually easier to sell a car if you establish

rapport. This guy and I got to talking, and he said something about playing the accordion and we established a great rapport because I play the accordion. He still drops in to see me every now and then.

Ladies also attempted to manipulate male management and co-workers through these stereotypical feminine traits. I watched saleswomen sew buttons on managers' and co-workers' shirts, bring them home cooked food, and do clerical chores such as locating cars, or assisting with paperwork. These Ladies were still seen as outsiders, different from the group, and less than equal; but they had become non-threatening, like older sisters or mothers, and they were respected. Mary played big sister:

> Salesmen come to me for advice with their love life. They don't treat me like I'm one of the guys. They watch their mouths. They are very careful about talking dirty or swearing or anything like that. They treat me like a lady.

Tough Guys

Some women went directly from Innocents to Tough Guys, where they attempted to adapt the aggressive, competitive male model of sales. Generally these women said they took on this role because they were told to "toughen up or get out." To toughen up means to block feelings. To Tough Guys this was interpreted as being able to handle verbal abuse in order to become "one of the boys." Once Sheila became insensitive toward the use of profanity and sexual innuendos, she was allowed to join the men:

> At first I used to break down and cry and show them I was scared or frightened of them. Then they just kept on more. They teased me, called me a 'bimbo' and asked me if it was that time of the month when I got depressed. At home, we never swore; we showed respect. I had to toughen up. Me, I'm just like one of the guys. They use profanity; I do too.

This woman not only accepted harassment; she had been socialized to use it against others. Most Tough Guys worked at high-volume dealerships they labeled "Revolving Door," "Beat 'Em up," and "Slam Dunk 'Em" stores. Generally, women at these agencies had to make enough sales to meet a high quota and were continually worried about being fired. Therefore, they learned to "fight for the door" [grab persons who walk in the door before other salespersons got to them], and pushed hard on these would-be customers, often intimidating them in order to make quick sales. This style of selling resulted in many negative interactions which Tough Guys blamed on customers.

Innocents and Ladies labeled customers too, but Tough Guys were more extreme in their antagonism. Innocents viewed customers as "knowledgeable about cars," but "rude" or "disrespectful." Tough Guys put customers in an "out-group" as "enemies" who needed to be conquered. Respondents described what they did using argot that depicted a wrestling match between themselves and the customer where they "pinned customers down." Tough Guy language became progressively more violent and warlike. Women claimed to "put customers away," and "do 'em in." Carol blamed the customer for causing the dishonesty and animosity in car sales:

> Some customers really want our vehicle, but they come here to see if they can rip you off, and they will. They lie about the condition of their trade-ins. They bring a car that they just brought to the repair shop and the mechanic said it was going to cost $700 to fix the damage. That's why they want to trade it in. They lie about their credit ratings, and they say they can get cars at other dealerships for less. The people who come in here can afford bucks. Probably, the more money they have, the harder it is to get it away from them.

Tough Guys valued most what the customer gave them, not what they could do for the customer. Gina defined a "good" customer as one who gave her lots of money, and a " bad" customer as one who tried to bargain:

> We have wonderful people like Mr. Smith. What a wonderful guy. He brought his wife with him. She picked out the car. They added every accessory on it imaginable. The first price that I gave him he bought the car at. So the dealership made millions of dollars on it, and I made millions of dollars on it. But other people are always trying to chew you down. They're whiners, complainers. They deserve nothing and wouldn't be happy under any circumstance.

Yet, even when Tough Guys sold at high volume dealerships, blamed the customer for dishonesty in the business, sold more aggressively, and distanced themselves from concern for customer needs, male co-workers felt female Tough Guys were not equal to salesmen in their competitive attitudes. Frank, a manager, said:

> The women, they're more laid back. They don't have what it takes, the "killer instinct." People will buy under pressure. They feel intimidated. I have the killer instinct. My first four months I was here every day, 12 hours a day, because I didn't want to miss anything. I wanted to have the most numbers. I just wanted to win. I wanted to be on top, to get every walk-in. Competitiveness. Just about every guy here now has it. They hate to lose.

I found that more than a few of the women informants—Innocents, Ladies, Reformers as well as Tough Guys, had to change their family and social life drastically in order to fit into the male work world and make a living wage. Married and single women had to curtail their social activities. Younger women even lived at home with their parents because they could not find the time to keep up an apartment. Not unexpectedly, divorced women like Fran, who were responsible for the care of young children, had the hardest time dividing their loyalties between work and family:

> Before, when I was married, I worked part-time at home doing typing. I was there when Billy came home from school and we did lots of things together. Now, I can only spend Sunday and Wednesday with him. I have no time for myself, and it's hard. I need to help him with homework, do chores like grocery shop and laundry, go to the dentist—things like that. It is very hard.

Yet Tough Guys, even those who found car sales hard work, did not fight for change. They continued to try and fit into the male model of work.

Reformers

Reformers believed that women were intrinsically better at selling than men. They generally began as Ladies who were motivated to change the way work was structured because of how they felt about what they did, and the conflict this brought them. Most Reformers were in conflict over the imposed priorities and resultant interactions between themselves and their customers. They wanted to be more client centered. Many wanted a life style that did not divide work from home so drastically.

Ladies who turned to Reform usually began by distancing themselves from male co-workers. They stopped mothering and nurturing them. Reformers usually continued to relate to customers through the role of Lady. Betty felt that most salesmen were crass, ignorant, and dishonest, and therefore, befriending them was dangerous:

> I am not like salesmen. We [women] are not even in the same business as they are. I am an educated professional. I smile, and am polite to them [male coworkers], but it is best to tell them nothing. They try to steal your customers. They lie to management about you.

Reformers who led Reform were very concerned with building trust. For this reason they were willing to risk effort and time in interactions that might not result in a sale. They spent more time with customers who were not easily sold, might need more time to consider their purchase, or wanted to "kick the tires," leave and perhaps return later. Reformers like Evelyn said patience and understanding bring in referrals because previous customers remember you:

> I come on very soft, and I spend a lot of time with people. If I'm not going to be able to make money, I still treat people nice and spend time with them, because down the road, I might get some business.

Lorber (1984) and Lunneborg (1990) found similar patterns in their studies. Medical women scheduled longer appointments with fewer patients in order to devote more time and energy to answering questions and listening to concerns. And, women stockbrokers spent more time learning about client's particular needs rather than attempting to push them into pre-arranged high-profit packages.

In addition to spending time developing trust, Reformers, more than any other category of saleswomen, fought for the stability needed to develop a work environment which encouraged trust. This was in opposition to the male sales model which defined success as a move to a higher volume and more lucrative dealership or a dealership that sold more expensive cars. Most salesmen moved from dealership to dealership, depending on where the "grass was greener," i.e., what cars were hotter sellers that season, where they thought they could make higher commissions, or where they were promised a contract for salary plus commission. In contrast, Nina managed to remain at her dealership for six years, and defined success in terms of stability, trust, and ongoing customer relationships as well as money gained:

> I have been here six years. Right now I'm not making as much money because the business is slow and the cars aren't selling as well as in the past, but I have repeaters and referrals and I still make a good living. If I move to another place, that place may not do so well in the long run. My boss trusts me, and it is a good place to work.

The concept of "trust" between management and salespersons was seldom found in this field, where upper management sometimes replaced complete sales forces overnight. When Reformers managed to be more stable, distrust was minimized for customers. Clients could expect to get to know their car salespersons and form ongoing trusting relationships concerning service or future dealings, as they do with doctors, dentists, or other tradepersons.

Some Reformers were willing to make less money to find time for family. A few women even fought for and achieved part-time status. Ann was ecstatic:

> After 12 years, I finally got management to let me work part-time. Now I have time for my grandchildren; I can go shopping with my daughter, and see some

friends. I have missed doing these things. I have been put on salary so I make less, but I'm doing okay. The owner knows my capabilities, and I have lots of steadies. They're willing to come in when I'm there.

Although Ann became a part-timer in 1990, she was fired six months later. Her boss complained she "did not fit with the team any longer" and had "lost her love for the work." She felt the real story was that "the car business is in a recession," and she was "fully vested" in a retirement program which was costing the dealership too much to keep her. Ann seemed very confused by the owner's singular disloyalty to her after 13 years because she made "good money" for the dealer over a long period of time, and her part-time pay was a relatively small salary of $100 a day. Yet, the mere fact that Reformers were continuing to demand and receive shorter hours, a concession rarely heard of in this field, changed the structure of the workplace and set important precedents.

Retreaters

Early on, many newcomers became disenchanted with car sales because they could find no role that allowed them to adapt to the changes they had to undergo to make a living at this work. Most Retreaters left the field because they felt the customer deserved better treatment—more honesty, lower prices, and less pressure to buy something he or she did not need. Retreaters could not distance themselves from their feelings, and did not "feel good" about what they had to do to build a career in car sales. Leah quit after a year:

> I told my manager I wanted to sell a lot of cars cheaper, and he screamed at me. I would say, "I'll sell a whole bunch for you, but I'm not going to make a whole lot of money on any one of them because I just couldn't do that, because I've got to shop with these people and live with them."

Mary, in the business for six months, was also leaving:

> I don't like the selling aspect of car sales. If you do well and you make your boss happy, you feel sick inside. I have a conscience. I am not the kind of individual who can gain your confidence and respect during the initial transaction of purchasing a car and then when it comes down to the dollars and cents, treat you like I never met you, which is to make the highest profit off of you. 90% of the men in this business have no conscience. When you purchase a car and come back, they'll start hiding. They pretend they don't know you for fear you're coming back to make a complaint, to address something that was not dealt with

properly in the first place. I don't like approaching people and having that look come over their faces and having to overcome that objection of, "No, I'm not a crook," and "Yes, I'll sell you a car cheap," knowing I can't because if you sell a car cheap the boss will say, "What are you doing, giving my cars away? Do you want to work here long?"

The sales culture's firmly established response to these self-recriminations was to encourage the salesperson's estrangement from a higher conscience (Prus 1989; Oakes 1990). Saleswomen were told to "toughen up or get out." They were expected to confine their emotions to feeling good about making a lot of money. If women complained to their bosses about their guilty consciences, they suffered negative sanctions. Complaints about having to overcharge or pressure customers resulted in ridicule, taunts, or they were sent home for the day. Such women were told they were weak and could not "make it" in car sales. On the other hand, saleswomen were praised and rewarded for how much over-invoice they could sell a car. A really big sale was talked about throughout the area dealerships and the salesperson became a celebrity. This resulted in a lack of introspection on the part of many salespersons. They stopped reflecting about what they were doing and reasoned that this was the way things should be done in order to keep the dealer in business and to keep their jobs.

Male Roles Compared

Males also take on the Innocent, Tough Guy, Retreater, and even a "Mr. Nice Guy" role, which is comparable to that of the Lady, but my principal observation is that all men who remained in the field eventually became Tough Guys. For these men, this role was not as much of an act as it appeared to be for the women. It is a role representing the behavior expected of salesmen by their peers. It seems to be a natural consequence, in the heat of the sales arena, for men eventually to become hard boiled. Men said that they wanted to be tough.

When men or women enter the field, they are forced into the role of the Innocent. However, none of the men interviewed in this study were without previous sales experience. So the Innocent role for men appears to be transient. Unlike women, who would cultivate the role of innocence, men wanted to shed any such appellation as soon as possible.

The Tough Guy role for men seemed to be something that became part of their personality over time. In contrast, the roles for women often appeared to be masks to hide their true identities and feelings—feelings which were often quite disparate from those they chose to express.

The Retreater men and the Retreater women were quite similar when interviewed. They were people who were unable to feel comfortable meeting management's expectations. One of the men who left car sales went into consumer electronic sales at a bargain center, where the prices were fixed and haggling was absent. He, as did the women, wanted more respect in his sales interactions.

Discussion

Interactions between salespersons and customers are becoming more positive through the moderating effect of women in the sales force. Their continued introspection and gendered values have exerted a subtle but significant influence. Car saleswomen's definition of success seemed to include more factors than mere profit. Quality of life, both at work and in the home, [was] more important to them than mere gain. Reformers defined success to include a stable work environment where trust could be built, and a home life which could include a family. These gendered values, reflected in the classification scheme used in my work, show that sales tactics based on these ethics help women to remain reflective, as well as to build success. The linking between the Reformer and the Lady categories is an argument in favor of the idea that the expression of even stereotypical female behavior may exert a positive influence in improving relations in the workplace.

However, changes that did take place depended upon the strategies adopted by the women, and the philosophy of the dealership where they worked. Often changes were not permanent. Yet, the fact that Reformers were usually top-volume sellers made them enviable examples to men they worked with. They showed men that profit need not be sacrificed in order to obtain other rewards such as job stability, trustful relations with customers, and shorter work hours to accommodate family life. These rewards, often thought to be unobtainable, may lure men to emulate women's examples. Because women are increasingly entering male fields where humaneness in relations has been devalued, their ability to construct role models combining profit-making with concern for others needs future study.

References

Chodorow, Nancy. 1978. *The Reproduction of Mothering*. Berkeley: The University of California Press.

Dinnerstein, Dorothy. 1976. *The Mermaid and the Minotaur: Sexual Arrangements and Human Malaise*. New York: Harper Colophon.

Gilligan, Carol. 1982. *In a Different Voice.* Cambridge: Harvard University Press.

Hughes, Everett C. 1962. "Good People and Dirty Work." *Social Problems* 10:3–11.

Kanter, Rosabeth. 1977. *Men and Women of the Corporation.* New York: Basic Books.

Leidner, Robin. 1991. "Serving Hamburgers and Selling Insurance: Gender, Work, and Identity in Interactive Service Jobs." *Gender and Society* 5:154–177.

Lorber, Judith. 1984. *Women as Physicians: Careers, Status and Power.* New York: Tavistock.

Lunneborg, Patricia. 1990. *Women Changing Work.* New York: Bergin & Garvey.

Mead, George Herbert. 1934. *Mind, Self and Society.* Chicago: University of Chicago Press.

Oakes, Guy. 1990. *The Soul of the Salesman.* New Jersey: Humanities Press International.

Oda, Massami. 1983. "Predicting Sales Performance of Car Salesmen by Personality Traits." *Japanese Journal of Psychology* 54:73–80.

Prus, Robert. 1989. *Pursuing Customers: An Ethnography of Market Activities.* California: Sage.

Rustad, Michael L. 1984. "Female Tokenism in the Volunteer Army." In F. Fisher and C. Sirianni (eds), *Critical Studies in Organization and Bureaucracy.* Philadelphia: Temple University Press.

Turner, R.H. 1990. "Role Change." *Annual Review of Sociology* 16:87–110.

18 Behavior in Pubic Places: The Sociology of the Vaginal Examination

JAMES M. HENSLIN
MAE A. BIGGS

All of us depend on others for the successful completion of the roles we play. In many ways, this makes cooperation the essence of social life (with due apologies to my conflict-theorist friends). Without teamwork, performances fall apart, people become disillusioned, jobs don't get done—and, ultimately, society is threatened. Accordingly, much of our socialization centers on learning to be good team players.

The work setting lends itself well to examining cooperative interaction and to seeing how people develop ways of handling differences—"working arrangements" that defuse threats to fragile social patterns. For example, instructors often accept from students excuses that they know do not match reality. For their part, students often publicly accept what instructors teach, even though they privately disagree with those interpretations. Not only is confrontation unpleasant, and therefore preferable to avoid, but also it is a threat to the continuity of interaction. Thus both instructors and students generally allow one another enough leeway to "get on with business" (which some might say is education, while others—more cynical— might say is the one earning a living and the other a degree).

One can gain much insight into the nature of society by trying to identify the implicit understandings that guide our interactions in everyday life. In this selection, Henslin and Biggs draw on Goffman's dramaturgical framework as they focus on the vaginal examination. Note how much teamwork is required to make the definition stick that nothing sexual is occurring.

GENITAL BEHAVIOR IS PROBLEMATIC for most of us. We are socialized at a very early age into society's dictates concerning the situations, circumstances, and purposes of allowable and unallowable genital exposure.

Our thanks to Erving Goffman for commenting on this paper while it was in manuscript form and for suggesting the title, a play on his book, *Behavior in Public Places*. Because the physicians in this study are men, the pronoun "he" is used.

After a U.S. female has been socialized into her society's expectations regarding the covering and privacy of specified areas of her body, especially her vagina, exposure of her pubic area becomes something that is problematic for her. Even for a woman who has overcome feelings of modesty and perhaps of shame at genital exposure in the presence of her sexual partner, the problem frequently recurs during the vaginal examination. Although her exposure is supposed to be nonsexual, the vaginal examination can be so threatening that for many women it not only punctures their feelings of modesty but it also threatens their self, their feelings of who they are.

Because emotions become associated with the genital area through the learning of meanings and taboos, the vaginal examination is an especially interesting process; it is an elaborately ritualized form of social interaction designed to desexualize the sexual organs. From a sociological point of view, what happens during such interaction? Since a (if not *the*) primary concern of the persons involved is that all the interaction be defined as nonsexual, with even the hint of sexuality to be avoided, what structural restraints on behavior operate? How does the patient cooperate in maintaining this definition of nonsexuality? In what ways are the roles of doctor, nurse, and patient performed such that each contributes to this definition?

This analysis is based on a sample of 12,000 to 14,000 vaginal examinations. Biggs served as an obstetrical nurse in hospital settings and as an office nurse for general practitioners for fourteen years, giving us access to this area of human behavior which ordinarily is not sociologically accessible. Based on these observations, we have divided the interaction of the vaginal examination into five major scenes. Let's examine what occurs as each of these scenes unfolds.

The setting for the vaginal examination may be divided into two areas (see Figure 18.1). Although there are no physical boundaries that demarcate the two areas, highly specific and ritualized interaction occurs in each. Area 1, where Scenes I and V are played, includes that portion of the "office-examination" room which is furnished with a desk and three chairs. Area 2, where Scenes II, III, and IV take place, contains an examination table, a swivel stool, a gooseneck lamp, a table for instruments, and a sink with a mirror above it.

Scene I: The Personalized Stage: The Patient as Person

The interaction flow of Scene I is as follows: (a) the doctor enters the "office-examination" room; (b) greets the patient; (c) sits down; (d) asks the patient why she is there; (e) questions her on specifics; (f) decides on a course of action, specifically whether a pelvic examination is needed or not; (g) if he

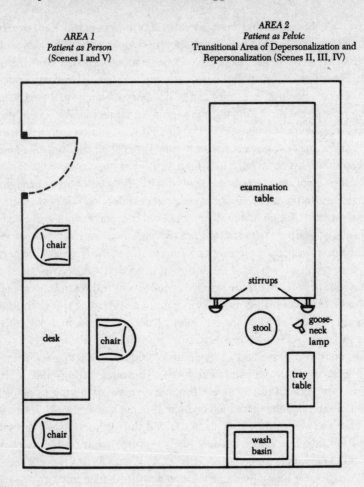

AREA 1
Patient as Person
(Scenes I and V)

AREA 2
Patient as Pelvic
Transitional Area of Depersonalization and
Repersonalization (Scenes II, III, IV)

Figure 18.1 The Doctor's Office—Examination Room

thinks a pelvic is needed, he signals the nurse on the intercom and says, "I want a pelvic in room (X)"; (h) he gets up; and (i) leaves the room.

During this scene, the patient is treated as a full person; that is, the courtesies of middle-class conversation are followed, and, in addition to gathering medical information, if the doctor knows the patient well he may intersperse his medical queries with questions about her personal life. The following interaction that occurred during Scene I demonstrates the doctor's treatment of his patient as a full person:

DOCTOR (upon entering the room): Hello, Joyce, I hear you're going to Southern Illinois University.

PATIENT: Yes, I am. I've been accepted, and I have to have my health record completed.

The doctor then seated himself at his desk and began filling out the health record that the patient gave him. He interspersed his questions concerning the record form with questions about the patient's teaching, about the area of study she was pursuing, about her children, their health and their schooling. He then said, "Well, we have to do this right. We'll do a pelvic on you." He then announced via the intercom, "I want to do a pelvic on Joyce in room 1." At that point he left the room.

This interaction sequence is typical of the interaction that occurs in Scene I between a doctor and a patient he knows well. When the doctor does not know the patient well, he does not include his patient's name, either her first or last name, in his announcement to the nurse that she should come into the room. In such a case, he simply says, "I want to do a pelvic in room 1," or, "Pelvic in room 1." The doctor then leaves the room, marking the end of the scene.

Scene II: The Depersonalized Stage: Transition from Person to Pelvic

When at the close of Scene I the doctor says, "Pelvic in room (X)," he is in effect announcing the transition of the person to a pelvic. It is a sort of advance announcement, however, of a coming event, because the transition has not yet been effected. The doctor's signal for the nurse to come in is, in fact, a signal that the nurse should now help the patient make the transition from a person to a pelvic. Additionally, it also serves as an announcement to the patient that she is about to undergo this metamorphosis.

The interaction flow which accomplishes the transition from person to pelvic is as follows: Upon entering the room, the nurse, without preliminaries, tells the patient, "The doctor wants to do a vaginal examination on you. Will you please remove your panties?" While the patient is undressing, the nurse prepares the props. She positions the stirrups of the examination table and arranges the glove, the lubricant, and the speculum (the instrument which, when inserted into the vagina, allows visual examination of the vaginal tract). She then removes the drape sheet from a drawer and directs the patient onto the table, covers the patient with the drape sheet, assists her in placing her feet into the stirrups, and positions her hips, putting her into the lithotomy position (lying on her back with knees flexed and out).

MEANING OF THE DOCTOR'S ABSENCE

The doctor's exiting just before this scene means that the patient will be undressing in his absence. This is not accidental. In many cases, the doctor may leave because another patient is waiting, but even if there are no waiting patients, the doctor always exits at the end of Scene I. His leaving means that he will not witness the patient undressing, thereby successfully removing any suggestion that a striptease is being performed, or that he is acting as a voyeur. From the patient's point of view, this greatly reduces embarrassment and other problems that would occur if she were to undress in front of the doctor. When the doctor returns, only a particularized portion of the woman's body will be exposed for the ensuing interaction. As we shall see, at that point the doctor is no longer dealing with a person, but he is, rather, facing a "pelvic."

THE PROBLEM OF UNDERCLOTHING

Undressing and nudity are problematic for the patient since she has been socialized into not undressing before strangers.[1] Almost without exception, when the woman undresses in Scene II, she turns away from the nurse and the door, even though the door is closed. She removes only her panties in the typical case, but a small number of patients also remove their shoes.

After the patient has removed her pantie, she faces the problem of what to do with them. Underclothing does not have the same meaning as other items of clothing, such as a sweater, that can be casually draped around the body or strewn on furniture. Clothing is considered to be an extension of the self (Gross and Stone 1964), and clothing often comes to represent the particular part of the body that it covers. In this case, this means that panties represent to women their "private area." Comments made by patients that illustrate the problematics of panty exposure include: "The doctor doesn't want to look at these," "I want to get rid of these before he comes in," and, "I don't want the doctor to see these old things."

Some patients seem to be at a loss in solving this problem and turn to the nurse for guidance, asking her what they should do with their underclothing. Most patients, however, do not ask for directions, but hide their panties in some way. The favorite hiding or covering seems to be in or under the purse.[2] Other women put their panties in the pocket of their coat or in the folds of a coat or sweater, some cover them with a magazine, and some cover them with their own body on the examination table. It is rare that a woman leaves her panties exposed somewhere in the room.[3]

THE DRAPE SHEET

Another problematic area in the vaginal examination is what being undressed can signify. Disrobing for others frequently indicates preparation for sexual relations. Since sexuality is the very thing that this scene is oriented toward removing, a mechanism is put into effect to eliminate sexuality—the drape sheet. After the patient is seated on the table, the nurse places a drape sheet from just below her breasts (she still has her blouse on) to over her legs. Although the patient is draped by the sheet, when she is positioned on the table with her legs in the stirrups, her pubic region is exposed. Usually it is not necessary for the doctor even to raise a fold in the sheet in order to examine her genitals.

Since the drape sheet does not cover the genital area, but, rather, leaves it exposed, what is its purpose? The drape sheet depersonalizes the patient. It sets the pubic area apart, letting the doctor view the pubic area in isolation, separating the pubic area from the person. The pubic area or female genitalia becomes an object isolated from the rest of the body. Because of the drape sheet, the doctor, in his position on the low stool, does not see the patient's face. He no longer sees or needs to deal with a person, just the exposed genitalia marked off by the drape sheet. Yet, from the patient's point of view in her supine position, her genitals are covered! When *she* looks down at her body, she does not see exposed genitalia. The drape sheet effectively hides her pubic area *from herself* while exposing it to the doctor.

THIGH BEHAVIOR

U.S. girls are given early and continued socialization in "limb discipline," being taught at a very early age to keep their legs close together while they are sitting or while they are retrieving articles from the ground. They receive such instructions from their mothers as, "Keep your dress down," "Put your legs together," and "Nice girls don't let their panties show." Evidence of socialization into "acceptable" thigh behavior shows up in the vaginal examination while the women are positioned on the examination table and waiting for the doctor to arrive. They do not let their thighs fall outwards in a relaxed position, but they try to hold their upper or mid-thighs together until the doctor arrives. They do this even in cases where it is very difficult for them to do so, such as when the patient is in her late months of pregnancy.

Although the scene has been carefully orchestrated to desexualize the ensuing interaction, and although the patient is being depersonalized such that when the doctor returns he primarily has a pelvic to deal with and not a person, at this point in the interaction sequence the patient's "proper" thigh behavior shows that she is still holding onto her sexuality and "personality." Only later, when the doctor reenters the scene, will she fully consent to the desexualized and depersonalized role and let her thighs fall outwards.

After the props are ready and the patient is positioned, the nurse announces to the doctor via intercom that the stage is set for the third scene, saying, "We're ready in room (X)."

Scene III: The Depersonalized Stage: The Person as Pelvic

FACE-TO-PUBIC INTERACTION

The interaction to this point, as well as the use of props, has been structured to project a singular definition of the situation—that of legitimate doctor–patient interaction and, specifically, the nonsexual examination of a woman's vaginal region by a man. To support this definition, team performance is vital (Goffman 1959:104). Although the previous interaction has been part of an ongoing team performance, it has been sequential, leading to the peak of the performance, the vaginal examination itself. At this time, the team goes into a tandem cooperative act, utilizing its resources to maintain the legitimation of the examination. The combined performance reinforces the specific role of each team member. The doctor, while standing, places a disposable latex glove on his right hand, again symbolizing the depersonalized nature of the action: By using the glove, he is saying that he will not himself be actually touching the "private area," that the glove will serve as an insulator.[4] It is at this point that he directs related questions to the patient regarding such things as her bowels or bladder. Then, while he is still in this standing position, the nurse in synchronization actively joins the performance by squeezing a lubricant onto his outstretched gloved fingers, and the doctor inserts the index and middle fingers of his right hand into the patient's vagina while externally palpating (feeling) the uterus. He then withdraws his fingers from the vagina, seats himself on the stool, inserts a speculum, and while the nurse positions the gooseneck lamp behind him, he visually examines the cervix.

Prior to this third scene, the interaction has been dyadic only, consisting of nurse and patient in Scene II and doctor and patient in Scene I. In this scene, however, the interaction becomes triadic, with the doctor, nurse, and patient simultaneously involved in the performance. The term triadic, however, does not even come close to accurately describing the role-playing of this scene. Since the patient has essentially undergone a metamorphosis from a person to an object—having been objectified or depersonalized—the focus of the interaction is now on a specific part of her body. The positioning of her legs, the use of the drape sheet, the shining of the light, and the doctor's location on the stool have made the patient's pubic region the focus of interaction. This location of actors and arrangement and use of props also blocks out the "talk lines" between the doctor and patient, physically obstructing their exchange of glances (Goffman 1963:161). Interaction between the doctor and the patient is no longer "face-to-face," being perhaps now more accurately described as "face-to-pubic" interaction.

BREASTS AS NONSEXUAL OBJECTS

To project and maintain the definition of nonsexuality in the vaginal examination also requires the desexualization of the woman's breasts, since they are attributed to have sexual meaning in our culture. When the breasts are to be examined in conjunction with a vaginal examination, a rather interesting ritual is employed. The goal of this ritual—like that of the vaginal ritual—is to objectify the breasts by isolating them from the rest of the body, permitting the doctor to see the breasts apart from the person. In this ritual, after the patient has removed her upper clothing, a towel is placed across her breasts, and the drape sheet is then placed on top of the towel. Since the towel in and of itself more than sufficiently covers the breasts, we can only conclude that the purpose of the drape sheet is to enhance the definition of nonsexual interaction. Additionally, the doctor first removes the sheet from the breasts, exposing the towel. He then lifts the towel from *one* breast, makes his examination, and *replaces* the towel over that breast. He then examines the other breast in exactly the same way, again replacing the towel after the examination.

THE NURSE AS CHAPERONE

That the interaction in Scene III is triadic is not accidental, nor is it instrumentally necessary. It is, rather, designed to help desexualize the vaginal examination. Instrumentally, the nurse functions merely to lubricate the doctor's fingers and to hand him the speculum. He obviously could do these things himself. It becomes apparent, then, that doing these things is not the purpose of the nurse's presence, that she plays an entirely different role in this scene. That role is chaperone, the person assigned to be present when an unmarried man and woman come together in order to give assurance to interested persons that no sexual acts take place. Although the patient has been depersonalized, or at least this is the definition that the team has been attempting to project and maintain, the possibility exists that the vaginal examination can erupt into a sexual scene. Because of this possibility (or the potential accusation that sexual behavior has taken place), the nurse is always present. Interestingly, with contemporary sexual mores so vastly different from those of a century ago, this medical setting is one of the few remaining examples of the chaperone in our society.[5] It is a significant role, for it helps the performance to be initiated and to continue smoothly to its logical conclusion.

THE PATIENT AS A NONPERSON TEAM MEMBER

With this definition of objectification and desexualization, the patient represents a vagina disassociated from a person. She has been dramaturgically transformed for the duration of this scene into a nonperson (Goffman 1959:152).[6] This means that while he is seated and performing the vaginal examination, the doctor need not interact with the patient as a person; he no longer needs to carry on a conversation nor to maintain eye contact with her. Furthermore, this means that he now is permitted to carry on a "side conversation" with the person with whom he does maintain eye contact, his nurse. For example, during one examination the doctor looked up at the nurse and said: "Hank and I really caught some good-sized fish while we were on vacation. He really enjoyed himself." He then looked at his "work" and announced, "Cervix looks good; no inflammation—everything appears fine down here." Ordinarily, for middle-class interactions such ignoring of the presence of a third person would constitute a breach of etiquette, but *in this case there really isn't a third person present.* The patient has been "depersonalized," to such an extent that the rules of conversation have changed, and no breach of etiquette has taken place.[7]

Although she has been defined as an object, the patient is actually the third member of the team. Her assignment is to "play the role of an object"; that is, she contributes to the flow of the interaction by acting as an object and not as a person. Through studied alienation from the interaction, she demonstrates what is known as dramaturgical discipline (Goffman 1959:216–18). She studiously gazes at the ceiling or wall, only occasionally allowing herself the luxury (or is it the danger?) of fleeting eye contact with the nurse. Eye contact with the doctor, of course, is prevented by the position of her legs and the drape sheet.

After the doctor tells the patient to get dressed, he leaves the room, and the fourth scene is ready to unfold.

Scene IV: The Repersonalizing Stage: The Transition from Pelvic to Person

During this stage of the interaction the patient undergoes a demetamorphosis, dramaturgically changing from vaginal object to person. Immediately after the doctor leaves, the nurse assists the patient into a sitting position, and she gets off the table. The nurse then asks the patient if she would like to use a towel to cleanse her genital area, and about 80 percent of the patients accept the offer. In this scene, it is not uncommon for patients to make some statement concerning their relief that the examination is over. Statements such as "I'm glad that's over with" seem to indicate the patient's overt recognition of the changing scene, to acknowledge that she is now entering a different phase of the drama.

During this repersonalizing stage, the patient is concerned with regrooming and recostuming. Patients frequently ask if they look all right, and the common question "My dress isn't too wrinkled, is it?" appears to indicate the patient's awareness of and desire to be ready for the resumption of roles other than vaginal object. Her dress isn't too wrinkled for what? It must be that she is asking whether it is too wrinkled for (1) her resumption of the role of (patient as) person and (2) her resumption of nonpatient roles.

Modesty continues to operate during this scene, and it is interesting that patients who have just had their genital area thoroughly examined both visually and tactually by the doctor are concerned that this same man will see their underclothing. ("He won't be in before I get my underwear on, will he?") They are now desiring and preparing for the return to the feminine role. They apparently fear that the doctor will reenter the room as they literally have one foot in and one foot out of their panties. They want to have their personal front reestablished to their own satisfaction before the return of this man and the onset of the next scene. For this, they strive for the poise and composure that they deem fitting the person role for which they are now preparing, frequently using either their own pocket-mirror or the mirror above the sink to check their personal front.

During this transitional role, patients indicate by their comments to the nurse that they are to again be treated as persons. While they are dressing, they frequently speak about their medical problems, their aches and pains, their fight against gaining weight, or feelings about their pregnancy. In such ways they are reasserting the self and are indicating that they are again entering "personhood."

The patient who best illustrates awareness that she had undergone a process of repersonalization is the woman who, after putting on her panties, said, "There! Just like new again." She had indeed moved out of her temporary and uncomfortable role as object, and her reappearance as person matched her self-concept.

After the patient has recostumed and regroomed, the nurse directs the patient to a chair alongside the doctor's desk. She then announces via intercom to the doctor, "The patient is dressed," or, "The patient is waiting." It is significant that at this point the woman is referred to as "patient" in the announcement to the doctor and not as "pelvic" as she was at the end of the second scene. Sometimes the patient is also referred to by name in this announcement. The patient has completed her demetamorphosis at this point, and the nurse, by the way she refers to her, is officially announcing the transition.

The nurse then leaves the room, and her interaction with the patient ceases.

Scene V: The Repersonalized Stage: The Patient as Person Once Again

When the doctor makes his third entrance, the patient has again resumed the role of person and is interacted with on this basis. The doctor makes eye contact with her, speaks to her, and listens to her. During this fifth scene, the patient's whole personal front is visible. The doctor informs the patient of the results of her examination, he may prescribe medications, and, wherever indicated, he suggests further care. He also tells the patient whether or not she need see him again.

For us, the significance of the interaction of Scene V is that the patient is again allowed to interact *as a person within the role of patient.* The doctor allows room for questions that the patient might have about the results of the examination, and he also gives her the opportunity to ask about other medical problems that she might be experiencing.

Interaction between the doctor and patient terminates as the doctor gets up from his chair and moves toward the door.

Conclusion: Desexualization of the Sacred

In concluding this analysis, we shall briefly indicate that conceptualizing the vagina as a sacred object yields a perspective that appears to be of value in analyzing the vaginal examination. A sacred object is surrounded by rules protecting the object from being profaned, rules governing who may approach the "sacred," under what circumstances it may be approached, and what may and may not be done during such an approach (Durkheim 1965:51–59). If these rules are followed, the "sacred" will lose none of its "sacredness," but if they are violated, the sacred will be profaned.

Apart from the husband and significant others,[8] except in a medical setting and by the actors about whom we are speaking, no one else may approach the vagina other than the self and still have it retain its sacred character.[9] Because of this, the medical profession has taken great pains to establish a dramaturgical ritual that will ensure the continued sacredness of the vaginas of its female patients, one that will avoid even the imputation of taboo violation. Accordingly, by dramaturgically desexualizing the vagina by dissociating it from the person, and by elaborately defining it as just another organ of the body, this ritual of the vaginal examination allows the doctor to approach the sacred without profaning it or violating taboos. The vaginal examination is a fascinating example of how reality is socially constructed, in this instance of how physicians are able to handle a woman's vagina and yet maintain a definition of nonsexuality.

Notes

1. With a society that is as clothing and bodily conscious as is ours, undressing and nudity are problematic for many, but perhaps more for females than for males since males are more likely to experience structured situations in which they undress and are nude before others, such as showering after high school physical education classes, while females in the same situation are often afforded a greater degree of privacy with, for example, private shower stalls in place of the mass showers of the males. This is not always the case, however, and Theresa France (private communication) reports that in her classes the girls also had communal showers.

2. From a psychiatric orientation this association of the panties with the purse is fascinating, given the Freudian interpretation that the purse signifies the female genitalia.

3. In some examination rooms, the problem of where to put the undergarments is solved by the provision of a special drawer for them located beneath the examination table.

4. It is true, of course, that the glove also serves instrumental purposes, such as protecting the physician from diseases that might be transmitted by means of digital–vaginal contact—and patients from diseases the physician might transmit from one patient to another.

5. It is interesting to note that even the corpse of a female is defined as being in need of such chaperonage. Erving Goffman, on reading this paper in manuscript form, commented that hospital etiquette dictates that "when a male attendant moves a female stiff from the room to the morgue he be accompanied by a female nurse."

6. Compare what Goffman (1959:104) has to say about secrets shared by team members. Remember that the patient in this interaction is not simply a member of the audience. She is also a team member, vitally interested in projecting and maintaining the definition of nonsexuality. Another reader of this paper, who wishes to remain anonymous, reports that during one of her pregnancies she had a handsome, young, and unmarried Hungarian doctor and that during vaginal examinations with him she would "concentrate on the instruments being used and the uncomfortableness of the situation" so as not to become sexually aroused.

7. While "playing the role" of an object, the patient is still able to hear verbal exchange, of course, and she could enter the interaction if she so desired. As such, side comments between doctor and nurse must be limited. In certain other doctor-patient situations, however, the patient completely leaves the "person role," such as when the patient is anesthetized, which allows much freer banter among medical personnel. In delivery rooms of hospitals, for example, it is not uncommon for the obstetrician to comment while stitching the episiotomy, "She's like a new bride now,"

or, when putting in the final stitch, to say, "This is for the old man." Additionally, while medical students are stitching their first episiotomy, instructing doctors have been known to say, "It's not tight enough. Put one more in for the husband."

8. Consensual approaches by boyfriends certainly run less risk of violating the sacred than at earlier periods in our history, yet this depends a good deal on the individual's religion and age.

9. It is perhaps for this reason that prostitutes ordinarily lack respect: They have profaned the sacred. And in doing so, not only have they failed to limit vaginal access to culturally prescribed individuals, but they have added further violation by allowing vaginal access on a monetary basis. They have, in effect, sold the sacred.

Many obstetricians do not want prostitutes to be their patients. The greater incidence of diseases among prostitutes may be part of the reason for this, but so is their derided status.

References

Durkheim, Emile (1965). *The Elementary Forms of the Religious Life.* New York: The Free Press (1915 copyright by George Allen & Unwin Ltd.).

Goffman, Erving (1959). *The Presentation of Self in Everyday Life.* Garden City, NY: Doubleday Anchor Books.

Goffman, Erving (1963). *Behavior in Public Places: Notes on the Social Organization of Gatherings.* New York: The Free Press.

Gross, Edward, and Gregory Stone (1964). "Embarrassment and the Analysis of Role Requirements," *American Journal of Sociology 70:* 1–15.

19 Diary of a Homeless Man

JOHN R. COLEMAN

Can you imagine yourself being without a home? Think of what it must be like not to have a house or apartment, not to have your own room or even one you must share with a sibling. No living room with television, no kitchen with a refrigerator you can "raid" whenever you want. Night falls, and you don't know where you'll sleep. Day breaks, and you have no place to go, nothing to do—and on top of this, no one who cares.

Such is life for some people in our society—the discards of the advanced technological society, those who have been left behind in our culturally mandated frenetic pursuit after material wealth. Like others, Coleman, the president of a small, private college, had seen these strange, disheveled, and forsaken looking people on the streets of the city. Like others, he had passed them by, occasionally wondering what their life was like. But unlike most others, he decided to find out first hand—by directly experiencing their world. He left his comfortable, upper–middle-class home and joined the street people. This is his engrossing account of that experience.

Wednesday, 1/19

SOMEHOW, 12 DEGREES at 6 A.M. was colder than I had counted on. I think of myself as relatively immune to cold, but standing on a deserted sidewalk outside Penn Station with the thought of ten days ahead of me as a homeless man, the immunity vanished. When I pulled my collar closer and my watch cap lower, it wasn't to look the part of a street person; it was to keep the wind out.

My wardrobe wasn't much help. I had bought my "new" clothes—flannel shirt, baggy sweater, torn trousers, the cap and the coat—the day before on Houston Street for $19. "You don't need to buy shoes," the shopkeeper had said. "The ones you have on will pass for a bum's." I was hurt; they were shoes I often wore to the office.

Having changed out of my normal clothes in the Penn Station men's room and stowed them in a locker, I was ready for the street. Or thought so.

Was I imagining it, or were people looking at me in a completely different way? I felt that men, especially the successful-looking ones in their forties and over, saw me and wondered. For the rest, I wasn't there.

At Seventh Avenue and 35th Street, I went into a coffee shop. The counterman looked me over carefully. When I ordered the breakfast special—99 cents plus tax—he told me I'd have to pay in advance. I did (I'd brought $40 to see me through the ten days), but I noticed that the other customers were given checks, and paid only when they left.

By 9:30, I had read a copy of the *Times* retrieved from a trash basket; I had walked most of the streets around the station; I had watched the construction at the new convention center. There was little else to do.

Later, I sat and watched the drug sales going on in Union Square. Then I went into the Income Maintenance Center on 14th Street and watched the people moving through the welfare lines. I counted the trucks on Houston Street.

I vaguely remembered a quote to the effect that "idleness is only enjoyable when you have a lot to do." It would help to be warm, too.

There was ample time and incentive to stare at the other homeless folk on the street. For the most part, they weren't more interesting than the typical faces on Wall Street or upper Madison Avenue. But the extreme cases caught and held the eye. On Ninth Avenue, there was a man on the sidewalk directing an imaginary (to me) flow of traffic. And another, two blocks away, tracing the flight of planes or birds—or spirits—in the winter sky. And there was a woman with gloves tied to her otherwise bare feet.

Standing outside the Port Authority Bus Terminal was a man named Howard. He was perhaps my age, but the seasons had left deeper marks on his face. "Come summertime, it's all going to be different," he told me. "I'm going to have a car to go to the beach. And I'm going to get six lemons and make me a jug of ice-cold lemonade to go with the car.

"This whole country's gone too far with the idea of one person being at the top. It starts with birthday parties. Who gets to blow out the candle? One person. And it takes off from there. If we're ever going to make things better, we gotta start with those candles."

Was there any chance of people like us finding work?

"Jobs are still out there for the young guys who want them," Howard said. "But there's nothing for us. Never again. No, I stopped dreaming about jobs a long time ago. Now I dream about cars. And lemonade."

Drugs and alcohol are common among the homeless. The damage done by them was evident in almost every street person I saw. But which was cause, and which was effect? Does it matter, once this much harm has been done?

My wanderings were all aimless. There was no plan, no goal, no reason to be anywhere at any time. Only hours into this role, I felt a useless part of the city streets. I wasn't even sure why I was doing this. . . .

A weathered drifter told me about a hideaway down in the bowels of the station, where it was warm and quiet. I found my way there and lay down on some old newspapers to sleep.

How long did I sleep? It didn't seem long at all. I was awakened by a flashlight shining in my eyes, and a voice, not an unkind one, saying, "You can't sleep here. Sorry, but you have to go outside."

I hadn't expected to hear that word "sorry." It was touching.

I left and walked up to 47th Street, between Fifth and Madison Avenues, where I knew there was a warm grate in the sidewalk. (I've been passing it every morning for over five years on my way to work.) One man was asleep there already. But there was room for two, and he moved over.

Thursday, 1/20

When you're spending the night on the street, you learn to know morning is coming by the kinds of trucks that roll by. As soon as there are other than garbage trucks—say, milk or bread trucks—you know the night will soon be over.

I went back to Penn Station to clean up in the washroom. The care with which some of the other men with me bathed themselves at the basins would have impressed any public-health officer. And I couldn't guess from the appearance of their clothes who would be the most fastidious.

I bought coffee and settled back to enjoy it out of the main traffic paths in the station. No luck. A cop found me and told me to take it to the street.

After breakfast ($1.31 at Blimpie), I walked around to keep warm until the public library opened. I saw in a salvaged copy of the *Times* that we had just had our coldest night of the year, well below zero with the windchill factor, and that a record 4,635 people had sought shelter in the city's hostels.

The library was a joy. The people there treated me the same as they might have had I been wearing my business suit. To pass the time, I got out the city's welfare reports for 50 years ago. In the winter of 1933, the city had 4,524 beds available for the homeless, and all were said to be filled every night. The parallel to 1983 was uncanny. But, according to the reports, the man in charge of the homeless program in 1933, one Joseph A. Manning, wasn't worried about the future. True, the country was in the midst of a depression. But there had been a slight downturn in the numbers served in the shelters in the two months immediately preceding his report. This meant, wrote Manning, that "the depression, in the parlance of the ring, is K.O.'d."

Already, I notice changes in me. I walk much more slowly. I no longer see a need to beat a traffic light or to be the first through a revolving door.

Force of habit still makes me look at my wrist every once in a while. But there's no watch there, and it wouldn't make any difference if there were. The thermometer has become much more important to me now than any time-piece could be. . . .

The temperature rose during the day. Just as the newspaper headlines seem to change more slowly when you're on the streets all day long, so the temperature seems to change more rapidly and tellingly.

At about 9 P.M., I went back to the heated grate on 47th Street. The man who had been there last night was already in place. He made it clear that there was again room for me.

I asked him how long he had been on the streets.

"Eleven years, going on twelve," he said.

"This is only my second night."

"You may not stick it out. This isn't for every man."

"Do you ever go into the shelters?"

"I couldn't take that. I prefer this anytime."

Friday, 1/21

When I left my grate mate—long before dawn—he wished me a good day. I returned the gesture. He meant his, and I meant mine.

In Manhattan's earliest hours, you get the feeling that the manufacture and removal of garbage is the city's main industry. So far, I haven't been lucky or observant enough to rescue much of use from the mounds of trash waiting for the trucks and crews. The best find was a canvas bag that will fit nicely over my feet at night.

I'm slipping into a routine: Washing up at the station. Coffee on the street. Breakfast at Blimpie. A search for the *Times* in the trash baskets. And then a leisurely stretch of reading in the park.

Some days bring more luck than others. Today I found 20 cents in a pay-phone slot and heard a young flutist playing the music of C.P.E. Bach on Sixth Avenue between 9th and 10th streets. A lot of people ignored her, even stepped over her flute case as if it were litter on the sidewalk. More often than not, those who put money in the case looked embarrassed. They seemed to be saying, "Don't let anyone see me being appreciative."

By nightfall, the streets were cruelly cold once again. . . .

I headed for the 47th Street grate again but found my mate gone. There was no heat coming up through it. Do they turn it off on Friday nights? Don't we homeless have any rights?

On the northwest corner of Eighth Avenue and 33rd Street, there was a blocked-off subway entrance undergoing repair. I curled up against the wall there under some cardboard sheets. Rain began to fall, but I stayed reasonably dry and was able to get to sleep.

At some point, I was awakened by a man who had pulled back the upper piece of cardboard.

"You see my partner here. You need to give us some money."

I was still half-asleep. "I don't have any."

"You must have something, man."

"Would I be sleeping here in the rain if I did?"

His partner intervened. "C'mon. Leave the old bastard alone. He's not worth it."

"He's got something. Get up and give it to us."

I climbed to my feet and began fumbling in my pocket. Both men were on my left side. That was my chance. Suddenly I took off and ran along 33rd Street toward Ninth Avenue. They gave no chase. And a good thing, too, because I was too stiff with cold to run a good race.

Saturday, 1/22

A man I squatted next to in a doorway on 29th Street said it all: "The onliest thing is to have a warm place to sleep. That and having somebody care about you. That'd be even onlier."

He had what appeared to be rolls of paper toweling wrapped around one leg and tied with red ribbon. But the paper, wet with rain by now, didn't seem to serve any purpose.

I slept little. The forecast was for more rain tomorrow, so why wish the night away?

The morning paper carried news of Mayor Koch's increased concern about the homeless.

But what can he do? He must worry that the more New York does to help, the greater the numbers will grow. At the moment he's berating the synagogues for not doing anything to take street people in.

Watching people come and go at the Volvo tennis tournament at Madison Square Garden, I sensed how uncomfortable they were at the presence of the homeless. Easy to love in the abstract, not so easy face to face.

It's no wonder that the railway police are under orders to chase us out of sight.

Perhaps a saving factor is that we're not individuals. We're not people anybody knows. So far I've had eye contact with only three people who know me in my other life. None showed a hint of recognition. One was the senior auditor at Arthur Andersen & Company, the accounting firm that handles the Clark Foundation, my employer. One was a fellow lieutenant in the Auxiliary

Police Force, a man with whom I had trained for many weeks. And one was an owner in the cooperative apartment where I live. . . .

Early in the evening I fell asleep on the Seventh Avenue steps outside the Garden. Three Amtrak cops shook me awake to ask if two rather good-looking suitcases on the steps were mine. I said that I had never seen them.

One cop insisted that I was lying, but then a black man appeared and said they belonged to a friend of his. The rapid-fire questioning from two of the cops soon made that alibi rather unlikely. The third cop was going through the cases and spreading a few of the joints he found inside on the ground.

As suddenly as it had begun, the incident was over. The cops walked away, and the man retrieved the bags. I fell back to sleep. Some hours later when I woke up again, the black man was still there, selling.

Sunday, 1/23

A new discovery of a warm and dry, even scenic, place to sit on a rainy day: the Staten Island Ferry.

For one 25-cent fare, I had four crossings of the harbor, read all I wanted of the copy of the Sunday *Times* I'd found, and finished the crossword puzzle.

When I got back to the Garden, where the tennis tournament was in its last hours, I found the police were being extra diligent in clearing us away from the departing crowds. One older woman was particularly incensed at being moved. "You're ruining my sex life," she shouted. "That's what you're doing. My sex life. Do you hear?"

A younger woman approached me to ask if I was looking for love. "No, ma'am. I'm just trying to stay out of the rain." . . .

So, back to the unused subway entrance, because there was still no heat across town on the 47th Street grate.

The night was very cold. Parts of me ached as I tried to sleep. Turning over was a chore, not only because the partially wet cardboard had to be re-arranged with such care, but also because the stiffer parts of my body seemed to belong to someone else. Whatever magic there was in those lights cutting down through the fog was gone by now. All I wanted was to be warm and dry once more. Magic could wait.

Monday, 1/24

Early this morning I went to the warren of employment agencies on 14th Street to see if I could get a day's work. There was very little action at most of these last-ditch offices, where minimum wages and sub-minimum conditions are the rule.

But I did get one interview and thought I had a dishwashing job lined up. I'd forgotten one thing. I had no identification with me. No identification, no job.

There was an ageless, shaggy woman in Bryant Park this morning who delivered one of the more interesting monologues I've heard. For a full ten minutes, with no interruption from me beyond an occasional "Uh huh," she analyzed society's ills without missing a beat.

Beginning with a complaint about the women's and men's toilets in the park being locked ("What's a poor body to do?"), she launched into the strengths of the Irish, who, though strong, still need toilets more than others, and the weaknesses of the English and the Jews, the advantages of raising turkeys over other fowl, and the wickedness of Eleanor Roosevelt in letting the now Queen Mother and that stuttering king of hers rave so much about the hot dogs served at Hyde Park that we had no alternative but to enter World War II on their side. The faulty Russian satellite that fell into the Indian Ocean this morning was another example of shenanigans, she said. It turns out the Russians and Lady Diana, "that so-called Princess of Wales," are in cahoots to keep us so alarmed about such things far away from home that we don't get anything done about prayer in schools or the rest of it. But after all, what would those poor Protestant ministers do for a living if the children got some real religion in school, like the kind we got from the nuns, God bless them?

That at least was the gist of what she said. I know I've missed some of the finer points.

At 3:30 P.M., with more cold ahead, I sought out the Men's Shelter at 8 East 3rd Street. This is the principal entry point for men seeking the city's help. It provides meals for 1,300 or so people every day and beds for some few of those. I had been told that while there was no likelihood of getting a bed in this building I'd be given a meal here and a bed in some other shelter.

I've seen plenty of drawings of London's workhouses and asylums in the times of Charles Dickens. Now I've seen the real thing, in the last years of the twentieth century in the world's greatest city.

The lobby and the adjacent "sitting room" were jammed with men standing, sitting, or stretched out in various positions on the floor. It was as lost a collection of souls as I could have imagined. Old and young, scarred and smooth, stinking and clean, crippled and hale, drunk and sober, ranting and still, parts of another world and parts of this one. The city promises to take in anyone who asks. Those rejected everywhere else find their way to East 3rd Street.

The air was heavy with the odors of Thunderbird wine, urine, sweat, and, above all, nicotine and marijuana. Three or four Human Resources Administration police officers seemed to be keeping the violence down to tolerable levels, but barely so.

After a long delay, I got a meal ticket for dinner and was told to come back later for a lodging ticket.

It was time to get in line to eat. This meant crowding into what I can only compare to a cattle chute in a stockyard. It ran along two walls of the sitting room and was already jammed. A man with a bullhorn kept yelling at us to stand up and stay in line. One very old and decrepit (or drunk?) man couldn't stay on his feet. He was helped to a chair, from which he promptly fell onto the floor. The bullhorn man had some choice obscenities for him, but they didn't seem to have any effect. The old man just lay there; and we turned our thoughts back to the evening meal.

I made a quick, and probably grossly unfair, assessment of the hundreds of men I could see in the room. Judging them solely by appearance, alertness, and body movements, I decided that one-quarter of them were perfectly able to work; they, more likely than not, were among the warriors who helped us win the battle against inflation by the selfless act of joining the jobless ranks. Another quarter might be brought back in time into job-readiness by some counseling and some caring for them as individuals. But the other half seemed so ravaged by illness, addiction, and sheer neglect that I couldn't imagine them being anything but society's wards from here on out to—one hopes—a peaceful end.

At the appointed hour, we were released in groups of twenty or thirty to descend the dark, filthy steps to the basement eating area. The man with the bullhorn was there again, clearly in charge and clearly relishing the extra power given to his voice by electric amplification. He insulted us collectively and separately without pause, but because his vocabulary was limited it tended to be the same four-letter words over and over.

His loudest attack on me came when I didn't move fast enough to pick up my meal from the counter. His analysis of certain flaws in my white ancestry wasn't hard to follow, even for a man in as much of a daze as I was.

The shouting and the obscenities didn't stop once we had our food. Again and again we were told to finish and get out. Eating took perhaps six minutes, but those minutes removed any shred of dignity a man might have brought in with him from the street.

Back upstairs, the people in charge were organizing the people who were to go to a shelter in Brooklyn. Few had volunteered, so there was more haranguing.

In the line next to the one where I was waiting for my lodging ticket a fight suddenly broke out. One man pulled a long knife from his overcoat pocket. The other man ran for cover, and a police officer soon appeared to remove the man with the knife from the scene. The issue, it seems, was one of proper places in the line.

There still weren't enough Brooklyn volunteers to suit the management, so they brought in their big gun: Mr. Bullhorn. "Now, listen up," he barked. "There aren't any buses going to Ft. Washington [another shelter] until 11:30, so if you want to get some sleep, go to Brooklyn. Don't ask me any questions. Just shut up and listen. It's because you don't listen up that you end up in a place like this."

I decided to ask a question anyway, about whether there would still be a chance for me to go to Brooklyn once I got my lodging ticket. He turned on me and let me have the full force of the horn: "Don't ask questions, I said. You're not nobody."

The delays at the ticket-issuing window went on and on. Three staff members there seemed reasonably polite and even efficient. The fourth and heaviest one—I have no idea whether it was a man or woman—could not have moved more slowly without coming to a dead halt. The voice of someone who was apparently a supervisor came over the public-address system from time to time to apologize for the delay in going to the Ft. Washington shelter, which was in an armory, but any good he did from behind the scenes was undone by the staff out front and a "see-no-work, hear-no-work, do-no-work" attendant in the office.

As 11:30 approached, we crowded back into the sitting room to get ready to board the buses. A new martinet had appeared on the scene. He got as much attention through his voice, cane, and heavy body as Mr. Bullhorn had with his amplifying equipment. But this new man was more openly vile and excitable; he loved the power that went with bunching us all up close together and then ordering us to stretch out again in a thinner line. We practiced that routine several times. . . .

Long after the scheduled departure, the lines moved. We sped by school buses to the armory at Ft. Washington Avenue and 168th Street. There we were met, just before 2:30 A.M., by military police, social workers, and private guards. They marched us into showers (very welcome), gave us clean underwear, and sent us upstairs to comfortable cots arranged in long rows in a room as big as a football field.

There were 530 of us there for the night, and we were soon quiet.

Tuesday, 1/25

We were awakened at 6 A.M. by whistles and shouting, and ordered to get back onto the buses for the return trip to lower Manhattan as soon as possible.

Back at 8 East 3rd Street, the worst of the martinets were off duty. So I thought breakfast might be a bit quieter than dinner had been. Still, by eight, I had seen three incidents a bit out of the ordinary for me.

A man waiting for breakfast immediately ahead of me in the cattle chute suddenly grabbed a chair from the adjoining area and prepared to break it over his neighbor's head. In my haste to get out of the way, I fell over an older man sleeping against the wall. After some shouts about turf, things cooled off between the fighters, and the old man forgave me.

In the stairwell leading down to the eating area, a young man made a sexual advance to me. When I withdrew from him and stupidly reached for my coat pocket, he thought I was going for a weapon. He at once pinned me against the wall and searched my pockets; there was nothing there.

As I came out of the building onto East 3rd Street, two black Human Resources Administration policemen were bringing two young blacks into the building. One officer had his man by the neck. The other officer had his man's hands cuffed behind his back and repeatedly kicked him hard in the buttocks.

My wanderings were still more aimless today. I couldn't get East 3rd Street out of my mind. What could possibly justify some of that conduct? If I were a staff member there, would I become part of the worst in that pattern? Or would I simply do as little, and think as little, as possible?

At day's end I can't recall much of where I went or why I went there.

Only isolated moments remain with me. Like . . . staring at the elegant crystal and silver in the shops just north of Madison Square Park and wondering what these windows say to the people I'd spent the night with.

Much too soon it was time to go back to the shelter for dinner and another night. At first I thought I didn't have the guts to do it again. Does one have to do *this* to learn who the needy are? I wanted to say, "Enough! There's only so much I need to see."

But I went back to the shelter anyway, probably because it took more guts to quit than it did to go ahead.

A man beside me in the tense dinner line drove one truth of this place home to me. "I never knew hell came in this color," he said.

I was luckier in my assignment for the night. I drew the Keener Building, on Wards Island, a facility with a capacity of 416 men. The building was old and neglected, and the atmosphere of a mental hospital, which it once was, still hung over it. But the staff was polite, the rooms weren't too crowded (there were only twelve beds in Room 326), the single sheet on each bed was clean, and there was toilet paper in the bathroom.

There were limits and guards and deprivations, but there was also an orderliness about the place. Here, at least, I didn't feel I had surrendered all of my dignity at the door.

Wednesday, 1/26

. . . Back to the shelter on East 3rd Street for dinner.

There is simply no other situation I've seen that is so devoid of any graces at all, so tense at every moment, or so empty of hope. The food isn't bad, and the building is heated; that's all it has going for it.

The only cutlery provided is a frail plastic spoon. With practice you can spread hard oleo onto your bread with the back of one. If there's liver or ham, you don't have to cut it; just put it between the two pieces of bread that go with each meal. Everything else—peas, collard greens, apple pudding, plums—can be managed with the spoon. And talk over dinner or sipping, rather than gulping, coffee isn't all that important.

What is hardest to accept is the inevitable jungle scene during the hour you stand in line waiting to eat. Every minute seems to be one that invites an explosion. You know instinctively that men can't come this often to the brink without someone going over. One person too many is going to try to jump ahead in line. One particular set of toes is going to be stepped on by mistake. And the lid is going to blow.

The most frightening people here are the many young, intensely angry blacks. Hatred pours out in all of their speech and some of their actions. I could spend a lot of time imagining how and why they became so completely angry—but if I were the major, the counselor, or the man with the bullhorn, I wouldn't know how to divert them from that anger any more. Hundreds and hundreds of men here have been destroyed by alcohol or drugs. A smaller, but for me more poignant, number are being destroyed by hate.

Their loudest message—and because their voices are so strong it is very loud indeed—is "Respect me, man." The constant theme is that someone or some group is putting them down, stepping on them, asking them to conform to a code they don't accept, getting in their way, writing them off.

So most of the fights begin over turf. A place in line. A corner to control. The have-nots scrapping with the have-nots. . . .

Tonight, I chose the Brooklyn shelter because I thought the buses going there would leave soonest. The shelter, a converted school, is on Williams Avenue and has about 400 beds.

We left in fairly good time but learned when we got to the shelter that no new beds would be assigned until after 11 P.M. We were to sit in the auditorium until then.

At about ten, a man herded as many of us newcomers as would listen to him into a corner of the auditorium. There he delivered an abusive diatribe outlining the horror that lay ahead for our possessions and our bodies during the night to come. It made the ranting at East 3rd Street seem tame.

It's illustrative of what the experience of homelessness and helplessness does to people that all of us—regardless of age, race, background, or health—listened so passively.

Only at midnight, when some other officials arrived, did we learn that this man had no standing whatsoever. He was just an underling who strutted for his time on the stage before any audience cowed enough to take what he dished out. . . .

Thursday, 1/27

Back on the street this morning, I became conscious of how little time I had left to live this way. There seemed so much still to do, and so little time in which to do it.

One part of me tells me I have been fully a part of this. I know I walk with slower steps and bent shoulders. . . . I know I worry a lot more about keeping clean.

But then I recall how foolish that is, I'm acting. This will end tomorrow night. I can quit any time I want to. And unlike my mate from 47th Street, I haven't the slightest idea of what eleven years of sleeping on a grate amount to.

Early this afternoon, I went again to the Pavilion restaurant, where I had eaten five times before. I didn't recognize the man at the cash register.

"Get out," he said.

"But I have money."

"You heard me. Get out." His voice was stronger.

"That man knows me," I said, looking toward the owner in the back of the restaurant.

The owner nodded, and the man at the register said, "Okay, but sit in the back."

If this life in the streets had been real, I'd have gone out the door at the first "Get out." And the assessment of me as not worthy would have been self-fulfilling; I'd have lost so much respect for myself that I wouldn't have been worthy of being served the next time. The downward spiral would have begun.

Until now I haven't understood the extent of nicotine addiction. Dependencies on drugs and alcohol have been around me for a long time, but I thought before that smoking was a bad habit rather easy to overcome.

How many times have I, a nonsmoker, been begged for a cigarette in these days? Surely hundreds. Cigarettes are central. A few folks give them away, a small number sell them for up to 8 cents apiece, and almost all give that last pathetic end of a butt to the first man who asks for what little bit is left. I know addiction now as I didn't before.

Tonight, after a repeat of the totally degrading dinner-line scene at East 3rd Street, I signed up for Keener once again. No more Brooklyn for me.

Sitting upstairs with the other Keener-bound men, I carelessly put my left foot on the rung of the chair in front of me, occupied by a young black.

"Get your foot off, yo."

("Yo" means "Hey, there," "Watch yourself," "Move along," and much more.)

I took it off. "Sorry," I said.

But it was too late. I had broken a cardinal rule. I had violated the man's turf. As we stood in the stairwell waiting for the buses, he told a much bigger, much louder, much angrier friend what I had done.

That man turned on me.

"Wait till we get you tonight, whitey. You stink. Bad. The worst I've ever smelled. And when you put your foot on that chair, you spread your stink around. You better get yourself a shower as soon as we get there, but it won't save you later on. . . . And don't sit near me or him on the bus. You hear, whitey?"

I didn't reply.

The bombardment went on as we mounted the bus. No one spoke up in my defense. Three people waved me away when I tried to sit next to them. The next person, black and close to my age, made no objection when I sat beside him.

The big man continued to tirade for a while, but he soon got interested in finding out from the driver how to go about getting a bus-driver's license. Perhaps he had come down from a high.

I admit I was scared. I wrote my name, address, and office telephone number on a piece of paper and slipped it into my pocket. At least someone would know where to call if the threats were real. I knew I couldn't and wouldn't defend myself in this setting.

While we stood in line on Wards Island waiting for our bed assignments, there were plenty of gripes about the man who was after me. But no one said anything directly to him. Somehow it didn't seem that this was the night when the meek would inherit the earth.

I slept fitfully. I don't like lying with the sheet hiding my face.

Friday, 1/28

I was up and out of Keener as early as possible. That meant using some of my little remaining money for a city-bus ride back to Manhattan, but it was worth it to get out of there.

After breakfast on East 3rd Street, I was finished with the public shelters. That was an easy break for me to make, because I had choices and could run.

The day was cold and, for the early hours, clear. I washed the memory of the big man at 3rd Street out of my mind by wandering through the Fulton Fish Market. I walked across the Brooklyn Bridge and even sang as I realized how free I was to relax and enjoy its beauty.

With a cup of coffee and the *Times,* I sat on a cinder block by the river and read. In time, I wandered through the Wall Street district and almost learned the lay of some of the streets.

I walked up to the Quaker Meeting House at Rutherford Place and 15th Street. Standing on the porch outside, I tried hard to think how the doctrine that "there is that of God in every person" applied to that man last night and to some of the others I had encountered in these ten days. I still think it applies, but it isn't always easy to see how. . . .

Darkness came. I got kicked out of both the bus terminal and Grand Central. I got my normal clothes out of the locker at Penn Station, changed in the men's room, and rode the AA train home.

My apartment was warm, and the bed was clean.

That's the onliest thing.

20 Handling the Stigma of Handling the Dead

WILLIAM E. THOMPSON

Life expectancy used to be short. As a result, at an early age people became personally acquainted with death. In 1900, the average American died by the age of 40, and children were likely to witness the death of one of their parents. Death seemed to hover over them, ready to intrude at any time. Consider a popular child's prayer from a few generations back. Each night as they went to bed, little Christian children, as young as two and three years, would kneel at their bedside, and say this prayer:

> Now I lay me down to sleep.
> I pray the Lord my soul to keep.
> If I should die before I wake,
> I pray the Lord my soul to take.

Death was also a family affair. Not only did people die at home, but also their mothers, wives, and sisters washed and dressed the body and the men made the coffin. Wakes (grieving ceremonies) were also held at home, with the body put on display in the "parlor," where family, friends, and neighbors "paid their last respects."

Today, in contrast, our life expectancy is almost double what it was, and we try to insulate ourselves from death. People die in hospitals, attended by strangers. Other strangers deliver the body to a funeral home. There, still more strangers prepare the body for burial by draining its blood and replacing it with embalming fluids. Afterward, these strangers dress the body in clothing selected by relatives, comb the hair, put makeup on the face, and place the body on display in a room reserved for this purpose (sometimes called "the eternal slumber room"). These strangers also transport the body in a special vehicle to the graveyard. Who are these "death specialists" who handle dead bodies, and how do they handle the stigma that comes from handling the dead? This is the focus of Thompson's article.

IN A COMPLEX, industrialized society a person's occupation or profession is central to his or her personal and social identity. As Pavalko (1988) pointed out, two strangers are quite ". . . likely to 'break the ice' by indicating the kind of work they do." As a result, individuals often made a number of initial judgments about others based on preconceived notions about particular occupations.

This study examines how morticians and funeral directors handle the stigma associated with their work. Historically, stigma has been attached to those responsible for caring for the dead, and the job typically was assigned to the lower classes (e.g., the Eta of Japan and the Untouchables in India), and in some cases, those who handled the dead were forbidden from touching the living.

Morticians and funeral directors are fully aware of the stigma associated with their work, so they continually strive to enhance their public image and promote their social credibility. They must work to shift the emphasis on their work from the dead to the living, and away from sales and toward service. As Aries (1976, 99) noted:

> In order to sell death, it had to be made friendly . . . since 1885 . . . [funeral directors have] presented themselves not as simple sellers of services, but as "doctors of grief" who have a mission . . . [which] consists in aiding the mourning survivors to return to normalcy.

Couched within the general theoretical framework of symbolic interactionism, there are a variety of symbolic and dramaturgical methods whereby morticians and funeral directors attempt to redefine their occupations and minimize and/or neutralize negative attitudes toward them and what they do.

Method

This study reflects over 2 years of qualitative fieldwork. Extensive ethnographic interviews were conducted with 19 morticians and funeral directors in four states: Kansas, Missouri, Oklahoma, and Texas. The funeral homes included both privately owned businesses and branches of large franchise operations.

Interviewees included people from different age groups, both sexes, and both whites and nonwhites. There were 16 males and 3 females interviewed for this study, ranging in age from 26 to 64 years.

The Stigma of Handling the Dead

Until [about 1900] in this country, people died at home and friends and family members prepared the bodies for burial (Lesy, 1987). As medical knowledge and technology progressed and became more specialized, more and more deaths occurred outside the home—usually in hospitals. Death became something to be handled by a select group of highly trained professionals—doctors, nurses, and hospital staff. As fewer people witnessed death firsthand, it became surrounded with more mystery, and physically handling the dead became the domain of only a few.

Members or friends of the family relinquished their role in preparing bodies for disposal to an *undertaker,* ". . . a special person who would 'undertake'. responsibility for the care and burial of the dead" (Amos, 1983, 2). Most states began licensing embalmers around the end of the nineteenth century (Amos, 1983). These licensed embalmers were viewed as unusual, if not downright weird. They were not family members or friends of the deceased faced with the unsavory but necessary responsibility for disposing of a loved one's body, but strangers who *chose* to work with dead bodies—for compensation. Although most welcomed the opportunity to relinquish this chore they also viewed those who willingly assumed it with some skepticism and even disdain.

Sudnow (1967, 51–64) underscored the negative attitudes toward people who work with the dead in describing how those who work in a morgue, for example, are "death-tainted" and work very hard to rid themselves of the social stigma associated with their jobs. Morticians and funeral directors cannot escape from this "taint of death" and they must constantly work to "counteract the stigma" directed at them and their occupations.

Are morticians and funeral directors really that stigmatized? After all, they generally are well-known and respected members of their communities. In small communities and even many large cities, local funeral homes have been owned and operated by the same family for several generations. These people usually are members of civic organizations, have substantial incomes, and live in nice homes and drive nice automobiles. Most often they are viewed as successful business people. On the other hand, their work is surrounded by mystery, taboos, and stigma, and they often are viewed as cold, detached, and downright morbid for doing it. All the respondents in this study openly acknowledged that stigma was associated with their work. Some indicated that they thought the stigma primarily came from the "misconception" that they were "getting rich" off other people's grief; others believed it simply came from working with the dead. Clearly these two aspects of their work—handling the dead and profiting from death and grief—emerged as the two most stigmatizing features of the funeral industry according to respondents.

Managing Stigma

Erving Goffman wrote the most systematic analysis of how individuals manage a "spoiled" social identity in his classic work, *Stigma* (1963). He described several techniques, such as "passing," "dividing the social world," "mutual aid," "physical distance," "disclosure," and "covering," employed by the *discredited* and *discreditable* to manage information and conceal their stigmatizing attributes (41–104). Although these techniques work well for the physically scarred, blind, stammerers, bald, drug addicted, ex-convicts, and many other stigmatized categories of people, they are less likely to be used by morticians and funeral directors.

Except perhaps when on vacation, it is important for funeral directors to be known and recognized in their communities and to be associated with their work. Consequently, most of the morticians and funeral directors studied relied on other strategies for reducing the stigma associated with their work. Paramount among these strategies were: symbolic redefinition of their work, role distance, professionalism, emphasizing service, and enjoying socioeconomic status over occupational prestige. This was much less true for licensed embalmers who worked for funeral directors, especially in chain-owned funeral homes in large cities. In those cases the author found that many embalmers concealed their occupation from their neighbors and others with whom they were not intimately acquainted.

SYMBOLIC REDEFINITION

One of the ways in which morticians and funeral directors handle the stigma of their occupations is through symbolically negating as much of it as possible. Woods and Delisle (1978, 98) revealed how sympathy cards avoid the use of the terms "dead" and "death" by substituting less harsh words such as "loss," "time of sorrow," and "hour of sadness." This technique is also used by morticians and funeral directors to reduce the stigma associated with their work.

Words that are most closely associated with death are rarely used, and the most harsh terms are replaced with less ominous ones. The term *death* is almost never used by funeral directors; rather, they talk of "passing on," "meeting an untimely end," or "eternal slumber." There are no *corpses* or *dead bodies;* they are referred to as "remains" "the deceased," "loved one," or more frequently, by name (e.g., "Mr. Jones"). Use of the term *body* is almost uniformly avoided around the family. Viewing rooms (where the embalmed body is displayed in the casket) usually are given serene names such as "the sunset room," "the eternal slumber room," or, in one case, "the guest room." Thus, when friends or family arrive to view the body, they are likely to be told that "Mr. Jones is lying in repose in the eternal slumber room." This language contrasts sharply with that used by morticians and funeral directors in "backstage" areas (Goffman, 1959, 112) such as the embalming room where drowning victims often are called "floaters," burn victims are called "crispy critters," and others are simply referred to as "bodies" (Turner and Edgley, 1976).

All the respondents indicated that there was less stigma attached to the term *funeral director* than *mortician* or *embalmer,* underscoring the notion that much of the stigma they experienced was attached to physically handling the dead. Consequently, when asked what they do for a living, those who acknowledge that they are in the funeral business (several indicated that they often do not) referred to themselves as "funeral directors" even if all they did was the embalming. *Embalming* is referred to as "preservation" or "restoration," and in order to be licensed, one must have studied "mortuary arts" or "mortuary science." Embalming no longer takes place in an *embalming room,* but in a "preparation room," or in some cases the "operating room."

Coffins are now "caskets," which are transported in "funeral coaches" (not *hearses*) to their "final resting place" rather than to the *cemetery* or worse yet, *graveyard,* for their "interment" rather than *burial.* Thus, linguistically, the symbolic redefinition is complete, with death verbally redefined during every phase, and the stigma associated with it markedly reduced.

All the morticians and funeral directors in this study emphasized the importance of using the "appropriate" terms in referring to their work. Knowledge of the stigma attached to certain words was readily acknowledged, and all indicated that the earlier terminology was stigma-laden, especially the term "undertaker," which they believed conjured up negative images in the mind of the public. For example, a 29-year-old male funeral director indicated that his father still insisted on calling himself an "undertaker." "He just hasn't caught up with [modern times]," the son remarked. Interestingly, when asked why he did not refer to himself as an undertaker, he replied "It just sounds so old-fashioned [pause] plus, it sounds so morbid."

In addition to using language to symbolically redefine their occupations, funeral directors carefully attempt to shift the focus of their work away from the care of the dead (especially handling the body), and redefine it primarily in terms of caring for the living. The dead are deemphasized as most of the funeral ritual is orchestrated for the benefit of the friends and family of the deceased (Turner and Edgley, 1976). By redefining themselves as "grief therapists," or "bereavement counselors" their primary duties are associated with making funeral arrangements, directing the services, and consoling the family in their time of need.

ROLE DISTANCE

Because a person' sense of self is so strongly linked to occupation, it is common practice for people in undesirable or stigmatized occupations to practice role distance. Although the specific role-distancing techniques vary across different occupations and among different individuals within an occupation, they share the common function of allowing individuals to violate some of the role expectations associated with the occupation, and express their individuality within the confines of the occupational role. Although the funeral directors and morticians in this study used a variety of role-distancing techniques, three common patterns emerged: emotional detachment, humor, and countering the stereotype.

Emotional Detachment.   One of the ways that morticians and funeral directors overcome their socialization regarding death taboos and the stigma associated with handling the dead is to detach themselves from the body of the work. Charmaz (1980) pointed out that a common technique used by coroners and funeral directors to minimize the stigma associated with death work is to routinize the work as much as possible. When embalming, morticians focus on the technical aspects of the job rather than thinking about the person they are working on. One mortician explained:

> When I'm in the preparation room I never think about who *who* I'm working on; I only think about what has to be done next. When I picked up the body, it was a person. When I get done, clean and dress the body, and place it in the casket, it becomes a person again. But in here it's just something to be worked on. I treat it like a mechanic treats an automobile engine—with respect, but there's no emotion involved. It's just a job that has to be done.

Another mortician described his emotional detachment in the embalming room:

> You can't think too much about this process [embalming], or it'll really get to you. For example, one time we brought in this little girl. She was about four years old—the same age as my youngest daughter at the time. She had been killed in a wreck; had gone through the windshield; was really a mess.
>
> At first, I wasn't sure I could do that one—all I could think of was my little girl. But when I got her in the prep room, my whole attitude changed. I know this probably sounds cold, and hard I guess, but suddenly I began to think of the challenge involved. This was gonna be an open-casket service, and while the body was in pretty good shape, the head and face were practically gone. This was gonna take a lot of reconstruction. Also, the veins are so small on children that you have to be a lot more careful.
>
> Anyway, I got so caught up in the job, that I totally forgot about working on a little girl. I was in the room with her about six hours when—[his wife] came in and reminded me that we had dinner plans that night. I washed up and

went out to dinner and had a great time. Later that night, I went right back to work on her without even thinking about it.

It wasn't until the next day when my wife was dressing the body, and I came in, and she was crying, that it hit me. I looked at the little girl, and I began crying. We both just stood there crying and hugging. My wife kept saying "I know this was tough for you," and "yesterday must have been tough." I felt sorta guilty, because I knew what she meant, and it should've been tough for me, real tough emotionally, but it wasn't. The only "tough" part had been the actual work, especially the reconstruction—I had totally cut off the emotional part.

It sometimes makes you wonder. Am I really just good at this, or am I losing something. I don't know. All I know is, if I'd thought about the little girl the way I did that next day, I never could have done her. It's just part of this job—you gotta just do what has to be done. If you think about it much, you'll never make it in this business.

Humor.   Many funeral directors and morticians use humor to detach themselves emotionally from their work. The humor, of course, must be carefully hidden from friends and relatives of the deceased, and takes place in backstage areas such as the embalming room, or in professional group settings such as at funeral directors' conventions.

The humor varies from impromptu comments while working on the body to standard jokes told over and over again. Not unexpectedly, all the respondents indicated a strong distaste for necrophilia jokes. One respondent commented, "I can think of nothing less funny—the jokes are sick, and have done a lot of damage to the image of our profession."

Humor is an effective technique of diffusing the stigma associated with handling a dead body, however, and when more than one person is present in the embalming room, it is common for a certain amount of banter to take place, and jokes or comments are often made about the amount of body fat or the overendowment, or lack thereof, of certain body parts. For example, one mortician indicated that a common remark made about males with small genitalia is, "Well, at least he won't be missed."

As with any occupation, levels of humor varied among the respondents. During an interview one of the funeral directors spoke of some of the difficulties in advertising the business, indicating that because of attitudes toward death and the funeral business, he had to be sure that his newspaper advertisements did not offend anyone. He reached into his desk drawer and pulled out a pad with several "fake ads" written on it. They included:

"Shake and Bake Special—Cremation with No Embalming"

"Business Is Slow, Somebody's Gotta Go"

"Try Our Layaway Plan—Best in the Business"

"Count on Us, We'll Be the Last to Let You Down"
"People Are Dying to Use Our Services"
"Pay Now, Die Later"
"The Buck Really Does Stop Here"

He indicated that he and one of his friends had started making up these fake ads and slogans when they were doing their mortuary internships. Over the years, they occasionally corresponded by mail and saw each other at conventions, and they would always try to be one up on the other with the best ad. He said, "Hey, in this business, you have to look for your laughs where you can find them."

Countering the Stereotype.   Morticians and funeral directors are painfully aware of the common negative stereotype of people in their occupations. The women in this study were much less concerned about the stereotype, perhaps because simply being female shattered the stereotype anyway. The men, however, not only acknowledged that they were well aware of the public's stereotypical image of them, but also indicated that they made every effort *not* to conform to it.

One funeral director, for instance, said:

> People think we're cold, unfriendly, and unfeeling. I always make it a point to be just the opposite. Naturally, when I'm dealing with a family I must be reserved and show the proper decorum, but when I am out socially, I always try to be very upbeat—very alive. No matter how tired I am, I try not to show it.

Another indicated that he absolutely never wore gray or black suits. Instead, he wore navy blue and usually with a small pinstripe. "I might be mistaken for the minister or a lawyer," he said, "but rarely for an undertaker."

The word "cold," which often is associated with death came up in a number of interviews. One funeral director was so concerned about the stereotype of being "cold," that he kept a handwarmer in the drawer of his desk. He said, "My hands tend to be cold and clammy. It's just a physical trait of mine, but there's no way that I'm going to shake someone's hand and let them walk away thinking how cold it was." Even on the warmest of days, he indicated that during services, he carried the handwarmer in his right-hand coat pocket so that he could warm his hand before shaking hands with or touching someone.

Although everyone interviewed indicated that he or she violated the public stereotype, each one expressed a feeling of being atypical. In other words, although they believed that they did not conform to the stereotype, they felt that many of their colleagues did. One funeral director was wearing jeans, a short-sleeved sweatshirt and a pair of running shoes during the interview. He had just finished mowing the lawn at the funeral home. "Look at me," he said, "Do I look like a funeral director? Hell, _____ [the funeral director across the street] wears a suit and tie to mow his grass!—or, at least he would if he didn't hire it done."

Others insisted that very few funeral directors conform to the public stereotype when out of public view, but feel compelled to conform to it when handling funeral arrangements, because it is an occupational role requirement. "I always try to be warm and upbeat," one remarked, "But, let's face it, when I'm working with a family, they're experiencing a lot of grief—I have to respect that, and act accordingly." Another indicated that he always lowered his voice when talking with family and friends of the deceased, and that it had become such a habit, that he found himself speaking softly almost all the time. "One of the occupational hazards, I guess," he remarked.

The importance of countering the negative stereotype was evident, when time after time, persons being interviewed would pause and ask "I'm not what you expected, am I?" or something similar. It seemed very important for them to be reassured that they did not fit the stereotype of funeral director or mortician.

PROFESSIONALISM

Another method used by morticians and funeral directors to reduce occupational stigma is to emphasize professionalism. Amos (1983, 3) described embalming as:

> . . . an example of a vocation in transition from an occupation to a profession. Until mid-nineteenth century, embalming was not considered a profession and this is still an issue debated in some circles today.

Most morticians readily admit that embalming is a very simple process and can be learned very easily. In all but two of the funeral homes studied, the interviewees admitted that people who were not licensed embalmers often helped with the embalming process. In one case, in which the funeral home was owned and operated by two brothers, one of the brothers was a licensed funeral director and licensed embalmer. The other brother had dropped out of high school and helped their father with the funeral business while his brother went to school to meet the educational requirements for licensure. The licensed brother said:

> By the time I got out of school and finished my apprenticeship, _____ [his brother] had been helping Dad embalm for over three years—and he was damned good at it. So when I joined the business, Dad thought it was best if I

concentrated on handling the funeral arrangements and pre-service needs. After Dad died, I was the only licensed embalmer, so "officially" I do it all—all the embalming and the funeral arrangements. But, to tell you the truth, I only embalm every now and then when we have several to do, 'cause _____ usually handles most of it. He's one of the best—I'd match him against any in the business.

Despite the relative simplicity of the embalming process and the open admission by morticians and funeral directors that "almost anyone could do it with a little practice," most states require licensure and certification for embalming. The four states represented in this study (Kansas, Oklahoma, Missouri, and Texas) have similar requirements for becoming a licensed certified embalmer. They include a minimum of 60 college hours with a core of general college courses (English, mathematics, social studies, etc.) plus 1 year of courses in the "mortuary sciences," or "mortuary arts." These consist of several courses in physiology and biology, and a 1-year apprenticeship under a licensed embalmer. To become a licensed funeral director requires the passing of a state board examination, which primarily requires a knowledge of state laws related to burial, cremation, disposal of the body, and insurance.

Although the general consensus among them was that an individual did not need a college education to become a good embalmer, they all stressed the importance of a college education for being a successful funeral director. Most thought that some basic courses in business, psychology, death and dying, and "bereavement counseling" were valuable preparation for the field. Also, most of the funeral directors were licensed insurance agents, which allowed them to sell burial policies.

Other evidence of the professionalization of the funeral industry includes state, regional, and national professional organizations that hold annual conventions and sponsor other professional activities; professional journals; state, regional, and national governing and regulating boards; and a professional code of ethics. Although the funeral industry is highly competitive, like most other professions, its members demonstrate a strong sense of cohesiveness and in-group identification.

One of the married couples in this study indicated that it was reassuring to attend national conventions where they met and interacted with other people in the funeral industry because it helps to "reassure us that we're not weird." The wife went on to say:

A lot of people ask us how we can stand to be in this business—especially because he does all of the embalming. They act like we must be strange or something. When we go to the conventions and meet with all of the other people there who are just like us—people who like helping other people—I feel normal again.

All these elements of professionalization—educational requirements, exams, boards, organizations, codes of ethics, and the rest—lend an air of credibility and dignity to the funeral business while diminishing the stigma associated with it. Although the requirements for licensure and certification are not highly exclusive, they still represent forms of boundary maintenance, and demand a certain level of commitment from those who enter the field. Thus, professionalization helped in the transition of the funeral business from a vocation that can be pursued by virtually anyone to a profession that can be entered only by those with the appropriate qualifications. As Pine (1975, 28) indicated:

> Because professionalization is highly respected in American society, the word "profession" tends to be used as a symbol by occupations seeking to improve or enhance the lay public's conception of that occupation, and funeral directing is no exception. To some extent, this appears to be because the funeral director hopes to overcome the stigma of "doing death work."

"By claiming professional status, funeral directors claim prestige and simultaneously seek to minimize the stigma they experience for being death workers involved in 'dirty work.' "

THE SHROUD OF SERVICE

One of the most obvious ways in which morticians and funeral directors neutralize the stigma associated with their work is to wrap themselves in a "shroud of service." All the respondents emphasized their service role over all other aspects of their jobs. Although their services were not legally required in any of the four states included in this study, all the respondents insisted that people desperately needed them. As one funeral director summarized, "Service, that's what we're all about—we're there when people need us the most."

Unlike the humorous fantasy ads mentioned earlier, actual advertisements in the funeral industry focus on service. Typical ads for the companies in this study read:

> "Our Family Serving Yours for Over 60 Years"
> "Serving the Community for Four Generations"
> "Thoughtful Service in Your Time of Need"

The emphasis on service, especially on "grief counseling" and "bereavement therapy," shifts the focus away from the two most stigmatizing elements of funeral work: the handling and preparation of the body, which already has been discussed at length; and retail sales, which are widely interpreted as profiting from other people's grief. Many of the funeral directors indicated that they believed the major reason for negative public feelings toward their occupation was not only that they handled dead bodies, but the fact that they made their living off the dead, or at least, off the grief of the living.

All admitted that much of their profit came from the sale of caskets and vaults, where markup is usually a minimum of 100%, and often 400–500%, but all played down this aspect of their work. The Federal Trade Commission requires that funeral directors provide their customers with itemized lists of all charges. The author was provided with price lists for all merchandise and services by all the funeral directors in this study. When asked to estimate the "average price" of one of their funerals, respondents' answers ranged from $3,000 to $4,000. Typically, the casket accounted for approximately half of the total expense. Respondents indicated that less than 5% of their business involved cremations, but that even then they often encouraged the purchase of a casket. One said, "A lot of people ask about cremation, because they think it's cheaper, but I usually sell them caskets even for cremation; then, if you add the cost of cremation and urn, cremation becomes more profitable than burial."

Despite this denial of the retail aspects of the job, trade journals provide numerous helpful hints on the best techniques for displaying and selling caskets, and great care is given to this process. In all the funeral homes visited, one person was charged with the primary responsibility for helping with "casket selection." In smaller family-operated funeral homes, this person usually was the funeral director's wife. In the large chain-owned companies, it was one of the "associate funeral directors." In either case, the person was a skilled salesperson.

Nevertheless, the sales pitch is wrapped in the shroud of service. During each interview, the author asked to be shown the "selection room," and to be treated as if he were there to select a casket for a loved one. All the funeral directors willingly complied, and most treated the author as if he actually were there to select a casket. Interestingly, most perceived this as an actual sales opportunity and mentioned their "pre-need selection service" and said that if the author had not already made such arrangements, they would gladly assist him with the process. The words "sell," "sales," "buy," and "purchase," were carefully avoided.

Also, although by law the price for each casket must be displayed separately, most funeral homes also displayed a "package price" that included the casket and "full services." If purchased separately, the casket was always more expensive than if it was included in the package of services. This gave the impression that a much more expensive casket could be purchased for less money if bought as part of a service package. It also implied that the services provided by the firm were of more value than the merchandise.

The funeral directors rationalized the high costs of merchandise and funerals by emphasizing that they were a small price to pay for the services performed. One insisted, "We don't sell merchandise, we sell service!" Another asked "What is peace of mind worth?" and another "How do you put a price on relieving grief?"

Another rationalization for the high prices was the amount involved in arranging and conducting funeral services. When asked about the negative aspects of their jobs, most emphasized the hard work and long hours involved. In fact, all but two of the interviewees said that they did not want their children to follow in their footsteps, because the work was largely misunderstood (stigmatized), too hard, the hours too long, and "the income not nearly as high as most people think."

In addition to emphasizing the service aspect of their work, funeral directors also tend to join a number of local philanthropic and service organizations (Pine, 1975, 49). Although many businessmen find that joining such organizations is advantageous for making contacts, Stephenson (1985, 223) contended that the small-town funeral director "may be able to counter the stigma of his or her occupation by being active in the community, thereby counteracting some of the negative images associated with the job of funeral directing."

SOCIOECONOMIC STATUS VERSUS OCCUPATIONAL PRESTIGE

It seems that what funeral directors lack in occupational prestige, they make up for in socioeconomic status. Although interviewees were very candid about the number of funerals they performed every year and the average costs per funeral, most were reluctant to disclose their annual incomes. One exception was a 37-year-old funeral home owner, funeral director, and licensed embalmer in a community of approximately 25,000 who indicated that in the previous year he had handled 211 funerals and had a gross income of just under $750,000. After deducting overhead (three licensed embalmers on staff, a receptionist, a gardener, a student employee, insurance costs, etc.), he estimated his net income to have been "close to $250,000." He quickly added, however, that he worked long hours, had his 5-day vacation cut to two (because of a "funeral call that he had to handle personally") and despite his relatively high income (probably one of the two or three highest incomes in the community), he felt morally, socially, and professionally obligated to hide his wealth in the community. "I have to walk a fine line," he said, "I can live in a nice home, drive a nice car, and wear nice suits, because people know that I am a successful businessman—but, I have to be careful not to flaunt it."

One of the ways he reconciles this dilemma was by enjoying "the finer things in life" outside the community. He owned a condominium in Vail where he took ski trips and kept his sports car. He also said that none of his friends or neighbors there knew that he was in the funeral business. In fact, when they inquired about his occupations he told them he was in insurance (which technically was true because he also was a licensed insurance agent who sold burial policies). When asked why he did not disclose his true occupational identity, he responded:

> When I tell people what I really do, they initially seem "put off," even repulsed. I have literally had people jerk their hands back during a handshake when somebody introduces me and then tells them what I do for a living. Later, many of them become very curious and ask a lot of questions. If you tell people you sell insurance, they usually let the subject drop.

Although almost all the funeral directors in this study lived what they characterized as fairly "conservative lifestyles," most also indicated that they enjoyed many of the material things that their jobs offered them. One couple rationalized their recent purchase of a very expensive sailboat (which both contended they "really couldn't afford"), by saying, "Hey, if anybody knows that you can't take it with you, it's us—we figured we might as well enjoy it while we can." Another commented, "Most of the people in this community would never want to do what I do, but most of them would like to have my income."

Summary and Conclusion

This study describes and analyzes how people in the funeral industry attempt to reduce and neutralize the stigma associated with their occupations. Morticians and funeral directors are particularly stigmatized, not only because they perform work that few others would be willing to do (preparing dead bodies for burial), but also because they profit from death. Consequently, members of the funeral industry consciously work at stigma reduction.

Paramount among their strategies are symbolically redefining their work. This especially involves avoiding all language that reminds their customer of death, the body, and retail sales; morticians and funeral directors emphasize the need for their professional services of relieving family grief and bereavement counseling. They also practice role distance, emphasize their professionalism, wrap themselves in a "shroud of service," and enjoy their relatively high socioeconomic status rather than lament their lower occupational prestige.

References

Amos, E. P. 1983. *Kansas Funeral Profession Through the Years*. Topeka: Kansas Funeral Directors' Association.

Aries, P. 1976. *Western Attitudes Toward Death: From the Middle Ages to the Present*. Trans. P. M. Ranum. Baltimore: Johns Hopkins University Press, p. 99.

Charmaz, K. 1980. *The Social Reality of Death: Death in Contemporary America*. Reading, MA: Addison-Wesley.

Goffman, E. 1959. *The Presentation of Self in Everyday Life*. Garden City, NY: Anchor Doubleday.

Lesy, M. 1987. *The Forbidden Zone*. New York: Farrar, Straus & Giroux.

Pavalko, R. M. 1988. *Sociology of Occupations and Profession*, 2nd ed. Itasca, IL: Peacock.

Pine, V. R. 1975. *Caretaker of the Dead: The American Funeral Director*. New York: Irvington.

Stephenson, J. S. 1985. *Death, Grief and Mourning: Individual and Social Realities*. New York: Free Press.

Sudnow, D. 1967. *Passing On: The Social Organization of Dying*. Englewood Cliffs, NJ: Prentice-Hall.

Turner, R. E., and D. Edgley. 1976. "Death as Theater: A Dramaturgical Analysis of the American Funeral." *Sociology and Social Research, 60* (July): 377–392.

Woods, A. S., and R. G. Delisle. 1978. "The Treatment of Death in Sympathy Cards." Pp. 95–103 in C. Winick (ed.), *Deviance and Mass Media*. Beverly Hills, CA: Sage.

PART VI

Deviance and Social Control

F OR SOCIETY TO EXIST, people must be able to know what to expect of others. If they couldn't do this, the world would be in chaos. Because the behavior of humans is not controlled by instincts, people develop *norms* (standards, rules, or expectations) to provide regularity, or patterns, to social life. Norms provide a high degree of certainty in what, without them, would be a hopelessly disoriented world. If everyone followed his or her own inclinations and no one knew what to expect of others, we would have chaos.

The confidence we can place in others is only relative, however, because not everyone follows all the rules all the time. In fact *deviance*, the violation of rules and expectations, is universal. All members of society violate some of the expectations that others have of them. In this sense, all of us are deviants.

Because the word *deviant* in common usage is equivalent to perverted, dirty, twisted, and nasty, to say that all of us are deviants may strike you as strange. It is important to stress that as the word is used in sociology, *deviance is not a term of negative judgment*, as it is when used by nonsociologists. To sociologists, the term simply refers to activities that violate the expectations of others. Unlike common usage, in sociology this term is neutral, passing judgment neither on the merit of the rules nor on those who violate them.

The norms that people develop to control one another cover a fascinating variety of human behavior. They include rules and expectations concerning our appearance, manner, and conduct.

1. *Appearance* (what we look like): the norms concerning clothing, make-up, hairstyle, and other such presentational aspects of our body, including its cleanliness and odors. These rules also cover the *social extensions of the person*, those objects thought to represent the individual in some way, such as the person's home, car, and, often, even the individual's pet.

2. *Manner* (our style of doing things): people's expectations about how we will express ourselves, such as our facial expressions, gestures, and other body language. Manner includes *personal style* (gruff and direct-to-the-point; pleasant and charming), the expectations others have of us because of how we acted in the past. Manner also includes *group style*, expectations attached to us because of our membership in a social group (race–ethnic, gender, occupation, age, and so on—"the way those kind of people are").

3. *Conduct* (what we say, what we do): rules covering the rest of human behavior, specifying what we can and cannot do or say, as well as the circumstances that require or forbid that we say or do something. These include rules of *authority* (who has the right to give which order to whom), rules of *obligation* (who has the responsibility to do what for whom), and rules of *account giving* (what we are expected to say when we are asked for an explanation). Account-giving rules even specify the degree to which we are expected to be honest, to go into detail, or to avoid implicating others.

These everyday rules of appearance, manner, and conduct are sliced very fine. They specify the circumstances that apply, how we must phrase what we say, such as with how much respect or informality, even our facial expressions and eye contact when we do or say it. In other words, hardly a single aspect of our lives goes untouched by rules made by others—most of whom are long ago dead. None of us is a free agent, able to do as we please. Rather, *social control* is a basic fact of social life, enveloping all of us in its pervasive net of expectations.

Norms also follow social status. That is, they differ according to the social positions we occupy, especially those watershed identities of age, gender, occupation, and social class. For example, as you know, the rules of conduct, appearance, and manner differ for convicts, CEOs, students, children, old people, men and women. Looking at this list, you can see that expectations (or rules) depend on reputation, prestige, wealth, occupation, age, and gender. In some instances, they also vary according to race–ethnicity.

The rules also change as we switch audiences. For example, as teenagers know so well, their parents' expectations usually aren't even close to what their friends expect of them. Similarly, we are expected to act one way when we are with members of our own age, gender, or racial–ethnic group, but differently when we are with others. Our everyday norms even dictate distinct clothing for different audiences (or as we are more likely to phrase it, for different occasions)—for a college classroom, for a formal dance, for the beach, and so on. In short, to change physical locations is to transform stages and audiences, bringing distinct expectations of how we are to present the self.

These complex expectations define *in* and define *out*: Those who conform to the norms are accorded the status of members-in-good-standing, while those who deviate from them are usually defined as outsiders of some sort. Often objects of suspicion, sometimes of derision and hostility, deviants are reacted to in a number of ways. They may be given more attention in order to bring them back into line, or they may be ostracized or kicked out of the group. For mild deviations, they may simply be stared at. People may also gossip about them, joke about them, divorce them, strike their names from guest lists, or demote or fire them. In more extreme cases of rule violations, the offender may be shunned or physically attacked. In the most extreme cases, they are tried and imprisoned—or even put to death.

This list of some of the social reactions to deviance indicates that people are extremely concerned with rule-following and rule-breaking behaviors. Challenging fundamental expectations about how social life is run, deviants are often seen as a threat to people's welfare. With such a stake in the conformity of others, then, people react to deviants—sharply and negatively if they consider the deviance threatening, but tolerantly and perhaps even with amusement if they believe it to be mild.

In Part VI, we examine both deviance and social control. The opening selection is a forceful reminder of the situational grounding of our morality. Janet Ruane and Karen Cerulo remind us that although honesty is the expectation that surrounds our interactions, too much honesty is deviant. As Philip Meyer recounts Stanley Milgram's classic experiment, we come face to face with the power of social groups—they are so potent they can get us to participate in acts we know are evil. In the next selection, I tell the story of an airplane crash in the Andes—looking at how social control operated among the survivors, who ate their deceased friends and relatives. Then William Chambliss turns the focus on how community reactions to delinquents have far-reaching effects on their adult lives. Philip Zimbardo then describes his intriguing experiment, in which he uncovered structural bases for the hostile relationships between prisoners and prison guards. David Rosenhan closes Part VI by asking the intriguing question of whether or not we can tell the sane from the insane.

21 Is Honesty Really Our Policy?

JANET M. RUANE
KAREN A. CERULO

As children, we learn that we should not lie. Most of us also learn that honesty is the best policy. "What would the world be like if everyone told lies?" seems to be the common assumption behind such taken-for-granted teachings. Yet, as Ruane and Cerulo point out, at the same time that we are taught not to lie, we are also taught *how* to lie. In fact, it may be that society itself is built on a structure of lies. That is, if we did not lie when we are expected to, the social interaction that we take for granted could not continue.

An interesting idea. But I need to warn you: Although instructors like students to apply what they learn, this does not give you the right to say that you need to make up a sociology test because your grandmother died. Ah, yes, acceptable versus unacceptable lying.

"HONESTY IS THE BEST POLICY," wrote Ben Franklin. From an early age, parents and teachers urge us to embrace this sentiment. We learn cultural fables and tales that verify the value of truthfulness—remember Pinocchio or George Washington and the cherry tree? Similarly, religious doctrines turn honesty into law with lessons such as "Thou shalt not lie." In civics class, individuals learn that perjury—lying while under oath—is an illegal act.

Prohibitions against lying are among the earliest norms to which individuals are socialized. *Norms* are social rules or guidelines that direct behavior. They are the "shoulds" and "should nots" of social action, feelings, and thought. These lessons continue throughout life. As we grow older, we witness firsthand the ways in which dishonesty can lead to the downfall of individuals, families, careers, communities—even presidencies. Indeed, many social commentators identify the Watergate incident, and the high-level lying that accompanied it, as the basis for today's widespread public distrust of the U.S. government.

The conventional wisdom on honesty is strong; yet it is interesting to note that almost as early as we learn prohibitions against lying, we also learn how to rationalize the telling of lies. We learn that "little white lies" are not as serious as "real lies." We learn that context matters: Lying to strangers is not as serious as lying to friends; lying to peers is more excusable than lying to parents or authorities. We learn that lies don't count if we cross our fingers or wink while telling them. And we learn that lies told under duress are not as awful as premeditated or "bald-faced lies."

Thus, despite conventional wisdom to the contrary, lying stands as a ubiquitous social practice. Children lie to parents, and parents lie to grandparents. Employees lie to employers, and employers lie to regulators. Presidents lie to Congress and the public, and governments lie to their people. Indeed, there may be no social sphere to which lying is a stranger.

What explains the prevalence of lies when conventional wisdom so strongly supports honesty? What accounts for the discrepancies between what we say about lies and what we do? Is lying wrong? Is it deviant or not?

Society's contradictory stance towards lies illustrates a crucial point about the overriding issue of deviance. *Deviance* is typically defined as any act that violates a social norm. Definitions of deviance are rarely "black and white." Rather, determining what is deviant is a relative process because norms can vary with time, setting, or public consciousness. Thus, today's deviant behaviors may be tomorrow's convention. (Think of some "deviant behaviors" that subsequently entered the realm of conformity: long hair on men, jeans on students, smoking among women.)

Because lying, like all deviant acts, is variable, sociologists distinguish between two types of lies: deviant lies and normal lies. *Deviant lies* are falsehoods always judged to be wrong by a society; they represent a socially unacceptable practice, one that can devastate the trust that enables interaction within a complex society of strangers. *Normal lies* are a socially acceptable practice linked to productive social outcomes. Individuals rationalize and legitimate normal lies as the means to a noble end: the good of one's family, colleagues, or country. A lie's relative deviancy or normalcy depends on who tells it; when, where, and why it is told; to whom it is told; and the outcome of its telling.

For example, withholding your AIDS diagnosis from your elderly mother may be viewed as an act of mercy. In contrast, withholding the diagnosis from a sex partner would probably be viewed as immoral or potentially criminal. Similarly, lying about one's age to engage a new romantic interest is likely to be defined as significantly less offensive than lying about one's age to secure Social Security benefits. As with all forms of deviance, lie classification is based on context. We cannot classify a lie as deviant or normal on the basis of objectively stated criteria.

Although deviant lies can destroy social relations, normal lies can function as a strategic tool in the maintenance of social order. Normal lies become a "lubricant" of social life; they allow both the user and receiver of lies to edit social reality. Normal lies can facilitate ongoing interaction. If our boss misses a lunch date with us, we tell her or him it was "no big deal," even if the missed appointment led to considerable inconvenience in our day. Similarly, we tell a soldier's parents that their son or daughter died a painless death even if circumstances suggest otherwise. In both of these cases, the normal lie represents a crucial mechanism for preserving necessary social routines.

In the same way, normal lies also are important in maintaining civil social environments. Thus, when a truthful child announces someone's obesity, foul smell, or physical disability while on a shopping trip at the mall, parents are quick to instruct him or her in the polite albeit deceptive practices of less-than-honest tact. Similarly, the daily contact between neighbors inherent in most city and suburban layouts leads us to tell a rather bothersome neighbor that she or he is "really no trouble at all." In both of these cases, honesty would surely prove a socially destructive policy—the normal lie allows individuals to preserve the interaction environment.

What processes allow us to normalize an otherwise deviant behavior such as lying? In a classic article, sociologists Gresham Sykes and David Matza (1957) identify five specific techniques of neutralization that prove useful in this regard. *Techniques of neutralization* are methods of rationalizing deviant behavior. In essence, these techniques allow actors to suspend the control typically exerted by social norms. Freed from norms in this way, social actors can engage in deviance. Using the techniques of neutralization—denial of responsibility, denial of injury, denial of victim, condemning the condemner, and appealing to higher loyalties—individuals effectively explain away the deviant aspects of a behavior such as lying. Individuals convince themselves that their actions, even if norm violating, were justified given the circumstance. Once an individual has learned to use these techniques, she or he can apply them to any deviant arena, thereby facilitating an array of deviant behaviors: stealing, fraud, vandalism, personal violence, and so on.

Employing Sykes and Matza's techniques, then, one might *deny responsibility* for a lie, attributing the action to something beyond one's control: "My boss forced me to say he wasn't in." One might *deny injury* of the lie, arguing that the behavior caused no real harm: "Yes, I lied about my age. What's the harm?" One might *deny the victim* of the lie by arguing that the person harmed by the lie deserves such a fate: "I told her that her presentation was perfect. I can't wait for it to bomb; she deserves it." *Condemning one's condemner* allows an individual to neutralize a lie by shifting the focus to how often one's accuser lies: "Yes, I lied about where I was tonight, but how often have you lied to me about that very thing?" Finally, *appealing to higher loyalties* neutralizes lying by connecting it to some greater good: "I didn't tell my wife I was unfaithful because I didn't want to jeopardize our family."

Just as individuals learn to neutralize certain lies, they also learn appropriate reactions to normal lies. With time and experience, individuals learn that challenging normal lies can be counterproductive. Such challenges can disrupt the social scripts that make collective existence possible. *Social scripts* document the shared expectations that govern those interacting within a particular setting or context. If the social audience wishes to maintain smooth social exchange, then each member must learn to tolerate certain lies. By doing so, individuals downplay deviations from the social script. Like actors on a stage, individuals ignore momentary lapses and faux pas so that the "performance" can continue.

The U.S. military policy of "Don't ask, don't tell," for example, is built on such logic. Military officials look the other way in order to avoid the potential disruption embodied in a truthful response to the question of homosexuality. Similarly, the spouse who fails to question a partner's change in routine or habit may do so in an effort to shield the marriage from the threat posed by potential truths.

A variety of social settings require that we take someone at their word or accept things at face value. We learn to listen with "half an ear," to take things "with a grain of salt," or to recognize that people don't always "say what they mean or mean what they say." All such options are strategies of interaction maintenance—strategies that demand tolerance for the normal lie.

When it comes to norms on lying, or any other social behavior, conformity may be, as conventional wisdom suggests, the best policy. However, when we understand the complexity involved in the workings of norm violations, we cannot help but note that deviating from the "best policy" may not be all that deviant after all.

Reference

Sykes, Gresham, and Matza, David. 1957. "Techniques of Neutralization: A Theory of Delinquency." *American Sociological Review*, 22: 664–670.

22 If Hitler Asked You to Electrocute a Stranger, Would You? Probably

PHILIP MEYER

Let's take the title of this selection seriously for a moment. Suppose that Hitler did ask you to electrocute a stranger, would you? "Of course, I wouldn't" is our immediate response. "*I* wouldn't even *hurt* a stranger just because someone asked me, much less electrocute the person."

Such an answer certainly seems reasonable, but unfortunately it may not be true. Consider two aspects of the power of groups over our lives. First, we all do things that we prefer not to—from going to work and taking tests when we really want to stay in bed to mowing the grass or doing the dishes when we want to watch television. Our roles and relationships require that we do them, and our own preferences become less important than fulfilling the expectations of others. Second, at least on occasion, most of us feel social pressures so strongly that we do things that conflict with our morals. Both these types of behavior are fascinating to sociologists, for they indicate how *social structure*—the way society is organized—shapes our lives.

But electrocute someone? Isn't that carrying the point a little too far? One would certainly think so. The experiments described by Meyer, however, indicate that people's positions in groups are so significant that even "nice, ordinary" people will harm strangers upon request. You may find the implications of authority and roles arising from these experiments disturbing. Many of us do.

IN THE BEGINNING, Stanley Milgram was worried about the Nazi problem. He doesn't worry much about the Nazis anymore. He worries about you and me, and perhaps, himself a little bit too.

Stanley Milgram is a social psychologist, and when he began his career at Yale University in 1960 he had a plan to prove, scientifically, that Germans are different. The Germans-are-different hypothesis had been used by historians, such as William L. Shirer, to explain the systematic destruction of the Jews by the Third Reich. One madman could decide to destroy the Jews and even create a master plan for getting it done. But to implement it on the scale that Hitler did meant that thousands of other people had to go along with the scheme and help to do the work. The Shirer thesis, which Milgram set out to test, is that Germans have a basic character flaw which explains the whole thing, and this flaw is a readiness to obey authority without question, no matter what outrageous acts the authority commands.

The appealing thing about this theory is that it makes those of us who are not Germans feel better about the whole business. Obviously, you and I are not Hitler, and it seems equally obvious that we would never do Hitler's dirty work for him. But now, because of Stanley Milgram, we are compelled to wonder. Milgram developed a laboratory experiment which provided a systematic way to measure obedience. His plan was to try it out in New Haven on Americans and then go to Germany and try it out on Germans. He was strongly motivated by scientific curiosity, but there was also some moral content in his decision to pursue this line of research, which was in turn colored by his own Jewish background. If he could show that Germans are more obedient than Americans, he could then vary the conditions of the experiment and try to find out just what it is that makes some people more obedient than others. With this understanding, the world might, conceivably, be just a little bit better.

But he never took his experiment to Germany. He never took it any farther than Bridgeport. The first finding, also the most unexpected and disturbing finding, was that we Americans are an obedient people: not blindly obedient, and not blissfully obedient, just obedient. "I found so much obedience," says Milgram softly, a little sadly, "I hardly saw the need for taking the experiment to Germany."

There is something of the theater director in Milgram, and his technique, which he learned from one of the old masters in experimental psychology, Solomon Asch, is to stage a play with every line rehearsed, every prop carefully selected, and everybody an actor except one person. That one person is the subject of the experiment. The subject, of course, does not know he is in a play. He thinks he is in real life. The value of this technique is that the experimenter, as though he were God, can change a prop here, vary a line there, and see how the subject responds. Milgram eventually had to change a lot of the script just to get people to stop obeying. They were obeying so much, the experiment wasn't working—it was like trying to measure oven temperature with a freezer thermometer.

The experiment worked like this: If you were an innocent subject in Milgram's melodrama, you read an ad in the newspaper or received one in the mail asking for volunteers for an educational experiment. The job would take about an hour and pay $4.50. So you make an appointment and go to an old Romanesque stone structure on High Street with the imposing name of The Yale

Interaction Laboratory. It looks something like a broadcasting studio. Inside, you meet a young, crew-cut man in a laboratory coat who says he is Jack Williams, the experimenter. There is another citizen, fiftyish, Irish face, an accountant, a little overweight, and very mild and harmless looking. This other citizen seems nervous and plays with his hat while the two of you sit in chairs side by side and are told that the $4.50 checks are yours no matter what happens. Then you listen to Jack Williams explain the experiment.

It is about learning, says Jack Williams in a quiet, knowledgeable way. Science does not know much about the conditions under which people learn and this experiment is to find out about negative reinforcement. Negative reinforcement is getting punished when you do something wrong, as opposed to positive reinforcement which is getting rewarded when you do something right. The negative reinforcement in this case is electric shock. You notice a book on the table, titled, *The Teaching-Learning Process,* and you assume that this has something to do with the experiment.

Then Jack Williams takes two pieces of paper, puts them in a hat, and shakes them up. One piece of paper is supposed to say, "Teacher," and the other, "Learner." Draw one and you will see which you will be. The mild-looking accountant draws one, holds it close to his vest like a poker player, looks at it, and says, "Learner." You look at yours. It says, "Teacher." You do not know that the drawing is rigged, and both slips say "Teacher." The experimenter beckons to the mild-mannered "learner."

"Want to step right in here and have a seat, please?" he says. "You can leave your coat on the back of that chair . . . roll up your right sleeve, please. Now what I want to do is strap down your arms to avoid excessive movement on your part during the experiment. This electrode is connected to the shock generator in the next room.

"And this electrode paste," he says, squeezing some stuff out of a plastic bottle and putting it on the man's arm, "is to provide a good contact and to avoid a blister or burn. Are there any questions now before we go into the next room?"

You don't have any, but the strapped-in "learner" does.

"I do think I should say this," says the learner. "About two years ago, I was in the veterans' hospital . . . they detected a heart condition. Nothing serious, but as long as I'm having these shocks, how strong are they—how dangerous are they?"

Williams, the experimenter, shakes his head casually. "Oh, no," he says. "Although they may be painful, they're not dangerous. Anything else?"

Nothing else. And so you play the game. The game is for you to read a series of word pairs: for example, blue-girl, nice-day, fat-neck. When you finish the list, you read just the first word in each pair and then a multiple-choice list of four other words, including the second word of the pair. The learner, from his remote, strapped-in position, pushes one of four switches to indicate which of the four answers he thinks is the right one. If he gets it right, nothing happens and you go on to the next one. If he gets it wrong, you push a switch that buzzes and gives him an electric shock. And then you go on to the next word. You start with 15 volts and increase the number of volts by 15 for each wrong answer. The control board goes from 15 volts on one end to 450 volts on the other. So that you know what you are doing, you get a test-shock yourself, at 45 volts. It hurts. To further keep you aware of what you are doing to that man in there, the board has verbal descriptions of the shock levels, ranging from "Slight Shock" at the left-hand side, through "Intense Shock" in the middle, to "Danger: Severe Shock" toward the far right. Finally, at the very end, under 435- and 450-volt switches, there are three ambiguous X's. If, at any point, you hesitate, Mr. Williams calmly tells you to go on. If you still hesitate, he tells you again.

Except for some terrifying details, which will be explained in a moment, this is the experiment. The object is to find the shock level at which you disobey the experimenter and refuse to pull the switch.

When Stanley Milgram first wrote this script, he took it to 14 Yale psychology majors and asked them what they thought would happen. He put it this way: Out of one hundred persons in the teacher's predicament, how would their break-off points be distributed along the 15- to 450-volt scale? They thought a few would break off very early, most would quit someplace in the middle, and a few would go all the way to the end. The highest estimate of the number out of 100 who would go all the way to the end was three. Milgram then informally polled some of his fellow scholars in the psychology department. They agreed that very few would go to the end. Milgram thought so too.

"I'll tell you quite frankly," he says, "before I began this experiment, before any shock generator was built, I thought that most people would break off at 'Strong Shock' or 'Very Strong Shock.' You would get only a very, very small proportion of people going out to the end of the shock generator, and they would constitute a pathological fringe."

In his pilot experiments, Milgram used Yale students as subjects. Each of them pushed the shock switches, one by one, all the way to the end of the board.

So he rewrote the script to include some protests from the learner. At first, they were mild, gentlemanly, Yalie protests, but "it didn't seem to have as much effect as I thought it would or should," Milgram recalls. "So we had more violent protestation on the part of the person getting the shock. All of the time, of course, what we were trying to do was not to create a macabre situation, but simply to generate disobedience. And that was one of the first findings. This was not only a technical deficiency of the experiment, that we didn't get disobedience. It really was the first finding: that obedience would be much greater than we had assumed it would be and disobedience would be much more difficult than we had assumed."

As it turned out, the situation did become rather macabre. The only meaningful way to generate disobedience was to have the victim protest with great anguish, noise, and vehemence. The protests were tape-recorded so that all the teachers ordinarily would hear the same sounds and nuances, and they started with a grunt at 75 volts, proceeded through a "Hey, that really hurts," at 125 volts, got desperate with, "I can't stand the pain—don't do that," at 180 volts, reached complaints of heart trouble at 195, an agonized scream at 285, a refusal to answer at 315, and only heartrending, ominous silence after that.

Still, 65 percent of the subjects, 20- to 50-year-old American males, everyday, ordinary people, like you and me, obediently kept pushing those levers in the belief that they were shocking the mild-mannered learner, whose name was Mr. Wallace, and who was chosen for the role because of his innocent appearance, all the way up to 450 volts.

Milgram was not getting enough disobedience so that he had something he could measure. The next step was to vary the circumstances to see what would encourage or discourage obedience. There seemed very little left in the way of discouragement. The victim was already screaming at the top of his lungs and feigning a heart attack. So whatever new impediment to obedience reached the brain of the subject had to travel by some route other than the ear. Milgram thought of one.

He put the learner in the same room with the teacher. He stopped strapping the learner's hand down. He rewrote the script so that at 150 volts the learner took his hand off the shock plate and declared that he wanted out of experiment. He rewrote the script some more so that the experimenter then told the teacher to grasp the learner's hand and physically force it down on the plate to give Mr. Wallace his unwanted electric shock.

"I had the feeling that very few people would go on at that point, if any," Milgram says. "I thought that would be the limit of obedience that you would find in the laboratory."

It wasn't.

Although [years have] gone by, Milgram still remembers the first person to walk into the laboratory in the newly rewritten script. He was a construction worker, a very short man. "He was so small," says Milgram, "that when he sat on the chair in front of the shock generator, his feet didn't reach the floor.

When the experimenter told him to push the victim's hand down and give the shock, he turned to the experimenter, and he turned to the victim, his elbow went up, he fell down on the hand of the victim, his feet kind of tugged to one side, and he said, 'Like this, boss?' Zzumph!"

The experiment was played out to its bitter end. Milgram tried it with 40 different subjects. And 30 percent of them obeyed the experimenter and kept on obeying.

"The protests of the victim were strong and vehement, he was screaming his guts out, he refused to participate, and you had to physically struggle with him in order to get his hand down on the shock generator," Milgram remembers. But 12 out of 40 did it.

Milgram took his experiment out of New Haven. Not to Germany, just 20 miles down the road to Bridgeport. Maybe, he reasoned, the people obeyed because of the prestigious setting of Yale University. If they couldn't trust a learning center that had been there for two centuries, whom could they trust? So he moved the experiment to an untrustworthy setting.

The new setting was a suite of three rooms in a run-down office building in Bridgeport. The only identification was a sign with a fictitious name: "Research Associates of Bridgeport." Questions about professional connections got only vague answers about "research for industry."

Obedience was less in Bridgeport. Forty-eight percent of the subjects stayed for the maximum shock, compared to 65 percent at Yale. But this was enough to prove that far more than Yale's prestige was behind the obedient behavior.

[Since the experiments] Stanley Milgram has been trying to figure out what makes ordinary American citizens so obedient. The most obvious answer—that people are mean, nasty, brutish, and sadistic—won't do. The subjects who gave the shocks to Mr. Wallace to the end of the board did not enjoy it. They groaned, protested, fidgeted, argued, and in some cases, were seized by fits of nervous, agitated giggling.

"They even try to get out of it," says Milgram, "but they are somehow engaged in something from which they cannot liberate themselves. They are locked into a structure, and they do not have the skills or inner resources to disengage themselves. . . ."

"The results, as seen and felt in the laboratory," he has written, "are disturbing. They raise the possibility that human nature, or more specifically the kind of character produced in American democratic society, cannot be counted on to insulate its citizens from brutality and inhumane treatment at the direction of malevolent authority. A substantial proportion of people do what they are told to do, irrespective of the content of the act and without limitation of conscience, so long as they perceive that the command comes from a legitimate authority. If, in this study, an anonymous experimenter can successfully command adults to subdue a 50-year-old man and force on him painful electric shocks against his protest, one can only wonder what government, with its vastly greater authority and prestige, can command of its subjects. . . ."

Stanley Milgram has his problems, too. He believes that in the laboratory situation, he would not have shocked Mr. Wallace. His professional critics reply that in his real-life situation he has done the equivalent. He has placed innocent and naive subjects under great emotional strain and pressure in selfish obedience to his quest for knowledge. When you raise this issue with Milgram, he has an answer ready. There is, he explains patiently, a critical difference between his naive subjects and the man in the electric chair. The man in the electric chair (in the mind of the naive subject) is helpless, strapped in. But the naive subject is free to go at any time.

Immediately after he offers this distinction, Milgram anticipates the objection.

"It's quite true," he says. "that this is almost a philosophic position, because we have learned that some people are psychologically incapable of disengaging themselves. But that doesn't relieve them of the moral responsibility."

The parallel is exquisite. "The tension problem was unexpected," says Milgram in his defense. But he went on anyway. The naive subjects didn't expect the screaming protests from the strapped-in learner. But they went on.

"I had to make a judgment," says Milgram. "I had to ask myself, was this harming the person or not? My judgment is that it was not. Even in the extreme cases, I wouldn't say that permanent damage results."

Sound familiar? "The shocks may be painful," the experimenter kept saying, "but they're not dangerous."

After the series of experiments was completed, Milgram sent a report of the results to his subjects and a questionnaire, asking whether they were glad or sorry to have been in the experiment. Eighty-three and seven-tenths percent said they were glad and only 1.3 percent were sorry; 15 percent were neither sorry nor glad. However, Milgram could not be sure at the time of the experiment that only 1.3 percent would be sorry.

Kurt Vonnegut, Jr., put one paragraph in the preface to *Mother Night,* in 1966, which pretty much says it for the people with their fingers on the shock-generator switches, for you and me, and maybe even for Milgram. "If I'd been born in Germany," Vonnegut said, "I suppose I would have *been* a Nazi, bopping Jews and gypsies and Poles around, leaving boots sticking out of snow-banks, warming myself with my sweetly virtuous insides. So it goes."

Just so. One thing that happened to Milgram back in New Haven during the days of the experiment was that he kept running into people he'd watched from behind the one-way glass. It gave him a funny feeling, seeing those people going about their everyday business in New Haven and knowing what they would do to Mr. Wallace if ordered to. Now that his research results are in and you've thought about it, you can get this funny feeling too. You don't need one-way glass. A glance in your own mirror may serve just as well.

23 Eating Your Friends Is the Hardest: The Survivors of the F-227

JAMES M. HENSLIN

A theme running through our previous readings is that each culture provides guidelines for how to view the world, even for how we determine right and wrong. The perspective we learn envelops us much as a fish is enveloped by water. Almost all the world's cultures uphold the idea that it is wrong to eat human flesh. (Some exceptions do apply, such as warriors who used to eat the heart or kidneys of slain enemies in an attempt to acquire the source of their strength or courage.) Thus it is safe to say that nowhere in the world is there a culture whose members regularly consume people as food. Yet, in the unusual situation recounted here, this is precisely what these people did.

Note how, even in the midst of reluctantly committing acts they themselves found extremely repugnant—and ones they fully knew that the world condemns—this group developed norms to govern their behavior. This was crucial for these survivors, because group support, along with its attendant norms, is crucial for maintaining sanity and a sense of a "good" self. At the conclusion of the article, Henslin shows how this event is more than simply an interesting story—that it represents the essence of social life.

LOCATED BETWEEN BRAZIL AND ARGENTINA, near Buenos Aires, is tiny Uruguay. On October 12, 1972, a propeller-driven Fairchild F-227 left Uruguay's capital, Montevideo, bound for Santiago, Chile—a distance of about 900 miles. On board were 15 members of an amateur rugby team from Uruguay, along with 25 of their relatives and friends. The pilots, from the Uruguayan Air Force, soon became concerned about turbulence over the Andes Mountains. Winds blowing in from the Pacific were colliding with air currents coming from the opposite direction, creating a turbulence that could toss a plane around like a scrap of paper in a wind storm.

Since the threat was so great, the pilots decided to land in Mendoza, Argentina, where everyone spent the night. The next day, with the weather only slightly improved, the crew debated about turning back. Several of the rugby players taunted them, saying they were cowards. When the captain of a plane which had just flown over the Andes reported that the F-227 should be able to fly over the turbulence, the Fairchild's pilots decided to continue the trip. Once again airborne, the young passengers laughed about its being Friday the 13th as some threw a rugby ball around and others played cards. Many of them still in their teens, and all of them from Uruguay's upper class (two were nephews of the president of Uruguay), they were in high spirits.

Over the Andes the plane flew into a thick cloud, and the pilots had to fly by instrument. Amid the turbulence they hit an "air pocket," and the plane suddenly plunged 3,000 feet. When the passengers abruptly found themselves below the cloud, one young man turned to another and said, "Is it normal to fly so close?" He was referring to the mountainside just 10 feet off the right wing.

With a deafening roar, the right wing sheared off as it hit the side of the mountain. The wing whipped over the plane and knocked off the tail. The steward, the navigator, and three of the rugby players still strapped in their seats were blown out of the gaping hole. Then the left wing broke off and, like a toboggan going 200 miles an hour, the fuselage slid on its belly into a steep, snow-covered valley.

As night fell, the survivors huddled in the wreckage. At 12,000 feet the cold, especially at night, was brutal. There was little fuel, because not much wood is used in the construction of airplanes. They had almost no food—basically some chocolate that the passengers had bought on their overnight stay in Mendoza. There were a few bottles of wine, and the many cartons of cigarettes they had purchased at a duty-free shop.

The twenty-seven who survived the crash expected to be rescued quickly. At most, they thought, they would have to spend the night on the mountain top. Seventy days later, only sixteen remained alive.

The chocolate and wine didn't go very far, and provided little nourishment. The plane, off course by a hundred miles or so and painted white, was not only difficult to track, but virtually invisible against the valley's deep layer of snow: Search planes were unable to locate the wreckage.

As the days went by, the survivors' spirits seemed to be sucked into a hopeless pit. Hunger and starvation began to bear down on them. They felt cold all the time. They became weaker and had difficulty keeping their balance. Their skin became wrinkled, like that of old people. Although no one mentioned it, several of the young men began to realize that their only chance to survive was to eat the bodies of those who died in the crash. The corpses lay strewn in the snow around the plane, perfectly preserved by the bitter cold.

The thought of cutting into the flesh of their friends was too ghastly a prospect to put into words. Finally, however, Canessa, a medical student, brought up the matter with his friends. He asserted that the bodies were no longer people. The soul was gone, he said, and the body was simply meat—and essential to their survival. They were growing weaker, and they could not survive without food. And what food was there besides the corpses? "They are no more human beings than the dead flesh of the cattle we eat at home," he said.

Days later, the topic moved from furtive discussion in a small group to open deliberation among all the survivors. Inside the plane, arguing the matter, Canessa reiterated his position. His three closest friends supported him, adding, "We have a duty to survive. If we don't eat the bodies, it is a sin. We must do this not just for our own sakes but also for our families. In fact," they continued, "God wants us to survive, and He has provided these bodies so we can live." Some, however, just shook their heads, the thought too disturbing to even contemplate.

Serbino pushed the point. He said, "If I die, I want you to eat my body. I want you to use it." Some nodded in agreement. In an attempt to bring a little humor to the black discussion, he added, "If you don't, I'll come back and give you a swift kick in the butt." Some said that while they did not think it would be wrong to eat the bodies, they themselves could never do it. The arguments continued for hours.

Four of the young men went outside. Near the plane, the buttocks of a body protruded from the snow. No one spoke as they stared at it. Wordlessly, Canessa knelt and began to cut with the only instrument he had found, a piece of broken glass. The flesh was frozen solid, and he could cut only slivers the size of matchsticks. Canessa laid the pieces on the roof of the plane, and the young men went back inside. They said that the meat was drying in the sun. The others looked mutely at one another. No one made a move to leave the plane.

Canessa decided that he would have to be the first. Going outside, he picked up a sliver of meat. Staring at it, almost transfixed, he became as though paralyzed. He simply couldn't make his hand move to his mouth. Summoning every ounce of courage, he forced his hand upwards. While his stomach recoiled, he pushed the meat inside his mouth and forced himself to swallow. Later, Serbino took a piece. He tried to swallow, but the sliver hung halfway down his throat. Quickly grabbing some snow, he managed to wash it down. Canessa and Serbino were joined by others, who also ate.

The next morning, on the transistor radio they had struggled so hard to get working, their hearts plunged when they heard that the air force had called off the search. The survivors knew that this announcement almost sealed their fate. The only way out, if there was one, was on their own. They held a meeting and decided that the fittest should try to seek help—even though no one knew where to seek it. But none was strong enough to try. With the snow's crust breaking under every step, even to walk was exhausting. There was only one way to regain strength, and, without giving the thought words, everyone knew what it was.

Canessa and Strauch went outside. The corpse was in the same position as before. They took a deep breath and began to hack meat off the bone. They laid the strips on the plane to thaw in the sun. The knowledge that no rescuers were looking for them encouraged others to join in eating the human flesh. They forced themselves to swallow—their consciences, seconded by their stomachs, accusing them of extreme wrongdoing. Still, they forced the flesh down, telling themselves over and over that there was no other way to survive.

Some, however, could not. Javier and Liliana Methol, husband and wife, though they longed to return to their children, could not eat human flesh. They said that the others could do as they liked, but perhaps God wanted them to choose to die.

The survivors began to organize. Canessa took charge of cutting up the bodies, while a group of the younger ones had the job of preventing the corpses from rotting by keeping them covered with snow. Another group had the task of seeing that the plane was kept in order. Even the weakest had a job to do: They were able to hold pieces of aluminum in the sun to melt snow for drinking water.

The first corpses they ate were those of the crew, strangers to them.

One day, when it was too cold to melt snow, they burned wooden Coca-Cola crates that they had found in the luggage compartment. After they had water, they roasted some meat over the embers. There was only enough heat to brown the pieces, but they found the flavor better—tasting, as they said, like beef, but softer. Canessa said they should never do this again, for heat destroys proteins. "You have to eat it raw to get its full value," he argued. Rejecting his advice, the survivors cooked the meat when they had the chance, about once or twice a week. Daily, the recurring question was, "Are we cooking today?"

Liliana told Javier that after they got back home she wanted to have another baby. He agreed. As they looked at one another, though, they saw eyes sunken into their sockets and bones protruding from their cheeks. They knew there was no hope, unless. . . . Liliana and Javier shuddered as they picked up a piece of meat.

Some never could eat. Although the others argued with them, they never could overcome their feelings of revulsion. They continued to refuse, and so day by day grew weaker. Others, however, grew accustomed to what they were doing. They became able to cut meat from a body before everyone's eyes. They could even eat larger pieces, which they had to chew and taste.

As time went on, they developed a set of rules. They would not eat the women's bodies. No one had to eat. The meat would be rationed, and no one could eat more than his or her share. The three who were going to leave in search of help could eat more than the others. One corpse would always be finished before another would be started. (It was overlooked when those who had the disagreeable job of cutting the corpses ate a little as they cut.)

They refused to eat certain parts of the body—the lungs, the skin, the head, and the genitals.

There were some things they never could get used to, such as cutting up a close friend. When they dug a corpse out of the snow, it was preserved just as it had been at the moment of death. If the eyes had been open when the friend died, they were still open, now staring back at them. Everyone understood that no one had to eat a friend or relative.

Survival work became more organized. Those who could stomach it would cut large chunks from a body and pass them to another team, who would slice them with razor blades into smaller pieces. This was not as disagreeable a task, for, separated from the body, the meat was easier to deal with.

The sheets of fat from a body lay outside the rules. They were dried in the sun until a crust formed. Anyone could eat as much as they wished. But the fat wasn't as popular as the meat.

Also outside the rationing system were the pieces of the first carcasses they had cut up, before they developed the rules. Those pieces lay about the snow, and anyone who wanted could scavenge them. Some could never stomach the liver, others the heart or kidneys, and many could not eat the intestines of the dead. Three young men refused the red meat of the muscles.

The dead became part of their lives. One night, Inciarte reached up to get something from the hat rack and was startled when an icy hand brushed against his cheek. Apparently someone had sneaked it in as a late snack.

Constipation was an unexpected complication of their diet. As day after day went by without defecation, they began to worry that their insides would burst. Eventually they developed a sort of contest, wondering who would be the last hold-out. After 28 days, only two had not defecated. At 32, only one. Finally, on the 34th day, Bobby François joined the others.

The three who had been selected to go in search of rescuers had to solve the problem of preventing their feet from freezing. The skin of the dead provided the solution. By cutting an arm just above and below the elbow, and slowly pulling, the skin came away with its subcutaneous layers of fat. Sewing up the lower end made an insulated pair of socks.

Their bland diet became boring. As their bodies and minds cried out for variety, they began to seek new tastes. After eating the meat from a bone, they would crack it open and scoop out the marrow. Everyone liked the marrow. Some sought out the blood clots from around the heart. Others even ate parts of bodies that had started to rot. Many were revolted by this, but, as time went on, more of the survivors did the same.

Canessa, Parrado, and Vizintin were selected to go in search of help. Before they left, Parrado took aside a couple of friends and said that they might run short of food before help could arrive. "I prefer you don't," he whispered, "but I'll understand if you eat my mother and sister."

Ten days after the expeditionaries set out, they stumbled into a shepherd's hut. The news of their survival, long after they had been given up for dead, came as a shock to their friends and relatives. Those still waiting on the mountain were rescued by helicopter—just four days before Christmas.

Although the survivors felt a compulsive need to talk about what they had done, at first physicians and government officials kept the cannibalism a secret. When the news leaked out, however, it made headlines around the world. One survivor explained, "It was like a heart transplant. The dead sustained the living." Another said, "It was like holy communion. God gives us the body and blood of Christ in holy communion. God gave us these bodies and blood to eat."

All were Roman Catholics, and they asked forgiveness. The priests replied that they did not need forgiveness, for they had done nothing wrong. There was no soul in the bodies, the priests explained, and in extreme conditions, if there is no other way to survive, it is permissible to eat the dead. After consultation with relatives, it was decided to bury what was left of the dead at the crash site.

The young men, rejoining their families, became celebrities. They shunned the spotlight, however, banded together, and thought of themselves as special people. As persons who had survived the impossible, they felt that they had a unique purpose in life.

The world's reaction to the events in the Andes was shock and horror— mixed with fascination. As one Chilean paper asked in its headlines, "What would *you* have done?"

The Social Construction of Reality

I was going to let the story stop here, but I was told by a person very influential in my life that I really ought to make the sociology explicit. So let's see what sociological lessons we can derive from this tragedy in the Andes.

First, the main lesson, one from which the other points follow, comes from the symbolic interactionists, who stress that *our world is socially constructed.* By this, they mean that nothing contains built-in meanings. In other words, whatever meaning something has is arbitrary: We humans have given it a particular meaning, but we could just as well have given it a different meaning. *Second,* it is through a social process that we determine meanings; that is, people jointly decide on the meanings to assign events and objects. *Third,* because meanings (or what things symbolize to people) are arbitrary, people can change them. I am aware that these statements may sound extremely vague, but they should become clear as we look at how these survivors constructed their reality.

We might begin by asking what the meaning of a human body is. As with other aspects of life, a group can assign to a body any meaning that it wishes, for, by itself, a body has no meaning. These survivors did not begin to develop their definitions from scratch, however, for they brought to the Andes meanings that they had learned in their culture—basically that a body, while not a person, is still human, and must be treated with respect. A related meaning they had learned is that a human body is "not food." Such an understanding may seem natural to us because it matches our own cultural definitions—which obscures the arbitrary nature of the definition.

Fourth, when circumstances change, definitions can become outmoded—even definitions about fundamental aspects of life. *Fifth,* even though definitions no longer "work," changes in basic orientations do not come easily. *Sixth,* anyone who suggests such changes is likely to be seen as a threatening deviant. Shock, horror, or ridicule may be the reactions, and—for persons who persist on a disorienting course—shunning, ostracism, and violence may result. *Seventh,* the source of radical new ideas is extremely significant in determining whether or not they gain acceptance. *Eighth,* if an individual can drum up group support, then there exists a *social* basis for the new, competing definition. *Ninth,* if the group that offers the new definition can get enough others to accept it, then the common definition of reality will change. *Tenth,* changed circumstances make people more open to accepting new definitions of reality.

In this case, Canessa did not want to appear as a deviant, so he furtively proposed a new definition—entrusting it at first to only a few close friends. Even there, however, since it violated basic definitions acquired in early socialization, it was initially met with resistance. But the friends had high respect for Canessa, who had completed a year of medical school, and they were won over. This small group then proposed their new definition of human bodies to the larger group. Eventually, in the growing realization that death was imminent, this definition won out.

Eleventh, behavior follows definitions. That is, definitions of reality are not just abstract ideas; they also indicate the boundaries of what is allowable. We tend to do what our definitions allow. In this case, when the definition of human bodies changed, so did the survivors' behavior: The changed definition allowed them to eat human corpses.

Twelfth, definitions also follow behavior. That is, as people engage in an activity, they tend to develop ideas that lend support to what they are doing. In this instance, the eating of human flesh—especially since it was a group activity—reinforced the initial definition that had been only tentatively held, that the flesh was no longer human. Eventually, at least for many, the flesh indeed became meat—so much so that some people were even able to take a human hand to bed for a late-night snack.

Thirteenth, for their very survival, all groups must have norms. By allowing people to know what to expect in a given situation, norms provide a basic structure for people's relationships with one another. Without norms, anarchy and chaos would reign.

This principle also applies to groups that make deviance part of their activities. Although a superficial view from the outside may make such groups appear disorganized and without rules, they are in fact very normative. Groups of outlaw motorcyclists, for example, share an elaborate set of rules about what they expect from one another, most of which, like those of other groups, are not in written form. In short, norms cover even deviant activities, for, without them, how can group members know what to expect of one another?

The Andes survivors developed a basic set of norms to provide order to their deviant activity. Some of those norms were:

1. No one had to violate his or her conscience. If someone did not wish to eat human flesh, no one would force them.
2. Some bodies were "off limits."
3. Meat was rationed, with a specified amount for each person:
   a. Fat was outside the rationing system, and
   b. Leftover parts from the first bodies were outside the rationing system.
4. Meat was distributed according to an orderly system, namely:
   a. Everyone who wished to could eat, and
   b. Designated parts of the body could be "wasted."

Fourteenth, human groups tend to stratify, that is, to sort themselves out on a basis of inequality, with some getting more of a group's resources, some less. A norm concerning eating human flesh that I did not mention above illustrates this principle: Those persons deemed most valuable to the group were allowed to eat more. These were persons who were going in search of rescue and those who performed the disagreeable task of cutting up the bodies. This unequal division of resources represents the formation of a basic system of social stratification.

Fifteenth, human groups tend to organize themselves. In this instance, the survivors did not just randomly cut away at the bodies, but specific tasks were assigned. Teamwork developed to coordinate tasks, with some individuals performing specialized jobs in making the meat edible. Even the weakest had a part to play. The incipient social stratification just mentioned is another example of organization, one that sociologists call the division of labor. *Sixteenth,* an essential part of the human tendency to organize is the emergence of leadership—to direct and coordinate the activities of others. In this case, Canessa stands out.

Seventeenth, people attempt to maintain a respectable sense of self. These survivors were conforming individuals in that they had accepted the norms of their society and were striving for a respectable place within it. They wanted to continue to think of themselves as good people. Yet, they had to make a decision about doing an activity that went beyond the bounds of what they looked at as normal—one they even knew that "everyone" defined as wrong.

Eighteenth, it is possible to maintain a "good" self-image and still engage in deviant activities. Because the essence of human society is the social construction of reality, so the key to the self also lies in how reality is defined. If you can redefine an activity to make it "not deviant," then it does not threaten your sense of a "good" self. In this present instance, the Andes survivors looked on eating human flesh as part of their "duty to survive." To do a duty is a good thing, and, accordingly, the acts required by it cannot be "bad." In fact, they must be "good." (The most infamous example of the use of this basic principle was Hitler's SS, who looked on killing Jews as necessary for the survival of the "Aryan" race and culture. They even termed the slaughter a "good" act and their participation in it as patriotic and self-sacrificing.)

This principle helps many people get through what otherwise would be excruciatingly painful nights—for they would toss sleeplessly owing to a gnawing conscience. Redefinition, by keeping one's sense of self intact, allows people to participate in a variety of acts condemned by society—even those disapproved by the self. For most people, redefinition involves much less dramatic acts than eating human flesh, such as a college student cheating on a test or a boss firing a worker.

Nineteenth, some people participate in deviant acts even though they remain unconvinced about such redefinitions. (Some do not even attempt to redefine them.) They may do so from a variety of motives—from what they consider "sheer necessity" to the desire to reach a future goal. Liliana and Javier, who decided that they wanted a baby, are an example. Such persons have greater difficulty adjusting to their acts than those who redefine them as "good." (Even the latter may have difficulty, for redefinitions may be only partial, especially in the face of competing definitions.)

Twentieth, people feel they must justify their actions to others. This process of justifying the self involves clothing definitions of reality in forms thought to be acceptable to others. In order for definitions to be accepted, they must be made to fit into the others' already-existing definitional framework. In this case, the survivors first justified their proposed actions by redefining the bodies as meat and by saying that they had a duty to survive. After their rescue—speaking to a Roman Catholic audience—they used the analogy of holy communion to justify their act.

Twenty-first, to gain institutional support is to secure a broad, solid base for one's definitions of reality. Then one no longer stands alone, which is to invite insanity, nor is one a member of a small group, which is to invite ridicule and may require cutting off oneself from the larger group. In this case, institutional support was provided by the Roman Catholic Church, which, while not accepting the survivors' analogy of cannibalism as communion, allowed them to avoid the label of sin by defining their actions as allowable under the circumstances.

Finally, note that these principles are fundamental to human life. They do not simply apply to the Andes survivors—or to deviants in general—but they underlie human society. For all of us, reality is socially constructed, and the story of the Andes survivors contains the essence of human society.

24 The Saints and the Roughnecks

WILLIAM J. CHAMBLISS

When people deviate from what is expected of them, other people react. But on what do their reactions depend? Do they depend simply on the nature of the deviance itself, or is more involved? If so, what sorts of things?

It is these fascinating questions that Chambliss examines in this study of two groups of delinquents in the same high school. He found that although both groups were involved in serious and repetitive delinquent acts, one was perceived as a group of saints, the other was viewed as a bunch of roughnecks. After analyzing what influenced people's perceptions, and hence their reactions to the boys, Chambliss examines the far-reaching effects of those reactions. He indicates that in the case of the roughnecks, people's reactions helped lock the boys into behaviors that continued after high school, eventually leading to prison or to low-paying jobs. In contrast, social reactions to the saints set them on a life-course that not only meant staying out of prison but also entering well-paying positions of prestige.

EIGHT PROMISING YOUNG MEN—children of good, stable, white upper-middle-class families, active in school affairs, good pre-college students—were some of the most delinquent boys at Hanibal High School. While community residents knew that these boys occasionally sowed a few wild oats, they were totally unaware that sowing wild oats completely occupied the daily routine of these young men. The Saints were constantly occupied with truancy, drinking, wild driving, petty theft, and vandalism. Yet no one was officially arrested for any misdeed during the two years I observed them.

This record was particularly surprising in light of my observations during the same two years of another gang of Hanibal High School students, six lower-class white boys known as the Roughnecks. The Roughnecks were constantly in trouble with police and community even though their rate of delinquency was about equal with that of the Saints. What was the cause of this disparity? the result? The following consideration of the activities, social class, and community perceptions of both gangs may provide some answers.

The Saints from Monday to Friday

The Saints' principal daily concern was with getting out of school as early as possible. The boys managed to get out of school with minimum danger that they would be accused of playing hookey through an elaborate procedure for obtaining "legitimate" release from class. The most common procedure was for one boy to obtain the release of another by fabricating a meeting of some committee, program, or recognized club. Charles might raise his hand in his 9:00 chemistry class and ask to be excused—a euphemism for going to the bathroom. Charles would go to Ed's math class and inform the teacher that Ed was needed for a 9:30 rehearsal of the drama club play. The math teacher would recognize Ed and Charles as "good students" involved in numerous school activities and would permit Ed to leave at 9:30. Charles would return to his class, and Ed would go to Tom's English class to obtain his release. Tom would engineer Charles's escape. The strategy would continue until as many of the Saints as possible were freed. After a stealthy trip to the car (which had been parked in a strategic spot), the boys were off for a day of fun.

Over the two years I observed the Saints, this pattern was repeated nearly every day. There were variations on the theme, but in one form or another, the boys used this procedure for getting out of class and then off the school grounds. Rarely did all eight of the Saints manage to leave school at the same time. The average number avoiding school on the days I observed them was five.

Having escaped from the concrete corridors the boys usually went either to a pool hall on the other (lower-class) side of town or to a café in the suburbs. Both places were out of the way of people the boys were likely to know (family or school officials), and both provided a source of entertainment. The pool hall entertainment was the generally rough atmosphere, the occasional hustler, the sometimes drunk proprietor and, of course, the game of pool. The café's entertainment was provided by the owner. The boys would "accidentally" knock a glass on the floor or spill cola on the counter—not all the time, but enough to be sporting. They would also bend spoons, put salt in sugar bowls and generally tease whoever was working in the café. The owner had opened the café recently and was dependent on the boys' business which was, in fact, substantial since between the horsing around and the teasing they bought food and drinks.

The Saints on Weekends

On weekends the automobile was even more critical than during the week, for on weekends the Saints went to Big Town—a large city with a population of over a million 25 miles from Hanibal. Every Friday and Saturday night most of the Saints would meet between 8:00 and 8:30 and would go into Big Town. Big Town activities included drinking heavily in taverns or nightclubs, driving drunkenly through the streets, and committing acts of vandalism and playing pranks.

By midnight on Fridays and Saturdays the Saints were usually thoroughly high, and one or two of them were often so drunk they had to be carried to the cars. Then the boys drove around town, calling obscenities to women and girls; occasionally trying (unsuccessfully so far as I could tell) to pick girls up; and driving recklessly through red lights and at high speeds with their lights out. Occasionally they played "chicken." One boy would climb out the back window of the car and across the roof to the driver's side of the car while the car was moving at high speed (between 40 and 50 miles an hour); then the driver would move over and the boy who had just crawled across the car roof would take the driver's seat.

Searching for "fair game" for a prank was the boys' principal activity after they left the tavern. The boys would drive alongside a foot patrolman and ask directions to some street. If the policeman leaned on the car in the course of answering the question, the driver would speed away, causing him to lose his balance. The Saints were careful to play this prank only in an area where they were not going to spend much time and where they could quickly disappear around a corner to avoid having their license plate number taken.

Construction sites and road repair areas were the special province of the Saints' mischief. A soon-to-be-repaired hole in the road inevitably invited the Saints to remove lanterns and wooden barricades and put them in the car, leaving the hole unprotected. The boys would find a safe vantage point and wait for an unsuspecting motorist to drive into the hole. Often, though not always, the boys would go up to the motorist and commiserate with him about the dreadful way the city protected its citizenry.

Leaving the scene of the open hole and the motorist, the boys would then go searching for an appropriate place to erect the stolen barricade. An "appropriate place" was often a spot on a highway near a curve in the road where the barricade would not be seen by an oncoming motorist. The boys would wait to watch an unsuspecting motorist attempt to stop and (usually) crash into the wooden barricade. With saintly bearing the boys might offer help and understanding.

A stolen lantern might well find its way onto the back of a police car or hang from a street lamp. Once a lantern served as a prop for a reenactment of the "midnight ride of Paul Revere" until the "play," which was taking place at 2:00 A.M. in the center of a main street of Big Town, was interrupted by a police car several blocks away. The boys ran, leaving the lanterns on the street, and managed to avoid being apprehended.

Abandoned houses, especially if they were located in out-of-the-way places, were fair game for destruction and spontaneous vandalism. The boys would break windows, remove furniture to the yard and tear it apart, urinate on the walls, and scrawl obscenities inside.

Through all the pranks, drinking, and reckless driving the boys managed miraculously to avoid being stopped by police. Only twice in two years was I aware that they had been stopped by a Big Town policeman. Once was for speeding (which they did every time they drove whether they were drunk or sober), and the driver managed to convince the policeman that it was simply an error. The second time they were stopped they had just left a nightclub and were walking through an alley. Aaron stopped to urinate and the boys began making obscene remarks. A foot patrolman came into the alley, lectured the boys and sent them home. Before the boys got to the car one began talking in a loud voice again. The policeman, who had followed them down the alley, arrested this boy for disturbing the peace and took him to the police station where the other Saints gathered. After paying a $5.00 fine, and with the assurance that there would be no permanent record of the arrest, the boy was released.

The boys had a spirit of frivolity and fun about their escapades. They did not view what they were engaged in as "delinquency," though it surely was by any reasonable definition of that word. They simply viewed themselves as having a little fun and who, they would ask, was really hurt by it? The answer had to be no one, although this fact remains one of the most difficult things to explain about the gang's behavior. Unlikely though it seems, in two years of drinking, driving, carousing, and vandalism no one was seriously injured as a result of the Saints' activities.

The Saints in School

The Saints were highly successful in school. The average grade for the group was "B," with two of the boys having close to a straight "A" average. Almost all of the boys were popular and many of them held offices in the school. One of the boys was vice president of the student body one year. Six of the boys played on athletic teams.

At the end of their senior year, the student body selected ten seniors for special recognition as the "school wheels"; four of the ten were Saints. Teachers and school officials saw no problem with any of these boys and anticipated that they would all "make something of themselves."

How the boys managed to maintain this impression is surprising in view of their actual behavior in school. Their technique for covering truancy was so successful that teachers did not even realize that the boys were absent from school much of the time. Occasionally, of course, the system would backfire and then the boy was on his own. A boy who was caught would be most contrite, would plead guilty and ask for mercy. He inevitably got the mercy he sought.

Cheating on examinations was rampant, even to the point of orally communicating answers to exams as well as looking at one another's papers. Since none of the group studied, and since they were primarily dependent on one another for help, it is surprising that grades were so high. Teachers contributed to the deception in their admitted inclination to give these boys (and presumably others like them) the benefit of the doubt. When asked how the boys did in school, and when pressed on specific examinations, teachers might admit that they were disappointed in John's performance, but would quickly add that they "knew that he was capable of doing better," so John was given a higher grade than he had actually earned. How often this happened is impossible to know. During the time that I observed the group, I never saw any of the boys take homework home. Teachers may have been "understanding" very regularly.

One exception to the gang's generally good performance was Jerry, who had a "C" average in his junior year, experienced disaster the next year, and failed to graduate. Jerry had always been a little more nonchalant than the others about the liberties he took in school. Rather than wait for someone to come get him from class, he would offer his own excuse and leave. Although he probably did not miss any more class than most of the others in the group, he did not take the requisite pains to cover his absences. Jerry was the only Saint whom I ever heard talk back to a teacher. Although teachers often called him a "cut up" or a "smart kid," they never referred to him as a troublemaker or as a kid headed for trouble. It seems likely, then, that Jerry's failure his senior year and his mediocre performance his junior year were consequences of his not playing the game the proper way (possibly because he was disturbed by his parents' divorce). His teachers regarded him as "immature" and not quite ready to get out of high school.

The Police and the Saints

The local police saw the Saints as good boys who were among the leaders of the youth in the community. Rarely, the boys might be stopped in town for speeding or for running a stop sign. When this happened the boys were always polite, contrite, and pled for mercy. As in school, they received the mercy they asked for. None ever received a ticket or was taken into the precinct by the local police.

The situation in Big Town, where the boys engaged in most of their delinquency, was only slightly different. The police there did not know the boys at all, although occasionally the boys were stopped by a patrolman. Once they were caught taking a lantern from a construction site. Another time they were stopped for running a stop sign, and on several occasions they were stopped for speeding. Their behavior was as before: contrite, polite, and penitent. The urban police, like the local police, accepted their demeanor as sincere. More important, the urban police were convinced that these were good boys just out for a lark.

The Roughnecks

Hanibal townspeople never perceived the Saints' high level of delinquency. The Saints were good boys who just went in for an occasional prank. After all, they were well dressed, well mannered, and had nice cars. The Roughnecks were a different story. Although the two gangs of boys were the same age, and both groups engaged in an equal amount of wild-oat sowing, everyone agreed that the not-so-well-dressed, not-so-well-mannered, not-so-rich boys were heading for trouble. Townspeople would say, "You can see the gang members at the drugstore, night after night, leaning against the storefront (sometimes drunk) or slouching around inside buying cokes, reading magazines, and probably stealing old Mr. Wall blind. When they are outside and girls walk by, even respectable girls, these boys make suggestive remarks. Sometimes their remarks are downright lewd."

From the community's viewpoint, the real indication that these kids were in trouble was that they were constantly involved with the police. Some of them had been picked up for stealing, mostly small stuff, of course, "but still it's stealing small stuff that leads to big time crimes." "Too bad," people said. "Too bad that these boys couldn't behave like the other kids in town; stay out of trouble, be polite to adults, and look to their future."

The community's impression of the degrees to which this group of six boys (ranging in age from 16 to 19) engaged in delinquency was somewhat distorted. In some ways the gang was more delinquent than the community thought; in other ways they were less.

The fighting activities of the group were fairly readily and accurately perceived by almost everyone. At least once a month, the boys would get into some sort of fight, although most fights were scraps between members of the group or involved only one member of the group and some peripheral hanger-on. Only three times in the period of observation did the group fight together: once against a gang from across town, once against two blacks, and once against a group of boys from another school. For the first two fights the group went out "looking for trouble"—and they found it both times. The third fight followed a football game and began spontaneously with an argument on the football field between one of the Roughnecks and a member of the opposition's football team.

Jack has a particular propensity for fighting and was involved in most of the brawls. He was a prime mover of the escalation of arguments into fights.

More serious than fighting, had the community been aware of it, was theft. Although almost everyone was aware that the boys occasionally stole things, they did not realize the extent of the activity. Petty stealing was a frequent event for the Roughnecks. Sometimes they stole as a group and coordinated their efforts; other times they stole in pairs. Rarely did they steal alone.

The thefts ranged from very small things like paperback books, comics, and ballpoint pens to expensive items like watches. The nature of the thefts varied from time to time. The gang would go through a period of systematically lifting items from automobiles or school lockers. Types of thievery varied with the whim of the gang. Some forms of thievery were more profitable than others, but all thefts were for profit, not just thrills.

Roughnecks siphoned gasoline from cars as often as they had access to an automobile, which was not very often. Unlike the Saints, who owned their own cars, the Roughnecks would have to borrow their parents' cars, an event which occurred only eight or nine times a year. The boys claimed to have stolen cars for joy rides from time to time.

Ron committed the most serious of the group's offenses. With an unidentified associate the boy attempted to burglarize a gasoline station. Although this station had been robbed twice previously in the same month, Ron denied any involvement in either of the other thefts. When Ron and his accomplice approached the station, the owner was hiding in the bushes beside the station. He fired both barrels of a double-barreled shotgun at the boys. Ron was severely injured; the other boy ran away and was never caught. Though he remained in critical condition for several months, Ron finally recovered and served six months of the following year in reform school. Upon release from reform school, Ron was put back a grade in school, and began running around with a different gang of boys. The Roughnecks considered the new gang less delinquent than themselves, and during the following year Ron had no more trouble with the police.

The Roughnecks, then, engaged mainly in three types of delinquency: theft, drinking, and fighting. Although community members perceived that this gang of kids was delinquent, they mistakenly believed that their illegal activities were primarily drinking, fighting, and being a nuisance to passersby.

278 / *William J. Chambliss*

Drinking was limited among the gang members, although it did occur, and theft was much more prevalent than anyone realized.

Drinking would doubtless have been more prevalent had the boys had ready access to liquor. Since they rarely had automobiles at their disposal, they could not travel very far, and the bars in town would not serve them. Most of the boys had little money, and this, too, inhibited their purchase of alcohol. Their major source of liquor was a local drunk who would buy them a fifth if they would give him enough extra to buy himself a pint of whiskey or a bottle of wine.

The community's perception of drinking as prevalent stemmed from the fact that it was the most obvious delinquency the boys engaged in. When one of the boys had been drinking, even a casual observer seeing him on the corner would suspect that he was high.

There was a high level of mutual distrust and dislike between the Roughnecks and the police. The boys felt very strongly that the police were unfair and corrupt. Some evidence existed that the boys were correct in their perception.

The main source of the boys' dislike for the police undoubtedly stemmed from the fact that the police would sporadically harass the group. From the standpoint of the boys, these acts of occasional enforcement of the law were whimsical and uncalled for. It made no sense to them, for example, that the police would come to the corner occasionally and threaten them with arrest for loitering when the night before the boys had been out siphoning gasoline from cars and the police had been nowhere in sight. To the boys, the police were stupid on the one hand, for not being where they should have been and catching the boys in a serious offense, and unfair on the other hand, for trumping up "loitering" charges against them.

From the viewpoint of the police, the situation was quite different. They knew, with all the confidence necessary to be a policeman, that these boys were engaged in criminal activities. They knew this partly from occasionally catching them, mostly from circumstantial evidence ("the boys were around when those tires were slashed"), and partly because the police shared the view of the community in general that this was a bad bunch of boys. The best the police could hope to do was to be sensitive to the fact that these boys were engaged in illegal acts and arrest them whenever there was some evidence that they had been involved. Whether or not the boys had in fact committed a particular act in a particular way was not especially important. The police had a broader view: their job was to stamp out these kids' crimes; the tactics were not as important as the end result.

Over the period that the group was under observation, each member was arrested at least once. Several of the boys were arrested a number of times and spent at least one night in jail. While most were never taken to court, two of the boys were sentenced to six months' incarceration in boys' schools.

The Roughnecks in School

The Roughnecks' behavior in school was not particularly disruptive. During school hours they did not all hang around together, but tended instead to spend most of their time with one or two other members of the gang who were their special buddies. Although every member of the gang attempted to avoid school as much as possible, they were not particularly successful and most of them attended school with surprising regularity. They considered school a burden—something to be gotten through with a minimum of conflict. If they were "bugged" by a particular teacher, it could lead to trouble. One of the boys, Al, once threatened to beat up a teacher and, according to the other boys, the teacher hid under a desk to escape him.

Teachers saw the boys the way the general community did, as heading for trouble, as being uninterested in making something of themselves. Some were also seen as being incapable of meeting the academic standards of the school. Most of the teachers expressed concern for this group of boys and were willing to pass them despite poor performance, in the belief that failing them would only aggravate the problem.

The group of boys had a grade point average just slightly above "C." No one in the group failed either grade, and no one had better than a "C" average. They were very consistent in their achievement or, at least, the teachers were consistent in their perception of the boys' achievement.

Two of the boys were good football players. Herb was acknowledged to be the best player in the school, and Jack was almost as good. Both boys were criticized for their failure to abide by training rules, for refusing to come to practice as often as they should, and for not playing their best during practice. What they lacked in sportsmanship they made up for in skill, apparently, and played every game no matter how poorly they had performed in practice or how many practice sessions they had missed.

Two Questions

Why did the community, the school, and the police react to the Saints as though they were good, upstanding, nondelinquent youths with bright futures but to the Roughnecks as though they were tough, young criminals who were headed for trouble? Why did the Roughnecks and the Saints in fact have quite different careers after high school—careers which, by and large, lived up to the expectations of the community?

The most obvious explanation for the differences in the community's and law enforcement agencies' reactions to the two gangs is that one group of boys was "more delinquent" than the other. Which group was more delinquent? The answer to this question will determine in part how we explain the differential responses to these groups by the members of the community and, particularly, by law enforcement and school officials.

In sheer number of illegal acts, the Saints were the more delinquent. They were truant from school for at least part of the day almost every day of the week. In addition, their drinking and vandalism occurred with surprising regularity. The Roughnecks, in contrast, engaged sporadically in delinquent episodes. While these episodes were frequent, they certainly did not occur on a daily or even a weekly basis.

The difference in frequency of offenses was probably caused by the Roughnecks' inability to obtain liquor and to manipulate legitimate excuses from school. Since the Roughnecks had less money than the Saints, and teachers carefully supervised their school activities, the Roughnecks' hearts may have been as black as the Saints', but their misdeeds were not nearly as frequent.

There are really no clear-cut criteria by which to measure qualitative differences in antisocial behavior. The most important dimension is generally referred to as the "seriousness" of the offenses.

If seriousness encompasses the relative economic costs of delinquent acts, then some assessment can be made. The Roughnecks probably stole an average of about $5.00 worth of goods a week. Some weeks the figure was considerably higher, but these times must be balanced against long periods when almost nothing was stolen.

The Saints were more continuously engaged in delinquency, but their acts were not for the most part costly to property. Only their vandalism and occasional theft of gasoline would so qualify. Perhaps once or twice a month they would siphon a tankful of gas. The other costly items were street signs, construction lanterns, and the like. All of these acts combined probably did not quite average $5.00 a week, partly because much of the stolen equipment was abandoned and presumably could be recovered. The difference in cost of stolen property between the two groups was trivial, but the Roughnecks probably had a slightly more expensive set of activities than did the Saints.

Another meaning of seriousness is the potential threat of physical harm to members of the community and to the boys themselves. The Roughnecks were more prone to physical violence; they not only welcomed an opportunity to fight; they went seeking it. In addition, they fought among themselves frequently. Although the fighting never included deadly weapons, it was still a menace, however minor, to the physical safety of those involved.

The Saints never fought. They avoided physical conflict both inside and outside the group. At the same time, though, the Saints frequently endangered their own and other people's lives. They did so almost every time they drove a car, especially if they had been drinking. Sober, their driving was risky; under the influence of alcohol it was horrendous. In addition, the Saints endangered the lives of others with their pranks. Street excavations left unmarked were a very serious hazard.

Evaluating the relative seriousness of the two gangs' activities is difficult. The community reacted as though the behavior of the Roughnecks was a problem, and they reacted as though the behavior of the Saints was not. But the members of the community were ignorant of the array of delinquent acts that characterized the Saints' behavior. Although concerned citizens were unaware of much of the Roughnecks' behavior as well, they were much better informed about the Roughnecks' involvement in delinquency than they were about the Saints'.

Visibility

Differential treatment of the two gangs resulted in part because one gang was infinitely more visible than the other. This differential visibility was a direct function of the economic standing of the families. The Saints had access to automobiles and were able to remove themselves from the sight of the community. In as routine a decision as to where to go to have a milkshake after school, the Saints stayed away from the mainstream of community life. Lacking transportation, the Roughnecks could not make it to the edge of town. The center of town was the only practical place for them to meet since their homes were scattered throughout the town and any noncentral meeting place put an undue hardship on some members. Through necessity the Roughnecks congregated in a crowded area where everyone in the community passed frequently, including teachers and law enforcement officers. They could easily see the Roughnecks hanging around the drugstore.

The Roughnecks, of course, made themselves even more visible by making remarks to passersby and by occasionally getting into fights on the corner. Meanwhile, just as regularly, the Saints were either at the café on one edge of town or in the pool hall at the other edge of town. Without any particular realization that they were making themselves inconspicuous, the Saints were able to hide their time-wasting. Not only were they removed from the mainstream of traffic, but they were almost always inside a building.

On their escapades the Saints were also relatively invisible, since they left Hanibal and traveled to Big Town. Here, too, they were mobile, roaming the city, rarely going to the same area twice.

Demeanor

To the notion of visibility must be added the difference in the responses of group members to outside intervention with their activities. If one of the Saints was confronted with an accusing policeman, even if he felt he was truly innocent of a wrongdoing, his demeanor was apologetic and penitent. A Roughneck's attitude was almost the polar opposite. When confronted with a threatening adult authority, even one who tried to be pleasant, the Roughneck's hostility and disdain were clearly observable. Sometimes he might attempt to put up a veneer of respect, but it was thin and was not accepted as sincere by the authority.

School was no different from the community at large. The Saints could manipulate the system by feigning compliance with the school norms. The availability of cars at school meant that once free from the immediate sight of the teacher, the boys could disappear rapidly. And this escape was well enough planned that no administrator or teacher was nearby when the boys left. A Roughneck who wished to escape for a few hours was in a bind. If it were possible to get free from class, downtown was still a mile away, and even if he arrived there, he was still very visible. Truancy for the Roughnecks meant almost certain detection, while the Saints enjoyed almost complete immunity from sanctions.

Bias

Community members were not aware of the transgressions of the Saints. Even if the Saints had been less discreet, their favorite delinquencies would have been perceived as less serious than those of the Roughnecks.

In the eyes of the police and school officials, a boy who drinks in an alley and stands intoxicated on the street corner is committing a more serious offense than is a boy who drinks to inebriation in a nightclub or a tavern and drives around afterwards in a car. Similarly, a boy who steals a wallet from a store will be viewed as having committed a more serious offense than a boy who steals a lantern from a construction site.

Perceptual bias also operates with respect to the demeanor of the boys in the two groups when they are confronted by adults. It is not simply that adults dislike the posture affected by boys of the Roughneck ilk; more important is the conviction that the posture adopted by the Roughnecks is an indication of their devotion and commitment to deviance as a way of life. The posture becomes a cue, just as the type of the offense is a cue, to the degree to which the known transgressions are indicators of the youths' potential for other problems.

Visibility, demeanor, and bias are surface variables which explain the day-to-day operations of the police. Why do these surface variables operate as they do? Why did the police choose to disregard the Saints' delinquencies while breathing down the backs of the Roughnecks?

The answer lies in the class structure of American society and the control of legal institutions by those at the top of the class structure. Obviously, no representative of the upper class drew up the operational chart for the police which led them to look in the ghettos and on street corners—which led them to see the demeanor of lower-class youth as troublesome and that of upper-middle-class youth as tolerable. Rather, the procedures simply developed from experience—experience with irate and influential upper-middle-class parents insisting that their son's vandalism was simply a prank and his drunkenness only a momentary "sowing of wild oats"—experience with cooperative or indifferent, powerless, lower-class parents who acquiesced to the law's definition of their son's behavior.

Adult Careers of the Saints and the Roughnecks

The community's confidence in the potential of the Saints and the Roughnecks apparently was justified. If anything, the community members underestimated the degree to which these youngsters would turn out "good" or "bad."

Seven of the eight members of the Saints went on to college immediately after high school. Five of the boys graduated from college in four years. The sixth one finished college after two years in the army, and the seventh spent four years in the air force before returning to college and receiving a B.A. degree. Of these seven college graduates, three went on for advanced degrees. One finished law school and is now active in state politics, one finished medical school and is practicing near Hanibal, and one boy is now working for a Ph.D. The other four college graduates entered submanagerial, managerial, or executive training positions with larger firms.

The only Saint who did not complete college was Jerry. Jerry had failed to graduate from high school with the other Saints. During his second senior year, after the other Saints had gone on to college, Jerry began to hang around with what several teachers described as a "rough crowd"—the gang that was heir apparent to the Roughnecks. At the end of his second senior year, when he did graduate from high school, Jerry took a job as a used-car salesman, got married, and quickly had a child. Although he made several abortive attempts to go to college by attending night school, when I last saw him (ten years after high school) Jerry was unemployed and had been living on unemployment for almost a year. His wife worked as a waitress.

Some of the Roughnecks have lived up to community expectations. A number of them were headed for trouble. A few were not.

Jack and Herb were the athletes among the Roughnecks, and their athletic prowess paid off handsomely. Both boys received unsolicited athletic scholarships to college. After Herb received his scholarship (near the end of his senior year), he apparently did an about-face. His demeanor became very similar to that of the Saints. Although he remained a member in good standing of the Roughnecks, he stopped participating in most activities and did not hang out on the corner as often.

Jack did not change. If anything, he became more prone to fighting. He even made excuses for accepting the scholarship. He told the other gang members that the school had guaranteed him a "C" average if he would come to play football—an idea that seems far-fetched, even in this day of highly competitive recruiting.

During the summer after graduation from high school, Jack attempted suicide by jumping from a tall building. The jump would certainly have killed most people trying it, but Jack survived. He entered college in the fall and played four years of football. He and Herb graduated in four years, and both are teaching and coaching in high schools. They are married and have stable families. If anything, Jack appears to have a more prestigious position in the community than does Herb, though both are well respected and secure in their positions.

Two of the boys never finished high school. Tommy left at the end of his junior year and went to another state. That summer he was arrested and placed on probation on a manslaughter charge. Three years later he was arrested for murder; he pleaded guilty to second degree murder and is serving a 30-year sentence in the state penitentiary.

Al, the other boy who did not finish high school, also left the state in his senior year. He is serving a life sentence in a state penitentiary for first degree murder.

Wes is a small-time gambler. He finished high school and "bummed around." After several years he made contact with a bookmaker who employed him as a runner. Later he acquired his own area and has been working it ever since. His position among the bookmakers is almost identical to the position he had in the gang; he is always around, but no one is really aware of him. He makes no trouble, and he does not get into any. Steady, reliable, capable of keeping his mouth closed, he plays the game by the rules, even though the game is an illegal one.

That leaves only Ron. Some of his former friends reported that they had heard he was "driving a truck up north," but no one could provide any concrete information.

Reinforcement

The community responded to the Roughnecks as boys in trouble, and the boys agreed with that perception. Their pattern of deviancy was reinforced, and breaking away from it became increasingly unlikely. Once the boys acquired an image of themselves as deviants, they selected new friends who affirmed that self-image. As that self-conception became more firmly entrenched, they also became willing to try new and more extreme deviances. With their growing alienation came freer expression of disrespect and hostility for representatives of the legitimate society. This disrespect increased the community's negativism, perpetuating the entire process of commitment to deviance. Lack of a commitment to deviance works the same way. In either case, the process will perpetuate itself unless some event (like a scholarship to college or a sudden failure) external to the established relationship intervenes. For two of the Roughnecks (Herb and Jack), receiving college athletic scholarships created new relations and culminated in a break with the established pattern of deviance. In the case of one of the Saints (Jerry), his parents' divorce and his failing to graduate from high school changed some of his other relations. Being held back in school for a year and losing his place among the Saints had sufficient impact on Jerry to alter his self-image and virtually to assure that he would not go on to college as his peers did. Although the experiments of life can rarely be reversed, it seems likely in view of the behavior of the other boys who did not enjoy this special treatment by the school that Jerry, too, would have "become something" had he graduated as anticipated. For Herb and Jack outside intervention worked to their advantage; for Jerry it was his undoing.

Selective perception and labeling—finding, processing, and punishing some kinds of criminality and not others—means that visible, poor, nonmobile, outspoken, undiplomatic "tough" kids will be noticed, whether their actions are seriously delinquent or not. Other kids, who have established a reputation for being bright (even though underachieving), disciplined, and involved in respectable activities, who are mobile and monied, will be invisible when they deviate from sanctioned activities. They'll sow their wild oats—

perhaps even wider and thicker than their lower-class cohorts—but they won't be noticed. When it's time to leave adolescence most will follow the expected path, settling into the ways of the middle class, remembering fondly the delinquent but unnoticed fling of their youth. The Roughnecks and others like them may turn around, too. It is more likely that their noticeable deviance will have been so reinforced by police and community that their lives will be effectively channeled into careers consistent with their adolescent background.

25 The Pathology of Imprisonment

PHILIP G. ZIMBARDO

Why are our prisons such powder kegs? To most people, this is not a difficult question and the answer is obvious—because of the kind of people who are locked up in prisons: They are criminals, antisocial, and disposed to violence. If not that, then they hate the guards, the food, or the restrictions of prison life (which is what they deserved in the first place!). Similarly, people have little difficulty explaining why prison guards are brutal: It is either the type of people with whom the guards must deal ("animals") or the type of people who are attracted to being prison guards in the first place ("sadistic types"). Such reasons are commonly cited to explain prison violence. It turns out, however, that much more fundamental social processes are involved. As Zimbardo's remarkable experiment uncovered, the structuring of relationships within the prison lays the foundation for prison brutality and violence.

    While reading this fascinating account, you may begin to think about how prisons could be improved in order to minimize violence. To reach such a goal, what changes would you suggest that we make in the social structure of prisons?

I was recently released from solitary confinement after being held therein for 37 months [months!]. A silent system was imposed upon me and to even whisper to the man in the next cell resulted in being beaten by guards, sprayed with chemical mace, blackjacked, stomped and thrown into a strip-cell naked to sleep on a concrete floor without bedding, covering, wash basin or even a toilet. The floor served as toilet and bed, and even there the silent system was enforced. To let a moan escape your lips because of the pain and discomfort . . . resulted in another beating. I spent not days, but months there during my 37 months in solitary. . . . I have filed every writ possible against the administrative acts of brutality. The state courts have all denied the petitions. Because of my refusal to let the things die down and forget all that happened during my 37 months in solitary . . . I am the most hated prisoner in [this] penitentiary, and called a "hardcore incorrigible."

    Maybe I am an incorrigible, but if true, it's because I would rather die than to accept being treated as less than a human being. I have never complained of my prison sentence as being unjustified except through legal means of appeals. I have never put a knife on a guard's throat and demanded my release. I know that thieves must be punished and I don't justify stealing, even though I am a thief myself. but now I don't think I will be a thief when I am released. No, I'm not rehabilitated. It's just that I no longer think of becoming wealthy by stealing. I now only think of killing—killing those who have beaten me and treated me as if I were a dog. I hope and pray for the sake of my own soul and future life of freedom that I am able to overcome the bitterness and hatred which eats daily at my soul, but I know to overcome it will not be easy.

THIS ELOQUENT PLEA FOR PRISON REFORM—for humane treatment of human beings, for the basic dignity that is the right of every American—came to me secretly in a letter from a prisoner who cannot be identified because he is still in a state correctional institution. He sent it to me because he read of an experiment I recently conducted at Stanford University. In an attempt to understand just what it means psychologically to be a prisoner or a prison guard, Craig Haney, Curt Banks, Dave Jaffe, and I created our own prison. We carefully screened over 70 volunteers who answered an ad in a Palo Alto city newspaper and ended up with about two dozen young men who were selected to be part of this study. They were mature, emotionally stable, normal, intelligent college students from middle-class homes throughout the United States and Canada. They appeared to represent the cream of the crop of this generation. None had any criminal record and all were relatively homogeneous on many dimensions initially.

Half were arbitrarily designated as prisoners by a flip of a coin, the others as guards. These were the roles they were to play in our simulated prison. The guards were made aware of the potential seriousness and danger of the situation and their own vulnerability. They made up their own formal rules for maintaining law, order, and respect, and were generally free to improvise new ones during their eight-hour, three-man shifts. The prisoners were unexpectedly picked up at their homes by a city policeman in a squad car, searched, handcuffed, fingerprinted, booked at the Palo Alto station house, and taken blindfolded to our jail. There they were stripped, deloused, put into a uniform, given a number, and put into a cell with two other prisoners where they expected to live for the next two weeks. The pay was good ($15 a day), and their motivation was to make money.

We observed and recorded on videotape the events that occurred in the prison, and we interviewed and tested the prisoners and guards at various points throughout the study. Some of the videotapes of the actual encounters between the prisoners and guards were seen on the NBC News feature "Chronolog" on November 26, 1971.

At the end of only six days we had to close down our mock prison because what we saw was frightening. It was no longer apparent to most of the subjects (or to us) where reality ended and their roles began. The majority had indeed become prisoners or guards, no longer able to clearly differentiate between role playing and self. There were dramatic changes in virtually every aspect of their behavior, thinking, and feeling. In less than a week the experience of imprisonment undid (temporarily) a lifetime of learning; human values were suspended, self-concepts were challenged, and the ugliest, most base, pathological side of human nature surfaced. We were horrified because we saw some boys (guards) treat others as if they were despicable animals, taking pleasure in cruelty, while other boys (prisoners) became servile, dehumanized robots who thought only of escape, of their own individual survival, and of their mounting hatred for the guards.

We had to release three prisoners in the first four days because they had such acute situational traumatic reactions as hysterical crying, confusion in thinking, and severe depression. Others begged to be paroled, and all but three were willing to forfeit all the money they had earned if they could be paroled. By then (the fifth day) they had been so programmed to think of themselves as prisoners that when their request for parole was denied, they returned docilely to their cells. Now, had they been thinking as college students acting in an oppressive experiment, they would have quit once they no longer wanted the $15 a day we used as our only incentive. However, the reality was not quitting an experiment but "being paroled by the parole board from the Stanford County Jail." By the last days, the earlier solidarity among the prisoners (systematically broken by the guards) dissolved into "each man for himself." Finally, when one of their fellows was put into solitary confinement (a small closet) for refusing to eat, the prisoners were given a choice by one of the guards: give up their blankets and the incorrigible prisoner would be let out, or keep their blankets and he would be kept in all night. They voted to keep their blankets and to abandon their brother.

About a third of the guards became tyrannical in their arbitrary use of power, in enjoying their control over other people. They were corrupted by the power of their roles and became quite inventive in their techniques of breaking the spirit of the prisoners and making them feel they were worthless. Some of the guards merely did their jobs as tough but fair correctional officers, and several were good guards from the prisoners' point of view since they did them small favors and were friendly. However, no good guards ever interfered with a command by any of the bad guards; they never intervened on the side of the prisoners, they never told the others to ease off because it was only an experiment, and they never even came to me as prison superintendent or experimenter in charge to complain. In part, they were good because the others were bad; they needed the others to help establish their own egos in a positive light. In a sense, the good guards perpetuated the prison more than the other guards because their own need to be liked prevented them from disobeying or violating the implicit guards' code. At the same time, the act of befriending the prisoners created a social reality which made the prisoners less likely to rebel.

By the end of the week the experiment had become a reality, as if it were a Pirandello play directed by Kafka that just keeps going after the audience has left. The consultant for our prison, Carlo Prescott, an exconvict with 16 years of imprisonment in California's jails, would get so depressed and furious each time he visited our prison, because of its psychological similarity to his experiences, that he would have to leave. A Catholic priest who was a former prison chaplain in Washington, D.C., talked to our prisoners after four days and said they were just like the other first-timers he had seen.

But in the end, I called off the experiment not because of the horror I saw out there in the prison yard, but because of the horror of realizing that *I* could have easily traded places with the most brutal guard or become the weakest prisoner full of hatred at being so powerless that I could not eat, sleep, or go to the toilet without permission of the authorities. *I* could have become Calley at My Lai, George Jackson at San Quentin, one of the men at Attica, or the prisoner quoted at the beginning of this article.

Individual behavior is largely under the control of social forces and environmental contingencies rather than personality traits, character, will power, or other empirically unvalidated constructs. Thus we create an illusion of freedom by attributing more internal control to ourselves, to the individual, than actually exists. We thus underestimate the power and pervasiveness of situational controls over behavior because: (a) they are often nonobvious and subtle, (b) we can often avoid entering situations where we might be so controlled, (c) we label as "weak" or "deviant" people in those situations who do behave differently from how we believed we would.

Each of us carries around in our heads a favorable self-image in which we are essentially just, fair, humane, and understanding. For example, we could not imagine inflicting pain on others without much provocation or hurting people who had done nothing to us, who in fact were even liked by us. However, there is a growing body of social psychological research which underscores the conclusion derived from this prison study. Many people, perhaps the majority, can be made to do almost anything when put into psychologically compelling situations—regardless of their morals, ethics, values, attitudes, beliefs, or personal convictions. My colleague, Stanley Milgram, has shown that more than 60 percent of the population will deliver what they think is a series of painful electric shocks to another person even after the victim cries for mercy, begs them to stop, and then apparently passes out. The subjects complained that they did not want to inflict more pain but blindly obeyed the command of the authority figure (the experimenter) who said that they must go on. In my own research on violence, I have seen mild-mannered co-eds repeatedly give shocks (which they thought were causing pain) to another girl, a stranger whom they had rated very favorably, simply by being made to feel anonymous and put in a situation where they were expected to engage in this activity.

Observers of these and similar experimental situations never predict their outcomes and estimate that it is unlikely that they themselves would behave similarly. They can be so confident only when they are outside the situation. However, since the majority of people in these studies do act in nonrational, nonobvious ways, it follows that the majority of observers would also succumb to the social psychological forces in the situation.

With regard to prisons, we can state that the mere act of assigning labels to people and putting them into a situation where those labels acquire validity and meaning is sufficient to elicit pathological behavior. This pathology is not predictable from any available diagnostic indicators we have in the social sciences, and is extreme enough to modify in very significant ways fundamental attitudes and behavior. The prison situation, as presently arranged, is guaranteed to generate severe enough pathological reactions in both guards and prisoners as to debase their humanity, lower their feelings of self-worth, and make it difficult for them to be part of a society outside of their prison.

For years our national leaders have been pointing to the enemies of freedom, to the fascist or communist threat to the American way of life. In so doing they have overlooked the threat of social anarchy that is building within our own country without any outside agitation. As soon as a person comes to the realization that he is being imprisoned by his society or individuals in it, then, in the best American tradition, he demands liberty and rebels, accepting death as an alternative. The third alternative, however, is to allow oneself to become a good prisoner—docile, cooperative, uncomplaining, conforming in thought, and complying in deed.

Our prison authorities now point to the militant agitators who are still vaguely referred to as part of some communist plot, as the irresponsible, incorrigible troublemakers. They imply that there would be no trouble, riots, hostages, or deaths if it weren't for this small band of bad prisoners. In other words, then, everything would return to "normal" again in the life of our nation's prisons if they could break these men.

The riots in prison are coming from within—from within every man and woman who refuses to let the system turn them into an object, a number, a thing, or a no-thing. It is not communist-inspired, but inspired by the spirit of American freedom. No man wants to be enslaved. To be powerless, to be subject to the arbitrary exercise of power, to not be recognized as a human being is to be a slave.

To be a militant prisoner is to become aware that the physical jails are but more blatant extensions of the forms of social and psychological oppression experienced daily in the nation's ghettos. They are trying to awaken the conscience of the nation to the ways in which the American ideals are being perverted, apparently in the name of justice but actually under the banner of apathy, fear, and hatred. If we do not listen to the pleas of the prisoners at Attica to be treated like human beings, then we have all become brutalized by our priorities for property rights over human rights. The consequence will not only be more prison riots but a loss of all those ideals on which this country was founded.

The public should be aware that they own the prisons and that their business is failing. The 70 percent recidivism rate and the escalation in severity of crimes committed by graduates of our prisons are evidence that current prisons fail to rehabilitate the inmates in any positive way. Rather, they are breeding grounds for hatred of the establishment, a hatred that makes every citizen a target of violent assault. Prisons are a bad investment for us taxpayers. Until now we have not cared; we have turned over to wardens and prison authorities the unpleasant job of keeping people who threaten us out of our sight. Now we are shocked to learn that their management practices have failed to improve the product and instead turn petty thieves into murderers. We must insist upon new management or improved operating procedures.

The cloak of secrecy should be removed from the prisons. Prisoners claim they are brutalized by the guards; guards say it is a lie. Where is the impartial test of the truth in such a situation? Prison officials have forgotten that they work for us, that they are only public servants whose salaries are paid by our taxes. They act as if it is their prison, like a child with a toy he won't share. Neither lawyers, judges, the legislature, nor the public is allowed into prisons to ascertain the truth unless the visit is sanctioned by authorities and until all is prepared for their visit. I was shocked to learn that my request to join a congressional investigating committee's tour of San Quentin and Soledad was refused, as was that of the news media.

There should be an ombudsman in every prison, not under the pay or control of the prison authority, and responsible only to the courts, the state legislature, and the public. Such a person could report on violations of constitutional and human rights.

Guards must be given better training than they now receive for the difficult job society imposes upon them. To be a prison guard as now constituted is to be put in a situation of constant threat from within the prison, with no social recognition from the society at large. As was shown graphically at Attica, prison guards are also prisoners of the system who can be sacrificed to the demands of the public to be punitive and the needs of politicians to preserve an image. Social scientists and business administrators should be called upon to design and help carry out this training.

The relationship between the individual (who is sentenced by the courts to a prison term) and his community must be maintained. How can a prisoner return to a dynamically changing society that most of us cannot cope with after being out of it for a number of years? There should be more community involvement in these rehabilitation centers, more ties encouraged and promoted between the trainees and family and friends, more educational opportunities to prepare them for returning to their communities as more valuable members of it than they were before they left.

Finally, the main ingredient necessary to effect any change at all in prison reform, in the rehabilitation of a single prisoner, or even in the optimal development of a child is caring. Reform must start with people—especially people with power—caring about the well-being of others. Underneath the toughest, society-hating convict, rebel, or anarchist is a human being who wants his existence to be recognized by his fellows and who wants someone else to care about whether he lives or dies and to grieve if he lives imprisoned rather than lives free.

26 On Being Sane in Insane Places

DAVID L. ROSENHAN

On the one hand, it is not uncommon for people who violate *explicit* rules written into law to find themselves enmeshed in a formal system that involves passing judgment on their fitness to remain in society. As we have just seen with the preceding selection, removing people's freedom can thrust them into a highly volatile situation. On the other hand, people who violate *implicit* rules (the assumptions about what characterizes "normal" people) also can find themselves caught up in a formal system that involves passing judgment on their fitness to remain in society. If found "guilty of insanity," they, too, are institutionalized—placed in the care of keepers who oversee almost all aspects of their lives.

The taken-for-granted assumption in institutionalizing people who violate implicit rules is that we are able to tell the sane from the insane. If we cannot do so, the practice itself would be insane! In that case, we would have to question contemporary psychiatry as a mechanism of social control. But what kind of question is this? Even most of us non-psychiatrists can tell the difference between who is sane and who is not, can't we? In a fascinating experiment, Rosenhan put to the test whether or not even psychiatrists can differentiate between the sane and the insane. As detailed in this account, the results contain a few surprises.

IF SANITY AND INSANITY EXIST . . . how shall we know them? The question is neither capricious nor itself insane. However much we may be personally convinced that we can tell the normal from the abnormal, the evidence is simply not compelling. It is commonplace, for example, to read about murder trials wherein eminent psychiatrists for the defense are contradicted by equally eminent psychiatrists for the prosecution on the matter of the defendant's sanity. More generally, there are a great deal of conflicting data on the reliability, utility, and meaning of such terms as "sanity," "insanity," "mental illness," and "schizophrenia."[1] Finally, as early as 1934, Benedict suggested that normality and abnormality are not universal.[2] What is viewed as normal in one culture may be seen as quite aberrant in another.

Thus, notions of normality and abnormality may not be quite as accurate as people believe they are.

To raise questions regarding normality and abnormality is in no way to question the fact that some behaviors are deviant or odd. Murder is deviant. So, too, are hallucinations. Nor does raising such questions deny the existence of the personal anguish that is often associated with "mental illness." Anxiety and depression exist. Psychological suffering exists. But normality and abnormality, sanity and insanity, and the diagnoses that flow from them may be less substantive than many believe them to be.

At its heart, the question of whether the sane can be distinguished from the insane (and whether degrees of insanity can be distinguished from each other) is a simple matter: Do the salient characteristics that lead to diagnoses reside in the patients themselves or in the environments and contexts in which observers find them? From Bleuler, through Kretschmer, through the formulators of the recently revised *Diagnostic and Statistical Manual* of the American Psychiatric Association, the belief has been strong that patients present symptoms, that those symptoms can be categorized, and, implicitly, that the sane are distinguishable from the insane. More recently, however, this belief has been questioned. Based in part on theoretical and anthropological considerations, but also on philosophical, legal, and therapeutic ones, the view has grown that psychological categorization of mental illness is useless at best and downright harmful, misleading, and pejorative at worst. Psychiatric diagnoses, in this view, are in the minds of the observers and are not valid summaries of characteristics displayed by the observed.[3,4,5]

Gains can be made in deciding which of these is more nearly accurate by getting normal people (that is, people who do not have, and have never suffered, symptoms of serious psychiatric disorders) admitted to psychiatric hospitals and then determining whether they were discovered to be sane and, if so, how. If the sanity of such pseudopatients were always detected, there would be *prima facie* evidence that a sane individual can be distinguished from the insane context in which he is found. Normality (and presumably abnormality) is distinct enough that it can be recognized wherever it occurs, for it is carried within the person. If, on the other hand, the sanity of the pseudopatients were never discovered, serious difficulties would arise for those who support traditional modes of psychiatric diagnosis. Given that the hospital staff was not incompetent, that the pseudopatient had been behaving as sanely as he had been outside of the hospital, and that it had never been previously suggested that he belonged in a psychiatric hospital, such an unlikely outcome would support the view that psychiatric diagnosis betrays little about the patient but much about the environment in which an observer finds him.

This article describes such an experiment. Eight sane people gained secret admission to twelve different hospitals.[6] Their diagnostic experiences constitute the data of the first part of this article; the remainder is devoted to a description of their experiences in psychiatric institutions. Too few psychiatrists and psychologists, even those who have worked in such hospitals, know what the experience is like. They rarely talk about it with former patients, perhaps because they distrust information coming from the previously insane. Those who have worked in psychiatric hospitals are likely to have adapted so thoroughly to the settings that they are insensitive to the impact of that experience. And while there have been occasional reports of researchers who submitted themselves to psychiatric hospitalization,[7] these researchers have commonly remained in the hospitals for short periods of time, often with the knowledge of the hospital staff. It is difficult to know the extent to which they were treated like patients or like research colleagues. Nevertheless, their reports about the inside of the psychiatric hospital have been valuable. This article extends those efforts.

Pseudopatients and Their Settings

The eight pseudopatients were a varied group. One was a psychology graduate student in his twenties. The remaining seven were older and "established." Among them were three psychologists, a pediatrician, a psychiatrist, a painter, and a housewife. Three pseudopatients were women, five were men. All of them employed pseudonyms, lest their alleged diagnoses embarrass them later. Those who were in mental health professions alleged another occupation in order to avoid the special attentions that might be accorded by staff, as a matter of courtesy or caution, to ailing colleagues.[8] With the exception of myself (I was the first pseudopatient and my presence was known to the hospital administrator and chief psychologist and, so far as I can tell, to them alone), the presence of pseudopatients and the nature of the research program were not known to the hospital staffs.[9]

The settings were similarly varied. In order to generalize the findings, admission into a variety of hospitals was sought. The twelve hospitals in the sample were located in five different states on the East and West coasts. Some were old and shabby; some were quite new. Some were research-oriented, others not. Some had good staff-patient ratios; others were quite understaffed. Only one was a strictly private hospital. All of the others were supported by state or federal funds, or in one instance, by university funds.

After calling the hospital for an appointment, the pseudopatient arrived at the admissions office complaining that he had been hearing voices. Asked what the voices said, he replied that they were often unclear, but as far as he could tell they said "empty," "hollow," and "thud." The voices were unfamiliar and were of the same sex as the pseudopatient. The choice of these symptoms was occasioned by their apparent similarity to existential symptoms. Such symptoms are alleged to arise from painful concerns about the perceived meaninglessness of one's life. It is as if the hallucinating person were saying, "My life is empty and hollow." The choice of these symptoms was also determined by the *absence* of a single report of existential psychoses in the literature.

Beyond alleging the symptoms and falsifying name, vocation, and employment, no further alterations of person, history, or circumstances were made. The significant events of the pseudopatient's life history were presented as they had actually occurred. Relationships with parents and siblings, with spouse and children, with people at work and in school, consistent with the aforementioned exceptions, were described as they were or had been. Frustrations and upsets were described along with joys and satisfactions. These facts are important to remember. If anything, they strongly biased the subsequent results in favor of detecting sanity, since none of their histories or current behaviors were seriously pathological in any way.

Immediately upon admission to the psychiatric ward, the pseudopatient ceased simulating *any* symptoms of abnormality. In some cases, there was a brief period of mild nervousness and anxiety, since none of the pseudopatients really believed that they would be admitted so easily. Indeed, their shared fear was that they would be immediately exposed as frauds and greatly embarrassed. Moreover, many of them had never visited a psychiatric ward; even those who had, nevertheless had some genuine fears about what might happen to them. Their nervousness, then, was quite appropriate to the novelty of the hospital setting, and it abated rapidly.

Apart from that short-lived nervousness, the pseudopatient behaved on the ward as he "normally" behaved. The pseudopatient spoke to patients and staff as he might ordinarily. Because there is uncommonly little to do on a psychiatric ward, he attempted to engage others in conversation. When asked by staff how he was feeling, he indicated that he was fine, that he no longer experienced symptoms. He responded to instructions from attendants, to calls for medication (which was not swallowed), and to dining-hall instructions. Beyond such activities as were available to him on the admissions ward, he spent his time writing down his observations about the ward, its patients, and the staff. Initially these notes were written "secretly," but as it soon became clear that no one much cared, they were subsequently written on standard tablets of paper in such public places as the dayroom. No secret was made of these activities.

The pseudopatient, very much as a true psychiatric patient, entered a hospital with no foreknowledge of when he would be discharged. Each was told that he would have to get out by his own devices, essentially by convincing the staff that he was sane. The psychological stresses associated with hospitalization were considerable, and all but one of the pseudopatients desired to be discharged almost immediately after being admitted. They were, therefore, motivated not only to behave sanely, but to be paragons of cooperation. That their behavior was in no way disruptive is confirmed by nursing reports, which have been obtained on most of the patients. These reports uniformly indicate that the patients were "friendly," "cooperative," and "exhibited no abnormal indications."

The Normal Are Not Detectably Sane

Despite their public "show" of sanity, the pseudopatients were never detected. Admitted, except in one case, with a diagnosis of schizophrenia,[10] each was discharged with a diagnosis of schizophrenia "in remission." The label "in remission" should in no way be dismissed as a formality, for at no time during any hospitalization had any question been raised about any pseudopatient's simulation. Nor are there any indications in the hospital records that the pseudopatient's status was suspect. Rather, the evidence is strong that, once labeled schizophrenic, the pseudopatient was stuck with that label. If the pseudopatient was to be discharged, he must naturally be "in remission"; but he was not sane, nor, in the institution's view, had he ever been sane.

The uniform failure to recognize sanity cannot be attributed to the quality of the hospitals, for, although there were considerable variations among them, several are considered excellent. Nor can it be alleged that there was simply not enough time to observe the pseudopatients. Length of hospitalization ranged from seven to fifty-two days, with an average of nineteen days. The pseudopatients were not, in fact, carefully observed, but this failure clearly speaks more to traditions within psychiatric hospitals than to lack of opportunity.

Finally, it cannot be said that the failure to recognize the pseudopatients' sanity was due to the fact that they were not behaving sanely. While there was clearly some tension present in all of them, their daily visitors could detect no serious behavioral consequences—nor, indeed, could other patients. It was quite common for the patients to "detect" the pseudopatients' sanity. During the first three hospitalizations, when accurate counts were kept, 35 of a total of 118 patients on the admissions ward voiced their suspicions, some vigorously. "You're not crazy. You're a journalist, or a professor [referring to the continual note-taking]. You're checking up on the hospital." While most of the patients were reassured by the pseudopatient's insistence that he had been sick before he came in but was fine now, some continued to believe that the pseudopatient was sane throughout his hospitalization.[11] The fact that the patients often recognized normality when staff did not raises important questions.

Failure to detect sanity during the course of hospitalization may be due to the fact that physicians operate with a strong bias toward what statisticians call the type 2 error.[5] This is to say that physicians are more inclined to call a healthy person sick (a false positive, type 2) than a sick person healthy (a false negative, type 1). The reasons for this are not hard to find: It is clearly more dangerous to misdiagnose illness than health. Better to err on the side of caution, to suspect illness even among the healthy.

But what holds for medicine does not hold equally well for psychiatry. Medical illnesses, while unfortunate, are not commonly pejorative. Psychiatric diagnoses, on the contrary, carry with them personal, legal, and social stigmas.[12] It was therefore important to see whether the tendency toward diagnosing the sane insane could be reversed. The following experiment was arranged at a research and teaching hospital whose staff had heard these findings but doubted that such an error could occur in their hospital. The staff was informed that at some time during the following three months, one or more pseudopatients would attempt to be admitted into the psychiatric hospital. Each staff member was asked to rate each patient who presented himself at admissions or on the ward according to the likelihood that the patient was a pseudopatient. A 10-point scale was used, with a 1 and 2 reflecting high confidence that the patient was a pseudopatient.

Judgments were obtained on 193 patients who were admitted for psychiatric treatment. All staff who had had sustained contact with or primary responsibility for the patient—attendants, nurses, psychiatrists, physicians, and psychologists—were asked to make judgments. Forty-one patients were alleged, with high confidence, to be pseudopatients by at least one member of the staff. Twenty-three were considered suspect by at least one psychiatrist. Nineteen were suspected by one psychiatrist and one other staff member. Actually, no genuine pseudopatient (at least from my group) presented himself during this period.

The experiment is instructive. It indicates that the tendency to designate sane people as insane can be reversed when the stakes (in this case, prestige and diagnostic acumen) are high. But what can be said of the nineteen people who were suspected of being "sane" by one psychiatrist and another staff member? Were these people truly "sane," or was it rather the case that in the course of avoiding the type 2 error the staff tended to make more errors of the first sort—calling the crazy "sane"? There is no way of knowing. But one thing is certain: Any diagnostic process that lends itself so readily to massive errors of this sort cannot be a very reliable one.

The Stickiness of Psychodiagnostic Labels

Beyond the tendency to call the healthy sick—a tendency that accounts better for diagnostic behavior on admission than it does for such behavior after a lengthy period of exposure—the data speak to the massive role of labeling in psychiatric assessment. Having once been labeled schizophrenic, there is nothing the pseudopatient can do to overcome the tag. The tag profoundly colors others' perceptions of him and his behavior.

From one viewpoint, these data are hardly surprising, for it has long been known that elements are given meaning by the context in which they occur. Gestalt psychology made this point vigorously, and Asch[13] demonstrated that there are "central" personality traits (such as "warm" versus "cold") which are so powerful that they markedly color the meaning of other information in forming an impression of a given personality.[14] "Insane," "schizophrenic," "manic-depressive," and "crazy" are probably among the most powerful of such central traits. Once a person is designated abnormal, all of his other behaviors and characteristics are colored by that label. Indeed, that label is so powerful that many of the pseudopatients' normal behaviors were overlooked entirely or profoundly misinterpreted. Some examples may clarify this issue.

Earlier I indicated that there were no changes in the pseudopatient's personal history and current status behond those of name, employment, and, where necessary, vocation. Otherwise, a veridical description of personal history and circumstances was offered. Those circumstances were not psychotic. How were they made consonant with the diagnosis of psychosis? Or were those diagnoses modified in such a way as to bring them into accord with the circumstances of the pseudopatient's life, as described by him?

As far as I can determine, diagnoses were in no way affected by the relative health of the circumstances of a pseudopatient's life. Rather, the reverse occurred: The perception of his circumstances was shaped entirely by the diagnosis. A clear example of such translation is found in the case of a pseudopatient who had had a close relationship with his mother but was rather remote from his father during his early childhood. During adolescence and beyond, however, his father became a close friend, while his relationship with his mother cooled. His present relationship with his wife was characteristically close and warm. Apart from occasional angry exchanges, friction was minimal. The children had rarely been spanked. Surely there is nothing especially pathological about such a history. Indeed, many readers may see a similar pattern in their own experiences, with no markedly deleterious consequences. Observe, however, how such a history was translated in the psychopathological context, this from the case summary prepared after the patient was discharged.

> This white 39-year-old male . . . manifests a long history of considerable ambivalence in close relationships, which begins in early childhood. A warm relationship with his mother cools during adolescence. A distant relationship to his father is described as becoming very intense. Affective stability is absent. His attempts to control emotionality with his wife and children are punctuated by angry outbursts and, in the case of the children, spankings. And while he says that he has several good friends, one senses considerable ambivalence embedded in those relationships also. . . .

The facts of the case were unintentionally distorted by the staff to achieve consistency with a popular theory of the dynamics of schizophrenic reaction.[15] Nothing of an ambivalent nature had been described in relations with parents, spouse, or friends. To the extent that ambivalence could be inferred, it was probably not greater than is found in all human relationships. It is true the pseudopatient's relationships with his parents changed over time, but in the ordinary context that would hardly be remarkable—indeed, it might very well be expected. Clearly, the meaning ascribed to his verbalizations (that is, ambivalence, affective instability) was determined by the diagnosis: schizophrenia. An entirely different meaning would have been ascribed if it were known that the man was "normal."

All pseudopatients took extensive notes publicly. Under ordinary circumstances, such behavior would have raised questions in the minds of observers, as, in fact, it did among patients. Indeed, it seemed so certain that the notes would elicit suspicion that elaborate precautions were taken to remove them from the ward each day. But the precautions proved needless. The closest any staff member came to questioning these notes occurred when one pseudopatient asked his physician what kind of medication he was receiving and began to write down the response. "You needn't write it," he was told gently. "If you have trouble remembering, just ask me again."

If no questions were asked of the pseudopatients, how was their writing interpreted? Nursing records for three patients indicate that the writing was seen as an aspect of their pathological behavior. "Patient engages in writing behavior" was the daily nursing comment on one of the pseudopatients who was never questioned about his writing. Given that the patient is in the hospital, he must be psychologically disturbed. And given that he is disturbed, continuous writing must be a behavioral manifestation of that disturbance, perhaps a subset of the compulsive behaviors that are sometimes correlated with schizophrenia.

One tacit characteristic of psychiatric diagnosis is that it locates the sources of aberration within the individual and only rarely within the complex of stimuli that surrounds him. Consequently, behaviors that are stimulated by the environment are commonly misattributed to the patient's disorder. For example, one kindly nurse found a pseudopatient pacing the long hospital corridors. "Nervous, Mr. X?" she asked. "No, bored," he said.

The notes kept by pseudopatients are full of patient behaviors that were misinterpreted by well-intentioned staff. Often enough, a patient would go "berserk" because he had, wittingly or unwittingly, been mistreated by, say, an attendant. A nurse coming upon the scene would rarely inquire even cursorily into the environmental stimuli of the patient's behavior. Rather, she assumed that his upset derived from his pathology, not from his present interactions with other staff members. Occasionally, the staff might assume that the patient's family (especially when they had recently visited) or other patients had stimulated the outburst. But never were the staff found to assume that one of themselves or the structure of the hospital had anything to do with a patient's behavior. One psychiatrist pointed to a group of patients who were sitting outside the cafeteria entrance half an hour before lunchtime. To a group of young residents, he indicated that such behavior was characteristic of the oral-acquisitive nature of the syndrome. It seemed not to occur to him that there were very few things to anticipate in the psychiatric hospital besides eating.

A psychiatric label has a life and an influence of its own. Once the impression has been formed that the patient is schizophrenic, the expectation is that he will continue to be schizophrenic. When a sufficient amount of time has passed, during which the patient has done nothing bizarre, he is considered to be in remission and available for discharge. But the label endures beyond discharge, with the unconfirmed expectation that he will behave as a schizophrenic again. Such labels, conferred by mental health professionals, are as influential on the patient as they are on his relatives and friends, and it should not surprise anyone that the diagnosis acts on all of them as a self-fulfilling prophecy. Eventually, the patient himself accepts the diagnosis, with all of its surplus meanings and expectations, and behaves accordingly.[15]

The inferences to be made from these matters are quite simple. Much as Zigler and Phillips have demonstrated that there is enormous overlap in the symptoms presented by patients who have been variously diagnosed,[16] so there is enormous overlap in the behaviors of the sane and the insane. The sane are not "sane" all of the time. We lose our tempers "for no good reason." We are occasionally depressed or anxious, again for no good reason. And we may find it difficult to get along with one or another person—again for no reason that we can specify. Similarly, the insane are not always insane. Indeed, it was the impression of the pseudopatients while living with them that they were sane for long periods of time—that the bizarre behaviors upon which their diagnoses were allegedly predicated constituted only a small fraction of their total behavior. If it makes no sense to label ourselves permanently depressed on the basis of an occasional depression, then it takes better evidence than is presently available to label all patients insane or schizophrenic on the basis of bizarre behaviors or cognitions. It seems more useful, as Mischel[17] has pointed out, to limit our discussions to *behaviors*, the stimuli that provoke them, and their correlates.

It is not known why powerful impressions of personality traits, such as "crazy" or "insane," arise. Conceivably, when the origins of and stimuli that give rise to a behavior are remote or unknown, or when the behavior strikes us as immutable, trait labels regarding the *behavior* arise. When, on the other hand, the origins and stimuli are known and available, discourse is limited to the behavior itself. Thus, I may hallucinate because I am sleeping, or I may hallucinate because I have ingested a peculiar drug. These are termed sleep-induced hallucinations, or dreams, and drug-induced hallucinations, respectively. But when the stimuli to my hallucinations are unknown, that is called craziness, or schizophrenia—as if that inference were somehow as illuminating as the others. . . .

The Consequences of Labeling and Depersonalization

Whenever the ratio of what is known to what needs to be known approaches zero, we tend to invent "knowledge" and assume that we understand more than we actually do. We seem unable to acknowledge that we simply don't know. The needs for diagnosis and remediation of behavioral and emotional problems are enormous. But rather than acknowledge that we are just embarking on understanding, we continue to label patients "schizophrenic," "manic-depressive," and "insane," as if in those words we had captured the essence of understanding. The facts of the matter are that we have known for a long time that diagnoses are often not useful or reliable, but we have nevertheless continued to use them. We now know that we cannot distinguish insanity from sanity. It is depressing to consider how that information will be used.

Not merely depressing, but frightening. How many people, one wonders, are sane but not recognized as such in our psychiatric institutions? How many have been needlessly stripped of their privileges of citizenship, from the right to vote and drive to that of handling their own accounts? How many have feigned insanity in order to avoid the criminal consequences of their behavior, and, conversely, how many would rather stand trial than live interminably in a psychiatric hospital—but are wrongly thought to be mentally ill? How many have been stigmatized by well-intentioned, but nevertheless erroneous, diagnoses? On the last point, recall again that a "type 2 error" in psychiatric diagnosis does not have the same consequences it does in medical diagnosis. A diagnosis of cancer that has been found to be in error is cause for celebration. But psychiatric diagnoses are rarely found to be in error. The label sticks, a mark of inadequacy forever.

Notes

1. P. Ash, *J. Abnorm. Soc. Psychol. 44*, 272 (1949); A. T. Beck, *Amer. J. Psychiat. 119*, 210 (1962); A. T. Boisen, *Psychiatry 2*, 233 (1938); N. Kreitman, *J. Ment. Sci. 107*, 876 (1961); N. Kreitman, P. Sainsbury, J. Morrisey, J. Towers, J. Scrivener, *ibid.*, p. 887; H. O. Schmitt and C. P. Fonda, *J. Abnorm. Soc. Psychol. 52*, 262 (1956); W. Seeman, *J. Nerv. Ment. Dis. 118*, 541 (1953). For an analysis of these artifacts and summaries of the disputes, see J. Zubin, *Annu. Rev. Psychol. 18*, 373 (1967); L. Phillips and J. G. Draguns, *ibid. 22*, 447 (1971).

2. R. Benedict. *J. Gen. Psychol. 10*, 59 (1934).

3. See in this regard H. Becker, *Outsiders: Studies in the Sociology of Deviance* (New York: Free Press, 1963); B. M. Braginsky, D. D. Braginsky, K. Ring, *Methods of Madness: The Mental Hospital as a Last Resort* (New York: Holt, Rinehart & Winston, 1969); G. M. Crocetti and P. V. Lemkau, *Amer. Sociol. Rev. 30*, 577 (1965); E. Goffman, *Behavior in Public Places* (New York: Free Press, 1964); R. D. Laing, *The Divided Self: A Study of Sanity and Madness* (Chicago: Quadrangle, 1960); D. L. Phillips, *Amer. Sociol. Rev. 28*, 963 (1963); T. R. Sarbin, *Psychol. Today 6*, 18 (1972); E. Schur, *Amer J. Sociol. 75*, 309 (1969); T. Szasz, *Law, Liberty and Psychiatry* (New York: Macmillan, 1963); *The Myth of Mental Illness: Foundations of a Theory of Mental Illness* (New York: Hoeber Harper, 1963). For a critique of some of these views, see W. R. Gove, *Amer. Sociol. Rev. 35*, 873 (1970).

4. E. Goffman. *Asylums* (Garden City, NY: Doubleday, 1961).

5. T. J. Scheff, *Being Mentally Ill: A Sociological Theory* (Chicago: Aldine, 1966).

6. Data from a ninth pseudopatient are not incorporated in this report because, although his sanity went undetected, he falsified aspects of his personal history, including his marital status and parental relationships. His experimental behaviors therefore were not identical to those of the other pseudopatients.

7. A. Barry, *Bellevue Is a State of Mind* (New York: Harcourt Brace Jovanovich, 1971); I. Belknap, *Human Problems of a State Mental Hospital* (New York: McGraw-Hill, 1956); W. Caudill, F. C. Redlich, H. R. Gilmore, E. B. Brody, *Amer J. Orthopsychiat. 22*, 314 (1952); A. R. Goldman, R. H. Bohr, T. A. Steinberg, *Prof. Psychol. 1*, 427 (1970); unauthored, *Roche Report 1* (No. 13), 8 (1971).

8. Beyond the personal difficulties that the pseudopatient is likely to experience in the hospital, there are legal and social ones that, combined, require considerable attention before entry. For example, once admitted to a psychiatric institution, it is difficult, if not impossible, to be discharged on short notice, state law to the contrary notwithstanding. I was not sensitive to these difficulties at the outset of the project, nor to the personal and situational emergencies that can arise, but later a writ of habeas corpus was prepared for each of the entering pseudopatients and an attorney was kept "on call" during every hospitalization. I am grateful to John Kaplan and Robert Bartels for legal advice and assistance in these matters.

9. However distasteful such concealment is, it was a necessary first step to examining these questions. Without concealment, there would have been no way to know how valid these experiences were; nor was there any way of knowing whether whatever detections occurred were a tribute to the diagnostic acumen of the staff or to the hospital's rumor network. Obviously, since my concerns are general ones that cut across individual hospitals and staffs, I have respected their anonymity and have eliminated clues that might lead to their identification.

10. Interestingly, of the twelve admissions, eleven were diagnosed as schizophrenic and one, with the identical symptomatology, as manic-depressive psychosis. This diagnosis has a more favorable prognosis, and it was given by the only private hospital in our sample. On the relations between social class and psychiatric diagnosis, see A. B. Hollingshead and F. C. Redlich, *Social Class and Mental Illness: A Community Study* (New York: Wiley, 1958).

11. It is possible, of course, that patients have quite broad latitudes in diagnosis and therefore are inclined to call many people sane, even those whose behavior is patently aberrant. However, although we have no hard data on this matter, it was our distinct impression that this was not the case. In many instances, patients not only singled us out for attention, but came to imitate our behaviors and styles.

12. J. Cumming and E. Cumming, *Community Ment. Health 1*, 135 (1965); A. Farina and K. Ring. *J. Abnorm. Psychol. 70*, 47 (1965); H. E. Freeman and O. G. Simmons, *The Mental Patient Comes Home* (New York: Wiley, 1963); W. J. Johannsen, *Mental Hygiene 53*, 218 (1969); A. S. Linsky, *Soc. Psychiat. 5*, 166 (1970).

13. S. E. Asch, *J. Abnorm. Soc. Psychol. 41*, 258 (1946); *Social Psychology* (New York: Prentice-Hall, 1952).

14. See also, I. N. Mensh and J. Wishner, *J. Personality 16*, 188 (1947); J. Wishner, *Psychol. Rev. 67*, 96 (1960); J. S. Bruner and R. Tagiuri, in *Handbook of Social Psychology*, G. Lindzey, ed. (Cambridge, MA: Addison-Wesley, 1954), vol. 2, pp. 634–54; J. S. Bruner, D. Shapiro, R. Tagiuri, in *Person Perception and Interpersonal Behavior*, R. Tagiuri and L. Petrullo, eds. (Stanford, CA: Stanford Univ. Press, 1958), pp. 277–88.

15. For an example of a similar self-fulfilling prophecy, in this instance dealing with the "central" trait of intelligence, see R. Rosenthal and L. Jacobson, *Pygmalion in the Classroom* (New York: Holt, Rinehart & Winston, 1968).

16. E. Zigler and L. Phillips, *J. Abnorm. Soc. Psychol. 63*, 69 (1961). See also R. K. Freudenberg and J. P. Robertson, *A.M.A. Arch. Neurol. Psychiatr. 76*, 14 (1956).

17. W. Mischel, *Personality and Assessment* (New York: Wiley, 1968).

Social Inequality

ALL SOCIETIES, PAST AND PRESENT, are marked by inequalities of some sort. Some people are stronger, learn more quickly, are swifter, shoot weapons more accurately, or have more of *whatever is considered important in that particular society*. Other inequalities, whatever form they take, may appear more contrived—such as distinctions of social rank based on wealth. But whether based on biological characteristics, social skills, or money, no system of dividing people into different groups is inevitable. Rather, each is arbitrary. Yet all societies rank their members, and whatever arbitrary criteria they use appear quite reasonable to them.

The primary social division in small, tribal groups is drawn along the line of gender. Sorted into highly distinctive groupings, men and women in these societies engage in separate activities—ones deemed "appropriate" for each sex. Indeed, in these small groups gender usually represents a cleavage that cuts across most of social life. These peoples also draw finer distinctions along much more individualistic lines of personality, skills, and reputation. Of all human groups, hunting and gathering societies—where most activities revolve around subsistence and there is little or no material surplus—appear to have the least stratification. These societies apparently also have the least *gender typing*, or division of activities by sex.

Perhaps the primary significance of a group's hierarchies and statuses—no matter what form they may take in a particular society—is that they surround the individual with *boundaries*. Setting limits and circumscribing one's possibilities in life, these social divisions establish the framework of socialization. They launch the individual onto the social scene by presenting to him or her an already existing picture of what he or she ought to expect from life.

None of us escapes this fundamental fact of social life, which sociologists call *social inequality* and *social stratification*. No matter into which society we are born, then, each of us inherits some system of social stratification. The boundaries and limits that come with social inequality have extensive consequences, for they envelop almost all aspects of our lives—our relationships with others, our behaviors, beliefs, and attitudes, our goals and aspirations, even our perception of the social world and of the self.

In analyzing the social inequality of contemporary society, sociologists focus on very large groupings of people. They call these groups *social classes*, which are determined by people's rankings on income, education, and occupation. The more income and education one has and the higher the prestige accorded one's work, the higher one's social class. Conversely, the lower one's income, education, and prestige of occupation, the lower one's social class.

On the basis of income, education, and occupation, one can divide Americans into three principle social classes: upper, middle, and lower. The *upper* are the very rich (several million dollars wouldn't even begin to buy your way in); the *middle*—primarily professionals, managers, executives, and other business people—is heavily rewarded with the material goods our society has to offer; and the *lower*, to understate the matter, receives the least.

Some sociologists add an upper and a lower to each of these divisions and say there are *six* social classes in the United States: an upper-upper and lower-upper, an upper-middle and lower-middle, and an upper-lower and lower-lower. Let's look at these.

Membership in the *upper-upper* class is the most exclusive of all, accorded not only on the basis of huge wealth but also according to how long that money has been in the family—the longer the better. Somehow or other, it is difficult to make many millions of dollars while remaining scrupulously honest in business dealings. It appears that many people who have entered the monied classes have cut moral corners, at least here and there. This "taint" to the money disappears with time, however, and the later generations of Vanderbilts, Rockefellers, Mellons, DuPonts, Chryslers, Kennedys, Morgans, Nashes, and so on are considered to have "clean" money simply by virtue of the passage of time. They can be philanthropic as well as rich. They have attended the best private schools and universities, the male heirs probably have entered law, and they protect their vast fortunes and economic empires with far-flung political connections and contributions.

And the *lower-upper* class? These people have money, but it is new, and therefore suspect. They lack "breeding" and proper social background. They have not gone to the right schools and cannot be depended on for adequate in-group loyalty. Unable themselves to make the leap into the upper-upper class, their hope for social supremacy lies in their children: If their children go to the right schools *and* marry into the upper-upper class, what has been denied the parents will be granted the children.

The *upper-middle* class consists primarily of people who have entered the professions or higher levels of management. They are doctors, professors, lawyers, dentists, pharmacists, and clergy. They are bank presidents and successful contractors and other business people. Their education is high, their income adequate for most of their needs.

The *lower-middle* class consists largely of lower-level managers, white-collar workers in the service industries, and the more highly paid and skilled blue-collar workers. Their education and income, as well as the prestige of their work, are correspondingly lower than those of their upper-middle class counterparts.

The *upper-lower* class is also known as the *working class*. (Americans find this term much more agreeable than the term "lower," as "lower" brings negative things to mind, while "working" elicits more positive images.) This class consists primarily of blue-collar workers who work regularly, not seasonally, at their jobs. Their education is limited, and little prestige is attached to their work. With the changes in wages and lifestyles of recent years, however, it often is difficult to distinguish this class from the lower-middle class above it.

At the bottom of the ladder of social inequality is the *lower-lower* class. This is the social class that gets the worst of everything society has to offer. Its members have the least education and the least income, and often their work is disdained, because, as with sharecropping and other menial labor, it usually requires few skills, is "dirty," and is the type of work that most people try to avoid. The main difference between the lower-lower and the upper-lower classes is that the upper-lower class works the year round while the lower-lower class doesn't. Members of the lower-lower class live on welfare, handouts, and occasional work. They generally are considered the ne'er-do-wells of society.

To illustrate social class membership in U.S. society, let's look at the automotive industry. The Fords, for example, own and control a global manufacturing and financial empire whose net worth is truly staggering. Their vast accumulation of wealth, like their accrued power, is now several generations old. Their children attend elite schools, know how to spend money in the "right" way, and can be trusted to make their family and class interests paramount in life. They are without question members of the upper-upper class.

Next in line come top Ford executives, who direct the company. With stock options and bonuses, they earn several million dollars annually. Because they are new to wealth and power, however, they remain on the rung below, and are considered members of the lower-upper class.

A husband and wife who own a successful Ford agency are members of the upper-middle class. Their income clearly sets them apart from the majority of

Americans, and they have an enviable reputation in the community. More than likely they also exert greater-than-average influence in community affairs, but find their capacity to wield power highly limited.

The sales staff, as well as those who work in the office, are members of the lower-middle class. Their income is less, their education is likely to be less, and people assign less prestige to their work than to that of the owners of the agency.

Mechanics who repair customers' cars would ordinarily be considered members of the upper-lower class. High union wages, however, have blurred this distinction, and they might more properly be classified as members of the lower-middle class. People who "detail" used cars (making them appear newer by washing and polishing them, painting their tires and floor mats, and so on) earn only minimum wage and are members of the upper-lower class.

Window washers and janitors who are hired to clean the agency during the busy season and then are laid off when business slacks off are members of the lower-lower class. (If they are year-round employees of the agency, they are members of the upper-lower class.) Their income is the least, as is their education, while the prestige accorded their work is also minimal.

It is significant to note that children are assigned the social class of their parents. For this reason, sociologists say we are born into a social class. Sociologists call this *ascribed membership* (compared with membership one earns or gains, which is called *achieved membership*). If a child of someone who "details" used cars for a living goes to college, works as a salesperson in the agency part-time and during vacations, and then eventually buys the agency, he or she experiences *upward social mobility*. The individual's new social class is said to be achieved membership. Conversely, if a child of the agency's owner becomes an alcoholic, fails to get through college, and takes a lower-status job, that person experiences *downward social mobility*. The resulting change in social class is also called *achieved membership*. (As you can see, "achieved" does not equal "achievement.")

You should note that this division into six social classes is not the only way that sociologists look at our social class system. In fact, sociologists have argued about this matter at length, and they have arrived at no single, standard, agreed-upon overview of the U.S. class system. Like others, this outline of classes is both arbitrary and useful, but it does not do justice to the nuances and complexities of our class system.

One view within sociology (called *conflict* or *Marxist*) holds that to understand social inequality we need focus only on income. What is the *source* of a person's income? Know this, and you know the person's social class. There are those with money and those without money. The monied class owns the means of production—the factories and machinery and buildings—and lives off their investments. The other class exchanges its labor to produce more money for the wealthy owners. In short, the monied class (the *capitalists*, or owners) is in the controlling sector of society, while those who sell their labor (the *workers*) are controlled by them. With society divided into the haves and the have-nots, insist conflict theorists, it is misleading to pay attention to the fine distinctions among those with or without money.

Be that as it may (and this debate continues among sociologists), society certainly is stratified. And the sociological (and personal) significance of social inequality is that it determines our *life chances*, the probabilities as to the fate we may expect in life. It is obvious that not everyone has the same chances in life, and the single most significant factor in determining a person's life chances in our society is money. Simply put, if you have money, you can do a lot of things you can't do if you do not have it. And the more money you have, the more control over life you have, and the more likely you are to find life pleasant.

Beyond this obvious point, however, lies a connection between social inequality and life chances that is not so readily evident. It involves such things as one's chances of dying during infancy; being killed by accident, fire, or homicide; becoming a drug addict; getting arrested; ending up in prison; dropping out of school; beating your spouse; getting divorced; becoming disabled; or, in old age, having a meager life, plagued by illness and supported only by Social Security. All vary inversely with social class; that is, the lower people's social class, the higher the chances that these things will happen to them. Conversely, the higher their social class, the smaller the risk of these events taking place.

As we examine social inequality in this Part, we consider some of its major dimensions and emphasize its severe and lifelong effects. Our opening article on physical appearance may seem to hit only a light note, but Sidney Katz points to implications that, ordinarily lying beyond our perception, have deep consequences for our lives. The next article by Patricia Martin and Robert Hummer on fraternities and rape at first blush may seem strikingly out of place. Its implications go far beyond the specific setting and events, however, for its focus is gender inequality, the broadest and largest-scale social inequality of all. We then turn our focus on race–ethnicity, an aspect of inequality in U.S. society that pervades so much of social life. The experiences recounted by Clarence Page give us insight not only into the process of developing a racial identity but also into the consequences of that identity. From here, we turn the focus on poverty, with Herbert Gans' claim that poverty is so functional for society that it can never be eliminated. Stephen Higley concludes this Part with a focus on an understudied group, the wealthy and powerful upper class, or as it is often called in sociology, the ruling class.

27 The Importance of Being Beautiful

SIDNEY KATZ

A chief characteristic of all societies is *social stratification,* a term that refers to a group's system of ranking. All of us find ourselves ranked according to a variety of dimensions, from our parents' social class when we are young to our own achievements, or lack thereof, when we grow older. Where we go to high school, if we attend college, and if so, where—make a difference in people's eyes. People rank us by our speech, by our walk, and even by things we own or display, from the car we drive to the clothing we wear.

Central to much of the ranking done on a face-to-face level is attractiveness. Because of appearance, we judge others—and are judged by them. This type of ranking is ordinarily thought to have little consequence beyond such temporary, individual matters as whether or not we can get a date this weekend—personally significant and intense, yes, but probably of little long-term consequence. As Katz points out, however, rankings based on attractiveness have significant consequences for our lives.

UNLIKE MANY PEOPLE, I was neither shocked nor surprised when the national Israeli TV network fired a competent female broadcaster because she was not beautiful. I received the news with aplomb because I had just finished extensive research into "person perception," an esoteric branch of psychology that examines the many ways in which physical attractiveness—or the lack of it—affects all aspects of your life.

Unless you're a 10—or close to it—most of you will respond to my findings with at least some feelings of frustration or perhaps disbelief. In a nutshell, you can't overestimate the importance of being beautiful. If you're beautiful, without effort you attract hordes of friends and lovers. You are given higher school grades than your smarter—but less appealing—classmates. You compete successfully for jobs against men or women who are better qualified but less alluring. Promotions and pay raises come your way more easily. You are able to go into a bank or store and cash a cheque with far less hassle than a plain Jane or John. And these are only a few of the many advantages enjoyed by those with a ravishing face and body.

313

"We were surprised to find that beauty had such powerful effects," confessed Karen Dion, a University of Toronto social psychologist who does person perception research. "Our findings also go against the cultural grain. People like to think that success depends on talent, intelligence, and hard work." But the scientific evidence is undeniable.

In large part, the beautiful person can attribute his or her idyllic life to a puzzling phenomenon that social scientists have dubbed the "halo effect." It defies human reason, but if you resemble Jane Fonda or Paul Newman it's assumed that you're more generous, trustworthy, sociable, modest, sensitive, interesting, and sexually responsive than the rest of us. Conversely, if you're somewhat physically unattractive, because of the "horns effect" you're stigmatized as being mean, sneaky, dishonest, antisocial, and a poor sport to boot.

The existence of the halo/horns effect has been established by several studies. One, by Dion, looked at perceptions of misbehavior in children.

Dion provided 243 female university students with identical detailed accounts of the misbehavior of a seven-year-old school child. She described how the youngster had pelted a sleeping dog with sharp stones until its leg bled. As the animal limped away, yelping in pain, the child continued the barrage of stones. The 243 women were asked to assess the seriousness of the child's offence and to give their impression of the child's normal behavior. Clipped to half of the reports were photos of seven-year-old boys or girls who had been rated "high" in physical attractiveness; the other half contained photos of youngsters of "low" attractiveness. "We found," said Dion, "that the opinions of the adults were markedly influenced by the appearance of the children."

One evaluator described the stone thrower, who in her report happened to be an angelic-looking little girl, in these glowing terms: "She appears to be a perfectly charming little girl, well mannered and basically unselfish. She plays well with everyone, but, like everyone else, a bad day may occur. . . . Her cruelty need not be taken too seriously." For the same offence, a homely girl evoked this comment from another evaluator: "I think this child would be quite bratty and would be a problem to teachers. She'd probably try to pick a fight with other children. . . . She would be a brat at home. All in all, she would be a real problem." The tendency throughout the 243 adult responses was to judge beautiful children as ordinarily well behaved and unlikely to engage in wanton cruelty in the future; the unbeautiful were viewed as being chronically antisocial, untrustworthy, and likely to commit similar transgressions again.

Dion found the implications of this study mind boggling. Every kid who was homely would be highly vulnerable in the classroom and elsewhere. Prejudged by his or her appearance, a vicious cycle is set in motion. The teacher views the child as having negative traits and treats him accordingly; the child responds by conforming to the teacher's expectations. Dion thinks that adults must realize to what extent their opinion of a child can be biased by the child's appearance: "When there's a question of who started a classroom disturbance, who broke the vase—adults are more likely to identify the unattractive child as the culprit."

The same standards apply in judging adults. The beautiful are assumed innocent. John Jurens, a colorful private investigator, was once consulted by a small Toronto firm which employed 40 people. Ten thousand dollars' worth of merchandise had disappeared, and it was definitely an inside job. After an intensive investigation, which included the use of a lie detector, Jurens was certain he had caught the thief. She was 24 years old and gorgeous—a lithe princess with high cheekbones, green eyes and shining, long black hair. The employer dismissed Jurens's proof with the comment, "You've made a mistake. It just can't be her." Jurens commented sadly, "A lot of people refuse to believe that beautiful can be bad."

David Humphrey, a prominent Ontario criminal lawyer, observed, "If a beautiful woman is on trial, you practically have to show the judge and jury a movie of her committing the crime in order to get a conviction." Another experienced lawyer, Aubrey Golden, has found it difficult defending a man charged with assault or wife-beating if he's a brutish-looking hulk. By the same token, a rape victim who happens to be stocky is a less credible witness than a slender, good-looking woman.

The halo and horns effect often plays an important role in sentencing by courts. After spending 17 days observing cases heard in an Ontario traffic court, Joan Finegan, a graduate psychology student at the University of Western Ontario, concluded that pleasant and neat-looking defendants were fined an average of $6.31 less than those who were "messy." The same pro-beauty bias was found by a British investigator in a series of simulated court cases. Physically appealing defendants were given prison terms almost three years less than those meted out to unattractive ones for precisely the same offence.

Beauty—or the lack of it—influences a person's entire life. The halo and horns effect comes into play beginning with birth and continues throughout the various stages of life.

Early Life

The flawless, seraphlike infant is irresistible. It receives an inordinate amount of attention and love. The child is constantly picked up, cuddled, and cooed to. In contrast, the unattractive baby may suffer neglect and rejection, which can have enduring effects on its personality and mental health. "When a child is unappealing because he's been born with a visible physical defect," said Dr. Ian Munro, a specialist in reconstructive facial surgery at the Hospital for Sick Children in Toronto, "parents are sometimes reluctant to touch, fondle, or give their child the normal displays of affection."

Later, when the baby attends nursery school, the halo and horns effect is even more potent. "Nursery school teachers," observed Dr. Ellen Berscheid, a psychologist who has conducted extensive person perception research at the University of Minnesota, "often insist that all children are beautiful, yet they can, when they're asked, rank their pupils by appearance." Even more noteworthy, the children themselves, despite their tender years, "behave in accordance with the adult ranking."

One nursery school study by Berscheid and Dion revealed that unattractive kids were not as well liked by their peers as the attractive ones. They were accused of "fighting a lot," "hitting other students," and "yelling at the teacher." Furthermore, other students labeled them "fraidy cats." They needed help to complete their work. When asked to name the person in class who scared them the most, the children usually nominated an unattractive classmate.

At School

It's sad but true that grade school teachers tend to judge their pupils largely on the basis of their looks. Consider the provocative study conducted by two American psychologists, Elaine Walster and Margaret Clifford: Four hundred grade five teachers were asked to examine identical report cards. They itemized the student's grades in various subjects, his or her work habits, attendance record, and attitudes. There was only one difference. Half of the report cards had the photo of an attractive boy or girl attached to the upper right-hand corner; half, the photo of a less attractive child. The teachers were then asked a number of specific questions based on the information provided. They concluded that the beautiful children had higher IQs, were more likely to go to college, and had parents who were more interested in education.

Parents should be concerned about these results. Because of an inflated opinion of the beautiful child, the teacher can be expected to give him more than his share of friendliness, encouragement, and time. And, consequently, the beautiful one will blossom—at the expense of his not-so-beautiful classmates.

The College Years

The beautiful person reaps an even richer harvest when he or she attends college. In one test, 60 male undergraduates were handed a 700-word essay on the effects of televised violence on the behavior of children. The authors, they were told, were freshmen coeds, and the undergrads were asked to assign a grade to the essay and to give their impression of the writer's abilities. Half of the students received an essay that was excellently written; the other half were given an essay that was a mishmash of clichés, grammatical errors, and sloppy writing. One-third of the papers had attached to them the photo of the alleged author—a young woman of striking beauty. Another third contained the likeness of an unappealing woman, while the remaining third were submitted without a photograph. When the evaluations were tallied, it was found that the beautiful person was consistently awarded a higher mark for her essay than the unattractive one. The essays without photos attached were usually given average marks. The investigators, David Landy and Harold Sigall, psychologists at the University of Rochester at the time of the study, concluded, "If you are ugly, you are not discriminated against as long as your performance is impressive. However, should performance be below par, attractiveness matters: you may be able to get away with inferior work if you are beautiful."

Not surprisingly, college students also preferred beauty when grading the desirability of a date. In interviews 376 young men and 376 young women assured investigators that it was "vulgar" to judge people by their appearance. They then proceeded to list the human qualities that they really valued; intelligence, friendliness, sincerity, "soul," and warmth. Yet when these same people were interviewed after going out on a blind date that was arranged by a computer, it became apparent that they were blind to everything *but* the physical appearance of their partners. The more beautiful the partner, the more he or she was liked. Features such as exceptional personality, high intelligence, and shared interests hardly seemed to count at all. "We were surprised to find that a *man's* physical attractiveness was the largest determinant of how well he was liked by a woman," observed Elaine Walster, one of the psychologists who conducted the study.

In addition to giving top marks to their beautiful classmates as dates, college students also predict glittering futures for them. In one study by Dion, Berscheid, and Walster, the opinion was almost unanimous that the physically appealing would contract better marriages, make better husbands and wives, and lead more fulfilling social and career lives. This finding is all the more impressive, Dion explained, because "the unattractive people in our sample were by no means at the extremes of unattractiveness—they possessed only a minor flaw to their beauty."

Marriage

It's logical that a beautiful person's marriage should be idyllic. An alluring woman, say, might have a busier social life than her less appealing sisters and therefore have a better chance of meeting a compatible mate. She's also apt to be more sexually responsive. Good-looking women fall in love more often and have more sexual experiences than others. "And," observed Berscheid, "since in almost all areas of human endeavor practice makes perfect, it may well be that beautiful women are indeed sexually warmer simply because of experience."

One thing is certain: the power of beauty is such that the status of even a homely man skyrockets if he marries a dazzling woman. People discover positive qualities in him they never before noticed: self-confidence, likability, friendliness. Sigall and Landy refer to this phenomenon as "a generalized halo effect" and offer this explanation: "People viewing individuals who are romantically linked to an attractive person try to make sense of the association. In effect, they may ask themselves, 'Why is *she,* desirable as she appears to be, involved with him?' The observers may answer the question by attributing favorable qualities to him."

Careers

If you're a good-looking male over six feet tall, don't worry about succeeding at your career.

A study of university graduates by the *Wall Street Journal* revealed that well proportioned wage earners who were six-foot-two or taller earned 12 percent more than men under six feet. "For some reason," explained Ronald Burke, a York University psychologist and industrial consultant, "tall men are assumed to be dynamic, decisive, and powerful. In other words, born leaders." A Toronto consultant for Drake Personnel, one of the largest employment agencies in Canada, recalled trying to find a sales manager for an industrial firm. He sent four highly qualified candidates, only to have them all turned down. "The fifth guy I sent over was different," said the consultant. "He stood six-foot-four. He was promptly hired."

The well favored woman also has a distinct edge when it comes to getting a job she's after. "We send out three prospects to be interviewed, and it's almost always the most glamorous one that's hired," said Edith Geddes of the Personnel Centre, a Toronto agency that specializes in female placements. "We sometimes feel bad because the best qualified person is not chosen." Dr. Pam Ennis, a consultant to several large corporations, observed, "Look at the photos announcing promotions in the *Globe and Mail* business section. It's no accident that so many of the women happen to be attractive and sexy-looking." Ennis, an elegant woman herself, attributes at least part of her career success to good looks. Her photograph appears on the brochures she mails out to companies soliciting new clients. "About eight out of 10 company presidents give me an appointment," she said. "I'm sure that many of them are curious to see me in person. Beauty makes it easier to establish rapport."

In an experiment designed to test the effect of stating or not stating an intent to change the listener's point of view, it was discovered that an attractive woman was more persuasive than an unattractive woman. In one session, an attractive woman disguised her good looks. Her dress was ill-fitting, she wore no makeup on her oily skin, her hair was a tattered mess, and the trace of a moustache was etched on her upper lip. She attempted to persuade a classroom of men that a general education was superior to a specialized one. Her arguments, in large part, failed to change their points of view.

The same woman then made herself as alluring as possible. She wore chic, tight-fitting clothes and tasteful makeup, and sported a fashionable coiffeur. Using the identical argument, she had little difficulty in persuading a second group of men to share her enthusiasm for a general education.

Every ugly duckling who has transformed herself into a Cinderella knows about the persuasive powers of beauty. Eleanor Fulcher, who runs a model and charm school in Toronto, says, "A woman can make things happen by improving her appearance. I've seen it hundreds of times."

Old Age

An elderly person's attractiveness influences the way in which he or she is treated in nursing homes and hospitals. Doctors and nurses give better care to the beautiful ones.

Lena Nordholm, an Australian behavioral scientist, presented 289 doctors, nurses, social workers, speech therapists, and physiotherapists with photos of eight attractive and unattractive men and women. They were asked to speculate about what kind of patients they would be. The good-lookers were judged to be more cooperative, better motivated, and more likely to improve than their less attractive counterparts. Pam Ennis, the consultant, commented,

"Because the doctor feels that beautiful patients are more likely to respond to his treatment, he'll give them more time and attention."

In the myths that shape modern civilization, beauty is equated with success. It has been that way since time began. In most of literature, the heroines are beautiful. Leo Tolstoy wrote, "It is amazing how complete is the delusion that beauty is goodness."

We like to think we have moved beyond the era when the most desirable woman was the beauty queen, but we haven't. Every day we make assumptions about the personality of the bank teller, the delivery man, or the waitress by their looks. The way in which we attribute good and bad characteristics still has very little to do with fact. People seldom look beyond a pleasing facade, a superficial attractiveness. But the professors of person perception are not discouraged by this. They want to educate us. Perhaps by arming us with the knowledge and awareness of why we discriminate against the unattractive, we'll learn how to prevent this unwitting bigotry. Just maybe, we can change human nature.

28 Fraternities and Rape on Campus

PATRICIA YANCEY MARTIN
ROBERT A. HUMMER

College certainly is a varied experience: challenging, with its many assignments, higher academic standards, and new vocabularies; frustrating, when concepts don't seem to sink in and instructors demand too much; fulfilling, with the satisfactions that come from forming new friendships and a sense of accomplishment as courses are passed and new ideas mastered; and, at the end, threatening, when the world of work and careers looms and, by comparison, college life suddenly appears so comfortable, almost serene.

On many campuses, fraternities are part of college life, a welcome respite from onerous classroom demands. They provide friendships, fun, diversion, sometimes even a test or paper to help pass a particularly grueling course. In some cases, bonds are formed that become significant for successful careers. There is a darker side to fraternities, however, a stress on hypermasculinity and calculated exploitation that destroys people. It is this dark side of fraternities that Martin and Hummer explore.

MANY RAPES, FAR MORE THAN COME to the public's attention, occur in fraternity houses on college and university campuses. . . .

The study reported here examined dynamics associated with the social construction of fraternity life, with a focus on processes that foster the use of coercion, including rape, in fraternity men's relations with women. We make no claims that all fraternities are "bad" or that all fraternity men are rapists. Our observations indicated, however, that rape is especially probable in fraternities because of the kinds of organizations they are, the kinds of members they have, the practices their members engage in, and a virtual absence of university or community oversight. . . . We conclude that unless fraternities change in fundamental ways, little improvement can be expected.

Methodology

We developed a conceptual framework from an initial case study of an alleged gang rape at Florida State University that involved four fraternity men and an eighteen-year-old coed. The group rape took place on the third floor of a fraternity house and ended with the "dumping" of the woman in the hallway of a neighboring fraternity house. According to newspaper accounts, the victim's blood-alcohol concentration, when she was discovered, was .349 percent, more than three times the legal limit for automobile driving and an almost lethal amount. One law enforcement officer reported that sexual intercourse occurred during the time the victim was unconscious. When the victim was found, she was comatose and had suffered multiple scratches and abrasions. Crude words and a fraternity symbol had been written on her thighs. When law enforcement officials tried to investigate the case, fraternity members refused to cooperate. This led, eventually, to a five-year ban of the fraternity from campus by the university and by the fraternity's national organization.

In trying to understand how such an event could have occurred, and how a group of over 150 members (exact figures are unknown because the fraternity refused to provide a membership roster) could hold rank, deny knowledge of the event, and allegedly lie to a grand jury, we analyzed newspaper articles about the case and conducted open-ended interviews with a variety of respondents about the case and about the fraternities, rapes, alcohol use, gender relations, and sexual activities on campus. Our data included over 100 newspaper articles on the initial gang rape case; open-ended interviews with Greek (social fraternity and sorority) and non-Greek (independent) students (N = 20); university administrators (N = 8, five men, three women); and alumni advisers to Greek organizations (N = 6). Open-ended interviews were held also with judges, public and private defense attorneys, victim advocates, and state prosecutors regarding the processing of sexual assault cases. . . .

Fraternities and the Social Construction of Men and Masculinity

Our research indicated that fraternities are vitally concerned—more than with anything else—with masculinity. They work hard to create a macho image and context and try to avoid any suggestion of "wimpishness," effeminacy, and homosexuality. Valued members display, or are willing to go along with, a narrow conception of masculinity that stresses competition, athleticism, dominance, winning, conflict, wealth, material possessions, willingness to drink alcohol, and sexual prowess vis-à-vis women.

VALUED QUALITIES OF MEMBERS

When fraternity members talked about the kind of pledges they prefer, a litany of stereotypical and narrowly masculine attributes and behaviors was recited and feminine or woman-associated qualities and behaviors were expressly denounced. Fraternities seek men who are "athletic," "big guys," good in intramural competition, "who can talk college sports." Males "who are willing to drink alcohol," "who drink socially," or "who can hold their liquor" are sought. Alcohol and activities associated with the recreational use of alcohol are cornerstones of fraternity social life. Non-drinkers are viewed with skepticism and rarely selected for membership.

Fraternities try to avoid "geeks," nerds, and men said to give the fraternity a "wimpy" or "gay" reputation. Art, music, and humanities majors, majors in traditional women's fields (nursing, home economics, social work, education), men with long hair, and those whose appearance or dress violate current norms are rejected. Clean-cut, handsome men who dress well (are clean, neat, conforming, fashionable) are preferred. . . .

One fraternity man, a senior, said his fraternity recruited "some big guys, very athletic" over a two-year period to help overcome its image of wimpiness. His fraternity had won the interfraternity competition for highest grade-point average several years running but was looked down on as "wimpy, dancy, even gay." With their bigger, more athletic recruits, "our reputation improved; we're a much more recognized fraternity now." Thus a fraternity's reputation and status depend on members' possession of stereotypically masculine traits. Good grades, campus leadership, and community service are "nice" but masculinity dominance—for example, in athletic events, physical size of members, athleticism of members—counts most.

One fraternity man, a junior, said: "We watch a guy [a potential pledge] talk to women . . . we want guys who can relate to girls." Assessing a pledge's ability to talk to women is, in part, a preoccupation with homosexuality and a conscious avoidance of men who seem to have effeminate manners or qualities. If a member is suspected of being gay, he is ostracized and informally drummed out of the fraternity. A fraternity with a reputation as wimpy or tolerant of gays is ridiculed and shunned by other fraternities. . . .

THE STATUS AND NORMS OF PLEDGESHIP

A pledge (sometimes called an associate member) is a new recruit who occupies a trial membership status for a specific period of time. The pledge period (typically ranging from ten to fifteen weeks) gives fraternity brothers an opportunity to assess and socialize new recruits. Pledges evaluate the fraternity also and decide if they want to become brothers. The socialization experience is structured partly through assignment of a Big Brother to each pledge. Big Brothers are expected to teach pledges how to become a brother and to support them as they progress through the trial membership period. Some pledges are repelled by the pledging experience, which can entail physical abuse; harsh discipline; and demands to be subordinate, follow orders, and engage in demeaning routines and activities, similar to those used by the military to "make men out of boys" during boot camp.

. . . One fraternity pledge who quit the fraternity he had pledged described an experience during pledgeship as follows:

> This one guy was always picking on me. No matter what I did, I was wrong. One night after dinner, he and two other guys called me and two other pledges into the chapter room. He said, "Here, X, hold this twenty-five-pound bag of ice at arm's length 'til I tell you to stop." I did it even though my arms and hands were killing me. When I asked if I could stop, he grabbed me around the throat and lifted me off the floor. I thought he would choke me to death. He cussed me and called me all kinds of names. He took one of my fingers and twisted it until it nearly broke. . . . I stayed in the fraternity for a few more days, but then I decided to quit. I hated it. Those guys are sick. They like seeing you suffer.

Fraternities' emphasis on toughness, withstanding pain and humiliation, obedience to superiors, and using physical force to obtain compliance contributes to an interpersonal style that de-emphasizes caring and sensitivity but fosters intragroup trust and loyalty. If the least macho or most critical pledges drop out, those who remain may be more receptive to, and influenced by, masculinist values and practices that encourage the use of force in sexual relations with women and the covering up of such behavior.

NORMS AND DYNAMICS OF BROTHERHOOD

Brother is the status occupied by fraternity men to indicate their relations to each other and their membership in a particular fraternity organization or group. Brother is a male-specific status; only males can become brothers, although women can become "Little Sisters," a form of pseudomembership. "Becoming a brother" is a rite of passage that follows the consistent and often lengthy display by pledges of appropriately masculine qualities and behaviors. Brothers have a quasi-familial relationship with each other, are normatively said to share bonds of closeness and support, and are sharply set off from nonmembers. Brotherhood is a loosely defined term used to represent the bonds that develop among fraternity members and the obligations and expectations incumbent upon them. . . .

Some of our respondents talked about brotherhood in almost reverential terms, viewing it as the most valuable benefit of fraternity membership. One senior, a business-school major who had been affiliated with a fairly high-status fraternity throughout four years on campus, said:

> Brotherhood spurs friendship for life, which I consider its best aspect, although I didn't see it that way when I joined. Brotherhood bonds and unites. It instills values of caring about one another, caring about community, caring about ourselves. The values and bonds [of brotherhood] continually develop over the four years [in college] while normal friendships come and go.

Despite this idealization, most aspects of fraternity practice and conception are more mundane. Brotherhood often plays itself out as an overriding concern with masculinity and, by extension, femininity. As a consequence, fraternities comprise collectivities of highly masculinized men with attitudinal qualities and behavioral norms that predispose them to sexual coercion of women. The norms of masculinity are complemented by conceptions of women and femininity that are equally distorted and stereotyped and that may enhance the probability of women's exploitation.

PRACTICES OF BROTHERHOOD

Practices associated with fraternity brotherhood that contribute to the sexual coercion of women include a preoccupation with loyalty, group protection and secrecy, use of alcohol as a weapon, and involvement in violence and physical force. . . .

Loyalty, Group Protection, and Secrecy. Loyalty is a fraternity preoccupation. Members are reminded constantly to be loyal to the fraternity and to their brothers. Among other ways, loyalty is played out in the practices of group protection and secrecy. The fraternity must be shielded from criticism. Members are admonished to avoid getting the fraternity in trouble and to bring all problems "to the chapter" (local branch of a national social fraternity) rather than to outsiders. Fraternities try to protect themselves from close scrutiny and criticism by the Interfraternity Council (a quasi-governing body composed of representatives from all social fraternities on campus), their fraternity's national office, university officials, law enforcement, the media, and the public. Protection of the fraternity often takes precedence over what is procedurally, ethically, or legally correct. Numerous examples were related to us of fraternity brothers' lying to outsiders to "protect the fraternity."

Group protection was observed in the alleged gang rape case with which we began our study. Except for one brother, a rapist who turned state's evidence, the entire remaining fraternity membership was accused by university and criminal justice officials of lying to protect the fraternity. Members consistently failed to cooperate even though the alleged crimes were felonies, involved only four men (two of whom were not even members of the local chapter), and the victim of the crime nearly died. According to a grand jury's findings, fraternity officers repeatedly broke appointments with law enforcement officials, refused to provide police with a list of members, and refused to cooperate with police and prosecutors investigating the case.

Secrecy, a priority value and practice in fraternities . . . is a boundary-maintaining mechanism, demarcating in-group from out-group, us from them. Secret rituals, handshakes, and mottos are revealed to pledge brothers as they are initiated into full brotherhood. Since only brothers are supposed to know a fraternity's secrets, such knowledge affirms membership in the fraternity and separates a brother from others. Extending secrecy tactics from protection of private knowledge to protection of the fraternity from criticism is a predictable development. Our interviews indicated that individual members knew the difference between right and wrong, but fraternity norms that emphasize loyalty, group protection, and secrecy often overrode standards of ethical correctness.

Alcohol as Weapon.   Alcohol use by fraternity men is normative. They use it on weekdays to relax after class and on weekends to "get drunk," "get crazy," and "get laid." The use of alcohol to obtain sex from women is pervasive—in other words, it is used as a weapon against sexual reluctance. According to several fraternity men whom we interviewed, alcohol is the major tool used to gain sexual mastery over women. . . . One fraternity man, a twenty-one-year-old senior, [said:] " . . . You have to buy them drinks or find out if she's drunk enough. . . . "

A similar strategy is used collectively. A fraternity man said that at parties with Little Sisters: "We provide them with 'hunch punch' and things get wild. We get them drunk and most of the guys end up with one." "Hunch punch" he said, "is a girls' drink made up of overproof alcohol and powdered Kool-Aid, no water or anything, just ice. It's very strong. Two cups will do a number on a female." He had plans in the next academic term to surreptitiously give hunch punch to women in a "prim and proper" sorority because "having sex with prim and proper sorority girls is definitely a goal." These women are a challenge because they "won't openly consume alcohol and won't get openly drunk as hell." Their sororities have "standards committees" that forbid heavy drinking and easy sex.

In the gang rape case, our sources said that many fraternity men on campus believed the victim had a drinking problem and was thus an "easy make." According to newspaper accounts, she had been drinking alcohol on the evening she was raped; the lead assailant is alleged to have given her a bottle of wine after she arrived at his fraternity house. Portions of the rape occurred in a shower, and the victim was reportedly so drunk that her assailants had difficulty holding her in a standing position. While raping her, her assailants repeatedly told her they were members of another fraternity under the apparent belief that she was too drunk to know the difference. Of course, if she was too drunk to know who they were, she was too drunk to consent to sex.

One respondent told us that gang rapes are wrong and can get one expelled, but he seemed to see nothing wrong in sexual coercion one-on-one. He seemed unaware that the use of alcohol to obtain sex from a woman is grounds for a claim that a rape occurred. Few women on campus (who also may not know these grounds) report date rapes, however; so the odds of detection and punishment are slim for fraternity men who use alcohol for "seduction" purposes.

Violence and Physical Force. Fraternity men have a history of violence. Their record of hazing, fighting, property destruction, and rape has caused them problems with insurance companies. Two university officials told us that fraternities "are the third riskiest property to insure behind toxic waste dumps and amusement parks." . . .

Fraternities' Commodification of Women

In claiming that women are treated by fraternities as commodities, we mean that fraternities knowingly, and intentionally, *use* women for their benefit. Fraternities use women as bait for new members, as servers of brothers' needs, and as sexual prey.

Women as Bait. Fashionably attractive women help a fraternity attract new members. As one fraternity man, a junior, said, "They are good bait." Beautiful, sociable women are believed to impress the right kind of pledges and give the impression that the fraternity can deliver this type of woman to its members. Photographs of shapely, attractive coeds are printed in fraternity brochures and videotapes that are distributed and shown to potential pledges. The women pictured are often dressed in bikinis, at the beach, and are pictured hugging the brothers of the fraternity. One university official says such recruitment materials give the message: "Hey, they're here for you, you can have whatever you want," and, "we have the best-looking women. Join us and you can have them, too." Another commented: "Something's wrong when males join an all-male organization as the best place to meet women. It's so illogical."

Fraternities compete in promising access to beautiful women. One fraternity man, a senior, commented that "the attraction of girls [i.e., a fraternity's success in attracting women] is a big status symbol for fraternities." One university official commented that the use of women as a recruiting tool is so well entrenched that fraternities that might be willing to forgo it say they cannot afford to unless other fraternities do so as well. One fraternity man said, "Look, if we don't have Little Sisters, the fraternities that do will get all the good pledges." Another said, "We won't have as good a rush [the period during which new members are assessed and selected] if we don't have these women around."

In displaying good-looking, attractive, skimpily dressed, nubile women to potential members, fraternities implicitly, and sometimes explicitly, promise sexual access to women. One fraternity man commented that "part of what being in a fraternity is all about is the sex" and explained how his fraternity uses Little Sisters to recruit new members:

> We'll tell the sweetheart [the fraternity's term for Little Sister], "You're gorgeous; you can get him." We'll tell her to fake a scam and she'll go hang all over him during a rush party, kiss him, and he thinks he's done wonderful and wants to join. The girls think it's great too. It's flattering for them.

Women as Servers. The use of women as servers is exemplified in the Little Sister program. Little Sisters are undergraduate women who are rushed and selected in a manner parallel to the recruitment of fraternity men. They are affiliated with the fraternity in a formal but unofficial way and are able, indeed required, to wear the fraternity's Greek letters. Little Sisters are not full-fledged fraternity members, however, and fraternity national offices and most universities do not register or regulate them. Each fraternity has an officer called Little Sister Chairman who oversees their organization and activities. The Little Sisters elect officers among themselves, pay monthly dues to the fraternity, and have well-defined roles. Their dues are used to pay for the fraternity's social events, and Little Sisters are expected to attend and hostess fraternity parties and hang around the house to make it a "nice place to be." One fraternity man, a senior, described Little Sisters this way: "They are very social girls, willing to join in, be affiliated with the group, devoted to the fraternity." Another member, a sophomore, said: "Their sole purpose is social—attend parties, attract new members, and 'take care' of the guys." . . .

Women as Sexual Prey. Little Sisters are a sexual utility. Many Little Sisters do not belong to sororities and lack peer support for refraining from unwanted sexual relations. One fraternity man (whose fraternity has 65 members and 85 Little Sisters) told us they had recruited "wholesale" in the prior year to "get lots of new women." The structural access to women that the Little Sister program provides and the absence of normative supports for refusing fraternity members' sexual advances may make women in this program particularly susceptible to coerced sexual encounters with fraternity men.

Access to women for sexual gratification is a presumed benefit of fraternity membership, promised in recruitment materials and strategies, and through brothers' conversations with new recruits. One fraternity man said: "We always tell the guys that you get sex all the time, there's always new girls. . . . After I became a Greek, I found out I could be with females at will." A university official told us that, based on his observations, "no one [i.e., fraternity men] on this campus wants to have 'relationships.' They just want to have fun [i.e., sex]." Fraternity men plan and execute strategies aimed at obtaining sexual gratification, and this occurs at both individual and collective levels.

Individual strategies include getting a woman drunk and spending a great deal of money on her. As for collective strategies, most of our undergraduate inteviewees agreed that fraternity parties often culminate in sex and that this outcome is planned. One fraternity man said fraternity parties often involve sex and nudity and can "turn into orgies." Orgies may be planned in advance, such as the Bowery Ball party held by one fraternity. A former fraternity member said of this party:

> The entire idea behind this is sex. Both men and women come to the party wearing little or nothing. There are pornographic pinups on the walls and usually porno movies playing on the TV. The music carries sexual overtones. . . . They just get schnockered [drunk] and, in most cases, they also get laid.

When asked about the women who come to such a party, he said: "Some Little Sisters just won't go. . . . The girls who do are looking for a good time, girls who don't know what it is, things like that."

Other respondents denied that fraternity parties are orgies but said that sex is always talked about among the brothers and they all know "who each other is doing it with." One member said that most of the time, guys have sex with their girlfriends "but with socials, girlfriends aren't allowed to come and it's their [members'] big chance [to have sex with other women]." The use of alcohol to help them get women into bed is a routine strategy at fraternity parties.

Conclusion

In general, our research indicated that the organization and membership of fraternities contribute heavily to coercive and often violent sex. Fraternity houses are occupied by same-sex (all men) and same-age (late teens, early twenties) peers whose maturity and judgment are often less than ideal. Yet fraternity houses are private dwellings that are mostly off-limits to, and away from scrutiny of, university and community representatives, with the result that fraternity house events seldom come to the attention of outsiders. Practices associated with the social construction of fraternity brotherhood emphasize a macho conception of men and masculinity, a narrow, stereotyped conception of women and femininity, and the treatment of women as commodities. Other practices contributing to coercive sexual relations and the cover-up of rapes include excessive alcohol use, competitiveness, and normative support for deviance and secrecy.

Some fraternity practices exacerbate others. Brotherhood norms require "sticking together" regardless of right or wrong; thus rape episodes are unlikely to be stopped or reported to outsiders, even when witnesses disapprove. The ability to use alcohol without scrutiny by authorities and alcohol's frequent association with violence, including sexual coercion, facilitate rape in fraternity houses. Fraternity norms that emphasize the value of maleness and masculinity over femaleness and femininity and that elevate the status of men and lower the status of women in members' eyes undermine perceptions and treatment of women as persons who deserve consideration and care. . . .

Our research led us to conclude that fraternity norms and practices influence members to view the sexual coercion of women, which is a felony crime, as sport, a contest, or a game. This sport is played not between men and women but between men and men. Women are the pawns or prey in the interfraternity rivalry game; they prove that a fraternity is successful or prestigious. The use of women in this way encourages fraternity men to see women as objects and sexual coercion as sport. Today's societal norms support young women's right to engage in sex at their discretion, and coercion is unnecessary in a mutually desired encounter. However, nubile young women say they prefer to be "in a relationship" to have sex while young men say they prefer to "get laid" without a commitment. In a fraternity context, getting sex without giving emotionally demonstrates "cool" masculinity. More important, it poses no threat to the bonding and loyalty of the fraternity brotherhood.

Unless fraternities' composition, goals, structures, and practices change in fundamental ways, women on campus will continue to be sexual prey for fraternity men. As all-male enclaves dedicated to opposing faculty and administration and to cementing in-group ties (i.e., fraternity members eschew any hint of homosexuality), their version of masculinity transforms women, and men with womanly characteristics, into the out-group. "Womanly men" are ostracized; feminine women are used to demonstrate members' masculinity. A case for or against fraternities cannot be made by studying individual members. The fraternity qua group and organization is at issue. Located on campus along with many vulnerable women, embedded in a sexist society, and caught up in masculinist goals, practices, and values, fraternities' violation of women—including forcible rape—should come as no surprise.

29 Showing My Color

CLARENCE PAGE

As you know, the circumstances we inherit at birth (sometimes called *social capital*) affect what happens to us in life. Some of us are born poor, others rich, and most of us in between. Some of us are born to single mothers, others to married parents; some to parents who are college graduates, others to parents who have not finished high school. Even our geography (South, West, rural, urban) sets up background factors that play a significant role in our orientations to life. Sociologists use the term *life chances* to refer to how the background factors that surround our birth affect our fate in life.

In the United States, race–ethnicity is a major divide. It opens and closes doors of opportunity and privilege. It is a primary source of identity, uniting us with some people, while separating us from others. Although race–ethnicity becomes a vital part of our identity, as with other concepts, we are not born with an awareness of our race or ethnicity. This we learn from others around us, which can be a jarring experience. In this selection, Page, a journalist, recounts how he learned that he was a black in a white society. He also shares examples of what this has meant for his life.

RACE HAS LONG HAD A RUDE PRESENCE in my life. While visiting relatives in Alabama as a child in the 1950s, I first saw water fountains marked "white" and "colored." I vaguely recall being excited. I rushed over to the one marked "colored" and turned it on, only to find, to my deep disappointment, that the water came out clear, just like the water back home in Ohio.

"Segregation," my dad said. I'd never heard the word before. My southern-born parents explained that it was something the white folks "down home" practiced. Some "home." Yet unpleasant experiences in the North already had taught me a more genteel, yet no less limiting, version.

"There are places white people don't want colored to go," my elders told me in their soft southern accents, "and white people make the rules."

We had plenty of segregation like that in the North. We just didn't have the signs, which made it cheaper and easier to deny. We could look out of my schoolhouse window to see a public swimming pool closed to nonwhites. We had to go across town to the separate-but-equal "pool for colored." The steel mill that was our town's biggest employer held separate picnics for colored and white employees, which seemed to be just fine with the employees. Everyone had a good time, separately and unequally. I think the colored folks, who today would be called the "black community," were just happy to have something to call their own.

When I was about six years old, I saw a television commercial for an amusement park near the southern Ohio factory town where I grew up.

I chose to go. I told my parents. They looked at each other sadly and informed me that "little colored kids can't go there." I was crushed.

"I wish I was white," I told my parents.

"No, you don't!" Mom snapped. She gave me a look terrible enough to persuade me instantly that no, I didn't.

"Well, maybe for a few minutes, anyway?" I asked. "Just long enough for me to get past the front gate?" Then I could show them, I thought. I remember I wanted to show them what a terrific kid I was. I felt sorry for the little white children who would be deprived of getting to know me.

Throughout our childhood years, my friendships with white schoolchildren (and with Pancho from the only Latino family in the neighborhood) proceeded without interruption. Except for the occasional tiff over some injudicious use of the N-word or some other slur we had picked up from our elders, we played in each other's backyards as congenially as Spanky, Buckwheat, and the rest of the gang on the old Hal Roach *Our Gang* comedies we used to watch on television.

Yet it quickly became apparent to me that my white friends were growing up in a different reality from the one to which I was accustomed. I could tell from the way one white friend happily discussed his weekend at LeSourdesville Lake that he did not have a clue of my reality.

"Have you been?" he asked.

"Colored can't go there," I said, somewhat astonished that he had not noticed.

"Oh, that can't be," he said.

For a moment, I perked up, wondering if the park's policy had changed. "Have you seen any colored people there?" I asked.

My white friend thought for a moment, then realized that he had not. He expressed surprise. I was surprised that he was surprised.

By the time I reached high school in the early 1960s, LeSourdesville Lake would relax its racial prohibitions. But the lessons of it stuck with me. It taught me how easily white people could ignore the segregation problem because, from their vantage point, it was not necessarily a problem. It was not necessarily an advantage to them, either, although some undoubtedly thought so. White people of low income, high insecurity, or fragile ego could always say that, no matter how badly off they felt, at least they were not black. Segregation helped them uphold and maintain this illusion of superiority. Even those white people who considered themselves to have a well-developed sense of social conscience could easily rationalize segregation as something that was good for both races. We played unwittingly into this illusion, I thought, when my friends and I began junior high school and, suddenly thrust into the edgy, high hormonal world of adolescence, quickly gravitated into social cliques according to tastes and race.

It became even more apparent to me that my white friends and I were growing up in *parallel realities,* not unlike the parallel universes described in the science fiction novels and comic books I adored—or the "parallel realities" experienced by Serbs, Bosnians, and Croatians as described years later by feminist writer Slavenka Drakulic in *The Balkan Express.* Even as the evil walls of legal segregation were tumbling down, thanks to the hard-fought struggles of the civil rights movement, it occurred to me that my reality might never be quite the same as that experienced by my white friends. We were doomed, I felt, to dwell in our parallel realities. Separated by thick walls of prejudice, we would view each other through windows of stained-glass perceptions, colored by our personal experiences. My parents had taught me well.

"Don't be showin' yo' color," my parents would admonish me in my youth, before we would go out in public, especially among white folks. The phrase had special meaning in Negro conversations. Imbued with many subtle meanings and nuances, the showing of one's "color" could be an expression of chastisement or warning, admonishment or adulation, satire or self-hatred, anger or celebration. It could mean acting out or showing anger in a loud and uncivilized way.

Its cultural origins could be traced to the Africa-rooted tradition of "signifying," a form of witty, deliberately provocative, occasionally combative word play. The thrill of the game comes from taking one's opponent close to the edge of tolerable insult. Few subjects—except perhaps sex itself—could be a more sensitive matter between black people than talk about someone else's "color." The showing of one's "color" then, connoted the display of the very worst stereotypes anyone ever dreamed up about how black people behaved. "White people are not really white," James Baldwin wrote in 1961, "but colored people can sometimes be extremely colored."

Sometimes you can still hear black people say in the heat of frustration, "I almost showed my color today," which is a way of saying they almost lost their "cool," "dropped the mask," or "went off." Losing one's cool can be a capital offense by black standards, for it shows weakness in a world in which spiritual rigor is one of the few things we can call our own. Those who keep their cool repress their "color." It is cool, in other words, to be colorless.

Showing My Color (the title of the book from which this reading is taken) emerged from my fuming discontent with the current fashions of *racial denial*, steadfast repudiations of the difference race continues to make in American life. Old liberals, particularly white liberals who have become new conservatives, charge that racial pride and color consciousness threaten to "Balkanize" American life, as if it ever was a model of unity. Many demand that we "get past race." But denials of a cancer, no matter how vigorous they may be, will not make the malignancy go away.

No less august a voice than the Supreme Court's conservative majority has taken to arguing in the 1990s for a "color-blind" approach to civil rights law, the area of American society in which color and gender consciousness have made the most dramatic improvement in equalizing opportunities.

The words of the Reverend Martin Luther King, Jr., have been perverted to support this view. Most frequently quoted is his oft-stated dream of the day when everyone would "not be judged by the color of their skin but by the content of their character." I would argue that King never intended for us to forget *all* about color. Even in his historic "I Have a Dream" speech, from which this line most often is lifted, he also pressed the less-often quoted but piquantly salient point about "the promissory note" America gave freed slaves, which, when they presented it, was returned to them marked "insufficient funds."

• • •

I would argue that too much has been made of the virtue of "color blindness." I don't want Americans to be blind to my color as long as color continues to make a profound difference in determining life chances and opportunities. Nor do I wish to see so significant a part of my identity denied. "Ethnic differences are the very essence of cultural diversity and national creativity," black social critic Albert Murray wrote in *The Omni-Americans* (1970). "The problem is not the existence of ethnic differences, as is so often assumed, but the intrusion of such differences into areas where they do not belong."

Where, then *do* they belong? Diversity is enriching, but race intrudes rudely on the individual's attempts to define his or her own identity. I used to be "colored." Then I was "Negro." Then I became "black." Then I became "African-American." Today I am a "person of color." In three decades, I have been transformed from a "colored person" to a "person of color." Are you keeping up with me?

Changes in what we black people call ourselves are quite annoying to some white people, which is its own reward to some black people. But if white people are confused, so are quite a few black people. There is no one way to be black. We are a diverse people amid a nation of diverse people. Some black people are nationalists who don't want anything to do with white people. Some black people are assimilationists who don't want anything to do with other black people. Some black people are integrationists who move in and out of various groups with remarkable ease. Some of us can be any of the three at any given time, depending on when you happen to run into us.

Growing up as part of a minority can expose the individual to horrible bouts of identity confusion. I used to think of myself as something of a *transracial man,* a figure no less frustrated than a transsexual who feels trapped in the body of something unfamiliar and inappropriate to his or her inner self.

These bouts were most torturous during adolescence, the period of life when, trembling with the shock of nascent independence from the ways of one's elders, the budding individual stitches together the fragile garments of an identity to be worn into adulthood. Stuttering and uncooperative motor skills left me severely challenged in dancing, basket shooting, and various social applications; I felt woefully inadequate to the task of being "popular" in the hot centers of black social activity at my integrated high school and college. "Are you black?" an arbiter of campus militancy demanded one day, when he "caught" me dining too many times with white friends. I had the skin pass, sure enough, but my inclinations fell well short of his standards. But I was not satisfied with the standards of his counterparts in the white world, either. If I was not "black" enough to please some blacks, I would never be "white" enough to please all whites.

Times have changed. Choices abound for black people, if we can afford them. Black people can now go anywhere they choose, as long as they can pay the bill when they get there. If anyone tries to stop them or any other minorities just because of their color, the full weight of the federal government will step in on the side of the minorities. I thank God and the hard-won gains of the civil rights revolution for my ability to have more choices. But the old rules of race have been replaced in many ways by new ones.

● ● ●

Today, I live a well-integrated life in the suburbs [of Montgomery County, Maryland, outside Washington, D.C.]. Black folks still tell me how to be "black" when I stray from the racial party lines, while white folks tell me how to be "color-blind." I still feel as frustrated in my attempts to transcend race as a reluctant lemming must feel while being rushed over the brink by its herd. But I find I have plenty of company in my frustration. Integration has not been a simple task for upwardly mobile African-Americans, especially for those of us who happen also to be parents.

A few years ago, after talking to black friends who were raising teenage boys, I realized that I was about to face dilemmas not unlike those my parents faced. My son was turning three years old. Everyone was telling me that he was quite cute, and because he was the spitting image of his dad, I was the last to argue.

But it occurred to me that in another decade he would be not three but thirteen. If all goes well, somewhere along the way he is going to turn almost overnight from someone who is perceived as cute and innocent into someone who is perceived as a menace, the most feared creature on America's urban streets today, a *young black male*. Before he, like me when I was barred from a childhood amusement park, would have a chance to let others get to know him, he would be judged not by the content of his character, but by the color of his skin. . . .

• • •

My mom is gone now, after helping set me up with the sort of education that has freed me to make choices. I have chosen to move my father to a nice, predominantly white, antiseptically tidy retirement village near me in Maryland with large golf courses and swimming pools. It is the sort of place he might have scrubbed floors in but certainly not have lived in back in the old days. It has taken him a while to get used to having so many well-off white people behaving so nicely and neighborly to him, but he has made the adjustment well.

Still the ugly specter of racism does not easily vanish. He and the other hundred or so African-American residents decided to form a social club like the other ethnically or religiously based social clubs in the village. One night during their meeting in the main social room, someone scrawled *KKK* on little sheets of paper and slipped them under the windshields of some of their cars in the parking lot. "We think maybe some of the white people wanted the blacks to socialize with the whites, not in a separate group," one lady of the club told me. If so, they showed an unusual method for extending the arms of brotherhood.

I live in a community that worships diversity like a state religion, although individuals sometimes get tripped up by it. The excellent Spanish "immersion" program that one of the county's "magnet" schools installed to encourage middle-class parents to stay put has itself become a cover for "white flight" by disgruntled white parents. Many of them, despite a lack of empirical evidence, perceive the school's regular English program as inferior, simply because it is 90 percent minority and mostly composed of children who come from a less-fortunate socioeconomic background. So the Spanish immersion classes designed to encourage diversity have become almost exclusively white and Asian America, while the English classes have become almost exclusively—irony of ironies—black and Latino, with many of the children learning English as a second language. Statistically, the school is "diverse" and "integrated." In reality, its student body is divided by an indelible wall, separate but supposedly equal. . . .

Despite all these color-conscious efforts to educate the country's children in a color-blind ideal of racial equality, many of our children seem to be catching on to race codes anyway, although with a twist suitable to the hip-hop generation. One local junior high school teacher, when he heard his black students referring to themselves as "bad," had the facts of racial life explained to him like this: They were not talking about the "bad means good" slang popularized by Michael Jackson's *Bad* album. They meant "bad" in the sense of misbehaving and poorly motivated. The black kids are "bad," the students explained, and the white kids are "good." The Asian kids are "like white," and the Latino kids "try to be bad, like the blacks." Anyone who tried to break out of those stereotypes was trying to break the code, meaning that a black or Latino who tried to make good grades was "trying to be white."

It is enough, as Marvin Gaye famously sang, to make you want to holler and throw up both your hands. Yet my neighbors and I hate to complain too loudly because, unlike other critics you may read or hear about, we happen to be a liberal community that not only believes in the dream of integration and true diversity, but actually is trying to live it. . . .

We see icons of black success—Colin Powell, Douglas Wilder, Bill Cosby, Oprah Winfrey, Bryant Gumbel, the two Michaels: Jordan and Jackson—not only accepted but adored by whites in ways far removed from the arm's-length way white America regarded Jackie Robinson, Willie Mays, Lena Horne, and Marian Anderson.

Yet, although the media show happy images of blacks, whites, Asians, and Hispanics getting along, amicably consuming the good life, a fog of false contentment conceals menacing fissures cracking the national racial landscape.

Despite the growth of the black middle class, most blacks and whites live largely separate lives. School integration actually peaked in 1967, according to a Harvard study, and has declined ever since. Economic segregation has proceeded without interruption, distancing poor blacks not only from whites but also from upwardly mobile blacks, making the isolation and misery of poor blacks worse. One out of every two black children lives below the poverty line, compared to one out of every seven white children. Black infants in America die at twice the rate of white infants. A record-setting million inmates crowd the nation's prisons, half of them black. The black out-of-wedlock birth rate has grown from about 25 percent in 1965 to more than 60 percent (more than 90 percent in the South Bronx and other areas of concentrated black poverty). . . .

The decline of industrial America, along with low-skill, high-pay jobs, has left much of black America split in two along lines of class, culture, opportunity and hope. The "prepared" join the new black middle class, which grew rapidly in the 1970s and early 1980s. The unprepared populate a new culture, directly opposed not only to the predominantly white mainstream, but also to any blacks who aspire to practice the values of hard work, good English, and family loyalty that would help them to join the white mainstream. The results of this spiritual decline, along with economic decline, have been devastating. Although more black women go to college than ever before, it has become a commonplace to refer to young black males as an endangered species. New anti-black stereotypes replace the old. Prosperous, well-dressed African Americans still complain of suffering indignities when they try to hail a taxicab. The fact that the taxi that just passed them by was driven by a black cabby, native born or immigrant, makes no difference. . . .

Behind our questions of race lurk larger questions of identity, our sense of who we are, where we belong, and where we are going. Our sense of place and peoplehood within groups is a perpetual challenge in some lives, particularly lives in America, a land where identity bubbles quite often out of nothing more than a weird alchemy of history and choice. "When I discover who I am, I'll be free," Ralph Ellison once wrote.

I reject the melting pot metaphor. People don't melt. Americans prove it on their ethnic holidays, in the ways they dance, in the ways they sing, in the culturally connected ways they worship. Displaced people long to celebrate their ethnic roots many generations and intermarriages after their ancestors arrived in their new land. Irish-American celebrations of St. Patrick's Day in Boston, Chicago, and New York City are far more lavish than anything seen on that day in Dublin or Belfast. Mexican-American celebrations of Cinco de Mayo, the Fifth of May, are far more lavish in Los Angeles and San Antonio than anything seen that day in Mexico City. It is as if holidays give us permission to expose our former selves as we imagine them to be. Americans of European descent love to show their ethnic cultural backgrounds. Why do they get nervous only when black people show their love for theirs? Is it that black people on such occasions suddenly remind white people of vulnerabilities black people feel quite routinely as a minority in a majority white society? Is it that white people, by and large, do not like this feeling, that they want nothing more than to cleanse themselves of it and make sure that it does not come bubbling up again? Attempts by Americans to claim some ephemeral, all-inclusive "all-American" identity reminds me of Samuel Johnson's observation: "Sir, a man may be so much of everything, that he is nothing of anything."

Instead of the melting pot metaphor, I prefer the mulligan stew, a concoction my parents tell me they used to fix during the Great Depression, when there was not a lot of food around the house and they "made do" with whatever meats, vegetables, and spices they had on hand. Everything went into the pot and was stirred up, but the pieces didn't melt. Peas were easily distinguished from carrots or potatoes. Each maintained its distinctive character. Yet each loaned its special flavor to the whole, and each absorbed some of the flavor from the others. That flavor, always unique, always changing, is the beauty of America to me, even when the pot occasionally boils over. . . .

African Americans are as diverse as other Americans. Some become nationalistic and ethnocentric. Others become pluralistic or multicultural, fitting their black identity into a comfortable niche among other aspects of themselves and their daily lives. Whichever they choose, a comfortable identity serves to provide not only a sense of belonging and protection for the individual against the abuses of racism, but also, ultimately, a sturdy foundation from which the individual can interact effectively with other people, cultures, and situations beyond the world of blackness.

"Identity would seem to be the garment with which one covers the nakedness of the self," James Baldwin wrote in *The Devil Finds Work,* "in which case, it is best that the garment be loose, a little like the robes of the desert, through which one's nakedness can always be felt, and, sometimes, discerned. This trust in one's nakedness is all that gives one the power to change one's robes."

The cloak of proud black identity has provided a therapeutical warmth for my naked self after the chilly cocoon of inferiority imposed early in my life by a white-exalting society. But it is best worn loosely, lest it become as constricting and isolating for the famished individual soul as the garment it replaced.

The ancestral desire of my ethnic people to be "just American" resonates in me. But I cannot forget how persistently the rudeness of race continues to intrude between me and that dream. I can defy it, but I cannot deny it. . . .

30 The Uses of Poverty: The Poor Pay All

HERBERT J. GANS

Some people think that poverty simply means having to tighten your belt, but the meaning of poverty is much more profound. Sociologists have documented that the poor confront social conditions so damaging that their marriages are more likely to break up, they are sicker than others, their children are more likely to drop out of school and get in trouble with the law, they are more likely to commit and to be victimized by violent crime. On average, they also die younger than most. It is difficult to romanticize poverty when one knows what its true conditions are.

In this selection, Gans does not document the degradation of the poor (although this is intrinsically present in his analysis), nor their failing health or troubled lives. Nor is his article a plea for social reform. Rather, from the observation that the poor are always present in society he concludes that this is because they perform vital services (functions) for society. (An essential assumption of *functionalism,* one of the theoretical perspectives in sociology, is that conditions persist in society only if they benefit—perform functions for—society or some of its parts.) In this selection, then, Gans tries to identify those functions.

Do you think the author has overlooked any "functions" of the poor? If his analysis, which many find startling, is not correct, what alternative explanation could you propose?

SOME YEARS AGO ROBERT K. MERTON applied the notion of functional analysis to explain the continuing though maligned existence of the urban political machine: If it continued to exist, perhaps it fulfilled latent—unintended or unrecognized—positive functions. Clearly it did. Merton pointed out how the political machine provided central authority to get things done when a decentralized local government could not act, humanized the services of the impersonal bureaucracy for fearful citizens, offered concrete help (rather than abstract law or justice) to the poor, and otherwise performed services needed or demanded by many people but considered unconventional or even illegal by formal public agencies.

Today, poverty is more maligned than the political machine ever was; yet it, too, is a persistent social phenomenon. Consequently, there may be some merit in applying functional analysis to poverty, in asking whether it also has positive functions that explain its persistence.

Merton defined functions as "those observed consequences [of a phenomenon] which make for the adaptation or adjustment of a given [social] system." I shall use a slightly different definition; instead of identifying functions for an entire social system, I shall identify them for the interest groups, socioeconomic classes, and other population aggregates with shared values that "inhabit" a social system. I suspect that in a modern heterogeneous society, few phenomena are functional or dysfunctional for the society as a whole, and that most result in benefits to some groups and costs to others. Nor are any phenomena indispensable; in most instances, one can suggest what Merton calls "functional alternatives" or equivalents for them, i.e., other social patterns or policies that achieve the same positive functions but avoid the dysfunction. (In the following discussion, positive functions will be abbreviated as functions and negative functions as dysfunctions. Functions and dysfunctions, in the planner's terminology, will be described as benefits and costs.)

Associating poverty with positive functions seems at first glance to be unimaginable. Of course, the slumlord and the loan shark are commonly known to profit from the existence of poverty, but they are viewed as evil men, so their activities are classified among the dysfunctions of poverty. However, what is less often recognized, at least by the conventional wisdom, is that poverty also makes possible the existence or expansion of respectable professions and occupations, for example, penology, criminology, social work, and public health. More recently, the poor have provided jobs for professional and para-professional "poverty warriors," and for journalists and social scientists, this author included, who have supplied the information demanded by the revival of public interest in poverty.

Clearly, then, poverty and the poor may well satisfy a number of positive functions for many nonpoor groups in American society. I shall describe 13 such functions—economic, social, and political—that seem to me most significant.

The Functions of Poverty

First, the existence of poverty ensures that society's "dirty work" will be done. Every society has such work: physically dirty or dangerous, temporary, dead-end and underpaid, undignified, and menial jobs. Society can fill these jobs by paying higher wages than for "clean" work, or it can force people who have no other choice to do the dirty work—and at low wages. In America, poverty functions to provide a low-wage labor pool that is willing—or, rather, unable to be *un*willing—to perform dirty work at low cost. Indeed, this function of the poor is so important that in some Southern states, welfare payments have been cut off during the summer months when the poor are needed to work in the fields. Moreover, much of the debate about the Negative Income Tax and the Family Assistance Plan has concerned their impact on the work incentive, by which is actually meant the incentive of the poor to do the needed dirty work if the wages therefrom are no larger than the income grant. Many economic activities that involve dirty work depend on the poor for their existence: restaurants, hospitals, parts of the garment industry, and "truck farming," among others, could not persist in their present form without the poor.

Second, because the poor are required to work at low wages, they subsidize a variety of economic activities that benefit the affluent. For example, domestics subsidize the upper-middle and upper classes, making life easier for their employers and freeing affluent women for a variety of professional, cultural, civic, and partying activities. Similarly, because the poor pay a higher proportion of their income in property and sales taxes, among others, they subsidize many state and local governmental services that benefit more affluent groups. In addition, the poor support innovation in medical practice as patients in teaching and research hospitals and as guinea pigs in medical experiments.

Third, poverty creates jobs for a number of occupations and professions that serve or "service" the poor, or protect the rest of society from them. As already noted, penology would be minuscule without the poor, as would the police. Other activities and groups that flourish because of the existence of poverty are the numbers game, the sale of heroin and cheap wines and liquors, pentecostal ministers, faith healers, prostitutes, pawn shops, and the peacetime army, which recruits its enlisted men mainly from among the poor.

Fourth, the poor buy goods others do not want and thus prolong the economic usefulness of such goods—day-old bread, fruit and vegetables that would otherwise have to be thrown out, secondhand clothes, and deteriorating automobiles and buildings. They also provide incomes for doctors, lawyers, teachers, and others who are too old, poorly trained, or incompetent to attract more affluent clients.

In addition to economic functions, the poor perform a number of social functions.

Fifth, the poor can be identified and punished as alleged or real deviants in order to uphold the legitimacy of conventional norms. To justify the desirability of hard work, thrift, honesty, and monogamy, for example, the defenders of these norms must be able to find people who can be accused of being lazy, spendthrift, dishonest, and promiscuous. Although there is some evidence that the poor are about as moral and law-abiding as anyone else, they are more likely than middle-class transgressors to be caught and punished when they participate in deviant acts. Moreover, they lack the political and cultural power to correct the stereotypes that other people hold of them and thus continue to be thought of as lazy, spendthrift, etc., by those who need living proof that moral deviance does not pay.

Sixth, and conversely, the poor offer vicarious participation to the rest of the population in the uninhibited sexual, alcoholic, and narcotic behavior in which they are alleged to participate and which, being freed from the constraints of affluence, they are often thought to enjoy more than the middle classes. Thus many people, some social scientists included, believe that the poor not only are more given to uninhibited behavior (which may be true, although it is often motivated by despair more than by lack of inhibition) but derive more pleasure from it than affluent people (which research by Lee Rainwater, Walter Miller, and others shows to be patently untrue). However, whether the poor actually have more sex and enjoy it more is irrelevant; so long as middle-class people believe this to be true, they can participate in it vicariously when instances are reported in factual or fictional form.

Seventh, the poor also serve a direct cultural function when culture created by or for them is adopted by the more affluent. The rich often collect artifacts from extinct folk cultures of poor people; and almost all Americans listen to the blues, Negro spirituals, and country music, which originated among the Southern poor. Recently they have enjoyed the rock styles that were born, like the Beatles, in the slums; and in the last year, poetry written by ghetto children has become popular in literary circles. The poor also serve as culture heroes, particularly, of course, to the left; but the hobo, the cowboy, the hipster, and the mythical prostitute with a heart of gold have performed this function for a variety of groups.

Eighth, poverty helps to guarantee the status of those who are not poor. In every hierarchical society someone has to be at the bottom; but in American society, in which social mobility is an important goal for many and people need to know where they stand, the poor function as a reliable and relatively permanent measuring rod for status comparisons. This is particularly true for the working class, whose politics is influenced by the need to maintain status distinctions between themselves and the poor, much as the aristocracy must find ways of distinguishing itself from the *nouveaux riches.*

Ninth, the poor also aid the upward mobility of groups just above them in the class hierarchy. Thus a goodly number of Americans have entered the middle class through the profits earned from the provision of goods and services in the slums, including illegal or nonrespectable ones that upper-class and upper-middle-class businessmen shun because of their low prestige. As a result, members of almost every immigrant group have financed their upward mobility by providing slum housing, entertainment, gambling, narcotics, etc., to later arrivals—most recently to blacks and Puerto Ricans.

Tenth, the poor help to keep the aristocracy busy, thus justifying its continued existence. "Society" uses the poor as clients of settlement houses and beneficiaries of charity affairs; indeed, the aristocracy must have the poor to demonstrate its superiority over other elites who devote themselves to earning money.

Eleventh, the poor, being powerless, can be made to absorb the costs of change and growth in American society. During the nineteenth century, they did the backbreaking work that built the cities; today, they are pushed out of their neighborhoods to make room for "progress." Urban renewal projects to hold middle-class taxpayers in the city and expressways to enable suburbanites to commute downtown have typically been located in poor neighborhoods, since no other group will allow itself to be displaced. For the same reason, universities, hospitals, and civic centers also expand into land occupied by the poor. The major costs of the industrialization of agriculture have been borne by the poor, who are pushed off the land without recompense; and they have paid a large share of the human cost of the growth of American power overseas, for they have provided many of the foot soldiers for Vietnam and other wars.

Twelfth, the poor facilitate and stabilize the American political process. Because they vote and participate in politics less than other groups, the political system is often free to ignore them. Moreover, since they can rarely support Republicans, they often provide the Democrats with a captive constituency that has no other place to go. As a result, the Democrats can count on their votes, and be more responsive to voters—for example, the white working class—who might otherwise switch to the Republicans.

Thirteenth, the role of the poor in upholding conventional norms (see the *fifth* point, above) also has a significant political function. An economy based on the ideology of laissez-faire requires a deprived population that is allegedly unwilling to work or that can be considered inferior because it must accept charity or welfare in order to survive. Not only does the alleged moral deviancy of the poor reduce the moral pressure on the present political economy to eliminate poverty, but socialist alternatives can be made to look quite unattractive if those who will benefit most from them can be described as lazy, spendthrift, dishonest, and promiscuous.

The Alternatives

I have described 13 of the more important functions that poverty and the poor satisfy in American society, enough to support the functionalist thesis that poverty, like any other social phenomenon, survives in part because it is useful to society or some of its parts. This analysis is not intended to suggest that because it is often functional, poverty *should* exist, or that it *must* exist. For one thing, poverty has many more dysfunctions than functions; for another, it is possible to suggest functional alternatives.

For example, society's dirty work could be done without poverty, either by automation or by paying "dirty workers" decent wages. Nor is it necessary for the poor to subsidize the many activities they support through their low-wage jobs. This would, however, drive up the costs of these activities, which would result in higher prices to their customers and clients. Similarly, many of the professionals who flourish because of the poor could be given other roles. Social workers could provide counseling to the affluent, as they prefer to do anyway; and the police could devote themselves to traffic and organized crime. Other roles would have to be found for badly trained or incompetent professionals now relegated to serving the poor, and someone else would have to pay their salaries. Fewer penologists would be employable, however. And pentecostal religion could probably not survive without the poor—nor would parts of the second- and third-hand-goods market. And in many cities, "used" housing that no one else wants would then have to be torn down at public expense.

Alternatives for the cultural functions of the poor could be found more easily and cheaply. Indeed, entertainers and adolescents are already serving as the deviants needed to uphold traditional morality and as devotees of orgies to "staff" the fantasies of vicarious participation.

The status functions of the poor are another matter. In a hierarchical society, some people must be defined as inferior to everyone else with respect to a variety of attributes, but they need not be poor in the absolute sense. One could conceive of a society in which the "lower class," though last in the pecking order, received 75 percent of the median income, rather than 15–40 percent, as is now the case. Needless to say, this would require considerable income redistribution.

The contribution the poor make to the upward mobility of the groups that provide them with goods and services could also be maintained without the poor's having such low incomes. However, it is true that if the poor were more affluent, they would have access to enough capital to take over the provider role, thus competing with, and perhaps rejecting, the "outsiders." (Indeed, owing in part to antipoverty programs, this is already happening in a number of ghettos, where white storeowners are being replaced by blacks.) Similarly, if the poor were more affluent, they would make less willing clients for upper-class philanthropy, although some would still use settlement houses to achieve upward mobility, as they do now. Thus "Society" could continue to run its philanthropic activities.

The political functions of the poor would be more difficult to replace. With increased affluence the poor would probably obtain more political power and be more active politically. With higher incomes and more political power, the poor would be likely to resist paying the costs of growth and change. Of course, it is possible to imagine urban renewal and highway projects that properly reimbursed the displaced people, but such projects would then become considerably more expensive, and many might never be built. This, in turn, would reduce the comfort and convenience of those who now benefit from urban renewal and expressways.

In sum, then, many of the functions served by the poor could be replaced if poverty were eliminated, but almost always at higher costs to others, particularly more affluent others. Consequently, a functional analysis must conclude that poverty persists not only because it fulfills a number of positive functions but also because many of the functional alternatives to poverty would be quite dysfunctional for the affluent members of society. A functional analysis thus ultimately arrives at much the same conclusion as radical sociology, except that radical thinkers treat as manifest what I describe as latent: that social phenomena that are functional for affluent or powerful groups and dysfunctional for poor or powerless ones persist; that when the elimination of such phenomena through functional alternatives would generate dysfunctions for the affluent or powerful, they will continue to persist; and that phenomena like poverty can be eliminated only when they become dysfunctional for the affluent or powerful, or when the powerless can obtain enough power to change society.

Postscript

Over the years, this article has been interpreted as either a direct attack on functionalism or a tongue-in-cheek satirical comment on it. Neither interpretation is true. I wrote the article for two reasons. First and foremost, I wanted to point out that there are, unfortunately, positive functions of poverty which have to be dealt with by antipoverty policy. Second, I was trying to show that functionalism is not the inherently conservative approach for which it has often been criticized, but that it can be employed in liberal and radical analyses.

31 The U.S. Upper Class

STEPHEN HIGLEY

Social inequality is a fact of life in all societies. Some people receive more of their society's goods and services, others far less. This is the way it has been in every known society of the past, is now, and—people's hopes to the contrary notwithstanding—likely always will be.

As much as many of us would wish it different, our own society is no exception. We, too, are marked by vast divisions, especially of wealth and power. Because the poor are the most accessible, research on social inequality usually focuses on them. (Note the immediately preceding three selections.) In this selection, in contrast, Higley examines the life situation of the rich. You might ask yourself in what ways your life would be different if you had been born into one of the families on which this article focuses. Obviously, your material circumstances would be different, but the distinction of wealth and power goes far beyond this obvious matter. It vitally affects our ideas of the world—and of our place in it.

FROM A CLASS PERSPECTIVE, the American upper class exhibits a class solidarity derived from the group awareness that they share a common fate. They consider one another equals, and their voting behavior in support of the Republican Party and their charitable efforts are the most obvious manifestations of their ability for joint action in the pursuit of common interests.

Those who are listed in the *Social Register* are chosen primarily for the style of life (and, implicitly, the system of values) they exhibit. The main purpose of the *Social Register* is to restrict social intercourse for the members by acting as a ready reference as to who is "in" and who is "out" of proper society. Although it is hard to confirm (because of the *Social Register's* policy of not responding to inquiries), the *Social Register* strives to "confine normal marriage to within the status circle" by requiring members who marry outside the *Register* to resubmit themselves and their bride or groom for membership. And the *Social Register* is but one element of the upper class's complete system of socialization. The American upper class has attempted to separate itself socially from the *hoi polloi* literally from birth to death—from favored maternity hospitals and attending physicians to specific retirement homes such as Dunwoody Village in Newtown Square, Pennsylvania, and Cathedral

Village in Washington, D.C. . . . Between birth and retirement is a full array of socializing institutions: prep schools, Ivy League schools, debutante balls, and metropolitan clubs, to name a few.

The upper-class families listed in the *Social Register* are direct descendants of the men who made great fortunes during the Gilded Age (1870– 1910). . . . The short-term and long-term economic success of the upper class is fundamentally important to maintaining the style of life that differentiates the upper class from the other classes in society. Once a family no longer has the economic resources to give its members the advantages that money can buy in the United States, the fall from social grace is swift and sure. The family that is reduced to "shabby gentility" is an often-used literary device that underlines the importance of liquid assets to continued good standing in American society.

The men and women who defined late-nineteenth- and early-twentieth-century American upper-class society were overwhelmingly white, Anglo-Saxon, and Protestant. As the personal, ethnic, and religious characteristics were unofficially codified, social and generational seasoning became equally important for acceptance into upper-class society. No amount of improperly socialized new money could buy its way into "proper" upper-class society. . . .

If one subscribes to the Weberian theory that status is ultimately dependent on economic control and wealth, there are clear implications that the influence of white, Anglo-Saxon Protestants will inevitably decline in the twenty-first century. Although "WASP" and "upper class" have been synonymous in the past, it is apparent that the ethnic definition of upper class will be transformed and redefined in the future.

The transformation, or de-WASPing, of the upper class that is now taking place in the United States is not easily evident to the casual observer. The status order will eventually reflect the economic order, although there are a multitude of cultural bulwarks that make the change slower and more subtle than [some] anticipate. There is a powerful WASP cultural inertia in the United States, and it will take decades to effect changes in the way Americans define themselves culturally. WASP culture is essentially derivative of the English nobility, and to this day, Anglophilia continues to pervade the American upper class. Because the upper class provides a value and consumptive role model for the American upper-middle class, upper-class values are in turn transmitted to the rest of American society—the upper-middle class being relatively large and visible to the rest of society. . . .

The Elements of Upper-Class Cohesion

The American upper class has a large number of institutions and associational arrangement that have made it possible for members to pass through life with very little significant contact with other social classes. This section reviews the most important of these institutions: private boarding schools (prep schools), colleges, metropolitan and country clubs, and the Episcopal and Presbyterian churches. The role of debutante balls, service organizations, and charitable organizations as contributing factors in maintaining upper-class cohesion will also be explored. Finally, an in-depth look at the *Social Register* will examine the role of neighborhood and community in upper-class cohesiveness.

PRIVATE PREPARATORY SCHOOLS

Of all of the institutions that inculcate upper-class values, private preparatory schools may have the greatest role (Cookson and Persell 1985, 13–30). The role of private education begins with upper-class day schools. Baltzell, in his examination of the role of education, termed the local institutions *provincial family surrogates* in that their outlooks were local in nature (Baltzell 1958, 292–300). Baltzell chronicles the changing role and fortunes of the Protestant Episcopal Academy, the first educator of large numbers of Philadelphia's young male upper class. The Episcopal Academy was founded in 1785 and began catering consciously to the upper class in 1846. The institution's move in 1921 to the suburban Main Line in pursuit of its clientele maintained its primacy in Philadelphia. The Episcopal Academy was not without competitors, however; other day schools were Haverford, Penn Charter, and Chestnut Hill. There were also day schools (such as Springside, Shipley, and Agnes Irwin) for upper-class girls in Philadelphia that served the same socializing functions as the boys' schools (Baltzell 1958, 300–301).

The day schools' popularity began to wane in the second half of the nineteenth century as boarding schools became the preferred method of educating young upper-class men and women. Boarding schools made it possible to completely control the social and educational environment of the students (Cookson and Persell 1985, 31–48). Parents could be assured that their child would be raised away from the distractions of the large cities and their hordes of newly arrived aliens. The prep schools were staffed with teachers who could be relied on to transmit the values of the upper class. The WASP ethic of civility, honesty, principle, and service was imparted within a totally structured environment. The schools, particularly the Episcopalian schools, were modeled after the public schools of England, complete with "forms" for grades and "headmasters" for principals.

The day schools increasingly turned to the nouveau riche to fill the slots left by the defections of some of their constituency. In his 1980 article, "The Rise of American Boarding Schools and the Development of a National Upper Class," Levine writes that the original purpose of the schools was to protect

the "old guard" of the upper class from the arrivistes, [the "newly arrived"—
people who only recently became rich] with their newly minted family fortunes created during the last quarter of the nineteenth century. He theorizes
that New England led the way in the creation of boarding schools as the
Boston Brahmins reacted to their imminent social eclipse by the much larger
fortunes the Gilded Age was producing. The elites of cities such as New York
and Philadelphia were able to participate in the industrialization of America,
whereas the Boston Brahmins, whose fortunes were grounded largely in the
trade from the Far East, were not as effective in gaining a share of the new
wealth. The boarding schools were but one of a series of institutions founded
during this era to create social distance between old money and new money.
Country clubs and metropolitan clubs were other examples. It was also during
this time that books such as the *Social Register* and various blue books were
published to provide a scorecard as to who was in and who was out of proper
society.

More important than the social distancing function prep schools provide
is the common socializing force they exert on young men and women of the
upper class. C. Wright Mills felt that prep schools were an essential element
in the calculus of preserving privilege. He wrote:

> As a selection and training place of the upper classes, both old and new, the pri-
> vate school is a unifying influence, a force for the nationalization of the upper
> classes. The less important the pedigreed family becomes in the careful trans-
> mission of moral and cultural traits, the more important the private school—
> rather than the upper-class family—as the most important agency for
> transmitting the traditions of the upper social classes and regulating the new
> admission of wealth and talent. It is the characterizing point in the upper-class
> experience. (Mills 1956, 64–65)

Although upper-class schools were originally conceived to buffer the old
guard from the nouveau riche, the need to infuse the upper class with new talent and money and the need to socialize the parvenus into the minutiae of
upper-class culture led to the acceptance of some newly moneyed families. As
sociologist Randall Collins notes, "Schools primarily teach vocabulary and in-
flection, styles of dress, aesthetic tastes, values and manners" (Collins 1971,
101). Levine's 1980 study found that, in general, it took one generation to socialize upper-class fortunes. The sons of fathers who acquired large fortunes
in the early twentieth century often placed their children in the most prestigious boarding schools. The fathers were not above building a new library
or class- room building to ensure their son's entrance. In most cases, the sons
went on to Ivy League schools and became members of the upper-class secret societies and eating clubs. They were also likely to be listed in the *Social*

Register. Gaining membership in upper-class secret societies and eating clubs would not present a problem because sponsorship would come easily from former schoolmates who were already members of the clubs.

Although there were literally hundreds of schools founded in the Gilded Age, a hierarchy of preferred schools quickly developed. At the top of the list in terms of prestige are the five Episcopalian boarding schools known collectively as St. Grottlesex (St. Paul's, St. Mark's, St. George's, Groton, and Middlesex). St. Paul's is often held up as the quintessential upper-class school (Domhoff 1983). Located in Concord, New Hampshire, it has a campus of eighty buildings (for six hundred students) and is situated on two thousand acres of woods and open land. In 1981, the student-faculty ratio was 6.3 to 1 and the average class size was twelve.

The second group of prestigious prep schools is represented by Choate, Hotchkiss, and Kent—nondenominational schools that were founded specifically to cater to the burgeoning market for private, exclusive education at the turn of the century.

The two oldest schools are usually put in a class by themselves. The Phillips Academy (commonly called Andover) and the Phillips Exeter Academy were founded originally to provide secondary education for a large array of students before the advent of the public school system. With the growth of the public school systems, Andover and Exeter became oriented strictly to preparing students for college. Both schools are larger and less aristocratic and have higher academic standards than the other boarding schools mentioned (Cookson and Persell 1985, 38).

In summary, boarding schools offered a place where the upper class could rest assured that class-supportive values would be instilled in their young. Their children would be exposed to only those nouveau riche children who were "acceptable" and to none of the perceived evils of the city. They would make valuable social and business friendships that would be nourished in college and in the world of private clubs during their adult lives.

AN UPPER-CLASS COLLEGE EDUCATION

Just as there are preferred upper-class boarding schools to attend, there are preferred universities for young men and women of the upper class. The three universities that are considered most desirable by upper class parents are Harvard, Yale, and Princeton. These three are followed by any other schools in the Ivy League (Brown University has become increasingly popular among students) or any number of small prestigious schools located primarily in New England (for example, Williams, Amherst, or Trinity). If an upper-class family lives in a state with an academically prestigious public university, such as

Wisconsin, Michigan, or California, it is increasingly considered appropriate to attend those universities. In addition, there are selected private regional universities that are considered acceptable as one's first choice. Examples of these schools are Duke, Stanford, and Northwestern.

FRATERNITIES AND EATING CLUBS

Once a young man has been accepted at Harvard, Princeton, or Yale, he is confronted with a large university that is dominated in numbers, if not tone, by members of other social classes. The solution to the problem of having to mix with the upper-middle class (or worse) is a system of private clubs similar to the fraternities and sororities found on many American campuses. The system of private clubs is best described in the words of Baltzell:

> An intricate system of exclusive clubs, like the fraternities on less rarefied American campuses, serve to insulate the members of the upper class from the rest of the students at Harvard, Princeton, and Yale. There are virtually "two nations" at Harvard. The private-school boys, with their accents, final clubs, and Boston debutante parties—about one-fifth of the student body—stand aloof and apart from the ambitious, talented, and less polished boys who come to Cambridge each year from public schools over the nation. (Baltzell 1958, 329–330)

The private eating clubs of Princeton were formed in the years following Woodrow Wilson's 1906 ban on fraternities. Juniors and Seniors joined eating clubs that had a "pecking order" based on social status. Upper-class young men usually joined the Ivy Club or the Cottage Club. The exclusivity of the eating clubs ended in the 1960s when the university compelled the clubs to accept all who had applied but had not been accepted.

At Harvard, Porcellian is the club of the most prestigious boarding schools such as St. Paul's and Groton. Other social clubs that are notable but of slightly less status are A.D., Fly, Spee, Delphic, and Owl. Porcellian's counterpart at Yale is the Fence Club. As at Harvard, there are a host of slightly prestigious clubs to join. Perhaps the senior societies are even more important than the social clubs at Yale. The two most important are the elite and meritorious Skull and Bones Club (of which former President George Bush is a member) and the more socially exclusive Scroll and Key Club. The purpose of these clubs is to build class solidarity and personal alliances that will be translated into lifetime friendships and business relationships at graduation (Baltzell 1958, 330–334).

At each critical juncture of a young person's life, the upper class has developed a series of supporting institutions to link individuals with a shared outlook and value system. By carefully molding young upper-class people into the established value system, the upper class assures its own continuity.

THE UPPER-CLASS WORLD OF PRIVATE CLUBS

On graduation, young men and women begin their careers with yet another array of private clubs that will act as an extended class-oriented family. One can differentiate between two types of private clubs, the metropolitan dining clubs and the more familiar suburban country clubs. Baltzell maintains that the metropolitan clubs are much more important than country clubs in terms of the social ascription of status.

Unlike the American middle classes, and resembling the lower classes, in fact, the Philadelphia upper class is largely male dominated and patriarchal. The social standing of the male family head, the best index of which is his metropolitan club affiliation, usually determines the social position of the family as a whole (Baltzell 1958, 336).

The first American metropolitan club, following the British experience with such clubs, grew out of an informal gathering of the leading citizens to discuss daily affairs over coffee. In the days before reliable newspapers, it was a way to pass on news and keep informed of current events. The first club formed in the United States was the Philadelphia Club in 1835. It was closely followed by the Union Club of New York City, which was founded in 1836 (Baltzell 1958, 335–363). The metropolitan club subculture, with its distinctive mores and value rituals, was perceptively outlined by Wecter:

> The social club in America has done a great deal to keep alive the gentleman in the courtly sense. Here is a peculiar asylum from the Pandemonium of commerce, the bumptiousness of democracy, and the feminism of his own household. Here he is technically invisible from the critical female eye—a state of bliss reflected in the convention that a gentleman never bows to a lady from a club window and does not, according to best form, discuss ladies there. The club is the Great Good Place with its comfortable and slightly shabby leather chairs, the pleasant malt-like effluvium of its bar, the newspaper room with a club servant to repair quickly the symptoms of disarray, the catholicity of magazines from highbrows to *La Vie Parisienne* which in less stately company would seem a trifle sophomoric, the abundant newspaper, the good cigars and hearty carnivorous menus. . . .
>
> With what Henry James called "a certain light of fine old gentlemenly prejudice to guide it," the preeminently social club welcomes the serious frivolity of horses, hounds, foxes, and boats, but not the effeminate frivolity of aestheticism. Pedantry is also frowned upon; except for the *Social Register*, the *World Almanac*, and *Lloyd's Register of American Yachts*, not a volume in the club

library has been taken down since the cross-word puzzle craze. It is comforting to think that one's sons and grandsons will sit in these same chairs, and firelight will flicker on the same steel engravings and oil portraits of past presidents—and though the stars may wheel in their courses and crowned heads totter to the guillotine, this little world will remain, so long as first mortgages and government bonds endure. (Wecter 1937, 253–255)

This evocative description of metropolitan clubs was written in 1937 and is dated in some details but still accurate in its main thrust.

There have been several recent legal challenges to the all-male membership policies of metropolitan clubs. The Supreme Court has ruled against the males-only policies of the clubs. The main argument made by female complainants was that women are excluded from important business transactions that are discussed in the clubs. Aldrich maintains that the women's victory will be mainly Pyrrhic because it is considered extremely bad form to discuss business in metropolitan clubs (Aldrich 1988, 122–123). However, Aldrich does not address the valuable alliances made in leisure that lead to business deals later, outside the confines of the club.

The suburban country club is less important than the metropolitan club, but it is significant in that the entire family are members and there are facilities and activities for all. The first American country club was established in 1882 in Brookline, Massachusetts; it is simply called The Country Club. These clubs are most frequently associated with golf, but they may include facilities for swimming, tennis, and, in some cases, polo. Americans are familiar with suburban country clubs, which have been enthusiastically established by the upper-middle class throughout the country.

As in the case of the metropolitan clubs, there is a status hierarchy among the country clubs. Because of the relatively small number of upper-class families, upper-class country clubs make up only a small portion of the private equity country clubs in the United States.

Yacht clubs are also an integral part of upper-class social life. Again, only a select few of the yacht clubs in America are favored by the American upper class. Similarly, there are a large number of historically oriented clubs, such as the well-known Daughters of the American Revolution and more obscure clubs such as the American Association of the Sovereign Military Order of Malta.

RELIGION AND THE UPPER CLASS

Observers of the American scene have long commented on the status differentiation of Protestant denominations. The upper class has had a long association with the Protestant Episcopal Church and to a lesser degree with the

Presbyterian Church. The Episcopalian connection is a logical extension of the Anglophilia of the American upper class because the church has a number of characteristics that make it attractive to upper-class men and women. The richness of the church's ritual, the classic traditionalism of most Episcopalian architecture, and the sophisticated, urbane, and intellectual nature of its leaders have great appeal to the upper class (Cookson and Persell 1985, 44–48). The Episcopalian Church was very close to an established church for some parts of colonial America and was, in fact, the established church of the state of Virginia until 1786. Although the church suffered during and immediately following the Revolutionary War because of its close association with England and her Loyalists, it quickly recovered its status as a church of the educated elite in the postwar period.

Baltzell confirmed the alliance statistically by analyzing the church membership of those people in the upper class who were in both the 1940 edition of *Who's Who in America* and the 1940 Philadelphia *Social Register*. *Who's Who*'s listing of church membership enabled Baltzell to determine religious affiliation for 226 upper-class heads of households. Although 35 percent did not acknowledge a church membership, 42 percent were affiliated with the Episcopalian Church (compared with 1.0 percent of the total U.S. population). An additional 13 percent of those in *Who's Who* listed the Presbyterian Church as their place of worship (compared to 1.2 percent of the general population). Because of the general privacy of religious information, it is difficult to verify Baltzell's findings. However, it is fair to say that the subjective information on the relationship is indeed overwhelming. Of course, not all Episcopalians are upper class. The actual number of upper-class families within the church is small compared to the total membership of Episcopalian churches; however, the church carries the distinctive imprint of upper-class support, philanthropy, and values.

DEBUTANTE BALLS

The debutante season consists of a series of parties, teas, and dances held by upper-class families to formally announce the arrival and availability of their daughters for suitable matrimonial partners. Each major city holds a grand ball that is the highlight of the season. Debutante "coming-out" parties are yet another means of reinforcing class solidarity because the young women and men who participate are carefully screened to ensure upper-class exclusivity. Because upper-class endogamy is highly valued, the debutante season is a formal process, the sole purpose of which is to encourage and create upper-class familial unions. Although there is often a philanthropic cause behind the tens of thousands of dollars spent for each coming out, none of the participants are under any illusion as to the real purpose behind the festivities. The debutante season strengthens the bonds of intermetropolitan upper-class social relationships just as shared summer resort holidays strengthen intermetropolitan alliances.

THE SOCIAL REGISTER

Before the Civil War, "society" in most large American cities, including New York City, was small enough that members of the upper class knew each other informally. Invitations to balls and other "serious" social events were handled either by personal secretaries or by the hostess herself. There were also self-appointed social arbiters whose dictates could help the unsure hostess in determining who was "in" and who was "out" of society.

The role of individual society kingmakers would soon be eclipsed with the appearance of the first *Social Register* in 1886. Hundreds of new fortunes were being made (and lost) during the last two decades of the nineteenth century, and a book was needed to take the place of personal knowledge as to a family's acceptability in polite society.

The first edition of the *Social Register* was a listing of society in Newport, Rhode Island. The next year, 1887, saw the first appearance of the New York City edition. It has been published continuously ever since that date. The *Social Register* was not the first of its kind; there were many books that purported to list society in the 1880s. The secret of success for the founder, Louis Keller, was the quality of his list and his refusal to clutter the book with advertisements for wine merchants, dressmakers, and the like.

Another component of Keller's success was a strict code of secrecy that has been conscientiously maintained to the present. The all-enveloping veil of secrecy has given the book a mystique that has made it all the more alluring to those who aspire to join. The aura of exclusivity is enhanced by the *Social Register's* policy of rarely speaking to the press or publicly commenting on itself in any way.

Keller incorporated his idea as the Social Register Association; new editions quickly followed the New York City volume in Philadelphia and Boston (1890), Baltimore (1892), Chicago (1893), Washington, D.C. (1903), St. Louis and Buffalo (1903), Pittsburgh (1904), San Francisco (1906), and Cleveland and Cincinnati-Dayton (1910). At its height in the 1920s, there were 24 volumes. Many of these editions failed during the Great Depression because of the lack of a large and sophisticated industrial elite and/or insufficient interest on the part of the local population. This would explain the absence of a large number of *Social Register* families from Detroit, a city that made its fortune in the 1920s, and the three post–World War II growth centers of

Dallas, Houston, and Los Angeles. The families that dominate the *Social Register* were created during the Gilded Age, and the sunbelt families would have to wait for their generational acculturation into upper-class mores.

The *Social Register* has remained the only social listing for the thirteen cities listed above since 1939. In 1977, the twelve editions were combined into one large book—a reflection of the national solidarity of the upper class and also of cost considerations (Birmingham 1978). The *Social Register* has subsequently become an address and telephone book for the American upper class. Along with this basic information, the *Register* also lists which boarding school and which university members attended, the year in which he or she graduated, and their club memberships. Members may also list their children and the schools they are attending or their current addresses. It has several useful appendices: "Married Maidens," a listing of the maiden names of the wives (very helpful in a divorce-prone culture), and "Dilatory Domiciles," for those who are late in returning their annual questionnaires. There is also a separate volume published each summer called the *Summer Social Register*. The summer edition lists summer homes and also has a yacht registry that lists the home port, tonnage, and year built for each yacht. As the upper class has added winter homes in the post–World War II period, they have tended to list those addresses in the main *Social Register*.

Getting into the *Social Register* and being dropped from the book have been subjects of endless speculation among the upper class and among gossip columnists. The best term to describe the process is *idiosyncratic.* There are three methods for obtaining membership. The most likely way to get in is to be born into it. The second is to marry into a listed family. However, a new bride or groom who is not in the *Register* must submit a new application to be accepted or rejected (without comment) by the "advisory committee." (The makeup of the committee has been the subject of much speculation, and some have questioned if there really is one.) The third way to gain a listing in the *Social Register* is to apply for membership. The prospective member fills out an application and if it passes initial review, he or she must then supply the committee with four or five recommendations from current listees. The application then goes to the advisory committee and the applicant is either accepted or rejected without comment. It is believed that the number that gain membership through this process is extremely limited (Winfrey 1980).

Even the ownership of the *Social Register* is veiled in mystery. When Keller died in 1924, he left the Association to several heirs. It was purchased by Malcolm Forbes in 1977 and remained in his family after his death in 1989, but who actually owns it is not known.

The reasons why members are dropped from the *Social Register* has also been the subject of much musing. Perhaps the surest way to guarantee elimination is to publicly disparage the *Social Register* or to be publicly disgraced. As long as one's personal foibles do not become public knowledge, one seems to be immune from being dropped. Another way to be banished is to marry an entertainer—one of the many groups of people who are *personae non gratae* in the *Social Register*.

The largest groups that are systematically excluded from the *Social Register* are Jews, African Americans, and Asian Americans. Although there are one known Black and several Jewish members, the *Social Register* remains a compendium that is overwhelming white, Anglo-Saxon, and Protestant American (*Newsday,* December 12, 1984, 10–11). A small percentage of the listees have French and Dutch surnames, but it is a challenge to find German, Scandinavian, or southern European surnames anywhere in the *Social Register*.

There are members of the upper class who have asked to have their names removed from the *Social Register* because of the *Register*'s discriminatory practices. Alfred Gwynne Vanderbilt and "Jock" Whitney were among the notable society people who asked to be deleted. It is politically astute for politicians to request that their names be deleted. George Bush had his name deleted before he received his complimentary listings as vice president and president. Former presidents and the chief justice of the Supreme Court are also given complimentary listings. There are many retired senators who are listed once it is "safe" to be associated with an organization that is so blatant in its discrimination.

[Summary]

The upper class has a distinct set of institutions that provide social and physical separation from the rest of society, and these institutions inculcate an intricate set of values and beliefs in both young and old. They affirm cultural and group solidarity within the upper class and clearly delineate class boundaries.

References

Aldrich, N. W., Jr. 1988. *Old Money: the Mythology of America's Upper Class.* New York: Knopf.

Baltzell, E. D. 1958. *Philadelphia Gentlemen: The Making of a National Upper Class.* New York: Free Press.

Birmingham, N. 1978. "Ask Me No Secrets." *Town and Country* vol. 132, October, 181.

Collins, R. 1971. "Functional and Conflict Theories of Educational Stratification." *American Sociological Review* 36: no.6, December 1,002–1,019.

Cookson, P. W., 3rd, and C. H. Persell, 1985. *Preparing for Power.* New York: Basic.

Domhoff, G. W. 1983. *Who Rules America Now?* New York: Touchstone.

Levine, S. B. 1980. "The Rise of American Boarding Schools and the Development of a National Upper Class." *Social Problems* 28, no.1: 63–94.

Mills, C. W. 1956. *The Power Elite.* London: Oxford University Press.

Social Register Association. 1986. *Social Register 1887, Facsimile Edition.* New York: Social Register Association.

Social Register Association. 1987. *Social Register 1988,* Vol. CII. New York: Social Register Association.

Social Register Association. 1987. *Social Register, Summer 1988,* Vol. CII. New York: Social Register Association.

Wecter, D. 1937. *The Saga of American Society.* New York: Charles Scribner's Sons.

Winfrey, C. 1980. "Society's 'In' Book: Does It Still Matter?," *New York Times,* 2 February.

PART
VIII Social Institutions

At FIRST GLANCE, the term *social institutions* appears far removed from everyday life. But in fact this term refers to concrete and highly relevant realities that profoundly affect our lives. Parents and their children, the basic family unit, constitute a social institution. So does the church, with its sacred books, clergy, and worship; and the law, with its police, lawyers, judges, courts, and prisons. Social institutions also means politics—running the full gamut of the U.S. political process, from campaign lies told with a straight face to the official acts of Congress, the president, and his cabinet. Too, social institutions means the economic order, with new plants opening and old ones closing, working for a living, or drawing unemployment or welfare or a pension. Schools, colleges, and universities—places where people are socialized (as sociologists phrase the matter) or where they go to learn (as most other people put it)—also are examples of a social institution. This term also refers to science, with its test tubes and experiments, interviewers and questionnaires. It means doctors and nurses and hospitals, as well as the patients they treat, and the Medicare and Blue Cross and Blue Shield that people struggle to pay for in order to keep the U.S. medical enterprise from destroying their present and future finances. And social institutions means the military, with its generals and privates and tanks and planes, and the whole war game that at times threatens to become too real. Far from being removed from life, then, social institutions means all these vital aspects of life in society—and more.

To understand social life, it is necessary to understand the institutions of a society. It is not enough to understand what people do when they are in one another's presence. This certainly is significant, but it is only part of the picture. The sociological (and personal) significance of social institutions is that *they provide the structure within which we live our lives*.

The characteristics of a society's institutions, in fact, dictate much of our interaction in everyday life. For example, because of the way our economic order is arranged, a common pattern is to work 8 hours a day, to be off 16, and to repeat this pattern five days a week. There is nothing natural about this pattern. Its regularity is but an arbitrarily imposed temporal arrangement for work, leisure, and personal concerns. Yet this one aspect of a single social institution has far-reaching effects on how we deal with our family and friends, how we meet our personal needs and nonwork obligations, and indeed on how we view time and even life itself.

Each social institution has similarly far-reaching effects on our lives and viewpoints. By shaping our society as a whole and establishing the context in which we live, these institutions give form to almost everything that is of concern to us. We can say, in fact, that if the social institutions of our society were different, we would be different people. We certainly could not be the same, for our ideas and attitudes and other orientations to the physical and social worlds would be changed.

Sociologists classify social institutions as primary and secondary. The *primary* U.S. social institutions are the economy, the political system, and the military establishment. According to conflict theory, these three social institutions dominate our society. Their top leaders make the major decisions that have the greatest impact on our society, and thereby on our own lives. With the dominant position of the United States in world affairs, these three social institutions are far-reaching, not only for our society but also for the rest of the world.

The *secondary* social institutions are the others: family, education, religion, sports, medicine, law, science, and the mass media. As the name implies, they are secondary in power, and, as conflict theorists stress, these secondary social institutions exist to serve the primary ones. According to conflict theory, the family produces workers (for the economy), voters and taxpayers (for the political system), and soldiers (for the military); education socializes children (and adults) into dominant values that support the present social class arrangement and trains workers for the ruling elite; the religious institution instills patriotism and acceptance of the current arrangement of power; sports take people's minds off social issues so they remain compliant workers; the medical institution patches workers up so they can continue to work; the law keeps the poor under its yoke so they don't rebel and upset current power arrangements; science produces knowledge that allows capitalists to exploit nature and produce wealth; and the mass media create desire for products so the capitalist class can become even wealthier.

To lead off this Part, Barbara Ehrenreich places the focus on economics, sharing her experiences as she attempted to live on a minimum wage. Arlie Hochschild then examines how attitudes toward work and family life are changing. Harry Gracey uses the conflict perspective to analyze kindergarten, viewing it as the means by which children learn to become conformists so they can take a "proper" place in life. In his analysis of sports, Stanley Eitzen makes it evident that sports is a vehicle of upward social mobility for only a few. Emily Martin's delightful analysis of how reproduction is presented in science reminds us that science has deep cultural roots and is far from objective. Jean Kilbourne then examines some of the far-reaching effects of the mass media, how they influence even our body images and sexual attitudes.

In the final four articles, we look at four more social institutions. Focusing on religion, Marvin Harris uses a functionalist lens to analyze the role of sacred cows in India. Daniel Chambliss then gives us a behind-the-scenes view of the medical institution, while Jennifer Hunt's inside report of police violence allows us to peer behind the scenes of the legal institution. The final article in this Part, which focuses on the military, allows us to continue to look behind closed doors. As Gwynne Dyer analyzes boot camp, we are able to see how the Marines successfully turn civilians into soldiers.

32 Nickel and Dimed

BARBARA EHRENREICH

Middle-class people have a difficult time understanding what life is like for the poor. Most people in the middle class enjoy health insurance, paid vacations, and sick leave. They have a late model car, credit cards, bank accounts, and closets full of clothing. If oranges go up a quarter a pound, or if the price of milk increases by fifty cents a gallon, it is an inconvenience, not a disaster. For the poor, in contrast, such a small price increase can mean that the poor must go without oranges and milk.

From their upper-middle-class vantage point, Ehrenreich and her editor were contemplating what it was like to live on a minimum wage. As they were relaxing over their $30 lunch at an upscale French restaurant, they wondered about the people lower on the social class ladder. "How are those many people who have come off the welfare rolls getting along?" they asked one another. When Ehrenreich said, "Someone should find out," her editor looked at her and said, "You should do it." She didn't expect her life to change so abruptly, but she took him up on the challenge. This selection describes some of her experiences.

AT THE BEGINNING of June 1998 I leave behind everything that normally soothes the ego and sustains the body—home, career, companion, reputation, ATM card—for a plunge into the low-wage workforce. There I become another, occupationally much diminished "Barbara Ehrenreich"—depicted on job-application forms as a divorced homemaker whose sole work experience consists of housekeeping in a few private homes. I am terrified, at the beginning, of being unmasked for what I am: a middle-class journalist setting out to explore the world that welfare mothers are entering, at the rate of approximately 50,000 a month, as welfare reform kicks in. Happily, though, my fears turn out to be entirely unwarranted during a month of poverty and toil, my name goes unnoticed and for the most part unuttered. In this parallel universe where my father never got out of the mines and I never got through college, I am "baby," "honey," "blondie," and most commonly, "girl."

My first task is to find a place to live. I figure that if I can earn $7 an hour—which, from the want ads, seems doable—I can afford to spend $500 on rent, or maybe, with severe economies, $600. In the Key West area, where I live, this pretty much confines me to flophouses and trailer homes—like the one, a pleasing fifteen-minute drive from town, that has no air-conditioning, no screens, no fans, no television, and, by way of diversion, only the challenge of evading the landlord's Doberman pinscher. The big problem with this place, though, is the rent, which at $675 a month is well beyond my reach. All right, Key West is expensive. But so is New York City, or the Bay Area, or Jackson Hole, or Telluride, or Boston, or any other place where tourists and the wealthy compete for living space with the people who clean their toilets and fry their hash browns. Still, it is a shock to realize that "trailer trash" has become, for me, a demographic category to aspire to.

So I decide to make the common trade-off between affordability and convenience, and go for a $500-a-month efficiency thirty miles up a two-lane highway from the employment opportunities of Key West, meaning forty-five minutes if there's no road construction and I don't get caught behind some sun-dazed Canadian tourists. I hate the drive, along a roadside studded with white crosses commemorating the more effective head-on collisions, but it's a sweet little place—a cabin, more or less, set in the swampy back yard of the converted mobile home where my landlord, an affable TV repairman, lives with his bartender girlfriend. Anthropologically speaking, a bustling trailer park would be preferable, but here I have a gleaming white floor and a firm mattress, and the few resident bugs are easily vanquished.

But is it really possible to make a living on the kinds of jobs currently available to unskilled people? Mathematically, the answer is no, as can be shown by taking $6 to $7 an hour, perhaps subtracting a dollar or two an hour for child care, multiplying by 160 hours a month, and comparing the result to the prevailing rents. According to the National Coalition for the Homeless, for example, in 1998 it took, on average nationwide, an hourly wage of $8.89 to afford a one-bedroom apartment and the Preamble Center for Public Policy estimates that the odds against a typical welfare recipient's landing a job at such a "living wage" are about 97 to 1. If these numbers are right, low-wage work is not a solution to poverty and possibly not even to homelessness.

It may seem excess to put this proposition to an experimental test. As certain family members keep unhelpfully reminding me, the viability of low-wage work could be tested, after a fashion, without ever leaving my study. I could just pay myself $7 an hour for eight hours a day, charge myself for room and board and total up the numbers after a month. Why leave the people and work that I love? But I am an experimental scientist by training. In that business, you don't just sit at a desk and theorize; you plunge into the everyday chaos of nature, where surprises lurk in the most mundane measurements.

On the morning of my first full day of job searching, I take a red pen to the want ads, which are suspiciously numerous. Everyone in Key West's booming "hospitality industry" seems to be looking for someone like me—trainable, flexible, and with suitably humble expectations as to pay. I decide on two rules: One, I cannot use any skills derived from my education or usual work—not that there are a lot of want ads for satirical essayists anyway. Two, I have to take the best-paid job that is offered me and of course do my best to hold it[.]

So I put on what I take to be a respectful-looking outfit of ironed Bermuda shorts and scooped-neck T-shirt and set out for a tour of the local hotels and supermarkets. Best Western, Econo Lodge, and HoJo's all let me fill out application forms, and these are, to my relief, interested in little more than whether I am a legal resident of the United States and have committed any felonies.

I lunch at Wendy's, where $4.99 gets you unlimited refills at the Mexican part of the Superbar, a comforting surfeit of refried beans and "cheese sauce." A teenage employee, seeing me studying the want ads, kindly offers me an application form, which I fill out, though here, too, the pay is just $6 and change an hour. Then it's off for a round of the locally owned inns and guesthouses. At "The Palms," let's call it, a bouncy manager actually takes me around to see the rooms and meet the existing housekeepers, who, I note with satisfaction, look pretty much like me—faded ex-hippie types in shorts with long hair pulled back in braids. Mostly, though, no one speaks to me or even looks at me except to proffer an application form. At my last stop, a palatial B&B, I wait twenty minutes to meet "Max," only to be told that there are no jobs now but there should be one soon, since "nobody lasts more than a couple weeks."

Three days go by like this, and, to my chagrin, no one out of the approximately twenty places I've applied calls me for an interview. I had been vain enough to worry about coming across as too educated for the jobs I sought, but no one even seems interested in finding out how overqualified I am. Only later will I realize that the want ads are not a reliable measure of the actual jobs available at any particular time. They are, as I should have guessed from Max's comment, the employers' insurance policy against turnover of the low-wage work force. Most of the big hotels run ads almost continually, just to build a supply of applicants to replace the current workers as they drift away or are fired, so finding a job is just a matter of being at the right place at the right time, and flexible enough to take whatever is being offered that day. This finally happens to me at one of the big discount hotel chains, where I go, as usual, for housekeeping and am sent, instead, to try out as a waitress at the attached "family restaurant," a dismal spot with a counter and about thirty tables that looks out on a parking garage and features such tempting fare as "Polish [sic] sausage and BBQ sauce" on 95-degree days. Philip, the dapper young West Indian who introduces himself as the manager, interviews me with about as much enthusiasm as if he were a clerk processing me for Medicare, the principal questions being what shifts can I work and when can I start. I mutter something about being woefully out of practice as a waitress, but he's already on to the uniform: I'm to show up tomorrow wearing black slacks and black shoes; he'll provide the rust-colored polo shirt with HEARTHSIDE embroidered on it, though I might want to wear my own shirt to get to work, ha ha. At the word "tomorrow," something between fear and indignation rises in my chest. I want to say, "Thank you for your time, sir, but this is just an experiment, you know, not my actual life."

So begins my career at the Hearthside, I shall call it, one small profit center within a global discount hotel chain, where for two weeks I work from 2:00 til 10:00 P.M. for $2.43 an hour plus tips. For the next eight hours, I run after the agile Gail, absorbing bits of instruction along with fragments of personal tragedy. All food must be trayed, and the reason she's so tired today is that she woke up in a cold sweat thinking of her boyfriend, who killed himself recently in an upstate prison. No refills on lemonade. And the reason he was in prison is that a few DUIs caught up with him, that's all, could have happened to anyone. Carry the creamers to the table in a monkey bowl, never in your hand. And after he was gone she spent several months living in her truck, peeing in a plastic pee bottle and reading by candlelight at night, but you can't live in a truck in the summer, since you need to have the windows down, which means anything can get in, from mosquitoes on up.

At least Gail puts to rest any fears I had of appearing overqualified. From the first day on, I find that of all the things I have left behind, such as home and identity, what I miss the most is competence. Not that I have ever felt utterly competent in the writing business, in which one day's success augurs nothing at all for the next. But in my writing life, I at least have some notion of procedure: do the research, make the outline, rough out a draft, etc. As a server, though, I am beset by requests like bees: more iced tea here, ketchup over there, a to-go box for table fourteen, and where are the high chairs, anyway? Of the twenty-seven tables, up to six are usually mine at any time, though on slow afternoons or if Gail is off, I sometimes have the whole place to myself. There is the touch-screen computer-ordering system to master, which is, I suppose, meant to minimize server-cook contact, but in practice requires constant verbal fine-tuning: "That's gravy on the mashed, okay? None on the meatloaf," and so forth—while the cook scowls as if I were inventing these refinements just to torment him. Plus, something I had forgotten in the years since I was eighteen: about a third of a server's job is "side work" that's invisible to customers—sweeping, scrubbing, slicing, refilling, and restocking. If it isn't all done, every little bit of it, you're going to face the 6:00 P.M. dinner rush defenseless and probably go down in flames. I screw up dozens of times at the beginning, sustained in my shame entirely by Gail's support—"It's okay, baby, everyone does that sometime"—because, to my total surprise and despite the scientific detachment I am doing my best to maintain, I care.

After a few days at the Hearthside, I feel the service ethic kick in like a shot of oxytocin, the nurturance hormone. The plurality of my customers are hard-working locals—truck drivers, construction workers, even housekeepers from the attached hotel—and I want them to have the closest to a "fine dining' experience that the grubby circumstances will allow. No "you guys" for me; everyone over twelve is "sir" or "ma'am." I ply them with iced tea and coffee refills; I return, mid-meal, to inquire how everything is; I doll up their salads with chopped raw mushrooms, summer squash slices, or whatever bits of produce I can find that have survived their sojourn in the cold-storage room mold-free.

• • •

Ten days into it, this is beginning to look like a livable lifestyle. I like Gail, who is "looking at fifty" but moves so fast she can alight in one place and then another without apparently being anywhere between them. I clown around with Lionel, the teenage Haitian busboy, and catch a few fragments of conversation with Joan, the svelte fortyish hostess and militant feminist who is the only one of us who dares to tell Jack to shut up. I even warm up to Jack when, on a low night and to make up for a particularly unwarranted attack on my abilities, or so I imagine, he tells me about his glory days as a young man at "coronary school"—or do you say "culinary"?—in Brooklyn, where he dated a knock-out Puerto Rican chick and learned everything there is to know about food. I finish up at 10:00 or 10:30, depending on how much side work I've been able to get done during the shift, and cruise home[.] * * * To bed by 1:30 or 2:00, up at 9:00 or 10:00, read for an hour while my uniform whirls around in the landlord's washing machine, and then it's another eight hours spent following Mao's central instruction, as laid out in the Little Red Book, which was: Serve the people.

I could drift along like this, in some dreamy proletarian idyll, except for two things. One is management. If I have kept this subject on the margins thus far it is because I still flinch to think that I spent all those weeks under the surveillance of men (and later women) whose job it was to monitor my behavior for signs of sloth, theft, drug abuse, or worse.

Managers can sit—for hours at a time if they want—but it's their job to see that no one else ever does, even when there's nothing to do, and this is why, for servers, slow times can be as exhausting as rushes. You start dragging out each little chore, because if the manager on duty catches you in an idle moment, he will give you something far nastier to do. So I wipe, I clean, I consolidate ketchup bottles and recheck the cheesecake supply, even tour the tables to make sure the customer evaluation forms are all standing perkily in their places—wondering all the time how many calories I burn in these strictly theatrical exercises. When, on a particularly dead afternoon, Stu finds me glancing at a *USA Today* a customer has left behind, he assigns me to vacuum the entire floor with the broken vacuum cleaner that has a handle only two feet long, and the only way to do that without incurring orthopedic damage is to proceed from spot to spot on your knees.

The other problem, in addition to the less-than-nurturing management style, is that this job shows no sign of being financially viable. You might imagine, from a comfortable distance, that people who live, year in and year out, on $6 to $10 an hour have discovered some survival stratagems unknown to the middle class. But no. It's not hard to get my co-workers to talk about their living situations, because housing, in almost every case, is the principal source of disruption in their lives, the first thing they fill you in on when they arrive for their shifts. After a week, I have compiled the following survey:

- Gail is sharing a room in a well-known downtown flophouse for which she and a roommate pay about $250 a week. Her roommate, a male friend, has begun hitting on her, driving her nuts, but the rent would be impossible alone.
- Claude, the Haitian cook, is desperate to get out of the two-room apartment he shares with his girlfriend and two other, unrelated, people. As far as I can determine, the other Haitian men (most of whom only speak Creole) live in similarly crowded situations.
- Annette, a twenty-year-old server who is six months pregnant and has been abandoned by her boyfriend, lives with her mother, a postal clerk.
- Marianne and her boyfriend are paying $170 a week for a one-person trailer.
- Jack, who is, at $10 an hour, the wealthiest of us, lives in the trailer he owns, paying only the $400-a-month lot fee.
- The other white cook, Andy, lives on his dry-docked boat, which, as far as I can tell from his living descriptions, can't be more than twenty feet long. He offers to take me out on it, once it's repaired, but the offer comes with inquiries as to my marital status, so I do not follow up on it.
- Tina and her husband are paying $60 a night for a double room in a Days Inn. This is because they have no car and the Days Inn is within

walking distance of the Hearthside. When Marianne, one of the breakfast servers, is tossed out of her trailer for subletting (which is against
the trailer-park rules), she leaves her boyfriend and moves in with Tina
and her husband.

- Joan, who has fooled me with her numerous and tasteful outfits (host-
esses wear their own clothes), lives in a van she parks behind a shopping center at night and showers in Tina's motel room. The clothes are
from thrift shops.

It strikes me, in my middle-class solipsism, that there is gross improvi-
dence in some of these arrangements. When Gail and I are wrapping silver-
ware in napkins—the only task for which we are permitted to sit—she tells me
she is thinking of escaping from her roommate by moving into the Days Inn
herself. I am astounded: How can she even think of paying between $40 and $60
a day? But if I was afraid of sounding like a social worker, I come out just sounding like a fool. She squints at me in disbelief, "And where am I supposed to get
a month's rent and a month's deposit for an apartment?" I'd been feeling pretty
smug about my $500 efficiency, but of course it was made possible only by the
$1,300 I had allotted myself for start-up costs when I began my low-wage life:
$1,000 for the first month's rent and deposit, $100 for initial groceries and cash
in my pocket, $200 stuffed away for emergencies. In poverty, as in certain
propositions in physics, starting conditions are everything.

There are no secret economies that nourish the poor; on the contrary,
there are a host of special costs. If you can't put up the two months' rent you
need to secure an apartment, you end up paying through the nose for a room
by the week. If you have only a room, with a hot plate at best, you can't save
by cooking up huge lentil stews that can be frozen for the week ahead. You eat
fast food, or the hot dogs and styrofoam cups of soup that can be microwaved
in a convenience store. If you have no money for health insurance—and the
Hearthside's niggardly plan kicks in only after three months—you go without
routine care or prescription drugs and end up paying the price.

• • •

My own situation, when I sit down to assess it after two weeks of work,
would not be much better if this were my actual life. The seductive thing
about waitressing is that you don't have to wait for payday to feel a few bills
in your pocket, and my tips usually cover meals and gas, plus something left
over to stuff into the kitchen drawer I use as a bank. But as the tourist business slows in the summer heat, I sometimes leave work with only $20 in tips
(the gross is higher, but servers share about 15 percent of their tips with the
bus boys and bartenders). With wages included, this amounts to about the
minimum wage of $5.15 an hour. Although the sum in the drawer is piling up,

at the present rate of accumulation it will be more than a hundred dollars short of my rent when the end of the month comes around. Nor can I see any expenses to cut. True, I haven't gone the lentil-stew route yet, but that's because I don't have a large cooking pot, pot holders, or a ladle to stir with (which cost about $30 at Kmart, less at thrift stores), not to mention onions, carrots, and the indispensable bay leaf. I do make my lunch almost every day—usually some slow-burning, high-protein combo like frozen chicken patties with melted cheese on top and canned pinto beans on the side. Dinner is at the Hearthside, which offers its employees a choice of BLT, fish sandwich, or hamburger for only $2. The burger lasts longest, especially if it's heaped with gut-puckering jalapenos, but by midnight my stomach is growling again.

So unless I want to start using my car as a residence, I have to find a second, or alternative, job. Jerry's, which is part of a well-known national family restaurant chain and physically attached here to another budget hotel chain, is ready to use me at once. The prospect is both exciting and terrifying, because, with about the same number of tables and counter seats, Jerry's attracts three or four times the volume of customers as the gloomy old Hearthside.

Picture a fat person's hell, and I don't mean a place with no food. Instead there is everything you might eat if eating had no bodily consequences— cheese fries, chicken-fried steaks, fudge-laden desserts—only here every bite must be paid for, one way or another, in human discomfort. The kitchen is a cavern, a stomach leading to the lower intestine that is the garbage and dishwashing area, from which issue bizarre smells combining the edible and the offal: creamy carrion, pizza barf, and that unique and enigmatic Jerry's scent—citrus fart. The floor is slick with spills, forcing us to walk through the kitchen with tiny steps[.] ° ° ° Put your hand down on any counter and you risk being stuck to it by the film of ancient syrup spills, and this is unfortunate, because hands are utensils here, used for scooping up lettuce onto salad plates, lifting out pie slices, and even moving hash browns from one plate to another. The regulation poster in the single unisex restroom admonishes us to wash our hands thoroughly and even offers instructions for doing so, but there is always some vital substance missing—soap, paper towels, toilet paper—and I never find all three at once. You learn to stuff your pockets with napkins before going in there, and too bad about the customers, who must eat, though they don't realize this, almost literally out of our hands.

I start out with the beautiful, heroic idea of handling the two jobs at once, and for two days I almost do it: the breakfast/lunch shift at Jerry's, which goes till 2:00, arriving at the Hearthside at 2:10, and attempting to hold out until 10:00. In the ten minutes between jobs, I pick up a spicy chicken sandwich at the Wendy's drive-through window, gobble it down in the car, and change from khaki slacks to black, from Hawaiian to rust polo. There is a problem, though.

When during the 3:00 to 4:00 P.M. dead time I finally sit down to wrap silver, my flesh seems to bond to the seat. I try to refuel with a purloined cup of soup, as I've seen Gail and Joan do dozens of times, but a manager catches me and hisses "No eating!" though there's not a customer around to be offended by the sight of food making contact with a server's lips.

I make friends, over time, with the other "girls" who work my shift: Nita, the tattooed twenty-something who taunts us by going around saying brightly, "Have we started making money yet?" Ellen, whose teenage son cooks on the graveyard shift and who once managed a restaurant in Massachusetts but won't try out for management here because she prefers being a "common worker" and not "ordering people around." Easy-going fiftyish Lucy, with the raucous laugh, who limps toward the end of the shift because of something that has gone wrong with her leg, the exact nature of which cannot be determined without health insurance. We talk about the usual girl things—men, children, and the sinister allure of Jerry's chocolate peanut-butter cream pie—though no one, I notice, every brings up anything potentially expensive, like shopping or movies. As at the Hearthside, the only recreation ever referred to is partying, which requires little more than some beer, a joint, and a few close friends. Still, no one here is homeless, or cops to it anyway, thanks usually to a working husband or boyfriend. All in all, we form a reliable mutual-support group: If one of us is feeling sick or overwhelmed, another one will "bev" a table or even carry trays for her. If one of us is off sneaking a cigarette or a pee, the others will do their best to conceal her absence from the enforcers of corporate rationality.

I make the decision to move closer to Key West. First, because of the drive. Second and third, also because of the drive: gas is eating up $4 to $5 a day, and although Jerry's is as high-volume as you can get, the tips average only 10 percent, and not just for a newbie like me. Between the base pay of $2.15 an hour and the obligation to share tips with the busboys and dishwashers, we're averaging only about $7.50 an hour. Then there is the $30 I had to spend on the regulation tan slacks worn by Jerry's servers—a setback it could take weeks to absorb. (I had combed the town's two downscale department stores hoping for something cheaper but decided in the end that these marked-down Dockers, originally $49, were more likely to survive a daily washing.) Of my fellow servers, everyone who lacks a working husband or boyfriend seems to have a second job: Nita does something at a computer eight hours a day; another welds. Without the forty-five minute commute, I can picture myself working two jobs and having the time to shower between them.

So I take the $500 deposit I have coming from my landlord, the $400 I have earned toward the next month's rent, plus the $200 reserved for emergencies, and use the $1,100 to pay the rent and deposit on trailer number 46 in the Overseas Trailer Park, a mile from the cluster of budget hotels that constitute Key West's version of an industrial park. Number 46 is about eight feet in width and shaped like a barbell inside, with a narrow region—because of the sink and the stove—separating the bedroom from what might optimistically be called the "living" area, with its two-person table and half-sized couch. The bathroom is so small my knees rub against the shower stall when I sit on the toilet, and you can't just leap out of the bed, you have to climb down to the foot of it in order to find a patch of floor space to stand on. Outside, I am within a few yards of a liquor store, a bar that advertises "free beer tomorrow," a convenience store, and a Burger King—but no supermarket or, alas, laundromat. By reputation, the Overseas park is a net of crime and crack, and I am hoping at least for some vibrant, multicultural street life. But desolation rules night and day, except for a thin stream of pedestrian traffic heading for their jobs at the Sheraton or 7-Eleven. There are not exactly people here but what amounts to canned labor, being preserved from the heat between shifts.

When my month-long plunge into poverty is almost over, I finally land my dream job—housekeeping. I do this by walking into the personnel office of the only place I figure I might have some credibility, the hotel attached to Jerry's, and confiding urgently that I have to have a second job if I am to pay my rent and, no, it couldn't be front-desk clerk. "All right," the personnel lady fairly spits, "So it's housekeeping," and she marches me back to meet Maria, the housekeeping manager, a tiny, frenetic Hispanic woman who greets me as "babe" and hands me a pamphlet emphasizing the need for a positive attitude. The hours are nine in the morning til whenever, the pay is $6.10 an hour, and there's one week of vacation a year. I don't have to ask about health insurance once I meet Carlotta, the middle-aged African-American woman who will be training me. Carla, as she tells me to call her, is missing all of her top front teeth.

On that first day of housekeeping and last day of my entire project—although I don't yet know it's the last—Carla is in a foul mood. We have been given nineteen rooms to clean, most of them "checkouts," as opposed to "stayovers," that require the whole enchilada of bed-stripping, vacuuming, and bathroom-scrubbing. For four hours without a break I strip and remake beds, taking about four and half minutes per queen-sized bed, which I could get down to three if there were any reason to. We try to avoid vacuuming by picking up the larger specks by hand, but often there is nothing to do but drag the monstrous vacuum cleaner—it weighs about thirty pounds—off our cart and try to wrestle it around the floor. Sometimes Carla hands me the squirt bottle of "BAM" (an acronym for something that begins, ominously, with "butyric"; the rest has been worn off the label) and lets me do the bathrooms. No service ethic challenges me here to new heights of performance. I just concentrate on removing the pubic hairs from the bathtubs, or at least the dark ones that I can see.

I had looked forward to the breaking-and-entering aspect of cleaning the stay-overs, the chance to examine the secret, physical existence of strangers. But the contents of the rooms are always banal and surprisingly neat—zipped up shaving kits, shoes lined up against the wall (there are no closets), flyers for snorkeling trips, maybe an empty wine bottle or two. It is the TV that keeps us going, from *Jerry* to *Sally* to *Hawaii Five-O* and then on to the soaps. If there's something especially arresting, like "Won't Take No for an Answer" on *Jerry,* we sit down on the edge of a bed and giggle for a moment as if this were a pajama party instead of a terminally dead-end job. The soaps are the best, and Carla turns the volume up full blast so that she won't miss anything from the bathroom or while the vacuum is on. In room 503, Marcia confronts Jeff about Lauren. In 505, Lauren taunts poor cuckolded Marcia. In 511, Helen offers Amanda $10,000 to stop seeing Eric, prompting Carla to emerge from the bathroom to study Amanda's troubled face. "You take it, girl," she advises. "I would for sure."

The tourists' rooms that we clean and, beyond them, the far more expensively appointed interiors in the soaps, begin after a while to merge. We have entered a better world—a world of comfort where every day is a day off, waiting to be filled up with sexual intrigue. We, however, are only gate-crashers in this fantasy, forced to pay for our presence with backaches and perpetual thirst. The mirrors, and there are far too many of them in hotel rooms, contain the kind of person you would normally find pushing a shopping cart down a city street—bedraggled, dressed in a damp hotel polo shirt two sizes too large, and with sweat dribbling down her chin like drool. I am enormously relieved when Carla announces a half-hour meal break, but my appetite fades when I see that the bag of hot-dog rolls she has been carrying around on our cart is not trash salvaged from a checkout but what she has brought for her lunch.

When I request permission to leave at about 3:30, another housekeeper warns me that no one has so far succeeded in combining housekeeping at the hotel with serving at Jerry's: "Some kid did it once for five days, and you're no kid." With that helpful information in mind, I rush back to number 46, down four Advils (the name brand this time), shower, stooping to fit into the stall, and attempt to compose myself for the oncoming shift. So much for what Marx terms the "reproduction of labor power," meaning the things a worker has to do just so she'll be ready to work again. The only unforeseen obstacle to the smooth transition from job to job is that my tan Jerry's slacks, which had looked reasonably clean by 40-watt bulb last night when I handwashed my Hawaiian shirt, prove by daylight to be mottled with ketchup and ranch-dressing stains. I spend most of my hour-long break between jobs attempting to remove the edible portions with a sponge and then drying the slacks over the hood of my car in the sun.

I can do this two-job thing, is my theory, if I can drink enough caffeine. At eight, Ellen and I grab a snack together standing at the mephitic end of the kitchen counter, but I can only manage two or three mozzarella sticks and lunch had been a mere handful of McNuggets. I am not tired at all, I assure myself, though it may be that there is simply no more "I" left to do the tiredness monitoring. What I would see, if I were more alert to the situation, is that the forces of destruction are already massing against me.

Then it comes, the perfect storm. Four of my tables fill up at once. Four tables is nothing for me now, but only so long as they are obligingly staggered. As I bev table 27, tables 25, 28, and 24 are watching enviously. As I bev 25, 24 glowers because their bevs haven't even been ordered. Twenty-eight is four yuppyish types, meaning everything on the side and agonizing instructions as to the chicken Caesars. Twenty-five is a middle-aged black couple, who complain, with some justice, that the iced tea isn't fresh and the tabletop is sticky. But table 24 is the meteorological event of the century: ten British tourists who seem to have made the decision to absorb the American experience entirely by mouth. Here everyone has at least two drinks—iced tea and milk shake, Michelob and water (with lemon slice, please)—and a huge promiscuous orgy of breakfast specials, mozz sticks, chicken strips, quesadillas, burgers with cheese and without, sides of hash browns with cheddar, with onions, with gravy, seasoned fries, plain fries, banana splits. Poor me! Because when I arrive with their first tray of food—after three prior trips just to refill bevs—Princess Di refuses to eat her chicken strips with her pancake-and-sausage special, since, as she now reveals, the strips were meant to be an appetizer. Maybe the others would have accepted their meals, but Di, who is deep into her third Michelob, insists that everything else go back while they work on their "starters." Meanwhile, the yuppies are waving me down for more decaf and the black couple looks ready to summon the NAACP.

Much of what happened next is lost in the fog of war. The little printer on the counter in front of him is spewing out orders faster than he can rip them off, much less produce the meals. Even the invincible Ellen is ashen from stress. I bring table 24 their reheated main courses, which they immediately reject as either too cold or fossilized by the microwave. When I return to the kitchen with their trays (three trays in three trips), Joy confronts me with arms akimbo: "What is this?" She means the food—the plates of rejected pancakes, hash browns in assorted flavors, toasts, burgers, sausages, eggs. "Uh, scrambled with cheddar." I try, "and that's . . ." "NO," she screams in my face. "Is it a traditional, a super-scramble, an eye-opener?" I pretend to study my check for a clue, but entropy has been up to its tricks, not only on the plates but in my head, and I have to admit that the original order is beyond reconstruction. "You don't know an eye-opener from a traditional?" she demands in outrage.

I leave. I don't walk out, I just leave. I don't finish my side work or pick up my credit-card tips, if any, at the cash register or, of course, ask Joy's permission to go. And the surprising thing is that you can walk out without permission, that the door opens, that the thick tropical night air parts to let me pass, that my car is still parked where I left it. There is no vindication in this exit, just an overwhelming, dark sense of failure pressing down on me and the entire parking lot. I had gone into this venture in the spirit of science, to test a mathematical proposition, but somewhere along the line, in the tunnel vision imposed by long shifts and relentless concentration, it became a test of myself, and clearly I have failed.

In one month, I had earned approximately $1,040 and spent $517 on food, gas, toiletries, laundry, phone, and utilities. If I had remained in my $500 efficiency, I would have been able to pay the rent and have $22 left over (which is $78 less than the cash I had in my pocket at the start of the month). During this time I bought no clothing except for the required slacks and no prescription drugs or medical care (I did finally buy some vitamin B to compensate for the lack of vegetables in my diet). Perhaps I could have saved a little on food if I had gotten to a supermarket more often, instead of convenience stores, but it should be noted that I lost almost four pounds in four weeks, on a diet weighted heavily toward burgers and fries.

How former welfare recipients and single mothers will (and do) survive in the low-wage workforce, I cannot imagine. Maybe they will figure out how to condense their lives—including child-raising, laundry, romance, and meals—into the couple of hours between full-time jobs. Maybe they will take up residence in their vehicles, if they have one. All I know is that I couldn't hold two jobs and I couldn't make enough money to live on with one. And I had advantages unthinkable to many of the long-term poor—health, stamina, a working car, and no children to care for and support. Certainly nothing in my experience contradicts the conclusion of Kathryn Edin and Laura Lein, in their book *Making Ends Meet: How Single Mothers Survive Welfare and Low-Wage Work*, that low-wage work actually involves more hardship and deprivation than life at the mercy of the welfare state. In the coming months and years, economic conditions for the working poor are bound to worsen, even without the almost inevitable recession. As mentioned earlier, the influx of former welfare recipients into the low-skilled workforce will have a depressing effect on both wages and the number of jobs available. A general economic downturn will only enhance these effects, and the working poor will of course be facing it without the slight, but nonetheless often saving, protection of welfare as a backup.

The thinking behind welfare reform was that even the humblest jobs are morally uplifting and psychologically buoying. In reality they are likely to be fraught with insult and stress. But I did discover one redeeming feature of the most abject low-wage work—the camaraderie of people who are, in almost all cases, far too smart and funny and caring for the work they do and the wages they're paid. The hope, of course, is that someday these people will come to know what they're worth, and take appropriate action.

33 When Work Becomes Home and Home Becomes Work

ARLIE RUSSELL HOCHSCHILD

Work and family are always interrelated. It used to be that work took place at home. Not only women but also men did their work there. Most men were farmers, and most women took care of the household *and* did farming chores. Husbands and wives produced most of the items they used—from their own clothing to the food they ate. From an early age, children were intricately involved in this survival process; they took care of younger children, fed animals, milked cows, and were responsible for a variety of other chores.

Then economic activity (making a living) moved to centralized locations called factories. This removed the husband from the home first. As nonhome production spread, a service industry for factories expanded, and more and more women left the home to work in offices. Today, despite a trend of using computers to work at home, most husbands and wives work outside the home.

To study the relationship between home and work life, Hochschild interviewed and observed working parents at a large company that she calls Amerco. What she found surprising was that the parents liked being at work—often more than they liked being at home. In this selection, she discusses what underlies this changing attitude toward work and family.

IT'S 7:40 A.M. WHEN Cassie Bell, 4, arrives at the Spotted Deer Child-Care Center, her hair half-combed, a blanket in one hand, a fudge bar in the other. "I'm late," her mother, Gwen, a sturdy young woman whose short-cropped hair frames a pleasant face, explains to the child-care worker in charge. "Cassie wanted the fudge bar so bad, I gave it to her," she adds apologetically.

"Please, can't you take me with you?" Cassie pleads.

"You know I can't take you to work," Gwen replies in a tone that suggests that she has been expecting this request. Cassie's shoulders droop. But she has struck a hard bargain—the morning fudge bar—aware of her mother's anxiety about the long day that lies ahead at the center. As Gwen explains later, she continually feels that she owes Cassie more time than she gives her—she has a "time debt."

Arriving at her office just before 8, Gwen finds on her desk a cup of coffee in her personal mug, milk no sugar (exactly as she likes it), prepared by a co-worker who managed to get in ahead of her. As the assistant to the head of public relations at a company I will call Amerco, Gwen has to handle responses to any reports that may appear about the company in the press—a challenging job, but one that gives her satisfaction. As she prepares for her first meeting of the day, she misses her daughter, but she also feels relief; there's a lot to get done at Amerco.

Gwen used to work a straight eight-hour day. But over the last three years, her workday has gradually stretched to eight and a half or nine hours, not counting the e-mail messages and faxes she answers from home. She complains about her hours to her co-workers and listens to their complaints—but she loves her job. Gwen picks up Cassie at 5:45 and gives her a long, affectionate hug.

At home, Gwen's husband, John, a computer programmer, plays with their daughter while Gwen prepares dinner. To protect the dinner "hour"—8:00–8:30—Gwen checks that the phone machine is on, hears the phone ring during dinner but resists the urge to answer. After Cassie's bath, Gwen and Cassie have "quality time," or "Q.T.," as John affectionately calls it. Half an hour later, at 9:30, Gwen tucks Cassie into bed.

There are, in a sense, two Bell households: the rushed family they actually are and the relaxed family they imagine they might be if only they had time. Gwen and John complain that they are in a time bind. What they say they want seems so modest—time to throw a ball, to read to Cassie, to witness the small dramas of her development, not to speak of having a little fun and romance themselves. Yet even these modest wishes seem strangely out of reach. Before going to bed, Gwen has to e-mail messages to her colleagues in preparation for the next day's meeting; John goes to bed early, exhausted—he's out the door by 7 every morning.

Nationwide, many working parents are in the same boat. More mothers of small children than ever now work outside the home. American men average 48.8 hours of work a week, and women 41.7 hours, including overtime and commuting. All in all, more women are on the economic train, and for many—men and women alike—that train is going faster.

But Amerco has "family-friendly" policies. If your division head and supervisor agree, you can work part time, share a job with another worker, work some hours at home, take parental leave or use "flex time." But hardly anyone uses these policies. In seven years, only two Amerco fathers have taken formal parental leave. Fewer than 1 percent have taken advantage of the opportunity to work part time. Of all such policies, only flex time—which rearranges but does not shorten work time—has had a significant number of takers (perhaps a third of working parents at Amerco).

Forgoing family-friendly policies is not exclusive to Amerco workers. A study of 188 companies conducted by the Families and Work Institute found that while a majority offered part-time shifts, fewer than 5 percent of employees made use of them. Thirty-five percent offered "flex place"—work from home—and fewer than 3 percent of their employees took advantage of it. And a Bureau of Labor Statistics survey asked workers whether they preferred a shorter workweek, a longer one or their present schedule. About 62 percent preferred their present schedule; 28 percent would have preferred longer hours. Fewer than 10 percent said they wanted a cut in hours.

Still, I found it hard to believe that people didn't protest their long hours at work. So I contacted Bright Horizons, a company that runs 136 company-based child-care centers associated with corporations, hospitals and Federal agencies in 25 states. Bright Horizons allowed me to add questions to a questionnaire they sent out to 3,000 parents whose children attended the centers. The respondents, mainly middle-class parents in their early 30s, largely confirmed the picture I'd found at Amerco. A third of fathers and a fifth of mothers described themselves as "workaholic," and 1 out of 3 said their partners were.

To be sure, some parents have tried to shorten their hours. Twenty-one percent of the nation's women voluntarily work part time, as do 7 percent of men. A number of others make under-the-table arrangements that don't show up on surveys. But while working parents say they need more time at home, the main story of their lives does not center on a struggle to get it. Why? Given the hours parents are working these days, why aren't they taking advantage of an opportunity to reduce their time at work?

The most widely held explanation is that working parents cannot afford to work shorter hours. Certainly this is true for many. But if money is the whole explanation, why would it be that at places like Amerco, the best-paid employees—upper-level managers and professionals—were the least interested in part-time work or job sharing, while clerical workers who earned less were more interested?

Similarly, if money were the answer, we would expect poorer new mothers to return to work more quickly after giving birth than rich mothers. But among working women nationwide, well-to-do new mothers are not much more likely to stay home after 13 weeks with a new baby than low-income new mothers. When asked what they look for in a job, only a third of respondents in a recent study said salary came first. Money is important, but by itself, money does not explain why many people don't want to cut back hours at work.

Were workers uninformed about the company's family-friendly policies? No. Some even mentioned that they were proud to work for a company that offered such enlightened policies. Were rigid middle managers standing in the way of workers using these policies? Sometimes. But when I compared Amerco employees who worked for flexible managers with those who worked for rigid managers, I found that the flexible managers reported only a few more applicants than the rigid ones. The evidence, however counterintuitive, pointed to a paradox: workers at the company I studied weren't protesting the time bind. They were accommodating to it.

Why? I did not anticipate the conclusion I found myself coming to: namely, that work has become a form of "home" and home has become "work." The worlds of home and work have not begun to blur, as the conventional wisdom goes, but to reverse places. We are used to thinking that home is where most people feel the most appreciated, the most truly "themselves," the most secure, the most relaxed. We are used to thinking that work is where most people feel like "just a number" or "a cog in a machine." It is where they have to be "on," have to "act," where they are least secure and most harried.

But new management techniques so pervasive in corporate life have helped transform the workplace into a more appreciative, personal sort of social world. Meanwhile, at home the divorce rate has risen, and the emotional demands have become more baffling and complex. In addition to teething, tantrums and the normal developments of growing children, the needs of elderly parents are creating more tasks for the modern family—as are the blending, unblending, reblending of new stepparents, stepchildren, exes and former in-laws.

This idea began to dawn on me during one of my first interviews with an Amerco worker. Linda Avery, a friendly, 38-year-old mother, is a shift supervisor at an Amerco plant. When I meet her in the factory's coffee-break room over a couple of Cokes, she is wearing blue jeans and a pink jersey, her hair pulled back in a long, blond ponytail. Linda's husband, Bill, is a technician in the same plant. By working different shifts, they manage to share the care of their 2-year-old son and Linda's 16-year-old daughter from a previous marriage. "Bill works the 7 A.M. to 3 P.M. shift while I watch the baby," she explains. "Then I work the 3 P.M. to 11 P.M. shift and he watches the baby. My daughter works at Walgreen's after school."

Linda is working overtime, and so I begin by asking whether Amerco required the overtime or whether she volunteered for it. "Oh, I put in for it," she replies. I ask her whether, if finances and company policy permitted, she'd be interested in cutting back on the overtime. She takes off her safety glasses, rubs her face and, without answering my question, explains: "I get home, and the minute I turn the key, my daughter is right there. Granted, she needs somebody to talk to about her day. . . . The baby is still up. He should have been in bed two hours ago, and that upsets me. The dishes are piled in the sink. My daughter comes right up to the door and complains about anything her stepfather said or did, and she wants to talk about her job. My husband is in the other room hollering to my daughter, 'Tracy, I don't ever get any time to talk to your mother, because you're always monopolizing her time before I even get a chance!' They all come at me at once."

Linda's description of the urgency of demands and the unarbitrated quarrels that await her homecoming contrast with her account of arriving at her job as a shift supervisor: "I usually come to work early, just to get away from the house. When I arrive, people are there waiting. We sit, we talk, we joke. I let them know what's going on, who has to be where, what changes I've made for the shift that day. We sit and chitchat for 5 or 10 minutes. There's laughing, joking, fun."

For Linda, home has come to feel like work and work has come to feel a bit like home. Indeed, she feels she can get relief from the "work" of being at home only by going to the "home" of work. Why has her life at home come to seem like this? Linda explains it this way: "My husband's a great help watching our baby. But as far as doing housework or even taking the baby when I'm at home, no. He figures he works five days a week; he's not going to come home and clean. But he doesn't stop to think that I work seven days a week. Why should I have to come home and do the housework without help from anybody else? My husband and I have been through this over and over again. Even if he would just pick up from the kitchen table and stack the dishes for me, that would make a big difference. He does nothing. On his weekends off, he goes fishing. If I want any time off, I have to get a sitter. He'll help out if I'm not here, but the minute I am, all the work at home is mine."

With a light laugh, she continues: "So I take a lot of overtime. The more I get out of the house, the better I am. It's a terrible thing to say, but that's the way I feel."

When Bill feels the need for time off, to relax, to have fun, to feel free, he climbs in his truck and takes his free time without his family. Largely in response, Linda grabs what she also calls "free time"—at work. Neither Linda nor Bill Avery wants more time together at home, not as things are arranged now.

How do Linda and Bill Avery fit into the broader picture of American family and work life? Current research suggests that however hectic their lives, women who do paid work feel less depressed, think better of themselves and are more satisfied than women who stay at home. One study reported that women who work outside the home feel more valued at home than housewives do. Meanwhile, work is where many women feel like "good mothers." As Linda reflects: "I'm a good mom at home, but I'm a better mom at work. At home, I get into fights with Tracy. I want her to apply to a junior college, but she's not interested. At work, I think I'm better at seeing the other person's point of view."

Many workers feel more confident they could "get the job done" at work than at home. One study found that only 59 percent of workers feel their "performance" in the family is "good or unusually good," while 86 percent rank their performance on the job this way.

Forces at work and at home are simultaneously reinforcing this "reversal." This lure of work has been enhanced in recent years by the rise of company cultural engineering—in particular, the shift from Frederick Taylor's principles of scientific management to the Total Quality principles originally set out by W. Edwards Deming. Under the influence of a Taylorist world view, the manager's job was to coerce the worker's mind and body, not to appeal to the worker's heart. The Taylorized worker was de-skilled, replaceable and cheap, and as a consequence felt bored, demeaned and unappreciated.

Using modern participative management techniques, many companies now train workers to make their own work decisions, and then set before their newly "empowered" employees moral as well as financial incentives. At Amerco, the Total Quality worker is invited to feel recognized for job accomplishments. Amerco regularly strengthens the familylike ties of co-workers by holding "recognition ceremonies" honoring particular workers or self-managed production teams. Amerco employees speak of "belonging to the Amerco family" and proudly wear their "Total Quality" pins or "High Performance Team" T-shirts, symbols of their loyalty to the company and of its loyalty to them.

The company occasionally decorates a section of the factory and serves refreshments. The production teams, too, have regular get-togethers. In a New Age recasting of an old business slogan—"The Customer Is Always Right"—Amerco proposes that its workers "Value the Internal Customer." This means: Be as polite and considerate to co-workers inside the company as you would be to customers outside it. How many recognition ceremonies for competent performance are being offered at home? Who is valuing the internal customer there?

Amerco also tries to take on the role of a helpful relative with regard to employee problems at work and at home. The education-and-training division offers employees free courses (on company time) in "Dealing With Anger," "How to Give and Accept Criticism," "How to Cope With Difficult People."

At home, of course, people seldom receive anything like this much help on issues basic to family life. There, no courses are being offered on "Dealing

With Your Child's Disappointment in You" or "How to Treat Your Spouse Like an Internal Customer."

If Total Quality calls for "re-skilling" the worker in an "enriched" job environment, technological developments have long been de-skilling parents at home. Over the centuries, store-bought goods have replaced homespun cloth, homemade soup and home-baked foods. Day care for children, retirement homes for the elderly, even psychotherapy are, in a way, commercial substitutes for jobs that a mother once did at home. Even family-generated entertainment has, to some extent, been replaced by television, video games and the VCR. I sometimes watched Amerco families sitting together after their dinners, mute but cozy, watching sitcoms in which television mothers, fathers and children related in an animated way to one another while the viewing family engaged in relational loafing.

The one "skill" still required of family members is the hardest one of all—the emotional work of forging, deepening or repairing family relationships. It takes time to develop this skill, and even then things can go awry. Family ties are complicated. People get hurt. Yet as broken homes become more common—and as the sense of belonging to a geographical community grows less and less secure in an age of mobility—the corporate world has created a sense of "neighborhood," of "feminine culture," of family at work. Life at work can be insecure; the company can fire workers. But workers aren't so secure at home, either. Many employees have been working for Amerco for 20 years but are on their second or third marriages or relationships. The shifting balance between these two "divorce rates" may be the most powerful reason why tired parents flee a world of unresolved quarrels and unwashed laundry for the orderliness, harmony and managed cheer of work. People are getting their "pink slips" at home.

Amerco workers have not only turned their offices into "home" and their homes into workplaces; many have also begun to "Taylorize" time at home, where families are succumbing to a cult of efficiency previously associated mainly with the office and factory. Meanwhile, work time, with its ever longer hours, has become more hospitable to sociability—periods of talking with friends on e-mail, patching up quarrels, gossiping. Within the long workday of many Amerco employees are great hidden pockets of inefficiency while, in the far smaller number of waking weekday hours at home, they are, despite themselves, forced to act increasingly time-conscious and efficient.

The Averys respond to their time bind at home by trying to value and protect "quality time." A concept unknown to their parents and grandparents, "quality time" has become a powerful symbol of the struggle against the growing pressures at home. It reflects the extent to which modern parents feel the flow of time to be running against them. The premise behind "quality time" is that the time we devote to relationships can somehow be separated from ordinary time. Relationships go on during quantity time, of course, but then we are only passively, not actively, wholeheartedly, specializing in our emotional ties. We aren't "on." Quality time at home becomes like an office appointment. You don't want to be caught "goofing off around the water cooler" when you are "at work."

Quality time holds out the hope that scheduling intense periods of togetherness can compensate for an overall loss of time in such a way that a relationship will suffer no loss of quality. But this is just another way of transferring the cult of efficiency from office to home. We must now get our relationships in good repair in less time. Instead of nine hours a day with a child, we declare ourselves capable of getting "the same result" with one intensely focused hour.

Parents now more commonly speak of time as if it is a threatened form of personal capital they have no choice but to manage and invest. What's new here is the spread into the home of a financial manager's attitude toward time. Working parents at Amerco owe what they think of as time debts at home. This is because they are, in a sense, inadvertently "Taylorizing" the house—speeding up the pace of home life as Taylor once tried to "scientifically" speed up the pace of factory life.

Advertisers of products aimed at women have recognized that this new reality provides an opportunity to sell products, and have turned the very pressure that threatens to explode the home into a positive attribute. Take, for example, an ad promoting Instant Quaker Oatmeal: it shows a smiling mother ready for the office in her square-shouldered suit, hugging her happy son. A caption reads: "Nicky is a very picky eater. With Instant Quaker Oatmeal, I can give him a terrific hot breakfast in just 90 seconds. And I don't have to spend any time coaxing him to eat it!" Here, the modern mother seems to have absorbed the lessons of Frederick Taylor as she presses for efficiency at home because she is in a hurry to get to work.

Part of modern parenthood seems to include coping with the resistance of real children who are not so eager to get their cereal so fast. Some parents try desperately not to appease their children with special gifts or smooth-talking promises about the future. But when time is scarce, even the best parents find themselves passing a system-wide familial speed-up along to the most vulnerable workers on the line. Parents are then obliged to try to control the damage done by a reversal of worlds. They monitor mealtime, homework time, bedtime, trying to cut out "wasted" time.

In response, children often protest the pace, the deadlines, the grand irrationality of "efficient" family life. Children dawdle. They refuse to leave places when it's time to leave. They insist on leaving places when it's not time to leave. Surely, this is part of the usual stop-and-go of childhood itself, but perhaps, too, it is the plea of children for more family time and more control over what time there is. This only adds to the feeling that life at home has become hard work.

Instead of trying to arrange shorter or more flexible work schedules, Amerco parents often avoid confronting the reality of the time bind. Some minimize their ideas about how much care a child, a partner or they themselves "really need." They make do with less time, less attention, less understanding and less support at home than they once imagined possible. They *emotionally downsize* life. In essence, they deny the needs of family members, and they themselves become emotional ascetics. If they once "needed" time with each other, they are not increasingly "fine" without it.

Another way that working parents try to evade the time bind is to buy themselves out of it—an approach that puts women in particular at the heart of a contradiction. Like men, women absorb the work-family speed-up far more than they resist it; but unlike men, they still shoulder most of the workload at home. And women still represent in people's minds the heart and soul of family life. They're the ones—especially women of the urban middle and upper-middle classes—who feel most acutely the need to save time, who are the most tempted by the new "time saving" goods and services—and who wind up feeling the most guilty about it. For example, Playgroup Connections, a Washington-area business started by a former executive recruiter, matches playmates to one another. One mother hired the service to find her child a French-speaking playmate.

In several cities, children home alone can call a number for "Grandma, Please!" and reach an adult who has the time to talk with them, sing to them or help them with their homework. An ad for Kindercare Learning Centers, a for-profit child-care chain, pitches its appeal this way: "You want your child to be active, tolerant, smart, loved, emotionally stable, self-aware, artistic and get a two-hour nap. Anything else?" It goes on to note that Kindercare accepts children 6 weeks to 12 years old and provides a number to call for the Kindercare nearest you. Another typical service organizes children's birthday parties, making out invitations ("sure hope you can come") and providing party favors, entertainment, a decorated cake and balloons. Creative Memories is a service that puts ancestral photos into family albums for you.

An overwhelming majority of the working mothers I spoke with recoiled from the idea of buying themselves out of parental duties. A bought birthday party was "too impersonal," a 90-second breakfast "too fast." Yet a surprising amount of lunchtime conversation between female friends at Amerco was devoted to expressing complex, conflicting feelings about the lure of trading time for one service or another. The temptation to order flash-frozen dinners or to call a local number for a homework helper did not come up because such services had not yet appeared at Spotted Deer Child-Care Center. But many women dwelled on the question of how to decide where a mother's job began and ended, especially with regard to babysitters and television. One mother said to another in the breakroom of an Amerco plant: "Damon doesn't settle down until 10 at night, so he hates me to wake him up in the morning and I hate to do it. He's cranky. He pulls the covers up. I put on cartoons. That way I can dress him and he doesn't object. I don't like to use TV that way. It's like a drug. But I do it."

The other mother countered: "Well, Todd is up before we are, so that's not a problem. It's after dinner, when I feel like watching a little television, that I feel guilty, because he gets too much TV at the sitter's."

As task after task falls into the realm of time-saving goods and services, questions rise about the moral meanings attached to doing or not doing such tasks. Is it being a good mother to bake a child's birthday cake (alone or together with one's partner)? Or can we gratefully save time by ordering it, and be good mothers by planning the party? Can we save more time by hiring a planning service, and be good mothers simply by watching our children have a good time? "Wouldn't that be nice!" one Amerco mother exclaimed. As the idea of the "good mother" retreats before the pressures of work and the expansion of motherly services, mothers are in fact continually reinventing themselves.

The final way working parents tried to evade the time bind was to develop what I call "potential selves." The potential selves that I discovered in my Amerco interviews were fantasy creations of time-poor parents who dreamed of living as time millionaires.

One man, a gifted 55-year-old engineer in research and development at Amerco, told how he had dreamed of taking his daughters on a camping trip in the Sierra Mountains: "I bought all the gear three years ago when they were 5 and 7, the tent, the sleeping bags, the air mattresses, the backpacks, the ponchos. I got a map of the area. I even got the freeze-dried food. Since then the kids and I have talked about it a lot, and gone over what we're going to do. They've been on me to do it for a long time. I feel bad about it. I keep putting it off, but we'll do it, I just don't know when."

Banished to garages and attics of many Amerco workers were expensive electric saws, cameras, skis and musical instruments, all bought with wages it took time to earn. These items were to their owners what Cassie's fudge bar was to her—a substitute for time, a talisman, a reminder of the potential self.

Obviously, not everyone, not even a majority of Americans, is making a home out of work and a workplace out of home. But in the working world, it is a growing reality, and one we need to face. Increasing numbers of women are discovering a great male secret—that work can be an escape from the pressures of home, pressures that the changing nature of work itself are only intensifying. Neither men nor women are going to take up "family-friendly" policies, whether corporate or governmental, as long as the current realities of work and home remain as they are. For a substantial number of time-bound parents, the stripped-down home and the neighborhood devoid of community are simply losing out to the pull of the workplace.

There are several broader, historical causes of this reversal of realms. The last 30 years have witnessed the rapid rise of women in the workplace. At the same time, job mobility has taken families farther from relatives who might lend a hand, and made it harder to make close friends of neighbors who could help out. Moreover, as women have acquired more education and have joined men at work, they have absorbed the views of an older, male-oriented work world, its views of a "real career," far more than men have taken up their share of the work at home. One reason women have changed more than men is the world of "male" work seems more honorable and valuable than the "female" world of home and children.

So where do we go from here? There is surely no going back to the mythical 1950s family that confined women to the home. Most women don't wish to return to a full-time role at home—and couldn't afford it even if they did. But equally troubling is a workaholic culture that strands both men and women outside the home.

For a while now, scholars on work-family issues have pointed to Sweden, Norway and Denmark as better models of work-family balance. Today, for example, almost all Swedish fathers take two paid weeks off from work at the birth of their children, and about half of fathers and most mothers take additional "parental leave" during the child's first or second year. Research shows that men who take family leave when their children are very young are more likely to be involved with their children as they grow older. When I mentioned this Swedish record of paternity leave to a focus group of American male managers, one of them replied, "Right, we've already heard about Sweden." To this executive, paternity leave was a good idea not for the U.S. today, but for some "potential society" in another place and time.

Meanwhile, children are paying the price. In her book *When the Bough Breaks: The Cost of Neglecting Our Children,* the economist Sylvia Hewlett claims that "compared with the previous generation, young people today are more likely to underperform at school; commit suicide; need psychiatric help; suffer a severe eating disorder; bear a child out of wedlock; take drugs; be the victim of a violent crime." But we needn't dwell on sledgehammer problems like heroin and suicide to realize that children like those at Spotted Deer need more of our time. If other advanced nations with two-job families can give children the time they need, why can't we?

34 Kindergarten as Academic Boot Camp

HARRY L. GRACEY

As we have seen in the preceding Parts, each society (and each group) maintains a vital interest in making its members conform to expectations. A major social institution for which conformity is a primary goal is education. Educators want to graduate people who are acceptable to the community, not only in terms of marketable skills but also in terms of their ideas, attitudes, and behaviors. Whether it be grade school, high school, or college, educational administrators want instructors to teach standard ideas and facts, to steer clear of radical politics, and to not stir up trouble in the school or community. *Then* the social institution can go about its business—and that business, when you probe beneath official utterances and uncover the *hidden curriculum*, is producing conformists who fit well in society.

Although Gracey's focus is kindergarten, this article was chosen to represent the educational institution because it focuses on this essential nature of education, training in conformity. The primary goal of kindergarten is to teach children to be students—so they can participate in conformity. If this is what education really is about, where are intellectual stimulation, the excitement of discovery, and creativity—long associated in the public mind with education? The answer is that they may occur so long as they are noncontroversial. In other words they, too, are expected to reflect the conformist nature of the educational institution.

Based on your own extensive experiences with education, how do you react to the idea that the essence of the educational institution is training into conformity?

EDUCATION MUST BE CONSIDERED one of the major institutions of social life today. Along with the family and organized religion, however, it is a "secondary institution," one in which people are prepared for life in society as it is presently organized. The main dimensions of modern life, that is, the nature of society as a whole, are determined principally by the "primary institutions," which today are the economy, the political system, and the military establishment. Education has been defined by sociologists, classical and contemporary, as an institution which serves society by socializing people into it through a formalized, standardized procedure. At the beginning of the last century Emile Durkheim told student teachers at the University of Paris that education "consists of a methodical socialization of the younger generation." He went on to add:

> It is the influence exercised by adult generations on those that are not ready for social life. Its object is to arouse and to develop in the child a certain number of physical, intellectual, and moral states that are demanded of him by the political society as a whole and by the special milieu for which he is specifically destined. . . . To the egotistic and asocial being that has just been born, [society] must, as rapidly as possible, add another, capable of leading a moral and social life. Such is the work of education.[1]

The education process, Durkheim said, "is above all the means by which society perpetually recreates the conditions of its very existence."[2] The contemporary educational sociologist Wilbur Brookover offers a similar formulation in his recent textbook definition of education:

> Actually, therefore, in the broadest sense education is synonymous with socialization. It includes any social behavior that assists in the induction of the child into membership in the society or any behavior by which the society perpetuates itself through the next generation.[3]

The educational institution is, then, one of the ways in which society is perpetuated through the systematic socialization of the young, while the nature of the society which is being perpetuated—its organization and operation, its values, beliefs, and ways of living—are determined by the primary institutions. The educational system, like other secondary institutions, *serves* the society which is *created* by the operation of the economy, the political system, and the military establishment.

Schools, the social organizations of the educational institution, are today for the most part large bureaucracies run by specially trained and certified people. There are few places left in modern societies where formal teaching and learning are carried on in small, isolated groups, like the rural, one-room schoolhouses of [the 1800s]. Schools are large, formal organizations which tend to be parts of larger organizations, local community School Districts. These School Districts are bureaucratically organized and their operations are supervised by state and local governments. In this context, as Brookover says:

> The term education is used . . . to refer to a system of schools, in which specifically designated persons are expected to teach children and youth certain types of acceptable behavior. The school system becomes a . . . unit in the

total social structure and is recognized by the members of the society as a separate social institution. Within this structure a portion of the total socialization process occurs.[4]

Education is the part of the socialization process which takes place in the schools; and these are, more and more today, bureaucracies within bureaucracies.

Kindergarten is generally conceived by educators as a year of preparation for school. It is thought of as a year in which small children, five or six years old, are prepared socially and emotionally for the academic learning which will take place over the next twelve years. It is expected that a foundation of behavior and attitudes will be laid in kindergarten on which the children can acquire the skills and knowledge they will be taught in the grades. A booklet prepared for parents by the staff of a suburban New York school system says that the kindergarten experience will stimulate the child's desire to learn and cultivate the skills he will need for learning in the rest of his school career. It claims that the child will find opportunities for physical growth, for satisfying his "need for self-expression," acquire some knowledge, and provide opportunities for creative activity. It concludes, "The most important benefit that your five-year-old will receive from kindergarten is the opportunity to live and grow happily and purposefully with others in a small society." The kindergarten teachers in one of the elementary schools in this community, one we shall call the Wilbur Wright School, said their goals were to see that the children "grew" in all ways: physically, of course, emotionally, socially, and academically. They said they wanted children to like school as a result of their kindergarten experiences and that they wanted them to learn to get along with others.

None of these goals, however, is unique to kindergarten; each of them is held to some extent by teachers in the other six grades at Wright School. And growth would occur, but differently, even if the child did not attend school. The children already know how to get along with others, in their families and their play groups. The unique job of the kindergarten in the educational division of labor seems rather to be teaching children the student role. The student role is the repertoire of behavior and attitudes regarded by educators as appropriate to children in school. Observation in the kindergartens of the Wilbur Wright School revealed a great variety of activities through which children are shown and then drilled in the behavior and attitudes defined as appropriate for school and thereby induced to learn the role of student. Observations of the kindergartens and interviews with the teachers both pointed to the teaching and learning of classroom routines as the main element of the student role. The teachers expended most of their efforts, for the first half of the year at least, in training the children to follow the routines which teachers created. The children were, in a very real sense, *drilled* in tasks and activities created by the teachers for their own purposes and beginning and ending quite arbitrarily (from the child's point of view) at the command of the teacher. One teacher remarked that she hated September, because during the first month "everything has to be done rigidly, and repeatedly, until they know exactly what they're supposed to do." However, "by January," she said, "they know exactly what to do [during the day] and I don't have to be after them all the time." Classroom routines were introduced gradually from the beginning of the year in all the kindergartens, and the children were drilled in them as long as was necessary to achieve regular compliance. By the end of the school year, the successful kindergarten teacher has a well-organized group of children. They follow classroom routines automatically, having learned all the command signals and the expected responses to them. They have, in our terms, learned the student role. The following observation shows one such classroom operating at optimum organization on an afternoon late in May. It is the class of an experienced and respected kindergarten teacher.

An Afternoon in Kindergarten

At about 12:20 in the afternoon on a day in the last week of May, Edith Kerr leaves the teachers' room where she has been having lunch and walks to her classroom at the far end of the primary wing of Wright School. A group of five- and six-year-olds peers at her through the glass doors leading from the hall cloakroom to the play area outside. Entering her room, she straightens some material in the "book corner" of the room, arranges music on the piano, takes colored paper from her closet and places it on one of the shelves under the window. Her room is divided into a number of activity areas through the arrangement of furniture and play equipment. Two easels and a paint table near the door create a kind of passageway inside the room. A wedge-shaped area just inside the front door is made into a teacher's area by the placing of "her" things there: her desk, file, and piano. To the left is the book corner, marked off from the rest of the room by a puppet stage and a movable chalkboard. In it are a display rack of picture books, a record player, and a stack of children's records. To the right of the entrance are the sink and clean-up area. Four large round tables with six chairs at each for the children are placed near the walls about halfway down the length of the room, two on each side, leaving a large open area in the center for group games, block building, and toy truck driving. Windows stretch down the length of both walls, starting about three feet from the floor and extending almost to the high ceilings. Under the windows are long shelves on which are kept all the toys, games, blocks, paper, paints, and other equipment of the kindergarten. The left rear corner of the room is a play store with shelves, merchandise, and cash register; the right rear corner is a play kitchen with stove, sink, ironing board, and bassinette with baby dolls in it. This area is partly shielded from the rest of the room by a large standing display rack for posters and children's art work. A sandbox is found against the back wall between these two areas. The room is light, brightly colored, and filled with things adults feel five- and six-year-olds will find interesting and pleasing.

At 12:25 Edith opens the outside door and admits the waiting children. They hang their sweaters on hooks outside the door and then go to the center of the room and arrange themselves in a semi-circle on the floor, facing the teacher's chair, which she has placed in the center of the floor. Edith follows them in and sits in her chair checking attendance while waiting for the bell to ring. When she has finished attendance, which she takes by sight, she asks the children what the date is, what day and month it is, how many children are enrolled in the class, how many are present, and how many are absent.

The bell rings at 12:30 and the teacher puts away her attendance book. She introduces a visitor, who is sitting against the wall taking notes, as someone who wants to learn about schools and children. She then goes to the back of the room and takes down a large chart labeled "Helping Hands." Bringing it to the center of the room, she tells the children it is time to change jobs. Each child is assigned some task on the chart by placing his name, lettered on a paper "hand," next to a picture signifying the task—e.g., a broom, a blackboard, a milk bottle, a flag, and a Bible. She asks the children who wants each of the jobs and rearranges their "hands" accordingly. Returning to her chair, Edith announces, "One person should tell us what happened to Mark." A girl raises her hand, and when called on says, "Mark fell and hit his head and had to go to the hospital." The teacher adds that Mark's mother had written saying he was in the hospital.

During this time the children have been interacting among themselves, in their semi-circle. Children have whispered to their neighbors, poked one another, made general comments to the group, waved to friends on the other side of the circle. None of this has been disruptive, and the teacher has ignored it for the most part. The children seem to know just how much of each kind of interaction is permitted—they may greet in a soft voice someone who sits next to them, for example, but may not shout greetings to a friend who sits across the circle, so they confine themselves to waving and remain well within understood limits.

At 12:35 two children arrive. Edith asks them why they are late and then sends them to join the circle on the floor. The other children vie with each other to tell the newcomers what happened to Mark. When this leads to a general disorder Edith asks, "Who has serious time?" The children become quiet and a girl raises her hand. Edith nods and the child gets a Bible and hands it to Edith. She reads the Twenty-third Psalm while the children sit quietly. Edith helps the child in charge begin reciting the Lord's Prayer; the other children follow along for the first unit of sounds, and then trail off as Edith finishes for them. Everyone stands and faces the American flag hung to the right of the door. Edith leads the pledge to the flag, with the children again following the familiar sounds as far as they remember them. Edith then asks the girl in charge what song she wants and the child replies, "My Country." Edith goes to the piano and plays "America," singing as the children follow her words.

Edith returns to her chair in the center of the room and the children sit again in the semi-circle on the floor. It is 12:40 when she tells the children, "Let's have boys' sharing time first." She calls the name of the first boy sitting on the end of the circle, and he comes up to her with a toy helicopter. He turns and holds it up for the other children to see. He says, "It's a helicopter." Edith asks, "What is it used for?" and he replies, "For the army. Carry men. For the war." Other children join in, "For shooting submarines." "To bring back men from space when they are in the ocean." Edith sends the boy back to the circle and asks the next boy if he has something. He replies "No" and she passes on to the next. He says "Yes" and brings a bird's nest to her. He holds it for the class to see, and the teacher asks, "What kind of bird made the nest?" The boy replies, "My friend says a rain bird made it." Edith asks what the nest is made of and different children reply, "mud," "leaves," and "sticks." There is also a bit of moss woven into the nest, and Edith tries to describe it to the children. They, however, are more interested in seeing if anything is inside it, and Edith lets the boy carry it around the semi-circle showing the children its insides. Edith tells the children of some baby robins in a nest in her yard, and some of the children tell about baby birds they have seen. Some children are asking about a small object in the nest which they say looks like an egg, but all have seen the nest now and Edith calls on the next boy. A number of children say, "I know what Michael has, but I'm not telling." Michael brings a book to the teacher and then goes back to his place in the circle of children. Edith reads the last page of the book to the class. Some children tell of books which they have at home. Edith calls the next boy, and three children call out, "I know what David has." "He always has the same thing." "It's a bang-bang." David goes to his table and gets a box which he brings to Edith. He opens it and shows the teacher a scale-model of an old-fashioned dueling pistol. When David does not turn around to the class, Edith tells him, "Show it to the children" and he does. One child says, "Mr. Johnson [the principal] said no guns." Edith replies, "Yes, how many of you know that?" Most of the children in the circle raise their hands. She continues, "That you aren't supposed to bring guns to school?"

She calls the next boy on the circle and he brings two large toy soldiers to her which the children enthusiastically identify as being from "Babes in Toyland." The next boy brings an American flag to Edith and shows it to the class. She asks him what the stars and stripes stand for and admonishes him to treat it carefully. "Why should you treat it carefully?" she asks the boy. "Because it's our flag," he replies. She congratulates him, saying, "That's right."

"Show and Tell" lasted twenty minutes and during the last ten one girl in particular announced that she knew what each child called upon had to show. Edith asked her to be quiet each time she spoke out, but she was not content, continuing to offer her comment at each "show." Four children from other classes had come into the room to bring something from another teacher or to ask for something from Edith. Those with requests were asked to return later if the item wasn't readily available.

Edith now asks if any of the children told their mothers about their trip to the local zoo the previous day. Many children raise their hands. As Edith calls on them, they tell what they liked in the zoo. Some children cannot wait to be called on, and they call out things to the teacher, who asks them to be quiet. After a few of the animals are mentioned, one child says, "I liked the spooky house," and the others chime in to agree with him, some pantomiming fear and horror. Edith is puzzled, and asks what this was. When half the children try to tell her at once, she raises her hand for quiet, then calls on individual children. One says, "The house with nobody in it"; another, "The dark little house." Edith asks where it was in the zoo, but the children cannot describe its location in any way which she can understand. Edith makes some jokes but they involve adult abstractions which the children cannot grasp. The children have become quite noisy now, speaking out to make both relevant and irrelevant comments, and three little girls have become particularly assertive.

Edith gets up from her seat at 1:10 and goes to the book corner, where she puts a record on the player. As it begins a story about the trip to the zoo, she returns to the circle and asks the children to go sit at the tables. She divides them among the tables in such a way as to indicate that they don't have regular seats. When the children are all seated at the four tables, five or six to a table, the teacher asks, "Who wants to be the first one?" One of the noisy girls comes to the center of the room. The voice on the record is giving directions for imitating an ostrich and the girl follows them, walking around the center of the room holding her ankles with her hands. Edith replays the record, and all the children, table by table, imitate ostriches down the center of the room and back. Edith removes her shoes and shows that she can be an ostrich too. This is apparently a familiar game, for a number of children are calling out, "Can we have the crab?" Edith asks one of the children to do a crab "so we can all remember how," and then plays the part of the record with music for imitating crabs by. The children from the first table line up across the room, hands and feet on the floor and faces pointing toward the ceiling. After they have "walked" down the room and back in this posture they sit at their table and the children of the next table play "crab." The children love this; they run from their tables, dance about on the floor waiting for their turns, and are generally exuberant. Children ask for the "inch worm," and the game is played again with the children squirming down the floor. As a conclusion Edith shows them a new animal imitation, the "lame dog." The children all hobble down the floor on three "legs," table by table to the accompaniment of the record.

At 1:30 Edith has the children line up in the center of the room: she says, "Table one, line up in front of me," and children ask, "What are we going to do?" Then she moves a few steps to the side and says, "Table two over here; line up next to table one," and more children ask, "What for?" She does this for table three and table four, and each time the children ask, "Why, what are we going to do?" When the children are lined up in four lines of five each, spaced so that they are not touching one another, Edith puts on a new record and leads the class in calisthenics, to the accompaniment of the record. The children just jump around every which way in their places instead of doing the exercises, and by the time the record is finished, Edith, the only one following it, seems exhausted. She is apparently adopting the President's new "Physical Fitness" program for her classroom.

At 1:35 Edith pulls her chair to the easels and calls the children to sit on the floor in front of her, table by table. When they are all seated she asks, "What are you going to do for worktime today?" Different children raise their hands and tell Edith what they are going to draw. Most are going to make pictures of animals they saw in the zoo. Edith asks if they want to make pictures to send to Mark in the hospital, and the children agree to this. Edith gives drawing paper to the children, calling them to her one by one. After getting a piece of paper, the children go to the crayon box on the righthand shelves, select a number of colors, and go to the tables, where they begin drawing. Edith is again trying to quiet the perpetually talking girls. She keeps two of them standing by her so they won't disrupt the others. She asks them, "Why do you feel you have to talk all the time?" and then scolds them for not listening to her. Then she sends them to their tables to draw.

Most of the children are drawing at their tables, sitting or kneeling in their chairs. They are all working very industriously and, engrossed in their work, very quietly. Three girls have chosen to paint at the easels, and having donned their smocks, they are busily mixing colors and intently applying them to their pictures. If the children at the tables are primitives and neo-realists in their animal depictions, these girls at the easels are the class abstract-expressionists, with their broad-stroked, colorful paintings.

Edith asks of the children generally, "What color should I make the cover of Mark's book?" Brown and green are suggested by some children "because Mark likes them." The other children are puzzled as to just what is going on and ask, "What book?" or "What does she mean?" Edith explains what she thought was clear to them already, that they are all going to put their pictures together in a "book" to be sent to Mark. She goes to a small table in the play-kitchen corner and tells the children to bring her their pictures when they are finished and she will write their message for Mark on them.

By 1:50 most children have finished their pictures and given them to Edith. She talks with some of them as she ties the bundle of pictures together—answering questions, listening, carrying on conversations. The children are playing in various parts of the room with toys, games, and blocks which they have taken off the shelves. They also move from table to table examining each other's pictures, offering compliments and suggestions. Three girls at a table are cutting up colored paper for a collage. Another girl is walking about the room in a pair of high heels with a woman's purse over her arm. Three boys are playing in the center of the room with the large block set, with which they are building walk-ways and walking on them. Edith is very much concerned about their safety and comes over a number of times to fuss over them. Two or three other boys are pushing trucks around the center of the room, and mild altercations occur when they drive through the block constructions. Some boys and girls are playing at the toy store, two girls are serving "tea" in the play kitchen, and one is washing a doll baby. Two boys have elected to clean the room, and with large sponges they wash the movable blackboard, the puppet stage, and then begin on the tables. They run into resistance from the children who are working with construction toys on the tables and do not want to dismantle their structures. The class is like a room full of bees, each intent on pursuing some activity, occasionally bumping into one another, but just veering off in another direction without serious altercation. At 2:05 the custodian arrives pushing a cart loaded with half-pint milk containers. He places a tray of cartons on the counter next to the sink, then leaves. His coming and going is unnoticed in the room (as, incidentally, is the presence of the observer, who is completely ignored by the children for the entire afternoon).

At 2:15 Edith walks to the entrance of the room, switches off the lights, and sits at the piano and plays. The children begin spontaneously singing the song, which is "Clean up, clean up. Everybody clean up." Edith walks around the room supervising the clean-up. Some children put their toys, the blocks, puzzles, games, and so on back on their shelves under the windows. The children making a collage keep right on working. A child from another class comes in to borrow the 45-rpm adaptor for the record player. At more urging from Edith the rest of the children shelve their toys and work. The children are sitting around their tables now, and Edith asks, "What record would you like to hear while you have your milk?" There is some confusion and no general consensus, so Edith drops the subject and begins to call the children, table by table, to come get their milk. "Table one," she says, and the five children come to the sink, wash their hands and dry them, pick up a carton of milk and a straw, and take it back to their table. Two talking girls wander about the room interfering with the children getting their milk and Edith calls out to them to "settle down." As the children sit, many of them call out to Edith the name of the record they want to hear. When all the children are seated at tables with milk, Edith plays one of these records called "Bozo and the Birds" and shows the children pictures in a book which go with the record. The record recites, and the book shows the adventures of a clown, Bozo, as he walks through a woods meeting many different kinds of birds who, of course, display the characteristics of many kinds of people or, more accurately, different stereotypes. As children finish their milk, they take blankets or pads from the shelves under the windows and lie on them in the center of the room, where Edith sits on her chair showing the pictures. By 2:30 half the class is lying on the floor on their blankets, the record is still playing, and the teacher is turning the pages of the book. The child who came in previously returns the 45-rpm adaptor, and one of the kindergartners tells Edith what the boy's name is and where he lives.

The record ends at 2:40. Edith says, "Children, down on your blankets." All the class is lying on blankets now. Edith refuses to answer the various questions individual children put to her because, she tells them, "it's rest time now." Instead she talks very softly about what they will do tomorrow. They are going to work with clay, she says. The children lie quietly and listen. One of the boys raises his hand and when called on tells Edith, "The animals in the zoo looked so hungry yesterday." Edith asks the children what they think about this and a number try to volunteer opinions, but Edith accepts only those offered in a "rest-time tone," that is, softly and quietly. After a brief discussion of animal feeding, Edith calls the names of the two children on milk detail and has them collect empty milk cartons from the tables and return them to the tray. She asks the two children on clean-up detail to clean up the room. Then she gets up from her chair and goes to the door to turn on the lights. At this signal, the children all get up from the floor and return their blankets and pads to the shelf. It is raining (the reason for no outside play this afternoon) and cars driven by mothers clog the school drive and line up along the street. One of the talkative little girls comes over to Edith and pointing out the window says, "Mrs. Kerr, see my mother in the new Cadillac?"

At 2:50 Edith sits at the piano and plays. The children sit on the floor in the center of the room and sing. They have a repertoire of songs about animals, including one in which each child sings a refrain alone. They know these by heart and sing along through the ringing of the 2:55 bell. When the song is finished, Edith gets up and coming to the group says, "Okay, rhyming words to get your coats today." The children raise their hands and as Edith calls on them, they tell her two rhyming words, after which they are allowed to go into the hall to get their coats and sweaters. They return to the room with these and sit at their tables. At 2:59 Edith says, "When you have your coats on, you may line up at the door." Half of the children go to the door and stand in a long line. When the three o'clock bell rings, Edith returns to the piano and plays. The children sing a song called "Goodbye," after which Edith sends them out.

Training for Learning and for Life

The day in kindergarten at Wright School illustrates both the content of the student role as it has been learned by these children and the processes by which the teacher has brought about this learning, or, "taught" them the student role. The children have learned to go through routines and to follow orders with unquestioning obedience, even when these make no sense to them. They have been disciplined to do as they are told by an authoritative person without significant protest. Edith has developed this discipline in the children by creating and enforcing a rigid social structure in the classroom through which she effectively controls the behavior of most of the children for most of the school day. The "living with others in a small society" which the school pamphlet tells parents is the most important thing the children will learn in kindergarten can be seen now in its operational meaning, which is learning to live by the routines imposed by the school. This learning appears to be the principal content of the student role.

Children who submit to school-imposed discipline and come to identify with it, so that being a "good student" comes to be an important part of their developing identities, *become* the good students by the school's definitions. Those who submit to the routines of the school but do not come to identify with them will be adequate students who find the more important part of their identities elsewhere, such as in the play group outside school. Children who refuse to submit to the school routines are rebels, who become known as "bad students" and often "problem children" in the school, for they do not learn the academic curriculum and their behavior is often disruptive in the classroom. Today schools engage clinical psychologists in part to help teachers deal with such children.

In looking at Edith's kindergarten at Wright School, it is interesting to ask how the children learn this role of student—come to accept school-imposed routines—and what, exactly, it involves in terms of behavior and attitudes. The most prominent features of the classroom are its physical and social structures. The room is carefully furnished and arranged in ways adults feel will interest children. The play store and play kitchen in the back of the room, for example, imply that children are interested in mimicking these activities of the adult world. The only space left for the children to create something of their own is the empty center of the room, and the materials at their disposal are the blocks, whose use causes anxiety on the part of the teacher. The room, being carefully organized physically by the adults, leaves little room for the creation of physical organization on the part of the children.

The social structure created by Edith is a far more powerful and subtle force for fitting the children to the student role. This structure is established by the very rigid and tightly controlled set of rituals and routines through which the children are put during the day. There is first the rigid "locating procedure" in which the children are asked to find themselves in terms of the month, date, day of the week, and the number of the class who are present and absent. This puts them solidly in the real world as defined by adults. The day is then divided into six periods whose activities are for the most part determined by the teacher. In Edith's kindergarten the children went through Serious Time, which opens the school day, Sharing Time, Play Time (which in clear weather would be spent outside), Work Time, Clean-up Time, after which they have their milk, and Rest Time, after which they go home. The teacher has programmed activities for each of these Times.

Occasionally the class is allowed limited discretion to choose between proffered activities, such as stories or records, but original ideas for activities are never solicited from them. Opportunity for free individual action is open only once in the day, during the part of Work Time left after the general class assignment has been completed (on the day reported the class assignment was drawing animal pictures for the absent Mark). Spontaneous interests or observations from the children are never developed by the teacher. It seems that her schedule just does not allow room for developing such unplanned events. During Sharing Time, for example, the child who brought a bird's nest told Edith, in reply to her question of what kind of bird made it, "My friend says it's a rain bird." Edith does not think to ask about this bird, probably because the answer is "childish," that is, not given in accepted adult categories of birds. The children then express great interest in an object in the nest, but the teacher ignores this interest, probably because the object is uninteresting to her. The soldiers from "Babes in Toyland" strike a responsive note in the children, but this is not used for a discussion of any kind. The soldiers are treated in the same way as objects which bring little interest from the children. Finally, at the end of Sharing Time the child-world of perception literally erupts in the class with the recollection of "the spooky house" at the zoo. Apparently this made more of an impression on the children than did any of the animals, but Edith is unable to make any sense of it for herself. The tightly imposed order of the class begins to break down as the children discover a universe of discourse of their own and begin talking excitedly with one another. The teacher is effectively excluded from this child's world of perception and for a moment she fails to dominate the classroom situation. She reasserts control, however, by taking the children to the next activity she has planned for the day. It seems never to have occurred to Edith that there might be a meaningful learning experience for the children in re-creating the "spooky house" in the classroom. It seems fair to say that this would have offered an exercise in spontaneous self-expression and an opportunity for real creativity on the part of the children. Instead, they are taken through a canned animal imitation procedure, an activity which they apparently enjoy, but which is also imposed upon them rather than created by them.

While children's perceptions of the world and opportunities for genuine spontaneity and creativity are being systematically eliminated from the kindergarten, unquestioned obedience to authority and rote learning of meaningless material are being encouraged. When the children are called to line up in the center of the room they ask "Why?" and "What for?" as they are in the very process of complying. They have learned to go smoothly through a programmed day, regardless of whether parts of the program make any sense to them or not. Here the student role involves what might be called "doing what you're told and never mind why." Activities which might "make sense" to the children are effectively ruled out, and they are forced or induced to participate in activities which may be "senseless," such as calisthenics.

At the same time the children are being taught by rote meaningless sounds in the ritual oaths and songs, such as the Lord's Prayer, the Pledge to the Flag, and "America." As they go through the grades children learn more and more of the sounds of these ritual oaths, but the fact that they have often learned meaningless sounds rather than meaningful statements is shown when they are asked to write these out in the sixth grade; they write them as groups of sounds rather than as a series of words, according to the sixth grade teachers at Wright School. Probably much learning in the elementary grades is of this character, that is, having no intrinsic meaning to the children, but rather being tasks inexplicably required of them by authoritative adults. Listening to sixth grade children read social studies reports, for example, in which they have copied material from encyclopedias about a particular country, an observer often gets the feeling that he is watching an activity which has no intrinsic meaning for the child. The child who reads, "Switzerland grows wheat and cows and grass and makes a lot of cheese" knows the dictionary meaning of each of these words but may very well have no conception at all of this "thing" called Switzerland. He is simply carrying out a task assigned by the teacher *because* it is assigned, and this may be its only "meaning" for him.

Another type of learning which takes place in kindergarten is seen in children who take advantage of the "holes" in the adult social structure to create activities of their own, during Work Time or out-of-doors during Play Time. Here the children are learning to carve out a small world of their own within the world created by adults. They very quickly learn that if they keep within permissible limits of noise and action they can play much as they please. Small groups of children formed during the year in Edith's kindergarten who played together at these times, developing semi-independent little groups in which they created their own worlds in the interstices of the adult-imposed physical and social world. These groups remind the sociological observer very much of the so-called "informal groups" which adults develop in factories and offices of large bureaucracies.[5] Here, too, within authoritatively imposed social organizations people find "holes" to create little subworlds which support informal, friendly, unofficial behavior. Forming and participating in such groups seems to be as much part of the student role as it is of the role of bureaucrat.

The kindergarten has been conceived of here as the year in which children are prepared for their schooling by learning the role of student. In the classrooms of the rest of the school grades, the children will be asked to submit to systems and routines imposed by the teachers and the curriculum. The days will be much like those of kindergarten, except that academic subjects will be substituted for the activities of the kindergarten. Once out of the school system, young adults will more than likely find themselves working in large-scale bureaucratic organizations, perhaps on the assembly line in the factory, perhaps in the paper routines of the white collar occupations, where they will be required to submit to rigid routines imposed by "the company" which may make little sense to them. Those who can operate well in this situation will be successful bureaucratic functionaries. Kindergarten, therefore, can be seen as preparing children not only for participation in the bureaucratic organization of large modern school systems, but also for the large-scale occupational bureaucracies of modern society.

Notes

1. Emile Durkheim, *Sociology and Education* (New York: The Free Press, 1956), pp. 71–72.

2. *Ibid.*, p. 123.

3. Wilbur Brookover, *The Sociology of Education* (New York: American Book Company, 1957), p. 4.

4. *Ibid.*, p. 6.

5. See, for example, Peter M. Blau, *Bureaucracy in Modern Society* (New York: Random House, 1956), Chapter 3.

35 Upward Mobility Through Sport

D. STANLEY EITZEN

The evidence is striking and seemingly undeniable. Turn on the radio or television, and you hear the crowds roar as the athletes run, kick, bounce, and throw balls. You see these athletes demonstrate their remarkable abilities as they try to outmaneuver one another on the playing field. The percentage of African American, and to a lesser extent Latino, players is also striking to anyone who watches professional sports. How can there even be a question that sports are a major way for children (especially boys) of the poor to climb the social class ladder? The poor know this is the way out of poverty, too, and they strive and succeed.

Such bountiful evidence of social mobility through sports is deceptive, however. As Eitzen shows in this article, the mirror throws off an inaccurate reflection. Despite their arduous efforts and remarkable talents, not many make it. The irony is that so many set their hearts and efforts on this highly limited avenue, while the broader avenues that practically guarantee social mobility are overlooked and, often, despised.

TYPICALLY, AMERICANS BELIEVE that sport is a path to upward social mobility. This belief is based on the obvious examples we see as poor boys and men (rarely girls and women) from rural and urban areas, whether white or black, sometimes skyrocket to fame and fortune through success in sports. Sometimes the financial reward has been astounding, such as the high pay that some African American athletes received in recent years. But while the possibility of staggering wealth and status through sport is possible, the reality is that dramatic upward mobility through sport is highly improbable. A number of myths, however, combine to lead us to believe that sport is a social mobility escalator.

Myth: Sport Provides a Free Education

Good high school athletes get college scholarships. These athletic scholarships are especially helpful to poor youth who otherwise would not be able to attend college because of the high costs. The problem with this assumption is that while true for some, very few high school athletes actually receive full scholarships. Football provides the easiest route to a college scholarship because Division I-A colleges have 85 football scholarships, but even this avenue is exceedingly narrow. In Colorado there were 3,481 male high school seniors who played football during the 1994 season. Of these, 31 received full scholarships at Division I-A schools (0.0089 percent).

Second, of all the male varsity athletes at all college levels only about 15 percent to 20 percent have full scholarships. Another 15 percent to 25 percent have partial scholarships, leaving 55 percent to 70 percent of all intercollegiate athletes without any sport related financial assistance. Third, as low as the chances are for men, women athletes have even less chance to receive an athletic scholarship. While women comprise about 52 percent of all college students, they make up only 35 percent of intercollegiate athletes with a similar disproportionate distribution of scholarships. Another reality is that if you are a male athlete in a so-called minor sport (swimming, tennis, golf, gymnastics, cross-country, wrestling), the chances of a full scholarship are virtually nil. The best hope is a partial scholarship, if that, since these sports are underfunded and in danger of elimination at many schools.

Myth: Sport Leads to a College Degree

College graduates exceed high school graduates by hundreds of thousands of dollars in lifetime earnings. Since most high school and college athletes will never play at the professional level, the attainment of a college degree is a crucial determinant of upward mobility through sport. The problem is that relatively few male athletes in the big time revenue producing sports, compared to their non-athletic peers, actually receive college degrees. This is especially the case for African American men who are over represented in the revenue producing sports. In 1996, for example, looking at the athletes who entered Division I schools in 1990, only 45 percent of African American football players and 39 percent of African American basketball players had graduated (compared to 56 percent of the general student body).

There are a number of barriers to graduation for male athletes. The demands on their time and energy are enormous even in the off-season. Many athletes, because of these pressures, take easy courses to maintain eligibility but do not lead to graduation. The result is either to delay graduation or to make graduation an unrealistic goal.

Another barrier is that they are recruited for athletic prowess rather than academic ability. Recent data show that football players in big time programs are, on average, more than 200 points behind their non-athletic classmates on SAT test scores. Poorly prepared students are the most likely to take easy courses, cheat on exams, hire surrogate test takers, and otherwise do the minimum.

A third barrier to graduation for male college athletes is themselves, as they may not take advantage of their scholarships to obtain a quality education. This is especially the case for those who perceive their college experience only as preparation for their professional careers in sport. Study for them is necessary only to maintain their eligibility. The goal of a professional career is unrealistic for all but the superstars. The superstars who do make it at the professional level, more likely than not, will have not graduated from college; nor will they go back to finish their degrees when their professional careers are over. This is also because even a successful professional athletic career is limited to a few years, and not many professional athletes are able to translate their success in the pros to success in their post-athletic careers.

Myth: A Sports Career Is Probable

A recent survey by the Center for the Study of Sport in Society found that two-thirds of African American males between the ages of 13 and 18 believe that they can earn a living playing professional sports (more than double the proportion of young white males who hold such beliefs). Moreover, African American parents were four times more likely than white parents to believe that their sons are destined for careers as professional athletes.

A career in professional sports is nearly impossible to attain because of the fierce competition for so few openings. In an average year there are approximately 1,900,000 American boys playing high school football, basketball, and baseball. Another 68,000 men are playing those sports in college, and 2,490 are participating at the major professional level. In short, one in 27 high school players in these sports will play at the college level, and only one in 736 high school players will play at the major professional level (0.14 percent). In baseball, each year about 120,000 players are eligible for the draft (high school seniors, college seniors, collegians over 21, junior college players, and foreign players). Only about 1,200 (1 percent) are actually drafted, and most of them will never make it to the major leagues. Indeed, only one in ten of those players who sign a professional baseball contract ever play in the major leagues for at least one day.

The same rigorous condensation process occurs in football. About 15,000 players are eligible for the NFL draft each year. Three hundred thirty-six are drafted and about 160 actually make the final roster. Similarly, in basketball and hockey, only about 40 new players are added to the rosters in the NBA and 60 rookies make the NHL each year. In tennis only about 100 men and 100 women make enough money to cover expenses.

Myth: Sport Is a Way Out of Poverty

Sport appears to be a major way for African Americans to escape the ghetto. African Americans dominate the major professional sports numerically. While only 12 percent of the population, African Americans comprise about 80 percent of the players in professional basketball, about 67 percent of professional football players, and 18 percent of professional baseball players (Latinos also comprise about 17 percent of professional baseball players). Moreover, African Americans dominate the list of the highest moneymakers in sport (salaries, commercial sponsorships). These facts, while true, are illusory.

While African Americans dominate professional basketball, football, and to a lesser extent baseball, they are rarely found in certain sports such as hockey, automobile racing, tennis, golf, bowling, and skiing. Moreover, African Americans are severely under-represented in positions of authority in sport—as head coaches, referees, athletic directors, scouts, general managers, and owners.

While the odds of African American males making it as professional athletes are more favorable than is the case for whites (about 1 in 3,500 African American male high school athletes, compared to 1 in 10,000 white male high school athletes) these odds remain slim. Of the 40,000 or so African American boys who play high school basketball, only 35 will make the NBA and only 7 will be starters. Referring to the low odds for young African Americans, Harry Edwards, an African American sociologist specializing in the sociology of sport, said with a bit of hyperbole: "Statistically, you have a better chance of getting hit by a meteorite in the next ten years than getting work as an athlete."

Despite these discouraging facts, the myth is alive for poor youth. As noted earlier, two-thirds of African American boys believe they can be professional athletes. Their parents, too, accept this belief (African American parents are four times more likely than white parents to believe that their children will be professional athletes). The film *Hoop Dreams* and Darcey Frey's book *The Last Shot: City Street, Basketball Dreams* document the emphasis that young African American men place on sports as a way up and their ultimate disappointments from sport. For many of them, sport represents their only hope of escape from a life of crime, poverty, and despair. They latch on to the dream of athletic success partly because of the few opportunities for middle-class success. They spend many hours per day developing their speed, strength, jumping height, or "moves" to the virtual exclusion of those abilities that have a greater likelihood of paying off in upward mobility such as reading comprehension, mathematical reasoning, communication skills, and computer literacy.

Sociologist Jay Coakley puts it this way: "My best guess is that less than 3,500 African Americans . . . are making their livings as professional athletes. At the same time there are about 30,015 black physicians and about 30,800 black lawyers currently employed in the U.S. Therefore, there are 20 times more blacks working in these two professions than playing top level professional sports. And physicians and lawyers usually have lifetime earnings far in excess of the earnings of professional athletes, whose playing careers, on average, last less than five years."

Harry Edwards posits that by spending their energies and talents on athletic skills, young African Americans are not pursuing occupations that would help them meet their political and material needs. Salim Muwakkil, an African American political analyst, argues that "If African Americans are to exploit the socio-economic options opened by varied civil rights struggles more fully, blacks must reduce the disproportionate allure of sports in their communities. Black leadership must contextualize athletic success by promoting other avenues to social status, intensifying the struggle for access to those avenues and better educating youth about those pot-holes on the road to the stadium."

John Hoberman in his book *Darwin's Athletes* also challenges the assumption that sport has progressive consequences. The success of African Americans in the highly visible sports gives white Americans a false sense of black progress and interracial harmony. But the social progress of African Americans in general has little relationship to the apparent integration that they have achieved on the playing fields.

Hoberman also contends that the numerical superiority of African Americans in sport, coupled with their disproportionate under-representation in other professions reinforces the racist ideology that African Americans, while physically superior to whites are inferior to them intellectually.

I do not mean to say that African Americans should not seek a career in professional sport. What is harmful is that the odds of success are so slim, making the extraordinary efforts over many years futile and misguided for the vast majority.

The allure of sport, however, remains strong and this has at least two negative consequences. First, ghetto youngsters who devote their lives to the pursuit of athletic stardom are, except for the fortunate few, doomed to failure in sport and in the real world where sports skills are essentially irrelevant

to occupational placement and advancement. The second negative consequence is more subtle but very important. Sport contributes to the ideology
that legitimizes social inequalities and promotes the myth that all it takes is
extraordinary effort to succeed. Sport sociologist George H. Sage makes this
point forcefully: "Because sport is by nature meritocratic—that is, superior
performance brings status and rewards—it provides convincing symbolic support for hegemonic [the dominant] ideology—that ambitious, dedicated, hard
working individuals, regardless of social origin, can achieve success and as-
cend in the social hierarchy, obtaining high status and material rewards, while
those who don't move upward simply didn't work hard enough. Because the
rags-to-riches athletes are so visible, the social mobility theme is maintained.
This reflects the opportunity structure of society in general—the success of
a few reproduces the belief in social mobility among the many."

36 The Romance Between the Egg and the Sperm

EMILY MARTIN

Science is objective. It is a search for truth. To be called a fact, something must be verified by experiment or controlled observation. Values, ideas, and opinions are irrelevant in this objective quest for Truth. This is the idealized view of science that we all learn in school. But is it really so?

Scientists do try to produce verifiable truth. But values and assumptions can go unrecognized, creeping in to distort perception and twist "facts." Those distortions, invisible to scientists, are then taken as truth. Martin demonstrates this process in her entertaining analysis of the romance between the egg and the sperm.

The theory of the human body is always a part of a world-picture
. . . . The theory of the human body is always a part of a *fantasy*.

—James Hillman[1]

As an anthropologist, I am intrigued by the possibility that culture shapes how biological scientists describe what they discover about the natural world. If this were so, we would be learning about more than the natural world in high school biology class; we would be learning about cultural beliefs and practices as if they were part of nature. In the course of my research I realized that the picture of egg and sperm drawn in popular as well as scientific accounts of reproductive biology relies on stereotypes central to our cultural definitions of male and female. The stereotypes imply not only that female biological processes are less worthy than their male counterparts but also that women are less worthy than men. Part of my goal in writing this article is to shine a bright light on the gender stereotypes hidden within the scientific language of biology. Exposed in such a light, I hope they will lose much of their power to harm us.

Egg and Sperm: A Scientific Fairy Tale

At a fundamental level, all major scientific textbooks depict male and female reproductive organs as systems for the production of valuable substances, such

411

as eggs and sperm.[2] In the case of women, the monthly cycle is described as being designed to produce eggs and prepare a suitable place for them to be fertilized and grown—all to the end of making babies. But the enthusiasm ends there. By extolling the female cycle as a productive enterprise, menstruation must necessarily be viewed as failure. Medical texts describe menstruation as the "debris" of the uterine lining, the result of necrosis, or death of tissue. The descriptions imply that a system has gone awry, making products of no use, not to specification, unsalable, wasted, scrap. An illustration in a widely used medical text shows menstruation as a chaotic disintegration of form, complementing the many texts that describe it as "ceasing," "dying," "losing," "denuding," "expelling."[3]

Male reproductive physiology is evaluated quite differently. One of the texts that sees menstruation as failed production employs a sort of breathless prose when it describes the maturation of sperm: "The mechanisms which guide the remarkable cellular transformation from spermatid to mature sperm remain uncertain. . . . Perhaps the most amazing characteristic of spermatogenesis is its sheer magnitude: the normal human male may manufacture several hundred million sperm per day."[4] In the classic *Medical Physiology*, edited by Vernon Mountcastle, the male/female, productive/destructive comparison is more explicit: "Whereas the female *sheds* only a single gamete each month, the seminiferous tubules *produce* hundreds of millions of sperm each day" (emphasis mine).[5] The female author of another text marvels at the length of the microscopic seminiferous tubules, which, if uncoiled and placed end to end "would span almost one-third of a mile!" She writes, "In an adult male these structures produce millions of sperm cells each day." Later she asks, "How is this feat accomplished?"[6] None of these texts expresses such intense enthusiasm for any female processes. It is surely no accident that the "remarkable" process of making sperm involves precisely what, in the medical view, menstruation does not: production of something deemed valuable.[7]

One could argue that menstruation and spermatogenesis are not analogous processes and, therefore, should not be expected to elicit the same kind of response. The proper female analogy to spermatogenesis, biologically, is ovulation. Yet ovulation does not merit enthusiasm in these texts either. Textbook descriptions stress that all of the ovarian follicles containing ova are already present at birth. Far from being *produced*, as sperm are, they merely sit on the shelf, slowly degenerating and aging like overstocked inventory: "At birth, normal human ovaries contain an estimated one million follicles [each], and no new ones appear after birth. Thus, in marked contrast to the male, the newborn female already has all the germ cells she will ever have. Only a few, perhaps 400, are destined to reach full maturity during her active productive life. All the others degenerate at some point in their development so that few, if any, remain by the time she reaches menopause at approximately 50 years of age."[8] Note the "marked contrast" that this description sets up between male and female: the male, who continuously produces fresh germ cells, and the female, who has stockpiled germ cells by birth and is faced with their degeneration.

Nor are the female organs spared such vivid descriptions. One scientist writes in a newspaper article that a woman's ovaries become old and worn out from ripening eggs every month, even though the woman herself is still relatively young: "When you look through a laparoscope . . . at an ovary that has been through hundreds of cycles, even in a superbly healthy American female, you see a scarred, battered organ."[9]

To avoid the negative connotations that some people associate with the female reproductive system, scientists could begin to describe male and female processes as homologous. They might credit females with "producing" mature ova one at a time, as they're needed each month, and describe males as having to face problems of degenerating germ cells. This degeneration would occur throughout life among spermatogonia, the undifferentiated germ cells in the testes that are the long-lived, dormant precursors of sperm.

But the texts have an almost dogged insistence on casting female processes in a negative light. The texts celebrate sperm production because it is continuous from puberty to senescence, while they portray egg production as inferior because it is finished at birth. This makes the female seem unproductive, but some texts will also insist that it is she who is wasteful.[10] In a section heading for *Molecular Biology of the Cell,* a best-selling text, we are told that "Oogenesis is wasteful." The text goes on to emphasize that of the seven million oogonia, or egg germ cells, in the female embryo, most degenerate in the ovary. Of those that do go on to become oocytes, or eggs, many also degenerate, so that at birth only two million eggs remain in the ovaries. Degeneration continues throughout a woman's life: by puberty 300,000 eggs remain, and only a few are present by menopause. "During the 40 or so years of a woman's reproductive life, only 400 to 500 eggs will have been released," the authors write. "All the rest will have degenerated. It is still a mystery why so many eggs are formed only to die in the ovaries."[11]

The real mystery is why the male's vast production of sperm is not seen as wasteful.[12] Assuming that a man "produces" 10 million (10^8) sperm per day (a conservative estimate) during an average reproductive life of sixty years, he would produce well over two trillion sperm in his lifetime. Assuming that a woman "ripens" one egg per lunar month, or thirteen per year, over the course of her forty-year reproductive life, she would total five hundred eggs in her lifetime. But the word "waste" implies an excess, too much produced. Assuming two or three offspring, for every baby a woman produces, she wastes only around two hundred eggs. For every baby a man produces, he wastes more than one trillion (10^{12}) sperm.

How is it that positive images are denied to the bodies of woman? A look at language—in this case, scientific language—provides the first clue. Take the egg and the sperm.[13] It is remarkable how "femininely" the egg behaves and how "masculinely" the sperm.[14] The egg is seen as large and passive.[15] It does not *move* or *journey*, but passively "is transported," "is swept,"[16] or even "drifts"[17] along the fallopian tube. In utter contrast, sperm are small, "streamlined,"[18] and invariably active. They "deliver" their genes to the egg, "activate the developmental program of the egg,"[19] and have a "velocity" that is often remarked upon.[20] Their tails are "strong" and efficiently powered.[21] Together with the forces of ejaculation, they can "propel the semen into the deepest recesses of the vagina."[22] For this they need "energy," "fuel,"[23] so that with a "whiplash-like motion and strong lurches"[24] they can "burrow through the egg coat"[25] and "penetrate" it.[26]

At its extreme, the age-old relationship of the egg and the sperm takes on a royal or religious patina. The egg coat, its protective barrier, is sometimes called its "vestments," a term usually reserved for sacred, religious dress. The egg is said to have a "corona,"[27] a crown, and to be accompanied by "attendant cells."[28] It is holy, set apart and above, the queen to the sperm's king. The egg is also passive, which means it must depend on sperm for rescue. Gerald Schatten and Helen Schatten liken the egg's role to that of Sleeping Beauty: "a dormant bride awaiting her mate's magic kiss, which instills the spirit that brings her to life."[29] Sperm, by contrast, have a "mission:"[30] which is to "move through the female genital tract in quest of the ovum."[31] One popular account has it that the sperm carry out a "perilous journey" into the "warm darkness," where some fall away "exhausted." "Survivors" "assault" the egg, the successful candidates "surrounding the prize."[32] Part of the urgency of this journey, in more scientific terms, is that "once released from the supportive environment of the ovary, an egg will die within hours unless rescued by a sperm."[33] The wording stresses the fragility and dependency of the egg, even though the same text acknowledges elsewhere that sperm also live for only a few hours.[34]

Bringing out another aspect of the sperm's autonomy, an article in the journal *Cell* has the sperm making an "existential decision" to penetrate the egg: "Sperm are cells with a limited behavioral repertoire, one that is directed toward fertilizing eggs. To execute the decision to abandon the haploid state, sperm swim to an egg and there acquire the ability to effect membrane fusion."[35] Is this a corporate manager's version of the sperm's activities—"executing decisions" while fraught with dismay over difficult options that bring with them very high risk?

There is another way that sperm, despite their small size, can be made to loom in importance over the egg. In a collection of scientific papers, an electron micrograph of an enormous egg and tiny sperm is titled "A Portrait of the Sperm."[36] This is a little like showing a photo of a dog and calling it a picture of the fleas. Granted, microscopic sperm are harder to photograph than eggs, which are just large enough to see with the naked eye. But surely the use of the term "portrait," a word associated with the powerful and wealthy, is significant. Eggs have only micrographs or pictures, not portraits.

The common picture—egg as damsel in distress, shielded only by her sacred garments; sperm as heroic warrior to the rescue—cannot be proved to be dictated by the biology of these events. While the "facts" of biology may not *always* be constructed in cultural terms, I would argue that in this case they are. The degree of metaphorical content in these descriptions, the extent to which differences between egg and sperm are emphasized, and the parallels between cultural stereotypes of male and female behavior and the character of egg and sperm all point to this conclusion.

New Research, Old Imagery

As new understandings of egg and sperm emerge, textbook gender imagery is being revised. But the new research, far from escaping the stereotypical representations of egg and sperm, simply replicates elements of textbook gender imagery in a different form. We need to understand the way in which the cultural content in scientific descriptions changes as biological discoveries unfold, and whether that cultural content is solidly entrenched or easily changed.

In all of the texts quoted above, sperm are described as penetrating the egg, and specific substances on a sperm's head are described as binding to the egg. Recently, this description of events was rewritten in a biophysics lab at Johns Hopkins University—transforming the egg from the passive to the active party.[37]

Prior to this research, it was thought that the zona, the inner vestments of the egg, formed an impenetrable barrier. Sperm overcame the barrier by mechanically burrowing through, thrashing their tails and slowly working their way along. Later research showed that the sperm released digestive enzymes that chemically broke down the zona; thus, scientists presumed that the sperm used mechanical *and* chemical means to get through to the egg.

In this recent investigation, the researchers began to ask questions about the mechanical force of the sperm's tail. (The lab's goal was to develop a contraceptive that worked topically on sperm.) They discovered, to their great surprise, that the forward thrust of sperm is extremely weak, which contradicts the assumption that sperm are forceful penetrators.[38] Rather than thrusting forward, the sperm's head was now seen to move mostly back and forth. The sideways motion of the sperm's tail makes the head move sideways with a force that is ten times stronger than its forward movement. So even if the overall force of the sperm were strong enough to mechanically break the zona, most of its force would be directed sideways rather than forward. In fact, its strongest tendency, by tenfold, is to escape by attempting to pry itself off the egg. Sperm, then, must be exceptionally efficient at *escaping* from any cell surface they contact. And the surface of the egg must be designed to trap the sperm and prevent their escape. Otherwise, few if any sperm would reach the egg.

The researchers at Johns Hopkins concluded that the sperm and egg stick together because of adhesive molecules on the surfaces of each. The egg traps the sperm and adheres to it so tightly that the sperm's head is forced to lie flat against the surface of the zona, a little bit, they told me, "like Br'er Rabbit getting more and more stuck to tar baby the more he wriggles." The trapped sperm continues to wiggle ineffectually side to side. The mechanical force of its tail is so weak that a sperm cannot break even one chemical bond. This is where the digestive enzymes released by the sperm come in. If they start to soften the zona just at the tip of the sperm and the sides remain stuck, then the weak, flailing sperm can get oriented in the right direction and make it through the zona—provided that its bonds to the zona dissolve as it moves in.

Although this new version of the saga of the egg and the sperm broke through cultural expectations, the researchers who made the discovery continued to write papers and abstracts as if the sperm were the active party who attacks, binds, penetrates, and enters the egg. The only difference was that sperm were now seen as performing these actions weakly.[39] Not until August 1987, more than three years after the findings described above, did these researchers reconceptualize the process to give the egg a more active role. They began to describe the zona as an aggressive sperm catcher, covered with adhesive molecules that can capture a sperm with a single bond and clasp it to the zona's surface.[40] In the words of their published account: "The innermost vestment, the *zona pellucida,* is a glycoprotein shell, which captures and tethers the sperm before they penetrate it. . . . The sperm is captured at the initial contact between the sperm tip and the *zona.* . . . Since the thrust [of the sperm] is much smaller than the force needed to break a single affinity bond, the first bond made upon the tip-first meeting of the sperm and *zona* can result in the capture of the sperm."[41]

Social Implications: Thinking Beyond

These revisionist accounts of egg and sperm cannot seem to escape the hierarchical imagery of older accounts. Even though each new account gives the egg a larger and more active role, taken together they bring into play another cultural stereotype: woman as a dangerous and aggressive threat. In the Johns Hopkins lab's revised model, the egg ends up as the female aggressor who "captures and tethers" the sperm with her sticky zona, rather like a spider lying in wait in her web.[42] The Schatten lab has the egg's nucleus "interrupt" the sperm's dive with a "sudden and swift" rush by which she "clasps the sperm and guides its nucleus to the center"[43] Wassarman's description of the surface of the egg "covered with thousands of plasma membrane-bound projections, called microvilli" that reach out and clasp the sperm adds to the spiderlike imagery.[44]

These images grant the egg an active role but at the cost of appearing disturbingly aggressive. Images of woman as dangerous and aggressive, the femme fatale who victimizes men, are widespread in Western literature and culture.[45] More specific is the connection of spider imagery with the idea of an engulfing, devouring mother.[46] New data did not lead scientists to eliminate gender stereotypes in their descriptions of egg and sperm. Instead, scientists simply began to describe egg and sperm in different, but no less damaging, terms.

One clear feminist challenge is to wake up sleeping metaphors in science, particularly those involved in descriptions of the egg and the sperm. Although the literary convention is to call such metaphors "dead," they are not so much dead as sleeping, hidden within the scientific content of texts—and all the more powerful for it.[47] Waking up such metaphors, by becoming aware of when we are projecting cultural imagery onto what we study, will improve our ability to investigate and understand nature. Waking up such metaphors, by becoming aware of their implications, will rob them of their power to naturalize our social conventions about gender.

References and Notes

1. James Hillman, *The Myth of Analysis* (Evanston, IL: Northwestern University Press, 1972), 220.

2. The textbooks I consulted are the main ones used in classes for undergraduate premedical students or medical students (or those held on reserve in the library for these classes) during the past few years at Johns Hopkins University. These texts are widely used at other universities in the country as well.

3. Arthur C. Guyton, *Physiology of the Human Body,* 6th ed. (Philadelphia: Saunders College Publishing, 1984), 624.

4. Arthur J. Vander, James H. Sherman, and Dorothy S. Luciano, *Human Physiology: The Mechanisms of Body Function,* 3d ed. (New York: McGraw Hill, 1980), 483–84.

5. Vernon B. Mountcastle, *Medical Physiology,* 14th ed. (London: Mosby, 1980), 2:1624.

6. Eldra Pearl Solomon, *Human Anatomy and Physiology* (New York: CBS College Publishing, 1983), 678.

7. For elaboration, see Emily Martin, *The Woman in the Body: A Cultural Analysis of Reproduction* (Boston: Beacon, 1987), 27–53.

8. Vander, Sherman, and Luciano, 568.

9. Melvin Konner, "Childbearing and Age," *New York Times Magazine* (December 27, 1987), 22–23, esp. 22.

10. I have found but one exception to the opinion that the female is wasteful: "Smallpox being the nasty disease it is, one might expect nature to have designed antibody molecules with combining sites that specifically recognize the epitopes on smallpox virus. Nature differs from technology, however: it thinks nothing of wastefulness. (For example, rather than improving the chance that a spermatozoon will meet an egg cell, nature finds it easier to produce millions of spermatozoa.)" (Niels Kaj Jerne, "The Immune System" *Scientific American* 229, no. 1 [July 1973]: 53). Thanks to a *Signs* reviewer for bringing this reference to my attention.

11. Bruce Alberts et al., *Molecular Biology of the Cell* (New York: Garland, 1983), 795.

12. In her essay "Have Only Men Evolved?" (in *Discovering Reality: Feminist Perspectives on Epistemology, Metaphysics, Methodology, and Philosophy of Science,* ed. Sandra Harding and Merrill B. Hintikka [Dordrecht: Reidel, 1983], 45–69, esp. 60–61), Ruth Hubbard points out that sociobiologists have said the female invests more energy than the male in the production of her large gametes, claiming that this explains why the female provides parental care. Hubbard questions whether it "really takes more 'energy' to generate the one or relatively few eggs than the large excess of sperms required to achieve fertilization." For further critique of how the greater size of eggs is interpreted in sociobiology, see Donna Haraway, "Investment Strategies for the Evolving Portfolio of Primate Females," in *Body/Politics,* eds. Mary Jacobus, Evelyn Fox Keller, and Sally Shuttleworth (New York: Routledge, 1990), 155–56.

13. The sources I used for this article provide compelling information on interactions among sperm Lack of space prevents me from taking up this theme here, but the elements include competition, hierarchy, and sacrifice. For a newspaper report, see Malcolm W. Browne, "Some Thoughts on Self Sacrifice," *New York Times* (July 5, 1988), C6. For a literary rendition, see John Barth, "Night-Sea Journey," in his *Lost in the Funhouse* (Garden City, NY: Doubleday, 1968), 3–13.

14. See Carol Delaney, "The Meaning of Paternity and the Virgin Birth Debate," *Man* 21, no. 3 (September 1986): 494–513. She discusses the difference between this scientific view that women contribute genetic material to the fetus and

the claim of long-standing Western folk theories that the origin and identity of the fetus comes from the male, as in the metaphor of planting a seed in soil.

15. For a suggested direct link between human behavior and purportedly passive eggs and active sperm, see Erik H. Erikson, "Inner and Outer Space: Reflections on Womanhood," *Daedalus* 93, no. 2 (Spring 1964): 582–606, esp. 591.

16. Guyton (n. 3 above), 619; and Mountcastle (n. 5 above), 1609.

17. Jonathan Miller and David Pelham, *The Facts of Life* (New York: Viking Penguin, 1984), 5.

18. Alberts et al., 796.

19. Ibid., 796.

20. See, e.g., William F. Ganong, *Review of Medical Physiology,* 7th ed. (Los Altos, CA.: Lange Medical Publications, 1975), 322.

21. Alberts et al. (n. 11 above), 796.

22. Guyton, 615.

23. Solomon (n. 6 above), 683.

24. Vander, Sherman, and Luciano (n. 4 above), 4th ed. (1985), 580.

25. Alberts et al., 796.

26. All biology texts quoted above use the word "penetrate."

27. Solomon, 700.

28. A. Beldecos et al., "The Importance of Feminist Critique for Contemporary Cell Biology," *Hypatia* 3, no. 1 (Spring 1988): 61–76.

29. Gerald Schatten and Helen Schatten, "The Energetic Egg," *Medical World News* 23 (January 23, 1984): 51–53, esp. 51.

30. Alberts et al., 796.

31. Guyton (n. 3 above), 613.

32. Miller and Pelham (n. 17 above), 7.

33. Alberts et al. (n. 11 above), 804.

34. Ibid., 801.

35. Bennett M. Shapiro, "The Existential Decision of a Sperm," *Cell* 49, no. 3 (May 1987): 293–94, esp. 293.

36. Lennart Nilsson, "A Portrait of the Sperm," in *The Functional Anatomy of the Spermatozoan,* ed. Bjorn A. Afzelius (New York: Pergamon, 1975), 79–82.

37. Jay M. Baltz carried out the research I describe when he was a graduate student in the Thomas C. Jenkins Department of Biophysics at Johns Hopkins University.

38. Far less is known about the physiology of sperm than comparable female substances, which some feminists claim is no accident. Greater scientific scrutiny of female reproduction has long enabled the burden of birth control to be placed on women. In this case, the researchers discovery did not depend on development of any new technology. The experiments made use of glass pipettes, a manometer, and a simple microscope, all of which have been available for more than one hundred years.

39. Jay Baltz and Richard A. Cone, "What Force Is Needed to Tether a Sperm?" (abstract for Society for the Study of Reproduction, 1985), and "Flagellar Torque on

the Head Determines the Force Needed to Tether a Sperm" (abstract for Biophysical Society, 1986).

40. Jay M. Baltz, David F. Katz, and Richard A. Cone, "The Mechanics of the Sperm-Egg Interaction at the Zona Pellucida," *Biophysical Journal* 54, no. 4 (October 1988): 643–54. Lab members were somewhat familiar with work on metaphors in the biology of female reproduction. Richard Cone, who runs the lab, is my husband, and he talked with them about my earlier research on the subject from time to time. Even though my current research focuses on biological imagery and I heard about the lab's work from my husband every day, I myself did not recognize the role of imagery in the sperm research until many weeks after the period of research and writing I describe. Therefore, I assume that any awareness the lab members may have had about how underlying metaphor might be guiding this particular research was fairly inchoate.

41. Ibid., 643, 650.

42. Baltz, Katz, and Cone (n. 42 above), 643, 650.

43. Schatten and Schatten, 53.

44. Wassarman, "The Biology and Chemistry of Fertilization," 557.

45. Mary Ellman, *Thinking about Women* (New York: Harcourt Brace Jovanovich, 1968), 140; Nina Auerbach, *Woman and the Demon* (Cambridge, MA: Harvard University Press, 1982), esp. 186.

46. Kenneth Alan Adams, "Arachnophobia: Love American Style," *Journal of Psychoanalytic Anthropology* 4, no. 2 (1981): 157–97.

47. Thanks to Elizabeth Fee and David Spain, who in February 1989 and April 1989, respectively, made points related to this.

37 Beauty and the Beast of Advertising

JEAN KILBOURNE

The most recent social institution to develop, and rapidly becoming one of the most powerful, is the mass media. The *mass media* consist of those forms of communication that reach mass audiences—radio, television, movies, newspapers, magazines, and books. The Internet is the most recent form of the mass media, with millions of people simultaneously reading the same news articles and ads transmitted via satellite across the world.

On a commonsense level, the primary functions of the media are to entertain and inform. Certainly, they do this. But have you noted the prevalence of advertising in the mass media (with the exception of most books)? There are those who claim that advertising has become *the* primary purpose of the mass media; the real reason for our entertaining and informative television programs, for example, is to round up an audience for the advertising. Perhaps so. The mass media are certainly a primary tool of business.

A second primary purpose of the media is social control. Seldom is this purpose so obvious as its heavy-handed use by Goebbels in Nazi Germany, Stalin in communist Russia, and Hussein in totalitarian Iraq. The social control function of *our* media, though more covert, is nonetheless similarly powerful. The mass media are used not only to keep us in line politically, but also to influence our ideas, attitudes, and behavior in all realms of life. As advertising continually bombards us, it plants ideas and massages our attitudes, giving them subtle shape and direction. That advertising is highly effective becomes apparent from Kilbourne's analysis of how it influences our ideas of beauty. (You may wish to compare this article with the findings Eder reported on middle-school girls in article 14 and Katz's observations in article 27.)

"YOU'RE A HALSTON WOMAN from the very beginning," the advertisement proclaims. The model stares provocatively at the viewer, her long blonde hair waving around her face, her bare chest partially covered by two curved bottles that give the illusion of breasts and a cleavage.

The average American is accustomed to blue-eyed blondes seductively touting a variety of products. In this case, however, the blonde is about five years old.

Advertising is an over $130 billion a year industry and affects all of us throughout our lives. We are each exposed to over 1500 ads a day, constituting perhaps the most powerful educational force in society. The average adult will spend one and one-half years of his/her life watching television commercials. But the ads sell a great deal more than products. They sell values, images, and concepts of success and worth, love and sexuality, popularity and normalcy. They tell us who we are and who we should be. Sometimes they sell addictions.

Advertising is the foundation and economic lifeblood of the mass media. The primary purpose of the mass media is to deliver an audience to advertisers.

Adolescents are particularly vulnerable, however, because they are new and inexperienced consumers and are the prime targets of many advertisements. They are in the process of learning their values and roles and developing their self-concepts. Most teenagers are sensitive to peer pressure and find it difficult to resist or even question the dominant cultural messages perpetuated and reinforced by the media. Mass communication has made possible a kind of nationally distributed peer pressure that erodes private and individual values and standards.

But what does society, and especially teenagers, learn from the advertising messages that proliferate in the mass media? On the most obvious level they learn the stereotypes. Advertising creates a mythical, WASP-oriented world in which no one is ever ugly, overweight, poor, struggling, or disabled either physically or mentally (unless you count the housewives who talk to little men in toilet bowls). And it is a world in which people talk only about products.

Housewives or Sex Objects

The aspect of advertising most in need of analysis and change is the portrayal of women. Scientific studies and the most casual viewing yield the same conclusion: Women are shown almost exclusively as housewives or sex objects.

The housewife, pathologically obsessed by cleanliness and lemon-fresh scents, debates cleaning products and worries about her husband's "ring around the collar."

The sex object is a mannequin, a shell. Conventional beauty is her only attribute. She has no lines or wrinkles (which would indicate she had the bad taste and poor judgment to grow older), no scars or blemishes—indeed, she has no pores. She is thin, generally tall and long-legged, and above all, she is young. All "beautiful" women in advertisements (including minority women), regardless of product or audience, conform to this norm. Women are constantly exhorted to emulate this ideal, to feel ashamed and guilty if they fail, and to feel that their desirability and lovability are contingent upon physical perfection.

Creating Artificiality

The image is artificial and can only be achieved artificially (even the "natural look" requires much preparation and expense). Beauty is something that comes from without: more than one million dollars is spent every hour on cosmetics. Desperate to conform to an ideal and impossible standard, many women go to great lengths to manipulate and change their faces and bodies. A woman is conditioned to view her face as a mask and her body as an object, as *things* separate from and more important than her real self, constantly in need of alteration, improvement, and disguise. She is made to feel dissatisfied with and ashamed of herself, whether she tries to achieve "the look" or not. Objectified constantly by others, she learns to objectify herself. (It is interesting to note that one in five college-age women has an eating disorder.)

"When *Glamour* magazine surveyed its readers in 1984, 75 percent felt too heavy and only 15 percent felt just right. Nearly half of those who were actually underweight reported feeling too fat and wanting to diet. Among a sample of college women, 40 percent felt overweight when only 12 percent actually were too heavy," according to Rita Freedman in her book *Beauty Bound*.

There is evidence that this preoccupation with weight begins at ever-earlier ages for women. According to a recent article in *New Age Journal*, "even grade-school girls are succumbing to stick-like standards of beauty enforced by a relentless parade of wasp-waisted fashion models, movie stars, and pop idols." A study by a University of California professor showed that nearly 80 percent of fourth-grade girls in the Bay Area are watching their weight.

A recent *Wall Street Journal* survey of students in four Chicago-area schools found that more than half the fourth-grade girls were dieting and three-quarters felt they were overweight. One student said, "We don't expect boys to be that handsome. We take them as they are." Another added, "But boys expect girls to be perfect and beautiful. And skinny."

Dr. Steven Levenkrom, author of *The Best Little Girl in the World*, the story of an anorexic, says his blood pressure soars every time he opens a magazine and finds an ad for women's fashions. "If I had my way," he said, "everyone one of them would have to carry a line saying, 'Caution: This model may be hazardous to your health.'"

Women are also dismembered in commercials, their bodies separated into parts in need of change or improvement. If a woman has "acceptable" breasts, then she must also be sure that her legs are worth watching, her hips slim, her feet sexy, and that her buttocks look nuder under her clothes ("like I'm not wearin' nothin' "). This image is difficult and costly to achieve and impossible to maintain—no one is flawless and everyone ages. Growing older is the great taboo. Women are encouraged to remain little girls ("because innocence is sexier than you think"), to be passive and dependent, never to mature. The contradictory message—"sensual, but not too far from innocence"—places women in a double bind: somehow we are supposed to be both sexy and virginal, experienced and naive, seductive and chaste. The disparagement of maturity is, of course, insulting and frustrating to adult women, and the implication that little girls are seductive is dangerous to real children.

Influencing Sexual Attitudes

Young people also learn a great deal about sexual attitudes from the media and from advertising in particular. Advertising's approach to sex is pornographic: it reduces people to objects and de-emphasizes human contact and individuality. This reduction of sexuality to a dirty joke and of people to objects is the real obscenity of the culture. Although the sexual sell, overt and subliminal, is at a fevered pitch in most commercials, there is at the same time a notable absence of sex as an important and profound human activity.

There have been some changes in the images of women. Indeed, a "new woman" has emerged in commercials in recent years. She is generally presented as superwoman, who manages to do all the work at home and on the job (with the help of a product, of course, not of her husband or children or friends); or as the liberated woman, who owes her independence and self-esteem to the products she uses. These new images do not represent any real progress but rather create a myth of progress, an illusion that reduces complex sociopolitical problems to mundane personal ones.

Advertising images do not cause these problems, but they contribute to them by creating a climate in which the marketing of women's bodies—the sexual sell and dismemberment, distorted body image ideal, and children as sex objects—is seen as acceptable.

This is the real tragedy, that many women internalize these stereotypes and learn their "limitations," thus establishing a self-fulfilling prophecy. If one accepts these mythical and degrading images, to some extent one actualizes them. By remaining unaware of the profound seriousness of the ubiquitous influence, the redundant message, and the subliminal impact of advertisements, we ignore one of the most powerful "educational" forces in the culture—one that greatly affects our self-images, our ability to relate to each other, and effectively destroys awareness and action that might help to change that climate.

38 India's Sacred Cow

MARVIN HARRIS

Although its form varies widely from one culture to another, religion is one of humanity's fundamental social institutions. A generation ago, some "experts" predicted that with the rise of science and the secularization of U.S. culture religion would fade quietly into the background. On the contrary, religion is as vital for Americans today as it was in the past. Church membership is even higher now than at any time in U.S. history. Tens of millions of Americans continue to seek solace in religion. They look to religion for answers to many of the perplexing questions that social life poses and that science cannot answer.

Like the other social institutions, religion is interconnected with the other parts of society. It sometimes is difficult to recognize these interconnections when we refer to our own religion, for we tend to focus on its smaller aspects, such as our own congregation, synagogue, or mosque. It often is easier to see this point, however, when we look at unfamiliar religions, those whose practices are far removed from our experiences. There, since we are not immersed in taken-for-granted assumptions, we may be prompted to ask basic questions. For example, why are cows allowed to wander India's city streets and country roads? Why don't deprived and hungry Indians eat them? Essential interconnections between religion and culture become evident as Harris analyzes such questions.

NEWS PHOTOGRAPHS that came out of India during the famine of the late 1960s showed starving people stretching out bony hands to beg for food while sacred cattle strolled behind undisturbed. The Hindu, it seems, would rather starve to death than eat his cow or even deprive it of food. The cattle appear to browse unhindered through urban markets eating an orange here, a mango there, competing with people for meager supplies of food.

By Western standards, spiritual values seem more important to Indians than life itself. Specialists in food habits around the world like Fred Simons at the University of California at Davis consider Hinduism an irrational ideology that compels people to overlook abundant, nutritious foods for scarcer, less healthful foods.

What seems to be an absurd devotion to the mother cow pervades Indian life. Indian wall calendars portray beautiful young women with bodies of fat white cows, often with milk jetting from their teats into sacred shrines.

Cow worship even carries over into politics. In 1966 a crowd of 120,000 people, led by holy men, demonstrated in front of the Indian House of Parliament in support of the All-Party Cow Protection Campaign Committee. In Nepal, the only contemporary Hindu kingdom, cow slaughter is severely punished. As one story goes, the car driven by an official of a United States agency struck and killed a cow. In order to avoid the international incident that would have occurred when the official was arrested for murder, the Nepalese magistrate concluded that the cow had committed suicide.

Many Indians agree with Western assessments of the Hindu reverence for their cattle, the zebu, or *Bos indicus,* a large-humped species prevalent in Asia and Africa. M.N. Srinivas, an Indian anthropologist, states: "Orthodox Hindu opinion regards the killing of cattle with abhorrence, even though the refusal to kill vast number of useless cattle which exist in India today is detrimental to the nation." Even the Indian Ministry of Information formerly maintained that "the large animal population is more a liability than an asset in view of our land resources." Accounts from many different sources point to the same conclusion: India, one of the world's great civilizations, is being strangled by its love for the cow.

The easy explanation for India's devotion to the cow, the one most Westerners and Indians would offer, is that cow worship is an integral part of Hinduism. Religion is somehow good for the soul, even it if sometimes fails the body. Religion orders the cosmos and explains our place in the universe. Religious beliefs, many would claim, have existed for thousands of years and have a life of their own. They are not understandable in scientific terms.

But all this ignores history. There is more to be said for cow worship than is immediately apparent. The earliest Vedas, the Hindu sacred texts from the second millennium B.C., do not prohibit the slaughter of cattle. Instead, they ordain it as part of sacrificial rites. The early Hindus did not avoid the flesh of cows and bulls; they ate it at ceremonial feasts presided over by Brahman priests. Cow worship is a relatively recent development in India; it evolved as the Hindu religion developed and changed.

This evolution is recorded in royal edicts and religious texts written during the last 3,000 years of Indian history. The Vedas from the first millennium B.C. contain contradictory passages, some referring to ritual slaughter and others to a strict taboo on beef consumption. A.N. Bose, in *Social and Rural Economy of Northern India*, 600 B.C.–200 A.D., concludes that many of the sacred-cow passages were incorporated into the texts by priests of a later period.

By 200 A.D. the status of Indian cattle had undergone a spiritual transformation. The Brahman priesthood exhorted the population to venerate the cow and forbade them to abuse it or to feed on it. Religious feasts involving the ritual slaughter and consumption of livestock were eliminated and meat eating was restricted to the nobility.

By 1000 A.D., all Hindus were forbidden to eat beef. Ahimsa, the Hindu belief in the unity of all life, was the spiritual justification for this restriction. But it is difficult to ascertain exactly when this change occurred. An important event that helped to shape the modern complex was the Islamic invasion, which took place in the eighth century A.D. Hindus may have found it politically expedient to set themselves off from the invaders, who were beefeaters, by emphasizing the need to prevent the slaughter of their sacred animals. Thereafter, the cow taboo assumed its modern form and began to function much as it does today.

The place of the cow in modern India is every place—on posters, in the movies, in brass figures, in stone and wood carvings, on the streets, in the fields. The cow is a symbol of health and abundance. It provides the milk that Indians consume in the form of yogurt and ghee (clarified butter), which contribute subtle flavors to much spicy Indian food.

This, perhaps, is the practical role of the cow, but cows provide less than half the milk produced in India. Most cows in India are not dairy breeds. In most regions, when an Indian farmer wants a steady, high-quality source of milk he usually invests in a female water buffalo. In India the water buffalo is the specialized dairy breed because its milk has a higher butterfat content than zebu milk. Although the farmer milks his zebu cows, the milk is merely a by-product.

More vital than zebu milk to South Asian farmers are zebu calves. Male calves are especially valued because from bulls come oxen, which are the mainstay of the Indian agricultural system.

Small, fast oxen drag wooden plows through late-spring fields when monsoons have dampened the dry, cracked earth. After harvest, the oxen break the grain from the stalk by stomping through mounds of cut wheat and rice. For rice cultivation in irrigated fields, the male water buffalo is preferred (it pulls better in deep mud), but for most other crops, including rainfall rice, wheat, sorghum, and millet, and for transporting goods and people to and from town, a team of oxen is preferred. The ox is the Indian peasant's tractor, thresher, and family car combined; the cow is the factory that produces the ox.

If draft animals instead of cows are counted, India appears to have too few domesticated ruminants, not too many. Since each of the 70 million farms in India require a draft team, it follows that Indian peasants should use 140 million animals in the fields. But there are only 83 million oxen and male water buffalo on the subcontinent, a shortage of 30 million draft teams.

In other regions of the world, joint ownership of draft animals might overcome a shortage, but Indian agriculture is closely tied to the monsoon rains of late spring and summer. Field preparation and planting must coincide with the rain, and a farmer must have his animals ready to plow when the weather is right. When the farmer without a draft team needs bullocks most, his neighbors are all using theirs. Any delay in turning the soil drastically lowers production.

Because of this dependence on draft animals, loss of the family oxen is devastating. If a beast dies, the farmer must borrow money to buy or rent an ox at interest rates so high that he ultimately loses his land. Every year foreclosures force thousands of poverty-stricken peasants to abandon the countryside for the overcrowded cities.

If a family is fortunate enough to own a fertile cow, it will be able to rear replacements for a lost team and thus survive until life returns to normal. If, as sometimes happens, famine leads a family to sell its cow and ox team, all ties to agriculture are cut. Even if the family survives, it has no way to farm the land, no oxen to work the land, and no cows to produce oxen.

The prohibition against eating meat applies to the flesh of cows, bulls, and oxen, but the cow is the most sacred because it can produce the other two. The peasant whose cow dies is not only crying over a spiritual loss but over the loss of his farm as well.

Religious laws that forbid the slaughter of cattle promote the recovery of the agricultural system from the dry Indian winter and from periods of drought. The monsoon, on which all agriculture depends, is erratic. Sometimes, it arrives early, sometimes late, sometimes not at all. Drought has struck large portions of India time and again in this century, and Indian farmers and the zebus are accustomed to these natural disasters. Zebus can pass weeks on end with little or no food and water. Like camels, they store both in their humps and recuperate quickly with only a little nourishment.

During drought the cows often stop lactating and become barren. In some cases the condition is permanent but often it is only temporary. If barren animals were summarily eliminated, as Western experts in animal husbandry have suggested, cows capable of recovery would be lost along with those entirely debilitated. By keeping alive the cows that can later produce oxen, religious laws against cow slaughter assure the recovery of the agricultural system from the greatest challenge it faces—the failure of the monsoon.

The local Indian governments aid the process of recovery by maintaining homes for barren cows. Farmers reclaim any animal that calves or begins to lactate. One police station in Madras collects strays and pastures them in a field adjacent to the station. After a small fine is paid, a cow is returned to its rightful owner when the owner thinks the cow shows signs of being able to reproduce.

During the hot, dry spring months most of India is like a desert. Indian farmers often complain they cannot feed their livestock during this period. They maintain the cattle by letting them scavenge on the sparse grass along the roads. In the cities the cattle are encouraged to scavenge near food stalls to supplement their scant diet. These are the wandering cattle tourists report seeing throughout India.

Westerners expect shopkeepers to respond to these intrusions with the deference due a sacred animal; instead, their response is a string of curses and the crack of a long bamboo pole across the beast's back or a poke at its genitals. Mahatma Gandhi was well aware of the treatment sacred cows (and bulls and oxen) received in India. "How we bleed her to take the last drop of milk from her. How we starve her to emaciation, how we ill-treat the calves, how we deprive them of their portion of milk, how cruelly we treat the oxen, how we castrate them, how we beat them, how we overload them" [Gandhi, 1954].

Oxen generally receive better treatment than cows. When food is in short supply, thrifty Indian peasants feed their working bullocks and ignore their cows, but rarely do they abandon the cows to die. When cows are sick, farmers worry over them as they would over members of the family and nurse them as if they were children. When the rains return and when the fields are harvested, the farmers again feed their cows regularly and reclaim their abandoned animals. The prohibition against beef consumption is a form of disaster insurance for all India.

Western agronomists and economists are quick to protest that all the functions of the zebu cattle can be improved with organized breeding programs, cultivated pastures, and silage. Because stronger oxen would pull the plow faster, they could work multiple plots of land, allowing farmers to share their animals. Fewer healthy, well-fed cows could provide Indians with more milk. But pastures and silage require arable land, land needed to produce wheat and rice.

A look at Western cattle farming makes plain the cost of adopting advanced technology in Indian agriculture. In a study of livestock production in the United States, David Pimentel of the College of Agriculture and Life Sciences at Cornell University, found that 91 percent of the cereal, legume, and vegetable protein suitable for human consumption is consumed by livestock. Approximately three quarters of the arable land in the United States is devoted to growing food for livestock. In the production of meat and milk, American ranchers use enough fossil fuel to equal more than 82 million barrels of oil annually.

Indian cattle do not drain the system in the same way. In a 1971 study of livestock in West Bengal, Stewart Odend'hal [1972] of the University of Missouri found that Bengalese cattle ate only the inedible remains of subsistence crops—rice straw, rice hulls, the tops of sugar cane, and mustard-oil cake. Cattle graze in the fields after harvest and eat the remains of crops left on the ground; they forage for grass and weeds on the roadsides. The food for zebu cattle costs the human population virtually nothing. "Basically," Odend'hal says, "the cattle convert the items of little direct human value into products of immediate utility."

In addition to plowing the fields and producing milk, the zebus produce dung, which fires the hearths and fertilizes the fields of India. Much of the estimated 800 million tons of manure produced annually is collected by the farmers' children as they follow the family cows and bullocks from place to place. And when the children see the droppings of another farmer's cattle along the road, they pick those up also. Odend'hal reports that the system operates with such high efficiency that the children of West Bengal recover nearly 100 percent of the dung produced by their livestock.

From 40 to 70 percent of all manure produced by Indian cattle is used as fuel for cooking; the rest is returned to the fields as fertilizer. Dried dung burns slowly, cleanly, and with low heat—characteristics that satisfy the household needs of Indian women. Staples like curry and rice can simmer for hours. While the meal slowly cooks over an unattended fire, the women of the household can do other chores. Cow chips, unlike firewood, do not scorch as they burn.

It is estimated that the dung used for cooking fuel provides the energy-equivalent of 43 million tons of coal. At current prices, it would cost India an extra 1.5 billion dollars in foreign exchange to replace the dung with coal. And if the 350 million tons of manure that are being used as fertilizer were replaced with commercial fertilizers, the expense would be even greater. Roger Revelle of the University of California at San Diego has calculated that 89 percent of the energy used in Indian agriculture (the equivalent of about 140 million tons of coal) is provided by local sources. Even if foreign loans were to provide the money, the capital outlay necessary to replace the Indian cow with tractors and fertilizers for the fields, coal for the fires, and transportation for the family would probably warp international financial institutions for years.

Instead of asking the Indians to learn from the American model of industrial agriculture, American farmers might learn energy conservation from the Indians. Every step in an energy cycle results in a loss of energy to the system. Like a pendulum that slows a bit with each swing, each transfer of energy from sun to plants, plants to animals, and animals to human beings involves energy losses. Some systems are more efficient than others; they provide a higher percentage of the energy inputs in a final, useful form. Seventeen percent of all energy zebus consume is returned in the form of milk, traction, and dung. American cattle raised on Western rangeland return only 4 percent of the energy they consume.

But the American system is improving. Based on techniques pioneered by Indian scientists, at least one commercial firm in the United States is reported to be building plants that will turn manure from cattle feedlots into combustible gas. When organic matter is broken down by anaerobic bacteria, methane gas and carbon dioxide are produced. After the methane is cleansed of the carbon dioxide, it is available for the same purposes as natural gas—cooking, heating, electric generation. The company constructing the biogasification plant plans to sell its product to a gas-supply company, to be piped through the existing distribution system. Schemes similar to this one could make cattle ranches almost independent of utility and gasoline companies; for methane can be used to run trucks, tractors, and cars as well as to supply heat and electricity. The relative energy self-sufficiency that the Indian peasant has achieved is a goal American farmers and industry are now striving for.

Studies of Odend'hal's understate the efficiency of the Indian cow, because dead cows are used for purposes that Hindus prefer not to acknowledge. When a cow dies, an Untouchable, a member of one of the lowest ranking castes in India, is summoned to haul away the carcass. Higher castes consider the body of the dead cow polluting; if they handle it, they must go through a rite of purification.

Untouchables first skin the dead animal and either tan the skin themselves or sell it to a leather factory. In the privacy of their homes, contrary to the teachings of Hinduism, untouchable castes cook the meat and eat it. Indians of all castes rarely acknowledge the existence of these practices to non-Hindus, but most are aware that beefeating takes place. The prohibition against beefeating restricts consumption by the higher castes and helps distribute animal protein to the poorest sectors of the population that otherwise would have no source of these vital nutrients.

Untouchables are not the only Indians who consume beef. Indian Muslims and Christians are under no restriction that forbids them beef, and its consumption is legal in many places. The Indian ban on cow slaughter is state, not national, law and not all states restrict it. In many cities, such as New Delhi, Calcutta, and Bombay, legal slaughterhouses sell beef to retail customers and to restaurants that serve steak.

If the caloric value of beef and the energy costs involved in the manufacture of synthetic leather were included in the estimate of energy, the calculated efficiency of Indian livestock would rise considerably. As well as the system works, experts often claim that its efficiency can be further improved. Alan Heston [et al., 1971], an economist at the University of Pennsylvania, believes that Indians suffer from an overabundance of cows simply because they refuse to slaughter the excess cattle. India could produce at least the same number of oxen and the same quantities of milk and manure with 30 million fewer cows. Heston calculates that only 40 cows are necessary to maintain a population of 100 bulls and oxen. Since India averages 70 cows for every 100 bullocks, the difference, 30 million cows, is expendable.

What Heston fails to note is that sex ratios among cattle in different regions of India vary tremendously, indicating that adjustments in the cow population do take place. Along the Ganges River, one of the holiest shrines of Hinduism, the ratio drops to 47 cows for every 100 male animals. This ratio reflects the preference for dairy buffalo in the irrigated sectors of the Gangetic Plains. In nearby Pakistan, in contrast, where cow slaughter is permitted, the sex ratio is 60 cows to 100 oxen.

Since the sex ratios among cattle differ greatly from region to region and do not even approximate the balance that would be expected if no females were killed, we can assume that some culling of herds does take place; Indians do adjust their religious restrictions to accommodate ecological realities.

They cannot kill a cow but they can tether an old or unhealthy animal until it has starved to death. They cannot slaughter a calf but they can yoke it with a large wooden triangle so that when it nurses it irritates the mother's udder and gets kicked to death. They cannot ship their animals to the slaughterhouse but they can sell them to Muslims, closing their eyes to the fact that the Muslims will take the cattle to the slaughterhouse.

These violations of the prohibition against cattle slaughter strengthen the premise that cow worship is a vital part of Indian culture. The practice arose to prevent the population from consuming the animal on which Indian agriculture depends. During the first millennium B.C., the Gange Valley became one of the most densely populated regions of the world.

Where previously there had been only scattered villages, many towns and cities arose and peasants farmed every available acre of land. Kingsley Davis, a population expert at the University of California at Berkeley, estimates that by 300 B.C. between 50 million and 100 million people were living in India. The forested Ganges Valley became a windswept semidesert and signs of ecological collapse appeared; droughts and floods became commonplace, erosion took away the rich topsoil, farms shrank as population increased, and domesticated animals became harder and harder to maintain.

It is probable that the elimination of meat eating came about in a slow, practical manner. The farmers who decided not to eat their cows, who saved them for procreation to produce oxen, were the ones who survived the natural disasters. Those who ate beef lost the tools with which to farm. Over a period of centuries, more and more farmers probably avoided beef until an unwritten taboo came into existence.

Only later was the practice codified by the priesthood. While Indian peasants were probably aware of the role of cattle in their society, strong sanctions were necessary to protect zebus from a population faced with starvation. To remove temptation, the flesh of cattle became taboo and the cow became sacred.

The sacredness of the cow is not just an ignorant belief that stands in the way of progress. Like all concepts of the sacred and the profane, this one affects the physical world; it defines the relationships that are important for the maintenance of Indian society.

Indians have the sacred cow, we have the "sacred" car and the "sacred" dog. It would not occur to us to propose the elimination of automobiles and dogs from our society without carefully considering the consequences, and we should not propose the elimination of zebu cattle without first understanding their place in the social order of India.

Human society is neither random nor capricious. The regularities of thought and behavior called culture are the principal mechanisms by which we human beings adapt to the world around us. Practices and beliefs can be rational or irrational, but a society that fails to adapt to its environment is doomed to extinction. Only those societies that draw the necessities of life from their surroundings without destroying those surroundings inherit the earth. The West has much to learn from the great antiquity of Indian civilization, and the sacred cow is an important part of that lesson.

References

Gandhi, Mohandas K. 1954. *How to Serve the Cow*. Bombay: Navajivan Publishing House.

Heston, Alan, et al. 1971. "An Approach to the Sacred Cow of India." *Current Anthropology* 12, 191–209.

Odend'hal, Stewart. 1972. "Gross Energetic Efficiency of Indian Cattle in Their Environment." *Journal of Human Ecology* 1, 1–27.

39 The World of the Hospital

DANIEL F. CHAMBLISS

To most of us, the distinction between professionals and non-professionals is vague. But not to sociologists, who view professionals as people who have been rigorously educated in the theory underlying their work. In addition, professionals are self-regulated; that is, they establish the criteria for entering the profession, oversee and evaluate the performance of their members, and discipline their rule breakers. Professionals also exercise authority over their clients: Being the expert, the professional tells the client what to do. Supposedly at least, professionals are also motivated by service to society rather than by self-interest. Certainly this is an idealized list of traits, and various groups of workers can be classified as having "more" or "less" of these characteristics.

Sociologists view medicine as the prime example of a profession, stressing how it exhibits these characteristics the best of any group. In this article, we get to look over the shoulder of medical professionals as they do their work. From this analysis, it becomes clear why the professional's view veers so sharply from that of the client. What for the patient is an emergency, is for physicians and nurses only routine—another part of their daily work. Chambliss' analysis helps us understand how, for professionals, even tragedy can become routine.

How the Hospital Is Different

... MUCH [IN A HOSPITAL] is the same as in other organizations: the daily round of paper processing, answering the phone, making staffing decisions, collecting bills, ordering supplies, stocking equipment rooms; there are fights between departments, arguments with the boss, workers going home tired or satisfied. And medical sociology has made much of these similarities, using its research to create broader theories of, for instance, deviance or of the structure of professions.

But in one crucial respect the hospital remains dramatically different from other organizations: *in hospitals, as a normal part of the routine, people suffer and die.* This is unusual. "[A] good working definition of a hospital is

434

that place where death occurs and no one notices; or, more sharply, the place where others agree to notice a death as a social fact only so far as it fits their particular purposes." Only combat military forces share this feature. To be complete, theories of hospital life need to acknowledge this crucial difference, since adapting themselves to pain and death is for hospital workers the most distinctive feature of their work. It is that which most separates them from the rest of us. In building theories of organizational life, sociologists must try to see how hospitals resemble other organizations . . . but we should not make a premature leap to the commonalities before appreciating the unique features of hospitals that make a nurse's task so different from that of a teacher or a businessman or a bureaucrat.

A quick survey of typical patients in one Surgical Intensive Care Unit on one Saturday evening should make the point. The words in brackets are additions to my original field notes:

Room 1. 64-year-old white woman with an aortic valve replacement: five separate IMEDs [intravenous drip-control devices] feeding in nitroglycerine, vasopressors, Versed [a pain killer which also blocks memory]. Chest tube [to drain off fluids]. On ventilator [breathing machine], Foley [catheter in the bladder], a pulse oximeter on her finger, a[rterial monitoring] line. Diabetic. In one 30-second period during the night, her blood pressure dropped from $^{160}/_{72}$ to $^{95}/_{50}$, then to $^{53}/_{36}$, before the nurse was able to control the drop. N[urse]s consider her "basically healthy."

Room 2. Man with pulmonary artresia, pulmonary valvotomy [heart surgery].

Room 3. Woman with CABG [coronary artery bypass graft; a "bypass operation"]. Bleeding out [i.e., hemorrhaging] badly at one point during the night, they sent her back to the OR [Operating Room]. On heavy vasopressors [to keep blood pressure up].

Room 4. Older woman with tumor from her neck up to her temple. In OR from 7 a.m. until 2 a.m. the next morning having it removed. Infarct [dead tissue] in the brain.

Room 5. 23-year-old woman. MVA [motor vehicle accident]. ICP [intracranial pressure—a measure of brain swelling] measured—terrible. Maybe organ donor. [Patient died next day.]

Room 6. Don't know.

Room 7.   Abdominal sepsis, possibly from surgery. DNR [Do Not Resuscitate] today.

Room 8.   Big belly guy [an old man with a horribly distended abdomen, uncontrollable. Staff says it's from poor sterile technique in surgery by Dr. M., who is notoriously sloppy. This patient died within the week.] [Field Notes]

This is a typical patient load for an Intensive Care Unit. Eight beds, three patients dead in a matter of days. "Patients and their visitors often find the ICU to be a disturbing, even terrifying place. Constant artificial light, ceaseless activity, frequent emergencies, and the ever-present threat of death create an atmosphere that can unnerve even the most phlegmatic of patients. Some are so sick that they are unaware of their surroundings or simply forget the experience, but for others the ICU is a nightmare remembered all too well," On floors—the larger, less critical care wards of the hospital—fatalities are less common, and patients are not so sick; even so, one-third of the patients may have AIDS, another one-third have cancer, and the rest suffer a variety of serious if not immediately lethal diseases. The ICUs just get patients whose deaths are imminent.

It is interesting that this density of disease presents one of the positive attractions of nursing. People don't become nurses to avoid seeing suffering or to have a quiet day. Everyday nurses respond to and share the most intense emotions with total strangers. "People you don't know are going through the most horrible things, and you are supposed to help them. That's intense," says one nurse. And another enthuses about coming home as the sun is coming up; the rest of the world thinks things are just starting, and here you're coming off a big emergency that lasted half the night: "[T]here's a real adrenaline kick in all this stuff. If you deny that, you're denying a big part of [nursing]."

The abnormality of the hospital scene liberates the staff from some niceties of everyday life and allows them a certain freedom. . . . Two small, even silly, examples may illustrate the point. (1) Many nurses wear scrub suits—the pajama-like pants and tops worn in operating rooms and on some units. Written on the suits are phone numbers, vital statistics, or even doodles drawn during surgery. It's more convenient than finding a piece of paper. One observer, Judith André, has commented, "It's like a childhood fantasy" to scribble things on your clothes. (2) During a "code," as a patient was being resuscitated, one nurse who was having her period began to leak menstrual fluid. She ran into the patient's bathroom to change her sanitary pad. When she came out, another nurse seeing the stain on her pants, yelled, "Well, J. got her period!"—a comment unthinkable in the everyday world.

But this isn't the everyday world. As Everett Hughes (1958: 79) wrote, "All occupations—most of all those considered professions and perhaps those of the underworld—include as part of their very being a licence to deviate in some measure from common modes of behavior." In this sense, the hospital is like a war zone, in which common niceties and rules of decorum are discarded in the pursuit of some more immediate, desperate objective. There is an excitement, and a pressure, that frees hospital workers in the "combat zone" from an array of normal constraints on what they say and do.

And yet, for them their work has become normal, routine. On a medical floor, with perhaps two-thirds of the patients suffering eventually fatal diseases, I say to a nurse, "What's happening?" and she replies, walking down the hall, "Same ol' same ol'. Nothing new, nothing exciting." Or an Intensive Care Unit in the same hospital, "What's going on?" The resident replies, with a little shrug of the shoulders, "People are living, people are dying." Again, no surprises, nothing new. The routine goes on.

As other writers have noted, the professional treats routinely what for the patient is obviously not routine. For the health worker, medical procedures happen to patients every day, and the hospital setting is quite comfortable: "The staff nurse . . . belongs to a world of relative health, youth, and bustling activity. She may not yet have experienced hospitalization herself for more than the removal of tonsils or the repair of a minor injury. Although she works in an environment of continuous sickness, she has been so conditioned to its external aspects that she often expresses surprise when someone suggests that the environment must be anxiety evoking." (Brown 1966: 202). Everett Hughes's (1958: 54, 88) formulation of this divergence of experience is classic: "In many occupations, the workers or practitioners . . . deal routinely with what are emergencies to the people who receive their services. This is a source of chronic tension between the two." Or, more precisely, "[O]ne man's routine of work is made up of the emergencies of other people."

To the patient, though, the hospital world is special, frightening, a jarring break from the everyday world. For the nurse, it's just the "same ol' same ol'." How extreme the gap is was observed in an ICU one evening:

> Three residents were attempting an LP [lumbar puncture—a "spinal tap" in which a long needle is inserted into the spinal column to draw out spinal fluid]. This is a very painful procedure and is difficult to perform. The television over the foot of the patient's bed was turned on, and "LA Law" was playing. While the resident was inserting the needle, she kept glancing up at the television, trying to simultaneously watch the show and do the LP. The patient, curled into the fetal position to separate the vertebrae, was unaware of this. The other two residents as well were glancing back and forth from procedure to television. The resident tried for several minutes drawing out blood instead of fluid. Eventually,

she called the head resident, who came in and successfully finished the LP. [Field Notes].

This illustrates how casual staff can become, to the point of malfeasance.

How do staff, nurses in particular, routinize the abnormal? Or more fundamentally, what do we even mean by routinization?

What Routinization Entails: The Operating Room

The most egregious violation of commonsense morality—the profound physical violation of another person's body—is made completely routine in the hospital operating room. To help the reader understand routinization, we will consider this example in some detail.

In large teaching hospitals like Northern General or Southwest Regional, there are some twelve to twenty operating rooms in the "OR suite," with the rooms organized in a long hallway around a central equipment and supply area. The entire suite is "sterile," that is, everyone coming in and out wears scrub suits and face masks, shoe covers, and hair bonnets. Each operating room is furnished with a narrow padded table on which the patient lies during surgery, as well as with huge movable overhead lights and rolling tables for equipment of all sorts. Certain rooms are typically reserved for cardiac, neurological, orthopedic, and other special types of surgery, and the peculiar equipment for each of these is always available in those rooms. There are also one or two "crash rooms," for emergency surgery of the sort associated with the automobile wrecks or shootings frequently seen in large urban medical centers. Each room may be scheduled for one to six operations in a day; several dozen surgeries are scheduled for the hospital each weekday morning, usually starting at 6:00 and running until 2:00 or so in the afternoon.

Nurses manage these rooms between operations, supervising the flow of patients and the resupply of equipment (sponges, surgical tools, clean linens, etc.), answering the telephone or intercom and letting the physicians know when it is time to begin. There are typically at least two such nurses, the "scrub nurse" who assists the surgeon, handing tools and dealing directly with the sterile field, and the "circulating nurse" who can move in and out of the OR, touch nonsterile areas (such as the telephone), and keep the supplies flowing as needed to the surgical team. The circulating nurse is a kind of stage manager and fills in as needed, solving problems arising outside the surgery itself.

During surgery, the circulating nurse has several duties. First, she must document everything that happens: the time when surgery begins, what specific procedures are being conducted, what personnel are participating, when the procedure is done and "closing" begins, and when the patient is wheeled out of the room. Working together with the scrub nurse, she repeatedly counts and recounts the number of "sponges" (absorbent pads) used in the operation (there may be dozens). She must account for all of them, both before and after the operation, to ensure that none are mistakenly left in the patient's body. She does the same for the surgical needles used, making certain that all are accounted for and disposed of properly, a serious concern since the advent of AIDS. The best circulating nurses, it would seem, are precise to the point of obsessiveness. The scrub nurse shares in these duties, counting sponges and accounting for all equipment, as well as passing to the surgeon, quickly and reliably, the specific tools needed at different stages of the operation. The scrub nurse also "preps" the patient: she drapes the patient with sterile cloths, leaving bare the shaved area to be cut open, disinfecting the body surface with an iodine solution, and covering the skin with a clear plastic film called "Opsite" which protects the uncut area. A screen of cloth is usually set up between the patient's head and the rest of the body, so conscious patients will not see what's going on. This also means that the operating area is detached from the patient as a person, an important feature of the scene. The nurses carry out routine tasks dozens of times in a single day—for instance, the one-by-one counting of sponges, carried with tongs from a table to a waste bucket, perhaps two dozen of them counted aloud. The failure to perform these tasks conscientiously could be disastrous.

Once both room and patient are "prepped," the medical team can begin. The patient's body, fundamentally, is transformed into an object. An anesthesiologist (a physician), or a nurse anesthetist, will administer either a spinal anesthetic, which numbs the body below the injection point on the spinal cord, or a general anesthetic, which puts the patient to sleep. From then on, the operative area, screened from the patient's head and deadened of all feeling, effectively becomes to the surgeons a piece of nonhuman meat. The target area is isolated and immobilized; the patient is either asleep or, with a spinal, may be chatting away up at the head of the table with the anesthesiologist. In one case, a man's leg was being removed at one end of the table while at the other he was telling the anesthesiologist about his recent vacation trip. Looking at the operating area, the skin being cut or bone being sawed, you think, "No one I know has ever looked like this." Anesthetized flesh doesn't respond as the flesh of a living human being would. In amputations, the flesh being removed is usually dead and looks it—dark, hard, lifeless. But living flesh, too, on the table, looks more like what it "objectively" is, that is, meat. Human fat looks like the chicken fat you see on the stove; human skin peels back the way a chicken's does when peeled. An old man's tanned skin, when cut, looks like leather—which, precisely speaking, it is: old, tanned, animal skin. Surgeons working inside the body cavity remind one of cooks stuffing the

Thanksgiving turkey, pulling open a section here, pushing a hand deep inside, feeling around for something there, stretching back tendons, trimming the fat, snipping pieces here and there with a small pair of scissors. The fine details of surgery are remarkably complex and refined, but its basic principles are brutally simple:

> To amputate this diabetic lady's toes, Dr. R., a small woman, used a thing like a big pair of bolt cutters to actually cut the bones, one toe at a time—with the big toe she had some difficulty, and she was almost lifted off the floor squeezing the big handles together before the "crunch" and the blades snapped through the toe. Then the last flesh was snipped away and five toes, all together, like a section of beef or chicken, came off in a single piece, and the scrub nurse laid it into a specimen tray. [Field Notes]

This primitive business is executed with simple tools: a razor-edge knife to cut open the skin (the scalpel); scissors to trim away flesh inside the body; smooth hooks to pull back the skin while the operation is under way (retractors); needle-nose pliers to shut off blood vessels (hemostats); and a small electric probe, essentially a soldering iron, used to cauterize the open ends of small blood vessels (the "Bovie"). Tools come in many sizes and specialized shapes, but this is the basic array. Orthopedic surgery adds its various saws, drills, and bits; the equipment table looks like a bench in an immaculate hobbyist's workshop, which in a sense it is.

To the senior staff, these tools and their uses become commonplace. During one routine orthopedic operation (routine for the staff, not for the patient), a group of young residents were working on a teenage patient's shoulder. The supervising attending physician, nominally in charge, popped in occasionally during the three-hour operation to see how things were going. On one visit he stopped for fifteen minutes to flip through the "swimsuit issue" of *Waterski* magazine, which one of the residents had brought. His pointed air of "no big deal" was more than casual; it seemed almost an assertion of his own power and sophistication, contrasted with the barely concealed anxiety of the residents he was monitoring. When he left, the residents visibly relaxed and resumed openly discussing how to perform the operation. One actually shuttled back and forth to a table against the wall to look at the diagrams in his textbook to see how the surgery should be done. Then the attending anesthesiologist came in to check on his resident and to sign a form ("So I'll get my cut," he said smiling) and walked out again. Music by popular musicians Phil Collins and Los Lobos was on a portable tape cassette player as the residents worked. The residents were learning to do highly skilled surgery and how to regard it as part of everyday life.

Routinization in the OR or elsewhere in the hospital seems to mean that actions are repeated, and that they violate normal taboos. Each operation is not the first of its kind; most in fact are done several times each day and hundreds of times each year, even by a single team of surgeons, nurses, and technical aides. What the team sees, they have seen many times. Gallbladder removals, hernia repairs and shoulder operations on athletes—these are all very common procedures in the major medical center.

And those repeated procedures take place against the even less dramatic background of the repeated daily events of the nurse's work: starting intravenous lines, taking blood pressure four times a day on every patient on the floor, drawing blood samples, charting vital signs, writing nurses' progress notes, passing food trays, helping patients on and off the bedpan. Both trivial and consequential activities are repeated over and over until each one becomes much like the next; indeed, as Hughes (1958: 54) says, the professional's "very competence comes from having dealt with a thousand cases of what the client likes to consider his unique experience." Says one nurse, "You get to the point where you don't really care for the patients anymore and one GI [gastrointestinal] bleeder gets to be the same as the next GI bleeder."

In a Medical Intensive Care Unit, death itself becomes an often-repeated event:

> Another MICU patient just coded and died; that's five in the past six days. Incredible. The docs are here one month—N[urse]s are here for good . . .
>
> I just came in unit; first N[urse] says, "You just missed it." They said that to me a few days ago. It's not that I "just miss," I think, but rather that so much [is] going on. You'll always "just miss" something. [Field Notes]

Death becomes a routinized part of daily life, incorporated into the flow. "Mr. Smith died last night," says one nurse to another. "Oh, that's too bad. He was such a nice man"; a casual exchange. One day is like another, if not for Mr. Smith, then at least for the rest of us. For the nurses, Mr. Smith will be replaced by another man, a Mr. Jones, with similar ailments and a similar end. . . .

After a middle-aged woman died late one night in room 5 of a medical ICU, her family, loudly crying and hugging each other, came into the room to see their dead mother. Outside the room, three nurses who had tried for thirty minutes to resuscitate the patient sat around a table eating corn chips and gossiping, as if nothing had happened. One of those nurses said to me, "We're pretty dehumanized, huh?" But it wasn't true: if she were dehumanized no such comment would even be made. She knew what was happening, and eating corn chips, even then, is in fact quite human. In a unit where three patients die each week, to get upset with every death would be humanly unacceptable.

Sometimes routinization goes beyond mere commonplace into an attitude of detachment, unconcern, or sheer boredom—one of the more common emotions of the nurse's life, to the surprise of laypersons. Indeed, one of the most frequent questions nurses asked me during my research was, "Aren't you bored?" . . .

How Routinization Is Accomplished: Creating Conditions for Ordinary Life

Thus, for the nurse, hospital life is ordinary—not extraordinary, or mystical, or even an object of thoughtful scrutiny. This is what we mean by saying the nurse has routinized the world of the hospital. Her life here has taken on a quality of mundane sameness, often to the point of sheer boredom.

> The first time I had to interview a patient in my first year of nursing school, he said he had a scar [on his chest]. I asked to see it, he just pulled up his gown [around his neck; she gestures to show how he was bare]. I was . . . [rolls her eyes, embarrassed] "Oh, my God." And now . . . [waves her hand, flutters eyes to indicate her totally blasé attitude]. [Field Notes]

No layperson would experience such exposure so casually. And nudity is simple; witnessing open heart surgery, or an endotracheal intubation, or CPR, is far more threatening to one's everyday reality. But nurses see these events every day, without becoming upset. The nurse's view—or more accurately, the nurse's very way of *living* here and dealing with such trauma—is different from ours.

How does this casual attitude develop? How does this abnormal become routine? The conventional answer is that "you just get used to it." This implies that over time, with enough exposure, one adapts, willy-nilly, to whatever is happening in the environment. This may be true, but it is insufficient. "Getting used to it" suggests that routinization is purely a matter of the passage of time, with repetition as the implied causative agent. Yes, routinization happens "over time," but time alone is insufficient to cause routinization. Some nurses never become accustomed, as we will see, to deformed newborns, or psychotic teenagers, or incontinent geriatric patients. Then, too, some people "get used to it" virtually immediately. Before my own first witnessing of surgery, I conscientiously followed all the head nurse's instructions to avoid physical or emotional upset: I rose early, ate a full breakfast, and was wide awake before going to the OR suite. After donning the scrub suit, bonnet, and shoe covers, I went into the OR and asked the circulating nurse what the first case would be, hoping for something "easy," maybe a wrist or ankle operation. She looked at the chart and said, without missing a beat, "leg amputation." I nearly panicked, but I stayed. To my own amazement, I was not in the least upset by the amputation or any of the surgeries I witnessed, including the repair of a ruptured ectopic pregnancy that drove at least two experienced nurses from the

OR in dismay. For some reason, there seemed to be no period of "getting used to it" at all. So repeated exposure as a means of routinization is insufficient; more is at work.

At least four phenomenological tasks go into the routinization of the hospital world: learning one's geographical surroundings, so that the routine is physically manageable; learning the language so one can meet and work with other people; learning the technique of the work being done (if you don't know how to start an IV, it's hard to be casual about it); and learning the "types" of patients and standard procedures for recognizing and dealing with them. . . . There is also, harder to define, a fifth task, a perceptual "leap," which I will describe after presenting these components. . . .

1. *Learning the geography*. The first step in the routinization of a world is simply to learn one's way around the physical setting. It's difficult to be casual when rooms are unfamiliar, hallways look long and forbidding, and one can't find the bathroom. Supplies are often kept in unexpected places, telephones sometimes work in strange ways ("You have to dial 8 first"), even chairs may have traditional claims on them (until recently in American hospitals, nurses stood while physicians sat). Hospital beds come in various models, and working them isn't always easy.

This geography has social meanings and implications too, which must be learned. One has to know that "this is Joanne's chair," or that the clerk always gets the phone, or that everyone cleans their own coffee cup. The physical setting, that is, must be known in its social ramifications. . . .

2. *Learning the language*. To move easily in the world of the hospital, the nurse must learn its peculiar language, the technical jargon, and the informal slang. The jargon is technically complex, even daunting. DNR: an order to Do Not Resuscitate a terminal patient when his or her breathing or heartbeat stops. CABG: pronounced "Cabbage," a coronary artery bypass graft, what the layperson calls bypass surgery. Or consider this description of the possible causes of one common symptom.

> [It is found] accompanying diaphragmatic pleurisy, pneumonia, uremia, or alcoholism . . . abdominal causes include disorders of the stomach, and esophagus, bowel diseases, pancreatitis, pregnancy, bladder irritation, hepatic metastases, or hepatitis. Thoracic and mediastinal lesions or surgery may be responsible. Posterior fossa tumors or infarcts may stimulate centers in the medulla oblongata . . . [Merck 1987: 1356–1357]

Pity the poor layperson who overhears such language to discuss his or her symptom—which in this case is hiccups.

Besides medical jargon, informal slang is highly developed, as the staff live in an experiential world far different than the layperson. Here, a dying patient is "going down the tubes," "circling the drain." The dead have "bought the farm," "straight-lined," or perhaps "Marshalled"—a reference to the name of the building that houses the morgue. An older patient who violently resists the nurses is "confused" and after drug sedation becomes much more "appropriate." Every emergency room has its "Gomers"—one of the most ubiquitous cases of hospital slang, derived from "Grand Old Man of the ER," or variants, and referring generically to old people with no treatable problems who are virtually permanent residents of the hospital. On the acute psychiatric unit, there is the "quiet room": what once was called a padded cell, where a suicidal teenage girl huddles in the corner, crying, visible through the peephole in the door. The patient is regularly technicized in discussions of "input" and "output" (of food and waste). Learning the peculiar language is a vital part of becoming an insider. To understand what people are talking about, much less to become comfortable here, you need to learn the slang. And even when no special jargon is used, the very matter-of-factness of the talk can be disarming: "Well, he had a stool; it was soft, but he said there was some diarrhea." Most of us simply don't talk in that way with fellow workers.

3. *Learning the techniques.* Routinization requires learning the techniques of one's work: the job itself must be familiar. One reason that I was immediately "used to" seeing surgery was that I was only observing it, not participating. Observing is a skill at which, as a sociologist, I have had much practice. There was no further technical learning necessary.

Nursing entails a great number of specific technical skills, and until one learns them the job can be overwhelming. "Being organized" is a prime job skill for nurses. The staff nurse dispenses hundreds of pills a day to dozens of patients, starts and maintains intravenous lines, gives bed baths, documents on paper virtually everything she does, monitors temperatures, blood pressures, and urine "outputs," delivers food trays, and responds more or less to all the miscellaneous patient and family requests that, from her point of view, often get in the way of her finishing her basic required work. Simply getting through an eight-hour shift without mistakenly giving Mrs. Jones the pills for Ms. Smith, or forgetting to check Mr. Martin's IV line, or not helping Miss Garcia eat her lunch is challenge enough. And these are the everyday, non-emergency tasks, the basics of the job.

4. *Learning the patients.* Patient types, too, become routine to the nurse. Despite an outsider's first impression of a multitude of different medical problems, most patients suffer one of a fairly small number of predictable

ailments: cancer, heart disease, COPD (chronic obstructive pulmonary disease, such as emphysema or bronchitis), and now AIDS. These cover most of the severe cases. Treatments are relatively predictable as well, from the nursing staff's perspective: surgery, intravenous therapy, the usual medications. In heart disease, there are perhaps a half-dozen routinely used drugs; for cancer, there is surgery and the usual chemotherapy or radiation. So patients quickly become typed: the COPD lady in room 8, the AIDS guy in 2. . . .

An advantage of being used to seeing pain is that one can then work with suffering people. The "detached concern" that Merton writes about allows a nurse to lose the embarrassment many of us feel in front of sick people and allows her to talk with sick or dying patients. A dying woman can tell a nurse her fears; she may hesitate to burden a friend with them. A nurse, one may believe, has seen it all, so seeing one more thing perhaps won't upset her. It's probably true. One nurse told me that a friend said to her, "My dad is on oxygen!" and she, the nurse, thought to herself, "What would these people think if they saw someone in the unit with IV lines, an NG [nasogastric] tube, chest tubes, a catheter stuck in the bladder, and another tube stuck up the rectum? Ye gods, everyone I *know* is on oxygen!" She has become familiar with the patients.

Having learned the geography of the hospital, the language, the techniques of work, and the types of patients, a nurse is well prepared to convert what was a chaos of disasters into a routine, well-organized round of daily activities.

5. *Routinization of the world.* But learning the specifics of the job—the geography, the jargon, the techniques, the patients—does not automatically produce an acceptance of the hospital world as normal. Some nurses learn the techniques but still never accept the daily disasters; they leave the profession, or move to less acute care settings, working in a school, a physician's office, or perhaps a home health care agency. More is demanded than simply accruing new information about work, or people, or the setting. Routinization itself demands a qualitative transformation in one's thinking, an entirely new way of relating to events and people. It can happen suddenly. Some nurses say that after six months or so on the job, having struggled through the heavy demands, often near to despair, one day they realize that the work no longer bothers them; they are "into" it.

> When I [first] walked into that unit, I had never seen any of these machines . . . there are 15,000 machines, they all have different alarms, they all have different ways to work them, different trouble-shooting things, and here you are expected to take care of this patient who's crumping every minute . . . it's just overwhelming.

And then all of a sudden, one day, you say, Gee, I've survived this shift, and all of these things happened, and it was OK. . . .

[So what happened that you got used to it?]

You know, I have absolutely no idea . . . You go in and you do it again and again, and your patient codes for the fifth time . . . I can't even tell you when it happens, it's different for different people . . .

Then the scary thing happens. You start to *like* it. [Field Notes]

What this nurse describes is not just a gradual transition over time, not a simple accumulation of experiences that finally equals "getting used to it." The accumulation of experiences is part of it, to be sure. But these only make possible the major shift, a qualitative transformation of consciousness, a *routinization of the world*. It is as if one takes the proverbial journey of a thousand single steps and discovers that the final step is in fact a fifteen-foot jump over a deep mountain gorge. Without the final leap, the journey is incomplete, almost a waste. But even that analogy doesn't quite fit, since many nurses "jump the gorge" without ever realizing what they have done. Usually, it just happens ("How did you get used to it?" "I have absolutely no idea."). Still, it is the nurse who "does" this happening, who makes the leap, even if subconsciously. . . .

References

Brown, Esther Lucille, "Nursing and Patient Care," in Fred Davis, *The Nursing Profession: Five Sociological Essays* (New York: John Wiley & Sons, 1966), p. 202.

Hughes, E. C., *Men and Their Work* (Westport, CT: Greenwood Press, 1958), p. 79.

The Merck Manual of Diagnosis and Therapy, 15th ed. (Rahway, NJ: Merck Sharp & Dohme Research Laboratories, 1987). pp. 1356–1357.

40 Police Accounts of Normal Force

JENNIFER HUNT

My personal contacts with the police have been infrequent and brief. Nevertheless, I have seen a policeman handcuff a rape suspect to a tree and then slap him in the face in front of a group of citizen-witnesses. I have heard another threaten the life of a suspect he was escorting near a stream, saying he wished the suspect would attempt to flee so he "could shoot her and watch her body float down the river." And in Mexico, after recovering my billfold and apprehending the two men who had picked my pocket, the secret police offered to hold the culprits while I beat them. They felt that I *ought* to beat them because, as they said, the men had caused me (and presumably them) so much trouble. (I didn't, in case you are wondering.)

These events have convinced me that police violence is no random matter but is a regular part of the occupation. Sociological research bears this out. Why should this be? Is it because the police recruit people with sadistic tendencies? As a sociologist, Hunt does not look for explanations lodged *within* people, such as "personality types." Rather, she examines the occupational culture, *external* conditions that affect people's orientations, in this instance how occupational norms influence the behavior and attitudes of recruits.

If you were a social reformer and you wanted to decrease police violence, where would you start? Keep in mind what Hunt found—the virtual absence of differences by gender, the distinction between formal and informal expectations, and the strong support for "normal" violence that is built into this occupation—and the lessons from the Zimbardo experiment in Part VI.

THE POLICE ARE REQUIRED to handle a variety of peacekeeping and law enforcement tasks including settling disputes, removing drunks from the street, aiding the sick, controlling crowds, and pursuing criminals. What unifies these diverse activities is the possibility that their resolution might require the use of force. Indeed, the capacity to use force stands at the core of the police mandate (Bittner, 1980). . . . The following research . . . explores how police themselves classify and evaluate acts of force as either legal, normal, or excessive. Legal force is that coercion necessary to subdue, control, and restrain a suspect in order to take him into custody. Although force not accountable in legal terms is technically labeled excessive by the courts and the public, the police perceive many forms of illegal force as normal. Normal force involves coercive acts that specific "cops" on specific occasions formulate as necessary, appropriate, reasonable, or understandable. Although not always legitimated or admired, normal force is depicted as a necessary or natural response of normal police to particular situational exigencies. . . . Brutality is viewed as illegal, illegitimate, and often immoral violence, but the police draw the lines in extremely different ways and at different points [from] either the court system or the public. . . .

The article is based on approximately eighteen months of participant observation in a major urban police department referred to as the Metro City P.D. I attended the police academy with male and female recruits and later rode with individual officers in one-person cars on evening and night shifts in high crime districts.[1] The female officers described in this research were among the first 100 women assigned to the ranks of uniformed patrol as a result of a discrimination suit filed by the Justice Department and a policewoman plaintiff.

Learning to Use Normal Force

The police phrase "it's not done on the street the way that it's taught at the academy" underscores the perceived contradiction between the formal world of the police academy and the informal world of the street. This contradiction permeates the police officer's construction of his world, particularly his view of the rational and moral use of force.

In the formal world of the police academy, the recruit learns to account for force by reference to legality. He or she is issued the regulation instruments and trained to use them to subdue, control, and restrain a suspect. If threatened with great bodily harm, the officer learns that he can justifiably use deadly force and fire his revolver. Yet the recruit is taught that he cannot use his baton, jack, or gun unnecessarily to torture, maim, or kill a suspect.

When recruits leave the formal world of the academy and are assigned to patrol a district, they are introduced to an informal world in which police recognize normal as well as legal and brutal force. Through observation and instruction, rookies gradually learn to apply force and account for its use in terms familiar to the street cop. First, rookies learn to adjust their arsenals to conform to street standards. They are encouraged to buy the more powerful weapons worn by veteran colleagues as these colleagues point out the inadequacy of a wooden baton or compare their convoy jacks to vibrators. They quickly discover that their department-issued equipment marks them as new recruits. At any rate, within a few weeks, most rookies have dispensed with the wooden baton and convoy jack and substituted . . . the more powerful plastic nightstick and flat-headed slapjack.[2]

Through experience and informal instruction, the rookie also learns the street use of these weapons. In school, for example, recruits are taught to avoid hitting a person on the head or neck because it could cause lethal damage. On the street, in contrast, police conclude that they must hit wherever it causes the most damage in order to incapacitate the suspect before they themselves are harmed. New officers also learn that they will earn the respect of their veteran co-workers not by observing legal niceties in using force, but by being "aggressive" and using whatever force is necessary in a given situation.

Peer approval helps neutralize the guilt and confusion that rookies often experience when they begin to use force to assert their authority. One female officer, for example, learned she was the object of a brutality suit while listening to the news on television. At first, she felt so mortified that she hesitated to go to work and face her peers. In fact, male colleagues greeted her with a standing ovation and commented, "You can use our urinal now." In their view, any aggressive police officer regularly using normal force might eventually face a brutality suit or civilian complaint. Such accusations confirm the officer's status as a "street cop" rather than an "inside man" who doesn't engage in "real police work."

Whereas male rookies are assumed to be competent dispensers of force unless proven otherwise, women are believed to be physically weak, naturally passive, and emotionally vulnerable.[3] Women officers are assumed to be reluctant to use physical force and are viewed as incompetent "street cops" until they prove otherwise. As a result, women rookies encounter special problems in learning to use normal force in the process of becoming recognized as "real street cops." It becomes crucial for women officers to create or exploit opportunities to display their physical abilities in order to overcome sexual bias and obtain full acceptance from co-workers. As a result, women rookies are encouraged informally to act more aggressively and to display more machismo than male rookies. . . .

For a street cop, it is often a graver error to use too little force and develop a "shaky" reputation than it is to use too much force and be told to calm down. Thus officers, particularly rookies, who do not back up their partners in appropriate ways or who hesitate to use force in circumstances where it is deemed necessary are informally instructed regarding their aberrant ways. If the problematic incident is relatively insignificant and his general reputation is good, a rookie who "freezes" one time is given a second chance before becoming generally known as an untrustworthy partner. However, such incidents become the subject of degrading gossip, gossip that pressures the officer either to use force as expected or risk isolation. Such talk also informs rookies about the general boundaries of legal and normal force.

For example, a female rookie was accused of "freezing" in an incident that came to be referred to as a "Mexican standoff." A pedestrian had complained that "something funny is going on in the drugstore." The officer walked into the pharmacy where she found an armed man committing a robbery. Although he turned his weapon on her when she entered the premises, she still pulled out her gun and pointed it at him. When he ordered her to drop it, claiming that his partner was behind her with a revolver at her head, she refused and told him to drop his.[4] He refused, and the stalemate continued until a sergeant entered the drugstore and ordered the suspect to drop his gun.

Initially, the female officer thought she had acted appropriately and even heroically. She soon discovered, however, that her hesitation to shoot had brought into question her competence with some of her fellow officers. Although many veterans claimed that "she had a lot a balls" to take her gun out at all when the suspect already had a gun on her, most contended "she shoulda shot him." Other policemen confirmed that she committed a "rookie mistake"; she had failed to notice a "lookout" standing outside the store and hence had been unprepared for an armed confrontation. Her sergeant and lieutenant, moreover, even insisted that she had acted in a cowardly manner, despite her reputation as a "gung-ho cop," and cited the incident as evidence of the general inadequacy of policewomen.

In the weeks that followed, this officer became increasingly depressed and angry. She was particularly outraged when she learned that she would not receive a commendation, although such awards were commonly made for "gun pinches" of this nature. Several months later, the officer vehemently expressed the wish that she had killed the suspect and vowed that next time she would "shoot first and ask questions later." The negative sanctions of supervisors and colleagues clearly encouraged her to adopt an attitude favorable to using force with less restraint in future situations. . . .

At the same time that male and female rookies are commended for using force under appropriate circumstances, they are reprimanded if their participation in force is viewed as excessive or inappropriate. In this way, rookies are instructed that although many acts of coercion are accepted and even demanded, not everything goes. They thereby learn to distinguish between normal and brutal force. . . .

Accounting for Normal Force

Police routinely normalize the use of force by two types of accounts: excuses and justifications. . . .

EXCUSES AND NORMAL FORCE

Excuses are accounts in which police deny full responsibility for an act but recognize its inappropriateness. Excuses therefore constitute socially approved vocabularies for relieving responsibility when conduct is questionable. Police most often excuse morally problematic force by referring to emotional or physiological states that are precipitated by some circumstances of routine patrol work. These circumstances include shootouts, violent fights, pursuits, and instances in which a police officer mistakenly comes close to killing an unarmed person.

Police work in these circumstances can generate intense excitement in which the officer experiences the "combat high" and "adrenaline rush" familiar to the combat soldier.[5] Foot and car pursuits not only bring on feelings of danger and excitement from the chase, but also a challenge to official authority. As one patrolman commented about a suspect: "Yeh, he got tuned up [beaten] . . . you always tune them up after a car chase." Another officer normalized the use of force after a pursuit in these terms:

> It's my feeling that violence inevitably occurs after a pursuit. . . . The adrenaline . . . and the insult involved when someone flees increases with every foot of the pursuit. I know the two or three times that I felt I lost control of myself . . . was when someone would run on me. The further I had to chase the guy the madder I got. . . . The funny thing is the reason for the pursuit could have been something as minor as a traffic violation or a kid you're chasing who just turned on a fire hydrant. It always ends in violence. You feel obligated to hit or kick the guy just for running.

Police officers also excuse force when it follows an experience of helplessness and confusion that has culminated in a temporary loss of emotional control. This emotional combination occurs most frequently when an officer comes to the brink of using lethal force, drawing a gun and perhaps firing, only to learn there were no "real" grounds for this action. The officer may then "snap out" and hit the suspect.[6] In one such incident, for example, two policemen picked up a complainant who positively identified a suspect as a man who just tried to shoot him. Just as the officers approached the suspect, he suddenly reached for his back pocket for what the officers assumed to be a gun. One officer was close enough to jump the suspect before he pulled his hand from his pocket. As it turned out, the suspect had no weapon, having dropped it several feet away. Although he was unarmed and under control, the suspect was punched and kicked out of anger and frustration by the officer who had almost shot him.

Note that in both these circumstances—pursuit and near-miss mistaken shootings—officers would concede that the ensuing force is inappropriate and unjustifiable when considered abstractly. But although abstractly wrong, the use of force on such occasions is presented as a normal, human reaction to an extreme situation. Although not every officer might react violently in such circumstances, it is understandable and expected that some will.

SITUATIONAL JUSTIFICATIONS

Officers also justify force as normal by reference to interactional situations in which an officer's authority is physically or symbolically threatened. [In contrast to excuses, which deny responsibility for the act but recognize that the act is blameworthy, justifications accept responsibility for the act but deny that the act is blameworthy.—Ed.] In such accounts, the use of force is justified instrumentally—as a means of regaining immediate control in a situation where that control has become tenuous. Here, the officer depicts his primary intent for using force as a need to reestablish immediate control in a problematic encounter, and only incidentally as hurting or punishing the offender.

Few officers will hesitate to assault a suspect who physically threatens or attacks them. In one case, an officer was punched in the face by a prisoner he had just apprehended for allegedly attempting to shoot a friend. The incident occurred in the stationhouse, and several policemen observed the exchange. Immediately, one officer hit the prisoner in the jaw and the rest immediately joined the brawl.

Violations of an officer's property such as his car or hat may signify a more symbolic assault on the officer's authority and self, thus justifying a forceful response to maintain control. Indeed, in the police view, almost any person who verbally challenges a police officer is appropriately subject to force. . . .

On rare occasions, women officers encounter special problems in these regards. Although most suspects view women in the same way as policemen, some seem less inclined to accord female officers *de facto* and symbolic control in street encounters, and on a few occasions seem determined to provoke direct confrontations with such officers, explicitly denying their formal authority and attempting none too subtly to sexualize the encounter. Women officers, then, might use force as a resource for rectifying such insults and for establishing control over such partially sexualized interactions. Consider the following woman officer's extended account providing such situational justifications for the use of force:

> . . . I'm sitting at Second Street, Second and Nassau, writing curfews up. And this silver Thunderbird . . . blows right by a stop sign where I'm sitting. And I look up and think to myself, "Now, do I want to get involved?" And I figure, it was really belligerent doing it right in front of me. So I take off after him, put my lights on and he immediately pulls over. So he jumps out of the car. I jump

out of the car right away and I say, "I'm stopping you for that stop sign you just blew through. . . . Let me see your cards, please." Then he starts making these lip smacking noises at me everytime he begins to talk. He said, (smack) "The only way you're seeing my cards is if you lock me up and the only way you're gonna lock me up is if you chase me." And I said to him, "Well, look, I will satisfy you on one account. Now go to your car because I will lock you up. . . . And just sit in your car. I'll be right with you." He smacks his lips, turns around and goes to his car and he sits. And I call a wagon at Second and Nassau. They ask me what I have. I say, "I've got one to go." So as the wagon acknowledges, the car all of a sudden tears out of its spot. And I get on the air and say, "I'm in pursuit." And I give them a description of the car and the direction I'm going. . . . And all of a sudden he pulls over about a block and a half after I started the pursuit. So I got on the air and I said, "I got him at Second and Washington." I jumped out of my car and as I jumped out he tears away again. Now I'm ready to die of embarrassment. I have to get back on the air and say no I don't have him. So I got on the air and said, "Look, he's playing games with me now. He took off again." I said, "I'm still heading South on Second Street." He gets down to Lexington. He pulls over again. Well, this time I pulled the police car in front of him. . . . I go over to the car and I hear him lock the doors. I pull out my gun and I put it right in his window. I say, "Unlock that door." Well, he looked at the gun. He nearly liked to shit himself. He unlocked the door. I holster my gun. I go to grab his arms to pull him out and all of a sudden I realize Anne's got him. So we keep pulling him out of the car. Throw him on the trunk of his car and kept pounding him back down on the trunk. She's punching his head. I'm kicking him. Then I take out my blackjack. I jack him across the shoulder. Then I go to jack him in the head and I jack Anne's fingers. . . . The next thing they know is we're throwing him bodily into the wagon. And they said, "Did you search him?" We go to the wagon, drag him out again. Now we're tearing through his pockets throwing everything on the ground. Pick him up bodily again, threw him in. . . . So I straightened it out with the sergeant. . . . I said, "What did you want me to do? Let any citizen on the street get stopped and pull away and that's the end of it?"

In this instance, a male suspect manages to convey a series of affronts to the officer's authority. These affronts become explicitly and insultingly sexual, turning the challenge from the claim that "no cop will stop me" to the more gender specific one, "no woman cop will stop me." Resistance ups the ante until the suspect backs down in the face of the officer's drawn revolver. The force to which the culprit was then subjected is normalized through all the accounts considered to this point—it is situationally justified as a means to reestablish and maintain immediate and symbolic control in a highly problematic encounter and it is excused as a natural, collective outburst following resolution of a dangerous, tension-filled incident. And finally, it is more implicitly justified as appropriate punishment, an account building upon standard police practices for abstract justification, to which I now turn.

ABSTRACT JUSTIFICATIONS

Police also justify the use of extreme force against certain categories of morally reprehensible persons. In this case, force is not presented as an instrumental means to regain control that has been symbolically or physically threatened. Instead, it is justified as an appropriate response to particularly heinous offenders. Categories of such offenders include: cop haters who have gained notoriety as persistent police antagonizers; cop killers or any person who has attempted seriously to harm a police officer (Westley, 1970:131); sexual deviants who prey on children and "moral women"; child abusers; and junkies and other "scum" who inhabit the street. The more morally reprehensible the act is judged, the more likely the police are to depict any violence directed toward its perpetrator as justifiable. Thus a man who exposes himself to children in a playground is less likely to experience police assault than one who rapes or sexually molests a child.

"Clean" criminals, such as high-level mafiosi, white-collar criminals, and professional burglars, are rarely subject to abstract force. Nor are perpetrators of violent and nonviolent street crimes who prey on adult males, prostitutes, and other categories of persons who belong on the street.[7] Similarly, the "psycho" or demented person is perceived as so mentally deranged that he is not responsible for his acts and hence does not merit abstract, punitive force (Van Maanen, 1978:233–34).

Police justify abstract force by invoking a higher moral purpose that legitimates the violation of commonly recognized standards. In one case, for example, a nun was raped by a seventeen-year-old male adolescent. When the police apprehended the suspect, he was severely beaten and his penis put in an electrical outlet to teach him a lesson. The story of the event was told to me by a police officer who, despite the fact that he rarely supported the use of extralegal force, depicted this treatment as legitimate. Indeed, when I asked if he would have participated had he been present, he responded, "I'm Catholic. I would have participated."

Excessive Force and Peer Responses

Although police routinely excuse and justify many incidents where they or their co-workers have used extreme force against a citizen or suspect, this does not mean that on any and every occasion the officer using such force is exonerated. Indeed, the concept of normal force is useful because it suggests that there are specific circumstances under which police officers will not condone the use of force by themselves or colleagues as reasonable and acceptable. Thus, officer-recognized conceptions of normal force are subject to restrictions of the following kinds:

1. Police recognize and honor some rough equation between the behavior of the suspect and the harmfulness of the force to which it is subject. There are limits, therefore, to the degree of force that is acceptable in particular circumstances. In the following incident, for example, an officer reflects on a situation in which a "symbolic assailant" (Skolnick, 1975:45) was mistakenly subject to more force than he "deserved" and almost killed:

> One time Bill Johnson and I . . . had a particularly rude drunk one day. He was really rude and spit on you and he did all this stuff and we even had to cuff him lying down on the hard stretcher, like you would do an epileptic. . . . So we were really mad. We said let's just give him one or two shots . . . slamming on the brakes and having him roll. But we didn't use our heads . . . we heard the stretcher go nnnnnBam and then nothing. We heard nothing and we realized we had put this man in with his head to the front so when we slammed on the brakes his stretcher. . . . I guess it can roll four foot. Well, it was his head that had hit the front. . . . So, we went to Madison Street and parked. It's a really lonely area. And we unlocked the wagon and peeked in. We know he's in there. We were so scared and we look in and there's not a sound and we see blood coming in front of the wagon and think " . . . we killed this man. What am I gonna do? What am I gonna tell my family?" And to make a long story short, he was just knocked out. But boy was I scared. From then on we learned, feet first.

2. Similarly, even in cases where suspects are seen as deserving some violent punishment, this force should not be used randomly and without control. Thus, in the following incident, an officer who "snapped out" and began to beat a child abuser clearly regarded his partner's attempt to stop the beating as reasonable.

> . . . I knock on the door and a lady answers just completely hysterical. And I say, "Listen, I don't know what's going on in here," but then I hear this, just this screeching. You know. And I figure well I'm just going to find out what's going on so I just go past the lady and what's happening is that the husband had. . . . The kid was being potty trained and the way they were potty training this kid, this two-year-old boy, was that the boyfriend of this girl would pick up this kid and he would sit him down on top of the stove. It was their method of potty training. Well, first of all you think of your own kids. I mean afterwards you do. I mean I've never been this mad in my whole life. You see this little two-year-old boy seated on the top of the stove with rings around it being absolutely scalding hot. And he's saying "I'll teach you to go. . . . " It just triggered something. An uncontrollable. . . . It's just probably the most violent I ever got. Well you just grab that guy. You hit him ten, fifteen times . . . you don't know how many. You just get so mad. And I remember my partner eventually came in and grabbed me

and said, "Don't worry about it. We got him. We got him." And we cuffed him and we took him down. Yeah that was bad.

Learning these sorts of restrictions on the use of normal force and these informal practices of peer control are important processes in the socialization of newcomers. This socialization proceeds both through ongoing observation and experience and, on occasion, through explicit instruction. For example, one veteran officer advised a rookie, "The only reason to go in on a pursuit is not to get the perpetrator but to pull the cop who gets there first offa the guy before he kills him."

Conclusion

The organization of police work reflects a poignant moral dilemma: For a variety of reasons, society mandates to the police the right to use force but provides little direction as to its proper use in specific, "real life" situations. Thus, the police, as officers of the law, must be prepared to use force under circumstances in which its rationale is often morally, legally, and practically ambiguous. This fact explains some otherwise puzzling aspects of police training and socialization.

The police academy provides a semblance of socialization for its recruits by teaching formal rules for using force. . . . [T]he full socialization of a police officer takes place outside the academy as the officer moves from its idealizations to the practicalities of the street. . . .

. . . [J]ustifications and excuses . . . conventionalize but do not reform situations that are inherently charged and morally ambiguous. In this way they simultaneously preserve the self-image of police as agents of the conventional order, provide ways in which individual officers can resolve their personal doubts as to the moral status of their action and those of their colleagues, and reinforce the solidarity of the police community.

Notes

1. Nonetheless masculine pronouns are generally used to refer to the police in this article, because the Metro P.D. remained dominated by men numerically, in style, and in tone. . . .

2. Some officers also substitute a large heavy duty flashlight for the nightstick. If used correctly, the flashlight can inflict more damage than the baton and is less likely to break when applied to the head or other parts of the body.

3. As the Metro City Police Commissioner commented in an interview: "In general, they [women] are physically weaker than males. . . . I believe they would be inclined to let their emotions all too frequently overrule their good judgment . . . there are periods in their life when they are psychologically unbalanced because of physical problems that are occurring within them."

4. The woman officer later explained that she did not obey the suspect's command because she saw no reflection of the partner in the suspect's glasses and therefore assumed he was lying.

5. The combat high is a state of controlled exhilaration in which the officer experiences a heightened awareness of the world around him. Officers report that perception, smell, and hearing seem acute; one seems to stand outside oneself, and the world appears extraordinarily vivid and clear. At the same time, officers insist that they are able to think rationally and instantly translate thoughts into action; when experienced, fear is not incapacitating but instead enhances the ability to act.

6. This police experience of fear and helplessness, leading to a violent outburst, may be analogized to a parent's reaction on seeing his child almost die in an accident. Imagine a scene in which a father is walking with his six-year-old son. Suddenly, the boy runs into the street to get a red ball on the pavement. The father watches a car slam on the brakes and miss the boy by two inches. He grabs his son and smacks him on the face before he takes him in his arms and holds him. . . .

7. The categories of persons who merit violence are not unique to the police. Prisoners, criminals, and hospital personnel appear to draw similar distinctions between morally unworthy persons; on the latter, see Sudnow (1967:105).

References

Bittner, E. (1980). *The Functions of the Police in Modern Society*. Cambridge, MA: Oelgeschlager, Gunn & Hain.

Hunt, J. (forthcoming). "The development of rapport through the negotiation of gender in field work among police." *Human Organization*.

Skolnick, J. (1975). *Justice Without Trial*. New York: John Wiley.

Sudnow, D. (1967). *Passing On: The Social Organization of Dying*. Englewood Cliffs, NJ: Prentice-Hall.

Van Maanen, J. (1978). "The asshole." In P. K. Manning and J. Van Maanen (eds.), *Policing: A View from the Street*. Santa Monica, CA: Goodyear.

Westley, W. A. (1970). *Violence and the Police: A Sociological Study of Law, Custom and Morality*. Cambridge, MA: MIT Press.

41 Anybody's Son Will Do

GWYNNE DYER

Perhaps the strangest social institution is the military. A notable characteristic is how separated it is from the society that it is set up to protect. Its bases are isolated from the rest of society—like a prison, armed guards control who enters and leaves. Like a prison, the military has the power to force its members to remain for years against their will. It can even lock them behind bars if they refuse orders. Many of its members live apart from the rest of society; they shop at their own stores, and go to doctors who serve only the military. They even play in their own recreational settings—the Department of Defense operates more bowling alleys than any other organization. The most visible sign of separateness is the dress—its members proudly set themselves apart by wearing uniforms that proclaim they are *not* one of us.

The strangest characteristic that sets the military apart from the rest of us, of course, is not these things, but that their business is killing. It becomes the military's task to turn civilians—who have learned contrasting values and ways of life—into soldiers. This means that civilians must learn to become killers. How does the military accomplish this? This is the question that Dyer answers in this selection.

You think about it and you know you're going to have to kill but you don't understand the implications of that, because in the society in which you've lived murder is the most heinous of crimes . . . and you are in a situation in which it's turned the other way round. . . . When you do actually kill someone, the experience, my experience, was one of revulsion and disgust. . . .

I was utterly terrified—petrified—but I knew there had to be a Japanese sniper in a small fishing shack near the shore. He was firing in the other direction at Marines in another battalion, but I knew as soon as he picked off the people there—there was a window on our side—that he would start picking us off. And there was nobody else to go . . . and so I ran towards the shack and broke in and found myself in an empty room. . . .

There was a door which meant there was another room and the sniper was in that—and I just broke that down. I was just absolutely gripped by the fear that this man would expect me and would shoot me. But as it turned out he was in a sniper harness and he couldn't turn around fast enough. He was entangled in the harness so I shot him with a .45, and I felt remorse and shame. I can remember whispering foolishly, "I'm sorry" and then just throwing up. . . . I threw up all over myself. It was a betrayal of what I'd been taught since a child.

—William Manchester

YET HE DID KILL THE Japanese soldier, just as he had been trained to—the revulsion only came afterward. And even after Manchester knew what it was like to kill another human being, a young man like himself, he went on trying to kill his "enemies" until the war was over. Like all the other tens of millions of soldiers who had been taught from infancy that killing was wrong, and had then been sent off to kill for their countries, he was almost helpless to disobey, for he had fallen into the hands of an institution so powerful and so subtle that it could quickly reverse the moral training of a lifetime.

The whole vast edifice of the military institution rests on its ability to obtain obedience from its members even unto death—and the killing of others. It has enormous powers of compulsion at its command, of course, but all authority must be based ultimately on consent. The task of extracting that consent from its members has probably grown harder in recent times, for the gulf between the military and the civilian worlds has undoubtedly widened: Civilians no longer perceive the threat of violent death as an everyday hazard of existence, and the categories of people whom it is not morally permissible to kill have broadened to include (in peacetime) the entire human race. Yet the armed forces of every country can still take almost any young male civilian and turn him into a soldier with all the right reflexes and attitudes in only a few weeks. Their recruits usually have no more than twenty years' experience of the world, most of it as children, while the armies have had all of history to practice and perfect their techniques.

> Just think of how the soldier is treated. While still a child he is shut up in the barracks. During his training he is always being knocked about. If he makes the least mistake he is beaten, a burning blow on his body, another on his eye, perhaps his head is laid open with a wound. He is battered and bruised with flogging. On the march . . . they hang heavy loads round his neck like that of an ass.
>
> —Egyptian, ca. 1500 B.C.

> The moment I talk to the new conscripts about the homeland I strike a land mine. So I kept quiet. Instead, I try to make soldiers of them. I give them hell from morning to sunset. They begin to curse me, curse the army, curse the state. Then they begin to curse together, and become a truly cohesive group, a unit, a fighting unit.
>
> —Israeli, ca. A.D. 1970

All soldiers belong to the same profession, no matter what country they serve, and it makes them different from everybody else. They have to be different, for their job is ultimately about killing and dying, and those things are not a natural vocation for any human being. Yet all soldiers are born civilians.

The method for turning young men into soldiers—people who kill other people and expose themselves to death—is basic training. It's essentially the same all over the world, and it always has been, because young men everywhere are pretty much alike.

Human beings are fairly malleable, especially when they are young, and in every young man there are attitudes for any army to work with: the inherited values and postures, more or less dimly recalled, of the tribal warriors who were once the model for every young boy to emulate. Civilization did not involve a sudden clean break in the way people behave, but merely the progressive distortion and redirection of all the ways in which people in the old tribal societies used to behave, and modern definitions of maleness still contain a great deal of the old warrior ethic. The anarchic machismo of the primitive warrior is not what modern armies really need in their soldiers, but it does provide them with promising raw material for the transformation they must work in their recruits.

Just how this transformation is wrought varies from time to time and from country to country. In totally militarized societies—ancient Sparta, the samurai class of medieval Japan, the areas controlled by organizations like the Eritrean People's Liberation Front today—it begins at puberty or before, when the young boy is immersed in a disciplined society in which only the military values are allowed to penetrate. In more sophisticated modern societies, the process is briefer and more concentrated, and the way it works is much more visible. It is, essentially, a conversion process in an almost religious sense—and as in all conversion phenomena, the emotions are far more important than the specific ideas. . . .

Armies know this. It is their business to get men to fight, and they have had a long time to work out the best way of doing it. All of them pay lip service to the symbols and slogans of their political masters, though the amount of time they must devote to this activity varies from country to country. . . . Nor should it be thought that the armies are hypocritical—most of their members really do believe in their particular national symbols and slogans. But their secret is that they know these are not the things that sustain men in combat.

What really enables men to fight is their own self-respect, and a special kind of love that has nothing to do with sex or idealism. Very few men have died in battle, when the moment actually arrived, for the United States of America or for the sacred cause of Communism, or even for their homes and families; if they had any choice in the matter at all, they chose to die for each other and for their own vision of themselves. . . .

The way armies produce this sense of brotherhood in a peacetime environment is basic training: a feat of psychological manipulation on the grand scale which has been so consistently successful and so universal that we fail to notice it as remarkable. In countries where the army must extract its recruits in their late teens, whether voluntarily or by conscription, from a civilian environment that does not share the military values, basic training involves a brief but intense period of indoctrination whose purpose is not really to teach the recruits basic military skills, but rather to change their values and their loyalties. "I guess you could say we brainwash them a little bit," admitted a U.S. Marine drill instructor, "but you know they're good people."

The duration and intensity of basic training, and even its major emphases, depend on what kind of society the recruits are coming from, and on what sort of military organization they are going to. It is obviously quicker to train men from a martial culture than from one in which the dominant values are civilian and commercial, and easier to deal with volunteers than with reluctant conscripts. Conscripts are not always unwilling, however; there are many instances in which the army is popular for economic reasons. . . .

It's easier if you catch them young. You can train older men to be soldiers; it's done in every major war. But you can never get them to believe that they like it, which is the major reason armies try to get their recruits before they are 20. There are other reasons too, of course, like the physical fitness, lack of dependents, and economic dispensability of teenagers, that make armies prefer them, but the most important qualities teenagers bring to basic training are enthusiasm and naiveté. Many of them actively want the discipline and the closely structured environment that the armed forces will provide, so there is no need for the recruiters to deceive the kids about what will happen to them after they join.

> There is discipline. There is drill. . . . When you are relying on your mates and they are relying on you, there's no room for slackness or sloppiness. If you're not prepared to accept the rules, you're better off where you are.
> —British army recruiting advertisement, 1976

> People are not born soldiers, they become soldiers. . . . And it should not begin at the moment a new recruit is enlisted into the ranks, but rather much earlier, at the time of the first signs of maturity, during the time of adolescent dreams.
> —*Red Star* (Soviet army newspaper), 1973

Young civilians who have volunteered and have been accepted by the Marine Corps arrive at Parris Island, the Corps's East Coast facility for basic training, in a state of considerable excitement and apprehension: Most are aware that they are about to undergo an extraordinary and very difficult experience. But they do not make their own way to the base; rather, they trickle in to Charleston airport on various flights throughout the day on which their training platoon is due to form, and are held there, in a state of suppressed but mounting nervous tension, until late in the evening. When the buses finally come to carry them the 76 miles to Parris Island, it is often after midnight—and this is not an administrative oversight. The shock treatment they are about to receive will work most efficiently if they are worn out and somewhat disoriented when they arrive.

The basic training organization is a machine, processing several thousand young men every month, and every facet and gear of it has been designed with the sole purpose of turning civilians into Marines as efficiently as possible. Provided it can have total control over their bodies and their environment for approximately three months, it can practically guarantee converts. Parris Island provides that controlled environment, and the recruits do not set foot outside it again until they graduate as Marine privates 11 weeks later.

> They're allowed to call home, so long as it doesn't get out of hand—every three weeks or so they can call home and make sure everything's all right, if they haven't gotten a letter or there's a particular set of circumstances. If it's a case of an emergency call coming in, then they're allowed to accept that call; if not, one of my staff will take the message. . . .
>
> In some cases I'll get calls from parents who haven't quite gotten adjusted to the idea that their son had cut the strings—and in a lot of cases that's what they're doing. The military provides them with an opportunity to leave home but they're still in a rather secure environment.
>
> —Captain Brassington, USMC

For the young recruits, basic training is the closest thing their society can offer to a formal rite of passage, and the institution probably stands in an unbroken line of descent from the lengthy ordeals by which young males in precivilized groups were initiated into the adult community of warriors. But in civilized societies it is a highly functional institution whose product is not anarchic warriors, but trained soldiers.

Basic training is not really about teaching people skills; it's about changing them so that they can do things they wouldn't have dreamt of otherwise. It works by applying enormous physical and mental pressure to men who have been isolated from their normal civilian environment and placed in one where the only right way to think and behave is the way the Marine Corps wants them to. The key word the men who run the machine use to describe this process is *motivation*.

> I can motivate a recruit and in third phase, if I tell him to jump off the third deck, he'll jump off the third deck. Like I said before, it's a captive audience and I can train that guy; I can get him to do anything I want him to

do. . . . They're good kids and they're out to do the right thing. We get some bad kids, but you know, we weed those out. But as far as motivation—here, we can motivate them to do anything you want, in recruit training.

—USM drill instructor, Parris Island

The first three days the raw recruits spend at Parris Island are actually relatively easy, though they are hustled and shouted at continuously. It is during this time that they are documented and inoculated, receive uniforms, and learn the basic orders of drill that will enable young Americans (who are not very accustomed to this aspect of life) to do everything simultaneously in large groups. But the most important thing that happens in "forming" is the surrender of the recruits' own clothes, their hair—all the physical evidence of their individual civilian identities.

During a period of only 72 hours, in which they are allowed little sleep, recruits lay aside their former lives in a series of hasty rituals (like being shaven to the scalp) whose symbolic significance is quite clear to them even though they are quite deliberately given absolutely no time for reflection, or any hint that they might have the option of turning back from their commitment. The men in charge of them know how delicate a tightrope they are walking, though, because at this stage the recruits are still newly caught civilians who have not yet made their ultimate inward submission to the discipline of the Corps.

Forming Day One makes me nervous. You've got a whole new mob of recruits, you know, 60 or 70 depending, and they don't know anything. You don't know what kind of a reaction you're going to get from the stress you're going to lay on them, and it just worries me the first day. . . .

Things could happen, I'm not going to lie to you. Something might happen. A recruit might decide he doesn't want any part of this stuff and maybe take a poke at you or something like that. In a situation like that it's going to be a spur-of-the-moment thing and that worries me.

—USMC drill instructor

But it rarely happens. The frantic bustle of forming is designed to give the recruit no time to think about resisting what is happening to him. And so the recruits emerge from their initiation into the system, stripped of their civilian clothes, shorn of their hair, and deprived of whatever confidence in their own identity they may previously have had as 18-year-olds, like so many blanks ready to have the Marine identity impressed upon them.

The first stage in any conversion process is the destruction of an individual's former beliefs and confidence, and his reduction to a position of helplessness and need. It isn't really as drastic as all that, of course, for three days cannot cancel out 18 years; the inner thoughts and the basic character are not erased. But the recruits have already learned that the only acceptable behavior is to repress any unorthodox thoughts and to mimic the character the Marine Corps wants. Nor are they, on the whole, reluctant to do so, for they *want* to be Marines. From the moment they arrive at Parris Island, the vague notion that has been passed down for a thousand generations that masculinity means being a warrior becomes an explicit article of faith, relentlessly preached: To be a man means to be a Marine.

There are very few 18-year-old boys who do not have highly romanticized ideas of what it means to be a man, so the Marine Corps has plenty of buttons to push. And it starts pushing them on the first day of real training. The officer in charge of the formation appears before them for the first time, in full dress uniform with medals, and tells them how to become men.

> The United States Marine Corps has 205 years of illustrious history to speak for itself. You have made the most important decision in your life . . . by signing your name, your life, your pledge to the Government of the United States, and even more importantly, to the United States Marine Corps—a brotherhood, an elite unit. In 10.3 weeks you are going to become a member of that history, those traditions, this organization—if you have what it takes. . . .
>
> All of you want to do that by virtue of your signing your name as a man. The Marine Corps says that we build men. Well, I'll go a little bit further. We develop the tools that you have—and everybody has those tools to a certain extent right now. We're going to give you the blueprints, and we are going to show you how to build a Marine. You've got to build a Marine—you understand?
>
> —Captain Pingree, USMC

The recruits, gazing at him in awe and adoration, shout in unison, "Yes, sir!" just as they have been taught. They do it willingly, because they are volunteers—but even conscripts tend to have the romantic fervor of volunteers if they are only 18 years old. Basic training, whatever its hardships, is a quick way to become a man among men, with an undeniable status, and beyond the initial consent to undergo it, it doesn't even require any decisions.

> I had just dropped out of high school and I wasn't doing much on the street except hanging out, as most teenagers would be doing. So they gave me an opportunity—a recruit picked me up, gave me a good line, and said that I could make it in the Marines, that I have a future ahead of me. And since I was living with my parents, I figured that I could start my own life here and grow up a little.
>
> —USMC recruit

I like the hand-to-hand combat and . . . things like that. It's a little rough going on me, and since I have a small frame I would like to become deadly, as I would put it. I like to have them words, especially the way they've been teaching me here.

—USMC recruit (from Brooklyn), Parris Island

The training, when it starts, seems impossibly demanding physically for most of the recruits—and then it gets harder week by week. There is constant barrage of abuse and insults aimed at the recruits, with the deliberate purpose of breaking down their pride and so destroying their ability to resist the transformation of values and attitudes that the Corps intends them to undergo. At the same time, the demands for constant alertness and for instant obedience are continuously stepped up, and the standards by which the dress and behavior of the recruits are judged become steadily more unforgiving. But it is all carefully calculated by the men who run the machine, who think and talk in terms of the stress they are placing on the recruits: "We take so many c.c.'s of stress and we administer it to each man—they should be a little bit scared and they should be unsure, but they're adjusting." The aim is to keep the training arduous but just within most of the recruits' capability to withstand. One of the most striking achievements of the drill instructors is to create and maintain the illusion that basic training is an extraordinary challenge, one that will set those who graduate apart from others, when in fact almost everyone can succeed.

There has been some preliminary weeding out of potential recruits even before they begin basic training, to eliminate the obviously unsuitable minority, and some people do "fail" basic training and get sent home, at least in peacetime. The standards of acceptable performance in the U.S. armed forces, for example, tend to rise and fall in inverse proportion to the number and quality of recruits available to fill the forces to the authorized manpower levels. But there are very few young men who cannot be turned into passable soldiers if the forces are willing to invest enough effort in it.

Not even physical violence is necessary to effect the transformation, though it has been used by most armies at most times.

It's not what it was 15 years ago down here. The Marine Corps still occupies the position of a tool which the society uses when it feels like that is a resort that they have to fall to. Our society changes as all societies do, and our society felt that through enlightened training methods we could still produce the same product—and when you examine it, they're right. . . . Our 100 c.c.'s of stress is really all we need, not two gallons of it, which is what used to be. . . . In some cases with some of the younger drill instructors it was more an initiation than it was an acute test, and so we introduced extra officers and we select our drill instructors to "fine-tune" it.

—Captain Brassington, USMC

There is, indeed, a good deal of fine-tuning in the roles that the men in charge of training any specific group of recruits assume. At the simplest level, there is a sort of "good cop-bad cop" manipulation of recruits' attitudes toward those applying the stress. The three younger drill instructors with a particular serial are quite close to them in age and unremittingly harsh in their demands for ever higher performance, but the senior drill instructor, a man almost old enough to be their father, plays a more benevolent and understanding part and is available for individual counseling. And generally offstage, but always looming in the background, is the company commander, an impossibly austere and almost godlike personage.

At least these are the images conveyed to the recruits, although of course all these men cooperate closely with an identical goal in view. It works: In the end they become not just role models and authority figures, but the focus of the recruits' developing loyalty to the organization.

> I imagine there's some fear, especially in the beginning, because they don't know what to expect. . . . I think they hate you at first, at least for a week or two, but it turns to respect. . . . They're seeking discipline, they're seeking someone to take charge, 'cause at home they never got it. . . . They're looking to be told what to do and then someone is standing there enforcing what they tell them to do, and it's kind of like the father-and-son game, all the way through. They form a fatherly image of the DI whether they want to or not.
>
> —Sergeant Carrington, USMC

Just the sheer physical exercise, administered in massive doses, soon has recruits feeling stronger and more competent than ever before. Inspections, often several times daily, quickly build up their ability to wear the uniform and carry themselves like real Marines, which is a considerable source of pride. The inspections also help to set up the pattern in the recruits of unquestioning submission to military authority: Standing stock-still, staring straight ahead, while somebody else examines you closely for faults is about as extreme a ritual act of submission as you can make with your clothes on.

But they are not submitting themselves merely to the abusive sergeant making unpleasant remarks about the hair in their nostrils. All around them are deliberate reminders—the flags and insignia displayed on parade, the military music, the marching formations and drill instructors' cadenced calls—of the idealized organization, the "brotherhood" to which they will be admitted as full members if they submit and conform. Nowhere in the armed forces are the military courtesies so elaborately observed, the staffs' uniforms so immaculate (some DIs change several times a day), and the ritual aspects of military life so highly visible as on a basic training establishment.

Even the seeming inanity of close-order drill has a practical role in the conversion process. It has been over a century since mass formations of men were of any use on the battlefield, but every army in the world still drills its troops, especially during basic training, because marching in formation, with every man moving his body in the same way at the same moment, is a direct physical way of learning two things a soldier must believe: that orders have to be obeyed automatically and instantly, and that you are no longer an individual, but part of a group.

The recruits' total identification with the other members of their unit is the most important lesson of all, and everything possible is done to foster it. They spend almost every waking moment together—a recruit alone is an anomaly to be looked into at once—and during most of that time they are enduring shared hardships. They also undergo collective punishments, often for the misdeed or omission of a single individual (talking in the ranks, a bed not swept under during barracks inspection), which is a highly effective way of suppressing any tendencies toward individualism. And, of course, the DIs place relentless emphasis on competition with other "serials" in training: There may be something infinitely pathetic to outsiders about a marching group of anonymous recruits chanting, "Lift your heads and hold them high, 3313 is a-passin' by," but it doesn't seem like that to the men in the ranks.

Nothing is quite so effective in building up a group's morale and solidarity, though, as a steady diet of small triumphs. Quite early in basic training, the recruits begin to do things that seem, at first sight, quite dangerous: descend by ropes from 50-foot towers, cross yawning gaps hand-over-hand on high wires (known as the Slide for Life, of course), and the like. The common denominator is that these activities are daunting but not really dangerous: The ropes will prevent anyone from falling to his death off the rappelling tower, and there is a pond of just the right depth—deep enough to cushion a falling man, but not deep enough that he is likely to drown—under the Slide for Life. The goal is not to kill recruits, but to build up their confidence as individuals and as a group by allowing them to overcome apparently frightening obstacles.

> You have an enemy here at Parris Island. The enemy that you're going to have at Parris Island is in every one of us. It's in the form of cowardice. The most rewarding experience you're going to have in recruit training is standing on line every evening, and you'll be able to look into each other's eyes, and you'll be able to say to each other with your eyes: "By God, we've made it one more day! We've defeated the coward."
>
> —Captain Pingree

Number on deck, sir, 45 . . . highly motivated, truly dedicated, rompin',
stompin', bloodthirsty, kill-crazy United States Marine Corps recruits, SIR!

—Marine chant, Parris Island

If somebody does fail a particular test, he tends to be alone, for the hurdles are deliberately set low enough that most recruits can clear them if they
try. In any large group of people there is usually a goat: someone whose intelligence or manner or lack of physical stamina marks him for failure and contempt. The competent drill instructor, without deliberately setting up this
unfortunate individual for disgrace, will use his failure to strengthen the solidarity and confidence of the rest. When one hapless young man fell off the
Slide for Life into the pond, for example, his drill instructor shouted the usual
invective—"Well, get out of the water. Don't contaminate it all day"—and
then delivered the payoff line: "Go back and change your clothes. You're useless to your unit now."

"Useless to your unit" is the key phrase, and all the recruits know that
what it means is "useless *in battle*." The Marine drill instructors at Parris Island know exactly what they are doing to the recruits, and why. They are not
rear-echelon people filling comfortable jobs, but the most dedicated and intelligent NCOs the Marine Corps can find; even now, many of them have
combat experience. The Corps has a clear-eyed understanding of precisely
what it is training its recruits for—combat—and it ensures that those who do
the training keep that objective constantly in sight.

The DIs "stress" the recruits, feed them their daily ration of synthetic
triumphs over apparent obstacles, and bear in mind all the time that the goal
is to instill the foundations for the instinctive, selfless reactions and the fierce
group loyalty that is what the recruits will need if they ever see combat. They
are arch-manipulators, fully conscious of it, and utterly unashamed. These
kids have signed up as Marines, and they could well see combat; this is the way
they have to think if they want to live.

I've seen guys come to Vietnam from all over. They were all sorts of people
that had been scared—some of them had been scared all their life and still
scared. Some of them had been a country boy, city boys—you know, all different kinds of people—but when they got in combat they all reacted the
same—99 percent of them reacted the same. . . . A lot of it is training here at
Parris Island, but the other part of it is survival. They know if they don't conform—conform I call it, but if they don't react in the same way other people
are reacting, they won't survive. That's just it. You know, if you don't react together, then nobody survives.

—USMC drill instructor, Parris Island

When I went to boot camp and did individual combat training they said if you walk into an ambush what you want to do is just do a right face—you just turn right or left, whichever way the fire is coming from, and assault. I said, "Man, that's crazy. I'd never do anything like that. It's stupid." . . .

The first time we came under fire, on Hill 1044 in Operation Beauty Canyon in Laos, we did it automatically. Just like you look at your watch to see what time it is. We done a right face, assaulted the hill—a fortified position with concrete bunkers emplaced, machine guns, automatic weapons—and we took it. And we killed—I'd estimate probably 35 North Vietnamese soldiers in the assault, and we only lost three killed. I think it was about two or three, and about eight or ten wounded. . . .

But you know, what they teach you, it doesn't faze you until it comes down to the time to use it, but it's in the back of your head, like, What do you do when you come to a stop sign? It's in the back of your head, and you react automatically.

—USMC sergeant

Combat is the ultimate reality that Marines—or any other soldiers, under any flag—have to deal with. Physical fitness, weapons training, battle drills, are all indispensable elements of basic training, and it is absolutely essential that the recruits learn the attitudes of group loyalty and interdependency which will be their sole hope of survival and success in combat. The training inculcates or fosters all of those things, and even by the halfway point in the 11-week course, the recruits are generally responding with enthusiasm to their tasks. . . .

In basic training establishments, . . . the malleability is all one way: in the direction of submission to military authority and the internalization of military values. What a place like Parris Island produces when it is successful, as it usually is, is a soldier who will kill because that is his job.

Social Change

W HAT IMAGERY SHOULD WE USE? We are in a small, drift-
ing boat on a tumultuous sea of social change. Like a mighty wind, unpre-
dictable events swirl around us, at times seeming to sweep us away. Like an
out-of-control fire, change threatens to devour us. Change is like a bullet un-
leashed from a rifle, which pierces whatever is in its path and cannot be
stopped until its energy is spent.

Regardless of the imagery, vast social change is a basic fact of contemporary life—and this change can be ominous, threatening to cast us into the
unknown. Nothing seems to remain the same. Familiar landmarks are torn
down and replaced, seemingly overnight, by a supermarket or another of an
endless chain of fast-food outlets. Farm fields and woods are paved over as
they sprout malls and shopping centers. Computers change so rapidly that
the one you bought a year or two ago seems hopelessly out of date. Afraid of
divorce—and of making a commitment—the young postpone marriage, opt-
ing instead to take refuge in the temporariness of cohabitation.

C-cash for purchases on the Internet. A plane propelled by human muscle-
power, and another that goes around the world without refueling. "Smart
cards" to control access and security. Interactive television and virtual reality. Long distance surgery, with patient and surgeon 3,000 miles apart. A wallet computer that functions as a credit/cash card, a checkbook, a fax, and an
e-mail communicator—and also dispenses tickets for airlines and concerts,
and, not incidentally, will pop a coke out of the soda machine.

471

Although change is an essential part of today's society, it is anything but new. Twenty-five hundred years ago, Heraclitus said, "Everything flows; nothing stands still." Six hundred years later, Marcus Aurelius Antoninus wrote, "The universe is change." A more recent observer of the social scene put it this way: "The only thing constant is the certainty of change."

Social change was indeed a part of past civilizations, too, but an essential difference distinguishes those changes and what we are experiencing today. Barring catastrophe in the form of human or natural disaster, change in ancient times was slow and orderly—sometimes so slow that even over generations its effects were barely perceptible. In all societies of the world, in fact, it was routinely the case that the father passed his occupation down to his son, who, in turn, passed it on to his son, and so on. Mothers, too, passed their occupation to their daughters. The society that children lived in was practically identical to that into which their parents had been born. Although the players had changed, the basic social institutions, with their routine ways of handling things, remained the same over generations.

The contrast with our situation is stark. Most children today take it for granted that they are different from their parents—some even being amazed if they notice similarities with them. Adolescents routinely assume that their parents will not understand them, for each represents a different world. With worlds so dissimilar, it is not uncommon for a grown child visiting his or her parents, following an absence of months or even years, to find that after "catching up"—about an hour or so—they have little or nothing left to talk about. Social change has sorted them into different worlds, their particular experiences imparting contrasting orientations to life and, in effect, making them different kinds of people.

"Adapt or die" may be the maxim under which living creatures exist. Only the organisms that adapt to changing circumstances survive, and humans are no exception. Confronted with challenge, humans adapt. They change their social institutions to match changing circumstances. The effects are highly visible as people modify their outward behaviors. But the consequences are hardly limited to the external, for they also penetrate people's inner life, changing their ideas, attitudes, and beliefs, their basic orientations to the world.

In the opening selection, Robin Leidner examines what is perhaps the broadest change affecting our lives today, the *McDonaldization of society*. This means that a rationalized efficiency is taking over many of the routine aspects of everyday life. Not everyone welcomes social change, of course. Jerry Savells focuses on the Amish, analyzing how this ethno-religious group resists social change in order to maintain its traditional way of life. Laura Miller then continues this theme by looking at men's resistance to the gender integration of the military. We close the book with an analysis by Kenneth Smith and

Linda Belgrave of how people adjust to natural disaster, a particularly unwelcome form of change.

In conclusion, I would like to add that you, the reader, are the future. Certainly you cannot escape being shaped by your experiences of the vast changes occurring in society. For you to make better sense of your transformative experiences, however, I highly recommend the sociological imagination—the idea with which we began this book.

42 Over the Counter at McDonald's

ROBIN LEIDNER

Rationalization means to make things efficient. It means to set up rules that reduce unexpected events, increase control and predictability, and lead to efficient outcomes. Rationalization has become a central part of life in U.S. society. We live in a world of fast-food restaurants, TV dinners, and instant oil changes. We know what to expect when we step inside a Burger King or a Taco Bell. We know what the decor will look like, what the employees will say to us, what items will be on the menu, even what our meal will taste like. Rationalization has led to almost identical experiences whether we visit one of these restaurants in Paris or in Muncie, Indiana.

    The epitome of rationalization, however, is McDonald's. Just as Henry Ford was to the assembly line of auto production so McDonald's is to the assembly line of food production. As you read Leidner's analysis of McDonald's, think of how other aspects of your life are being "McDonaldized," such as package tours, franchised gyms and work-out centers, and, at college, machine-graded multiple choice questions. This trend toward the rationalization of everyday life—which makes human experience uniform from one situation to another—is so solid that the term *the McDonaldization of society* has been coined to refer to it.

McDonald's

No ONE EVER WALKS into a McDonald's and asks, "So, what's good today?" except satirically. The heart of McDonald's success is its uniformity and predictability. Not only is the food supposed to taste the same every day everywhere in the world, but McDonald's promises that every meal will be served quickly, courteously, and with a smile. Delivering on that promise over 20 million times a day in 54 countries is the company's colossal challenge. Its strategy for meeting that challenge draws on scientific management's most basic tenets: Find the One Best Way to do every task and see that the work is conducted accordingly.

To ensure that all McDonald's restaurants serve products of uniform quality, the company uses centralized planning, centrally designed training programs, centrally approved and supervised suppliers, automated machinery and other specially designed equipment, meticulous specifications, and systematic inspections. To provide its customers with a uniformly pleasant "McDonald's experience," the company also tries to mass produce friendliness, deference, diligence, and good cheer through a variety of socialization and social control techniques. Despite sneers from those who equate uniformity with mediocrity, the success of McDonald's has been spectacular.

McFacts

The relentless standardization and infinite replication that inspire both horror and admiration are the legacy of Ray Kroc, a salesman who got into the hamburger business in 1954, when he was 52 years old, and created a worldwide phenomenon. His inspiration was a phenomenally successful hamburger stand owned by the McDonald brothers of San Bernardino, California. He believed that their success could be reproduced consistently through carefully controlled franchises, and his hamburger business succeeded on an unprecedented scale. The basic idea was to serve a very few items of strictly uniform quality at low prices. Over the years, the menu has expanded somewhat and prices have risen, but the emphasis on strict, detailed standardization has never varied. . . .

Enforcement of McDonald's standards has been made easier over the years by the introduction of highly specialized equipment. Every company-owned store in the United States now has an "in-store processor," a computer system that calculates yields and food costs, keeps track of inventory and cash, schedules labor, and breaks down sales by time of day, product, and worker. In today's McDonald's, lights and buzzers tell workers exactly when to turn burgers or take fries out of the fat, and technologically advanced cash registers, linked to the computer system, do much of the thinking for window workers. Specially designed ketchup dispensers squirt exactly the right amount of ketchup on each burger in the approved flower pattern. The french-fry scoops let workers fill a bag and set it down in one continuous motion and help them gauge the proper serving size.

The extreme standardization of McDonald's products, and its workers, is closely tied to its marketing. The company advertises on a massive scale. In fact, McDonald's is the single most advertised brand in the world. The national advertising assures the public that it will find high standards of quality, service, and cleanliness at every McDonald's store. The intent of the strict quality-control standards applied to every aspect of running a McDonald's outlet, from proper cleaning of the bathrooms to making sure the hamburgers are served hot, is to help franchise owners keep the promises made in the company's advertising.

The image of McDonald's outlets promoted in the company's advertising is one of fun, wholesomeness, and family orientation. Kroc was particularly concerned that his stores not become teenage hangouts, since that would discourage families' patronage. To minimize their attractiveness to teenage loiterers, McDonald's stores do not have jukeboxes, video games, or even telephones.

You Deserve a Break Today: Conditions of Employment

Although McDonald's does not want teenagers to hang out on its premises, it certainly does want them to work in the stores. Almost half of its U.S. employees are under 20 years old. In recent years, as the McDonald's chain has grown faster than the supply of teenagers, the company has also tried to attract senior citizens and housewives as workers. What people in these groups have in common is a preference or need for part-time work, and therefore a dearth of alternative employment options. Because of this lack of good alternatives, and because they may have other means of support for themselves and their dependents, many people in these groups are willing to accept jobs that provide less than subsistence wages.

Traditionally, McDonald's has paid most of its employees the minimum wage, although labor shortages have now forced wages up in some parts of the country. Benefits such as health insurance and sick days are entirely lacking for crew people at most franchises. In fact, when the topic of employee benefits was introduced in a class lecture at McDonald's management training center, it turned out to refer to crew meetings, individual work-evaluation sessions, and similar programs to make McDonald's management seem accessible and fair.

The lack of more tangible benefits is linked to the organization of employment at McDonald's as part-time work. According to the manager of the franchise I studied, all McDonald's hourly employees are officially part-time workers, in that no one is guaranteed a full work week. The company's labor practices are designed to make workers bear the costs of uncertainty based on fluctuation in demand. McDonald's places great emphasis on having no more crew people at work at any time than are required by customer flow at that period, as measured in half-hour increments. Most workers therefore have fluctuating schedules, and they are expected to be flexible about working late or leaving early depending on the volume of business.

McDonald's wants both managers and workers to dedicate themselves to the values summed up in its three-letter corporate credo, "QSC." Quality, service, and cleanliness are the ends that the company's thousands of rules and specifications are intended to achieve. Kroc promised his customers QSC, and he believed firmly that if, at every level of the organization, McDonald's workers were committed to providing higher quality food, speedier service, and cleaner surroundings than the competition, the success of the enterprise was assured. McDonald's extraordinarily elaborate training programs are designed both to teach McDonald's procedures and standards and to instill and enforce corporate values.

Kroc approached his business with a zeal and dedication that even he regarded as religious: "I've often said that *I believe in God, family, and McDonald's—and in the office that order is reversed.*" Throughout the organization, Kroc is still frequently quoted and held up as a model, and nowhere is his ongoing influence more apparent than at Hamburger University.

Taking Hamburgers Seriously: Training Managers

McDonald's main management training facility is located on 80 beautifully landscaped acres in Oak Brook, Illinois, a suburb of Chicago. Its name, Hamburger University, captures the thoroughness and intensity with which McDonald's approaches management training, and it also suggests the comic possibilities of immersion in McDonald's corporate world. The company tries to produce managers "with ketchup in their veins," a common McDonald's phrase for people who love their work, take pride in it, and are extraordinarily hardworking, competitive, and loyal to McDonald's. A line I heard frequently at Hamburger U. was, "We take hamburgers very seriously here." Nothing I saw called this fixity of purpose into doubt.

Ensuring uniformity of service and products in its far-flung empire is a major challenge for McDonald's. In each McDonald's store, in regional training centers, and at Hamburger University, crew people, managers, and franchisees learn that there is a McDonald's way to handle virtually every detail of the business and that doing things differently means doing things wrong. Training begins in the stores, where crew people are instructed using materials provided by the corporation and where managers prepare for more advanced training. Management trainees and managers seeking promotion work with their store managers to learn materials in manuals and workbooks provided by the corporation. When they have completed the manual for the appropriate level, they are eligible for courses taught in regional training centers and at Hamburger University: the Basic Operations Course, the Intermediate

Operations Course, the Applied Equipment Course, and, finally, the Advanced Operations Course, taught only at Hamburger University. Altogether, the full training program requires approximately six hundred to one thousand hours of work. It is required of everyone who wishes to own a McDonald's store, and it is strongly recommended for all store managers. By the time trainees get to Hamburger University for the Advanced Operations Course, they have already put in considerable time working in a McDonald's store—two to three and a half years, on average—and have acquired much detailed knowledge about McDonald's workings.

The zeal and competence of franchisees and managers are of special concern to McDonald's, since they are the people responsible for daily enforcement of corporate standards. Their training therefore focuses as much on building commitment and motivation as on extending knowledge of company procedures. In teaching management skills, McDonald's also works on the personalities of its managers, encouraging both rigid adherence to routines and, somewhat paradoxically, personal flexibility. Flexibility is presented as a virtue both because the company wants to minimize resistance to adopting McDonald's ways of doing things and to frequent revision of procedures, and because managers must provide whatever responsiveness to special circumstances the system has, since crew people are allowed virtually no discretion. Hamburger University therefore provides a large dose of personal-growth cheerleading along with more prosaic skills training. . . .

The curriculum of the Advanced Operating Course includes inculcation with pride in McDonald's. Sessions are devoted to McDonald's history and McDonald's dedication to ever-improving QSC. Lectures are sprinkled with statistics attesting to McDonald's phenomenal success. Students hear the story of Ray Kroc's rise to wealth and prominence, based on his strength of character and willingness to work hard, and are assigned his autobiography, *Grinding It Out*. Kroc is quoted frequently in lectures, and students are encouraged to model themselves on him. They are told repeatedly that they have all proven themselves "winners" by getting as far as they have at McDonald's. The theme throughout is "We're the best in the world, we know exactly what we're doing, but our success depends on the best efforts of every one of you."

About 3,500 students from all over the world attend classes at Hamburger University each year. Those who complete the course receive diplomas proclaiming them Doctors of Hamburgerology. The course lasts two weeks and is extremely rigorous. Class time is about evenly divided between work in the labs and lectures on store operations and personnel management. In the labs, trainees learn the mechanics of ensuring that McDonald's food is of consistent quality and its stores in good working order. They learn to check the equipment and maintain its properly so that fries cook at precisely the right temperature, shakes are mixed to just the right consistency, and ice cubes are uniform. "Taste of Quality" labs reinforce McDonald's standards for food quality. For instance, in a Condiments Lab, trainees are taught exactly how to store vegetables and sauces, what the shelf lives of these products are, and how they should look and taste. Samples of "McDonald's quality" Big Mac Special Sauce are contrasted with samples that have been left too long unrefrigerated and should be discarded. The importance of serving only food that meets McDonald's standards is constantly emphasized and, a trainer pointed out, "McDonald's has standards for everything, down to the width of the pickle slices." . . .

LEARNING THE JOB

As a manager at Hamburger University explained to me, the crew training process is how McDonald's standardization is maintained, how the company ensures that Big Macs are the same everywhere in the world. The McDonald's central administration supplies franchisees with videotapes and other materials for use in training workers to meet the company's exacting specifications. The company produces a separate videotape for each job in the store, and it encourages franchisees to keep their tape libraries up-to-date as product specifications change. The Hamburger University professor who taught the Advanced Operating Course session on training said that, to keep current, franchisees should be buying 10 or 12 tapes a year. For each work station in the store, McDonald's also has a "Station Operation Checklist" (SOC), a short but highly detailed job description that lays out exactly how the job should be done: how much ketchup and mustard go on each kind of hamburger, in what sequence the products customers order are to be gathered, what arm motion is to be used in salting a batch of fries, and so on. . . .

THE ROUTINE

McDonald's had routinized the work of its crews so thoroughly that decision making had practically been eliminated from the jobs. As one window worker told me, "They've tried to break it down so that it's almost idiot-proof." Most of the workers agreed that there was little call for them to use their own judgment on the job, since there were rules about everything. If an unusual problem arose, the workers were supposed to turn it over to a manager.

Many of the noninteractive parts of the window workers' job had been made idiot-proof through automation. The soda machines, for example, automatically dispensed the proper amount of beverage for regular, medium, and large cups. Computerized cash registers performed a variety of functions handled elsewhere by human waitresses, waiters, and cashiers, making some kinds of skills and knowledge unnecessary. As a customer gave an order, the window worker simply pressed the cash register button labeled with the name of the selected product. There was no need to write the orders down, because the buttons lit up to indicate which products had been selected. Nor was there any need to remember prices, because the prices were programmed into the machines. Like most new cash registers, these added the tax automatically and told workers how much change customers were owed, so the window crew did not need to know how to do those calculations. The cash registers also helped regulate some of the crew's interactive work by reminding them to try to increase the size of each sale. For example, when a customer ordered a Big Mac, large fries, and a regular Coke, the cash register buttons for cookies, hot apple pies, ice cream cones, and ice cream sundaes would light up, prompting the worker to suggest dessert. It took some skill to operate the relatively complicated cash register, as my difficulties during my first work shift made clear, but this organizationally specific skill could soon be acquired on the job.

In addition to doing much of the workers' thinking for them, the computerized cash registers made it possible for managers to monitor the crew members' work and the store's inventory very closely. For example, if the number of Quarter Pounder with Cheese boxes gone did not match the number of Quarter Pounders with Cheese sold or accounted for as waste, managers might suspect that workers were giving away or taking food. Managers could easily tell which workers had brought in the most money during a given interval and who was doing the best job of persuading customers to buy a particular item. The computerized system could also complicate what would otherwise have been simple customer requests, however. For example, when a man who had not realized the benefit of ordering his son's food as a Happy Meal came back to the counter to ask whether his little boy could have one of the plastic beach pails the Happy Meals were served in, I had to ask a manager what to do, since fulfilling the request would produce a discrepancy between the inventory and the receipts. Sometimes the extreme systematization can induce rather than prevent idiocy, as when a window worker says she cannot serve a cup of coffee that is half decaffeinated and half regular because she would not know how to ring up the sale.

The interactive part of window work is routinized through the Six Steps of Window Service and also through rules aimed at standardizing attitudes and demeanors as well as words and actions. The window workers were taught that they represented McDonald's to the public and that their attitudes were therefore an important component of service quality. Crew people could be reprimanded for not smiling, and often were. The window workers were supposed to be cheerful and polite at all times, but they were also told to be themselves while on the job. McDonald's does not want its workers to seem like robots, so part of the emotion work asked of the window crew is that they act naturally. "Being yourself" in this situation meant behaving in a way that did not seem stilted. Although workers had some latitude to go beyond the script, the short, highly schematic routine obviously did not allow much room for genuine self-expression.

McDonald's window workers' routines were not intended to give them much leverage over customers' behavior, however. The window workers interacted only with people who had already decided to do business with McDonald's and who therefore did not need to be persuaded to take part in the service interaction. Furthermore, almost all customers were familiar enough with McDonald's routines to know how they were expected to behave. For instance, I never saw a customer who did not know that she or he was supposed to come up to the counter rather than sit down and wait to be served. This customer training was accomplished through advertising, spatial design, customer experience, and the example of other customers.

Additional cues about expected customer behavior are provided by the design of the restaurants. For example, the entrances usually lead to the service counter, not to the dining area, making it unlikely that customers will fail to realize that they should get in line, and the placement of waste cans makes clear that customers are expected to throw out their own trash. Most important, the majority of customers have had years of experience with McDonald's, as well as with other fast-food restaurants that have similar arrangements. The company estimates that the average customer visits a McDonald's 20 times a year and it is not uncommon for a customer to come in several times per week. For many customers, then, ordering at McDonald's is as routine an interaction as it is for the window worker.

Not surprisingly, then, most customers at the McDonald's I studied knew what was expected of them and tried to play their part well. They sorted themselves into lines and gazed up at the menu boards while waiting to be served. They usually gave their orders in the conventional sequence: burgers or other entrees, french fries or other side orders, drinks, and desserts. Hurried customers with savvy might order an item "only if it's in the bin," that is, ready to be served. Many customers prepared carefully so that they could give their orders promptly when they got to the counter. This preparation sometimes became apparent when a worker interrupted to ask, "What kind of dressing?" or "Cream and sugar?", flustering customers who could not deliver their orders as planned.

McDonald's routines work most efficiently when all customers accept their products exactly as they are usually prepared; indeed, the whole business is based on this premise. Since, however, some people give special instructions for customized products, such as "no onions," the routine allows for these exceptions. At the franchise I studied, workers could key the special requests into their cash registers, which automatically printed out "grill slips" with the instructions for the grill workers to follow. Under this system, the customer making the special order had to wait for it to be prepared, but the smooth flow of service for other customers was not interrupted. Another type of routine difficulty was customer dissatisfaction with food quality. Whenever a customer had a complaint about the food—cold fries, dried-out burger—window workers were authorized to supply a new product immediately without consulting a supervisor.

These two kinds of difficulties—special orders and complaints about food—were the only irregularities window workers were authorized to handle. The subroutines increased the flexibility of the service system, but they did not increase the workers' discretion, since procedures were in place for dealing with both situations. All other kinds of demands fell outside the window crew's purview. If they were faced with a dispute about money, an extraordinary request, or a furious customer, workers were instructed to call a manager; the crew had no authority to handle such problems.

Given the almost complete regimentation of tasks and preemption of decision making, does McDonald's need the flexibility and thoughtfulness of human workers? As the declining supply of teenagers and legislated increases in the minimum wage drive up labor costs, it is not surprising that McDonald's is experimenting with electronic replacements. So far, the only robot in use handles behind-the-scenes work rather than customer interactions. ARCH (Automated Restaurant Crew Helper) works in a Minnesota McDonald's where it does all the frying and lets workers know when to prepare sandwich buns, when supplies are running low, and when fries are no longer fresh enough to sell. Other McDonald's stores (along with Arby's and Burger King units) are experimenting with a touch-screen computer system that lets customers order their meals themselves, further curtailing the role of the window worker.

Overview

McDonald's pioneered the routinization of interactive service work and remains an exemplar of extreme standardization. Innovation is not discouraged at McDonald's; the company favors experimentation, at least among managers and franchisees. Ironically, though, "the object is to look for new, innovative ways to create an experience that is exactly the same no matter what McDonald's you walk into, no matter where it is in the world." Thus, when someone in the field comes up with a good idea—and such McDonald's

success stores as the Egg McMuffin and the Big Mac were store-level inspi-
rations—the corporation experiments, tests, and refines the idea and finally
implements it in a uniform way systemwide.

McDonald's . . . does promise uniform products and consistent service,
and to provide them the company has broken down virtually every task required to run a store into detailed routines with clear instructions and standards. For those routines to run smoothly, conditions must be relatively
predictable, so McDonald's tries to control as many contingencies as possible, including the attitudes and behavior of workers, managers, and customers.
The company uses a wide array of socialization and control techniques to ensure that these people are familiar with McDonald's procedures and willing
to comply with them.

Most McDonald's work is organized as low-paying, low-status, part-time
jobs that give workers little autonomy. Almost every decision about how to do
crew people's tasks has been made in advance by the corporation, and many
of the decisions have been built into the stores' technology. Why use human
workers at all, if not to take advantage of the human capacity to respond to circumstances flexibly? McDonald's does want to provide at least a simulacrum
of the human attributes of warmth, friendliness, and recognition. For that
reason, not only worker's movements but also their words, demeanor, and attitudes are subject to managerial control.

Although predictability is McDonald's hallmark, not all factors can be
controlled by management. One of the most serious irregularities that store
management must deal with is fluctuation in the flow of customers, both expected and unexpected. Since personnel costs are the most manipulable variable affecting a store's profitability, managers want to match labor power to
consumer demand as exactly as possible. They do so by paying all crew people by the hour, giving them highly irregular hours based on expected sales—
sometimes including split shifts—and sending workers home early or keeping
them late as conditions require. In other words, the costs of uneven demand
are shifted to workers whenever possible. Since most McDonald's crew people cannot count on working a particular number of hours at precisely scheduled times, it is hard for them to make plans based on how much money they
will earn or exactly what times they will be free. Workers are pressured to be
flexible in order to maximize the organization's own flexibility in staffing levels. In contrast, of course, flexibility in the work process itself is minimized.

Routinization has not made the crew people's work easy. Their jobs, although highly structured and repetitive, are often demanding and stressful.
Under these working conditions, the organization's limited commitment
to workers, as reflected in job security, wages, and benefits, makes the task
of maintaining worker motivation and discipline even more challenging. A

variety of factors, many orchestrated by the corporation, keeps McDonald's crew people hard at work despite the limited rewards. Socialization into McDonald's norms, extremely close supervision (both human and electronic), individual and group incentives, peer pressure, and pressure from customers all play their part in getting workers to do things the McDonald's way.

Because franchisees and store-level managers are responsible for enforcing standardization throughout the McDonald's system, their socialization includes a more intensive focus on building commitment to and pride in the organization than does crew training. In fact, it is the corporate attempt at transforming these higher-level McDonald's people by making them more loyal, confident, flexible, and sensitive to others, as well as more knowledgeable about company procedures, that makes the extreme rigidity of the crew training workable. The crew people do not have to be trusted with decision-making authority, because all unusual problems are referred to managers. Their more extensive training gives them the knowledge and attitudes to make the kinds of decisions the corporation would approve. . . . In addition to thorough socialization, McDonald's managers and franchisees are subjected to close corporate oversight. Every aspect of their stores' operations is rated by corporate staff, and they are sanctioned accordingly.

Despite elaborate socialization and social controls, McDonald's stores do not, of course, carry out every corporate directive exactly as recommended. In the store I studied, managers did not always provide their workers with the mandated support and encouragement, crew trainers did not always follow the Six Steps of Window Service with the required eye contact and smile. There were many kinds of pressures to deviate from corporate standards. Nonetheless, the benefits of standardization should not be underestimated. As every Durkheimian knows, clear rules and shared standards provide support and coherence as well as constraint. Although some aspects of the routines did strike the participants as overly constraining, undignified, or silly, the approved routines largely worked.

Obtaining the cooperation of workers and managers is not enough to ensure the smooth functioning of McDonald's relatively inflexible routines. Customers must be routinized as well. Not only do customers have to understand the service routine and accept the limited range of choices the company offers, they also must be willing to do some kinds of work that are done for them in conventional restaurants, including carrying food to the table and throwing out their trash. Experience, advertising, the example set by other customers, and clear environmental cues familiarize customers with McDonald's routines, and most want to cooperate in order to speed service.

43 Social Change Among the Amish

JERRY SAVELLS

With change in contemporary society so common, and so extensive, how is it possible to hold it back? Most of us are engulfed in social change so vast that it sweeps over us like a tide. Like it or not, we have little choice but to adapt. Isn't this the situation for everyone who lives in an industrialized or post-industrialized society? Vast changes occur, and rapidly so. Our only choice seems to be how to adapt.

But not so for everybody. The Amish are an outstanding exception. This group of people, who broke from the Swiss-German Mennonite church in the late 1600s and settled in Pennsylvania around 1727, can now be found in about twenty states and Ontario, Canada. About 75 percent, however, live in just three states: Pennsylvania, Ohio, and Indiana. To protect their values, the Amish strategically control change. They maintain customs of dress, music, transportation, and morality from the 1600s and continue to reject "worldly ways." How do they manage to resist such pressure? That is the focus of Savells' article.

THE AUTHOR VISITED EIGHT Amish communities in six states from 1982 to 1986: Berne and Milroy, Indiana; Ethridge, Tennessee; Intercourse and Bird-in-Hand, Pennsylvania; Kalona, Iowa; Plain City, Ohio; and Montezuma, Georgia. Face-to-face interviews were conducted with a select number of the local Amish population and some of the non-Amish population who have frequent contact with the Amish, i.e., local merchants who sell to the Amish, craftpersons, farmers, mail carriers, drivers of the local milk trucks who travel to Amish farms almost daily, and others. A structured twelve-page questionnaire has been used to collect research data using a stratified random sample selected from the New American Almanac (1983) and the Ohio Amish Directory (1981). At this time, 130 questionnaires and/or personal interviews have been completed with selected Amish families. An additional fifty interviews have also been completed among so-called "conservative Mennonite" families for future comparisons.

Although the sample is small, it is encouraging since the Old Order Amish have spurned many efforts from the scientific community to investigate their lifestyle. This particular effort gave new meaning to the term "field research," since it represents approximately 6,500 miles of driving, spread over thirty months.

The Amish interviewees were polite and cordial, but they typically do not welcome outsiders intruding into their lives. They were both retiring and private in their demeanor, since they have not been socialized to desire interaction with strangers. Their lifestyle and religion promote voluntary isolation and this has been a major obstacle to anyone intent on collecting research data via personal interviews. Since the religious concerns of the Amish hold top priority, they would not engage intentionally in any activity that would have the potential of embarrassing members in the same church district.

Sociological Considerations

A brief visit to the public library will reinforce the observation that the Amish cherish many social values once widely embraced in our agrarian society of the Colonial period—values which are largely the antithesis of those that emerged in a modern urban, industrialized society. The Amish typically emphasize the importance of humility, modesty, strong obedience to God, and social conformity; they abhor pride, social snobbery, individualism, and winning through competition. Family bonds and their faith are indeed the cornerstones of the Amish lifestyle.

Unfortunately, what limited information is available to the lay public about the Old Order Amish is often sensationalized and distorted. Yet, there is a distinct feeling of "separateness" and "difference" with numerous references to their horse-and-buggy transportation, somewhat drab clothing, and their aloofness (or overt resistance) to those things considered "trendy" or fashionable.

The Amish are very ethnocentric with a strong sense of social solidarity. There is a consciousness-of-kind evident in their thinking and quick sanctions directed toward the non-believer or those displaying evidence of weakness in their faith. Indeed, some sociologists might argue that the Amish practice of insularity—with a limited tolerance of any deviation—is a major reason why they have survived as a model of the extended family of the past.

In his professional writing, journalist Alvin Toffler has pointed out the disastrous consequences of modern materialism, self-serving lifestyles, hedonistic behavior, the transience and rootlessness of this culture, and extreme emphasis upon competition, money, and careerism to determine one's self-worth. The latter suggest experiences both alien and repulsive to Amish tradition; they abhor the concept of personal achievement rather than seeking to express God's will, the modern habit of "powerbrokering" to gain social advantages, and mutual manipulation. . . . Social change is evident—but carefully controlled and monitored. They work to preserve traditions of the past, emphasize the importance of humility and divine guidance in controlling their own destiny, and maintain a strong posture of serving God rather than the interests of humanity.

An Operational Definition of Change

The Amish do not live within a social vacuum. They are surrounded by accelerating currents of social, political, and economic changes which directly influence their quality of life. One reasonably expects the Amish to be vulnerable to pressures toward modernization. For example, many have been asked to sell their land for commercial development at inflated prices. The changing economic climate in these eight communities and the frustration of competing in a money market where "megabucks" and agri-business threaten the small farmer are having a definite impact upon the Amish way of life.

Amish farmers and the future of their children are often adversely affected by soaring land prices, and the foreign trade imbalance can mean a restricted market for some of their farm exports. Furthermore, when the Amish farmer needs to borrow money for spring planting, the interest rate at the local bank can be especially painful for the small farmer with a limited cash flow.

The Amish are forced to compete in a "money market" where agribusiness and the profit motive often threaten some of their most cherished values. For example, our society promotes maximum efficiency, quality control through standardization, the accumulation of capital or wealth, competition among workers for career advancement, and the merits of mass production—basic trends essentially alien to the Amish pursuit of "devotedness, simplicity, and peace."

The Amish strongly advocate the "therapeutic value of real work." They believe that physical labor is good for mind, body, and soul in keeping with the biblical admonition of earning one's bread by the sweat of one's brow. Their work is labor-intensive, in contrast to the national marketplace dominated by the forces of technology and profit margins. Thus, the Amish do not view every new labor-saving device as desirable or progressive. . . .

Since life in any Amish community is ongoing, it is not possible or practical to totally isolate units of analysis, i.e., families, without the influence of outside variables. The Amish do not constitute an experimental group in a laboratory situation. Hence, one must be careful not to treat all indicators of social change as evidence of modernity. Some changes may be basically unique to one church district or community, and cannot be considered universal to all Amish. For example, the New Order Amish in both Kalona and Intercourse have accepted the practice of having closer contact with the outside world; some own cottage industries that cater to tourists and some have given their business cards to this researcher. In many Old Order communities this behavior would be unacceptable.

Pressures That Influence Modernization

The five major social institutions—family, religion, economics, education, and politics—were studied in this sample of Amish interviewees as an ethnographic method to identify and document patterns of modernity. Caution is both recommended and prudent to avoid the pitfalls of making global generalizations regarding the Amish lifestyle, since rules of behavior may vary among church districts or regions. The Amish define the behavioral expectations and boundaries of their communities through the *Ordnung*, the official rules of the Amish community. Any member found to have disobeyed the *Ordnung* would be subject to *Meidung*, or shunning. It is a measure of social and religious control still considered an acceptable practice by over eighty percent of the respondents in this study. This has the avowed purpose of encouraging the offender to seek forgiveness from God and other members of the church district as quickly as possible.

FAMILY

This institution is still greatly cherished by the Amish. It is not unusual to see three generations living together in either of the eight research sites. The average Amish family in this sample had seven children, but this researcher talked with some Amish families that had as many as thirteen children. Family size would appear to be more a reflection of age and economic security than sheer desire, since almost all Amish parents profess to want large families. Modern means of contraception are forbidden, unless medically prescribed to protect the health of the mother.

Several Amish parents were concerned that economic factors beyond their control represent a serious challenge to their children and may cause many of their youth to accept employment in occupations provided by outsiders. In Milroy, Indiana, several of the young married males commuted to Indianapolis with the assistance of a non-Amish driver to work as carpenters in the building industry—a situation that forces them to accommodate the expectations of a non-Amish employer. Being away from hearth and home was clearly not their first choice; it reduces the opportunities and time to share family activities. The subtle pressures of this experience can undermine cherished Amish values in the name of economic survival.

Amish parents prefer that their families remain self-supporting, since the daily sharing of work assignments tends to give prolonged contact between parent and child, with a "solidifying effect." The Amish still grow much of their food, provide for their own energy needs, and assume responsibility for their own well-being, rather than relying upon insurance companies, welfare programs, or Social Security to shield them from the hazards of life.

To help preserve this family-centered focus, Amish parents are careful to shield their children from the information explosion of our technological society—particularly as it is disseminated by the mass media and in the public schools. However, where outside employment is essential for survival, accommodation may become necessary through learning new skills or pursuing an advanced education.

The Amish family is still strongly patriarchal. The women's liberation movement has made very few incursions into any of these eight Amish communities. However, Amish women today are by no means totally subservient in a traditional sense. This researcher discovered that Amish women in some church districts can accept modest change without severe reprisals or shunning. For example, in Berne, it was a common practice for Amish women to use polyester cloth rather than 100 percent cotton for their family's clothing. Also, many of these clothes are now purchased, rather than handsewn. Some of the Amish wives in Berne used Mary Kay cosmetics, but only the creams, not the make-up. The latter is considered too "worldly."

RELIGION

The Amish in this sample show some gradual change in their religious practices. Over ten percent of the respondents had changed their religious preference from Old Order to New Order within the context of one generation. This change will definitely have a ripple effect for their children, grandchildren, and great-grandchildren. . . .

The Old Order Amish prohibit ownership of automobiles, telephones, and electricity in the home. However, farm tractors are now being used by the New Order Amish in some areas; in Kalona, tractors were acceptable if they had steel wheels, not rubber tires. The adoption of the latter would create too much mobility.

In both Plain City and Intercourse, diesel generators are now considered an acceptable innovation to supply the barn (not the house) with electricity.

The Amish dairy farmer—like all other dairy farmers—must meet state health standards regarding proper refrigeration of milk which is sold commercially. Hence, it is very difficult to pinpoint where the Old Order Amish religious practices actually end and their lifestyle begins since the two are often "one and the same."

A few of the Amish in Berne are now beginning to use cameras, especially to photograph their children, a practice that would have brought immediate censure a few years ago. Even when this practice is known to other family members, it is regarded as a taboo topic for everyday conversation. Most of the Old Order Amish interviewed in Berne still believe that the Bible forbids taking "graven images" of persons.

ECONOMIC CHANGES

The economic security in some of the families interviewed appeared to be more fragile than that of previous generations. Wherever possible parents are still subdividing their farms so that their children will have the chance to enjoy the fruit of their labor in farming. However, with a shortage of affordable and available land for farming, the younger generation has found itself increasingly dependent upon ties with the non-Amish sector of the local economy. In Berne and Intercourse, some of the local Amish men work in craft-related industries, such as factories that manufacture furniture (mostly handcrafted), coal or wood burning stoves, and carriages. In Kalona some of the Amish girls work in a local cheese factory that purchases the bulk milk produced on Amish farms. The waitresses in some of the local restaurants are also members of the local Amish community.

This trend toward outside employment leaves the Amish especially vulnerable to forces of economic recession and a stagnant national economy. Since the Old Order Amish prohibit their members from pursuing an advanced education which would make them more competitive in the national job market, they are often underskilled in jobs that require moderate levels of technological sophistication.

The Amish are also forbidden to accept employment where joining a labor union is a condition of the workplace; thus, they have minimal job security in a formal sense. However, the Amish in this sample remained cheerful and optimistic that God would provide for their daily needs.

EDUCATION

As one moves from the environment of the Old Order Amish to the New Order Amish, one expects that the number of years of formal education might increase with each successive generation. There is a definite trend in that direction, since some of the New Order Amish want to develop marketable skills at a trade school or by taking correspondence courses. In Montezuma this researcher interviewed a young female from a New Order Amish family who is a registered nurse.

The Old Order Amish still maintain their own schools in most of the communities studied. In Berne the Old Order Amish can send their children to the eighth grade in an Amish school where funds for operating the school are provided by the parents of the children who attend, and an Amish teacher is provided, or they are permitted to send their children to a public school in Berne—only through the ninth grade.

Very few of the children in Old Order Amish families remain in school after reaching age sixteen—the age at which they can quit according to most state laws. In order to comply with legal requirements some Amish children voluntarily repeat the ninth grade—a sacrifice to the expectations of their Amish parents.

One Old Order Amish mother of several children indicated that she wanted her sons and daughters to consider going to college, preferably a Mennonite college, where they could receive training to become a member of a "noble" profession. Then they could serve the Amish community directly in professions such as teaching, and medical or veterinary practice.

This researcher found that most of the Amish adults were reasonably well informed about news events on a global scale. Some Amish families subscribe to both *The Budget*, an Amish-related newspaper, and a local or regional newspaper. Some have subscriptions to such mass circulation magazines as *Time*, *Newsweek*, *U.S. News and World Report*, *Reader's Digest*, and *National Geographic*. Most of the Amish adults do travel out-of-state to visit relatives and for recreation. In Montezuma, one respondent had recently returned from a trip to Australia.

POLITICS

The Old Order Amish in each of these eight communities do not permit their members to pursue or hold public office. To say that the Old Order Amish are politically uninvolved is not accurate. For example, they have petitioned the Congress of the United States to be exempt from payment of Social Security taxes since they do not allow their members to collect Social Security benefits. They have also sought a favorable hearing in the courts to have their children exempt from both mandatory attendance at public secondary schools and conscription into the military service.

The Old Order Amish in this sample showed an aloofness to affiliation with either major political party. Less than fifteen percent of the male interviewees had voted in either the 1980 or 1984 United States presidential election, when one of the most conservative candidates in recent history was representing the Republican Party. The Amish fear that politics with either party would certainly invite reprisals from the opposite party. Thus, it is in their best interest to remain neutral—a strong statement for the separation of church and state.

MODERNIZATION

This researcher found that the majority of the social changes that are occurring in these eight Amish communities are the result of very careful, selective, conscious deliberation, i.e., planned change. . . . One respondent added a word of caution regarding their non-use of so-called modern technology: "We do not feel that electricity, the telephone, and the automobile are evil in themselves; rather, our non-use helps us to keep from being drawn into the mainstream of the world."

Thomas Foster, a respected scholar of the Old Order Amish, has suggested that one of the most significant factors reinforcing Amish self-sufficiency is their reliance upon appropriate technologies that complement their lifestyle and religious beliefs, i.e., their sustained, practical use of human labor and power from wind, water, horses, wood, and the sun. These small-scale, labor-intensive technologies greatly reduce the need for large capital investments while keeping a lid on operating costs compared to their non-Amish peers. Foster maintains that in Ohio, for example, the Old Order Amish can earn profits on 75 to 150 acres of land at a time when Ohio's non-Amish farmers, who use diesel tractors and other costly equipment, have difficulty making a decent profit on acreage twice as large.

Social Change Among the Amish

Change has been regarded as neither evil nor good among the Amish. It can work for betterment, or it can create havoc. The Amish perceive that much of what is regarded as "modern" or "progress" by contemporary standards remains a source of temptation for their young, and potential conflict and disharmony for their communities if not kept at a proper distance. For example, the Amish do not believe electricity, telephones, and driving an automobile are inherently evil, but they realize that these so-called modern conveniences would alter the Amish lifestyle and that of future generations. The effects of this technology, e.g., high mobility with an automobile, would offer too much temptation and less concern for maintaining tradition.

Simply speaking, the Amish prefer not to become dependent upon these inventions, but prefer to maintain a quiet and simple life unfettered with the high-level complications of the modern world. Some outsiders feel the Amish have essentially avoided the acceptance of social change in order to maintain the pursuit of a Nirvana or heaven on earth. The Amish, on the other hand, rarely convey that they feel cheated by denying themselves in this life. . . .

Historians and sociologists have been aware that in other historical periods, religious ideology and practice have fueled powerful motivations for creating change—as seen in the kinship between the growth of Protestantism and industrialism in the Western World. Yet, the Amish have cited their religion as one of the most important reasons why they have essentially and successfully avoided much of the social change identified with the Industrial Revolution. Change is *not* welcome if it adversely affects their religious beliefs, their family stability, their nonresistant lifestyle, or if it creates too much conflict.

Where change has been accepted—and this can be measured figuratively more in inches than yards—it has ordinarily been seen as either an improvement of their ability to provide economically for their families or as reasonable for public safety and the public good. Two examples of the latter were the adoption in some states of batteries on horsedrawn transportation to provide flashing taillights at night as a safety precaution, and the adoption in some districts of diesel generators in their barns, primarily to cool and agitate milk in bulk tanks. To the Amish this is a preference, not a paradox. If it confuses outsiders, they do not feel a need to explain.

Although the vast majority of my sample had routine (daily or weekly) contact with outsiders, most felt that the average outsider did not understand their Amish lifestyle or values and the religious justification for the way they prefer to live. Thus, from an outsider's perspective, the Amish are resisting change simply to preserve tradition—but the Amish understand their actions to be "the will of God."

Summary and Conclusions

. . . Each generation experiences a certain amount of trial and error in finding norms and values that will best serve their unique needs. Tradition for the sake of tradition is hardly an answer to the complex problems facing the Amish. Although the Amish honor important traditions regarding their faith and their people, they also recognize that social and economic survival necessitates that some acceptance of change will be both normal and inevitable.

As one Old Order Amish man remarked, "You cannot put a ship in the middle of the ocean and expect the deck to always stay dry."

Acculturation *is* occurring in the majority of Old Order Amish communities visited by this researcher, but it is neither rampant nor whimsical. Rather, social change has consistently been scrutinized carefully and accepted gradually—where the results could be monitored for any possible unwanted side effects. The Old Order Amish enclave is not so much a model of "paradise lost" as it is a model of "evasive innovation" to save and protect a small, but significant, religious minority who wish to be "in the world, but not of the world."

44 Women in the Military

LAURA L. MILLER

That we are immersed in rapid social change has become a taken-for-granted assumption of contemporary life. But the pinch of change is not felt to the same degree by everyone. A change may affect one person's life profoundly, while for others that same change merely provides an interesting topic of conversation. Some change is so moderate that we can adjust to the new aspect of life with little difficulty. Other change upsets us because it challenges our taken-for-granted assumptions about the way the world is and should be. Some people gain by change, and like what is happening; others lose, and can't stand it. With perspectives so vastly different in our pluralistic society, some view the same change as long overdue; others insist that it should never have come about in the first place.

The women's movement represents profound social change. It has challenged taken-for-granted assumptions and brought deep consequences for our lives. But, as with other social change, not everyone has been touched in the same way. In this article we look at the integration of women in the military, where women now occupy positions from which they were excluded just a generation ago. Miller focuses on how men react to the presence of women in formerly all-male jobs, noting that they are using techniques of resistance more commonly associated with the protests of minorities.

THE DATA PRESENTED HERE are taken from multiple stages of field research on active-duty Army soldiers from early 1992 to late 1994. I used a multimethod strategy to capture both large-scale attitudinal patterns and individual viewpoints. To collect the data, I traveled to eight stateside Army posts and two national training centers, where soldiers conduct war games on a simulated battlefield. I also lived with Army personnel for 10 days in Somalia during Operation Restore Hope, for seven days in Macedonia during Operation Able Sentry, and for six days in Haiti during Operation Uphold Democracy. . . .

Given the military context and the sensitive nature of some of the issues, [in my discussion groups and interviews] I relied on written notes rather than tape-recording. . . . I also collected large-scale survey data in order to analyze the relationships between soldiers' demographics and their attitudes on a wide array of issues. The ethnographic data were cross-validated by multiple stages of questionnaires totaling more than 4,100. . . .

In *Domination and the Arts of Resistance,* James C. Scott (1990) provides an extensive historical analysis explaining how powerless groups resist and subvert the efforts of those with power over them. His work demonstrates that people's fear of negative sanctions often drives them to resist in ways that cannot be traced to the initiator, or are lost in the anonymity of crowds. The greater the power exerted from above, the more fully masked the resistance from below. Scott provides numerous examples of the art of political disguise, including gossip, rumor, grumbling, folktales, possession by spirits, mass defiance, anonymous threats, symbolic inversion of the social order, and rituals of reversal such as carnival. Like much of the research on which he draws, Scott continues the Marxist tradition of dividing the world in two: those with economic power (the bourgeoisie, landlords, kings, the ruling class, employers) and those who depend on them or must serve them (the proletariat, peasants, serfs, slaves, workers). . . .

Scott's examples closely parallel behavior that I found in gender relations in the Army, except for one very significant anomaly: It is the structurally dominant group, Army men, who employ the strategies of resistance that are generally seen as the weapons of the weak. My research shows that some men devote a great deal of energy to resisting their women coworkers and commanders through methods such as sabotage, name-calling, foot-dragging, and spreading rumors. Women, paradoxically, do not appear to be using any of these strategies of the weak to gain power from men, according to either their accounts or men's.

What explains the use of weapons of the weak by the structurally dominant group but not by the subordinate minority? My investigation led me to social psychological studies of power. In this literature it is argued that people act according to perceptions of power based on their own experiences and knowledge, not according to some objective analysis of resources. . . . Frequently military men described themselves as unjustly constrained or controlled by military women. Furthermore, these men tend to believe that women's power is usually gained illegitimately and that women take advantage of their gender to promote their own careers. . . .

For example, enlisted men may not enjoy the privileges of their sex as much as men at the higher command levels, particularly in relation to women officers; also, in this era of organizational downsizing, male career officers sometimes blame their limited opportunities on increased participation by women. Thus not all military men experience male privilege, and even some of the more privileged members are constrained within the organization. . . .

In this article I first describe men's resistance in the form of gender harassment. Then I examine who is likely to oppose expanded or even current roles for women soldiers, and why gender harassment is a product of this opposition. I conclude with the implications of this case for gender and other minority relations as well as for the study of power and resistance.

Gender Harassment

DISTINGUISHING GENDER HARASSMENT FROM SEXUAL HARASSMENT

> Sexual harassment implies that you can only be harassed through sexual means. Women can also be harassed through the job in other ways. If your commander doesn't like you, you will encounter harassment, i.e., the shit details, made to work later than everyone else, constant field problems, low efficiency ratings, etc. It's more prejudice than harassment towards females in the Army. (black NCO [Non-Commissioned Officer] in administrative support)

Sexual harassment is not an analytically useful category because it may refer to situations as disparate as sexual assault, discrimination in promotion or assignment, sexual comments, and gender harassment. . . . In my analysis, I limit the term *sexual harassment* to unwanted sexual comments or advances.

Gender harassment refers to harassment that is not sexual, and is used to enforce traditional gender roles, or in response to the violation of those roles. This form of harassment also may aim to undermine women's attempts at gaining power or to describe that power as illegitimately obtained or exercised. Examples include men proclaiming "Women can't drive trucks" in the presence of female drivers or refusing to follow a superior's directives simply because that superior is a woman. Many Army women report that gender harassment on the job is more prevalent than sexual harassment.

Gender harassment also can be used against men who violate gender norms. For example, men who fail to live up to the "masculine ideal" by showing insecurity or hesitation during maneuvers may be called "fags" or "girls" by their comrades. . . . Because behavior that conflicts with one's gender role is stereotypically associated with homosexuality, both heterosexuality and traditional gender roles are enforced through gender harassment.

Because of the prevalence of gender harassment, workshops and policies that address only sexual harassment miss much of the picture. Women report that gender harassment can be just as disruptive in their lives as sexual harassment: It can interfere with their ability to do their work, with their private lives, and with their opportunities to receive some recognition and promotions. Gender harassment is often difficult to attribute to individuals, may not be recognized by command as a problem, and is often invisible in debates about harassment of women in the military. . . .

Gender harassment is hardly unique to military men and women; it is found in many studies of women in sex-atypical work. Examples of what I call gender harassment are scattered throughout studies of job climate, male coworkers' reactions to women, and subtle or covert sex discrimination:

> [We] also face another pervasive and sinister kind of harassment which is gender-based, but may have nothing to do with sex. It is a harassment aimed at us simply because we are women in a "man's" job, and its function is to discourage us from staying in our trades. (M. Martin 1988: 10)

SOME FORMS OF GENDER HARASSMENT

Below are some illustrative examples of gender harassment.

Resistance to Authority.   Women who are officers or NCOs commonly complained of male subordinates, especially older enlisted men, who "just don't like answering to a woman." When given orders, they feign ignorance about what is expected of them, or engage in foot-dragging. This method is effective because the men do not risk the official reprimand warranted by an outright refusal to obey orders; yet they challenge women's authority by not complying completely. As one white NCO hypothesized, "Men are intimidated by women superiors and most try to undermine their work." Several women leaders reported having to "pull rank" more often than their male counterparts to get things done. . . .

Constant Scrutiny.   Hostile men use constant scrutiny to catch individual women making mistakes, and then use the mistakes to criticize the abilities of women in general. Because of this scrutiny women often feel obligated to work harder than those under less supervision. Women report that they experience such scrutiny as relentless harassment, and that it can make them feel self-conscious and extremely stressed.

Both enlisted and officer women report that as women they are subject to closer scrutiny than men. When women are singled out for observation by suspicious peers and superiors, they often feel they have to work harder than their coworkers just to be accepted as equal members of the unit. . . .

The behavior of a few women is often projected onto the entire gender, but the same is not true for men. To illustrate, some women soldiers serving in the early phases of operations in Haiti pointed out that if the three soldiers who committed suicide there had been women, a discussion would have ensued: People would have asked whether women could handle the stress of deployments or separation from their families. Yet because they were "just men," they were reported as *soldiers*, and the suicides were not interpreted as saying anything about men in general. . . .

Women leaders are rendered less flexible than men because of the constant scrutiny. Sometimes they believe that the people watching them are waiting for them to make mistakes or deviate from regulations; this is a disconcerting environment in which to make decisions. As a result, some men as well as some women classify female superiors as unfair or "too hard." They prefer to serve under men, who have more freedom to bend the rules in favor of their troops: "Women seem to feel they have something to prove. They do, but should not abuse their soldiers [in the process]" (white enlisted man in electronics).

Scrutiny as a harassment strategy is particularly safe in the military because it fits into the functioning of the organization. One cannot be punished for seeking out and correcting errors, and it would be quite difficult to prove that women are being watched more closely than men.

Gossip and Rumors.   Army women are often the subject of untrue gossip about their sex lives. Repeatedly I heard that if a woman dates more than one man in the Army, she is labeled a "slut." If she doesn't date, she is labeled a "dyke." Unlike men, women who are promoted quickly or who receive coveted assignments are often rumored to have "slept their way to the top." At every post I visited, soldiers had heard the rumor (which has never been verified) that a few women soldiers in the Persian Gulf War made a fortune by setting up a tent and serving as prostitutes for their male counterparts.

Young Army women in particular feel that their personal lives are under intense scrutiny at all times, and that ridiculous lies can emerge from the rumor mill for no apparent reason. One enlisted woman was shocked when her commander took her aside one day and said, "Look, I know you're sleeping with all the guys in your unit." She could not imagine why he said that to her; who would have started such a rumor, or why; or why fellow soldiers—her friends—would have contributed to spreading the stories. . . .

Because rumors are usually untraceable, they cannot be addressed through a formal complaint system. Scott discusses the power of such strategies:

> Gossip is perhaps the most familiar and elementary form of disguised popular aggression. Though its use is hardly confined to attacks by subordinates on their superiors, it represents a relatively safe social sanction. Gossip, almost by definition, has no identifiable author, but scores of eager retellers who can claim they are just passing on the news. Should the gossip—and here I have in mind malicious gossip—be challenged, everyone can disavow responsibility for having originated it. . . .

The character of gossip that distinguishes it from rumor is that gossip consists typically of stories that are designed to ruin the reputation of some identifiable person or persons. If the perpetrators remain anonymous, the victim is clearly specified. There is, arguably, something of a disguised democratic voice about gossip in the sense that it is propagated only to the extent that others find it in their interest to retell the story. If they don't, it disappears. (1990:142)

Sabotage.   I found evidence of sabotage, as a form of gender harassment, only in work fields that are nontraditional for women. Because these nontraditional occupations can be strenuous and dangerous, the sabotage of equipment can be quite threatening. . . . .

In one instance of sabotage from my research, two women new to an all-male vehicle maintenance and repair unit arrived at work every morning to find that the heavy, difficult-to-change track had been removed from their assigned vehicle. After a few weeks, during which they patiently replaced the track each day, the harassment ended. They had earned the men's respect by proving their skills and their willingness to work hard. The men's doubts were dispelled when they decided that the women's abilities had earned them a position in the unit, and that they would not use their gender to exempt themselves from dirty and difficult work.

Sabotage of equipment and tools was reported by women in mechanical fields, but I never heard of sabotage in the form of disappearing files, erased computer data, jammed typewriters, hidden medical supplies, or misplaced cooking utensils.

Indirect Threats.   Some soldiers reported that some of their fellow men would rape women who dared to enter infantry or armor units. The comments written on surveys include these remarks by a black enlisted man in the combat arms:

> The majority of men in the Army are sexist. I know, because I'm a man. Women in combat units would be harassed, if not raped. I say this because I've seen it and have nothing to hide. If you want the truth about issues, don't ask NCOs or officers. They'll tell you everything is all peaches and cream!! If you want the truth ask an E4 that's been in about 5 years. Women only have a fair shake as cooks or nurses. They'll be extremely harassed, if not molested, if they enter combat arms. I know, trust me.

Another infantryman echoed that assessment, although he proposed that male violence toward women is due to the conditions of deployments, not to sexism:

> In a situation where times are hard—less food, no showers, road marching, with 70–100 lbs ruck on your back, and [you] don't know when the next supply shipment will be in, the male soldiers will start thinking of sex and the female soldiers may be raped or something.

Why Gender Harassment? Perceptions of Power and Limited Forms of Protest

Some men resort to gender harassment to protect changing gender norms, either because they personally prefer traditional norms or because they think that men and women are not capable of successfully working outside traditional roles. Many of these men believe that women's attempts to claim equality have resulted in favorable treatment for women who have been largely unwilling or unable to fully meet the demands of being a soldier. Gender harassment is an attempt to push women back into their more "natural" roles, restore the meritocratic order of the organization, and ensure that all soldiers on the battlefield can do their jobs and assist the wounded in times of war. Certainly these views are considered sexist by many, and potentially could cause problems for any soldier who expresses them openly in mixed company. Thus gender harassment is preferred as an often unattributable way to protest the expansion of women's roles and to attempt to balance scales that are perceived to be tilted in women's favor.

HOSTILE PROPONENTS AND ANOTHER VERSION OF EQUALITY

"Women should be given totally equal treatment and standards. But I don't see it happening." This assertion by a male Army captain expresses the views of many Army men. Rather than championing women's rights, however, this officer is among the men who feel that women, not men, are the privileged and powerful group in the military. These men oppose expanding women's opportunities because they believe that women already enjoy too many advantages in the organization and have not yet met the requirements of the roles they already fill.

Some men believe that women use the term *equality* to advance their personal interests, and that they would object if true equality were offered:

> My opinion is that if women want the right to be in combat roles, they should have to register with selective service. Also, if women want to be treated and have the same rights as men, they should be treated equally all of the time and not just when it is convenient for them. (white enlisted man)

Interview data reveal that most of the men who favor opening combat roles to women on the same terms as men do so only because they are confident that women will fail in those roles. I term this group "hostile proponents" of women in combat. Such hostile proponents reason that the issue of women in the combat arms will not be put to rest until women have been given the opportunity to prove their incompetence. For example, a male driver agreed that women should be allowed to volunteer for combat roles—until he dropped off the female officer who was traveling with us. As soon as she left our group, he added that he thought women should be allowed into combat because they would see how hard the combat arms really are, and no one would have to listen any longer to their complaints about wanting to be included. This "treat women the same to watch them fail" attitude was expressed in writing by a white NCO in the combat arms:

> My feelings are that women just want a door open that is closed. If they want to be totally equal with us, shave their head in basic training [and] give them the same [physical training] test as men. Women in the infantry would ruin male bonding and get soldiers killed or hurt trying to cover for them in combat. Try an all female infantry basic training and [advanced individual training] with the exact same standards as males.

These hostile proponents have found that they can voice their objections by appropriating the language of the feminist activists. Arguments that women should stay home and raise children can be denounced as sexist; agreeing with activists that women and men are "equal" and should be expected to be treated equally cannot. When women are kept out of certain occupations, feminists can continue to argue that women, given the chance, could perform as well as men. Hostile proponents believe that admitting women is a better strategy for reducing the credibility of such arguments because, they insist, the reality will prove the arguments false.

One resistant male soldier provided the formula "(Equal pay = equal job = equal responsibility = equal risk) = equal opportunity" to stress that equality should be sought across the board, not only in pay or opportunity. He was one of the many men who believed that the differential policies actually work in women's favor, disrupt the meritocratic order, and are likely to imperil soldiers in times of war.

A few combat soldiers in my survey were motivated by self-interest to support admitting women to their Military Occupational Specialties (MOSs). One such man, a black NCO, wrote:

> If women are allowed in combat they should be made to shave their heads like men, or let men grow their hair like women. And if women are allowed, field duty would become better for men, because of [women's] needs. So therefore, I'm for them in combat. Yes, let them in.

MEN'S PERCEPTIONS OF WOMEN'S PRIVILEGES

Why do some Army men perceive themselves, and not women, to be the disadvantaged gender in the military? Although other respondents offer counterarguments to these men's opinions, I focus here on the viewpoint of men who regard themselves as underdogs. In this section I demonstrate how a structurally dominant group can perceive itself to be a disadvantaged group, and therefore resort to the types of resistance strategies that Scott attributes to the weak. The unifying theme of these examples is the belief that most military women do not take the same risks or work as hard as do military men, and yet are promoted more quickly than men because of their gender.

Easier Physical Training Standards. Both men and women reported that women's physical training requirements are not only different from men's, but easier for most women to meet than men's are for most men. Although this training is supposed to maintain physical fitness, most soldiers interpret it as a measure of strength. That the women's requirements are easier than the men's is seen by many as proof that women are less well qualified for physically strenuous work:

> I can't be adamant enough. There is no place for women in the infantry. Women do not belong in combat units. If you haven't been there, then you wouldn't understand. As far as equal rights, some women say they are as physically strong as a man. Then why are the [physical training] standards different? (white NCO in the combat arms)

Thus some soldiers argue that only one standard should exist for men and for women, and that such a standard should reflect the requirements of the job. A white lieutenant in intelligence and communications explained his view:

> The standards are never the same for men and women. The [Army Physical Fitness Test] is a perfect example. [W]hat most junior leaders feel (that I have discussed the topic with) . . . there should be no difference for either sex. [The Department of the Army] has established minimum standards and they should apply across the board, regardless of sex. Which means the female standards would have to go out the window. A man who can only do 18 pushups is unfit for service, so it should be [the same] for females. If a female can meet the same standards as me, I will gladly serve with, for, or over her. But if she can't I will also gladly chapter her out of the Army as unfit for service. I've seen action in Grenada and Iraq and know there are females who could've done my job. Few, but some. However my wife, who went to Saudi, is 104 lbs., 5'4" and couldn't carry my 201 lbs. across the living room, much less the desert if I was wounded. Whose standards should apply?

In deployments and field exercises, the differences are most apparent. Some commanders find them difficult to know how to handle:

> The topic about women in combat MOS's has finally cleared up with me, I have completed [platoon leadership training], and found that the women on my patrol

team could not perform their squad duties. For example, being a 60-gunner, or radio operator I was patrol leader. I assigned the females on my team the 60 and the radio. After about 2 miles of patrolling, the females could not do their jobs. I was accused of being sexist, but when it came down to it, men had to take those assigned jobs in my squad from these women. I'm sure that there are some females that could "keep up" or "hang" with the men, but the fact is that women are not physically strong enough. (white enlisted man in the combat arms)

Pregnancy as an Advantage.   Some men find it unfair that women have an honorable option out of the service, deployments, or single barracks that men do not have: pregnancy. A white enlisted man in intelligence and communications wrote:

> There seems to be a trend that females in the Army take advantage of free medical and have kids while serving. The 9 months of pregnancy limits them to no physical labor and is bad on morale. They are still a soldier, but they are only working at about 30% of their potential, forcing men or non-pregnant women to compensate.

A white lieutenant in the medical field noted, "I am currently in a unit with female soldiers, about 60–75% are pregnant or on some type of profile." "Profile" is a standing in which soldiers' physical abilities are limited; therefore they are exempt from physically strenuous tasks, including daily physical training. Pregnant women are among the most common sources of resentment and thus are targets of harassment. Pregnancy then, is another way in which some men feel that women are receiving equal pay and promotion, but are not doing equal work and not taking equal risks and responsibilities.

Better Educational Opportunities.   Many men feel that restrictions on women's roles are unfair not because they limit women, but because they appear to give women opportunities to receive more schooling than men, thus improving their chances for promotion. A white enlisted man wrote, "Most women are in rear units and have the chance to go to school and complete correspondence courses." A black NCO viewed these opportunities as tipping the balance in women's favor in competitions for promotion: "Of most of the units that I've served, the female soldier is more apt to attend schools, i.e., military and civilian. This constant trend allows them better opportunities for career progression."

Some men feel that with this extra training, women will be more qualified than men, with the result that "Most women are promoted above their peers" (white NCO). One white enlisted man expressed the view that it is wasteful to allow women to take coveted slots in combat-related training to help their careers when they are currently restricted from performing those tasks in the event of a real war:

Each person male or female will perform according to his or her gifts. We cannot make that determination. Congress needs to get off its lazy butt and make a decision one way or the other. Until that time, it remains a waste of time and taxpayer's money to send women to combat related schools (jump schools and air assault, etc.) just for the sake of being "stylish" and to appease those women who whine about discrimination when they're not allowed to do something a male soldier does.

Exemption from Combat Arms as a Way to Faster Promotion, Better Assignments, and "Cushy" Jobs. In some units there is a hierarchy of assignments, which is sometimes disrupted by the way women are integrated. The lowest jobs are often the "grunt work"—hard, mindless labor. Some men protested to me that when women are assigned to such a unit, they are spared the grunt work and placed (often by male superiors) ahead of men for more desirable assignments. Not only are they excused from doing what men have to do; they also delay men's progress into better positions and sometimes have authority over the men they have bumped. A white lieutenant cited an example of the problems created because a man in a signal MOS can be assigned to a combat unit and required to do grunt work, but a woman is always assigned elsewhere:

> Currently, females in combat support roles (e.g., signal, chemical, [military police], medical services) can not hold a designated position in Combat Units. For example, females are allowed to serve in the signal corps, but they are not allowed to serve as a signal [platoon leader] in a combat arms unit. There is too much animosity towards females in a specific branch if they can't hold the same positions that their male counterparts [do]. The females are seen as getting the "cushy" jobs and interesting jobs as the males have to fulfill the combat roles. If a female can not hold a position in their designated specialty, they should not be allowed in that specific specialty.

These men view women not only as obtaining easier work, but as jumping up the hierarchy without earning it. As a white lieutenant explains, this can breed resentment:

> Chemical corps: females should not be allowed in this branch if they cannot serve in all positions. For example, they get sent to this division, but cannot serve in the infantry, armor, or forward artillery units. This leaves very few slots for them to fill. [The Army] does not manage this very [well] at all. As a new lieutenant, we must put in our time at the battalion staff level, first, then we are awarded a platoon at the chem company. (One company per division). [The Department of the Army] sends us more females than we have slots for, so they wind up being platoon leaders at the company ahead of the males who have put in their time at the battalions. A lot of hard feelings about this. They (females) should not be branched chemical or some of the other combat support branches.

Men complained that women are not required to do the heaviest or dirtiest part of any job, and that they can get away with it without reprimand because of their sex. Although men may find it humorous when Beetle Bailey shirks his assignments, they may become resentful when women have an unfair advantage based on their sex. One black enlisted man wrote: "Today all you hear in the Army is that we are equal, but men do all the hard and heavy work whether it's combat or not."

According to some men, women's current behavior is proof that most are unable or unwilling to do the work required of soldiers in the combat arms. Thus they resist putting their lives on the line with such soldiers: "I feel women are useless to the Army, most do not do their part when it comes to real work! Most won't change a tire, or pick up a box if it weighs more than 5 lbs. I would not go to war with women in or out of a combat role." Some of these conclusions are based on experience in the States:

> When given the same opportunity, most [women] look for excuses not to do the work. You in your position can not see it. However, I am exposed to it daily. The majority of females I know are not soldiers. They are employed. Anything strenuous is avoided with a passion. I would hate to serve with them during combat! I would end up doing my job and $2/3$ of theirs just to stay alive. (black NCO in administrative work)

> I feel as if women in the military are ordered to do less work, get out of doing things such as field problems, and when it comes to doing heavy work, they just stand around and watch the work until it is completed. This is part of the reason I feel they could not handle a combat role because of a weaker physical and mental capability under such a stressful situation. I say this because it is proved in an everyday day of work. (black enlisted man in a technical field)

Women's gender identity traditionally has been tied to "delicacy," while men's identity has been tied to the ability to be tough and strong. So men may try to avoid work in general, but avoiding heavy labor in particular would make them look weak, cast doubt on their masculinity, and draw ridicule from other men about their "femininity." Thus many men resent that women can avoid a great deal of dirty, heavy work and still succeed in the military, while men's lives are considerably tougher. Although men tend to lay most of the blame for "getting by" on women, this behavior could not persist unless the leaders allowed it.

Paternalism Allowing Women to Get Away With More.   Both men and women may try to bend the rules, but when women succeed because of their gender, male coworkers may hold it against them. Several times women told me how they could avoid certain duties by complaining of cramps to particular male commanders. At the first mention of anything "menstrual" their commander would grimace and wave them away. (This did not work with women superiors, who sent them to sick call if they thought the cramps were serious.) Two women told me that they could hide off-limits items such as candy by placing tampons or underwear on top of the contents of their lockers or drawers. During inspections, their male commander took one look at their belongings, saw the personal items, and moved on, apparently too embarrassed to examine the rest of the contents.

As another example, one man wrote on his survey.

> I don't think women can withstand not being able to take showers for as long as men. When I was in the Gulf, we were ordered to use the water that we had only for drinking. But after one week the women were using our drinking water to take bird baths. This made me very upset.

This problem is framed as a matter of women's behavior, not the command's enforcement of rules.

Male commanders enforce rules differently for women, for several reasons. In the case of the water, the leader may have made this exception for women because he perceived them as more fragile than men, or felt that some sort of chivalry was appropriate. Padavic and Reskin (1990) call such behavior "paternalism," which they measured in their study of blue-collar workers according to whether women "had been relieved of some hard assignments, whether male coworkers had given them special treatment because of their sex, and whether their supervisors had favored them because of their sex" (p. 618).

Men in command positions sometimes fear disciplining women or pushing them to excel. These men worry that they will be accused of harassing women soldiers because of their gender, or of being insensitive to women's needs or limitations. Also, some are too embarrassed about women's underwear or hygiene to perform the ritual invasion of privacy men must undergo. As a result, even when sensitivity to women is intended, women receive privileges that men do not; this situation breeds disdain for women soldiers among some of the men.

In the military, some believe that male leaders' unwillingness to push women to excel creates a weakness among the troops that could have grave consequences during a war:

> The more fundamental question is whether women should be in the military at all. They have served well, but are victims of a male dominated system which has always demanded less of them than they would (hopefully) of themselves. If every soldier in the U.S. Army today had been trained at the same low level of expectation that female soldiers routinely are, the U.S. Army today would either be dead or in Prisoner of War camps. (an "other race" major)

Quotas, Sex, and Other Paths to the Top. As noted earlier, some men believe that women can "sleep their way" to the top, and that quotas allow women to receive undeserved promotions and assignments because of their minority status. Some men also believe that women can and do challenge poor performance reviews by claiming discrimination, and that they can use false harassment claims to punish or remove men they do not like. The perception is that women usually are believed over men in harassment cases; as a result, men's careers are ruined by the whims of ambitious or vengeful women.

Most of these perceptions reinforce the view that women want the prestige and promotions that come with serving in the combat arms, but do not intend to make the same efforts as men: "They want equal rights, but don't want to do what it takes to become equal" (white enlisted man in administration).

LIMITED FORMS OF PROTEST

When I asked men who opposed women in combat roles what they thought would happen in the future, they all asserted that integration was inevitable. They concluded that women eventually would "have their way" despite any reasonable objections. Perhaps because women's gains have been made gradually over the years, men perceive this progression not as a series of slow, incremental change toward one goal but as a string of victories for women over men.

One white major said, "As minorities, women have advantages." White men were likely to have a similar attitude about race; for example, they tended to think that nonwhite soldiers unfairly charge racial discrimination to challenge negative performance reviews. One white NCO spoke for many of his comrades in defining himself as a member of the oppressed minority: "I feel that the white enlisted male has more prejudice against him than any other sector in the military." He specified not only his gender but also his race and rank as contributing to his position.

Scott analyzes both the micro interactional forms of resistance by subjugated people and the outward rebellion of the powerless that occurs when "an entire category of people suddenly finds its public voice no longer stifled" (1990:210). I found the reverse among military men: a category of people who have assumed and enjoyed gender privilege, and who rebel because their public voice has been deemed sexist and has been silenced.

Because of the nature of the military organization, many forms of protest are not realistic options for men who contend that they are disadvantaged. Army men cannot strike, circulate petitions, organize rallies or demonstrations, walk out during the workday, or quit collectively in response to a policy change. (Before quitting they would have to meet their enlistment obligations or complete time-consuming formal exit procedures and paperwork.) Boycotts and "client preference" arguments are generally irrelevant here. Thus men who are silent in mixed-sex environments may be channeling their frustrations into underground grumbling.

I experienced firsthand evidence of men's perception that they must hide their opinions. Often the men who eventually voiced their objections to working with women were not initially forthright. When asked about gender issues, they first told me what they imagined I wanted to hear, or recited the "party line" that would keep them out of trouble should any statements be attributed to them. After calculating my opinion on the basis of my status as a young civilian woman conducting research on military women, they hesitated at my opening questions and then said reluctantly that they thought women should and could serve in any military roles. Then, when I raised an opposing argument (such as "So you don't see any problem with close contact between men and women serving in tanks together?"), their true feelings burst forth.[1]

In mixed-sex groups (particularly groups of officers), some of the men squirmed, rolled their eyes, or shook their heads, but did not speak up during discussions about gender. After I dismissed the group, I privately asked those men to stay behind, and asked them why they were silent but seemingly dissatisfied. They revealed that they refrained from participating because they believed that organizational constraints prohibited them from stating their true opinions, particularly in the presence of officer women. In this way I learned which arguments were considered legitimate in the organization (at least when women were present) and which would be censured. The opportunity to write anonymous comments on the formal questionnaires may have been particularly appreciated by soldiers who felt their views were controversial. Men were concerned that they would be held accountable for any statements that could be considered sexist; they feared an official reprimand and negative consequences for their career.

These soldiers' perceptions are evidence that the Army has made some headway in controlling men's willingness to make openly sexist statements. (Soldiers' self-censorship about gender contrasted sharply with their comments about allowing open gays and lesbians to serve in the military; men did not hesitate to make loud, violent threats against any gays they might discover.) Many of these men resent the inability to speak their minds. They believe that even if they could speak candidly, their concerns would not be addressed formally because they think women have the advantage in

---

[1]Men who I believe truly support women in combat roles responded to this probing technique with assertions such as "No. I don't think it would be a problem. Men and women can work together without having sex all the time: I've seen it."

gender-based disputes. Therefore they express their resentment in ways that the institution cannot control.

Male soldiers interpret the "suppression" of some arguments against women as proof that those arguments are valid and that women have no legitimate counterargument. Thus some men are angry because they perceive women as having gained their power in the military illegitimately or as having taken advantage of that power. Others simply object to changing gender norms and increasing participation of women in non-traditional roles. This tension is exacerbated by the perceived prohibition against expressing their dissatisfaction. Therefore many men hold their tongues in public, but complain among themselves and retaliate with gender harassment. Although grumbling is certainly a part of military culture, the resistance strategies I found directed against women are rarely employed for similar complaints against male leaders or fellow soldiers in general.

Implications of Gender Harassment

The Army's formal sexual harassment [policies] in the 1990s have taught many men the definitions and the possible consequences of this behavior.

Yet improvements in controlling sexual harassment do not necessarily mean that women are now working in a supportive or even a tolerant environment. Although women can be hurt by public sexist comments that express doubts about their abilities, it is also debilitating when such comments are forced underground, where they cannot be challenged. In addition, because many men perceive themselves as unable to safely voice their concerns about women as coworkers, some men feel that gender harassment is a justified means of registering their complaints.

As previously disadvantaged groups gain some power in legislating discriminatory behavior, their opponents may come to rely on forms of resistance that are difficult to regulate. These implications go beyond gender and affect areas such as race, ethnicity, and sexual orientation. Even as minorities enjoy increased success in controlling overt harassment, they must recognize that people will seek other ways to express hostility. When minority groups call for equality, they should be prepared to be informed about inequities that favor them, and to learn how the language of equality might be used against them.

Underlying the cases in the resistance literature is the assumption that the reader is sympathetic to the oppressed groups; groups claiming oppression in fact are oppressed and are justified in their resistance. Resistance, then, has been treated as something constructive, which preserves human dignity and may lead to the overthrow of an unjust system. Thus nobody has asked how to eliminate the "hidden transcript" and dismantle underground forms of resistance. In the traditional dichotomous framework of resistance studies, that question would have been asked only by oppressors seeking compliance—seeking to use their power for manipulation or indoctrination.

But what do we say when the resisting group is not entirely powerless and does not wish to relinquish one of the realms in which it holds power? The powerful can appropriate for themselves the language and framework used to explain dominance and resistance. They can portray themselves as victims, as "silenced," when *they* suddenly are required to monitor their behavior in the presence of others. Is the attempt to regulate racist, sexist, and homophobic speech and behavior equivalent to the past suppression of minority groups' voices? Are we to be sympathetic when previously powerful groups develop underground resistance because their behavior is suppressed?

In this paper I have sought to demonstrate that in order to effectively examine power dynamics, studies of resistance must supplement cultural and structural analyses. Future work must recognize the importance of perceptions of power because such perceptions do not necessarily correspond to objective measures of power. These perceptions, however, strongly influence people's attitudes and behavior. In the military, soldiers' experience of gender varies according to rank, age, race, and occupational specialty.

Resistance studies also must move beyond seeing the world in terms of only two classes: the oppressors and the oppressed. This dichotomy cannot fully explain the dynamics of a world in which multiple hierarchies can make people simultaneously powerful and powerless relative to others. Future research must account for people's multiple statuses which result in a much more varied distribution of power than a dichotomous model would allow. The behavior of some military men toward women soldiers demonstrates that researchers must look for "weapons of the weak" in the hands of people at all levels of both perceived and structurally measured power.

References

Martin, Molly, ed. 1988. *Hard Hatted Women: Stories of Struggle and Success in the Trades.* Seattle: Seal Press.

Padavic, Irene, and Barbara F. Reskin. 1990. "Men's Behavior and Women's Interest in Blue-Collar Jobs." *Social Problems,* 37:613–628.

Scott, James C. 1990. *Domination and the Arts of Resistance: Hidden Transcripts.* New Haven: Yale University Press.

45 After Hurricane Andrew

KENNETH J. SMITH
LINDA LISKE BELGRAVE

Collective behavior is a catch-all term that refers to a wide variety of human activity. It is often used to refer to groups of people who are doing extraordinary things, such as participating in riots and lynchings. This term is so broad, however, that it also refers to fads, even to a food fight in a cafeteria. Its breadth makes collective behavior one of the less useful terms in sociology, as it lumps together young women who get ankle tattoos with an enraged mob bent on lynching someone. The term is so unsatisfactory that even to try to make the extraordinary its common element fails, for it also includes fashions, often not unusual at all.

As you can see, however, despite its limitations, collective behavior refers to some of the most interesting of human activities. One of the many topics encompassed by this term is the behavior of people following a disaster. In this article, we examine the aftermath of a devastating hurricane in Florida. Smith and Belgrave focus on how people attempted to rebuild their normal realities, the obstacles they encountered, and how lives were changed by this catastrophic event. If you consider the findings reported here of how people's lives were changed, the significance of the twin themes of this book—social structure and social interaction—will become apparent.

AT MIDNIGHT, August 24, the winds hit Miami. The high winds are 140 miles an hour and gusting to 180 miles an hour. In every inhabited South Dade County home, people are hiding in closets, hallways, and bathrooms. By 8 AM Monday, people were coming out of their shelters and homes. The storm had cut a twenty-by-twenty-mile swath of destruction through the inhabited part of South Dade County. A total of 63,000 houses were destroyed, 250,000 people were homeless, and 39 people were dead (Lyskowski et al. 1992; Christie 1992). . . .

Theoretical Considerations

Natural (Mount St. Helena) and technological (Chernobyl) disasters destroy, at least temporarily, the rituals and routines that make up everyday life. They impose the necessity of reorienting and reorganizing the responses to the primary world of family and neighbors and the secondary world of community relationships (Goode 1992).

Quarantelli and Dynes (1985) note that the primary and secondary interactions of disaster victims can be viewed, over time, as moving through three phases: a disaster phase, transition from disaster to normality, and a postdisaster recovery period. If one views this formulation as proceeding through three phases at two different levels of interaction, one can describe the process in the following way. The initial phase is the disaster as an event requiring an extraordinary mobilization of available energy and resources to face the onslaught or sequelae of the event itself. Following the disruption and dislocation caused by the disaster is a transition toward normality where "approximate versions" of the work, school, shopping, and other routines of the antedisaster period are reinstated. This transition to normality leads to a postdisaster recovery period. In this third period, new routines and rituals of everyday life are reconstructed to redefine the new meaning of everyday life. Recovery, however, does not mean returning to the status quo ante. The hurricane's impact can be a lasting one and can affect life course changes as well as gender role relations and generational relationships. The focus of this article is on the transition and recovery periods rather than on the disaster itself.

Research Design

Our data consist of forty accounts collected during the weeks and months following Hurricane Andrew. These accounts include twenty-one individual interviews, two focus group interviews involving eight people, three first-person accounts, and eight interviews conducted by our students for a special class project. The interviews were in-depth and lasted approximately two hours. They were taperecorded (with permission) and transcribed verbatim, thereby preserving the respondents' own use of language. . . .

The majority of respondents were selected from a list of University of Miami employees and from the staff of a nearby community mental health center who had suffered some hurricane damage. Respondents were chosen so as to include administrators, faculty, and staff. Acquaintances of the authors (and their students) from other social settings whose stories included additional features of the hurricane experience were also interviewed. . . .

Time Out from Everyday Life: Getting By and Digging Out

Time out from everyday life is a period of unreality that follows the destruction of everyday life and continues until the establishment of a new taken-for-granted reality is under way. While this was in some ways a hiatus, it also involved tasks for which many had little or no preparation. During the first few days after the hurricane, those who suffered significant damage devoted much of their energy to simply getting by. *Getting by* is the process of obtaining the basic necessities for survival (water, food, shelter), which became a major undertaking. For some, words such as "adventure" and "pioneering" were used to describe their situations. Not everyone, however, was successful at getting by beyond mere survival. Alternating with getting by is a process that we have described as *digging out*. By this expression, we mean the initial attempts to reconstruct the intimate territory of everyday life. The hiatus and disorientation of getting by merges into a more future-oriented set of tasks designed to reestablish a normal and continuing everyday life.

Basic survival needs that had been part of the mundane world the day before could no longer be taken for granted . . . The water supply was contaminated and was not potable for as long as six weeks in some areas. Some had no running water at all. One respondent, Paul, reported,

> The water we had to drink and the water that was outside could have been contaminated, so we couldn't go for a swim or anything. People were actually dumping sewage into it because they couldn't use their toilets. . . . I think that was the worst part, not even being able to get cleaned up after you were doing all the things you were doing.

Some had no food but were able to get to open stores. Others had food but could not wash, cook, or store it. For those who had come through the storm with well-stocked freezers, the concern was what to do with it:

> We had a freezer full of food with no power, and so I spent a lot of that first day sorting the refrigerator and we cooked what we thought would perish. . . . We did everything to lengthen the life of this food and make it ready to eat at a moment's notice. So we ate some really neat stuff those first few days. (Wendy)

Loading up supplies on a trip north was common. It was not unusual to see someone arrive home, open the car's trunk, and call the neighbors over to get what they needed. In the heavily damaged areas, people were dependent on friends or relatives who lived further north to supply them with food and other necessities. Sharing, accepting, and even requesting food from friends and neighbors quickly became normal.

Even for those who had the means to cook, such as Dixie, "Just the little bit of cooking you did became a major problem." Potable water was purchased from the store. Others used tapwater after boiling it or treating it with bleach for washing or cooking food. One solution was to rely on open restaurants. Another was to subsist on foods that did not require cooking. An adequate but boring diet had some drawbacks. As one respondent exclaimed, "I thought if I saw another can of tuna fish or peanut butter and jelly, I would scream."

Hurricane Andrew left 250,000 people homeless (Lyskowski et al. 1992). While some defined shelter as their most pressing concern, others made do with whatever they had left even though it might be uninhabitable. Rachel's family had few options:

> We were so tired and so cold, so wet and filthy. And all we could do was lay down and go to sleep. We went and laid down in all the debris. . . . [We] tried to get some comforters, and of course they were all soaking wet. And we just went to sleep.

The day after the hurricane, they went to stay with a relative who lived in Fort Myers.

The need for alternative housing, combined with the destruction of rental units, created tremendous difficulties for those who did decide to look for temporary housing. Moves were generally to smaller, less desirable housing or into shared housing. Dean's family, forced by their contractor to vacate their house, moved twice: "We rented a place on Miami Beach, a little one-bedroom apartment. . . . That was just much too small, so we [found] a place a month and a half later in Key Biscayne which is still small, but much better."

Those with fewer resources moved in with family, friends, or even strangers, and families were separated. Thelma and her three children, whose apartment was destroyed, first moved into her ex-husband's one-bedroom apartment. A few days later, she and her oldest son moved in with a neighbor she had just met in her complex's laundry room while her daughter moved to a friend's home and her younger son stayed with his father. Two weeks later, her landlord found her a small apartment. Thelma, her three children, and a friend of her daughter moved into it with no furniture except a twin bed. The daughter's friend, whose own family had only a few inhabitable rooms in their apartment, stayed with Thelma until after Christmas.

For those in devastated areas, the processes of getting by and digging out focused on the present and immediate future, and the tasks involved meeting basic needs. Despite the difficulties of getting by, it could hold a certain appeal and a test of individual resourcefulness:

> We thought we were pioneers. . . . I almost began to love the lifestyle because it was so simple. It was just survival. I must get water to these animals. And then I found I could wash all my clothes in the horse tub and stomp on the clothes. . . . If I stretched fifty foot of hose and let it lay all day in the sun, I could have hot water for a bath. (Barrie)

Of course, not everyone found "roughing it" to be charming. Although she survived, Rachel was not successful at getting by. In describing severe marital problems during the first few weeks after the hurricane, she explained,

He kept on riding me. "Why don't you have this place liveable? Why don't you clean this place up? Why don't you cook? . . . I lost thirteen pounds in three weeks. I didn't eat at all. . . . I wasn't drinking anything at that time either, no water or soda. I was dehydrated. My lips were starting to crack. . . . My husband said I looked as if I'd been drinking. I know that is why he accused me of it; I looked so bad. . . . I looked like a banshee and I had no self-esteem and I kind of felt the way I used to feel in my drinking days.

Digging out emerged alongside efforts required for getting by. Activities tended to be centered around cleaning up and salvaging belongings, although some were dealing with insurance almost immediately. Almost everyone who had suffered substantial damage reported cleaning up as a top-priority task. Despite the everydayness of the terms used, this cleaning up was far removed from the mundane, as indicated by Wendy's colorful description of the process. Her family "used a shovel and went and threw the living room out in the front yard."

In addition to cleaning up, there was the task of salvaging anything that could be saved. Those often involved "scrounging" or even literally digging through the remains of one's home to find whatever might be left. While many focused on salvaging items that had more personal meaning than material value, for those who faced virtually total loss items with neither material value nor personal meaning could become important. Rachel recalled, "We had so few things that made it through the storm that no matter what it was, even a bath brush, I was going to take it 'cause it meant that much to me."

Whatever activities one engaged in were undertaken with unusual constraints. The lack of electricity meant more than an inability to use labor-saving devices, many of which would have been useless for the tasks at hand. A vacuum cleaner is of no help when the carpeting is under water. The loss of electric light meant that everything had to be done during daylight hours. Sam explained, "We'd work, eat dinner, and go to bed. There was no electricity and no flashlights, so after sunset just about everybody in the area was going to bed." The lack of supplies, combined with the number of people needing them, increased greatly the effort required for many tasks. One respondent noted that "everywhere you went you had to wait forever." As Angela explained,

There was nothing that was easy to do. If you attempted anything, there was difficulty. You didn't have nails. The store did not have nails. So you would ask your neighbor, "Could you spare three nails?" So everything was hard.

Time out from everyday life did not end abruptly but began to dissolve as the "unreal" became routinized and people returned to at least some of their prior daily routines. Thus aspects of the unreality of the time-out phase continued even after the hiatus ended.

Life in "the Zone"

Life in "the zone" is an expression of one of our informants that seemed an apt way of describing the contrast between everyday life prior to Hurricane Andrew and in undamaged areas compared to the cultural ambience that was established as a result of the hurricane. Essentially, life in the zone consists of emergent ways of doing daily life in the absence of the usual supports that maintain taken-for-granted reality; it is routinization of the nonroutine. . . .

Life in the zone was the daily trek to buy ice and bottled water, dealing with contractors, being apprehensive about transient construction workers who roam the countryside, and living out the day in the unrelenting sunshine and dust (alternating with mud) in a country flattened by a devastating hurricane. . . .

Individuals and families in their automobiles gawking at the misery of others for their own entertainment and the continual helicopters (media or relief going elsewhere) were also a part of the problem:

> They didn't bring us food. . . . They didn't come down and say, "May we help you?" or something. They were just rubbernecking and I wanted to, if I had a bazooka I'd have blown them out of the sky. They just made me so mad, one after the other, providing no assistance, no nothing. We got nothing. (Marie)

This frequent linking of the offensiveness of being observed with the observers' neglect to bring help suggests that the tourists might have been better tolerated had they carried down needed supplies. This was not a short-term problem. During the Christmas holidays, the height of the tourist season for South Florida, a local radio personality brought the wrath of the community on himself by suggesting to listeners that the devastation in South Dade County was something you just had to see for yourself.

In the face of extensive devastation, interruption of services, and changed living arrangements, people developed new routines for handling what had once been mundane tasks. Communication was particularly problematic yet important enough for extensive efforts. In some areas, neighborhood mail delivery was interrupted for six weeks. Martha recalled, "You had to go down and wait in line for two or three hours to get your mail. [I went] once a week, on Saturday. How often do you have three hours to wait for your mail?" Likewise, telephone service was unavailable for months in some areas:

> Every Sunday morning, we'd go someplace to use a pay phone and call both sets of relatives. It was part of the routine. We would go to the grocery store then. The first month or so, it was a pain 'cause there weren't any restaurants open, but afterward we would go and have breakfast and call. (Ed)

The return of services that were once taken for granted was sometimes treated as a major event; their expressed importance helped characterize people's situations. Dixie's response to the return of electricity was not unusual:

> We were waiting for them to get it plugged in, you know, to fix the line. That was a night of absolute celebration. I mean, now you could vacuum. Your refrigerator would get cold. Watch television. All these modern, wonderful things. . . .

A continuing thread running through people's attempts to endure was the desire, or even need, to talk about their experiences. This need was not always easily met:

> I feel like it was yesterday. I cry almost every night. I can't cry in front of my husband because he can't take it. I don't care if people don't want to talk about it at all. That's all I can think about. I came to work every day and I talked there. We all did, though. For about a month, none of us worked. We all just talked about it. (Rachel)

After a while, those who wanted to talk about the storm began to experience disapproval for this behavior. According to Bridget, "We were in the bathroom and talking about the hurricane, and this one lady said, 'I can't believe it! Six weeks after the storm, and they are still talking about it.' "

Dixie, who still wanted to talk about the storm in January, explained that it depends on how badly you were damaged: "The ones that got a lot of damage are all the same way. The ones that didn't get any damage are probably bored with this conversation." Efforts to reconstruct a social reality, especially with those who did not experience the intensity of the hurricane, were met with a lack of empathy, if not outright hostility, perhaps because the non-victims lived in a different social world. Such impatience with hurricane conversation was, if not a flat-out denial of victims' subjective reality, at least a refusal to help validate it. . . .

The Return to Work

For some, the return to work took on unusual importance. Dixie reported that going back to work felt "wonderful! It was so nice to get back to something that was normal. . . . It was a saving grace to go back to familiar jobs." This sentiment was echoed by Bob, even though he had been all but dragged back by his employer:

> They said, "Hey, you got to come back to work . . ." and I was happy 'cause that was like coming to civilization. One week later, there was electricity here. There was running water; you couldn't drink it, but that was pretty close.

Similarly, Derry reported that at first she "spent more time at work than normally I would, but I didn't do much work. [I just wanted] to be there because it was so much more comfortable than at home."

Even some of those who were not personally employed outside the home commented on the impact of the return to work. In reference to her husband, one woman reported, "Once he went back to work, he was a little bit better 'cause he could be around his friends at work and talk and [it was] more of a normal routine for him." . . .

For those living in hard-hit areas, the return to work took place within the context of on-going digging out and getting by. New routines emerged, routines that involved not only continual movement between devastation and normal life but often conflicting demands between these two worlds. Child care was a primary concern. One subject, May, said, "I didn't come back full-time. I came in a little at a time because we didn't have power and I had a lot of problems with finding daycare for Katya." Joe, who along with his wife was putting in twelve- and thirteen-hour days, said, "I sent my daughter over to my mother, who lives in Deland [approximately 100 miles north of Dade County], and she stayed there for about ten or twelve days." Many found that the demands of rebuilding interfered with their ability to meet their own standards for job performance even when those around them were understanding of the difficulties:

> She's always been like my best friend, and she is so supportive. But no matter how great or wonderful your boss is, you have this horrible guilt all the time because I am always saying, "Do you mind if I leave work early? I've got to be there or they won't deliver the tar paper." I feel like I'm always having to ask, and I hate that because I am very conscious of wanting to do a good job. (Barrie)

And a professor echoed similar sentiments:

> Because you are trying to keep on top of everything and keep your appointments and keeping track of tests and classes, and you are also trying to think, "What do I need? I need plywood, and where should I get it?"—because it wasn't always easy to get. . . . I am telling you, I have taught two semesters poorly, and I am not proud of it. (Ed)

Altered Lives

. . . Some of our respondents talked about the impact of Hurricane Andrew in initiating and retarding critical decisions that altered former lives or interfered with desired, anticipated changes in future lives. For example, Ruben was unable to put his former life back together again. The economic burden of rebuilding the prehurricane life was too expensive:

I would say I go there three to four times a week. It has been very painful; part of the difficulty in selling the house was the neighborhood. The kids had friends there; they were used to walking down the street, talking to the neighbors, and knowing the place. That's probably why we hung on to it as long as we did. When people started talking about the six-month anniversary of the hurricane, that is, when we realized this is the time we were supposed to be back in this house and none of this [had] happened. There is no way we can carry two mortgages and a lease for another six months. . . . So it was painful, but economics drove the decision to sell our house. We do feel a tremendous amount of guilt for having sold the house.

Rachel succeeded in restoring the physical and domestic aspects of her life but was acutely disappointed with the result. Many of her neighbors moved. Homes were sold to speculators, who in turn rented the houses. Even though Rachel rebuilt her house, many of her neighbors did not:

If I'd known that we [would] have to still be looking at this mess and not having friendly neighbors and having a whole different group of people [neighborhood], I wouldn't have [rebuilt]. . . . Well, we know that we are going to sell this in a year or two anyway and leave. . . . Yeah, we have already decided that. It's just that we don't have the same feeling about this house as we did when we first moved in.

For others, posthurricane circumstances altered responses to existing or anticipated family relationships and life-course situations. . . . In one instance, we found a significant change in the relationship between a mother and her son:

About five weeks after the hurricane . . . David, my son, had a car accident. . . . I dumped [responsibility for] the whole thing on him. It's his accident, it's his license, his ticket, his driver's school, his insurance, and his problem to get the car fixed. My [only] contribution is that I'm going to a car rental agency to sign some papers so that he has wheels to drive while the car is in the shop. I'll always be his mother. But if the hurricane hadn't happened, then I would have been right in there minding his business for him. [The hurricane] moved things along a little quicker. I have the definite feeling that we crammed about eighteen months of living into the last three months. (Wendy)

. . . It must not be assumed that the problem and complexity of re-creating an everyday life of routines, plans, and goals is the same for the whole family. One's prehurricane life-course situation could be a critical factor in whether the trajectory of the former life was maintained or altered. Talking about his wife eighteen months after the hurricane, Lance explained,

I think the problem, big problem, is that my wife was just finishing her internship. She is trying to get a degree, a Ph.D. in psychology. She was just finishing her internship at Miami Children's Hospital, and she had to write her dissertation; she had finished all her exams. . . . She had various arrangements for offices and contacts and this and that and [had] plans for what she was going to work out for her dissertation, and the hurricane destroyed all of that. I think a lot of the papers got wrecked because [in] the room she had things in, [the papers] just blew out of the window and we found things floating in the neighbor's pool. So all her connections were ruined, especially since for two months we weren't even in Dade County. So I think that the effect on her, the real effect—I'm not talking about just the psychological effect—was much bigger than on me. . . . It wasn't just a year, because . . . everything was built up to a point and then it was [destroyed]. It wasn't that you were at the same point for a year and you went back another year. So maybe it wiped out two years of her life.

Conclusions

The experience of our respondents highlights dramatically the destruction of the taken-for-granted world and the profound alteration of identity and self. Hurricane Andrew not only destroyed the physical environment but also undermined the plausibility of reality itself. Those who endured the full catastrophe had to rebuild their sense of reality as well as their homes.

The alteration of identity and sense of self was illustrated in reports of stressed and conflicted relationships between our respondents and their spouses, children, and friends. Old relationships and assumptions were blown away by the wind. The trust that had been built up between a recovering alcoholic wife and her husband was challenged by accusations of drinking. Parents redefined their relationships with their children. One's emotional ties to neighbors and homes were changed significantly. Dangerous traffic and fear of looters and strangers turned familiar neighborhoods into hostile places.

Those who remained in South Dade County to reconstruct their social worlds experienced the alienating impact of being identified as "victims," or as estranged others, at whom the "real" people gawked as they drove by in their air-conditioned cars. People who thought of themselves as competent and independent found their resources strained to the limit as they struggled to put food on their tables. Most of the people interviewed were employed both before and after the hurricane. Many, for the first time in their lives, were fearful about their next meals. In their topsy-turvy world, the work and workplace became the context of recreation and relaxation. Home was a place of drudgery, stress, and unrelenting demands.

In attempts to reconstruct and reintegrate the reality of their lives, the hurricane was the principal theme in all of their conversations. Those who shared the experience empathized with and valorized each other's experiences. They needed to talk about it; they exchanged information about contractors, food preparation, and where to buy lumber. To communicate, they drove miles to find working telephones and stood in line for hours in post offices. Those whose sense of reality was not challenged and undermined by the hurricane remained aloof and uninvolved. It was as though they did not understand the language that was being spoken.

Large-scale disasters destroy fundamental aspects of everyday life and the taken-for-granted reality on which it is based, leaving survivors in an untenable situation. The reconstruction of reality is not primarily an intentional process but rather emerges as new routines are developed to deal with the changed situation. In the face of overwhelming destruction of their physical environment and taken-for-granted social structures, disaster victims go to extraordinary lengths to reestablish some semblance of their past routines. Such efforts provide evidence of the tenacity of socially constructed reality, once internalized.

References

Christie, John, ed. 1992. *Andrew: Savagery from the sea.* Orlando, FL: Tribune Publishing. (Collection of published articles)

Goode, E. 1992. *Collective behavior.* Fort Worth, TX: Harcourt Brace Jovanovich.

Lyskowski, Roman, et al. 1992. *Hurricane Andrew: The big one.* Kansas City, MO: Andrews & McMeel. (Collection of published articles)

Quarantelli, E., and R. R. Dynes. 1985. Community responses to disasters. In *Disasters and mental health,* (pp. 158–68), ed. B. J. Sowder. Washington, DC: U.S. Department of Health and Human Services, Public Health Service, Alcohol, Drug Abuse, and Mental Health Administration.

Glossary

Account One's version of an incident; often an excuse or justification for unexpected or inappropriate behavior. See *Excuse* and *Justification*.

Achieved status A person's position or ranking achieved at least partly through personal efforts (such as becoming a college student) or failings (such as becoming a skid row alcoholic).

Aggregate People grouped together for the purpose of social research because of characteristics they have in common. An example is U.S. females between the ages of 18 and 23 who wear contact lenses.

Alienation Used in a couple of different meanings. The first is Weberian, a sense of separation, of not belonging, of being estranged. This meaning includes the idea that one has little control over the social world; may also include the feeling that one's world is meaningless. The second is Marxian, a sense of being separated from and not identifying with the product of one's labor.

Anomie Normlessness; conflict between norms, weakened respect for norms, or absence of norms.

Anticipatory socialization Learning the perspectives of a role before entering it. See *Role* and *Socialization*.

Ascribed status A person's position or ranking assigned on the basis of standards over which the individual has little or no control, such as age, race, or sex.

Authority Power that is regarded as legitimate or proper by those over whom it is exercised.

Background expectancies (or **assumptions**)   The taken-for-granted assumptions people have about the way the world is. See *Social construction of reality*.

Belief   An idea about some part of the natural or social world; a view of reality.

Body language   Giving and receiving messages through the movement or positioning of the body; includes gestures and facial expressions.

Bureaucracy   A form of organization that has several layers of authority, usually depicted by a pyramid. Decisions flow downward, accountability for fulfilling orders goes upward, rules are explicit, emphasis is placed on written records, resources are directed toward efficiently reaching the goals of the organization, the "bottom line" is of utmost concern, and the personal is kept separate from that which belongs to the organization. The reality of any particular organization does not necessarily match this *Ideal type*.

Case study   An in-depth investigation of a single event, experience, organization, or situation in order to better understand that case or to abstract principles of human behavior.

Charisma   Extraordinary personal qualities that attract followers. It varies from simply a "magnetic" personality to qualities so extraordinary that they are assumed to be supernatural.

Charismatic authority   Leadership exercised on the basis of charisma. See *Charisma* and *Traditional authority*.

Class   See *Social class*.

Class conflict   Karl Marx's term for the struggle between social classes; generally thought of as the struggle between the rich (and powerful) and the poor (and powerless), or those who own the means of economic production and those who do not.

Coding   Fitting data into classifications so they can be more easily analyzed.

Collective behavior   Relatively spontaneous, unstructured, and transitory ways of thinking, feeling, and acting that develop among a large number of people.

Community   Its primary meaning is that of people who inhabit the same geographical area and share common interests and feel a sense of "belonging." From this sense comes a derived meaning of people who share common interests and have a sense of "belonging" but who do not inhabit the same geographical area, such as in the phrase "a community of scholars."

Conflict theory   The theoretical view (or school) which emphasizes conflict as the inevitable outcome in society due to its various groups competing for limited resources. See *Functionalism* and *Symbolic interactionism*.

Conformity   Following social norms or expectations.

Conspicuous consumption   Thorstein Veblen's term for a change from an orientation toward saving in the Protestant ethic to showing off wealth by the elaborate consumption of goods.

Content analysis   The classification of the content of documents in order to identify its themes; such as presidential speeches, a series of medical novels, situation comedies, and so on.

Control group   The subjects in an experiment who are *not* exposed to the independent variable, as opposed to the experimental group who are subjected to this variable. See *Experiment*, *Experimental group*, *Independent variable*, and *Variable*.

Covert participant observation   See *Participant observation*.

Crime   An act prohibited by law.

Cultural diffusion   The process by which items (or behavior, beliefs, and attitudes) from one culture are adopted by members of another culture.

Cultural relativity   The view that one cannot judge the characteristics of any culture to be morally superior to those of another. See its opposite, *Ethnocentrism*.

Culture   A way of life, or shared ways of doing things; includes nonmaterial culture (such as norms, beliefs, values, and language) and material culture (such as art, tools, weapons, and buildings). See *Ideal culture* and *Real culture*.

Culture lag (Cultural lag)   A term developed by William F. Ogburn to refer to the material culture changing more rapidly than the nonmaterial culture. Thought to be a primary factor in social change.

Culture of poverty   The distinctive culture said to exist among the poor of industrialized societies; its central features of defeatism, dependence, and a present time orientation are thought to trap people in poverty and to perpetuate it from one generation to the next.

Culture shock   The disorienting effect that immersion in a strange culture has on a visitor as he or she encounters markedly different norms, values, beliefs, customs, and other basic expectations of social life. No longer is the individual able to rely on the basics of his or her socialization.

Data   The information scientists gather in their studies.

Definition of reality   A view of what the world or some part of the world is like. See *Social construction of reality*.

Dehumanization   The act or process of reducing people to objects that do not deserve the treatment given humans.

Demography   The study of the size, distribution, composition, and change in human populations.

Dependent variable   That which is being explained as the result of other factors; a variable or social phenomenon thought to be changed or influenced by another variable. See *Independent variable*.

Deviance   Violation of social norms or expectations.

Deviant   One who violates social norms or expectations. As used by sociologists, a neutrally descriptive rather than a negative term.

Deviant career   The main course of events during someone's involvement in deviance; generally refers to people who are habitually, or at least for a period of time heavily, involved in some deviant activity.

Differential association   If a person associates with one group of people, he or she will learn one set of attitudes, ideas, and norms; associating with a different group teaches a different approach to life. Thus such differential association is highly significant in influencing people either to conform or to deviate.

Diffusion   The spread of an invention or discovery from one area or group to another.

Disclaimer   An excuse or justification for inappropriate behavior that is *about* to take place. Examples are: "Now don't get me wrong, but . . . ;" and "Let me play the devil's advocate for a minute."

Discrimination   The denial of rights, privileges, or opportunities to others on the basis of their group membership. See *Minority group*, *Racism*, and *Sexism*.

Division of labor   A concept developed by Emile Durkheim to refer to the work specializations in a society (the various ways in which work is divided, with some people specializing in financing or production, others in advertising or distribution, teaching or learning, and so on).

Documents   In its narrow sense, written sources that provide data; in its extended sense, archival material of any sort, including photographs, movies, and so on.

Double standard   More stringent expectations being applied to one group than to another. *The* double standard refers to attitudes and ideas more favorable to males than to females—often to males being allowed more sexual freedom.

Downsizing   A fancy way of saying that to reduce costs a company is firing workers.

Downward social mobility   Movement from a higher to a lower social position. See *Social class*.

Dramaturgical analysis   Developed by Erving Goffman, this term refers to viewing human interaction as a theatrical performance. People are seen as actors, their clothing as costumes, what they do as parts they play, what they say as the delivery of lines, where they interact as a stage, and so on.

Dramaturgy   Refers to theatrical performances. The same as *Dramaturgical analysis*.

Ecology   The study of reciprocal relationships between organisms and their environment.

Education   One of the primary institutions of society, it is designed to transmit values, skills, and knowledge from one generation to the next.

Ego   Commonly used as a term to refer to the self; technically, Freud's term for the conscious, rational part of an individual.

Endogamy   A cultural pattern of marrying *within* one's own social group. See *Exogamy*.

Ethnic cleansing   A recent term for killing people because of their ethnicity, with the goal of "cleaning out" an entire area for one's own ethnic group to inhabit.

Ethnic group   A group of people with a sense of common ancestry, who generally share similar cultural traits and regard themselves as distinct from others.

Ethnic stratification   Groups of people who are stratified on the basis of their ethnic group membership. See *Social stratification*.

Ethnocentrism   Using the standards of one's own group, culture, or subculture to evaluate the characteristics of other groups, cultures, or subcultures, generally from the point of view that one's own are superior. See its opposite, *Cultural relativity*.

Ethnography   A report or study that details the major characteristics of the way of life of a group of people; can be of an entire tribe, an entire village, or a smaller group within a large society, such as urban cabdrivers.

Ethnomethodology   Developed by Harold Garfinkel, this term refers to the study of people's worlds of reality, their taken-for-granted background assumptions, and the ways by which they make sense out of their experiences.

Excuse   An account of an event in which someone acknowledges that an act is blameworthy, but denies responsibility for the act. See *Account* and *Justification*.

Exogamy   A cultural pattern of marrying *outside* one's social group. See *Endogamy*.

Experiment   A study in which the researcher manipulates one or more variables (independent variables) in order to measure the results on other variables (dependent variables). See *Variable*.

Experimental group   The subjects in an experiment who are exposed to the independent variable, as opposed to the control group who do not experience this variable. See *Experiment*.

Extended family   A family consisting of two or more generations; they are *extended* beyond the nuclear family. See *Nuclear family*.

False consciousness   A term developed by Karl Marx to refer to people's understanding of their social class membership that does not square with objective facts; often used to refer to members of the working class identifying with capitalists.

Family   People who are related by ancestry, marriage, or adoption, who generally live together and form an economic unit, and whose adult members assume responsibility for the young. The form of the family varies remarkably from one culture to another.

Family of orientation   The family into which one is born. See *Family* and *Family of procreation*.

Family of procreation   The family that is created by marriage. See *Family* and *Family of orientation*.

Femininity   Our behaviors and orientations as females. Assumed in sociology to be an expression not of biology but of cultural or social learning. See *Masculinity*.

Feral children Children who have been found in the wilderness, supposedly raised by animals. Not only do they possess no language, but also they exhibit few behaviors that we ordinarily associate with humans.

Field research Another term for *Participant observation*.

Field study Another term for *Participant observation*.

Fieldwork Another term for *Participant observation*.

Folk society A term developed by Robert Redfield to refer to small, traditional societies in which there is little social change.

Folkways Developed by William G. Sumner, this term refers to norms people are expected or encouraged to follow, but whose violation is not considered immoral; the ordinary rules, usages, conventions, and expectations of everyday life, such as, in U.S. society, the use of deodorant. See *Mores*.

Formal organization A social group that is brought into existence to reach specific goals; often utilizes a bureaucratic mode of operation to achieve those objectives. See *Bureaucracy*.

Formal sanction A social reward or punishment that is formally applied; often a part of ritual recognition for achievement (such as receiving a passing grade in school, or being promoted at work) or failure (such as receiving a failing grade in school, or being fired from one's job). See *Informal sanction* and *Sanction*.

Functionalism The theoretical view (or school) that stresses how the parts of a society or social group are interrelated. Emphasis is placed on the contributions (functions) that one part makes for the adjustment or well-being of other parts. Each part, working properly, is seen as contributing to the stability of the whole. See *Symbolic interactionism* and *Conflict theory*.

Future shock A term developed by Alvin Toffler to refer to the dizzying disorientation brought on by the rapid arrival of the future.

Gender The social expectations attached to a person on account of that person's sex. Sex is biological, while gender is social. See *Femininity* and *Masculinity*.

Gender socialization Learning one's gender. See *Gender*.

Generalize To conclude that the research findings from a sample apply to a broader group.

Generalized other The ideas we have of the expectations of a major reference group, or even of society in general.

Genocide Killing an entire population, usually because of the group's biological and cultural traits.

Gentrification The process by which the relatively affluent move to decaying urban neighborhoods, renovate buildings, and displace the poor.

Gestures The movement and positioning of the body to communicate meaning. See *Body language*.

Heterosexuality   Sexual acts or feelings toward members of the opposite sex. See *Homosexuality*.

Hidden curriculum   The unwritten goals of schools, such as teaching obedience to authority and conformity to cultural norms.

Holocaust   The Nazi destruction, in death camps and by means of death squads, of Jews, gypsies, Slavs, homosexuals, the mentally retarded, and others considered threats to the purity of the so-called Aryan race.

Homosexuality   Sexual acts or feelings toward members of the same sex. See *Heterosexuality*.

Horizontal mobility   Movement from one social position to another that is approximately equivalent.

Human ecology   The reciprocal relationships between people and their environment.

Hypothesis   A prediction about how two or more variables are related. See *Variable*.

Ideal culture   The way of life represented by people's values and norms, rather than by their actual practices. See *Real culture*.

Ideal type   Developed by Max Weber, this term refers to a model or description of something that is derived from examining real cases and abstracting what appear to be the essential characteristics of those cases.

Identity formation   The process by which we develop a personal identity; our internalization of social expectations. The end result is that we come to think of ourselves in a certain way; that is, as we internalize people's reactions to us, we develop a "self."

Ideology   Statements or beliefs (especially of reasons and purposes) that justify a group's actions or interests; they buttress, uphold, or legitimate the existing social order.

Incest   Sexual intercourse with forbidden categories of kinfolk. See *Incest taboo*.

Incest taboo   A prohibition against sexual intercourse with specific categories of kinfolk. See *Incest*.

Independent variable   That which is thought to affect or to cause change in some other factor; the variable thought to influence another variable. See *Dependent variable*.

Informal sanction   A social reward or punishment that is informally applied, includes spontaneous gestures of approval or disapproval. Examples include staring, smiling, and gossip. See *Formal sanction* and *Sanction*.

Ingroup   The group to which an individual belongs, identifies, and feels loyalty. See *Outgroup*.

Institution   See *Social institution*.

Institutional(ized) racism   The use of social institutions to discriminate, exploit, or oppress a racial (or ethnic) group. See *Discrimination* and *Racism*.

Institutional(ized) sexism   The use of social institutions to discriminate, exploit, or oppress either males or females as a group. See *Discrimination* and *Sexism*.

Interaction   See *Social interaction*.

Interactional sociology   An emphasis on the study of social interaction. See *Participant observation*, *Qualitative sociology*, and *Structural sociology*.

Internalization   Experiences becoming part of one's "internal" consciousness.

Interview   Asking a respondent questions; can be face-to-face, by writing, or by some form of electronic communication such as by telephone or fax. See *Respondent*.

Interviewer bias   Effects that interviewers have on respondents that tilt answers in some direction.

Involuntary associations   Groups to which people belong, but about which they have little or no choice. Examples include grade school for youngsters and military service during periods of conscription. See *Voluntary associations*.

Justification   An account of an event in which one accepts responsibility for an act, while denying that the act is blameworthy. See *Account* and *Excuse*.

Kin   People who are related by birth, adoption, or marriage.

Kinfolk   See *Kin*.

Kinship   The network of people who are related to one another by birth, adoption, or marriage.

Labeling theory (or **perspective**)   This perspective, which focuses on the effects of labels (or terms) on people, stresses that acts are not inherently deviant (or criminal) but are such only because those acts have been so labeled (or defined). Deviants are those on whom the label of deviant has been successfully applied.

Life chances   The likelihood that an individual or group will benefit from their society's opportunities, goods and services, and other satisfactions in life.

Life course   The stages of our life as we go from birth to death.

Life expectancy   The average number of years a person can expect to live.

Looking-glass self   Charles Horton Cooley's term for the process by which people see themselves through the eyes of others. As people act, others react. In those reactions, people see themselves reflected. Perceiving this, they interpret its meaning, which yields a particular self-image.

Masculinity   Our behaviors and orientations as males. Generally assumed in sociology to be an expression not of biology but of cultural or social learning. See *Femininity*.

Mass media   Forms of communication that reach a large audience, with no personal contact between the senders and receivers of the message. Examples are movies, radio, television, newspaper, magazines, plays, books, and the Internet.

Master status (or **trait**)   A social role (or achieved or ascribed status) that cuts across most other social roles and provides a major basis for personal and public identity.

Material culture   See *Culture*.

Meanings   The significance that something has to someone. Also called symbols, mental constructs, ideas, and stereotypes. See *Qualitative sociology*.

Methodology (Methods)   The procedures scientists use to conduct their studies.

Military-industrial complex   The relationships between top leaders of the Pentagon and U.S. corporations by which they reciprocally support one another and thereby influence political decisions on their behalf.

Minority group   A group of people who are treated unequally because of their physical or cultural characteristics. See *Discrimination*.

Mores   (Pronounced MORE-rays) Developed by William G. Sumner, this term refers to norms whose violation is considered a moral transgression. Examples are the norms against murder and theft. See *Folkways*.

Negative sanction   Punishment for disapproved behavior. See *Sanction*.

Neutralization (techniques of)   Words and ways of thinking that help to deflect social norms and avoid social disapproval. An example is saying, "The circumstances required it" or, "I didn't know what I was doing."

Nonmaterial culture   See *Culture*.

Nonverbal communication   Communication by the use of symbols other than language. Examples are *Body language* and traffic lights.

Norms   Rules concerning appropriate and inappropriate behavior by which people are judged and sanctions applied. See *Sanction*.

Nuclear family   A family that consists of a husband, wife, and their children. See *Extended family*.

Operational definition   The way in which a variable in a hypothesis is measured.

Organization   A social unit established for the purpose of attaining some agreed-upon goals.

Outgroup   A group toward which an individual feels hostility, tension, or dislike. See *Ingroup*.

Overt participant observation   See *Participant observation*.

Participant observation   A method of studying social groups in which the researcher participates in the group being studied. If the people being studied know the researcher is in their midst, this method is called *overt participant observation*; if they do not know they are being studied, it is called *covert participant observation*.

Peer group   People who occupy a similar social status and who are usually close in age. Examples are one's playmates as a child and workmates as an adult.

Personal identity   Our ideas of who we are. Roughly equivalent to self concept. See *Public identity* and *Self*.

Personality   An individual's tendency over time to act (and think and feel) in ways similar to those he or she did in the past; the stable behavior patterns we come to expect of people.

Population   The target group to be studied.

Positive sanction   A reward for approved behavior. See *Sanction*.

Power   The ability to get your way, even over the objections of others.

Power elite   C. Wright Mills' term to refer to a small group of powerful people who have interlocking interests, and who make a nation's most important political decisions.

Prejudice   Attitudes, ideas, and feelings, often negative and about people one does not know. See *Discrimination* and *Ethnocentrism*.

Prestige   Favorable evaluation, respect, or social recognition.

Primary group   People whose relationship is intimate, face-to-face, expressive, and extended over time. Examples are one's family and close friends.

Prostitution   The exchange of sexual favors for some gain, usually money.

Public identity   The ideas that others have of what we ought to be like. Roughly equivalent to the public social roles we play. See *Personal identity* and *Self*.

Qualitative sociology   Studies of social life in which the emphasis is on the *meanings* of people's experiences. The goal is to determine how people construct their worlds, develop their ideas and attitudes, communicate these with one another, and how their meanings affect their behavior, ideas about the self, and relationships to one another. See *Meanings* and *Quantitative sociology*.

Quantitative sociology   Studies of social life in which the emphasis is on precise measurement, or numbers. Sociologists who have this orientation stress that to understand human behavior we must use statistical techniques. See *Qualitative sociology*.

Questionnaire   An interview by means of a written form.

Race   A large number of people who share physical characteristics on the basis of which they regard themselves as a biological unit and are similarly regarded by others.

Racism   One racial or ethnic group dominating or exploiting another, generally based on seeing those they exploit as inferior. See *Discrimination* and *Ethnocentrism*.

Random sample   A sample in which everyone in the target population has the same chance of being included in the study.

Rapport   A feeling of trust and communication between people.

Rationalization (of society)   Weber's term for the process by which a society or other group adopts a bureaucratic orientation, with emphasis on efficiency, impersonal relations, and the bottom line.

Real culture A people's actual way of life, as contrasted with the way of life that is expressed by their ideals. See *Ideal culture*.

Reference group A group to which people refer when they evaluate themselves, their behavior, or actions they are considering.

Relative deprivation Feeling deprived relative to what others have; a sense of unjustice regarding the gap between the resources or rewards that one has and what others have.

Reliability The extent to which studies produce consistent results.

Replication The repetition of a study in order to test its findings.

Research methods See *Methodology*.

Resocialization Learning norms, values, and behaviors that contrast with one's previous experiences.

Respondent A person who has been interviewed or who has filled out a questionnaire. (He or she has *responded* to the request for data.)

Rising expectations A situation in which people who have accepted existing conditions in the past now feel they have a right to better conditions.

Rites of passage Formal rituals that mark someone's transition from one social status to another. Examples include bar mitzvahs, confirmations, first communions, weddings, graduation ceremonies, and funerals. Also known as *rites de passage*.

Role The part played by a person who occupies a particular status. See *Status*.

Role conflict If a person finds himself or herself torn between conflicting demands of two or more roles, that person is said to be experiencing role conflict. Examples include a student wanting to date on the same night that he or she is supposed to study for a final examination.

Role taking Putting yourself in the shoes of someone else and seeing how things look from that perspective.

Sample The individuals who are intended to represent the population to be studied.

Sanction A social reward for approved behavior, or punishment for disapproved behavior. See *Negative sanction* and *Positive sanction*.

Secondary analysis The analysis of data that have already been collected by other researchers.

Secondary group The more formal, impersonal, and transitory groups to which people belong, such as an introductory course in sociology.

Self The sense of identity that individuals have of themselves as a distinct person; this sense, idea, or conception is acquired through social interaction. See *Identity formation*.

Self-fulfilling prophecy A false definition of a situation ("The bank is in trouble") that causes people to change their behavior ("People rush to the bank to withdraw their savings") and makes the originally false statement come true ("The bank is now in trouble as it does not have enough cash on hand to meet the unexpected demand for immediate withdrawals"). (If the "prophecy" had not been made, it would not have come true.)

Sex role The behaviors and characteristics that a male or female is expected to demonstrate, based on cultural concepts of masculinity or femininity; assigned on the basis of one's sex organs.

Sex role socialization Learning one's sex role. See *Sex role*.

Sexism Males or females dominating or exploiting the other, with the exploitation generally based on seeing the other as inferior; usually used to refer to males dominating females. See *Discrimination* and *Ethnocentrism*.

Social change Alteration in society, in its patterns of social structure, social institutions (or some small part of them), culture, and people's behavior.

Social class A large number of people who have about the same amount of social power. In our society, some sociologists (Weberian) see the primary bases as the amount of people's income and education and the prestige of their occupation. Other sociologists (Marxian) see the essential difference as people's relationship to the means of production—whether they are capitalists (own the means of production) or workers (work for capitalists).

Social class mobility Changing one's social class, usually in relationship to that of one's parents. See *Social mobility*.

Social construction of reality The process by which definitions of reality (views of what some part of the world is like) are socially created, objectified, internalized, and then taken for granted.

Social control The techniques used to keep people in line or, if they step out, to bring them back into line. Examples include persuasion, coercion, ridicule, education, and punishment. See *Sanction*.

Social group Any human group.

Social inequality Any inequality between or among groups of people; sometimes used to refer to *social stratification*.

Social institution Standardized practices (clustered around a set of norms, values, beliefs, statuses, and roles) that develop around the attempt to meet a basic need of society. Examples include government and politics (for social order), education (for training in conformity and the transmission of skills and knowledge), and the military (for protection from external enemies and the implementation of foreign policy).

Social interaction People acting and reacting to one another; as they do so, they influence each other's feelings, attitudes, and actions.

Social mobility Movement from one social position to another. See *Downward*, *Horizontal*, and *Upward social mobility*.

Social stratification Large groups of people who are ranked in a hierarchy that gives them different access to the rewards their society has to offer.

Social structure The ways in which the basic components of a group or society are related to one another.

Socialization Refers to learning; the process of social interaction by which people learn the way of life of their society, or learn to play specific roles.

Society A group of individuals who share the same territory and participate in a common culture.

Sociobiology The study of the biological bases of human behavior.

Sociology The study of human society and social behavior; the study of how groups influence people and how people influence groups.

Status One's position in a group or society, such as woman, mother, and plumber.

Stereotypes A generalization (or idea) about people (or even animals and objects); a mental image that summarizes what is believed to be typical about these people.

Stigma An indelible mark of social disgrace.

Stratification See *Social stratification*.

Structural sociology The emphasis is on the influence of social structure on human behavior, with a focus on social institutions and other group memberships. See *Aggregates, Qualitative sociology,* and *Social structure*.

Structured interview An interview that uses closed-ended questions.

Subculture A group that shares in the overall culture of a society but also has its own distinctive values, norms, beliefs, and life style. Examples include cabdrivers, singles, prostitutes, muggers, and physicians.

Subjective interpretation See *Verstehen*.

Survey The collection of data by having people answer a series of questions.

Symbol Any act, object, or event that represents something, such as a traffic light, a gesture, or this definition. See *Symbolic interactionism*.

Symbolic interaction People's interaction based on symbols. See *Symbolic interactionism*.

Symbolic interactionism Developed by Herbert Blumer, this term refers to the school of thought (or theoretical perspective) that focuses on symbols as the basis of human behavior—the signs, gestures, and language by which people communicate with one another and change or refine their courses of action in anticipation of what others might do. See *Conflict theory* and *Functionalism*.

Techniques of neutralization See *Neutralization*.

Technology Tools or items used to accomplish tasks.

Theory A statement that organizes a set of concepts in a meaningful way by explaining the relationship between them.

Total institution Erving Goffman's term to refer to a place in which people are confined, cut off from the rest of society, and under the almost absolute control of the people in charge. Examples include prisons, the military, and convents.

Traditional authority Authority that is legitimated by custom and practice. The explanation for something is, "We have always done it this way." See *Charismatic authority*.

Trust The willingness to accept the definition that someone offers of oneself or of a situation and to play a corresponding role based on that definition.

Unobtrusive measures Techniques of observing people who do not know they are being studied.

Unstructured interview An interview that uses open-ended questions.

Upward social mobility Movement from a lower to a higher social position.

Validity The extent to which an *operational definition* measures what it is intended to measure.

Value conflict Disagreement over goals, ideals, policies, or other expressions of values.

Value judgment A subjective opinion based on one's own set of values.

Values Ideas about what is worthwhile.

Variable Any condition or characteristic that varies from one situation or person or group to another. Examples include age, occupation, beliefs, and attitudes. See *Dependent variable*, *Experiment*, and *Independent variable*.

Verstehen A term used by Max Weber to refer to the subjective interpretation of human behavior; that is, because we are members of a group or culture, we gain insight and understanding into what others are experiencing, allowing us to interpret those experiences. See *Qualitative sociology*.

Vertical social mobility Movement to a higher or a lower social position.

Voluntary associations Groups that people join voluntarily, often because they wish to promote some goal or to be with like-minded people. Examples include a church, a college class, and a bowling league. See *Involuntary associations*.

War Armed confict between nations or politically distinct groups.

White-collar crime Crimes committed by "respectable" persons of high status, frequently during the course of their occupation.

Appendix
Correlation Chart

To help you integrate this twelfth edition with whatever main text you may be using, I have matched the articles with 27 chapter themes found in introductory texts. Some selections in *Down to Earth Sociology* have more than one theme, and they may be listed for more than a single chapter. To make it easier for you to produce your syllabus, for each article I have listed its number, title, author, and the page number on which it begins.

Some instructors build their introductory course around the articles in *Down to Earth Sociology*. They supplement the *Down to Earth* selections with a few chapters of what is usually the main text. In this way, their students concentrate on primary sociological materials, rather than on secondary analyses. Regardless of your approach, because of the inherent interest of most of these readings, they help make sociology come alive. Instructors report that *Down to Earth* helps them give their students a more engaging introduction to sociology. I hope this is your experience, too.

I have also prepared an instructor's manual for this edition. I have written not only the usual multiple choice, essay, and true-false questions, but also suggestions for in-class activities. These activities are designed to make your class more lively, to arouse your students' interest in sociology, and to stimulate their sociological imagination. You may wish to try some of these exercises, for from the feedback that I have received from instructors, they accomplish their purpose. I welcome any suggestions you might have for other in-class activities.

Again, my best wishes for your classroom success.

Jim Henslin

Collective Behavior

Culture

Deviance and Social Control

Law

Marriage and Family

Mass Media

Medicine

Social Class

Social Groups

Social Interaction

Social Movements

Social Stratification

Socialization

The Sociological Perspective

Sports

Urbanization and Urban Life

Work and Occupations

Name Index

Subject Index